For Victoria

Animal Learning & Cognition,

An Introduction

Third Edition

John M. Pearce

Cardiff University

Ψ Psychology Press
Taylor & Francis Group

HOVE AND NEW YORK

Published in 2008
by Psychology Press
27 Church Road, Hove, East Sussex, BN3 2FA

Simultaneously published in the USA and Canada
by Psychology Press
711 Third Avenue, New York, NY 10017

*Psychology Press is an imprint of the Taylor & Francis Group,
an informa business*

British Library Cataloguing in Publication Data
A catalogue record for this book is available from the British Library

Library of Congress Cataloging-in-Publication Data
Pearce, John M.
    Animal learning and cognition: an introduction / John M. Pearce.
        p. cm.
    Includes bibliographical references and index.
    ISBN 978–1–84169–655–3—ISBN 978–1–84169–656–0
     1. Animal intelligence. I. Title.

    QL785.P32 2008
    591.5'13—dc22   2007034019

ISBN: 978–1–84169–655–3 (hbk)
ISBN: 978–1–84169–656–0 (pbk)

Typeset by Newgen Imaging Systems (P) Ltd, Chennai, India

Contents

Preface

In preparing the third edition of this book, my aim, as it was for the previous editions, has been to provide an overview of what has been learned by pursuing one particular approach to the study of animal intelligence. It is my belief that the intelligence of animals is the product of a number of mental processes. I think the best way of understanding these processes is by studying the behavior of animals in an experimental setting. This book, therefore, presents what is known about animal intelligence by considering experimental findings from the laboratory and from more naturalistic settings.

I do not attach any great importance to the distinction between animal learning and animal cognition. Research in both areas has the common goal of elucidating the mechanisms of animal intelligence and, very often, this research is conducted using similar procedures. If there is any significance to the distinction, then it is that the fields of animal learning and animal cognition are concerned with different aspects of intelligence. Chapters 2 to 6 are concerned predominantly with issues that fall under the traditional heading of animal learning theory. My main concern in these chapters is to show how it is possible with a few simple principles of associative learning to explain a surprisingly wide range of experimental findings. Readers familiar with the previous edition will notice that apart from a new chapter devoted to extinction, there are relatively few changes to this part of the book. This lack of change does not mean that researchers are no longer actively investigating the basic learning processes in animals. Rather, it means that the fundamental principles of learning are now reasonably well established and that current research is directed towards issues that are too advanced to be considered in an introductory text book.

The second half of the book covers material that is generally treated under the heading of animal cognition. My overall aim in these chapters is to examine what has been learned from studying animal behavior about such topics as memory, the representation of knowledge, navigation, social learning, communication, and language. I also hope to show that the principles developed in the earlier chapters are of relevance to understanding research that is reviewed in the later chapters. It is in this part of the book that the most changes have been made. Research on animal cognition during the last 10 years has headed in many new directions. I have tried to present a clear summary of this research, as well as a balanced evaluation of its theoretical implications.

Those who wish to study the intelligence of animals face a daunting task. Not only are there numerous different species to study, but there is also an array of intellectual skills to be explored, each posing a unique set of challenging theoretical problems. As a result, many of the topics that I discuss are still in their infancy. Some readers may therefore be disappointed to discover that we are still trying to answer many of the interesting questions that can be asked about the intelligence of animals. On the other hand, it is just this lack of knowledge that makes the study of animal learning and cognition so exciting. Many fascinating discoveries remain to be made once the appropriate experiments have been conducted.

One of the rewards for writing a book is the opportunity it provides to thank the many friends and colleagues who have been so generous with the help they have given me. The way in which this book is organized and much of the material it contains have been greatly influenced by numerous discussions with A. Dickinson, G. Hall, N. J. Mackintosh, and E. M. Macphail. Different chapters have benefited greatly from the critical comments on earlier versions by A. Aydin, N. Clayton, M. Haselgrove, C. Heyes, V. LoLordo, A. McGregor, E. Redhead, and P. Wilson. A special word of thanks is due to Dave Lieberman, whose thoughtful comments on an earlier draft of the present edition identified numerous errors and helped to clarify the manner in which much of the material is presented. The present edition has also greatly benefited from the detailed comments on the two previous editions by N. J. Mackintosh.

I should also like to express my gratitude to the staff at Psychology Press. Without the cajoling and encouragement of the Assistant Editor, Tara Stebnicky, it is unlikely that I would have embarked on this revision. I am particularly grateful to the Production Editor, Veronica Lyons, who, with generous amounts of enthusiasm and imagination, has done a wonderful job in trying to transform a sow's ear into a silk purse. Thanks are also due to the colleagues who were kind enough to send me photographs of their subjects while they were being tested. Finally, there is the pleasure of expressing gratitude to Victoria, my wife, who once again patiently tolerated the demands made on her while this edition was being prepared. In previous editions I offered similar thanks to my children, but there is no need on this occasion now that they have left home. Even so, Jess, Alex, and Tim would never forgive me if I neglected to mention their names.

While preparing for this revision I read a little about Darwin's visit to the Galapagos Islands. I was so intrigued by the influence they had on him that I felt compelled to visit the islands myself. During the final stages of preparing this edition, Veronica and Tania, somewhat reluctantly, allowed me a two-week break to travel to the Galapagos Islands. The holiday was one of the highlights of my life.

The sheer number of animals, and their absolute indifference to the presence of humans, was overwhelming. The picture on the previous page shows me trying unsuccessfully to engage a giant tortoise in conversation. This, and many other photographs, were taken without any elaborate equipment and thus reveal how the animals allowed me to approach as close as I wished in order to photograph them. I came away from the islands having discovered little that is new about the intelligence of animals, but with a deeper appreciation of how the environment shapes not only their form, but also their behavior.

John M. Pearce
October, 2007

CHAPTER 1

CONTENTS

The study of animal intelligence

1

A book dedicated to the study of animal learning and cognition is, in the broadest sense, concerned with understanding animal intelligence. Thus the present book will address questions of the following kind: What is animal intelligence? How does it differ from human intelligence? If there is a difference between the intelligence of humans and animals, why should this be? In what way do species of animals differ in their intelligence? How can animal intelligence be measured? None of these is an easy question to answer, and it is partly the difficulty of answering the first that makes it so difficult to answer all others.

This book examines a particular account of animal intelligence. It presumes that animals, like humans, possess a number of mental or cognitive processes and that these collectively contribute to an animal's intelligence. Thus the way animals remember, learn, reason, solve problems, communicate, and so forth will be examined in some detail. One advantage of this approach is that it permits relatively straightforward answers to the questions posed earlier. For instance, a scale of intelligence might be constructed by ranking animals according to the number of the intellectual abilities they possess. Alternatively, it might turn out that it would be nonsensical to construct any such scale because a species better endowed than another with one of these abilities might be less well endowed with a second. In addition, as this account is based on a human model, it should readily permit the comparison of human and animal intelligence. The chapters that follow examine in some detail the various intellectual capacities that have been revealed in animals and—to a lesser extent—look at the way animals differ in their possession of these capacities. The purpose of the present chapter is to provide a background to this discussion by considering a number of preliminary issues:

1. A popular view of animal intelligence is that there is a growth of this capacity with evolutionary development; apes are therefore seen by many as being more intelligent than most other animals. Although common, this view deserves critical analysis, as it rests on questionable assumptions.
2. The study of animal intelligence is of interest in its own right, but this might be seen as insufficient justification for devoting a book to the topic. The study of human intelligence might be considered a more proper part of psychology. It is therefore worth identifying some of the benefits that can derive from the study of the mental life of animals.
3. The study of mental processes in animals is difficult because the subject matter is not available for direct observation. It is impossible at present to point at any event that can be regarded as a mental process in animals. As a result, special methods must be employed for the study of animal cognition, and the rationale for these needs discussion.
4. Much of the research discussed in this book relates to work conducted during the last thirty years or so, but the study of animal intelligence in the laboratory has

now been pursued for over a hundred years. By way of providing a historical background to the rest of the book, the final section of the chapter presents a brief review of the dominant theoretical themes of this work.

THE DISTRIBUTION OF INTELLIGENCE

Nakajima, Arimitsu, and Lattal (2002) asked university students in both Japan and the USA to rank the intelligence of a variety of animals relative to that of humans (who were assigned 100 points). The results from the survey, which can be seen in Table 1.1, revealed that chimpanzees were regarded as being the most intelligent animal and amoeba the least. The implication of this study is that most of us assume there is a progressive development of intelligence throughout the animal kingdom, culminating with our own species being the most intelligent.

I shall examine two popular justifications for the assumption that intelligence is distributed in this way. One is based on an interpretation of evolution that presumes that animals can be arranged in a sequence according to their phylogenetic status. The other is derived from the assumption that there is a relationship between intelligence and brain size. In fact, neither of these justifies the views expressed by the students questioned by Nakajima et al. (2002).

The role of evolution

Since the time of Aristotle (384–322 BC), attempts have been made to represent the animal kingdom in an orderly sequence. Such a sequence has been referred to as the **scala naturae** or the "great chain of being". Typically, the lower rankings of these scales are occupied by formless creatures like sponges, whereas the upper echelons are reserved for humans. Ascending through the intermediate range of these scales

TABLE 1.1 The rank order of the 56 animals students were asked by Nakajima et al. (2002) to score on intelligence, together with the means score assigned to each species. The maximum score was 100

Animal	Score	Animal	Score	Animal	Score	Animal	Score
Chimpanzee	77	Kangaroo	50	Penguin	40	Tuna	25
Orangutan	72	Panda	48	Rabbit	39	Octopus	24
Dolphin	72	Hawk	48	Ostrich	38	Lizard	24
Gorilla	68	Parrot	48	Crocodile	37	Ant	23
Dog	61	Sea lion	48	Rat	35	Frog	23
Baboon	60	Crow	46	Pigeon	33	Carp	22
Whale	57	Cow	45	Sparrow	32	Crab	20
Wolf	56	Giraffe	44	Quail	31	Cockroach	19
Cat	55	Owl	44	Fowl	31	Goldfish	19
Lion	54	Shark	43	Mole	31	Butterfly	17
Bear	52	Sheep	42	Snake	30	Jellyfish	15
Horse	52	Bat	41	Salmon	29	Earthworm	10
Fox	51	Koala	41	Turtle	28	Slug	10
Elephant	50	Pig	41	Honeybee	28	Ameba	8

can be found insects, fish, amphibians, reptiles, and various mammals. According to Aristotle, elephants were placed just below humans. Although these scales generally end with our own species, this has by no means been a universal practice. Occasionally the "great chain" has extended beyond humans to include angels and, ultimately, God.

Various justifications have been proposed for such a simple ordering. Aristotle based his scheme on whether the animals possessed blood and on the number of their legs. More recently, evolutionary terms have been used to justify what is now referred to as the phyletic or **phylogenetic scale**. Since the publication of Darwin's *On the origin of species by means of natural selection, or the preservation of favoured races in the struggle for life*, in 1859, it has become accepted that all existing species have descended or evolved from different, earlier species. As a result, it is possible to envisage a chain of evolution in which the earliest animals are placed at the bottom, and the species they led to are placed above them in the order of their appearance. *Homo sapiens* appeared some 100,000 years ago and would be very near the top of this scale. Most would accept that humans are vastly more intelligent than the protozoa to which we are distantly related, and so it is not difficult to regard the phyletic scale as roughly corresponding to the intellectual development of the species ordered along it. This interpretation could hardly be more incorrect.

While on his voyage around South America on HMS Beagle, Darwin noted that the iguanas on the Galapagos Islands were different from those on the mainland in that only the former ate seaweed and swam in the sea. To explain this difference between such closely related species, he developed the principle of natural selection, which is based on two observations:

1. Many more animals are born than achieve reproductive success; some die before reaching sexual maturity, others might fail to find a mate.
2. The individuals of a given species are not identical but differ from one another in a variety of ways.

It follows from these observations that certain members of a species will be better suited than others to survive in a given environment, and will be more likely to mature sexually and to leave offspring. If we assume that offspring resemble their parents, it further follows that better-adapted characteristics will spread through a population at the expense of less well-adapted characteristics. If members of the same species should occupy different environments, the different demands they face will favor the reproduction of animals with slightly different characteristics. Eventually, their characteristics might have diverged to such an extent that they can no longer interbreed successfully, and they will constitute separate species.

Presumably, then, the ancestors of the iguanas observed by Darwin on the Galapagos Islands and on the mainland of South America were of the same stock. However, the radically different nature of these two environments—an abundance of seaweed and a dearth of vegetation on the islands, and a proliferation of vegetation on the mainland—would have favored the gradual development of different characteristics in successive generations of offspring from the common ancestor.

One important implication of this account is that the notion of a phylogenetic scale is a gross oversimplification of the history of **evolution**. Instead of one species evolving from another in a strict sequence, as the "great chain of being" suggests, it is now accepted that evolution has resulted in animals being related by a sort of

KEY TERMS

Phylogenetic scale
A sequence in which all livings things are ordered according to their complexity. The scale has, at times, been justified erroneously on evolutionary grounds.

Evolution
The change in the inherited characteristics of a species from one generation to the next.

Darwin's observation of the differences between the Galapagos iguana and its relatives inspired his theory of natural selection, where factors such as environmental adaptation were instrumental in the survival of a species.

family tree. The roots and trunk of the tree are composed of the early life forms. The species that have evolved from these origins can be regarded as separate branches, which themselves branch out as later generations of their offspring evolve into new species. The contrast between this view of evolution with that which assumes humans are the pinnacle of a great chain is captured very well by Gould (1996), who regards our species as "a tiny twig on the floridly arborescent bush of life" (Gould, 1996, p. 18).

Figure 1.1 shows the trunk and principal branches of a simplified version of the evolutionary tree. To give some idea of the time-scale involved, the fossil record provides evidence of animal life as long as 2600 million years ago, yet it was not until about 450–500 million years ago that the first true vertebrates came into existence. Figure 1.2 shows the outer branches for the four families of primates: prosimians, monkeys, apes, and us.

The tree of evolution is interesting in its own right, but of more relevance to the present discussion is the fact that it is impossible to organize the relationship among the various species into any simple linear scale. Mammals and birds have both evolved from reptiles, and many of the reptiles that are alive today are only distant relatives of the reptiles that were ancestral to the birds and mammals. Given such a relationship, it is extremely difficult to imagine how the present-day animals could be ranked in a sequence that mimics their evolutionary history. Evolution provides an explanation for the diversity of species—it does not provide any grounds for ranking animals according to their intelligence or, for that matter, any other characteristic.

Several authors have pursued this line of argument one step further to conclude that the evolutionary process will render futile any attempt to find common mechanisms of intelligence among animals (Hinde & Stevenson-Hinde, 1973; Shettleworth, 1998). It is not just the physical characteristics of animals that are shaped

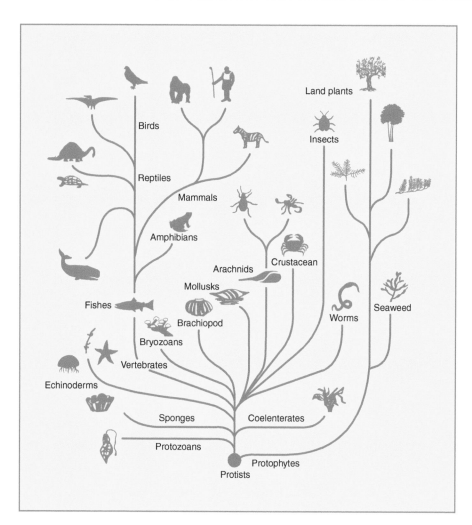

FIGURE 1.1 A simplified version of the tree of life.

by evolution, but also their intellectual processes. Thus it might be expected that different species, if they inhabit different environments, will differ radically in the nature of their intelligence. For example, the habitat of a bird like the arctic tern, which spends most of its time flying between the polar regions, has very little in common with the sewer in which a rat might live. It is possible that animals occupying such contrasting environments possess very different intellectual processes. Furthermore, because the last common ancestor of the rat and the arctic tern was probably alive 200 million years ago, there has been ample time for the evolution of different mental capacities. If this argument is correct, then it is no more possible to conclude that one species is more intelligent than another than it is to say that one is more evolved than the other. All that can be said is that the species have developed different intellectual abilities that enable them to survive in their particular environments.

There is certainly some merit in this argument. Chapter 11 describes how birds that migrate great distances possess the ability to navigate by the stars. One would hardly expect to discover this skill in the sewer rat. But, at the same time, there are good grounds for believing that animals might have much in common intellectually

FIGURE 1.2 A family tree of the primates; the details of the tree are still a matter for debate.

(Bitterman, 2000). Despite living in radically different environments, animals face a number of common problems. Many animals must learn which foods are nutritious and which are poisonous. They must learn to identify their predators and where they can be found. They must learn the location of plentiful rather than lean supplies of food, and where water can be located. If the animals raise their young in a specific location, they must remember its position in respect to local landmarks. Given such a collection of common problems, it is at least plausible that different species employ the same intellectual processes for solving them.

Animals might, for example, have the ability to learn about recurring sequences of events, particularly when one of them is of biological significance. This would enable them, in a sense, to expect future events and to behave adaptively in anticipation of them. A simple example would be the ability to learn about the taste of a food and its ultimate gastric consequences. Animals that can learn about this relationship would then be able to restrict their diet to foods that are not harmful. There is also an obvious advantage—for virtually all animals—in being able to learn about the consequences of their actions: It will permit behavior that has beneficial consequences to be repeated, and that which has harmful ones to be withheld.

Many species might also benefit by possessing the capacity to communicate and to solve problems. The purpose of this discussion is not to argue that all animals should possess these and other abilities. Instead, my aim is to indicate that although evolution will result in animals possessing very different characteristics, the common intellectual problems that confront many species might perhaps result in their sharing the same methods for solving them. If this is correct, then there could be a considerable degree of similarity in the intellectual processes of different species. Of course, whether this is true can be discovered only by studying the animals directly.

Brain size

One obvious candidate for providing an independent index of the intelligence of a species is its brain size. However intelligence is defined, few would dispute that the organ responsible for this capacity is the brain. It is thus reasonable to expect the species with the larger brains to possess the greater potential for intelligence. Perhaps this rationalization was responsible for the replies to the questionnaire reported in the study by Nakajima et al. (2002). There is certainly a high correlation between their ranking of intelligence and the brain size of the animals concerned, as Figure 1.3 demonstrates. Is it possible to rank the intelligence of species according to their brain size?

A problem that is encountered when attempting to relate intelligence to brain size becomes apparent when it is appreciated that elephants possess much heavier brains than humans. Few would accept that this relationship accurately indicates the relative intelligence of these species, and a moment's reflection should reveal the fallacy in the argument. The concern of the brain is not solely with such high matters as intelligence, but also with more basic activities such as respiration, digestion, reproduction, and movement—in short, all the somatic and vegetative processes of the body. Thus, the bigger the animal, the larger the volume of the brain that will be required to control these processes, and it is unrealistic to expect the size of the brain in absolute terms to provide an index of intelligence. A more plausible candidate is the ratio of the size of the brain to the body. If two species possess the same body size but one has a considerably larger brain, then it is likely that this extra brain will enable its owner to be the more intelligent.

Figure 1.4 shows the brain weights (vertical axis) and the body weights (horizontal axis) of a variety of species, plotted in log–log coordinates. This scale is necessary because of the extremely wide range of values that must be considered. On the basis of what has just been said, it can be concluded (with some relief) that our own species should be more intelligent than the ostrich. Both have the same body weight but the ostrich brain weighs less than ours. The main problem is in deciding how species with different body weights should be compared.

One simple method is to draw polygons around the points for a collection of related species. In Figure 1.4, Jerison (1973), from whose book this account is taken, has drawn two polygons, one around the "higher" vertebrates (birds and mammals), the other enclosing the "lower" vertebrates (reptiles, amphibians, fish). Because the polygons do not overlap, it is possible

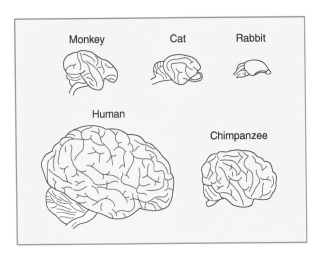

FIGURE 1.3 The brain size of a variety of species.

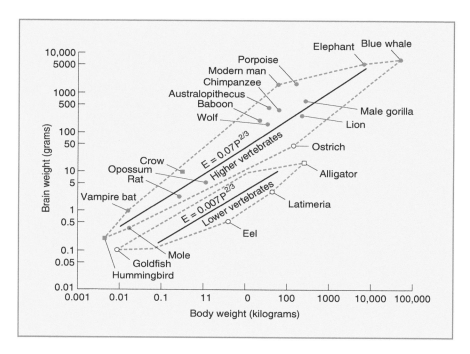

FIGURE 1.4 The brain weights (vertical axis) and body weights (horizontal axis) of a number of vertebrates (from Jerison, 1969). Copyright © 1969 The University of Chicago Press. Reproduced with permission.

to conclude that, in general, the weight of the brain for a given body weight is greater for the higher vertebrates. In other words, the "higher" vertebrates might be expected to have a greater potential for intelligence than the "lower" vertebrates.

More precise comparisons between species can be made by computing a **cephalization index** (K). This essentially represents the ratio of the brain weight (E) to body weight (P), and the larger its value-we might assume-the greater the intelligence of the species concerned. Jerison (1973) rejects the use of a simple ratio of the form E/P for determining the cephalization index and recommends, instead, the use of the ratio $E/P^{2/3}$.[1]

The solid lines in Figure 1.4 pass through the brain and body weights that yield a K value of 0.07 (upper polygon) and 0.007 (lower polygon). Jerison (1973) assumes that all the species that lie on one of these lines possess an equivalent neural capacity for intelligence, irrespective of their body size. The magnitude of the displacement from these lines indicates the K value for a given species. Humans and porpoises possess K values that are furthest above the 0.07 line, which suggests they should be the two most intelligent species, with humans possessing a slight superiority.

Thus, by computing a cephalization index it may be possible to rank different species according to the volume of brain they have available for intelligence. Table 1.2 indicates that this ranking is not too unlike that proposed by the students in the Nakajima et al. (2002) study. On this scale, the elephant has a rather average potential for intelligence.

The ranking in Table 1.2 might accord with the popular conception of the way intelligence is distributed throughout the animal kingdom, but it does not confirm

[1] One justification for this ratio is the assumption that body area is the major determinant for the amount of brain required for somatic processes. As the volume of an animal is related to the cube of its length, whereas its area is related to the square of its length, it follows that for larger animals the proportion of the brain required for somatic control is less than for smaller animals. The exponent 2/3 captures this relationship.

KEY TERM

Cephalization index
A measure of the size of the brain relative to the size of the body.

TABLE 1.2 The cephalization index (K) for 21 mammals arranged in descending order

Mammal	Score	Mammal	Score
Man	0.89	Dog	0.14
Dolphin	0.64	Squirrel	0.13
Chimpanzee	0.30	Wild pig	0.12
Squirrel monkey	0.28	Cat	0.12
Rhesus monkey	0.25	Horse	0.10
Elephant	0.22	Sheep	0.10
Whale	0.21	Ox	0.06
Marmoset	0.21	Mouse	0.06
Fox	0.19	Rat	0.05
Walrus	0.15	Rabbit	0.05
Camel	0.14		

Adapted from Russell (1979).

this view. The most that this ranking could indicate is that some animals have less brain available for intelligence than others, once account has been taken of its remaining functions. What is needed is a detailed investigation of the intellectual abilities of animals to determine whether they correspond with the order summarized in Table 1.2. This in turn depends on a satisfactory definition of animal intelligence, and it is with this issue that the next section is concerned.

Before studying this problem, it is worth stating that not all authors maintain that Table 1.2 reflects accurately the distribution of animal intelligence. As early as about 500 BC, the Ionian philosopher Anaxagoras proposed that all living things possess a substance, *nous*, which is equivalent to mind. This substance has power over all things that have life: It is infinite, self-ruled, and just as good in animals as in humans. In more mundane terms, Anaxagoras was claiming that all animals are equally intelligent. Any apparent intellectual differences between animals were said to be due to variations in the way they can express themselves. Hence, he might have argued that worms are intelligent, but unfortunately they lack the necessary appendages to demonstrate this capacity fully. Among Anaxagoras' other novel ideas is the proposal that snow is, in part, black.

Over twenty years ago Macphail (1982) concluded, after an extremely thorough review of a vast body of experimental evidence, that there is no difference in the intellectual capacity of vertebrates other than humans. This **null hypothesis of intelligence** is based on the results of direct tests of animal intelligence, and thus merits serious attention. We shall see from time to time throughout this book that, even today, Macphail's claim is remarkably difficult to disprove.

DEFINING ANIMAL INTELLIGENCE

Adaptability

Many authors consider that the defining characteristic of intelligence is that it enables animals to behave adaptively. Thus in a book entitled *Instinct and intelligence*, the zoologist Barnett (1970, p. 59), proposed that "intelligence here means the ability to adapt behavior to circumstances". There can surely be little to disagree with in this definition. None the less, its limitations become evident when attempts are made to compare the intelligence of different species. How it could be determined whether a rat or a dog is better at adapting its behavior to the prevailing circumstances is not immediately apparent. Nor does this definition tell us anything about the mechanisms that enable an animal to adapt its behavior.

One solution to this problem is to acknowledge that an animal that can profit from its experiences is likely to be better at adapting to a new environment than one lacking this capacity. For example, once the location of food, water, and predators has been identified, being able to remember where they were encountered will considerably facilitate survival. Accordingly, the animal that is faster at **learning** and better at remembering may be regarded as the more adaptable and hence the more intelligent. Indeed, Warren (1973) has suggested that this type of argument formed the rationale for much of the work in comparative psychology conducted during the first half of the twentieth century.

Learning

Learning is surprisingly hard to define satisfactorily. For the present discussion, it can be said to take place when some experience results in a relatively permanent change in the reaction to a situation (see Domjan, 1998, pp.13–16). Since the dawn of the twentieth century there has been an enormous number of experimental studies of learning, using animals ranging from protozoa to humans, and a variety of tasks. One clear conclusion that can be drawn from this work is that there is definitely no relationship between the speed at which an animal learns and its cephalization index. Evidence supporting this claim will be presented throughout the book, but at this juncture several examples will serve to make the point. Skard (1950) compared the speed at which rats and humans mastered a complex maze and found no difference whatsoever in the number of trials required to attain errorless performance. Warren (1965) reported that there was no difference in the rate at which goldfish, chickens, cats, horses, and rhesus monkeys learned a discrimination in which they were required to approach one of two stimuli to gain reward.

Equally surprising are the results of Angermeier (1984), who conducted a thorough series of experiments at the University of Cologne. Various animals were required to perform a simple response to obtain food: Mammals had to press a lever, birds peck a disc, and fish push a rod that was hanging vertically into their tank. Subjects were placed into the apparatus when hungry, and food was delivered only when the response had been performed. As his measure of learning, Angermeier (1984) recorded the number of rewards delivered before subjects reached a criterion of responding at a constant rate. The results from his studies are presented in Table 1.3, which also includes the results of other researchers using 5-month-old human infants, rewarded with food for turning their heads (Papousek, 1977), and bees rewarded for discriminating between different colors (Menzel & Erber, 1978). The remarkable feature of these data is that they are precisely the opposite of that expected if the cephalization index of a species corresponded with its intelligence, as revealed by the speed of learning. Whatever the explanation for these intriguing results, they suggest that it would be unwise to look to speed of learning as an index of animal intelligence.

KEY TERM

Learning
A long-lasting change in behavior that results from experience.

TABLE 1.3 Number of rewards delivered before criterion was reached in a simple learning task for 11 animals arranged in ascending order

Animal	No. rewards	Animal	No. rewards
Bees	2	Pigeons	10
Triggerfish	4	Rats	22
Koi carp	4	Raccoons	24
Silverbarb	4	Rabbits	24
Quail	8	Human infants	28
Hybrid chickens	10		

Adapted from Angermeier (1984).

Another reason for being wary of using speed of learning as a measure of intelligence comes from studies showing that, for a given species, the speed of learning is greatly influenced by the means used to assess it. Bolles (1971) has shown that rats will readily learn to press a lever for food, yet they have considerable difficulty in learning to perform the same response to avoid electric shock. This difficulty does not reflect an inability to perform avoidance responses, as rats find it easy to learn to jump onto a ledge or to run from one compartment to another to avoid shock (Baum, 1966; Theios, Lynch, & Lowe, 1966). Similarly, in one of my experiments (Pearce, Colwill, & Hall, 1978) rats were shown to be much better at learning to press a lever than to scratch themselves for food. One of the clearest demonstrations of this type of effect was reported by Garcia and Koelling (1966), using an extremely simple technique known as **taste aversion conditioning**. Thirsty rats were allowed to drink salt-flavored water from a tube in the presence of a distinctive exteroceptive stimulus comprising a light and a clicker. For one group, drinking was followed by an injection of a mild poison that induced illness; for another group the consequence of drinking was electric shock. After several sessions of this training the subjects were returned to the apparatus for a number of test trials; on some trials drinking salt-free water was accompanied by the light and clicker, on others these stimuli were omitted but the water contained salt. Animals that had previously been shocked showed a marked aversion to drinking in the presence of the light and clicker but they were quite happy to drink the salty water by itself. Conversely, the animals that had been made ill freely drank water accompanied by the light and clicker but rejected it when it was flavored with salt.

This aversion to drinking on certain test trials is generally attributed to animals learning about the relationships between the stimuli and their consequences. What is important to note is that the ease of this learning depended critically on the combination of these events. Certain pairings resulted in poor learning (salt with shock, noise and light with illness), whereas others produced very good learning (salt with illness, noise and light with shock). On the basis of these findings it is impossible to say whether rats are good or bad at learning, because this depends

KEY TERM

Taste aversion conditioning
A technique by which an aversion is acquired to an attractive flavor by making an animal ill after consuming it.

critically on the way in which they are tested. This conclusion is also true for many other species.

But these are not the only problems with using speed of learning as a measure of intelligence. The inherent differences between species make it very hard to devise a task that poses exactly the same demands on them. For example, where a subject must learn to respond for food, the speed at which it does so is likely to be influenced by its perceptual, motivational, and motor processes. Bitterman (1965) refers to such factors as **contextual variables** and, as they will undoubtedly vary from one species to another, they may be responsible for any differences in learning that are exhibited. This point can be emphasized by returning to Angermeier's (1984) findings. He observed that rats learned more slowly than fish to perform a response for food. This might reflect the inferior learning ability of rats, but it could equally well be due to a more trivial factor—perhaps the reward given to the fish was more effective than that given to the rats, or perhaps the fish found it easier to locate the object they were required to operate. Unless we can be certain that these and many other factors were equated, it would be unwise to draw any firm conclusions from Angermeier's (1984) study about the relative intelligence of the animals concerned.

To deal with this sort of problem, Bitterman (1965) suggested the use of a technique known as systematic variation. This method, in essence, involves training animals from different species on the same task across a wide range of conditions. These conditions might involve variations in reward size, in the level of deprivation, in the nature of the stimuli employed, and so on. If it could be shown that, despite all these manipulations, one species is uniformly better at learning than another, then it would suggest that this species is the more intelligent. In principle this method should be successful, but in practice it is extremely challenging to implement. Identifying the important procedural details of an experiment is not easy, and it is therefore difficult to be sure that the relevant manipulations have been conducted. In addition, there is the practical problem that this method dictates the use of a large number of subjects being run in many possibly time-consuming experiments. Few psychologists have either the facilities or the patience to pursue this approach to the study of animal intelligence. Even so, unless account is taken of contextual variables, it will always be dangerous to draw conclusions from attempts to compare the intelligence of different species, however intelligence is defined.

One final reason for being wary of using learning as a means for assessing the intelligence of animals is that it may direct attention away from other important intellectual capacities. In addition to being able to learn, animals must be able to remember what they have learned until it is needed; they may also be capable of reasoning, of solving problems, and so on. These and other abilities should be regarded as attributes of intelligence, yet until recently they have received relatively little study. We now turn to an alternative view of animal intelligence, which takes account of such abilities.

Information processing

The study of human cognition is characterized by the way it regards people as if they are sophisticated processors of information. Throughout our lives we are surrounded by information about the environment in which we live. Not only does this information emanate from such artificial sources as books or the radio, it is also

KEY TERM

Contextual variables
The sensory, motivational, and motor processes that influence the speed at which learning takes place, and which make it difficult to compare the intelligence of different species by studying speed of learning.

provided by our interaction with the natural world. This information is received by all the senses, and its reception is essential for our survival. Of paramount importance is the fact that we do not receive this information passively. Of all the information that is available, we attend selectively only to a portion, and that which gains our attention may then be transformed as it passes through a variety of stages. The information may be retained so that it can be recalled on some subsequent occasion, or it may be forgotten. It may be integrated with other information, or it may be stored as a relatively discrete unit. Alternatively, it may be used as a step in a complex reasoning process. Ultimately, after passing through these stages, the information may produce a response. Given such a framework, the task of the cognitive psychologist is to identify as precisely as possible the nature and properties of the various information-processing stages. There is no good reason for confining this approach to the study of humans. Animals, too, are surrounded by information that is relevant to their survival, and it is plausible that they also possess a variety of mechanisms for analyzing and storing it. We shall shortly take a brief look at some of the different methods that can be used to study how animals process information. First, it is worth considering why the study of animal intelligence is worthwhile.

WHY STUDY ANIMAL INTELLIGENCE?

Intellectual curiosity

A major source of motivation for any scientific enterprise is the satisfaction of intellectual curiosity; the study of animal intelligence is no different in this respect. As pets, as sources of food, or in the wild, animals often play a prominent role in our lives, and for this reason alone it is natural to wonder about their intelligence. This curiosity is enhanced by the occasional reports of apparently sophisticated

intellectual skills being displayed by animals. About a hundred years ago, there was considerable interest in a horse named Clever Hans, who, it was claimed, could count. More recently, television programs have shown dolphins allegedly engaged in a complicated dialog that enabled one to tell the other how to obtain food. There have also been claims that apes are capable of communicating with humans, and vice versa. Pigeons are said to be able to perform remarkable feats of navigation to return home from a distant and unfamiliar site of release; indeed, this topic has been the subject of correspondence to newspapers and popular scientific magazines (see pages 17 and 18). Reports such as these are bound to arouse in many a genuine curiosity concerning the mental abilities of animals, and the only way to satisfy this curiosity is to investigate further the nature of animal intelligence.

Reports that dolphins possess sophisticated skills, such as the ability to communicate complicated messages to each other, heighten our interest in the true intellectual capacity of animals.

Relevance to humans

The study of animal cognition is further justified by an interest in the intelligence of our own species. In a book on human cognition, Anderson (2005) considered the

Quicker by Tube (a selection of letters and a cartoon from the *New Scientist*)

I travel regularly on the London underground from Paddington into the City. The other morning I was waiting at the platform, the train arrived and everyone got on as normal, except that on this occasion the passengers included a pigeon. The bird hopped on rather nonchalantly and began to peck around inside the carriage. True to form none of the other commuters seemed to notice.

The doors then shut and I expected the pigeon to panic, knowing how birds normally react to being in a small space. But this truly urban bird didn't appear to notice, even when the train moved off from the station. A few minutes later we arrived at the next stop. The doors opened and the pigeon hopped out quite calmly.

As the pigeon seemed so unconcerned I can only imagine that it had done this little journey before. With their renowned navigational abilities is it possible the pigeon knew where it was going? I'd be interested to know if any other readers have observed these avian fare-dodgers.

Rachel Robson
Bayswater, London

EXTRAORDINARY! THEY SEEM TO KNOW WHERE TO GET OFF.

During 1974--76, I regularly encountered a single pigeon of light reddish colouring boarding the underground at Paddington and disembarking at the next station. Could it be the same bird that Robson saw — perhaps now having graduated to a senior citizen's pass? Or has the habit been passed on to the next generation. And if the latter, is there a genetic component in this?

Jim Brock
London

A pigeon, calm as you please, hopped into my Northern Line carriage at King's Cross and stood quite calmly near the door. The tourists did the cooing, not the pigeon; they thought it was an added London attraction and tried to tempt it with crisps, but unusually, the bird wasn't interested. It appeared to know where it was going and as soon as the doors opened at Euston, it flew out.

The second occasion was during a Piccadilly Line journey to Heathrow three weekends ago. This time the pigeon waddled in at an overground station, Hounslow Central. A bird-phobic passenger shooed it out, whereupon it repeatedly walked back in, to be hustled out again every time. The bird appeared quite determined to make its journey and when it was shooed out for a final time, just before the doors closed, it made one final frantic swoop towards the door, rather in the manner in which some human passengers launch themselves at tube doors just before they close.

From observing the birds, I feel quite sure that travel, not food, was their purpose. Pigeons are intelligent and easily trained and I see no reason why they should not have cottoned on to the fact that travel by tube saves their wings, especially as there are so many deformed and crippled pigeons in the city.

Lorna Read
London

Passenger Pigeons (a selection of letters to the *Times*)

From Lord Greenhill of Harrow

Sir

Mr Price's letter (September 10 draws attention to the intelligence of pigeons. My wife wrote similarly in your columns in December 1968, and received supporting evidence in letters from all over the world.

May I offer a further example? Some years ago I observed a flock of racing pigeons from Calais to Dover. At about mid-point a single pigeon at the rear detached itself from the flock and alighted on a lifeboat davit. It remained resting until shortly before Dover when it rejoined, no doubt considerably refreshed, its fellow competitors. I could think of no way of betraying its intelligent deceit.

Yours
GREENHILL of HARROW
House of Lords
September 10

From Vice-Admiral Sir Anthony Troup

Sir

I don't know about yachting pigeons (Michael Greville's letter of September 24) but I do know about submarine pigeons.

In 1948 I took three pigeons to sea in a submarine from Gosport as an experiment. Submerging in mid-channel for several hours and after turning many circles at depth, we surfaced and released them at thirty miles, well out of sight of land.

After release they circled the submarine three times and then flew straight home to Gosport

Yours faithfully
TONY TROUP
Bridge Gardens
Hungerford
Berkshire
September 25

From Mr Michael Greville

Sir

Until I read Lord Greenhill's observations in his letter to you today (September 17) on the apparently common tactics of racing pigeons, I had thought of my experience two years ago as unique.

I was sailing a 34ft yacht from Fecamp towards Beachy Head when, shortly after dropping the French coast, a number of these birds passed and one of them proceeded to join me on watch in the cockpit.

For six hours he kept me company, refusing all offers of hospitality (biscuits and beer) and declining to indulge in conversation, until he alighted from his perch, circled the mast head, presumably in appreciation, and flew off.

Within ten minutes the Royal Sovereign Tower was sighted, and soon Beachy Head itself.

I was most impressed by this display of constructive idleness and accurate dead reckoning to boot, but not so by the mess left on the tiller.

Yours faithfully
MICHAEL GREVILLE
79a Milson Road, W14

success of the study of artificial intelligence (AI) to mimic human intelligence. He concluded (p. 2):

> *Although this field has been an active one for half a century and there have been many notable successes, AI researchers still do not know how to create a program that matches human intelligence. No existing programs can recall facts, solve problems, reason, learn, and process language with human facility. This lack of success has occurred not because computers are inferior to human brains but because we do not yet know in sufficient detail how intelligence is organized in the brain.*

Humans have evolved from animals, and it thus seems likely that the intelligence of humans has at least something in common with the intelligence of animals. As progress is made in understanding animal intelligence we may well gain valuable insights into the mechanisms of human intelligence. For example we shall see in Chapter 13 that animals in their natural environment do not appear to communicate by means of language. The role that human language plays in problem solving is a matter of considerable debate. If it could be shown that animals possess sophisticated problem-solving skills without complex linguistic skills, then this would at least lend support to the view that human problem solving does not always depend on language.

To make a rather different point: The human brain is estimated to contain 100 billion cells, each of which is in contact with many others. Rather little is known about how this complex collection of neurons and synapses controls our thoughts, actions, sensations, and experiences. One approach to understanding the way in which the human brain functions is to study the simpler brains of animals. But unless brain researchers have a clear understanding of the cognitive processes of animals, the effects of their various experimental manipulations will be difficult to assess. In other words, it is essential to know what the animal brain is capable of achieving intellectually before it is possible to know at a physiological level how it is achieved. As this knowledge is acquired with animals, it is likely that considerable insights into the working of the human brain will follow.

Animal welfare

Another justification for studying the intelligence of animals is that it will assist us in making informed decisions about caring for them if they are to be kept in captivity. To help make this point, we shall consider briefly the welfare of chimpanzees. Our understanding of the intelligence of chimpanzees is far from complete and there is a debate about the extent to which it is similar to that of human intelligence. Some researchers (e.g. Macphail, 1982; Povinelli, 2000) maintain that there is a radical difference between the intelligence of chimpanzees and humans, whereas others are conducting studies that, if successful, will imply that the difference between chimpanzees and humans is relatively small. They are asking whether chimpanzees can communicate with humans through language (see Chapter 13), whether they are self aware (see Chapter 12), and whether they have theories about the minds of other animals (see Chapter 12). As this research progresses we are bound to gain a fuller understanding of the true nature of chimpanzee intelligence, and we will then be in a better position to make informed decisions about how best to care for them when they are held in captivity.

The only method for improving our understanding of the intelligence of a particular species is to conduct research, often using experiments, with the animals concerned. The use of experiments may raise questions as to whether the animals will suffer as a consequence. In fact, there is no reason why the majority of experiments should cause distress to the subjects, and most researchers make a considerable effort to design studies that are as benign as possible. There are several reasons why researchers are keen to minimize the suffering experienced by their subjects. First, it is unlikely that an animal will reveal its full capacity for intelligence if a test should cause it distress. Second, no normal person, including scientists, enjoys making an animal suffer. Finally, research with animals is governed by strict legal guidelines that ensure an experiment causes the minimum of distress to its subjects. These three reasons together ensure that the research in which animals are engaged is generally as harmless as possible in order to achieve the scientific goals of the research.

METHODS FOR STUDYING ANIMAL INTELLIGENCE

Physiological techniques

One route for understanding how animals process information is to investigate the nervous system directly. Accordingly, for about a hundred years now, researchers have been trying to identify the role that the brain plays when animals are confronted with a variety of tests of learning, memory, and problem solving. Despite the many advances that have been made, there is still a great deal to learn before the relationship between animal intelligence and brain function is fully understood.

One line of enquiry has been to identify the changes that take place in the nervous system during relatively straightforward learning tasks (see Macphail, 1993). Some experiments on this topic have been conducted with invertebrates because their relatively simple nervous systems are more tractable for physiological investigation than those of vertebrates. This research is based on the plausible assumption that the knowledge gained from studying simple nervous systems will prove invaluable in helping to unravel the secrets of the vastly more complex nervous systems of vertebrates. An example of what has been learned by adopting this strategy is considered in the next chapter.

Of course, a complete understanding of the vertebrate nervous system will require it to be studied directly and a considerable amount of research has already been conducted with this aim in mind. One area of interest has been to study changes that take place in the nervous system during relatively simple learning tasks, such as **Pavlovian conditioning** where a neutral stimulus signals an event of importance such as food or shock. Evidence suggests that this training makes it easier for one neuron to activate another in the cerebellum (Thompson, 1986; Tracy, Thompson, Krupa, & Thompson, 1998). It also appears that the important event excites certain neurons to a greater extent during the early than the later stages of conditioning (Schultz & Dickinson, 2000). This finding is consistent with theories of learning considered in Chapter 3, which assume that important events have their maximal impact when they are unexpected, such as at the outset of conditioning.

Another area of interest has been to identify the various intellectual functions that are carried out by different regions of the brain. By damaging the relevant regions, or by monitoring activity within them, considerable gains have been made in this respect.

A hint of the fruits of this research will be revealed in Chapter 11, where a region known as the hippocampus is shown to be involved in navigation. But progress has also been made with other intellectual skills. Different regions of the brain are believed to be important for storing different types of information (Kesner, Bolland, & Dakis, 1993). As far as retrieving information from memory is concerned, recollecting a previous event has been shown to involve a different neural system to one concerned with recognizing an event as being familiar (Aggleton & Brown, 1999). It is also believed that such regions of the brain as the amygdala (Gallagher & Holland, 1994), the hippocampus (Kaye & Pearce, 1987), and the prefrontal lobes (Dias, Robbins, & Roberts, 1996), focus attention on stimuli that are important to the animal.

As might be expected, given the complexity of the vertebrate brain, these and many other findings are fraught with interpretative problems. As a result, the precise role that a given brain region plays in a particular task is far from being fully understood. Furthermore, very little is known about the changes that occur at a cellular level during any task with vertebrates, which would constitute a complete physiological understanding of animal intelligence (see Bliss, Collingridge, & Morris, 2003, for an account of progress in this area). The use of physiological techniques will without doubt be of help in unraveling the mechanisms of vertebrate cognition, but it will take many years before we have a complete understanding of the relationship between brain and intelligence.

The study of unobservable processes

One alternative to studying the nervous system directly is to assume that an animal's brain constructs a perceptual world that corresponds to its environment (cf. Jerison, 1973). This then implies that information processing by the brain can be regarded as two distinct but related processes. The first of these is perceptual processing, in which information provided by the senses is integrated into units that correspond to features of the animal's environment. Very little is said about this type of perceptual processing in this book, not because the topic is unimportant but simply because of limitations of space. The second type of processing concerns the manner in which the brain deals with the information in the perceptual world it has constructed. It is this type of processing that is the concern of this book.

Thus if an animal is presented with a tone that signals food, we shall ignore the processes underlying the perception of these events. It will be taken for granted that their perception takes place and results in the formation of internal, central representations of the tone and food. The main focus of concern will be with such issues as identifying what information is encoded in these representations and understanding the mechanisms that enable subjects to learn about the relationships between them. In a sense, then, a central representation of an environmental event constitutes an essential component of animal cognition. The task confronting a person interested in this topic is to show what these representations consist of and how they function.

The obvious problem in studying animal cognition from this perspective is that there is no direct way of observing a central representation. It is impossible to point to any feature of an animal and identify it as being a representation of food or any other event. Instead, the existence of such representations and their properties must be inferred, and for the present the animal's behavior provides the only medium by which this can be achieved. Consequently, psychologists interested in animal cognition conduct experiments in which it is hoped that subjects act in such a way as to demonstrate unambiguously the existence and operation of a central, internal mental process. Not surprisingly, this approach is not without its pitfalls. If the operation of a central process has to be inferred from an animal's behavior, then different theorists may well appeal to different mental processes to explain the same activity. How is it possible to choose between a variety of accounts when they refer to events that are not open to direct observation? In the following discussion of the historical background to the study of animal intelligence, some of the methods that have been proposed for answering this question will be revealed.

HISTORICAL BACKGROUND

Animal intelligence has been the subject of scientific study for over a century. By way of providing a background for the material that is presented in the following chapters, the remainder of the present chapter will provide a summary of the early attempts to study the intelligent behavior of animals. An excellent account of the early years of this work can be found in Boakes (1984).

Romanes (1848–1894)

Darwin did not restrict his views on evolution to the development of physical characteristics. In his book *The descent of man and selection in relation to sex* (1871) he raised the possibility that mental abilities were also shaped by evolutionary pressures. Darwin failed to pursue this idea in much detail, but it was taken up enthusiastically by Romanes, who believed that evolution resulted in a progressive development of intelligence, culminating in the intelligence of humans. He appreciated the need for evidence to support this claim and he therefore went about collecting anecdotal reports of the intelligent behavior of many different animals. His book, *Animal intelligence*, which was published in 1882, is a compendium of reports of the intelligent behavior of different species ranging from ants to monkeys. The quotation in Box 1.1 should give a flavor of the reports it contains, and of the florid style in which they were presented.

> **BOX 1.1 An account by Romanes (1882, pp. 457–458) of the events that led him to conclude that a terrier dog is capable of reasoning by analogy**
>
> "The terrier in question followed a conveyance from the house in which I resided in the country, to a town ten miles distant. He only did this on one occasion, and about five months afterwards was taken by train to the same town as a present to some friends there. Shortly afterwards I called upon these friends in a different conveyance from the one which the dog had previously followed; but the latter may have known that the two conveyances belonged to the same house. Anyhow, after I had put up the horses at an inn, I spent the morning with the terrier and his new masters, and in the afternoon was accompanied by them to the inn. I should have mentioned that the inn was the same as that at which the conveyance had been put up on the previous occasion, five months before. Now, the dog evidently remembered this, and reasoning from analogy, inferred that I was about to return. This is shown by the fact that he stole away from our party—although at what precise moment he did so I cannot say, but it was certainly after we had arrived at the inn, for subsequently we all

> remembered his having entered the coffee room with us. Now, not only did he infer from a single precedent that I was going home, and make up his mind to go with me, but he also further reasoned thus: 'As my previous master lately sent me to town, it is probable that he does not want me to return to the country; therefore, if I am to seize this opportunity of resuming my poaching life, I must now steal a march upon the conveyance. But not only so, my former master may possibly pick me up and return with me to my proper owners; therefore I must take care only to intercept the conveyance at a point sufficiently far without the town to make sure that he will not think it worth his while to go back with me.' Complicated as this train of reasoning is, it is the simplest one I can devise to account for the fact that slightly beyond the third milestone the terrier was awaiting me, lying right in the middle of the road with his face towards the town."
> (Romanes, 1882, pp. 457–458)

Credit must be given to Romanes for being the first to seek evidence in order to understand animal intelligence, but much of the detail of his endeavor has been criticized. As these criticisms are as valid today as they were more than a hundred years ago, it is worth taking time to review them. The first criticism relates to a point that was made earlier in this chapter. That is, Romanes was unjustified in concluding that evolution would result in a progressive increase in intelligence among animals with human intelligence at its pinnacle. There is no denying that evolution is responsible for any disparities that exist among the intelligence of different species. However, if one were to consider two present-day species, all that can be said in terms of evolution is that the development of these two species has followed different routes, and that they may therefore differ in their intelligence. It does not follow from evolutionary principles that one species will necessarily be more intelligent than the other.

A second criticism that can be leveled at the approach adopted by Romanes is the reliance on anecdotal evidence. His book contains many remarkable stories about the intelligence of a wide variety of animals, but it is impossible to know how seriously the anecdotes should be taken. It is possible that some of the reports were tinged by wishful thinking on behalf of the observer, and some may have been entirely fictitious. How can a reader of his book be confident that each report constitutes a true record of what actually occurred? This rhetorical question may seem harsh, but unless an example of an animal behaving intelligently is observed in carefully controlled conditions, the example does not constitute proper scientific evidence on which to base the study of animal intelligence.

A third criticism is that Romanes was too generous in the explanations he offered for the behavior recorded in the anecdotes. If the behavior of an animal resembled the way a human might behave in a similar situation, he believed the thought processes responsible for the human's behavior would also take place in the animal. This **anthropomorphic** strategy is clearly evident in the interpretation of the terrier's behavior offered in the quotation in Box 1.1, and there is a serious limitation with this type of explanation for an animal's behavior. An anthropomorphic explanation is based on an argument by analogy. That is, it is being assumed that because an animal behaves in a similar way to a human, then the explanation for their behavior will be similar. Arguments based on analogy are inductive arguments—the conclusion they lead to may be true, but not necessarily true. Thus the similarity between

KEY TERM

Anthropomorphic The use of anthropomorphism, which is the attribution of human thought processes to animals when they behave in a similar way to humans.

the behavior of an animal and a human allows us to conclude that the animal might have engaged in the same mental processes as the human, but it is also possible that these processes are very different. Anecdotes do not allow a choice to be made between these alternatives, what is needed, as will become evident throughout this book, is evidence from an experiment.

The temptation to attribute human feelings and experiences to animals remains to this day. Itani (2004, p. 228) provides the following quote from a psychologist called Roger Fouts, who works with chimpanzees and who communicates with them using sign language (see Chapter 13). The most famous of these chimpanzees is Washoe. Fouts (1997) states:

When I looked into Washoe's eyes she caught my gaze and regarded me thoughtfully, just like my own son did. There was a person inside that ape "costume". And in those moments of steady eye contact I knew that Washoe was a child.

To labor the point that has just been made, it is possible that Washoe has similar mental experiences to a child, but it is also possible that Washoe has a very different type of mental experience, or no mental experience at all. Gazing into her eyes will not resolve this issue.

Anthropomorphic accounts of animal behavior have their uses. On the one hand, they may point to new hypotheses about the nature of animal intelligence, but these hypotheses must then be tested scientifically. On the other hand, they serve to bring to life descriptions of behavior in a way that would be impossible if only the actions of the animal were recorded. With this in mind, I was unable to resist including in Box 1.2 a paragraph that was written by an early explorer of Antarctica after he encountered penguins for the first time. The penguins were on the edge of an ice floe. For readers who had never seen a penguin this description must have been particularly vivid but, of course, they would have been wrong to infer from it that this animal has "unchristian" thoughts, or any other thoughts.

BOX 1.2 An engaging description of the behavior of penguins by an early explorer of Antarctica

"The life of an Adelie penguin is one of the most unchristian and successful in the world. The penguin which went in for being a true believer would never stand the ghost of a chance. Watch them go to bathe. Some fifty or sixty agitated birds are gathered upon the ice-foot, peering over the edge, telling one another how nice it will be, and what a good dinner they are going to have. But this is all swank: they are really worried by a horrid suspicion that a sea-leopard is waiting to eat the first to dive. The really noble bird, according to our theories, would say, 'I will go first and if I am killed I shall at any rate have died unselfishly, sacrificing my life for my companions'; and in time all the most noble birds would be dead. What they really do is to try and persuade a companion of weaker mind to plunge; failing this, they hastily pass a conscription act and push him over. And then—bang, helter-skelter, in go all the rest" (Cherry-Garrard, 2003, p. 581, originally published, 1922).

Penguins must have been an unusual sight for early explorers of Antarctica. Even though anthropomorphic descriptions of their behavior would help readers at home imagine what penguins look like, they would reveal nothing about their mental lives.

KEY TERM

Trial and error learning A change in behavior that results from an animal making a response that, by chance, leads to reward.

Lloyd Morgan (1852–1936)

Shortly after Romanes published his book on animal intelligence, many of the shortcomings with his method of study were identified by Lloyd Morgan (1890), who attempted to bring more rigor to the study of animal intelligence. Morgan criticized the reliance on anecdotal evidence and urged the use of experiments. It must be admitted that not all of his experiments were of a high standard, but they made some important points. In one investigation he would throw a nine-inch stick over some railings that were six inches apart. His dog, Tony, would then retrieve the stick, but took many trials to learn how to negotiate the railings so that the stick did not get caught as he passed through them to return the stick to his master. If Tony had been capable of reasoning in the manner proposed by Romanes, then he should have inferred from the outset how to negotiate the railings without getting the stick caught. On another occasion, Morgan observed his dog as he put his put his head through the railings of a gate to gaze into the road. By chance Tony lifted his head, and the latch, and thereby opened the gate and was able to escape (Figure 1.5). During the course of the next three weeks, this performance improved gradually until Tony was able to go to the gate and open it efficiently. On the basis of these findings, Morgan concluded that animals do not solve problems through sophisticated reasoning processes. Instead, the gradual improvement in the performance of Tony led him to conclude that when animals encounter a problem they solve it by **trial and error learning**, which improves with practice. Additional support for this analysis can be found in the observation that Tony always raised the latch with the back of his head,

FIGURE 1.5 Lloyd Morgan's dog, Tony, using trial-and-error learning to open a gate (from Morgan, 1900).

rather than his muzzle, which might have been his preferred method if he had had the mental agility to decide upon the most efficient means of opening the gate.

There are, therefore, at least two different explanations for how animals open gates: One is based on the supposition that animals are capable of reasoning; the other on the supposition that animals solve problems through trial and error. In the absence of relevant experimental evidence, how can we choose between them? Another important contribution by Morgan was to provide a straightforward answer to this question which has come to be known as Lloyd Morgan's canon (Morgan, 1894, p. 53):

In no case may we interpret an action as the outcome of the exercise of a higher psychical faculty, if it can be interpreted as the outcome of one that stands lower in the psychological scale.

In other words, the best explanation is one that refers to the simplest psychological mechanisms. Few would disagree with the claim that solving a problem through trial and error depends on simpler mechanisms than solving it through reasoning, which means that the explanation offered by Morgan is to be preferred to the one offered by Romanes.

Morgan's contribution to the study of animal intelligence is reflected in the approach adopted by many investigators to this day. To understand a particular aspect of an animal's behavior a variety of explanations may be developed. They will be presented in the simplest possible terms, with little reference to sophisticated theoretical constructs. To test the explanations, experiments are conducted. Gradually, this process will yield a substantial body of experimental evidence that—with luck—supports a particular theory and, at the same time, contradicts a number of others.

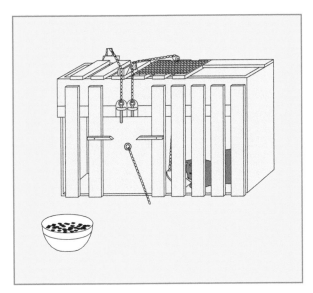

FIGURE 1.6 A sketch of a typical puzzle box used in experiments by Thorndike with cats (adapted from Thorndike, 1898).

Thorndike (1874–1949)

Without question, Morgan made a valuable contribution to the study of animal intelligence, but the sophistication of his experimental approach left something to be desired. As a response to this shortcoming, Thorndike, an American psychologist, embarked on a series of experiments to give the "*coup de grace* to the despised notion that animals reason" (Thorndike, 1898, p. 39). This research entailed the study of animals escaping from puzzle boxes, and the stimulus–response theory it led to was to exert a profound influence on the study of animal intelligence.

In a typical experiment, a cat was placed into a box with a bowl of food outside (Figure 1.6). To reach the food, the cat had to respond in a specified way to open a door, perhaps by pulling a lever. Initially, the cat would scratch and struggle in the box, and it was a considerable time before it responded correctly. Having made the correct response, the cat was allowed a few moments of access to food before being returned to the box for another trial. Thorndike's main concern was with the time it took the cat to escape from the apparatus across successive trials (Thorndike, 1911). The results from two cats are plotted in the learning curves in Figure 1.7. The vertical axis of each graph represents the time in seconds that a subject

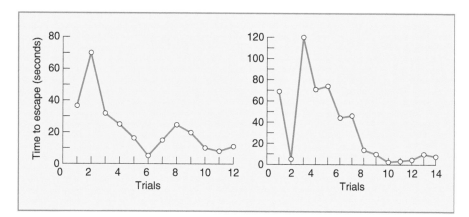

FIGURE 1.7 The time taken by two individual cats to escape from a puzzle box across successive trials (from Thorndike, 1898).

took to escape from the box on any trial. The horizontal axis represents successive trials. It is evident that the time, or latency, to escape decreased over trials. Thorndike (1911) regarded this change as evidence of learning, which raised two crucially important issues: On the one hand, Thorndike was concerned with identifying what the subject had learned; and on the other, he wanted to specify as carefully as possible the conditions that promoted this learning.

Thorndike (1911) placed a great deal of emphasis on the fact that in general the decline in the latency to escape with continued training was gradual. This, he maintained, was clear evidence that animals did not use reason or thought to solve the problem. If these processes had been employed, then the learning curve should drop suddenly at the point where the correct solution occurred to the cat. Prior to this there should have been little improvement in performance, because the subject would be ignorant of the solution to the problem. From his results, Thorndike (1911) argued that problem solving is achieved not by reasoning but by a process of trial and error. That is, after being placed into the box, the subject eventually, and quite by chance, performed the correct response—perhaps by accidentally knocking the lever—and was able to escape. The subsequent decline in escape latencies was attributed to the food serving to stamp in or strengthen the correct response. This strengthening process was held to be gradual, which accounted for the progressive decline in latencies.

To say that Thorndike (1911) regarded the response itself as being strengthened is an oversimplification. In fact, he proposed that the food served to strengthen a hypothetical connection between, on the one hand, the neural center responsible for the perception of the stimuli that were present immediately prior to the execution of the response and, on the other, the center responsible for the performance of the response itself. The greater the strength of this connection, or stimulus–response (S–R) association, the greater the likelihood of the animal responding correctly in the presence of the stimuli. These views were expressed as the Law of Effect (Thorndike, 1911, p. 244):

> *Of several responses made to the same situation, those which are accompanied or closely followed by satisfaction to the animal will, other things being equal, be more firmly connected with the situation.*

This law summarizes Thorndike's view of animal intelligence, and it is clear that he did not regard this capacity as involving sophisticated mental processes. The only reference to such processes is the proposal that learning consists of the gradual strengthening of a connection between neural centers concerned with the perception of a stimulus and the performance of a response. This approach is nowadays regarded as too simple, but at the time it was extremely influential and, together with the proposal that reward is essential for learning, set the stage for more than 50 years of vigorous research and theoretical debate.

The method employed by Thorndike to study animal intelligence is now referred to either as **instrumental or as operant conditioning**. It is characterized by the experimenter delivering an event such as food to an animal after it has responded in a certain way.

Watson (1878–1958)

The quotation in Box 1.1 makes it clear that Romanes was quite happy to view animals as having mental states that served as the impetus for their actions. Watson (1913, 1914) objected vigorously to this type of mentalistic explanation for behavior. He maintained that mental states are private experiences that cannot be measured objectively. One might, for example, explain the behavior of a rat running down an alley for food by saying that it is doing so because it desires food. However, it is impossible to perform any sort of experiment that can evaluate this hypothesis. I know what it means to desire food from my personal experiences, but there is no test that I can conduct to determine whether a rat experiences a similar mental state as it runs down an alley. Indeed, Watson argued that it is impossible to know whether rats, or any other animal, experience mental states at all. A rat may behave as if it desires food, but this does not mean it has the experience of desire. Such a conclusion is not permitted because it is impossible to get into the mind of a rat, if they have one, to learn about the nature of its conscious mental experience.

Watson (1913, 1914) advocated that psychologists should become behaviorists. This meant studying only what can be observed—behavior—and to eschew any reference to mentalistic terms. Once he had adopted this position he was forced to attack Thorndike's Law of Effect because it made reference to the mental state of satisfaction. The proposal that a dog will continue making a response that leads to satisfaction is impossible to evaluate because there is no method of knowing when a dog experiences satisfaction. Watson therefore suggested that two factors would determine the response that is most likely to occur in a given context. One factor is the frequency with which the response has occurred in that context; the other is whether the response was the last one to be made in that context.

To help clarify this principle of recency, consider again a cat that has been placed in a puzzle box. The response that leads to the door being opened is likely to be the last response that the cat makes in the box before it leaves to eat the food outside. According to Watson, this same response will now be more likely to occur when the cat is returned to the box. We shall see shortly in the discussion of the contribution made by Guthrie to the study of animal intelligence that there is some merit to the principle of recency as a replacement to the Law of Effect. We shall also see (in Chapter 4) that it is possible to provide a nonmentalistic definition of what constitutes satisfaction and retain the Law of Effect.

Pavlov (1849–1936)

At much the same time as Thorndike was conducting his studies, the Russian physiologist, Pavlov, was using a fundamentally different procedure to study learning in animals. Instead of waiting for his subjects to respond before delivering food, he delivered it independently of the animal's behavior whenever a particular signal had just been presented. This procedure is referred to as either "Pavlovian" or "classical" conditioning. The term **conditioned stimulus (CS)** refers to the signal; the term **unconditioned stimulus (US)** refers to the stimulus with which it is paired.

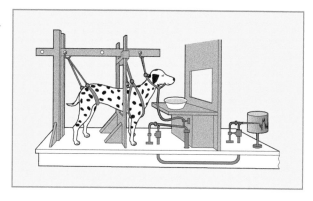

FIGURE 1.8 Diagram of the apparatus used by Pavlov for his study of classical conditioning with dogs (adapted from Yerkes & Morgulis, 1909).

The subjects in many of Pavlov's (1927) experiments were hungry dogs. They were lightly restrained in an experimental chamber, such as that depicted in Figure 1.8, and the CS—for example, the ticking of a metronome—was presented for a number of seconds before the delivery of the food US. At first the animal would show little reaction to the metronome but, as conditioning progressed, Pavlov (1927) noted that the dog salivated during the CS even before the food was delivered. This response was defined as the "conditioned response" (CR). Because dogs do not normally salivate when they hear a metronome, such a change in behavior can be regarded as evidence of learning.

The quotation in Box 1.3 provides an account of a typical experiment in Pavlov's laboratory as witnessed by a representative of the British Foreign Office in 1934. The lives of the dogs appear to have been more comfortable than for many of the citizens of Russia, who at that time were under the rule of Stalin. No doubt Watson would have objected, justifiably, to the mentalistic language that the dog learns "to expect" food, and "thinks" food is coming.

BOX 1.3 A description of one of Pavlov's experiment by a British diplomat who worked in Russia and who visited his laboratory in 1934

"We saw a dog in a lighted sound-proof chamber where he can be observed through a tiny window. A tube which acts in the same way as a dentist's drain passes through one cheek and draws off saliva from one of the three pairs of salivary glands. At five-minute intervals a signal is given in the chamber: a metronome ticks, a light appears, a musical note is sounded. Some of these mean that food is coming, some that food is not coming. For instance, food follows the ticking of a metronome at a certain rate, but not the ticking at half that rate. The dog learns when to expect food. When he thinks food is coming, the saliva necessary for digestion begins to form; one-third of it is drawn off, and the amount is shown by an instrument outside the chamber. The dog we saw was not very practised, and also, according to the observer, rather stupid. He produced some—though not much—saliva even when no food was coming. The dog seemed perfectly content, and looked quite indifferent when the tube was pulled out of the little hole in his cheek. He seemed fond of the professor and gave him a paw when asked to do so. We saw other dogs too who are used for the experiment, and they wagged their tails and seemed pleased to see the professor. The professor claimed that when they have been used for a certain time they are pensioned off and all the dogs eventually die of old age. They have a garden to themselves with a swimming-pool and other doggish delights" (Bullard & Bullard, 2000, pp. 254–255).

KEY TERMS

Conditioned stimulus (CS)
The neutral stimulus used for Pavlovian conditioning.

Unconditioned stimulus (US)
The biologically significant stimulus that is presented after a conditioned stimulus for Pavlovian conditioning. The pairing of the conditioned and unconditioned stimulus results in the former eliciting a conditioned response (CR).

At first sight, it may seem that not much can be gained for our understanding of animal intelligence from Pavlovian conditioning. After all, teaching a dog to salivate to a ticking metronome might be thought to reveal rather little about how animals cope with the many problems that confront their fight for survival. The method of conditioning developed by Pavlov will, however, be referred to frequently in the forthcoming chapters, where it will be shown to be an essential tool for studying the fundamental mechanisms of learning in animals.

It must also be said that when Pavlov's work became known outside Russia it had a widespread impact. The visit of the British Foreign Office official to his laboratory is evidence of this impact. A further indication of this impact can be found in a story reported by Catania and Laties (1999). Apparently, after hearing about the work of Pavlov, the author H. G. Wells considered the following hypothetical problem. He was asked to imagine standing on a pier, with the playwright George Bernard Shaw drowning on one side and Pavlov on the other. Given only one lifebelt, Wells had to decide to whom it should be thrown. According to Skinner (1976, p. 301), Wells replied that Pavlov:

> . . . is a star which lights the world shining above a vista hitherto unexplored. Why should I hesitate with the lifebelt for one moment?

I suspect that Shaw would have quickly found a good reason. Not only did the work of Pavlov make a deep impression on H. G. Wells, it also had a profound effect on the influential behaviorist B. F. Skinner who, on hearing Wells' reply, decided to abandon a career in literature and pursue one in behavioral science (Skinner, 1979).

The stimulus–response theorists

Following the publication of the work by Pavlov and Thorndike, a number of North American psychologists attempted to develop sophisticated accounts of behavior from the premise that all learning involves the formation of S–R connections. Thus, despite the different methods involved in Pavlovian and instrumental conditioning, they were both assumed to result in the formation of Thorndike's S–R connections. As far as Pavlovian conditioning is concerned, these connections were held to be between a representation of the CS and a component of the response elicited by the US.

Hull (1884–1952)

One attempt to address the weakness identified by Watson in Thorndike's Law of Effect was made by Hull (1943), who proposed that satisfaction can be regarded as a reduction in any of the animal's needs. This led him to develop a version of S–R theory that placed considerable importance on the way needs influence both what the animal learns and what it does. Hull suggested that all needs activate a single central motivational state that he termed **drive**. An S–R connection was supposed to be strengthened whenever a response was followed by a reduction in the level of drive. Hence it was only responses that led to a reduction in a need that could be learned.

Although they provide a clearer specification than Thorndike of when learning will occur, there are still problems with Hull's proposals. For instance, Olds and

KEY TERM

Drive
A theoretical state that was proposed by Hull to energize behavior. Drive is excited by the presence of any need.

Milner (1954) demonstrated that rats can be trained to press a lever if it results in the electrical stimulation of certain regions of the brain. The need that is reduced in these circumstances is hard to identify, yet learning has clearly occurred. A further property of drive is that it can energize whatever response the animal is currently performing. If it is pressing a lever for food, then the hungrier the animal is, the greater will be the level of drive and the more rapidly will it respond. Although this prediction has been confirmed (see Bolles, 1975, p. 95), other predictions from the theory have been proved wrong. For example, the level of drive of an animal that is both hungry and thirsty will be greater than that of one that is just hungry. According to Hull's theory, therefore, being thirsty should enhance the rate at which an animal responds for food. In fact it is generally found that thirst has the opposite effect (e.g. Capaldi, Hovancik, & Lamb, 1975).

Guthrie (1886–1959)

One of Guthrie's (1935) main concerns was Thorndike's (1911) claim that reward, however it is defined, is essential for strengthening an S–R connection. As a simpler alternative he offered the principle of contiguity, which stipulates that the mere pairing of a stimulus and a response is sufficient for learning to take place and result in the formation of an S–R connection:

> *A combination of stimuli which has accompanied a movement will on its recurrence tend to be followed by that movement (Guthrie, 1935, p. 36).*

Obviously, an animal in a test chamber will make a number of responses in addition to the one that leads to reward, and it is necessary to explain why only this last one shows a marked increase in frequency. Guthrie's (1935) solution to this problem was to follow Watson's lead and to suggest that a response will be connected to a set of stimuli only if it is the last one to occur in their presence. He further maintained that the delivery of reward will produce a marked environmental change, and this ensures that the instrumental response is connected to the stimuli that preceded its delivery. Support for this interpretation can be found in the surprising outcome of an experiment by Fowler and Miller (1963).

Hungry rats were trained to run down a straight alley for food. One group received only this treatment, whereas the others were given a mild shock to their feet as they were about to consume food in the goal box. For one group the shock was administered to the front paws, for the other group it was administered to the hind paws. The purpose of these different methods for delivering shock was to ensure that the shock induced different responses. When it was delivered to the front paws the rats lurched backwards, whereas they jumped forwards when the hind paws were shocked. Although the effect of such punishment in terms of the Law of Effect has not been considered, in keeping with common sense the law asserts that shock should disrupt running to the goal in both cases. By contrast, if Guthrie's (1935) claim that the mere pairing of a stimulus and a response is sufficient to strengthen an S–R connection is correct, then a different outcome is anticipated. While the rats are running down the alley for food, the lurch forward produced by shock to the hind paws will make them run faster. The pairing of this response with the apparatus cues will then strengthen an S (alley) R (rapid running) connection, so that when placed into the alley subjects would be likely to run rapidly even before the shock is administered.

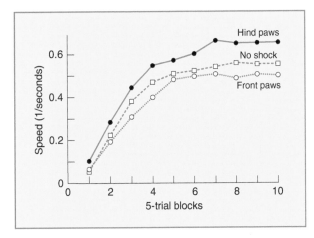

FIGURE 1.9 Speed of running down an alley for food by groups of rats that were shocked near the goal to either their front paws, or hind paws, or that received no shock in the alley (adapted from Fowler & Miller, 1963).

The results depicted in Figure 1.9 support this interpretation by showing that the group receiving the hind-paw shock actually ran faster down the alley than the group receiving only food in the goal box. The figure also shows that running, relative to the food-only group, was disrupted when the shock was administered to the front paws. In this instance the jerk backwards would be the response that became connected to the alley cues, and its performance prior to the shock should disrupt running.

These findings do not challenge Thorndike's claim that all learning consists of the formation of S–R connections. They do suggest, however, that reward or punishment is not essential for this learning to take place. In the aforementioned study it was found that the mere contiguity of the alley cues and the shock-elicited response was sufficient to influence what the rats learned. Many, more recent, studies also support this conclusion, and it is now accepted that reward, however it is defined, is by no means essential for learning to occur.

Tolman (1886–1959)

For Tolman, an essential feature of instrumental conditioning is that it results in behavior that is goal directed or purposive. If a rat has been trained to press a lever for food, then Tolman regards this response as being directed towards the goal of obtaining food. This seemingly obvious interpretation is completely lacking from S–R theory, which asserts that all an animal learns during instrumental conditioning is to respond in the presence of a given set of stimuli. It can even be said that because there is no mechanism in S–R theory that allows animals to anticipate the rewards of their behavior, then whenever reward is delivered, it comes as a complete surprise.

The S–R analysis of Pavlovian conditioning is similarly counterintuitive. When a CS and a US are repeatedly paired, the theory states that animals will learn to perform a response whenever the CS is presented. No additional learning is assumed that would enable the subject to expect, during the CS, the US that is soon to follow.

Tolman (1932) viewed these as grave shortcomings of animal learning theory and developed a purposive account of behavior, which rejected the S–R connection as the unit of learning. As far as Pavlovian conditioning is concerned, animals were assumed to learn a CS–US connection that made the CS a sign for the forthcoming US. For instrumental conditioning, the fundamental unit of learning was an S–R–US connection. The initial S–R link in this chain is similar to its counterpart in S–R theory, but the additional, final link permits the animal to know the consequences of its actions while it is responding. The precise manner in which these units operated is not of present concern; what should be stressed is that Tolman's (1932) formulation is a radical departure from S–R theory because it enables animals to anticipate stimuli that will soon be presented to them. Thus animals can be regarded as acquiring knowledge rather than responses, and it is this that marks Tolman's approach as cognitive rather than behavioral.

Tolman (1932) also objected to the claim of S–R theory that reward is essential for learning. Instead, rather like Guthrie, he suggested that for both CS–US and

S–R–US learning to take place, all that was necessary was the contiguous pairing of the appropriate stimuli and responses.

Animals were not regarded as passive learners simply acquiring a collection of CS–US and S–R–US units as they interacted with their environment. They were seen, instead, as active processors of information integrating previously gained knowledge, as the following quotation concerning the operation of the brain (central office) indicates (Tolman, 1948, p. 192):

> *We assert that the central office is far more like a map control room than it is like an old-fashioned telephone exchange. The stimuli which are allowed in are not connected by just one-to-one switches to the outgoing responses. Rather, the incoming impulses are usually worked over and elaborated in the central control room into a tentative cognitive-like map of the environment. And it is this tentative map, indicating routes and paths and environmental relationships, which finally determines what responses, if any, the animal will finally release.*

This excerpt captures the essence of an extremely original view of animal intelligence that anticipated by 25 years or so contemporary accounts of information processing in animals. Thus there is now abundant evidence that Pavlovian conditioning can result in the formation of CS–US connections, or associations, as they are now called (see Chapter 2). There is also evidence that, during instrumental conditioning, animals learn about the relationship between responses and their consequences (see Chapter 4). The notion that animals form cognitive maps is also growing in popularity (see Chapter 11). During his lifetime, however, Tolman's critique and experiments led to the refinement and increasing complexity of S–R theory rather than to its downfall.

In concluding this brief history, it is worth stating that the demise of S–R theory was not brought about by its failure to explain effects with which it was principally concerned, namely, instrumental conditioning. Instead, the decline in popularity of this theory was brought about by a resurgence of interest in the 1960s and 1970s in the mechanisms of Pavlovian conditioning. It soon became apparent that attempts to explain all the effects obtained with this technique in terms of S–R learning would be unsuccessful. As a consequence, more cognitive explanations were developed to explain these findings, and this has been accompanied by a growth of interest in the cognitive mechanisms underlying behavior in general.

CHAPTER 2

CONTENTS

Associative learning

In an animal's environment, one event will often reliably predict another. The ingestion of certain flavors will be followed by illness, whereas ingestion of others will lead to beneficial consequences. Some environments will frequently be visited by predators, others will not. In addition, the action of the animal itself may result in consistent consequences: Following a certain route might take it to food or water, whereas different paths might lead to danger. An animal that knows about these relationships will benefit because it will be able to anticipate future events and behave appropriately in preparation for them. But how can this knowledge be acquired? In an unchanging world animals could be born with it so that, for instance, contact with food of a certain flavor would automatically result in it being consumed or rejected. However, the world is not unchanging. At the very least, the location of food will change from generation to generation, and so too might the relationship between the taste or sight of food and its gastric consequences. Accordingly, animals must themselves discover which events reliably signal important events, and an important way of achieving this is by the process of associative learning.

Associative learning can be said to have taken place when there is a change in an animal's behavior as a result of one event being paired with another. Two different methods that have proved extremely useful for the study of associative learning were described in the historical survey at the end of Chapter 1. One method is exemplified by Pavlovian conditioning, where the two events that are paired together are a neutral conditioned stimulus (CS) and a biologically significant unconditioned stimulus (US). The other method is instrumental conditioning, in which a response made by the animal constitutes one event, and the outcome of that response constitutes the second event. In this chapter, and in Chapter 3, we concentrate on what Pavlovian conditioning has revealed about the mechanisms of associative learning. We will then turn to an examination of instrumental conditioning in Chapter 4.

At first sight there may seem to be little of interest in studying the process that enables a dog to salivate in the presence of a light paired with food, or a rabbit to blink whenever it hears a tone that signals a mild cheek shock. But once it is acknowledged that these conditioned responses (CRs) are a product of a process that is essential for learning about the sequential structure of the environment, then they take on a fundamentally important significance. Their occurrence allows us to study in detail a basic learning process.

The first part of this chapter describes some different **excitatory** and **inhibitory conditioning** techniques that have proved particularly useful for the study of associative learning. Both excitatory and inhibitory conditioning are believed to be effective because they result in a relatively permanent change within the animal. In the second part of this chapter we shall look at what is known about the nature of this change. The third, and final, part of the chapter will consider the factors that determine how an animal will react to a CS that has been paired with a US.

Animals must learn to adapt in line with environmental changes. The source of food for these elephants will change over time, as supplies are exhausted. Associative learning, therefore, becomes imperative to ensure survival.

CONDITIONING TECHNIQUES

Excitatory conditioning

Eye-blink conditioning

For eye-blink conditioning the subject, normally a rabbit, is restrained in a stock or harness, and a number of light-weight sensors are placed near its eye. Rabbits possess an outer and an inner eyelid, and the equipment can permit the recording of a small movement of either. Conditioning consists of the presentation of a relatively brief CS—say a 300-millisecond tone—followed by the delivery of a mild shock to the cheek. In most cases, the intensity of the shock is just sufficient to produce a blink. After a number of CS–US pairings, the CS, which by itself should not make the rabbit blink, is often found to elicit this response. The results from a typical study are presented in the left-hand side of Figure 2.1, which shows the percentage of trials on which a blink was detected during the CS across successive blocks of 100 trials. The right-hand side depicts the effects of **extinction** in which the CS is presented but is no longer followed by shock. A term that is frequently used in discussions of learning curves is the **asymptote**.

Moore (1972) describes an experiment, in which rabbits first received conditioning, in which a 1200-Hz tone signaled the delivery of shock. Test trials were then given in which the same tone was presented intermixed with tones of different frequencies.

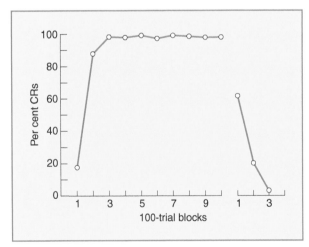

FIGURE 2.1 The acquisition and extinction of an eye-blink conditioned response (CR) to a tone conditioned stimulus (CS) by rabbits (adapted from Gibbs, Latham, & Gormezano, 1978).

The results from these test trials can be seen in Figure 2.2. The percentage of trials on which a CR was recorded was maximal for the 1200-Hz tone and, when other tones were presented, the likelihood of this response declined. The extent of this decline was greater for stimuli that were further removed from the training stimulus. The fact that responding occurs at all with conditions that differ from those present during training demonstrates **stimulus generalization**, and when the extent of this generalization is incomplete this is said to reflect generalization decrement.

Autoshaping

With autoshaping, a hungry pigeon is placed in a conditioning chamber such as that depicted in Figure 2.3. At intervals of about 1 minute a Perspex panel is illuminated for about 5 seconds and then food is delivered to a hopper. At first, subjects may be unresponsive to the panel, but after a few trials they will peck it rapidly whenever it is illuminated. Note this is not an example of instrumental conditioning as the pigeon does not have to peck the key to obtain food. Instead, it is an example of Pavlovian conditioning, as the mere pairing of the illuminated panel with food is sufficient to engender a CR of key pecking. A typical learning curve produced by this training is presented in Figure 2.4.

Conditioned suppression

In a procedure known either as conditioned suppression or conditioned emotional response (CER), subjects—very often rats—are first trained in an operant chamber in which they must press a lever to obtain food. Conditioning, which takes place in

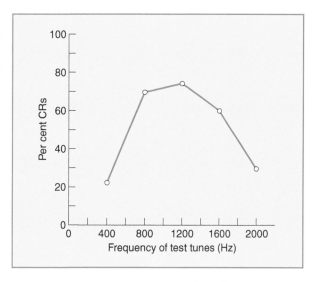

FIGURE 2.2 The strength of an eye-blink conditioned response (CR) to tones of different frequencies after conditioning with a tone of 1200 Hertz (adapted from Moore, 1972).

FIGURE 2.3 A typical conditioning chamber for pigeons.

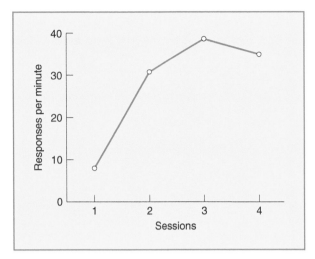

FIGURE 2.4 The rate of key-pecking by a group of pigeons for which the illumination of a response key by white light for 10 seconds signaled the delivery of food. There were ten conditioning trials in each session (unpublished study by Pearce).

this chamber while the subject is pressing the lever, consists of pairing a stimulus that lasts for about 1 minute with a relatively mild shock delivered through the grid floor. There may be four such trials in each session, which itself may last for an hour or more.

When it is first presented, the signal for shock will have little influence on the rate of lever pressing. But as conditioning trials continue, so a gradual decline in the rate of responding will be recorded until eventually the lever may not be pressed at all during the CS. As soon as the shock has been delivered, lever pressing recovers rapidly to its normal rate and remains at this level until the next trial. It is important to be aware that the cessation of lever pressing has no influence on the outcome of the trial, so that shock is presented irrespective of the animal's behavior. The decline in responding during the CS is regarded as evidence of successful Pavlovian conditioning.

The measure of conditioning is the extent to which the CS reduces the rate of lever pressing. The slower the response rate during the CS, the more effective conditioning is assumed to be. Because rats vary considerably in the rate at which they press a lever for food, it has not proved useful to look directly at the rate of responding during the CS as a measure of conditioning. Instead, a suppression ratio is computed according to the formula $a/(a + b)$. The value of a is determined by the rate of lever pressing during the CS, and b is the rate during a short interval immediately before the onset of the CS. A ratio of 0.50 indicates that these rates are equal and that conditioning is ineffective, whereas a ratio of 0.00 shows that no responses at all were performed during the CS and that conditioning has been maximally effective. Figure 2.5 (left-hand side) presents the results from a typical study in which the value of the average suppression ratio for a group of rats declines across successive trials. The right-hand side of this figure shows the effects of extinction, when the CS was no longer followed by the foot shock.

FIGURE 2.5 Acquisition and extinction of conditioned suppression by rats to a 60-second conditioned stimulus (CS) that was paired with foot shock (adapted from Hall & Pearce, 1979).

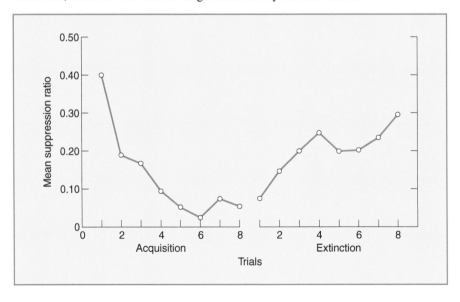

Taste aversion conditioning

The final example of a technique for Pavlovian conditioning was mentioned briefly in Chapter 1. If an animal is made ill after consuming a particular food, by being injected with a mild poison such as lithium chloride, it will develop a marked aversion to the flavor of that food. This technique has a number of characteristics that set it apart from many other methods of conditioning. It is often extremely effective with only a single trial, and intervals of several hours between the CS and the onset of illness can be employed with little detriment to learning. None the less, in most respects the effects of this procedure resemble those of other methods of conditioning, and for this reason it has proved an extremely useful tool for the study of the general principles of associative learning.

The need for control groups

The above examples give some indication of the methods that can be used to train an animal to produce a response to a CS. It was suggested in the introduction to this chapter that our interest in Pavlovian conditioning lies not so much in the opportunity it offers for changing an animal's behavior, but in the opportunity it provides for understanding how animals learn about regularly occurring sequences of stimuli. Although the results from the above examples imply that this learning has taken place, an experiment by Sheafor (1975) highlights the possibility that this may not be the case. Two groups of thirsty rabbits received training in which they were presented with a brief tone and a squirt of water into the mouth. For Group T–W the tone preceded the water, whereas for Group T/W the tone and water were separated by an interval of 12 minutes.

The results from this study are presented in Figure 2.6, which shows, for each group, the percentage of trials with the tone that were accompanied by a movement of the jaw. For Group T–W the frequency of this response increased to a substantial and consistent level across the first 48 sessions. As the tone preceded the delivery of water, this jaw movement could be regarded as a CR showing that subjects had detected the relationship between the two stimuli. From this point of view the results from Group T/W are surprising as the tone and water were unpaired and yet substantial jaw movement was also recorded during the tone.

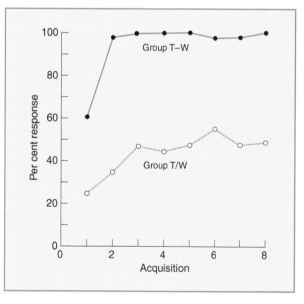

FIGURE 2.6 Percentage of trials on which a jaw movement was recorded in the presence of a tone, as a function of 6-day blocks, with 1 tone presentation each day. The tone was paired with water for Group T–W and unpaired with water for Group T/W (adapted from Sheafor, 1975).

The findings for Group T/W are worrying because they indicate that a response that can be considered to be a CR occurs to the tone, even when it is not paired with water. In these circumstances it would be unwise to regard the existence of jaw movement as evidence that rabbits had learned that the tone was a signal for water, and it becomes necessary to consider when a response can be safely used to indicate such learning.

One solution to this problem is to use a control group which would be treated in much the same way as Group T–W, by giving it the same amount of exposure to the tone and water, but these events should not be consistently paired. If pairing the tone and water enables animals to learn that the tone is a signal for water, then such training should produce a stronger CR than for the control group. According to Rescorla (1967), a useful control treatment is one that is referred to as the **truly random control**. An alternative method, which was employed for Group T/W is to ensure that the CS and US are never paired. The considerable level of responding by this group to the tone indicates that it would be unwise to attribute all the jaw movements elicited by this stimulus in Group T–W to associative learning. Nevertheless, the substantially greater level of responding by Group T–W than by Group T/W indicates that the pairing of the tone and water was responsible for at least some of the responding, and this is the necessary evidence to infer that associative learning has taken place.

The reasons for the jaw movements during the tone in Group T/W are not entirely clear but it may be of some interest to consider Sheafor's (1975) explanation. He proposed that the experience of water in the test chambers resulted in rabbits persistently expecting this US. Normally, this expectancy does not result in a response, but one can be readily triggered if a relatively salient stimulus such as a tone is presented.

Whatever the merits of this account, the point to stress is that a response that resembles a CR does not only occur when a CS and US are paired. Occasionally, such a response may be observed when the CS is presented, either alone or unpaired in respect to the US. In view of this possibility the best way of being certain that a response is a consequence of associative learning is to compare the level of responding produced by a conditioning schedule with that engendered by the appropriate control. Unfortunately the use of control groups is time-consuming, and they are not always employed. Yet, without them, the conclusions that can be drawn from an experiment will be limited.

Inhibitory conditioning

Excitatory conditioning was said to be of interest because it allows us to study the way in which animals are able to learn that one stimulus signals another. But in an animal's environment, stimuli may conceivably signal that important events will not occur. Such stimuli are of potential importance because they might indicate places that are free from danger, or regions where food and water are not found. If Pavlovian conditioning allows animals to learn that one stimulus signals another, then we might also expect the appropriate training will allow them to learn the opposite—that one stimulus indicates another will not occur. Inhibitory conditioning refers to any method of training in which a stimulus is used specifically to signal the omission of a US.

Hearst and Franklin (1977) placed pigeons into a chamber containing a food hopper and two response keys. The keys were illuminated one at a time for 20 seconds in a random sequence, with an interval averaging 80 seconds between successive illuminations. During this interval food was occasionally delivered to the hopper, but food was never available when a key was lit. The position of the subject in the chamber was monitored continuously throughout this training. As the training progressed, the pigeons displayed a marked tendency to move away from the key that was illuminated. This finding suggests that they are capable of learning that stimuli signal the omission of food and that they can withdraw from such stimuli. One technique, therefore, for inhibitory conditioning is to ensure that the US is delivered in the absence but not the presence of the CS.

The study of inhibitory conditioning did not start with the experiment by Hearst and Franklin (1977). Long before their study, Pavlov (1927) had devised an alternative method to study the effects of this type of conditioning. An example of

Pavlov's pioneering technique is provided by Zimmer-Hart and Rescorla (1974). In the first stage of their experiment, a tone signaled shock for conditioned suppression training. Trials in which the tone was paired with shock were then intermixed with trials in which the tone was accompanied by a light and not followed by shock. Initially, the magnitude of conditioned suppression during the compound was much the same as that during the tone (Figure 2.7) but, as training progressed, the presence of the light on compound trials counteracted the suppressive effects of the tone. This pattern of responding suggests animals learned that the light signaled the omission of shock and that this opposed the properties of the tone.

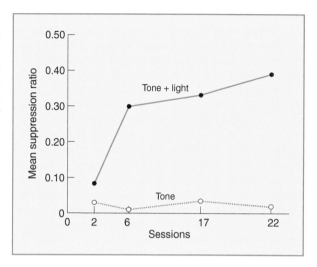

FIGURE 2.7 Mean suppression ratios for rats given excitatory conditioning with a tone intermixed among trials with a light-tone compound followed by nothing (adapted from Zimmer-Hart & Rescorla, 1974).

The detection of conditioned inhibition

A problem that occurs in many studies of conditioned inhibition is that it is not immediately apparent that animals have learned anything about the conditioned inhibitor—that is, the stimulus that signals the omission of the US. This is because conditioned inhibitors rarely elicit a CR on their own. The study by Hearst and Franklin (1977) is unusual in this respect because their subjects moved away from the key light, but frequently a conditioned inhibitor by itself has no effect at all on behavior. To return to the study by Zimmer-Hart and Rescorla (1974), had they presented the light alone rather than in compound with the tone, it would have had very little influence on the rate of lever pressing. How then can we be certain that animals have learned anything about this stimulus? One answer to this question, at least for the Zimmer-Hart and Rescorla (1974) study, would be to point to its effects on the compound trials. But on these trials it is possible that the subjects learned nothing about the light itself; they may merely have learned that the configuration of the light and tone together was followed by nothing. To refute this explanation, and to show that a conditioned inhibitor can have properties of its own, two techniques have been developed to reveal the existence of conditioned inhibition: the summation and the **retardation test** (Rescorla, 1969; Williams, Overmier, & LoLordo, 1992).

The retardation test

The retardation test involves pairing the conditioned inhibitor directly with the US. If the initial inhibitory conditioning has resulted in a stimulus being regarded as a signal for the absence of a US, then it should be difficult to convert this stimulus into a signal for the US. A formal explanation of this effect is elaborated in Chapter 3, but for the moment it should not be too surprising.

A demonstration of a successful retardation test is provided by Pearce, Nicholas, and Dickinson (1982). After receiving training similar to that employed by Zimmer-Hart and Rescorla (1974), an experimental group (Group E) was given conditioned suppression training in which the inhibitory CS was paired with shock. A control group (Group C) also received these pairings but without any prior training. The course of excitatory conditioning with the stimulus is depicted in Figure 2.8. Evidently the retardation test was successful because conditioning

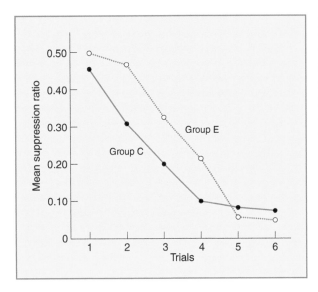

FIGURE 2.8 Acquisition of conditioned suppression to a conditioned stimulus (CS) that was novel (Group C) or one that had previously signaled the omission of shock (Group E) (adapted from Pearce et al., 1982).

progressed more slowly for Group E than Group C. One important point to note is that on the first test trial the CS had no influence at all on responding in Group E. On this basis there would be little reason for believing that it had acquired any special properties as a result of the prior training. This emphasizes the need for special tests to reveal the effects of inhibitory conditioning.

The summation test

The experiment by Zimmer-Hart and Rescorla (1974) revealed that the light counteracted the CR elicited by the tone. This effect was attributed to the stimulus serving as a signal for the omission of the US. If this is correct, then this property of a conditioned inhibitor should be evident whenever it is accompanied by a CS that has been paired with the US in question. A demonstration of this transfer can be found in another conditioned suppression study by Pearce et al. (1982).

Rats were first trained with three types of trial: a tone paired with shock, a clicker paired with the same shock, and a clicker–light compound followed by nothing. Eventually, a strong CR was observed in the presence of the tone and the clicker, but not during the clicker–light compound. To test whether the influence of the light on the clicker could transfer to the tone, a single test session was administered. Trials in which the tone was presented alone were intermixed among trials with a light–tone compound. The results in the right-hand pair of histograms of Figure 2.9 show that the strength of the CR, as indexed by the suppression ratio, was substantially greater to the tone than to the compound. For purposes of comparison, the left-hand pair of histograms shows the difference in responding to the clicker and the clicker–light compound for the final training session. Evidently the influence of the light transferred very well from the clicker to the tone, and this constitutes a successful **summation test** for conditioned inhibition.

For a variety of reasons, Rescorla (1969) has argued that the ideal method for determining whether a stimulus is a conditioned inhibitor is to conduct both the retardation and the summation tests. If the stimulus passes both of these tests, then it can be concluded with some confidence that it is a conditioned inhibitor and effectively serves as a signal for the absence of a US.

THE NATURE OF ASSOCIATIVE LEARNING

Both excitatory and inhibitory conditioning can result in a relatively permanent change in the way an animal reacts to an initially neutral stimulus. To be effective, therefore, these procedures must produce an equally permanent change within the animal. The purpose of this section is to elucidate the nature of this change. Few would deny that successful conditioning depends on modifications that take place within the nervous system. In the first part of this section we consider briefly what is known about the neural processes that underpin associative learning. In fact, rather little is known about these processes and a number of researchers have found it more useful to concentrate on identifying the knowledge that is acquired by an animal during the course of Pavlovian conditioning. The findings that have resulted from pursuing this line of enquiry are reviewed in the remainder of this section.

A neural model of excitatory learning

It might come as something of a surprise to discover that some of the more important advances in our understanding of the physiological basis of learning have derived from research with the rather unattractive animal shown in Figure 2.10. The figure shows two views of the large marine snail, *Aplysia californica* (the head is at the right-hand end). *Aplysia* lives on seaweed, individuals can weigh as much as 7 kilograms and can grow to about 1 meter in length.

In case the reader should wonder why anyone would want to study conditioning in this creature, the answer lies in part in the structure of its nervous system. This contains a rather small number (20,000) of relatively large (1 millimeter in diameter) neurons, which makes it easy to identify individual neurons, as well as neural pathways. These properties have made it possible to understand the changes that take place in the nervous system of *Aplysia* during Pavlovian conditioning.

If a stimulus is applied to the siphon, or the mantle shelf, of an *Aplysia* it will withdraw its respiratory organ, the gill (Carew, Pinsker, & Kandel, 1972). Of present interest is the finding that the strength of the withdrawal reflex is enhanced if stimulation of either the siphon or the mantle shelf is followed by an electric shock to the tail. For example, Carew, Hawkins, and Kandel (1983) presented a discrimination in which mild stimulation of the siphon of some animals, or the gills of others, was followed immediately by a tail shock for 1 second. After 2.5 minutes, the other region was then stimulated, but on this trial shock was not presented. For the sake of convenience, stimulation of the region that signaled shock will be referred to as CS+, whereas stimulation of the region that did not signal shock will be referred to as CS−.

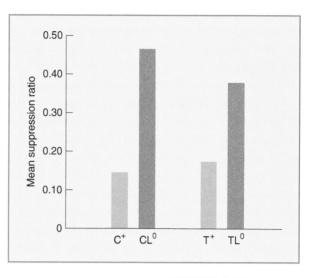

FIGURE 2.9 Mean suppression ratios on the final session of training for a group of rats that had received clicker–shock trials (C+) intermixed among trials in which a clicker–light compound was followed by nothing (CL⁰, left-hand pair of histograms), and on a test session when they were given a tone that had previously signaled shock (T+), and a compound composed of the tone and the light (TL⁰, right-hand pair of histograms) (adapted from Pearce et al., 1982).

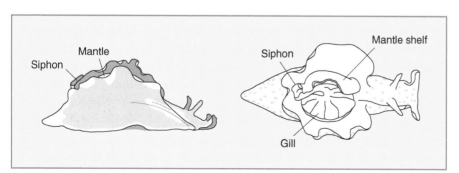

FIGURE 2.10 A view of *Aplysia californica* from (left) the side and (right) above.

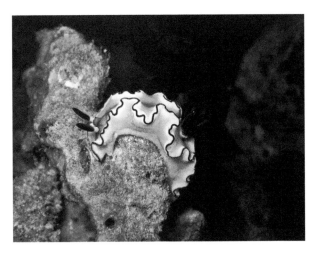

Aplysia (small marine gastropod molluscs of the suborder Anaspidea), display evidence of discrimination learning.

The histograms in Figure 2.11 show the duration of gill withdrawal on a test trial with each CS prior to conditioning and on a test trial after conditioning. Shock was not presented on these test trials. At first, both CS+ and CS− elicited gill withdrawal for about 5 seconds, but at the end of conditioning this response was considerably stronger in the presence of CS+. The slight increase in responding that occurred to CS− indicates that even the unpaired experience of this stimulus and the tail shock was sufficient to enhance the strength of the response elicited by CS−. However, the fact that the strength of responding to CS+ was very much greater than to CS− demonstrates the importance of the paired relationship between CS+ and the tail shock. In other words, the stronger responding to CS+ than to CS− provides a convincing demonstration of successful Pavlovian conditioning with *Aplysia*. In one respect, this demonstration of Pavlovian conditioning is unusual because it shows a strengthening of a response that was already elicited by the CS. This type of conditioning is referred to as **alpha conditioning**, and can be contrasted with the findings from many other studies where at least a component of the CR bears no resemblance to the responses initially elicited by the CS.

A sketch of one of the neural pathways involved in the conditioning that has just been described is shown in Figure 2.12 (Kandel & Hawkins, 1992; see also Hawkins & Kandel, 1984). The two sensory neurons can be excited by stimulating the siphon (upper neuron) or the mantle shelf (lower neuron). These neurons make synaptic contact with a motor neuron that is responsible for gill withdrawal. Thus, in normal circumstances, stimulating the siphon area will excite a sensory neuron that will then excite the motor neuron and cause the gill to withdraw. The figure also shows a third sensory neuron that can be excited by a shock to the tail. This neuron is in synaptic contact with a modulatory interneuron that in turn makes contact with synapses of the other sensory neurons. This sketch is a gross oversimplification of the actual circuitry as each neuron is in contact with many other neurons.

To identify the changes that take place in this circuit during conditioning, Hawkins et al. (1983) capitalized on the large size of the neurons, and placed stimulating electrodes in a sensory neuron for the siphon area and for the mantle shelf. Stimulation of a sensory neuron for the siphon (CS+) was followed immediately by a tail shock, whereas stimulation of a sensory neuron for the mantle shelf (CS−) was never followed by shock. In addition, a recording electrode was placed in a motor neuron that was in contact with the two selected sensory neurons. The level of activity in the motor neuron was recorded after CS+ and CS−

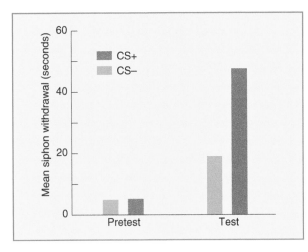

FIGURE 2.11 Mean duration of siphon withdrawal by *Aplysia* to a stimulus that was either paired with shock (CS+) or presented by itself (CS−) on test trials that were conducted before and after conditioning (adapted from Macphail, 1993).

on a pretest trial that was conducted prior to conditioning and on a test trial that was conducted after five conditioning trials with each stimulus. The results from the tests, expressed as a percentage of the activity recorded on the pretest trials are shown in Figure 2.13. The figure makes it clear that conditioning enabled CS+ to increase considerably the level of electrical activity in the motor neuron, whereas CS− had little effect on the activity in this neuron.

In essence, this experiment by Hawkins et al. (1983) demonstrates that when the stimulation of one sensory neuron is followed a short time later by a tail shock, then its ability to excite the motor neuron is increased. Kandel and Hawkins (1992) have argued that this enhanced influence of the sensory neuron is due to biochemical changes that take place at the synapse between the sensory and motor neuron. The catalyst for these changes is provided by the interneuron. Whenever shock is administered to the tail, the interneuron releases serotonin at its synapses with sensory neurons. If a sensory neuron should fire at much the same time as this release of serotonin, then a relatively permanent change takes place within the sensory neuron that enables it to release a greater amount of neurotransmitter than would normally occur. Subsequent stimulation of the sensory neuron will then release this abnormally large amount of neurotransmitter and result in a strong response in the motor neuron.

Thus the basis of associative learning appears to be an enhancement of the ease with which one neuron can excite another. There is no evidence to suggest that this learning depends on the growth of new neural connections, or synapses. Instead, learning simply depends on a change in the effectiveness of existing connections. We shall see over the course of the next few chapters that this finding is remarkably in keeping with current theoretical views about learning.

Stimulus generalization can also be explained with the sort of circuit shown in Figure 2.12. Instead of exciting a single sensory neuron, a CS is likely to excite a collection of sensory neurons, each of which could acquire the capacity to excite a motor neuron. The strength of the response to a CS would then be determined by the number of motor neurons it excites. The presentation of a slightly different CS will excite some, but not all, of the sensory neurons excited by the original CS. The new CS will thus elicit a CR, and provide evidence of stimulus generalization; but the strength of the CR will be weaker than to the original CS. If it is assumed that the degree of similarity between two stimuli determines the number of sensory neurons that they both excite, then this account correctly predicts that the amount of stimulus generalization will be determined by the similarity of the test and training stimuli.

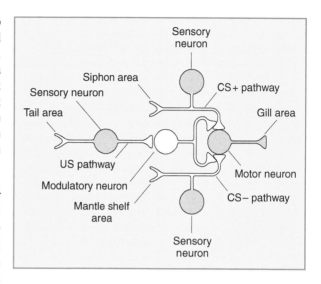

FIGURE 2.12 A simplified diagram of the neural pathways that are involved in conditioning with *Aplysia*.

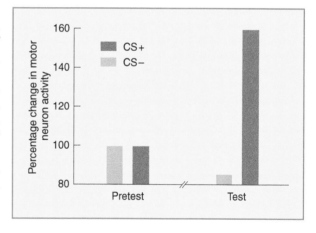

FIGURE 2.13 Mean percentage of change in motor neuron activity in *Aplysia* to stimulation of one sensory neuron that was paired with tail shock (CS+) and to another sensory neuron that was never followed by shock (CS−), on test trials that were conducted before and after conditioning (adapted from Macphail, 1993).

A memory model for associative learning

The nervous system of vertebrates is very much more complex than of invertebrates and we do not yet know if the physiological changes that have just been described also underlie associative learning in this group of animals. As a consequence, theorists with an interest in the changes responsible for learning in vertebrates tend not to talk in terms of physiological processes. Instead, they prefer to work within the framework provided by an information-processing model of conditioning. An example of such a model is shown in Figure 2.14.

Stimuli such as a CS or US can be detected by a sensory register that excites a representation of these events in a memory system. Activation of the representation of the US will lead to the activation of a center in a system concerned with response generation and thus elicit an unconditioned response. As a result of the repeated pairing of a CS and a US, there are two possible changes that can take place within this model. On the one hand, a CS–R connection might develop, so that whenever the CS is presented it will directly excite the US response center and lead to a response that mimics the one elicited by the US. In other words, this conceptualization is based on the assumption that Pavlovian conditioning results in the growth of S–R connections, or associations. These proposals are very much in keeping with the way in which the S–R theorists mentioned in Chapter 1 conceptualized the conditioning process. They are also consistent with the findings by Kandel with *Aplysia*. The sensory and motor neurons in these animals can be said to provide a rudimentary counterpart to the stimulus and response centers shown in Figure 2.14.

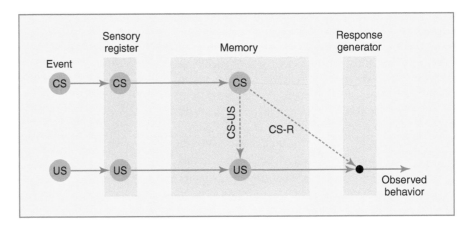

FIGURE 2.14 Two possible accounts of what is learned during Pavlovian conditioning; the solid arrows are permanent connections, the dashed arrows are a consequence of conditioning. A CS and US can be detected by the sensory register, which leads to representations of these events being activated in memory. Whenever the US representation is activated it will produce a response by activating a center in the system concerned with response generation. According to one account, conditioning will result in the growth of a CS–US association so that the CR will be an indirect consequence of the CS activating the US representation. The alternative S–R account assumes that conditioning strengthens a CS–R association and thus allows the CS to excite the CR directly. CR, conditioned response; CS, conditioned stimulus; R, response; S, stimulus; US, unconditioned stimulus.

FIGURE 2.15 A typical CR of magazine activity by a rat during a CS that signals the delivery of food.

Alternatively, Pavlovian conditioning could result in the growth of a connection between the CS and US representations. Subsequent presentations of the CS will then excite the representation of the US which will then excite a response. Although the findings with *Aplysia* do not support this possibility, experiments with vertebrates lend it considerable support.

The idea that the CS retrieves a memory of the US, which is then responsible for generating the CR, was tested by Colwill and Motzkin (1994). Hungry rats in a conditioning chamber were occasionally presented with a tone that signaled food pellets and a light that signaled sucrose solution. In fact, the design of this study was more complicated than is indicated here, but its details have been overlooked for the sake of simplifying the description of the experiment. The training by Colwill and Motzkin (1994) resulted in subjects performing a CR during either the tone or light of approaching the magazine where the two outcomes were delivered (an example of this response can be seen in Figure 2.15). The rats then received training in which they were allowed to consume food and sucrose in different sessions. Consumption of food was followed by an injection of lithium chloride to condition an aversion to it, but consumption of sucrose solution was not. After several sessions of this training, rats were extremely reluctant to eat the food, but they willingly consumed the sucrose solution. The critical aspect of the experiment was a test trial in which rats were again presented with the tone and light in the conditioning chamber, but on this occasion neither stimulus was followed by an outcome. The rats were much more willing to approach the magazine during the light than the tone. These results are depicted in Figure 2.16, which reveals the frequency with which magazine activity was observed to occur during the tone and light in the test session.

These results are entirely consistent with the proposal that Pavlovian conditioning results in the growth of CS–US associations. On the test session, the tone will activate a representation of food that has been rendered unattractive by

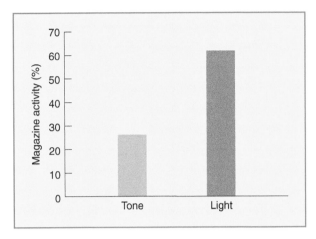

FIGURE 2.16 The frequency of magazine activity in the presence of the tone and light during the test session in the study by Colwill and Motzkin (1994).

the taste-aversion training. The activation of this representation by the tone will then be unlikely to excite magazine activity, because there is little point in going to a magazine for food that is undesirable. During the light, on the other hand, the representation that it activates of sucrose will still be attractive and thus encourage rats to approach the magazine.

We should also consider the implications of these results for an S–R analysis of conditioning. According to this theory, the initial training will result in an association being formed between each of the tone and light and the response of approaching the magazine, so that whenever either of these stimuli is presented it will automatically make the animal move towards the magazine. An important feature of S–R theory is that the responses elicited by a stimulus can be altered only by making the animal perform a different response in its presence. Because the tone was not presented in the second stage of the experiment, there was no opportunity for its influence to be altered and responding during the tone and light should have been similar during the test trials. The clear difference between the results for the tone and light in the final stage of the experiment is thus very difficult for S–R theory to explain. It would be a mistake to conclude, however, that no stimulus–response connections were formed during the initial stage of the experiment. Inspection of Figure 2.16 will show that during the test trials subjects would occasionally head towards the food magazine during the tone. If the taste aversion training had been completely effective, then the rats should make no effort at all to approach the magazine in the test stage because of a profound aversion to eating the food pellets. The responses during the tone on the test trials may thus have been a consequence of S–R associations that were formed during the initial training. If this is correct, then we must conclude that the training by Colwill and Motzkin (1994) resulted in both S–R and CS–US learning. Further evidence is presented shortly that shows that Pavlovian conditioning will, at least on occasion, permit the growth of S–R associations. But first, we shall examine two further studies that demonstrate that this training can also foster CS–US associations.

Table 2.1 summarizes the design of an ingenious experiment by Holland (1990). Hungry rats in a conditioning chamber occasionally heard either a tone or white noise for 10 seconds. The tone signaled the delivery of sucrose solution flavored with wintergreen, and the noise signaled a similar solution flavored with peppermint. As a result of this training, Holland (1990) hoped that the rats would anticipate wintergreen-flavored sucrose whenever they heard the tone, and peppermint-flavored sucrose whenever they heard the noise. The rats were then allowed to drink sucrose flavored with wintergreen for 5 minutes, in the absence any auditory stimulus, before being injected with the poison lithium chloride. The purpose of this treatment was to condition an aversion to the flavor of wintergreen. Finally, the animals were allowed to consume plain sucrose solution in the presence of each auditory stimulus. By carefully observing the animals, Holland discovered that they reacted very differently in the presence of the two stimuli. During the noise the rats showed a typical ingestive reaction, comprising rhythmic mouth movements, tongue protrusions, and paw licking. On the other hand, in the

> **TABLE 2.1** Summary of the design of an experiment involving a single group of rats by Holland (1990)
>
> | Stage 1 | Stage 2 | Test |
> | --- | --- | --- |
> | Tone → sucrose + wintergreen | Sucrose + wintergreen → lithium chloride | Tone + sucrose |
> | Noise → sucrose + peppermint | | Noise + sucrose |

presence of the tone they showed a marked aversive reaction, which consisted of gaping, chin rubbing, head shaking, and flailing of the forelimbs. Holland argued that this second response was due to the tone retrieving a memory of wintergreen-flavored sucrose. The rats then reacted as if this flavor, which had been made aversive by the second stage of training, were actually present. Holland (1990) cites a number of additional findings that lend considerable support to this conclusion.

These last results imply that activating a memory of a stimulus is in many respects equivalent to presenting the stimulus itself. If this is correct, then it should be possible to conduct conditioning with an activated memory of a stimulus in much the same way as it is possible to conduct conditioning with that stimulus. A remarkable experiment by Holland (1981) provides striking support for this prediction. Two groups of rats were first placed into a conditioning chamber where, every few minutes, a tone was presented for 10 seconds and then followed immediately by a distinctively flavored food pellet. In the next stage of the experiment, both groups again received the tone but this time it was not followed by food. For the experimental group, the tone was followed by an injection of lithium chloride, whereas for the control group these two events were presented in an unpaired fashion. Holland argued that during the second stage the tone should activate a memory of flavored food with which it had been paired and that, for the experimental group, once activated this memory would then become associated with the poison. A test of this proposal was conducted in a final session in which both groups had free access to the food. In keeping with Holland's predictions, the experimental rats revealed an acquired aversion to the food by eating rather little of it, relative to the controls.

STIMULUS–STIMULUS LEARNING

The results in the previous section show that, at least for vertebrates, Pavlovian conditioning can result in the growth of a connection between internal representations of the CS and US. There is no good reason, however, for believing that associative learning will be confined to those occasions when a US is presented. The following examples show that associations can develop between two stimuli, even when neither of them has any unconditioned properties.

Serial conditioning

In **serial conditioning**, a sequence of stimuli precedes the US—for example, a tone might be followed by a light, which would be followed by food. Despite being rather

> **KEY TERM**
>
> **Serial conditioning**
> Training in which two or more conditioned stimuli are presented in sequence and followed by a single unconditioned stimulus.

distant from the US, the initial element of the sequence will often elicit a CR, although it may be weaker than the response observed in the presence of the element that is closer to the US. An interesting feature of serial conditioning is revealed in a study by Holland and Ross (1981), who trained rats with the sequence light–tone–food. The normal conditioned response to a light that signals food is rearing or magazine approach; for a tone it is either head jerking or magazine approach. After a number of sessions of serial conditioning it was found that during the light there was little magazine activity but there was a considerable amount of head jerking. This led Holland and Ross (1981) to suggest that during serial conditioning the presence of the first element causes animals to anticipate the second one and to respond as if it were actually present.

Sensory preconditioning

A rather different demonstration for the development of stimulus–stimulus associations is provided by **sensory preconditioning**. In an experiment by Rizley and Rescorla (1972), rats first received the sequence of a light followed by a tone for a number of trials. The tone was then paired with shock and, finally, the light was found to elicit a substantial fear CR when it was presented for testing. The generally accepted explanation for this finding is that during the first stage subjects acquired a light–tone association, and in the second stage a tone–shock association. When the light was then presented alone it would activate a memory of the tone, which, in turn, would activate a memory of the shock and lead to an aversive CR.

Second-order conditioning

The final method that shows evidence of associations being formed between two stimuli is known as **second-order, or higher-order, conditioning**. We shall see that depending on certain details this training can result in different outcomes.

Two types of conditioning trial are administered for second-order conditioning. Initially, first-order conditioning is conducted in which a neutral stimulus, CS1, is paired with a US until a stable CR is recorded. At this point additional trials are introduced in which a new stimulus, CS2, precedes CS1 but the US is omitted. With the right amount of training, a CR can be observed during CS2 even though this stimulus itself is never paired with the US.

Pavlov (1927) was the first to report this effect, but a more recent example will be described (Rashotte, Griffin, & Sisk, 1977). Pigeons first received autoshaping in which the illumination of a key by white light for 6 seconds signaled food; additional trials were then introduced in which the key was illuminated by blue light for 6 seconds, followed by white light for the same amount of time. Food was not presented on these second-order conditioning trials. Figure 2.17 shows, for the second-order conditioning stage, the percentage of trials in any session on which at least one peck was directed towards these stimuli. The success of second-order conditioning is revealed by the increase in responding to CS2.

One explanation for successful second-order conditioning is that pairing a second-order CS (CS2), with one that has already been paired with a US (CS1) will foster a CS2–CS1 association. A subsequent occurrence of CS2 should then activate a representation of CS1, which should then activate a representation of the US and elicit a response. Some evidence supports this proposal, and some contradicts it.

KEY TERMS

Sensory preconditioning
Training in which two stimuli, A and B, are presented together before B is paired with an unconditioned stimulus.

Second-order, or higher-order, conditioning
Training in which two stimuli, A and B, are presented together after B has been paired with an unconditioned stimulus.

Evidence that favors this analysis can be found in a further stage of the study by Rashotte et al. (1977). An outline of the various stages of the experiment is shown in the upper half of Table 2.2. After second-order conditioning, Rashotte et al. (1977) gave Group E a series of extinction trials in which the white key light (CS1) was presented alone. This training was intended to abolish its association with food, and it was soon found that pecking at the white key declined to a very low level. When the blue key light (CS2) was again shown for the final test trials, it should still activate a representation of the white key, by virtue of the prior second-order conditioning. However, activation of this latter representation should no longer excite a memory of food, and pecking at blue should not take place. For Group C, which did not receive the extinction training with white, the presence of both an effective blue–white and a white–food association should allow blue to activate a representation of the food and engender a high rate of responding. In keeping with this analysis it was found on the test session that Group C responded significantly more rapidly than Group E in the presence of CS2.

Evidence to the contrary—that second-order conditioning does not enable CS2 to retrieve information about CS1—is provided by Rizley and Rescorla (1972). The design of their experiment is very similar to that of Rashotte et al. (1977) and is presented in the lower half of Table 2.2. The methods differed principally in that Rizley and Rescorla (1972) used conditioned suppression. Two groups of rats received first-order conditioning with a tone signaling shock, and second-order conditioning in which a light was followed by the tone and no shock. Group E was then given extinction training with the tone. Although this treatment abolished the CR to the tone, the subsequent presentation of the second-order light CS elicited a very strong CR, which did not differ in magnitude from that performed by Group C. This finding makes it difficult to believe that a light-tone association was formed during second-order conditioning, for if it had been, extinction with the tone should

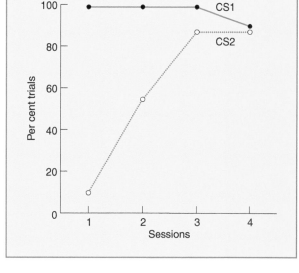

FIGURE 2.17 Number of trials in each second-order conditioning session for which at least one peck was recorded to the previously trained white CS1 and to the second-order blue CS2 (adapted from Rashotte et al., 1977).

TABLE 2.2 Summary of the stimuli used in the second-order conditioning studies by Rashotte, Griffin, and Sisk (1977) and by Rizley and Rescorla (1972)

	First-order conditioning	Second-order conditioning	Extinction	Test
Rashotte, Griffin, and Sisk (1977)				
Group E	White → Food	Blue → White	White	Blue
Group C	White → Food	Blue → White	–	Blue
Rizley and Rescorla (1972)				
Group E	Tone → Shock	Light → Tone	Tone	Light
Group C	Tone → Shock	Light → Tone	–	Light

have reduced the CR recorded during the light. Moreover, this outcome is not unique: Holland and Rescorla (1975) have obtained a similar effect with rats using appetitive conditioning.

One explanation for the findings by Rizley and Rescorla (1972) is that second-order conditioning resulted in an S–R association being formed between CS2 and the response elicited by CS1. Thus, as a result of the first-order conditioning, the tone may have aroused a CR of fear (for want of a better word), which was associated directly with the light. If this account is correct, then manipulations of the tone–shock association should not influence the light–fear association and hence leave unaffected the prior second-order conditioning.

What, then, determines the nature of the associations that are formed during second-order conditioning? According to Rescorla (1980), one answer to this question is the similarity of CS1 and CS2. When the stimuli are similar, such as the illumination of a key by different colors, then a CS2–CS1 association will be formed. When the stimuli are very different, for example if they are from different modalities, then CS2 will become associated with the response elicited by CS1. Of course, this account is incomplete. It does not explain why stimulus similarity should be so important in determining the outcome of second-order conditioning. And as it stands, it leads to the incorrect expectation that first-order conditioning will only permit S–R associations because the CS and US are so different.

THE NATURE OF US REPRESENTATIONS

Conditioned excitation

Thus far we have said that the CS is able to activate a memory or representation of the US, but what does this mean as far as animals are concerned? I do not wish to imply for one moment that when the CS is presented to a rat it has a mental experience of remembering the US in much the same way as we may remember what we ate for our last meal. There are simply no methods that would allow us to determine whether or not animals have this type of mental experience. Holland (1990) favors the proposal that, after conditioning, the CS is able to activate some of the perceptual mechanisms that are normally activated by the US. A similar idea has been proposed to account for certain aspects of human memory (e.g. Finke, 1980; Farah, 1985). One implication of this proposal is that whenever a CS is presented it will evoke a sort of hallucination of the US with which it is paired (Konorski, 1967). Whether this is true remains to be determined; for the present it is safe to conclude that at least in some circumstances a CS can activate, or retrieve, information about the US. All this means is that once information about the US is activated it can influence the animal's behavior, and enable further learning about the US even though it is absent.

Given such a conclusion, it then becomes meaningful to enquire about the nature of the information that is activated. According to Konorski (1967), unconditioned stimuli possess two different characteristics: specific and affective. Specific characteristics are those that make the US unique: the place where it is delivered, its duration, intensity, and so on. Affective characteristics, by contrast, are those that the US has in common with other stimuli and reflect its motivational quality. Thus food, water, and an opportunity to mate have the common appetitive characteristic that animals will actively search for them. Conversely, electric shock, illness, and loud noise possess the common aversive characteristic that animals will do their best to minimize their contact with them. For humans, this distinction can be summarized by saying that appetitive events arouse a state of satisfaction, whereas aversive events arouse an unpleasant state of discomfort or pain.

Konorski (1967) suspected that a CS may be capable of retrieving information about the specific or about the affective attributes of the US, or indeed about both simultaneously. We can return to the study by Holland (1990) for evidence that a CS can retrieve information about the specific attributes of the US. In that study, Holland found that pairing wintergreen-flavored solution with illness affected the responses during a tone that had been paired with the same flavored solution, but not during a noise that had been paired with a peppermint-flavored solution. Unless the noise and tone could retrieve specific information about the flavors of the solutions with which they had been paired, they should both have elicited the same responses on the test trials.

For evidence that a CS is capable of retrieving information about the affective characteristics of a US, we must consider the effects of an experimental manipulation known as **blocking**. In the first stage of an experiment by Kamin (1969) Group E, but not Group C, was given pairings of a noise with shock. For the second stage, both groups received a compound composed of the noise and a light that was repeatedly paired with shock. Finally, test trials involving the light by itself were given. On the test trials with the light there was virtually no evidence of a CR in Group E, whereas one of considerable strength was recorded for Group C. For Group E, therefore, the original training with the noise was somehow responsible for preventing, or blocking, learning about the light during compound conditioning.

The reason why blocking occurs will be considered in some detail in Chapter 3. For the present, it is important to note that blocking can be disrupted if the US is changed for the second stage of training. Thus Dickinson (1977) has found that blocking does not occur if the US is food in Stage 1 and shock in Stage 2. This type of finding has led to the informal suggestion that blocking will be most effective when the US that is delivered in Stage 2 corresponds to the memory of the US that was presented in Stage 1. But should this correspondence be between the affective or the specific properties of the US? This question is impossible to answer on the basis of the study by Dickinson, because both properties were changed. However, an experiment by Ganesan and Pearce (1988) found that blocking was not at all disrupted when the US was changed from water in Stage 1 to food in Stage 2. Such a finding suggests that blocking will be effective, provided that the general, affective properties of the US remain unchanged throughout the training stages of experiment. In other words, for blocking to have taken place in the study by Ganesan and Pearce (1988), the CS presented in Stage 1 must have become associated with a memory of the nonspecific, appetitive attributes of the water US (for a similar finding, see Williams, 1994).

A second reason for believing that a CS can activate an affective representation of the US comes from studies showing that conditioning can sometimes be facilitated if the CS has previously been paired with a different US of related affective value. Pearce, Montgomery, and Dickinson (1981), for instance, conducted rabbit eye-blink conditioning in which, for Group E, a brief light signaled shock to the cheek; Group C did not receive this training. Then, in the test phase of the experiment, both groups were conditioned with the light signaling shock to the opposite cheek. Acquisition of an eye-blink CR in these circumstances was considerably more rapid for Group E than Group C, which suggests that the original conditioning with the light resulted in it retrieving information that was not entirely specific to the cheek where the US was applied. The implication of this study—and this is certainly the view advocated by Konorski (1967)—is that once an association has been formed between a CS and the affective properties of a US, this facilitates the learning necessary for the occurrence of specific CRs, such as eye-blink, when the US is applied elsewhere.

There are, therefore, good reasons for believing that a CS can retrieve information about either the specific or the affective properties of a US. Unfortunately, rather little is known about the circumstances that promote learning about these different properties, and that determine when information about these properties will be effective. For example, prior to our experiment (Ganesan & Pearce, 1988) we were uncertain as to whether or not blocking would be effective when the US was switched from water to food.

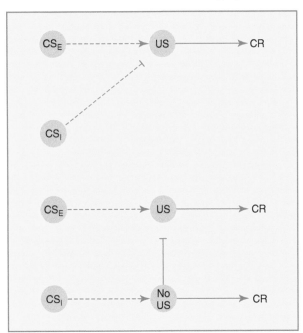

FIGURE 2.18 Two possible models of the learning that occurs during inhibitory conditioning. The arrows and stopped lines depict excitatory and inhibitory links, respectively; the solid lines depict permanent links; the dashed lines depict conditioned links; the circles denote representations in memory. CR, conditioned response; CS$_E$, excitatory conditioned stimulus; CS$_I$, inhibitory conditioned stimulus; US, unconditioned stimulus.

Conditioned inhibition

It is natural to assume in the case of excitatory conditioning that representations of the CS and US become associated, as these events are paired. But where inhibitory learning is concerned, the event associated with the inhibitory CS is less obvious. After all, this stimulus is not usually followed by any tangible event.

One possibility is that as a result of signaling the omission of a US, the presence of an inhibitory CS makes it more difficult to activate a representation of the US. This point of view has been expressed by Konorski (1948) and Rescorla (1979). Both assume that an excitatory CS is capable of activating a representation of the US with which it is paired. If this excitatory stimulus, CS$_E$, should be presented in compound with another stimulus and the US is withheld, an inhibitory link is assumed to be formed between the representation of the latter stimulus, CS$_I$, and the US representation excited by CS$_E$. This relationship is depicted in the upper half of Figure 2.18. The subsequent presentation of CS$_I$ will then serve to dampen the US representation that is activated by any excitatory CS with which it is concurrently paired. A consequence of this dampening will be to reduce the strength of the excitatory CR. If CS$_I$ should be paired with the US in a retardation test, then, although an association will grow between a representation of CS and the US; the existence of the inhibitory link will initially prevent the CS from activating the US representation, and a CR will not be recorded.

A crucial implication of this account is that a conditioned inhibitor should not have any response-eliciting properties of its own. An inhibitory link will serve only to modulate the strength of CRs whenever the US representation is activated. But we have seen that a conditioned inhibitor by itself may influence behavior. In the Hearst and Franklin (1977) experiment a conditioned inhibitor was shown to elicit withdrawal. Whereas in other studies it has been found that rats will consume relatively large volumes of a flavored solution that has previously signaled the omission of a lithium chloride injection (Batson & Best, 1981; Best, Dunn, Batson,

Meachum, & Nash, 1985). Findings such as these suggest the need for an alternative account of what is learned during inhibitory conditioning.

In his later theorizing, Konorski (1967; see also Pearce & Hall, 1980) proposed that inhibitory conditioning permits the growth of a conventional association between the CS and what Konorski (1967) called a no-US representation. The activation of this representation was deemed to have two effects: It can dampen any concurrently excited US representations and thus weaken excitatory CRs, and it may also elicit responses in its own right (see lower half of Figure 2.18). If this account is to be accepted, then it is essential to specify what constitutes a no-US representation.

Superficially, the notion of such a representation might seem strange, but a moment's reflection should reveal what is meant by this term. Being told that something is going to happen and then discovering that it will not, can often produce strong emotional reactions. The withdrawal of a promised reward, like a large sum of money, might result in frustration or disappointment, whereas an opposite reaction of relief or joy might accompany the news that something unpleasant, like a visit to the dentist, is no longer going to happen. Konorski (1967) proposed the no-US representation contained information about these diffuse reactions, and they are the counterpart to the affective representations formed of the US during excitatory conditioning. It is also conceivable that the no-US representation encodes precise information about the omitted US, and this would be equivalent to the specific component of a US representation. In fact there is evidence to support both proposals (e.g. Pearce et al., 1981; Cotton, Goodall, and Mackintosh, 1982).

THE CONDITIONED RESPONSE

Thus far, we have been concerned principally with identifying the kind of information that animals acquire during the course of Pavlovian conditioning. We now need to understand how this information is able to influence an animal's behavior. The discussion has already hinted at the way in which a simple CS–US association can control behavior. The presentation of a CS is believed to excite a representation of the US, which in turn will excite a response center that will then elicit a CR. On this basis, therefore, the CS might be expected to elicit a response that is very similar to the one elicited by the US. That is, the CS might be thought to serve as a substitute for the US.

There is certainly some evidence to support this stimulus-substitution account for the nature of the Pavlovian CR. Hungry pigeons direct eating responses towards a response key that signals the imminent delivery of food, whereas a thirsty pigeon will make drinking responses to the same key if it signals the delivery of water (Moore, 1973). But, as we shall see, the way in which the US determines the nature of the CR is more complex than has just been implied. We shall also see that the CS can have an influence on the responses that are performed in its presence.

Influence of the US on the CR

Consummatory CRs

Konorski (1967) believed that whenever a CS retrieved information about the specific properties of the US, then what he called a **consummatory CR** would be performed.

Normally, such a response was expected to mimic some aspect of the response to the US. Thus in the study by Moore (1973) that has just been mentioned, the different responses of pigeons to an illuminated key that signaled either food or water provide two clear examples of consummatory CRs. Other examples can be found in the salivation by dogs to a CS that is paired with either food or the delivery of a weak solution of acid into the mouth (Pavlov, 1927). And one further example can be found in experiments where a stimulus that is followed by a mild electric shock to the cheek will cause the eye to blink in a manner similar to that seen when the shock itself is presented (Gormezano, 1965).

Preparatory CRs

Konorski (1967) further proposed that when a CS retrieved information about the affective properties of a US, it would elicit what he called a **preparatory CR**. In contrast to consummatory CRs, a preparatory CR was assumed not to be intimately tied to the responses elicited by the US. An appetitive preparatory CR might consist of a general increase in activity, whereas for aversive conditioning it might consist of immobility. This is not to say that these CRs are without direction. Konorski (1967) argued that for appetitive conditioning the preparatory CR will consist of approaching the CS, and that the equivalent response for aversive conditioning is more likely to be withdrawal. Clear support for both claims can be found in a series of experiments by Karpicke, Christoph, Peterson, and Hearst (1977).

Rats were trained to press a lever for food in a chamber containing two light bulbs, one near the lever and one further away. While subjects were pressing the lever, the bulbs were occasionally illuminated, and this signaled the imminent delivery of either food (Experiment 1) or electric shock (Experiment 5). There was a decline in instrumental responding when the CS was presented in either study, but the magnitude of this effect was dependent on the position of the illuminated bulb. When the bulb nearer to the lever signaled food, there was less disruption of lever pressing than when the more distant bulb signaled this US. Presumably a preparatory CR of approaching an appetitive CS is likely to be most disruptive when the CS is far from the lever. By contrast, it was the illumination of the near light bulb that produced the greater reduction in lever pressing during aversive conditioning. In this instance, a tendency to withdraw from a light signaling shock will interfere most with instrumental responding when it is close to the lever.

Compensatory CRs

The results considered thus far are in keeping with the idea that the conditioned response will resemble the unconditioned response. There is, however, a body of evidence that, at first sight, shows that the CR will oppose or compensate for the unconditioned response. A good example of such a **compensatory CR** can be found in studies of **drug tolerance**. Originally it was thought that drug tolerance was a consequence of a reaction by the body to the onset of the drug, but over the last 30 years it has become evident that Pavlovian conditioning makes an important contribution to this effect (Ramsay & Woods, 1997; Siegel & Allan, 1998). The following experiment by Siegel (1977) was one of the first to make this point.

In each of the six sessions of the first stage of the experiment two groups of rats were injected with morphine. This drug has a pain-killing, or analgesic effect which Siegel (1977) tested by recording the weight a rat would allow to be placed on its paw before pulling the paw away. After the first injection rats did not react until a quite large weight had been applied, but with the repeated administration of morphine a weakening of its analgesic properties was revealed by a decline in the pressure that the rats were prepared to tolerate after each injection. This pattern of results, which is depicted in the left-hand side of Figure 2.19, demonstrates the development of a tolerance to the analgesic effects of morphine.

To explain the development of the tolerance, Siegel (1977) viewed each injection during the first stage of the experiment as a Pavlovian conditioning episode. The cues associated with the injection—being held by the experimenter in a particular fashion, the prick of the needle, etc.—were regarded as the CS, and the effects of the drug as the US. The critical contribution of Siegel's (1977) analysis was the additional claim that this treatment would result in the CS (the experience of being injected) eliciting a CR that would counteract the analgesic influence of morphine. The strength of this compensatory CR was expected to increase with repeated injections and result in a progressive reduction in analgesia

These proposals were tested in the two remaining stages of the experiment. For the next 12 sessions the groups were treated differently. Group Extinction was treated in much the same way as for the preceding sessions, except the daily injections contained saline instead of morphine. As a result of this treatment, the rats were again exposed to the CS of being picked up and being injected but the absence of morphine meant that the CS was no longer followed by the drug US. Each of these trials can therefore be regarded as an extinction trial that will reduce the capacity of the CS to elicit the compensatory CR. This prediction was tested in the third stage of the experiment by again injecting the rats with morphine during six daily sessions. If the treatment in Stage 2 had reduced the capacity of the injection treatment to elicit a compensatory CR, then the analgesic effect of morphine in Stage 3 should be restored to some extent. The right-hand half of Figure 2.19 reveals support for this prediction by showing that rats in the Extinction Group were prepared to tolerate

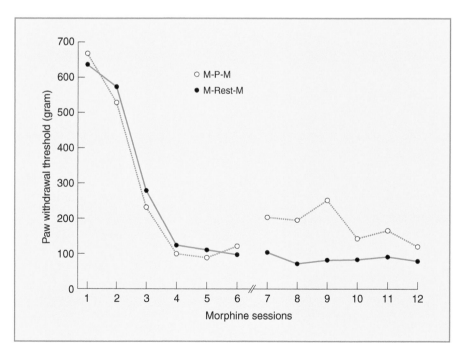

FIGURE 2.19 The mean weight that two groups of rats were prepared to tolerate on their paws shortly after an injection of morphine (M). The left-hand side shows the results for the first six daily trials, the right-hand side shows the results for a further six injections. During the interval between these stages Group M–P–M but not Group M–Rest–M had received saline placebo (P) injections (from Siegel, 1977).

a greater weight on their paws than at the end of the first stage of the experiment. In addition, this recovery of drug tolerance was not observed in the second group, Group Rest. This group did not receive any injections of either saline or morphine during Stage 2. There was thus no opportunity for the cues arising from the injection treatment to lose their capacity for exciting the compensatory CR and this group was not expected to show any change in tolerance to the drug.

The experiment by Siegel (1977), along with many others (e.g. Siegel, 1975; Crowell, Hinson, & Siegel, 1981; Hinson, Poulos, & Cappell, 1982) demonstrates the importance of Pavlovian conditioning for understanding drug tolerance. But, as noted above, this research raises questions about the factors that determine the nature of the conditioned response. If, as Pavlov (1927) asserted, the CS is a substitute for the US, then the conditioned response should resemble the unconditioned response. In the case of Siegel's (1977) study, however, the conditioned response to the act of being injected was opposite to the unconditioned response of analgesia. To resolve this paradox, Ramsay and Woods (1997) have suggested that when a drug is administered it will have a number of effects on the body and nervous system. In particular, the drug by itself might not only have an analgesic effect, but this effect might in turn cause the nervous system to send signals to counter the impact of the drug. If the cues arising from the act of being injected elicit a conditional response that is equivalent to this second effect on the nervous system, then these cues could be said to be a partial substitute for the morphine and at the same time counter the influence of the morphine.

Most researchers now accept this analysis for compensatory conditioned responses (e.g. Siegel & Allan, 1998), but it raises an obvious question. If morphine excites a wide array of responses, some of which counteract each other, what determines which of these responses will be selected as the CR that is excited by the cues surrounding the injection? Will the CR mimic the unconditioned analgesic effect of the drug, or will it mimic the unconditioned response that counters the analgesic influence? Unfortunately, we do not yet know the answer to these questions. Even if the answer was known, our knowledge of the factors that determine the nature of the conditioned response would still be incomplete. This is because the nature of the CS can also influence the conditioned response.

Influence of the CS on the CR

A dramatic example of the way in which the CS influences the CR can be found in a conditioned taste aversion study by Garcia, Rusiniak, and Brett (1977). Coyotes and wolves were made ill by feeding them chopped mutton that was laced with lithium chloride and wrapped in raw sheep hide. The effects of this conditioning episode were then examined by allowing the animals to approach live sheep. Rather than attacking them as they normally do, one coyote sniffed the sheep and then turned away retching; the reaction of the wolves was even more impressive, at first they:

> . . . charged the sheep and made oral contact several times with their characteristic flank attack but immediately released their prey. During the next half hour, the sheep became dominant as the wolves gave way whenever the sheep threatened with short charges. Gradually the wolves withdrew and responded to the sheep like submissive pups. (Garcia et al., 1977, pp. 281–282)

The response of retching by the coyote is to be expected if the US determined the CR, but the additional reactions of the wolves are clearly influenced by the fact that the CS paired with illness tasted and smelt of sheep, and that the live sheep, finding themselves not eaten by wolves, were prepared to attack their erstwhile predators.

In a different vein, Timberlake and Grant (1975) signaled the delivery of food to rats by inserting into the conditioning chamber for 10 seconds a platform on which another rat was strapped. As this event was always followed by food, an account of conditioning that assumes that the CS should elicit the same responses as the US leads to the expectation that the experimental subjects would attempt to eat the CS. Happily, there was no evidence of such cannibalism. Instead, whenever the CS was presented, the subject engaged in social behavior with the restrained rat. This activity included pawing, grooming, and anogenital sniffing. To emphasize the importance that the nature of the CS played in this experiment, it was found that social responses were not directed towards a block of wood when it served as the CS. A further finding from the experiment was that social behavior was not directed towards the rat on the platform, if its entry into the chamber was unrelated to the delivery of food. Thus the social response can be confidently said to be a consequence of conditioning, and it is determined by properties of the CS as well as the US.

The extraordinary submissive behavior of the wolves in Garcia et al.'s (1977) taste aversion experiment, demonstrates the clear influence of the conditioned stimulus (CS) on the conditioned response (CR).

Interpretation

By now, it should be evident that our understanding of the factors that determine the nature of a CR for a given conditioning task is far from complete. On some occasions the CR mimics the response to the US, on other occasions it appears to counter the response to the US, and in other tasks the CR is determined more by the properties of the CS. Clearly, the simple memory model of conditioning that was sketched on p. 46 is unable to explain this complex pattern of findings. In general, learning theorists have veered away from trying to specify the circumstances in which a particular CR will be performed, but this is not to say the problem has been ignored completely.

Several authors have proposed that the determinants of conditioned behavior are organized into functional systems that are concerned with such activities as feeding, mating, defense, and parenting (Davey, 1989; Timberlake, 1994, 2001). These systems are activated by the appropriate stimuli and serve to coordinate patterns of behavior that are both innate and learned. Each system is assumed to control a wide range of actions, the selection of which is determined by the stimuli that are present. Thus in the case of appetitive conditioning, many of the actions controlled by the feeding system are assumed to be available to serve as potential CRs.

To explain the finding by Timberlake and Grant (1975) that social behavior can serve as a CR, this behavior must be assumed to constitute one of the activities that lie within the feeding system. The question is then raised as to whether it is reasonable to suppose that social behavior belongs to the feeding system. Timberlake (1994) has justified this assumption by pointing out that young rats have a natural tendency to follow adult rats and to eat the food that they select. That is, social behavior with adults is an integral part of feeding in young rats. We might predict, therefore, that any animal that is a solitary feeder throughout its life will be unlikely to demonstrate social CRs when it is presented with a conspecific that signals the delivery of food. Timberlake (1983) has confirmed this prediction with hamsters that tend to eat by themselves. He actually found a decrease in social behavior in hamsters when they were exposed to another hamster immediately before food was delivered.

Whatever the merits of the details of this behavior systems approach to Pavlovian conditioning, there is no doubt that it has the benefit of attempting to come to terms with the complexity of the factors that determine the nature of the CR. For this reason alone, this approach deserves serious attention.

CONCLUDING COMMENT: THE REFLEXIVE NATURE OF THE CONDITIONED RESPONSE

A common claim concerning conditioned responding is that the CS elicits the CR quite automatically, just as an innate reflex will be triggered by the appropriate releasing stimulus. As a result, whereas properties of the CS and US can influence the form of the CR, this response is often quite unaffected by its consequences. In some circumstances this does not matter, because the CR will approximate behavior that is in the animal's best interests. Signals for food are generally found in close proximity to food itself, and a preparatory CR of approaching an appetitive CS may well lead a hungry animal to its goal. Alternatively, an animal that flees from a signal for an aversive event will very often be fleeing from that event as well. This is not to say that CRs will always benefit the animal; given the appropriate circumstances, as the following examples will show, the automatic occurrence of a CR can occasionally lead to maladaptive behavior.

In one study by Hearst and Jenkins (1974), pigeon autoshaping was conducted in a long conditioning chamber. The delivery of food was signaled by the illumination of a response key located more than 0.6 meters from the hopper. After a number of autoshaping trials, the pigeons would approach and peck the key as soon as it was illuminated. Pecking then continued until the key light was turned off, whereupon the pigeon frantically rushed down the box to collect the grain that was briefly available at the hopper. Not surprisingly, subjects got very little food to eat as a result of this training. In this example, then, the CS elicited the typical CRs of approach and pecking, and their occurrence prevented the more sensible response of going to the magazine. The automatic, or reflexive, nature of the CRs is revealed by the persistence with which they were performed, even though they interfered with the collection of grain.

A similar outcome has been demonstrated by Williams and Williams (1969) using what is known as an omission schedule for autoshaping. Pigeons were given conventional autoshaping in which the illumination of a response key signaled food. But if the birds pecked the key during a trial, the light was turned off and food was not presented. Given this arrangement, it would be in the pigeons' best interests never to peck the key. But it seems that the behavior of these birds is not always governed by their best interests: Even with extended training they all persisted in pecking the key to some extent, thereby receiving only a fraction of the food that was potentially available. The implication of this finding is that even the intermittent pairings of the CS and food were sufficient to sustain a key-light-food association. Illumination of the key would then activate a representation of food and automatically produce a consummatory peck CR and cancel the delivery of food.

The final example of the disruptive influence of CRs comes from a study by Breland and Breland (1961), who experienced considerable difficulty in training a raccoon to pick up a coin and insert it in a money box for food. The problem did not lie with making the subjects pick up the coin but with making them let go of it again. Boakes, Poli, Lockwood, and Goodall (1978) have suggested that this demonstration of "misbehavior" occurs because the coin became an appetitive CS as a result of being paired with food. Consequently, the subject will be compelled to approach the coin whenever it is visible (preparatory CR) and perhaps attempt to eat it (consummatory CR). On this basis it is quite understandable why the raccoons were unwilling to release the coin.

Pavlovian conditioning has the potential for allowing animals to learn a great deal about sequences of events that occur regularly in their environment. But if the only way this knowledge can influence behavior is through a restricted range of reflex-like responses, then, as the studies just discussed demonstrate, its full benefits could not be realized. It now seems that in addition to eliciting stereotyped CRs, Pavlovian conditioning can exert a more flexible influence on what an animal does by modulating the vigor of instrumental responses. But we must wait until we have examined the instrumental learning process in Chapter 4 before this possibility is investigated further. In the meantime we turn in the next chapter to an examination of the conditions that determine whether or not Pavlovian conditioning will take place.

CHAPTER 3

CONTENTS

The conditions for learning: Surprise and attention

An important conclusion to be drawn from Chapter 2 is that conditioning results in the growth of an association between representations of the conditioned stimulus (CS) and the unconditioned stimulus (US). Our task now is to identify—as precisely as possible—the circumstances responsible for this learning. The brief historical review of learning theories in Chapter 1 demonstrated that the formation of associations was believed to be governed by the principle of contiguity (e.g. Guthrie, 1935). According to this principle, the mere pairing of two events, such as a tone and shock, should be sufficient for conditioning to be effective, that is, for an association to develop between them. Evidence to be cited shortly shows that this principle is wrong. To be successful, conditioning is now believed to depend on the US being unexpected or surprising, and on the CS receiving the animal's full attention. In the first part of this chapter, one account of the way in which the surprisingness of the US influences conditioning is described. How changes in attention to the CS can affect conditioning is considered in the second part of the chapter.

The reason for believing that the surprisingness of the US influences conditioning rests with the discovery of blocking, which was mentioned briefly in the previous chapter. Table 3.1 outlines the stages of a blocking study by Kamin (1969) using conditioned suppression. In the first stage, Group E, but not Group C, was given pairings of a noise with shock. For the second stage, both groups received identical training for a number of trials in which a compound composed of the noise and a light was paired with shock. Finally, test trials involving the light by itself were given. The suppression ratios at the right-hand side of the table indicate that on the test trials with the light there was virtually no evidence of a conditioned response (CR) in Group E, whereas one of considerable strength was recorded for Group C. For Group E, therefore, the original training with the noise was somehow responsible for preventing, or blocking, learning about the light during compound conditioning.

If conditioning depended merely on the pairing of a CS and a US, then Stage 2 should have resulted in effective conditioning with the light for both groups. To explain his finding to the contrary with Group E, Kamin (1969) proposed that in the first stage of the experiment animals learned that the noise predicted the shock,

TABLE 3.1 Summary of the training given to the two groups in Kamin's (1969) study of blocking

	Stage 1	Stage 2	Test
Group E	Noise → Shock	Light + Noise → Shock	Light 0.45
Group C		Light + Noise → Shock	Light 0.05

and this led to the light being followed by an unsurprising US during compound conditioning. The importance of this relationship is made apparent by the following quote (Kamin, 1969, p. 59):

> *Perhaps, for an increment in an associative connection to occur, it is necessary that the US instigate some "mental work" on behalf of the animal. This mental work will occur only if the US is unpredicted—if it in some sense "surprises" the animal.*

This proposal led to the development of a number of formal theories of learning, all of which in various ways have stressed the importance of surprise in conditioning (Rescorla & Wagner, 1972; Wagner & Rescorla, 1972; Mackintosh, 1975a; Wagner, 1976, 1978, 1981; Pearce, 1994; Pearce & Hall, 1980). To demonstrate how these theories operate, we shall consider one of them—that proposed by Rescorla and Wagner (1972)—in detail. Some of its successors are discussed in the second part of this chapter. By way of introduction to the model, a simplified version of it is applied to conditioning with a single CS.

PART 1: SURPRISE AND CONDITIONING

CONDITIONING WITH A SINGLE CS

Figure 3.1 depicts the results from a rabbit eye-blink conditioning experiment in which a light was paired with a mild shock to the cheek (Kehoe, Horne, Horne, & Macrae, 1994). The measure of conditioning was the percentage of trials for which a response was observed in each daily session. At first, the likelihood of a response to the light was low, which is hardly surprising because of the absence of prior light–shock pairings. There was then a rapid increase in magnitude of the response, which diminished gradually as training progressed until there were no further increases in the measure of the CR. The shape of the learning curve in Figure 3.1 is typical of that found in many studies of conditioning.

In Chapter 2, we saw that conditioning results in the growth of an association between internal representations of the CS and US. An important assumption of the Rescorla–Wagner (1972) theory is that the strength of this association determines the strength of the CR. The implication of Figure 3.1 for this theory is that at the outset of the light–shock pairings the strength of the light–shock association was zero. The first few trials then resulted in a rapid growth of this association but, as training progressed, the amount by which the strength of the CS–US association increased in each session became less and less and eventually ceased. At this point, the strong CS–US association would ensure that a vigorous CR of fixed magnitude would be performed on every trial.

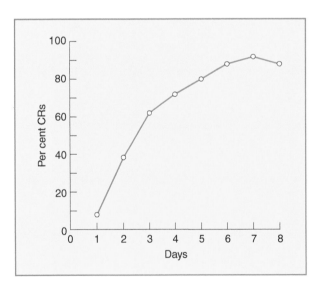

FIGURE 3.1 The acquisition of an eye-blink conditioned response (CR) during conditioning with rabbits in which a light was paired with a mild shock to the cheek (adapted from Kehoe et al., 1994).

At the heart of the Rescorla–Wagner (1972) theory lies an equation that is used to predict the change in the **associative strength** of a CS–US association that results from a conditioning trial. When a single CS is followed by a US then Equation 3.1 is used to predict these changes:

$$\Delta V = \alpha(\lambda - V) \tag{3.1}$$

The symbol ΔV refers to the change in associative strength on a particular trial. If this value is large it will mean that the CR on the next trial will be considerably stronger than on the current trial. The symbol, V, in the expression $(\lambda - V)$ refers to the strength of the CS–US association. The value of λ, is set by the magnitude of the US and reflects the maximum strength that the CS–US association can achieve. The parameter α does not vary during conditioning and has a value between 0 and 1; its function will be made evident shortly.

The application of Equation 3.1 is extremely simple. Assume for the present that α is 0.20 and λ is 100. On the first occasion that the CS is paired with the US it will possess no associative strength, and the value of V will be zero. For the first CS–US pairing, the growth in the association between them will be given by Equation 3.2, which is derived by substituting the values given into Equation 3.1:

$$\begin{aligned} \Delta V &= 0.20 \times (100 - 0) \\ &= 20 \end{aligned} \tag{3.2}$$

Thus, on the first conditioning trial there will be an increase of 20 units in associative strength. On the second trial, the increment in associative strength will be determined by a new set of values. Specifically, it will be determined by Equation 3.3, because the associative strength of the CS, V, will no longer be zero but will instead have a value of 20 units. The effect of this change will be to produce a smaller increment in associative strength on the second than on the first trial:

$$\begin{aligned} \Delta V &= 0.20 \times (100 - 20) \\ &= 16 \end{aligned} \tag{3.3}$$
$$\begin{aligned} \Delta V &= 0.20 \times (100 - 36) \\ &= 12.8 \end{aligned} \tag{3.4}$$

On the third trial (see Equation 3.4), the associative strength of the CS will be 36 (20 + 16) units, and this will result in an even smaller change than on the previous trials. Eventually, a point will be reached where the sum of the increments will equal 100; at this juncture, the expression $(\lambda - V)$ will equal 0 and, according to Equation 3.1, no further changes in associative strength will be possible. The equation thus predicts that the growth in associative strength—and hence increase in CR strength—will be extremely rapid on the initial trials but decline and eventually cease with continued training. In other words, the theory predicts the learning curve obtained by Kehoe et al. (1994) shown in Figure 3.1. To emphasize this point, the dotted line in the left-hand side of Figure 3.2 shows the growth in associative strength with repeated CS–US pairings that is predicted by Equation 3.1 when α is 0.20 and λ is 100. The similarity between this curve and that shown in Figure 3.1 should be obvious.

One advantage of Equation 3.1 is that it can provide a straightforward account for extinction when a CS is no longer followed by a US. Suppose there has been

KEY TERM

Associative strength
The strength of the connection between internal representations of the conditioned and unconditioned stimulus which determines the strength of the conditioned response.

FIGURE 3.2 The
changes in associative
strength predicted by
the Rescorla–Wagner
(1972) model during
conditioning with a
large unconditioned
stimulus (US) ($\lambda = 100$
units; dotted line) or a
small US ($\lambda = 50$ units;
solid line), and during
extinction for a
conditioned stimulus
(CS) that has been
paired with a large US.

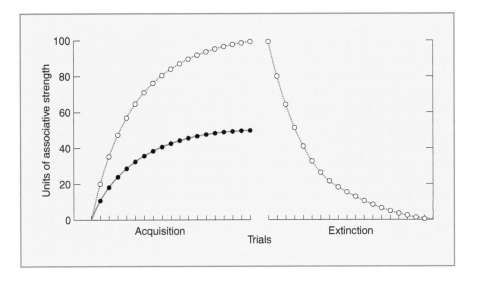

sufficient training to ensure that the strength of a CS–US association equals the value of λ (100 units). If we then present the CS without the US, what does Equation 3.1 predict? Before answering this question, the value to be substituted for λ on these nonreinforced trials must be decided. This term refers to the magnitude of the US, and a value of 0 is appropriate to indicate its absence. The associative strength of the CS, however, does have a value (100 units); the change in associative strength on the first extinction trial is given by Equation 3.5:

$$\Delta V = 0.20 \times (0 - 100)$$
$$= -20 \tag{3.5}$$

The first extinction trial will therefore result in the CS losing 20 units of associative strength. Repeatedly applying Equation 3.1 for extinction will, because of the declining value of V, produce progressively smaller losses in associative strength, and result in the curve depicted in the right-hand half of Figure 3.2. Extinction will be complete when the associative strength of the CS has fallen to zero.

The application of Equation 3.1 is not difficult. However, if you feel uncomfortable with this account of acquisition and extinction, then perform your own calculations to see the effects of changing the values of α and λ on the shape of the learning curve. This will help considerably with understanding what is to follow. A number of factors can influence the course of conditioning; some of these are now described and it is shown how they can be incorporated into the theoretical framework provided by Equation 3.1.

US intensity

Equation 3.1 might be objected to because it is hard to know what value should be assigned to λ. But this is not a serious problem, as the purpose of developing such equations is not to derive exact, quantitative predictions of the sort: "On Trial 4 the CR will be of such a magnitude". Instead, it is concerned more with qualitative statements where different methods of training are predicted to have different outcomes. Suppose we wished to predict the effects of changing the magnitude of the US on conditioning. The fact that we do not know the precise values of λ that should be assigned to USs when they vary in intensity does not matter. All that needs to be said is that this value will be greater for the stronger US. Thus, if λ for a strong US is set at 100 units, then a value of 50 units could be employed for one that is weaker.

Equation 3.1 predicts that on the first conditioning trial with the weak US the increment in associative strength will be $0.20 \times (50 - 0) = 10$ units (using the previously selected value for α). Future increments will decline progressively from this value, and conditioning will cease when their combined value is equal to 50. The solid line in Figure 3.2 portrays this predicted growth of associative strength. Comparing this curve with the dotted line, which was calculated with $\lambda = 100$ units, then allows us to conclude what the effects will be of conditioning with different magnitudes of US. Specifically, pairing a CS with a strong US should result in a stronger CR than if the CS is paired with a weaker US. This prediction will always be true no matter what values are ascribed to λ, providing that its value is greater for the stronger US.

The foregoing analysis is reasonably consistent with experimental findings. For instance, Annau and Kamin (1961), using conditioned suppression, found that both the rate of conditioning and the ultimate level of conditioned responding was greater with a strong than with a weak shock US. When examining Figure 3.3, which shows the results from their study, bear in mind that a suppression ratio of 0.50 indicates the absence of a CR, whereas one of 0.00 indicates a CR of maximum strength.

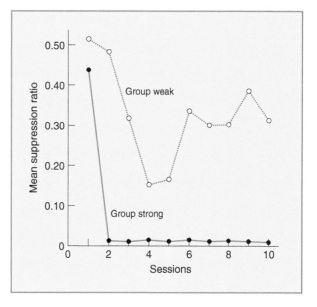

FIGURE 3.3 The acquisition of conditioned suppression to a noise conditioned stimulus (CS) by two groups of rats that received either a 0.49 milliamp (Group Weak) or a 0.85 milliamp (Group Strong) shock unconditioned stimulus (US) (adapted from Annau & Kamin, 1961).

CS intensity

Little has been said so far about the role of α in Equation 3.1. Conditioning is known to progress more rapidly with a strong than with a weak CS, and to accommodate this finding Rescorla and Wagner (1972) proposed that α is set according to the intensity of the CS. With a strong CS α should approach 1, but with a weaker stimulus α should tend towards 0. Figure 3.4 portrays the acquisition curves predicted by Equation 1 with α set at 0.8 (strong CS, solid line) and 0.2 (weak CS, dashed line). The value of λ was 100 units. The effect of changing the magnitude of α is to alter the rate of conditioning but not the ultimate level of conditioned responding. Because the influence of α is confined solely to determining the speed at which conditioning takes place, it is defined as a learning-rate parameter that reflects the **associability or conditionability** of the CS.

The results from a study by Kamin and Schaub (1963), which investigated the influence of CS intensity on the acquisition of conditioned suppression, are presented in Figure 3.5. Three groups were conditioned with the same magnitude of US but with different intensities of a white noise for the CS. For Group Strong the CS was 81 dB, for Group Medium it was 62.5 dB, and for Group Weak it was 49 dB.

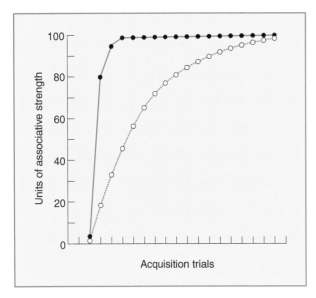

FIGURE 3.4 The change in associative strength predicted by the Rescorla–Wagner (1972) model during conditioning with a relatively intense conditioned stimulus (CS) ($\alpha = 0.8$; solid line) or a weak CS ($\alpha = 0.2$; dashed line).

The rate of conditioning was directly related to the CS intensity, but this factor did not influence at all the ultimate level of responding.

An important property of Equation 3.1 is that it characterizes the role of surprise in conditioning. As the associative strength of a CS grows, so the CS can be said to become a more accurate predictor of the US. Given this perspective, the discrepancy ($\lambda - V$) then becomes significant because it indicates the extent to which the US is unexpected or surprising. When V is much less than λ, the CS will be a poor predictor of the US and the occurrence of the US will be surprising. However, when the value of V is close to that of λ, the CS will be a good predictor of the US and the occurrence of the latter will not be surprising. We have seen that conditioning is predicted to be most rapid when ($\lambda - V$) has a large value, which is when the US is most unexpected or surprising. Thus, although Equation 3.1 is presented in mathematical terms, it expresses the psychological idea that animals learn most readily about USs that are surprising or unexpected. The next section will show how this idea can be applied when two or more CSs are presented together as a signal for the US.

CONDITIONING WITH A COMPOUND CS

When a compound containing two or more individual CSs is presented, Rescorla and Wagner (1972) proposed that the associative strengths of the individual stimuli will be added together. To capture this notion they suggested Equation 3.6, where V_A, $V_B \ldots V_X$ represent the associative strengths of the stimuli that are present on the trial. V_{ALL} is the sum of the associative strengths of all the CSs that are present on a trial, and indicates the extent to which they collectively predict the US. The value of V_{ALL} also determines the strength of the CR that can be expected in the presence of these stimuli:

$$V_{ALL} = V_A + V_B + \ldots V_X \qquad (3.6)$$

A number of experiments have demonstrated support for this equation. For instance, Kehoe et al. (1994) conducted eye-blink conditioning with rabbits in which a tone and a light each signaled the delivery of a mild shock to the cheek. For each subject, the measure of conditioning was percentage of trials on which an eye blink was recorded. Figure 3.6 shows

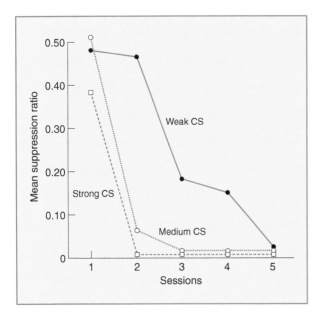

FIGURE 3.5 Acquisition of conditioned suppression by groups of rats trained with the same unconditioned stimulus (US) but with a conditioned stimulus (CS) that was weak, medium, or strong (adapted from Kamin & Schaub, 1963).

the results from a session containing not only the training trials but also test trials with the tone and light presented together. In support of the prediction that can be derived from Equation 3.6, eye blinks were more likely to be recorded during the compound than during either of the elements.

The overall associative strength of a compound, V_{ALL}, is important because it determines not only the strength of response that will occur on a particular trial but also the changes in associative strength that take place during conditioning. This influence was expressed by Rescorla and Wagner (1972) as Equation 3.7:

$$\Delta V_A = \alpha_A (\lambda - V_{ALL}) \qquad (3.7)$$

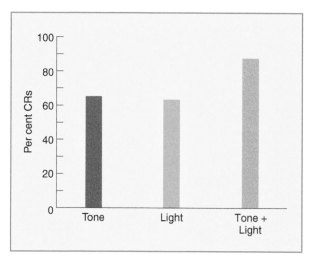

In Equation 3.7 the change in associative strength of a particular CS, A, is no longer determined by the discrepancy between its own associative strength and the value of λ. Instead, this change is determined by the discrepancy between the combined associative strength of all the stimuli present on the trial and λ. In other words, the equation retains the implication of Equation 3.1 that conditioning will be most effective with a surprising US, but it alters slightly the way in which surprisingness is determined. Surprise is no longer determined by how well a single CS predicts the occurrence of the US. Instead, the surprisingness of a US is determined by the difference between by how well all the stimuli present on a trial collectively predict the occurrence of the US.

FIGURE 3.6 The mean percentage of trials in which a conditioned response (CR) was recorded during rabbit eye-blink conditioning in which a tone and a light were separately paired with a mild shock to the cheek, and during test trials in which the light and tone were presented together (adapted from Kehoe et al., 1994).

Blocking

In the blocking experiment by Kamin (1969), which is summarized in Table 3.1, conditioning was conducted with a noise (N) prior to compound conditioning with the noise and a light (L). Subsequent testing revealed that despite being paired with shock during compound conditioning, the light virtually failed to elicit a response. According to Rescorla and Wagner (1972), the explanation for this blocking effect rests with the original training with the noise, which will ensure it has maximum associative strength when conditioning commences with the noise–light compound. At the outset of Stage 2, therefore, the associative strength of the noise will be at the asymptotic value of λ (100 units, say). To determine the increment in associative strength of the light on the first compound trial, Equation 3.7 should be rewritten as Equation 3.8. The novelty of the light will ensure that V_L is equal to 0 for this trial:

$$\begin{aligned} \Delta V_L &= \alpha_L[\lambda - (V_N + V_L)] \\ &= \alpha_L[100 - (100 + 0)] \\ &= 0 \end{aligned} \qquad (3.8)$$

On the first—or for that matter any—trial of Stage 2 there will be no change in the associative strength of the light. A rather different state of affairs will hold for the control group shown in Table 3.1 because on the first compound trial both the light and noise will be novel, and the values of V_L and V_N will be zero. Equations 3.9a and 3.9b describe the increments in associative strength that can be expected with these stimuli on the first trial:

$$\Delta V_L = \alpha_L[\lambda - (V_N + V_L)]$$
$$= \alpha_L[100 - (0 + 0)]$$
$$= \alpha_L \times 100 \tag{3.9a}$$
$$\Delta V_N = \alpha_N[\lambda - (V_N + V_L)]$$
$$= \alpha_N[100 - (0 + 0)]$$
$$= \alpha_N \times 100 \tag{3.9b}$$

For these subjects the noise and the light will both gain in associative strength, and the latter stimulus will elicit a stronger CR on the test trial than its counterpart in Group E. Put another way, the Rescorla–Wagner model predicts that blocking will occur because the pretraining with the noise ensure the US is accurately predicted by the compound. The lack of surprisingness of the US will then prevent the development of a light–US association.

Overshadowing

Further reflection on Equations 3.9a and 3.9b should reveal that conditioning with the noise and light will cease when their combined associative strengths equal λ. As a result, neither V_L nor V_N will alone reach this value, which they would do if they were paired independently with the US. The Rescorla–Wagner model thus predicts that when animals are conditioned with two stimuli in a compound, each will gain less associative strength than if they were separately paired with the same US. In these circumstances the presence of one CS is said to result in **overshadowing** with the other. Pavlov (1927) first reported this effect, and it has been demonstrated on many subsequent occasions (e.g. Kamin, 1969).

Inhibitory conditioning

One of the great advantages of the Rescorla–Wagner model is that it provides an elegant account for effects of inhibitory conditioning. Consider an experiment in which subjects are first given excitatory conditioning with a tone until its associative strength is at asymptotic value, λ (100 units). They then receive inhibitory conditioning in which tone–US trials are intermixed among presentations of a light-tone compound followed by nothing. What will happen to the associative strength of the light as a result of this training?

Equation 3.10 indicates the change in associative strength that can be expected on the first compound trial. The value of λ is zero because of the absence of the US. V_T is equal to 100 because of the pretraining with the tone, and V_L has a value of 0 due to the novelty of the light. The compound trial will thus reduce the associative strength of the light. Because this stimulus does not possess any strength to lose, we must conclude that the training will endow the light with negative associative strength. In fact, conditioning will continue until V_L is of a sufficient negative value to cancel out the positive strength of the tone, V_T:

$$\Delta V_L = \alpha_L[\lambda - (V_L + V_T)]$$
$$= \alpha_L[0 - (0 + 100)]$$
$$= -\alpha_L \times 100 \tag{3.10}$$

Wagner and Rescorla (1972) suggest that any stimulus that possesses negative associative strength will be a conditioned inhibitor, and it is easy to see why this should be. If a stimulus with negative associative strength is paired with a US, then conditioning will at first be without apparent effect, because a number of trials will be needed before the associative strength of the stimulus becomes positive and it can elicit a CR. This effect constitutes a retardation test for conditioned inhibition. As far as the summation test is concerned, bear in mind that Rescorla and Wagner (1972) assume that the associative strength of a compound is made up of the algebraic sum of the associative strengths of the elements (Equation 3.6). If one of the elements has negative associative strength, then the overall associative strength of the compound and the vigor of the CR that is performed in its presence will be less than if that stimulus is absent.

The CS–US contingency

A factor that exerts an extremely important influence on the associative strength acquired by a CS during excitatory conditioning is the **CS–US contingency**, as a study by Rescorla (1968) demonstrates. Rats were trained to press a lever for food in a conditioning chamber before being given a number of sessions in a different chamber where a 2-minute tone and shock were presented. The effect of these conditioning sessions was ultimately assessed by presenting the tone to the rats while they were again responding for food in the original chamber.

In each conditioning session, for all subjects the probability of the shock being presented during the tone was 0.4, that is, the shock was delivered on an average of 4 out of every 10 occasions that the tone was presented. The groups differed in the probability of being shocked during the interval, averaging 8 minutes, between successive tone trials. For Group 0 no shocks were presented in this interval. For Group 0.40 the probability of shock being presented in each 2-minute segment of the interval was 0.40, which meant that the probability of shock during the tone was the same as at any other time in the session. For the two remaining groups the probability of shock during a 2-minute segment of the interval was either 0.20 (Group 0.20), or 0.10 (Group 0.10). Thus, for these subjects there was a chance of being shocked at any time in the session, but shock was more likely in the presence than in the absence of the tone.

The effects of this training were revealed by the magnitude of conditioned suppression evoked by the tone in the four groups on the test session (Figure 3.7). The striking finding was that the strength of conditioning differed dramatically in the four groups, even though the tone–shock pairings were identical for all subjects. What appears to be an important determinant of conditioning, therefore, is the difference between the probability of shock when the CS is present and when it is absent. When this difference is large, as in the case of Group 0, conditioning is very effective. With a smaller difference between these probabilities conditioning is still effective but correspondingly weaker (Groups 0.20 and 0.10). Finally, when the likelihood of shock is the same whether or not the CS is present, conditioning does not occur (Group 0.40).

Findings such as these are said to demonstrate the importance of contingency in conditioning. When the probability of a shock given the presence of a tone is equal to that in the absence of this stimulus, then the contingency between the tone and shock is zero, and conditioning is ineffective. But when the shock is more likely in the presence than the absence of the tone, then there is a positive tone–shock

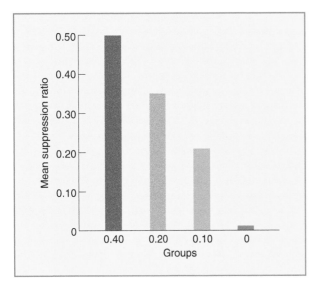

FIGURE 3.7 Mean suppression ratio to the tone conditioned stimulus (CS) on the test session for each of the four groups in the study by Rescorla (1968) (adapted from Rescorla, 1968).

contingency, and excitatory conditioning will take place. A negative contingency between the CS and US can also be envisaged in which the likelihood of the US is greater when the CS is absent than when it is present. An example of such a contingency is provided by the study of Hearst and Franklin (1977), discussed in Chapter 2, in which the probability of food was greater in the absence than in the presence of an illuminated key. The results from that study indicate that when there is a negative CS–US contingency it will result in inhibitory learning.

To account for the importance of the CS–US contingency in determining the outcome of conditioning, Rescorla and Wagner (1972) point out that a CS is necessarily presented in a **context** that itself can be construed as a stimulus. Even with a single CS, then, conditioning is conducted with a compound in which the experimental context provides the additional stimulus. To return to Rescorla's (1968) study, for some subjects shocks were delivered during the interval between successive presentations of the CS, and this will enable the contextual stimuli to acquire associative strength. The context should then function in a manner analogous to the pretrained element in the earlier example for blocking, and block conditioning to the CS whenever it is presented. It also follows from the model that the more associative strength the blocking stimulus has, the more effective it will be in restricting conditioning to the target CS. Hence the model correctly predicts that increasing the associative strength of the context by increasing the probability of shock in the absence of the CS will reduce conditioning to the CS.

EVALUATION OF THE RESCORLA–WAGNER MODEL

It would be most convenient if the discussion could be closed at this point with the conclusion that the Rescorla–Wagner model provides the ideal account of the conditions of learning. Unfortunately, the perfect learning theory has yet to be developed and this particular theory is unable to explain certain results (Miller, Barnet, & Grahame, 1995).

The model provides a good account of many of the facts of compound conditioning, but not all the effects associated with blocking and overshadowing are consistent with it. A summary of these and related findings can be found in Pearce (1987) and Pearce and Hall (1980). Of particular concern to the present discussion is the discovery that the model does not adequately account for the role of surprise in conditioning (e.g. Holland & Kenmuir, 2005). A blocking experiment, using conditioned suppression, by Dickinson, Hall, and Mackintosh (1976) was the first to reveal this shortcoming.

A summary of the design is presented in Table 3.2. In Stage 1, two groups received excitatory conditioning in which on every trial a light was followed immediately by two shocks separated by an interval of 8 seconds. Both groups were then given compound conditioning with the light and a clicker. For Group C the

TABLE 3.2 Summary of the training given to the two groups of rats in the study by Dickinson et al. (1976). The effects of blocking were reduced by the surprising omission of one of a pair of shocks (Sh) during compound conditioning

	Stage 1	Stage 2	Test
Group E	Light → Sh + Sh	Light + Clicker → Sh	Clicker 0.27
Group C	Light → Sh + Sh	Light + Clicker → Sh + Sh	Clicker 0.45

compound was followed by two shocks, again separated by 8 seconds, but for Group E only the first of each pair of shocks accompanied the compound. Apart from the use of double shocks, the method for Group C resembles the conventional blocking design and, in keeping with most blocking studies, the clicker on test trials was found to produce an insubstantial CR.

The outcome for Group E was rather different, because on the test trials the clicker elicited a reasonably strong CR. Blocking for Group E was thus attenuated, and this must have been due to the surprising omission of the second shock during Stage 2. According to the Rescorla–Wagner (1972) model, in this instance effective conditioning with the clicker should definitely not have taken place. In fact, the omission of one of the shocks during Stage 2 is predicted by the theory to weaken the associative strength of the clicker and to result in it becoming a conditioned inhibitor, rather than a conditioned excitor. One way in which this result can be explained is discussed in the second part of this chapter.

A further problem with the theory is the manner in which inhibition is conceptualized as negative associative strength. There is no objection to this proposal as far as accounting for the retardation and summation tests is concerned. However, we saw in Chapter 2 that occasionally a conditioned inhibitor can elicit its own CRs. How this can be explained by assuming that inhibition is nothing more than negative associative strength is hard to understand. Other problems with the theory will be revealed in later chapters: we shall discover in Chapter 5 that despite some notable successes, the account it provides for extinction is incomplete; and in Chapter 6 a problem will be revealed with the way in which this theory explains how certain discriminations are solved.

Despite the shortcomings of the Rescorla and Wagner (1972) theory, there are at least three reasons for taking it seriously. The first rests with the manner in which it is presented. Any attempt to describe the behavior of an animal with an equation might at first seem unduly optimistic. But once it is appreciated that the theory is concerned only with making qualitative predictions about the relative performance of animals that are treated differently, then the goals of theory can be seen as being reasonable. That is, by using the theory it is possible to predict a conditioned response will be stronger after one type of treatment than another. Even though this prediction was derived from an equation, it can then be tested with an experiment. Furthermore, by being expressed in such formal terms it has been possible to derive novel predictions from the model, and these have led to experiments that on more than one occasion have supported the theory. Even on those occasions when the predictions were not confirmed, the theory has been of value by prompting the development of alternative theories of learning. The Rescorla–Wagner (1972) model, in short, provides an outstanding example of the benefits of a particular style of theorizing.

The second reason for taking the theory seriously is that it can now be seen as an important, senior relative of a number of more recent theories of conditioning and associative learning (see Pearce and Bouton, 2001). Some of these theories will be encountered in the next part of this chapter, and in Chapter 6. By appreciating the strengths and weaknesses of the Rescorla–Wagner (1972) model, the reasons for the development of its descendants can be readily understood.

The third reason is that the influence of the Rescorla–Wagner (1972) theory extends well beyond the study of animal learning. Siegel and Allan (1996) show how this theory has enhanced our understanding in humans of verbal learning, category formation, causal judgments, reasoning, social psychology, perception and physiological regulation. As Siegel and Allan note, there are precious few theories in experimental psychology that have had such a widespread impact and for this reason alone the Rescorla–Wagner (1972) theory merits serious consideration.

PART 2: ATTENTION AND CONDITIONING

Cognitive psychologists have long acknowledged that selective attention plays an important role in the processing of information by humans. They have pointed out that we are often exposed to more sources of information than we can deal with at once, and that some sort of selection is necessary to enable information from one source to be attended to while other information is being ignored. For instance, while you read this textbook, paying attention to the words will probably lead to the sensations in your feet being ignored. But once these sensations have been mentioned, you may concentrate on them momentarily, and this transfer of attention away from the text will disrupt reading. An experimental demonstration of this effect is provided by Brown and Poulton (1961).

People were asked to listen to repeated strings of eight numbers. The same sequence was presented successively, except that a randomly selected member of the list was changed from one trial to the next. The task for the person was to listen to the sequence and identify the new item. Not surprisingly, performance was very accurate when this was all that subjects were required to do. But when they were asked to identify the changed number and at the same time drive a car through the rural lanes of Cambridgeshire, their accuracy declined considerably. Presumably these people were unable to attend to the task of driving as well as to the list of numbers, and one source of information had to be ignored. Fortunately for the pedestrians of Cambridgeshire, it was the numerical information that was rejected.

The suggestion has been made on more than one occasion that the attention that animals pay to stimuli can vary. Pavlov raised this possibility by monitoring what is now known as the **orienting response (OR)**. In his studies of conditioning, Pavlov (1927, p. 12) noted that novel stimuli often elicit an OR or, as he referred to it, an investigatory reflex that allows the animal to investigate any changes that occur in its environment. The implication of this proposal is that the OR is a consequence of the animal attending to the stimulus, and the vigor of this response may well provide an indication of the attention a stimulus receives. Other methods for determining the amount of attention that a stimulus receives are notably less direct. Hence it has been suggested that the conditionability of a stimulus is not solely determined by its intensity, as the Rescorla–Wagner (1972) model stipulates, but by the attention it receives.

If this is correct, then the conditionability of a CS, or its associability with a US, will provide an indication of the attention paid to it.

An experiment by Kaye and Pearce (1987) shows how the simple experience of being presented repeatedly with a stimulus might influence these measures of attention. Two groups of rats were placed into a conditioning chamber containing a light bulb and a food dispenser. For the first 12 sessions nothing happened for Group Novel, whereas for Group Familiar the bulb was illuminated for 10 seconds at a time at intervals in each session. Both groups were then given a single pretest session in which the light was occasionally illuminated for 10 seconds.

FIGURE 3.8 A typical orienting response by a rat to an illuminated bulb.

Figure 3.8 shows a typical OR to the light that was performed at the outset of training by Group Familiar. But as the left-hand side of Figure 3.9 reveals, there was evidence of **habituation** as the light was repeatedly illuminated across 12 sessions. The strength of the OR for both groups in the pretest session is presented to the right in this part of Figure 3.9. The OR was considerably more vigorous in Group Novel than in Group Familiar, which suggests that the groups differed in the amount of attention they paid to the light. All subjects were then conditioned with the light serving as a signal for food—the measure of conditioning was the frequency with which rats entered the food magazine during the light. If the repeated exposure to the light reduced the attention paid to it, then for Group Familiar conditioning should progress relatively slowly. The right-hand side of Figure 3.9 shows the frequency of

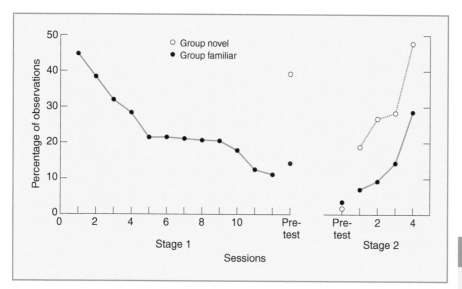

FIGURE 3.9 Left-hand side: shows the frequency of the orienting response (OR) by rats to a light during 12 sessions of exposure (Group Familiar) and during a single pretest session when this stimulus was first shown (Group Novel). Right-hand side: for both groups, the amount of magazine activity in the presence of the light that was recorded during the pretest session and during the next four conditioning sessions (adapted from Kaye & Pearce, 1987).

KEY TERM

Habituation
The waning of an unconditioned response, such as an OR, to a stimulus that is repeatedly presented.

magazine activity during the light for both groups on the pretest session, when there was no difference, and on each of the four sessions of conditioning. As predicted, conditioning was more rapid in Group Novel than in Group Familiar. This effect is known as **latent inhibition** (Lubow, 1973) and supports the claim that Group Familiar paid rather little attention to the light as a result of the preexposure stage.

The term "latent inhibition" might imply that the disruption in conditioning to which it refers is the same as that produced by conditioned inhibition. But this is incorrect for two reasons. In Chapter 2 it is proposed that inhibitory conditioning depends on the CS being followed by the omission of an expected US. Latent inhibition, on the other hand, can develop in the absence of an expectancy of a US. Furthermore, latent inhibition has been found to disrupt inhibitory conditioning (e.g. Reiss & Wagner, 1972). Such an outcome should not occur if latent and conditioned inhibition were the same. It is, however, entirely consistent with the view that latent inhibition reflects a loss of attention to the CS.

One way of characterizing attention is to assume that it is an all-or-none process. A stimulus might either be attended to fully or not at all. In fact, this is a relatively rare theoretical claim. An alternative view is that the amount of attention paid to a stimulus varies along a continuum, and this determines its effectiveness for conditioning as well as the strength of any ORs it might elicit. Such an assumption underlies each of the three theories that we shall now consider. The theories differ in the rules that are believed to govern changes in attention.

KEY TERM

Latent inhibition
The reduction in effectiveness of pairing a conditioned stimulus with an unconditioned stimulus, as a result of prior exposure to the conditioned stimulus.

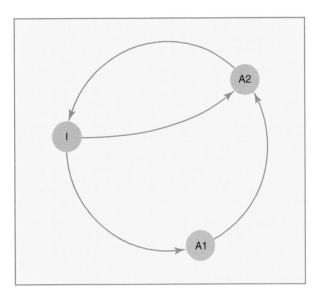

FIGURE 3.10 The relationship between the A1, A2, and inactive (I) states of a representation, as envisaged by the standard operating procedures (SOP) model. When in the inactive state, a representation can be excited to the A1 state by presenting the stimulus to which it corresponds. The A2 representation of a stimulus develops either as a result of decay from the A1 state (self-generated representation), or directly from the I state by presenting a stimulus with which it is associated (retrieval-generated representation). Representations are assumed to decay rapidly from the A1 to the A2 state, and then more slowly from the A2 to the inactive state (adapted from Wagner, 1981).

WAGNER'S THEORY

Over the course of a series of influential articles, Wagner has developed a complex and extremely comprehensive theory of the memory and learning processes in animals (Wagner, 1981; Wagner & Larew, 1985; Wagner & Brandon, 1989; Brandon & Wagner, 1998). The theory has the acronym SOP because it is concerned with the "Standard Operating Procedures" in memory. At the heart of this theory is the assumption that the representation, or memory, of a stimulus can be in three different states (Figure 3.10). There is an inactive state where the memory is not modifiable and is unable to influence an animal's behavior. The two remaining are referred to as A1 and A2. They are regarded as being active (A) because when a stimulus is in either one of them it can influence behavior. A stimulus in the A1 state could be said to be at the center of an animal's attention; when in the A2 state it will be at the periphery of the field of attention. In keeping with our earlier claim that a stimulus must be fully attended to if it is to be learned about readily, Wagner (1981) has proposed that excitatory and inhibitory conditioning is possible only when the CS is represented in the Al state. The OR to a stimulus will also presumably be strongest in these circumstances.

Information can reside more or less indefinitely in the inactive state, but only for a short while in the active states. A representation of a stimulus in the A1 state will transform rapidly to the A2 state and then revert rather more slowly to its inactive state. As a result of this relationship the model correctly predicts that conditioning will be more effective with an intermediate rather than short- or long-duration CS (e.g. Smith, 1968). When the CS is too short, conditioning will be poor because there will have been insufficient time for a representation of the CS to be excited from the inactive to the A1 state. When the CS is too long, the A1 representation that is essential for successful conditioning will have decayed into the A2 state and no longer be capable of entering into associations. Put informally, conditioning with an intermediate duration CS is successful because it is at this point that the stimulus will most fully occupy the animal's attention.

A further feature of the SOP model, and one of particular relevance to this chapter, is that there is only one route by which a representation can be excited to the Al state and that is from the inactive state. If an animal is shown a stimulus for which a representation already exists in the A2 state, then it will be impossible to activate an A1 representation of the stimulus and it will effectively be ignored. By contrast, there are two routes by which a stimulus can gain access to the A2 state, and hence influence an animal's sensitivity to a stimulus. The next two sections consider each of these routes separately.

Self-generated A2 representations

The first route for activating an A2 representation has already been mentioned and consists of presenting the stimulus by itself. When it first occurs, the stimulus will activate an A1 representation, which will then decay rapidly to the A2 representation and, as we have just seen, this A2 representation will then revert slowly to the inactive state. Despite the simplicity of this proposal, it has important implications for both habituation and conditioning.

Habituation is the decline in responsiveness to a stimulus as a result of its repeated presentation. Suppose that an animal is presented with the same stimulus twice, with a short interval between each presentation. On its first occurrence, the stimulus will be represented in the A1 state and it may elicit a strong response. This state will then decay to the A2 state and the theory predicts that strength of the response will show a corresponding decline. If the stimulus should be presented again while the A2 representation is still active then, because of the principles on which SOP is based, the stimulus will be unable to activate an A1 representation and it will be unable to evoke a strong response. In other words there should be evidence of habituation with the second presentation of the stimulus. However, if the interval between the two presentations of the stimulus is long, then by the time of its second occurrence, the A2 representation of the first occurrence will have decayed to the inactive state. In these conditions, the theory predicts that an A1 representation will be formed of the stimulus on its second appearance and it will elicit a strong response. Thus SOP predicts that habituation is more likely to occur on the second presentation of a stimulus, when the interval between the two presentations is short rather than long.

An experiment that tests these proposals was conducted by Whitlow (1975), who used vasoconstriction (a rapid constriction of the blood vessels) as the measure of responsiveness to a tone. Rabbits were presented with a tone on one occasion, when it elicited a strong response of vasoconstriction, and on a second occasion some time later.

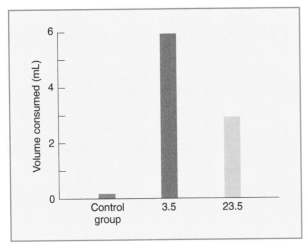

FIGURE 3.11 Mean volume of flavored solution consumed on a test trial that followed a single flavor aversion conditioning trial. Two groups were given a single exposure to the flavor either 3.5 or 23.5 hours before the conditioning trial; for the control group, conditioning was conducted with a novel flavor (adapted from Best & Gemberling, 1977).

In keeping with predictions from SOP, the response on the second trial was significantly stronger with a long rather than a short interval between the two tones.

The implications of this aspect of the SOP model for conditioning are revealed in an experiment by Best and Gemberling (1977). Two groups of rats were exposed to a flavor, which some time later was presented again and followed by illness for taste aversion conditioning. For Group 3.5, the interval between the flavors was 3.5 hours, and for Group 23.5 it was 23.5 hours. A third group, Group Control, received just the conditioning trial with no prior exposure to the flavor. On the following day, all subjects were given a test trial in which they were allowed to drink the flavored solutions. Figure 3.11 summarizes the results of this test by showing the amount of solution consumed by the three groups. Conditioning was evidently effective with the control group because it showed a considerable reluctance to drink the flavor. A rather similar result was found with the group exposed to the flavor 23.5 hours before conditioning. In comparison, taste aversion conditioning was far less effective for the group exposed to the flavor 3.5 hours before the conditioning trial, as this group was quite willing to consume the flavor at the time of testing. This poor conditioning, according to the SOP model, is due to the original exposure to the flavor leaving a memory trace in the A2 state that persisted until the conditioning trial. When the flavor was then presented for this trial, it would be unable to excite an A1 representation of itself, and conditioning should be ineffective. The results from Group 23.5 suggest, not surprisingly, that 23.5 hours is sufficient to allow the A2 trace to decay and permit conditioning when the flavor was again presented.

Retrieval-generated A2 representations

The second route by which a stimulus can gain access to the A2 state, and thus influence attention, is made possible by associative learning. For successful excitatory conditioning, the SOP model requires the simultaneous rehearsal of representations of the CS and the US while they are both in the A1 state. Once conditioning is completed, future presentations of the CS will then be able to excite a representation of the US directly into the A2 state. This is referred to as a retrieval-generated representation, as it is not excited by the US directly but by a CS with which it is associated.

An obvious example of the influence of retrieval-generated representations is provided by blocking. Suppose that a tone is paired with food, prior to trials in which a compound of the tone and a light together signal food. On trials with the tone and light, food will be unable to excite an A1 representation of itself because the presence of the tone will have already activated an A2 representation of this US. Conditioning with the light will then be impossible because it is paired with a representation of food that is in an unsuitable state for associative learning. What might perhaps be rather less obvious is that a similar account can be developed to explain latent inhibition. Repeatedly presenting a neutral stimulus in a conditioning chamber will, according to the SOP model, result in the growth of an association between the context and the stimulus. Consequently, whenever the animal is returned to the chamber, the sight of it will retrieve a representation of the stimulus to the A2 state.

Should the stimulus then be presented in conjunction with a US, learning about this relationship will be difficult because the representation of the CS will be in a state that does not allow excitatory conditioning.

The experiments by Whitlow (1975) and by Best and Gemberling (1977) have also revealed effects that can be attributed to the influence of retrieval-generated A2 representations. In his study with rabbits, Whitlow (1975) discovered that the response to a repeatedly presented tone was greater on the first than on subsequent sessions of testing. This relatively long-term effect was attributed to the growth of a context–tone association during the first session. Subsequent placement of the rabbits into the apparatus should then partially retrieve an A2 representation of the tone and make them less responsive to it whenever it occurred. Thus the SOP model predicts that habituation is the result of the interaction of both short-term (self-generated) and long-term (retrieval-generated) processes.

For the study by Best and Gemberling (1977), inspection of Figure 3.11 reveals that conditioning with Group 23.5 was somewhat less effective than for Group Control. The interval of 23.5 hours between the first exposure to the flavor and the conditioning trial makes it unlikely that this disruption was due to the influence of a self-generated representation. But the preexposure trial may well have fostered the growth of a context-flavor association. This would then disrupt conditioning somewhat by ensuring that at least a component of the representation of the flavor was in the A2 state at the time of conditioning (see Westbrook, Bond, & Feyer, 1981, for a similar finding).

Some novel predictions

A measure of the value of any theory is the degree to which it generates novel experimental research. In this respect, Wagner's theorizing has been most successful. A wide range of studies has been designed to test the theory, often with positive results.

We have seen that according to the theory the repeated experience of a stimulus in a specific context will result in the growth of a context-stimulus association and will be responsible for a loss of attention to that stimulus. But such a loss need not be permanent. Suppose the stimulus is subsequently presented in a different context with which it is not associated. The new context should not excite an A2 representation of the stimulus, and it should now be attended to fully. The theory predicts therefore that latent inhibition and habituation will be specific to the context in which the stimulus was exposed. Note that this prediction is confined to the influence of retrieval-generated representations. The more transient effects of self-generated A2 representations should be found in any context, as they depend simply on the recent occurrence of the stimulus concerned.

As far as both latent inhibition and habituation are concerned, there is evidence showing that these effects are specific to the context in which the stimulus was exposed. Lovibond, Preston, and Mackintosh (1984), for example, reported that exposure to a stimulus is more likely to disrupt future conditioning in the same than in a different chamber, whereas Jordan, Strasser, and McHale (2000) have shown that once habituation has occurred in one context, it is possible to observe a recovery from this effect—dishabituation—by presenting the stimulus in a different environment.

A related prediction concerns the influence of exposing animals to an experimental context after they have repeatedly been exposed to a stimulus in it. The original exposure will result in the development of a context-stimulus association. Then, just as presenting a CS without a US can weaken a previously formed CS–US association, so a context–stimulus association should be weakened by placing subjects in the apparatus without the stimulus. Such extinction will prevent the context from exciting an A2 representation of the stimulus, so that it should be attended to when it next occurs. In support of this prediction Wagner (1978, pp. 203–204) cites an experiment in which two groups of rabbits were exposed to a series of tones for a single habituation session. One group was then placed into the apparatus for two sessions, in the absence of the tone. Animals from the other group remained in their home cages for this stage. Finally, both groups were returned to the apparatus for a test of their reaction to the tone. Subjects given exposure to the context without the tone, which should have weakened the context–tone association, responded more on these test trials than did those that had spent the previous stage in their home cages.

The successes referred to can be contrasted with a number of failures to support the theory. Latent inhibition is said to be due to the growth of context–CS associations, so that a period of exposure to the apparatus alone after the prior exposure to the CS should weaken these associations and disrupt latent inhibition. Despite a number of tests of this prediction, it has met with very little success (Hall, 1991). In addition, habituating a stimulus and then presenting it in a new context should produce dishabituation, but this does not always occur (Jordan et al., 2000). Further results that are inconsistent with Wagner's theorizing will also be mentioned later in this chapter. Despite these conflicting findings, the success with which the theory accounts for many of the phenomena associated with latent inhibition and habituation means that it would be unwise to ignore it as an account for the attentional processes of animals.

"Hunting by search image" (Von Uexkull, 1934) describes the perceptual mechanism by which animals "zone in" on their intended prey (a salmon, in this eagle's case) at the expense of other targets.

STIMULUS SIGNIFICANCE

One class of stimuli to which an animal might be expected to attend is that which signals events of biological significance. The animal that rapidly detects a signal for food, for instance, is more likely to survive than one that ignores this stimulus. Given this line of reasoning, several authors have proposed that animals are likely to pay most attention to stimuli that predict important events.

Von Uexkull (1934) was one of the first to make this suggestion when he coined the phrase "hunting by search image". This was meant to imply that, when animals are searching for food, their perceptual systems are biased to facilitate the identification of a particular type of food at the expense of not recognizing other types. Provided that the food being attended to is in plentiful supply, this should be an efficient strategy for gaining nourishment.

Support for this proposal comes from an experiment by Bond (1983) who presented pigeons with a mixture of two different types of grain on a gravel-based background. When the grains were conspicuous in respect to the background, the birds showed no bias in their choice of grain. However, a marked bias for one type of grain over another was shown when they were both difficult to distinguish from the background. Thus, if identification of food is difficult, pigeons attend selectively to the features of a single food type to facilitate its discovery (see also Dawkins, 1971a,b).

In a related study, Plaisted (1997) required pigeons to identify a target that was hard to distinguish from the background. Two examples of the targets are presented in the upper row of Figure 3.12; examples of the backgrounds they were presented against are shown in the lower rows. The experiment started with the target presented against patterns of low crypticity (row A), but as the birds became proficient at finding the target it was presented against backgrounds of increasing complexity (rows B and C). The important finding from the study is that the target was easier to find when the interval between trials was 20 seconds then when it was 40 seconds. The implication of this finding is that hunting by search image will be effective only if the prey is relatively abundant and if it does not take too much time to find the next item of food once the previous one has been eaten. To explain this constraint, Plaisted (1997) suggested that once a target has been detected it leaves a gradually decaying trace of itself. If this trace should persist until the target is encountered again then it will facilitate the detection of the target. Although this explanation might be correct, it is at odds with the proposals by Wagner (1981) concerning the interaction between stimulus representations in the A1 and A2 state. According to the SOP theory, the presence of a decaying memory trace will make it harder, not easier, to react to a stimulus when it is presented again. Quite how Plaisted's findings, and her explanation for them, can be reconciled with this aspect of Wagner's theorizing remains to be determined.

FIGURE 3.12 Examples of the targets and the backgrounds for the study by Plaisted (1997). Copyright © American Psychological Association. Reprinted with permission.

Rather different evidence for the claim that animals concentrate on stimuli that signal events of biological significance comes from attempts to show that animals pay more attention to stimuli if they are relevant than if they are irrelevant to the solution of a discrimination. The results from early experiments that claimed to reveal such an effect (e.g. Lawrence, 1949, 1950) are open to interpretation in ways that do not rely on changes in attention (Siegel, 1967). More recent experiments that have compared the effects of what are known as **intradimensional shifts** and **extradimensional shifts** (IDS and EDS) have led to mixed results, but on balance their findings are consistent with the claim that, during a discrimination, animals learn to pay more attention to relevant than irrelevant stimuli (for reviews see Mackintosh, 1974, pp. 597–598; Hall, 1991, pp. 192–193).

To appreciate what is involved in studies of EDS and IDS, examine the patterns in the left-hand panel of Figure 3.13 (Stage 1) that depict stimuli used by George and Pearce (1999) for a discrimination involving two groups of pigeons. The stimuli were shown on a television screen behind a rectangular, clear Perspex response key and

KEY TERMS

Intradimensional shift (IDS)
The selection of two stimuli for a discrimination from a dimension that provided two stimuli for an earlier discrimination.

Extradimensional shift (EDS)
The selection of two stimuli for a discrimination from a different dimension to one that provided two stimuli for an earlier discrimination.

FIGURE 3.13 The stimuli used in an experiment by George and Pearce (1999) involving patterns composed of two squares that contained one of four different colors (depicted by the four levels of brightness) and four line orientations. Reward was delivered after responses to the patterns beneath the + sign, but not after responses to patterns beneath the − sign. EDS, extradimensional; IDS, intradimensional.

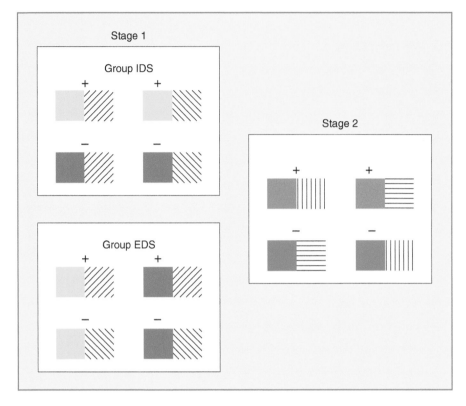

consisted of two squares. One of the squares was filled with either blue or yellow, and the other was filled with either forwards- or backwards-slanting black and white lines. Group IDS received the training displayed in the top half of the panel, with reward being delivered for pecking the Perspex panel when the colored square was yellow (indicated by + in Figure 3.13) but not when it was blue (− in the figure). Group EDS received the training displayed in the bottom half of the panel, with reward being delivered for pecking in the presence of forwards- (+) but not backwards-slanting lines (−). As a result of this arrangement, color was relevant and line orientation was irrelevant for Group IDS, whereas the opposite was true for Group EDS.

Once the birds had mastered the discrimination, both groups received a new discrimination with stimuli shown in the right-hand panel of the figure (Stage 2). On this occasion, the colors were red and green, and the lines were horizontal or vertical. Food was presented after pecks when the color in the square was red (+ in Figure 3.13) but not when it was green (− in the figure). For this stage, color but not line orientation was relevant to the solution of the discrimination. The new discrimination for Group IDS was based, therefore, on stimuli that belonged to a dimension that had been relevant during Stage 1, whereas for Group EDS the new discrimination was based on a dimension that had previously been irrelevant. If pigeons pay more attention to stimuli that are relevant than irrelevant to the solution of a discrimination then, as a result of the Stage-1 training, Group IDS should start Stage 2 by attending to color rather than line orientation, and learn the new discrimination rapidly. Conversely, Group EDS should start Stage 2 by paying more attention to line orientation than color, and find the new discrimination difficult.

The results confirmed this prediction. Similar findings have been reported using rats (Shepp & Eimas, 1964) and marmosets (Dias, Robbins, & Roberts, 1996).

Findings such as these have encouraged the development of a number of theories that assume that significant stimuli gain in the attention they are paid during the course of conditioning (Sutherland & Mackintosh, 1971; Mackintosh, 1975a; Moore & Stickney, 1980). The discussion that follows focuses on the most influential of these theories.

Mackintosh's theory

Mackintosh (1975a) based his theory on the claim that animals will pay attention to, and hence learn readily about, stimuli that are good predictors of significant events, such as food or shock. In other words, stimuli with high associative strength are likely to receive more attention than those with low associative strength. In fact, the theory is not quite this simple. To be attended to fully, a CS must not only be a good predictor of the US, it must be a better predictor than all the other stimuli that are present on a trial.

One important feature of Mackintosh's (1975a) theory is that it provides a different account of blocking to that considered hitherto. The Rescorla–Wagner (1972) model, as well as Wagner's (1981) SOP model, maintains that blocking is due to the US being fully predicted and thus incapable of entering into novel associations. Mackintosh (1975a) has challenged this claim by proposing that blocking is entirely a result of subjects ignoring the stimulus added for compound conditioning. To understand the application of his theory to blocking, it is essential to emphasize that Mackintosh (1975a) rejects the Rescorla–Wagner (1972) account of compound conditioning. As an alternative, the growth of associative strength to a CS is given by Equation 3.11, which is to be applied when the stimulus is presented either in isolation or in conjunction with other stimuli:

$$\Delta V_A = \alpha_A (\lambda - V_A) \qquad (3.11)$$

According to this equation, conditioning with a CS on any given trial is completely unaffected by the properties of the stimuli that accompany it. The value of α reflects the amount of attention that the stimulus receives; the greater its value, the more rapid will conditioning be. The way in which α is calculated need not concern us here, except to note that its value can vary during the course of conditioning. The value of α will approach 1 when the stimulus is a good predictor of the US relative to other stimuli, and when the stimulus is a relatively poor predictor of the US then it will approach 0.

According to Mackintosh (1975a), animals will pay attention to stimuli that are good predictors of events such as food and shock. These lemurs have learned to be on the look out for any warning signs of predators.

Consider now a blocking experiment in which a tone is paired with a US prior to conditioning with a light–tone compound. On the first compound trial, the attention paid to the light will be relatively high because of its novelty, and Equation 3.11 predicts that it will gain in associative strength. Animals will also have the opportunity of discovering on this trial that the light is a much poorer predictor of the US than the tone. The theory therefore predicts that on future conditioning trials they should pay very little attention to the light and further increments in associative strength to this stimulus will be slight. The difference between this account and that provided by the Rescorla–Wagner model for blocking is emphasized by the conflicting predictions they make. As we have seen, Mackintosh's (1975a) theory asserts that conditioning with the added CS should be normal on the first compound trial. It is only on later trials when the added CS is ignored that the effects of blocking should become evident. By contrast, the Rescorla–Wagner (1972) model predicts that provided the US is fully predicted on the first compound trial, conditioning with the added CS should be impossible.

In keeping with the prediction from his theory, Mackintosh (1975b) has shown that conditioning with the added CS is normal for the first compound-conditioning trial but that there was very little change in the associative strength of this stimulus on subsequent compound trials. Further support for this theory can be found in studies that have looked at the influence of surprise on blocking (Dickinson, Hall, & Mackintosh, 1976; Mackintosh, Bygrave, & Picton, 1977; Dickinson & Mackintosh, 1979). One of these studies was described earlier (see p. 73), where its results were shown to be incompatible with predictions from the Rescorla–Wagner (1972) model. Essentially, the study demonstrated that the surprising omission of one of a pair of shocks after each compound-conditioning trial was sufficient to disrupt blocking. According to Mackintosh's (1975a) theory, this outcome is due to the surprising omission of one shock arresting the decline in attention to the added stimulus, and hence allowing subjects to learn about its relationship with the shock that was presented. A more complete presentation of this explanation can be found in Dickinson and Mackintosh (1979), and findings that pose a challenge to the detail—but not the spirit—of the explanation for blocking offered by Mackintosh (1975a) can be found in Holland and Kenmuir (2005). Additional support for the proposals of Mackintosh (1975a) comes from a study by Holland and Fox (2003), who demonstrated a loss of associability by a stimulus that was introduced for the compound conditioning stage of a blocking experiment.

Selective association and learned irrelevance

In addition to enhancing our understanding of such effects as blocking, Mackintosh's (1975a) theory has the merit of pointing to a new way of looking at an effect known as **selective association**. An assumption that was once common to many theories of learning is that conditioning will be equally effective, no matter what stimuli are paired together. In a discussion of this topic Seligman and Hager (1972) referred to this claim as the principle of equipotentiality but, they argued, there is abundant evidence to contradict it. For example, Garcia and Koelling (1966) (see p. 14) found that rats associate illness more readily with a flavor than with an auditory–visual compound. This is not simply due to the interoceptive stimulus being more intense and hence a more effective CS than the exteroceptive compound, because the opposite pattern of results was found when the stimuli were paired with shock. Moreover, this pattern of results is not confined to tastes, illness, or rats. Shapiro, Jacobs, and LoLordo (1980) have demonstrated a similar outcome with pigeons, which have little trouble in learning that a red light signals food but which learn with difficulty when the same stimulus is used to signal shock. Conversely, conditioning with a tone progresses more readily when it signals an aversive rather than an appetitive US.

One explanation for selective association is that it is due to some stimuli, or stimulus dimensions, being more relevant to the occurrence of biologically significant events than others. In the case of the Garcia and Koelling (1966) study, for example, tastes are likely to provide more reliable information than sounds and lights about whether or not a certain food is poisonous. Given such naturally occurring relationships, it would be in the animal's best interests to learn about them rapidly. Animals may also benefit by being disposed to learn little or nothing at all about those relationships that are unlikely to occur in their natural environment (Seligman, 1970; Seligman & Hager, 1972).

Experiments on selective association thus suggest that during conditioning animals will attend most to those stimuli, or dimensions, that in the past have proved reliable predictors of the US concerned. But how do they know which cues are most relevant for a given US? According to Rozin and Kalat (1971), this knowledge is acquired as a result of evolutionary processes. That is, some members of a species may be innately disposed to learn rapidly about the relationship between tastes and illness and hence more likely to survive, and to pass on this characteristic, than those lacking in this respect.

The implication of this suggestion is that selective association will be evident from birth, which is supported by the findings of Gemberling and Domjan (1982). Rats were conditioned when they were only 24 hours old with either illness, induced by an injection of lithium chloride, or electric shock. When illness constituted the US, the consumption of saccharin—but not being placed into a cardboard box—was

KEY TERM

Learned irrelevance
The slower learning that takes place when a CS and US are paired if they have previously been presented randomly with respect to each other.

an effective CS. But when shock was the US, it was being placed into the box, rather than saccharin, that was the more effective CS. The rats are unlikely to have learned anything during their first 24 hours of life that would account for this pattern of results. Instead, the most likely explanation for these findings is that rats are genetically disposed to learn about some relationships more easily than about others.

In addition to innate factors, the discovery of an effect known as **learned irrelevance** suggests that an animal's experience may also contribute to selective association. In a typical study, Mackintosh (1973) exposed rats to random presentations of a CS and foot shock (Group Random). As the CS was no better a predictor of the US than the contextual stimuli, his theory predicts that attention to the CS will decline. To test this prediction, conditioned suppression training in which the CS and US were paired was then conducted. Figure 3.14 shows that conditioning for this group was considerably less effective than for Group Control, in which the CS and US were both novel at the start of conditioning. A third group, Group Water, was also included in this study. These subjects were given random presentations of the CS and water prior to conditioned suppression training in which the same CS was paired with shock. The intriguing finding from this group is that pretreatment with the CS had a much less disruptive influence on conditioning than for Group Random. The converse of this effect has also been demonstrated: Conditioning with water is disrupted to a greater extent by prior random presentations of the CS and water than of the CS and shock. Here then is an example of selective association that is due to the individual's experience, rather than to its evolutionary history.

To explain this pattern of findings, Mackintosh (1973; Bennett, Maldonado, & Mackintosh, 1995) proposed that the random pairings of a CS and a US will result

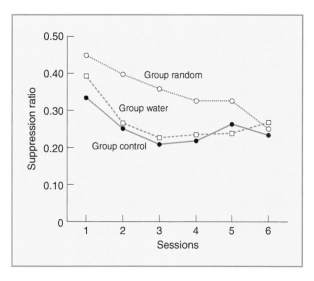

FIGURE 3.14 Acquisition of conditioned suppression by three groups of rats trained with a conditioned stimulus (CS) that was novel for the start of conditioning (Group Control) or had previously been presented in a random relationship with shock (Group Random) or with water (Group Water) (adapted from Mackintosh, 1973).

in a loss of attention to the CS that is US specific. Put informally, learning that a CS is irrelevant to the delivery of shock will result in animals ignoring it when these events are eventually paired. However, should the CS be used to signal a different US, such as water, then attention to it will be restored, and conditioning will progress more readily.

The results reported in this section again point to the importance of attentional factors in governing the behavior of animals. The principal theoretical claim that has been examined is that animals will pay attention to those stimuli that predict important events. We turn now to consider a theory that makes a rather different assumption about the factors that determine whether or not an animal will attend to a stimulus.

THE PEARCE–HALL THEORY

To introduce the third account of animal attention it may help to return to the experiment of Brown and Poulton (1961), in which people found it difficult to attend to a string of numbers while driving. An additional group in this study consisted of policemen with considerable driving experience. They, too, were required to identify the changed member of a list while driving, but they were able to do both tasks without difficulty, even in urban areas. Perhaps this result should not be too surprising, as the popularity of car radios attests to the ability of many people to drive and attend to an unrelated source of information at the same time. The challenge posed by such results is to provide an adequate theory of attention to explain them.

According to a number of authors, people have two modes of attention that can operate simultaneously. One of these is assumed to be of limited capacity and is directed towards tasks that are novel or require conscious control. This type of attention is referred to as controlled or deliberate (LaBerge & Samuels, 1974; Shiffrin & Schneider, 1977). An example of a task that might be appropriate to this type of attention is the number-identification task employed by Brown and Poulton (1961). The other type of attention is more automatic and directed towards tasks that are very well practiced and the performance of which is more or less habitual. When learning to drive, it can be assumed that the novelty of the task will demand controlled processing and that little spare capacity will be available for attending to numbers. With practice, however, automatic processes may be responsible for driving, freeing the controlled processing mechanisms to cope with other tasks.

It is within this framework that the Pearce–Hall (1980) model can be most readily understood. This model is based on the supposition that animals need to attend to a stimulus only while they are learning about its relationship with its consequences. With Pavlovian conditioning, for instance, attention must be paid to the CS to allow it to gain or lose associative strength. But once conditioning has reached a stable asymptote, there will be no further need for the subject to attend to the CS and it can be ignored, at least as far as learning is concerned. This type of attention is analogous to controlled processing in humans. Of course, once learning has ceased, the fact that the stimulus may no longer receive controlled processing does not mean that it will be without influence. Instead, it is assumed that once learning has reached a stable asymptote, the CS will be detected, and the appropriate CR triggered, by automatic processes.

According to Pearce and Hall (1980), therefore, controlled attention will be directed most to those stimuli that need to be learned about. But what sort of stimuli fall into this category? To answer this question we proposed that the surprisingness of the event that follows a CS will determine how much learning remains to be done with that CS. If learning about a CS has reached a stable asymptote then the US that follows it will not come as a surprise, and no further learning will be needed. By contrast, if learning about the CS–US relationship is still taking place then the US will to some extent be surprising after each presentation of the CS and thus indicate the need for additional learning. Hence, if the US is surprising on one conditioning trial, trial n, then on the next trial, trial $n + 1$, the CS should receive attention so that learning about its relationship with the US can continue. But if the US that accompanies a CS is entirely predictable, then there is little need for learning and hence little need for attention to be directed towards the CS on future trials.

To present these ideas formally we used the now familiar discrepancy $\lambda - V$ to describe the extent to which the US is surprising on trial n. The relationship between this discrepancy, and the amount of attention paid to the CS on the next trial, α_{n+1} is given by Equation 3.12

$$\alpha_{n+1} = |\lambda_n - V_n| \tag{3.12}$$

On trials when the US is surprising, the value of the discrepancy will be large, and attention to the CS will be high on the following trial. But as the CS becomes a better predictor of the US, there will be a smaller difference between λ and V, and attention to the CS will be reduced accordingly.

Implications for the orienting response

An experiment by Kaye and Pearce (1984) demonstrates the operation of these principles. The aim of the study was to test the Pearce–Hall (1980) theory by using the OR as an index of the attention paid to a light CS during conditioning. Three groups of rats received in a pretest session six presentations of the light, each lasting for 10 seconds, so that their reactions to it when novel could be assessed. Figure 3.15 indicates that attention to the light for this session was comparatively high. The conditions for the groups then differed for the test stage of the experiment, which

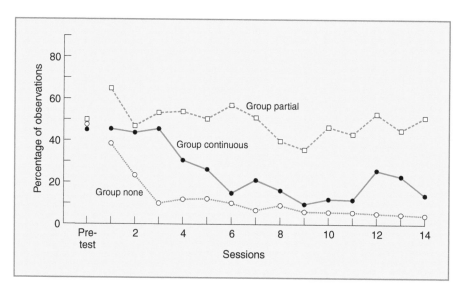

FIGURE 3.15 The frequency with which an orienting response (OR) to a light was recorded for three groups in a pretest session and during the next 14 sessions when the light signaled nothing (Group None), food on every trial (Group Continuous), or food on a randomly determined half of the trials (Group Partial) (adapted from Kaye & Pearce, 1984).

comprised 14 sessions. In each session, Group None was given a number of exposures to the light entirely in the absence of any US. In these circumstances, the events following the light will never be surprising, because from the outset it will not predict a US and none will occur. Accordingly, there will be no need for subjects to attend to the light, and it should very quickly be ignored. Figure 3.15 shows support for this prediction in a rapid decline in the frequency of the OR across sessions. The second group, Group Continuous, received the same number of presentations of the light as the previous group, but each one was followed by a pellet of food. Initially, the low associative strength of the light will ensure that the food with which it is paired is unexpected, and attention to the light should be considerable. As training progresses, however, the CS will gain in associative strength and, as it becomes a better predictor of the US, so attention to it will decline. Thus the model predicts that the OR to the light will be high at the start of conditioning but decline gradually thereafter. Once again, these predictions are supported by the results shown in Figure 3.15.

The final group, Group Partial, received the light followed by food on a random 50% of the trials, and on the remaining trials the light was followed by nothing. On this schedule, rats will be unable to predict what will follow the CS on each trial and, as a result, the occurrence of food—or its omission—will consistently be surprising. The effect of this should be to sustain attention to the light no matter how many times it is presented. In confirmation of this prediction Figure 3.15 shows that for Group Partial the OR to the light was as vigorous after 14 sessions (84 trials) as when it was novel.

Implications for conditioning

Pearce and Hall (1980) proposed that animals will pay least attention to, and hence learn most slowly about, those stimuli that have been followed by accurately predicted events; whereas stimuli that have been paired with surprising events should be attended to and learned about readily. To explain the rapid conditioning that often occurs with a novel CS, the theory accepts that the attention paid to a stimulus is high when it is first presented. But once conditioning has commenced, the CS will gain in associative strength and become a progressively more accurate predictor of the US. This will result in a gradual loss of attention to the CS, and the increments in associative strength will therefore be less on later than on earlier trials. Eventually the CS will accurately predict the US, whereupon it will be ignored completely and no further changes in associative strength will be possible. This relationship between attention and learning is summarized by Equation 3.13 in which α is given by Equation 3.12 and S is determined by the intensity of the CS:

$$\Delta V = \alpha \times S \times \lambda \tag{3.13}$$

Interpretation of the study by Kaye and Pearce (1984) points to the way in which the Pearce–Hall model explains latent inhibition. Attention was said to decline to a stimulus that is repeatedly presented by itself because it is an accurate predictor of nothing (Group None). If such a stimulus is then paired with a US, it will gain associative strength more slowly than if it were novel.

Blocking

The presentation of the Pearce–Hall model so far has been concerned exclusively with the effects of training with a single CS. When applied to compound conditioning, it is assumed that as long as the US is accurately predicted by one stimulus, or a collection of stimuli, then there is no further need for learning and thus no further need for attention to any of the stimuli present on that trial. As a consequence, Pearce and Hall (1980) stipulate that for conditioning with a compound, attention to each element will be determined by how accurately the US is predicted by all the stimuli that belong to the compound. To incorporate this stipulation into Equation 3.12, the value of V must be determined by the combined associative strength of all the stimuli that are present on a trial.

Quite surprisingly, given the differences between them, the Pearce–Hall model now makes exactly the same predictions about blocking as Mackintosh's theory. On the first compound-conditioning trial, the novelty of the added stimulus will ensure it receives attention and that it acquires some associative strength. The subject will also discover on this trial that the stimulus is followed by a US that is totally unsurprising, because its occurrence will be predicted by the other element of the compound. This discovery will ensure that the new stimulus is virtually ignored on the next trial, and further changes in its associative strength will be slight.

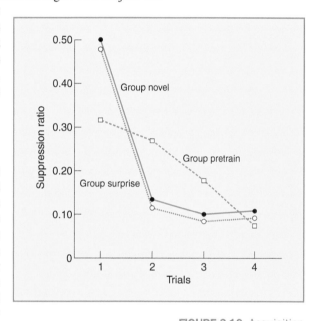

Latent inhibition of a CS

The difference between the theories of Mackintosh (1975a) and Pearce and Hall (1980) is brought out very clearly by another set of experiments (Hall & Pearce, 1979, 1982a,b; Pearce & Hall, 1979). In one of these (Hall & Pearce 1982a), three groups of rats received conditioned suppression training in which a tone was paired with a moderately strong shock. For Group Novel, the tone was novel at the outset of this stage, and conditioning with it was very rapid (Figure 3.16). Prior to conditioning with moderately strong shock, Group Pretrain experienced a large number of conditioning trials in which the tone was paired with a relatively weak shock. At the start of conditioning with the weak shock animals should attend to the tone as it gains in associative strength; but once conditioning has reached asymptote, the Pearce–Hall (1980) theory predicts that the tone should be ignored. This low level of attention to the tone should then ensure that conditioning progresses slowly when it is paired with the large shock for the test phase. In other words, the Pearce–Hall (1980) theory predicts that it should be possible to obtain latent inhibition by repeatedly pairing the CS with a US, as well as repeatedly presenting it by itself. In confirmation of this prediction Figure 3.16 shows that conditioning with Group Pretrain was slow for the test stage. Note that the low suppression ratio on the first trial was probably due to the pretraining with the weak shock.

Subjects in Group Pretrain eventually learned about the relationship between the tone and the large shock, albeit gradually, and this can be explained in the following manner. The low attention paid to the tone on the first trial will permit only a limited increment of associative strength. Of more importance, however, is that subjects will also be provided with the opportunity of discovering that the tone is again followed by a surprising US—in the recent past it accurately predicted a small US, and now

FIGURE 3.16 Acquisition of conditioned suppression to a tone by three groups of rats when it was paired with a strong shock for four test trials. The tone was novel at the outset of this training for Group Novel, but for Group Pretrain and Group Surprise it had previously been paired with a weak shock. Group Surprise additionally received two trials with the tone presented alone between the two conditioning stages (adapted from Hall & Pearce, 1982a).

suddenly it is followed by a large one. Attention to the tone should therefore be restored and enable better learning about the CS–strong shock relationship in the future. To test this account a third group was included in the study, Group Surprise. These subjects received the same initial training as Group Pretrain, but on the test session two surprise trials prior to conditioning with the large shock were included. These trials consisted simply of following the tone by nothing and were intended to alert animals to the fact that the CS is no longer an accurate predictor of shock. Such a manipulation should restore attention to the tone and facilitate conditioning with the larger shock in the final stage. The results confirmed this prediction by showing that Group Surprise conditioned more rapidly than Group Pretrain and at much the same rate as Group Novel. A similar finding, but using appetitive conditioning, has been reported by Wilson, Boumphrey and Pearce (1992).

Turning now to the theory of Mackintosh (1975a), pairing the tone with the weak shock in Group Pretrain should result in the tone eventually being the best available predictor of this US. The theory therefore predicts that the original training with the tone will ensure that it receives considerable attention, and conditioning will progress rapidly when it is paired with the larger shock. By failing to confirm this prediction, the results from Group Pretrain pose a serious challenge to perhaps the most important assumption of the theory. The idea that animals pay a lot of attention to stimuli that signal biologically important events is undoubtedly attractive. On the basis of the findings that have just been discussed, however, we must conclude that if a high level of attention is directed to such stimuli, then it is in order to ensure they elicit appropriate responses, rather than to determine their conditionability.

The results from Group Surprise also have a bearing on the theory developed by Wagner (1981). The way to restore attention to a stimulus according to this theory is to present it in a manner that ensures that it is not represented in the A2 state. We saw earlier that this may be achieved either by exposing subjects to the stimulus in a different context, or by adopting steps to weaken previously formed context–stimulus associations. In the case of Group Surprise, neither of these manipulations was adopted, yet a restoration of attention to the tone was recorded, as revealed by the rapid conditioning in the test phase relative to Group Pretrain. This finding strongly implies that it is how accurately the events following a stimulus are predicted that determines the attention it receives.

Before closing this discussion of the Pearce–Hall model, we should note, with regret, that even this theory has its shortcoming. A clear prediction from the theory is that once a stimulus is ignored, attention to it can be restored only by following it with a surprising event. However, in the discussion of Wagner's theory it was shown that attention to a stimulus can be restored in a number of other ways, for example, by presenting the stimulus in a new context or by placing the subject in the original context and withholding the stimulus for a number of sessions.

Another problem for the theory is posed by Mackintosh's (1973) discovery of learned irrelevance, in which random pairings of a CS and US were found to retard conditioning when they were eventually paired. By being randomly related to the US, the CS can be considered to be an inaccurate predictor of its occurrence. Hence, according to the theory, attention should remain at a high level to this stimulus and facilitate conditioning in the test phase. One possible explanation for the failure to confirm this prediction can be based on the fact that the random presentations of the CS and US will result in the growth of a context–US association. As a consequence, whenever the US is, by chance, paired with the CS, it will be accurately predicted by the contextual stimuli, and attention to the CS will decline because it is followed by an accurately predicted event. A final problem is posed by experiments showing that animals pay more attention to stimuli that are relevant than irrelevant to the solution of a discrimination (George & Pearce, 1999).

CONCLUDING COMMENTS

The great pity when considering the aforementioned three theories of attention is that not one of them can explain all the relevant experimental findings. Perhaps we should conclude, therefore, that there is a grain of truth in each of these different theories, and that the attentional processes in animals are more complex than has hitherto been acknowledged. Indeed, a recent theory of learning proposed by LePelley (2004) is based on just this conclusion and incorporates the attentional rules proposed by Mackintosh (1975a) and by Pearce and Hall (1980). This theory also assumes that changes in associative strength are governed by a rule similar to that advocated by Rescorla and Wagner (1972). One of the many intriguing implications of LePelley's (2004) theory is that blocking will be a consequence of the interaction of two factors. One factor is a loss of effectiveness by the US because it is no longer surprising. The other factor is a loss of attention, and hence associability, by the added stimulus because it is a relatively poor predictor of the US. Support for this hybrid account of blocking is revealed in an experiment by Holland and Fox (2003). They were able to demonstrate, on the one hand that blocking can reduce the associability of the added stimulus and, on the other hand, that blocking can take place even when steps are taken to prevent any changes in associability. Such changes were prevented by lesioning the hippocampus.

There has been a marked imbalance in the comparative study of attention. A large number of studies have shown habituation in a wide range of species. By contrast, there have been remarkably few attempts to discover whether changes in the conditionability of stimuli can be obtained with species other than mammals. Lubow (1973) reviews experiments showing latent inhibition in goats, dogs, sheep, rats, and rabbits, but beyond this, studies of latent inhibition are rare. There have been several attempts to demonstrate latent inhibition in pigeons, but these have led to conflicting findings (Mackintosh, 1973; Tranberg & Rilling, 1978); others have had no success in their attempts to show latent inhibition in honey-bees (Bitterman, Menzel, Fietz, & Schafer, 1983) or goldfish (Shishimi, 1985). If future research should confirm that changes in attention, as indexed by changes in conditionability, are unique to mammals, then this will be an important discovery. Perhaps selective attention, or some aspects of it, is one capacity that will allow us to differentiate between the cognitive processes of species.

Finally, the experiments described in this chapter demonstrate forcefully that conditioning does not occur automatically whenever the CS and US are paired together. Experiments designed to test the Rescorla–Wagner (1972) theory, as well as Wagner's (1981) theory, demonstrate that a US can be effective for conditioning in some circumstances but not others. Likewise, the experiments considered in the second section of this chapter demonstrate that certain experiences with a CS can alter its effectiveness for conditioning. If future theories of learning are to be successful they must take account of these changes in the properties of both the CS and the US.

CHAPTER 4

CONTENTS

Instrumental conditioning

Behavior is affected by its consequences. Responses that lead to reward are repeated, whereas those that lead to punishment are withheld. Instrumental conditioning refers to the method of using reward and punishment in order to modify an animal's behavior. The first laboratory demonstration of instrumental conditioning was provided by Thorndike (1898) who, as we saw in Chapter l, trained cats to make a response in order to escape from a puzzle box and earn a small amount of fish. Since this pioneering work, there have been many thousands of successful demonstrations of instrumental conditioning, employing a wide range of species, and a variety of experimental designs. Skinner, for example, taught two pigeons, by means of instrumental conditioning, to play ping-pong with each other.

From the point of view of understanding the mechanisms of animal intelligence, three important issues are raised by a successful demonstration of instrumental conditioning. We need to know what information an animal acquires as a result of its training. Pavlovian conditioning was shown to promote the growth of stimulus–stimulus associations, but what sort of associations develop when a response is followed by a reward or punishment? Once the nature of the associations formed during instrumental conditioning has been identified, we then need to specify the conditions that promote their growth. Surprise, for example, is important for successful Pavlovian conditioning, but what are the necessary ingredients to ensure the success of instrumental conditioning? Finally, we need to understand the factors that determine when, and how vigorously, an instrumental response will be performed.

Before turning to a detailed discussion of these issues, we must be clear what is meant by the term **reinforcer**. This term refers to the events that result in the strengthening of an instrumental response. The events are classified as either positive reinforcers, when they consist of the delivery of a stimulus, or negative reinforcers, when it involves the removal of a stimulus.

THE NATURE OF INSTRUMENTAL LEARNING

Historical background

Thorndike (1898) was the first to propose that instrumental conditioning is based on learning about responses. According to his Law of Effect, when a response is followed by a reinforcer, then a stimulus–response (S–R) connection is strengthened. In the case of a rat that must press a lever for food, the stimulus might be the lever itself and the response would be the action of pressing the lever. Each successful lever press would thus serve to strengthen a connection between the sight of the lever and the response of pressing it. As a result, whenever the rat came across the lever in the future, it would be likely to press it and thus gain reward. This analysis of instrumental conditioning has formed the basis of a number of extremely influential theories of learning (e.g. Hull, 1943).

KEY TERM

Reinforcer
An event that increases the probability of a response when presented after it. If the event is the occurrence of a stimulus, such as food, it is referred to as a positive reinforcer; but if the event is the removal of a stimulus, such as shock, it is referred to as a negative reinforcer.

A feature of the Law of Effect that has proved unacceptable to the intuitions of many psychologists is that it fails to allow the animal to anticipate the goal for which it is responding. The only knowledge that an S–R connection permits an animal to possess is the knowledge that it must make a particular response in the presence of a given stimulus. The delivery of food after the response will, according to the Law of Effect, effectively come as a complete surprise to the animal. In addition to sounding implausible, this proposal has for many years conflicted with a variety of experimental findings.

One early finding is reported by Tinkelpaugh (1928), who required monkeys to select one of two food wells to obtain reward. On some trials the reward was a banana, which was greatly preferred to the other reward, a lettuce leaf. Once the animals had been trained they were occasionally presented with a lettuce leaf when they should have received a banana. The following quote, which is cited in Mackintosh (1974), provides a clear indication that the monkey expected a more attractive reward for making the correct response (Tinkelpaugh, 1928, p. 224):

She extends her hand to seize the food. But her hand drops to the floor without touching it. She looks at the lettuce but (unless very hungry) does not touch it. She looks around the cup and behind the board. She stands up and looks under and around her. She picks the cup up and examines it thoroughly inside and out. She had on occasion turned toward the observers present in the room and shrieked at them in apparent anger.

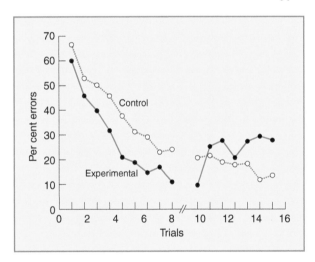

FIGURE 4.1 The mean number of errors made by two groups of rats in a multiple-unit maze. For the first nine trials the reward for the control group was more attractive than for the experimental group, but for the remaining trials both groups received the same reward (adapted from Elliott, 1928).

A rather different type of finding that shows animals anticipate the rewards for which they are responding can be found in experiments in which rats ran down an alley, or through a maze, for food. If a rat is trained first with one reward which is then changed in attractiveness, there is a remarkably rapid change in its performance on subsequent trials. Elliott (1928) found that the number of errors in a multiple-unit maze increased dramatically when the quality of reward in the goal box was reduced. Indeed, the animals were so dejected by this change that they made more errors than a control group that had been trained throughout with the less attractive reward (Figure 4.1). According to S–R theory, the change in performance by the experimental group should have taken place more slowly, and should not have resulted in less accurate responding than that shown by the control group. As an alternative explanation, these findings imply that the animals had some expectancy of the reward they would receive in the goal that allowed them to detect when it was made less attractive.

Tolman (1932) argued that findings such as these indicate that rats form R–unconditioned stimulus (US) associations as a result of instrumental conditioning. They are assumed to learn that a response will be followed by a particular outcome. There is no doubt that the results are consistent with this proposal, but they do not force us to accept it. Several S–R theorists have pointed out that the anticipation of reward could have been based on conditioned stimulus (CS)–US, rather than R–US associations. In Elliott's (1928) experiment, for example, the animal consumed the reward in the goal box. It is possible that the stimuli created by this part of the apparatus served as a CS that became associated with food. After a number of training trials, therefore, the sight of the goal box would activate a representation of the reward and thereby permit the animal to detect when its value was changed. Both Hull (1943) and Spence (1956) seized on this possibility and proposed that the strength of instrumental responding is influenced by the Pavlovian properties of the context in which the response is performed.

The debate between S–R theorists and what might be called the expectancy (R–US) theorists continued until the 1970s (see for example, Bolles, 1972). In the last 20 years or so, however, experiments have provided new insights into the nature of the associations that are formed during instrumental conditioning. To anticipate the following discussion, these experiments show that both the S–R and the expectancy theorists were correct. The experiments also show that these theorists underestimated the complexity of the information that animals can acquire in even quite simple instrumental conditioning tasks.

Evidence for R–US associations

To demonstrate support for an expectancy theory of instrumental conditioning, Colwill and Rescorla (1985) adopted a **reinforcer devaluation** design (see also Adams & Dickinson, 1981). A single group of rats was trained in the manner summarized in Table 4.1. In the first (training) stage of the experiment subjects were able to make one response (R1) to earn one reinforcer (US1) and another response (R2) to earn a different reinforcer (US2). The two responses were lever pressing or pulling a small chain that was suspended from the ceiling, and the two reinforcers were food pellets or sucrose solution. After a number of sessions of this training, an aversion was formed to US1 by allowing subjects free access to it and then injecting them with a mild poison (lithium chloride; LiCl). This treatment was so effective that subjects completely rejected US1 when it was subsequently presented to them. For the test trials subjects were again allowed to make either of the two responses, but this time neither response led to the delivery of a reinforcer. The results from the experiment are shown in Figure 4.2, which indicates that R2 was performed more vigorously than R1. The figure also shows a gradual decline in the strength of R2, which reflects the fact that neither response was followed by reward. This pattern of results can be most readily explained by assuming that during their training rats formed R1–US1 and R2–US2 associations. They would then be reluctant to perform R1 in the test phase because of their knowledge that this response produced a reinforcer that was no longer attractive.

KEY TERM

Reinforcer devaluation
A technique in which the positive reinforcer for an instrumental response is subsequently devalued, normally by pairing its consumption with illness.

TABLE 4.1 Summary of the training given to a single group of rats in an experiment by Colwill and Rescorla (1985)

Training	Devaluation	Test
R1 → US1	US1 → LiCl	R1 versus R2
R2 → US2		

LiCl, lithium chloride; R, response; US, unconditioned stimulus.

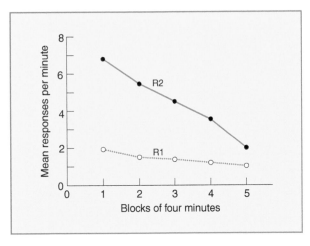

FIGURE 4.2 The mean rates at which a single group of rats performed two responses, R1 and R2, that had previously been associated with two different rewards. Before the test sessions, the reward for R1, but not R2, had been devalued. No rewards were presented in the test session (adapted from Rescorla, 1991).

Evidence for S–R associations

The evidence that instrumental conditioning results in the development of S–R associations is perhaps less convincing than that concerning the development of R–US associations. A re-examination of Figure 4.2 reveals that after the devaluation treatment there remained a tendency to perform R1. This tendency was sustained even though the response never resulted in the delivery of a reinforcer and, more importantly, it was sustained even though the devaluation training resulted in a complete rejection of US1. The fact that an animal is willing to make a response, even though it will reject the reinforcer that normally follows the response, is just what would be expected if the original training resulted in the growth of an S–R connection. In other words, because an S–R connection does not allow an animal to anticipate the reward it will receive for its responses, once such a connection has formed the animal will respond for the reward even if it is no longer attractive. Thus the results of the experiment by Colwill and Rescorla (1985) indicate that during the course of their training rats acquired both R–US and S–R associations.

Readers who are struck by the rather low rate at which Rl was performed might conclude that the S–R connection is normally of little importance in determining responding. Note, however, that for the test trials there was the opportunity of performing either R1 or R2. Even a slight preference for R2 would then have a suppressive effect on the performance of R1. On the basis of the present results, therefore, it is difficult to draw precise conclusions concerning the relative contribution S–R and R–US associations to instrumental responding.

To complicate matters even further, it seems that the relative contribution of S–R and R–US associations to instrumental behavior is influenced by the training given. Adams and Dickinson (1981) conducted a series of experiments in which rats had to press a lever for food. An aversion to the food was then conditioned using a technique similar to that adopted by Colwill and Rescorla (1985). If a small amount of instrumental training had been given initially, then subjects showed a marked reluctance to press the lever in a final test session. But if extensive instrumental training had been given initially, there was little evidence of any effect at all of the devaluation treatment. Adams and Dickinson (1981) were thus led to conclude that R–US associations underlie the acquisition and early stages of instrumental training, but with extended practice this learning is transformed into an S–R habit. There is some debate about the reasons for this change in influence of the two associations, or whether it always takes place (see Dickinson & Balleine, 1994).

Evidence for S–(R–US) associations

Animals can thus learn to perform a particular response in the presence of a given stimulus (S–R learning), they can also learn that a certain reinforcer will follow a response (R–US learning). The next question to ask is whether this information can be integrated to provide the knowledge that in the presence of a certain stimulus a certain response will be followed by a certain outcome. Table 4.2 summarizes

---

TABLE 4.2 Summary of the training given to a single group of rats in an experiment by Rescorla (1991)

Discrimination training	Devaluation	Test
SI: R1 → US1 and R2 → US2		S1: R1 > R2
	US2 → LiCl	
S2: R1 → US2 and R2 → US1		S2: R2 > RI

LiCl, lithium chloride; R, response; S, stimulus; US, unconditioned stimulus.

---

the design of an experiment by Rescorla (1991) that was conducted to test this possibility.

A group of rats first received discrimination training in which a light or a noise (S1 or S2) was presented for 30 seconds at a time. During each stimulus the rats were trained to perform two responses (pulling a chain or pressing a lever), which each resulted in a different reinforcer (food pellets or sucrose solution). The design of conditioning experiments is rarely simple and, in this case, it was made more difficult by reversing the response–reinforce relationships for the two stimuli. Thus in S1, R1 led to US1 and R2 led to US2; but in S2, R1 led to US2 and R2 led to US1. For the second stage of the experiment, the reinforcer devaluation technique was used to condition an aversion to US2. Finally, test trials were conducted in extinction in which subjects were provided with the opportunity of performing the two responses in the presence of each stimulus. The result from these test trials was quite clear. There was a marked preference to perform R1, rather than R2, in the presence of S1; but in the presence of S2 there was a preference to perform R2 rather than R1. These findings cannot be explained by assuming that the only associations acquired during the first stage were S–R, otherwise the devaluation technique would have been ineffective. Nor can the results be explained by assuming that only R–US associations developed, otherwise devaluation treatment should have weakened R1 and R2 to the same extent in both stimuli. Instead, the results can be most readily explained by assuming that the subjects were sensitive to the fact that the devalued reinforcer followed R2 in S1, and followed R1 in S2. Rescorla (1991) has argued that this conclusion indicates the development of a hierarchical associative structure that he characterizes as S–(R–US). Animals are first believed to acquire an R–US association, and this association in its entirety is then assumed to enter into a new association with S. Whether it is useful to propose that an association can itself enter into an association remains to be seen. There are certainly problems with this type of suggestion (see, for example, Holland, 1992). In addition, as Dickinson (1994) points out, there are alternative ways of explaining the findings of Rescorla (1991). Despite these words of caution, the experiment demonstrates clearly that animals are able to anticipate the reward they will receive for making a certain response in the presence of a given stimulus.

THE CONDITIONS OF LEARNING

There is, therefore, abundant evidence to show that animals are capable of learning about the consequences of their actions. We turn now to consider the conditions that enable this learning to take place.

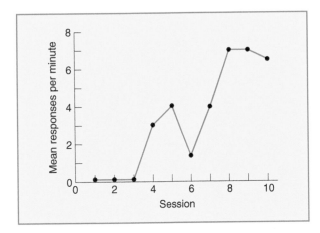

FIGURE 4.3 The mean rate of pressing a lever by a single rat when food was presented 30 seconds after a response (adapted from Lattal & Gleeson, 1990).

Temporal contiguity is an important factor in the effectiveness of instrumental conditioning. This golden retriever's obedience training will be much more effective if the owner rewards his dog with a treat straight after the desired response.

Contiguity

A fundamental principle of the early theories of learning was that instrumental conditioning is most effective when the response is contiguous with or, in other words, followed immediately by the reinforcer. An early demonstration of this influence of contiguity on instrumental conditioning was made by Logan (1960), who trained rats to run down an alley for food. He found that the speed of running was substantially faster if the rats received food as soon as they reached the goal box, as opposed to waiting in the goal box before food was made available. This disruptive effect of waiting was found with delays from as little as 3 seconds. Moreover, the speed of running down the alley was directly related to the duration of the delay in the goal box. This effect, which is referred to as the **gradient of delay**, has been reported on numerous occasions (e.g. Dickinson, Watt, & Griffiths, 1992).

It is apparent from Logan's (1960) study that even relatively short delays between a response and a reinforcer disrupt instrumental conditioning. Once this finding has been established, it then becomes pertinent to consider by how much the reinforcer can be delayed before instrumental conditioning is no longer possible. The precise answer to this question remains to be sought, but a study by Lattal and Gleeson (1990) indicates that it may be greater than 30 seconds. Rats were required to press a lever for food, which was delivered 30 seconds after the response. If another response was made before food was delivered then the timer was reset and the rat had to wait another 30 seconds before receiving food. This schedule ensured that the delay between any response and food was at least 30 seconds. Despite being exposed to such a demanding method of training, each of the three rats in the experiment showed an increase in the rate of lever pressing as training progressed. The results from one rat are shown in Figure 4.3. The remarkable finding from this experiment is that rats with no prior experience of lever pressing can increase the rate of performing this response when the only response-produced stimulus change occurs 30 seconds after a response has been made.

It should be emphasized that the rate of lever pressing by the three rats was relatively slow, and would have been considerably faster if food had been presented immediately after the response. Temporal contiguity is thus important for instrumental conditioning, but such conditioning is still effective, albeit to a lesser extent, when there is a gap between the response and the delivery of reward.

Response–reinforcer contingency

We saw in Chapter 3 that the CS–US contingency is important for Pavlovian conditioning because learning is more effective when the US occurs only in the presence of the CS than when the US also occurs both in the presence and absence of the CS. An experiment by Hammond (1980) makes a similar point for instrumental behavior, by demonstrating the importance of the **response–reinforcer contingency** for effective conditioning. The training schedule was quite complex and required that the experimental session was divided into 1-second intervals. If a response occurred in any interval then, for three groups of thirsty rats, water was delivered at the end of the interval with a probability of 0.12. The results from a group that received only this training, and no water in the absence of lever pressing (Group 0), are shown in the left-hand histogram of Figure 4.4. By the end of training this group was responding at more than 50 responses a minute. For the remaining two groups, water was delivered after some of the 1-second intervals in which a response did not occur. For Group

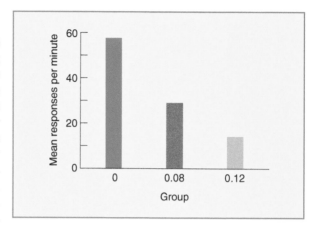

FIGURE 4.4 The mean rates of lever pressing for water by three groups of thirsty rats in their final session of training. The groups differed in the probability with which free water was delivered during the intervals between responses. Group 0 received no water during these intervals, Group 0.08 and Group 0.12 received water with a probability of 0.08 and 0.12, respectively, at the end of each period of 1 second in which a response did not occur (adapted from Hammond, 1980).

0.08, the probability of one of these intervals being followed by water was 0.08, whereas for Group 0.12 this probability was 0.12. The remaining two histograms show the final response rates for these two groups. Both groups responded more slowly than Group 0, but responding was weakest in the group for which water was just as likely to be delivered whether or not a response had been made. The contingency between response and reinforcer thus influences the rate at which the response will be performed. We now need to ask why this should be the case. In fact, there are two answers to this question.

One answer is based on a quite different view of instrumental conditioning to that considered thus far. According to this account, instrumental conditioning will be effective whenever a response results in an increase in the rate of reinforcement (e.g. Baum, 1973). Thus there is no need for a response to be followed closely by reward for successful conditioning, all that is necessary is for the overall probability of reward being delivered to increase. In other words, the contingency between a response and reward is regarded as the critical determinant for the outcome of instrumental conditioning. This position is referred to as a **molar theory of reinforcement** because animals are assumed to compute the rate at which they make a response over a substantial period of time and, at the same time, compute the rate at which reward is delivered over the same period. If they should detect that an increase in the rate of responding is correlated with an increase in the rate of reward delivery, then the response will be performed more vigorously in the future. Moreover, the closer the correlation between the two rates, the more rapidly will the response be performed. Group 0 of Hammond's (1980) experiment demonstrated a high correlation between the rate at which the lever was pressed and the rate at which reward was delivered, and this molar analysis correctly predicts that rats will learn to respond rapidly on the lever. In the case of Group 0.12, however, the rate of lever pressing had some influence on the rate at which reward was delivered, but this influence was slight because the reward would be delivered even if a rat refused to press the lever. In these circumstances,

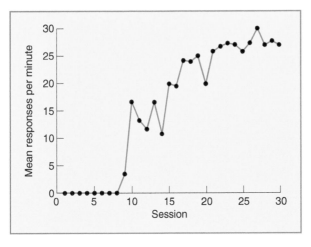

FIGURE 4.5 The total number of lever presses recorded in each session for a rat in the experiment by Thomas (1981).

responding is predicted to be slow and again the theory is supported by the findings.

The molar analysis of instrumental behavior has received a considerable amount of attention and generated a considerable body of experimental research, but there are good reasons for believing that it may be incorrect. In an experiment by Thomas (1981), rats in a test chamber containing a lever were given a free pellet of food once every 20 seconds, even if they did nothing. At the same time, if they pressed the lever during any 20-seconds interval then the pellet was delivered immediately, and the pellet at the end of the interval was cancelled. Subsequent responses during the remainder of the interval were without effect. This treatment ensured that rats received three pellets of food a minute whether or not they pressed the lever. Thus lever pressing in this experiment did not result in an increase in the rate of food delivery and, according to the molar point of view, the rate of making this response should not increase. The mean rate of responding during successive sessions is shown for one rat in Figure 4.5. Although the rat took some time to press the lever, it eventually pressed at a reasonably high rate. A similar pattern of results was observed with the other rats in the experiment, which clearly contradicts the prediction drawn from a molar analysis of instrumental behavior.

Thomas (1981) reports a second experiment, the design of which was much the same as for the first experiment, except that lever pressing not only resulted in the occasional, immediate delivery of food but also in an overall reduction of food by postponing the start of the next 20-second interval by 20 seconds. On this occasion, the effect of lever pressing was to reduce the rate at which food was delivered, yet each of six new rats demonstrated an increase in the rate of lever pressing as training progressed. The result is opposite to that predicted by a molar analysis of instrumental conditioning.

Although molar theories of instrumental behavior (e.g. Baum, 1973) are ideally suited to explaining results such as those reported by Hammond (1980), it is difficult to see how they can overcome the problem posed by the findings of Thomas (1981). It is therefore appropriate to seek an alternative explanation for the influence of the response–reinforcer contingency on instrumental conditioning. One alternative, which by now should be familiar, is that instrumental conditioning depends on the formation of associations. This position is referred to as a **molecular theory of reinforcement** because it assumes that the effectiveness of instrumental conditioning depends on specific episodes of the response being paired with a reinforcer. The results from the experiment can be readily explained by a molecular analysis of instrumental conditioning, because contiguity between a response and a reinforcer is regarded as the important condition for successful conditioning. Each lever press that resulted in food would allow an association involving the response to gain in strength, which would then encourage more vigorous responding as training progressed.

At first glance, Hammond's (1980) results appear to contradict a molecular analysis because the response was paired with reward in all three groups and they would therefore be expected to respond at a similar rate, which was not the case. It is, however, possible to reconcile these results with a molecular analysis of instrumental conditioning by appealing to the effects of associative competition, as the following section shows.

KEY TERM

Molecular theory of reinforcement
The assumption that the rate of instrumental responding is determined by response–reinforcer contiguity.

Associative competition

If two stimuli are presented together for Pavlovian conditioning, the strength of the conditioned response (CR) that each elicits when tested individually is often weaker than if they are presented for conditioning separately. This overshadowing effect is explained by assuming the two stimuli are in competition for associative strength so that the more strength acquired by one the less is available for the other (Rescorla & Wagner, 1972). Overshadowing is normally assumed to take place between stimuli but, if it is accepted that overshadowing can also occur between stimuli and responses that signal the same reinforcer, then it is possible for molecular theories of instrumental behavior to explain the contingency effects reported by Hammond (1980). In Group 0 of his study, each delivery of water would strengthen a lever-press–water association and result eventually in rapid lever pressing. In the other groups, however, the delivery of free water would allow the context to enter into an association with this reinforcer. The delivery of water after a response will then mean that it is signaled by both the context and the response, and theories of associative learning predict that the context–water association will restrict, through overshadowing, the growth of the response–water association. As the strength of the response–water association determines the rate at which the response is performed, responding will be slower when some free reinforcers accompany the instrumental training than when all the reinforcers are earned. Furthermore, the more often that water is delivered free, the stronger will be the context–water association and the weaker will be the response–water association. Thus the pattern of results shown in Figure 4.4 can be explained by a molecular analysis of instrumental conditioning, providing it is assumed that responses and stimuli compete with each other for their associative strength. The results from two different experiments lend support to this assumption.

The first experiment directly supports the claim that overshadowing is possible between stimuli and responses. Pearce and Hall (1978) required rats to press a lever for food on a variable interval schedule, in which only a few responses were followed by reward. For an experimental group, each rewarded response was followed by a brief burst of white noise before the food was delivered. The noise, which accompanied only rewarded responses, resulted in a substantially lower rate of lever pressing by the experimental than by control groups that received either similar exposure to the noise (but after nonrewarded responses) or no exposure to the noise at all (Figure 4.6). Geoffrey Hall and I argued that the most plausible explanation for these findings is that instrumental learning involves the formation of R–US associations and that these were weakened through overshadowing by a noise–food association that developed in the experimental group.

The second source of support for a molecular analysis of the effect of contingency on instrumental responding can be found in contingency experiments in which a brief stimulus signals the delivery of each free reinforcer. The brief stimulus should itself enter into an association with the reinforcer and thus overshadow the

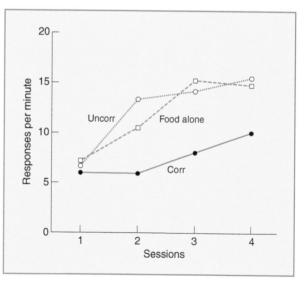

FIGURE 4.6 The mean rates of lever pressing by three groups of rats that received a burst of noise after each rewarded response (Corr), after some nonrewarded responses (Uncorr), or no noise at all (Food alone) (adapted from Pearce & Hall, 1978).

development of an association between the context and the reinforcer. Whenever a response is followed by the reinforcer it will now be able to enter a normal R–US association, because of the lack of competition from the context. Responding in these conditions should thus be more vigorous than if the free US is not signaled. In support of this argument, both Hammond and Weinberg (1984) and Dickinson and Charnock (1985) have shown that free reinforcers disrupt instrumental responding to a greater extent when they are unsignaled than when they are signaled. These findings make a particularly convincing case for the belief that competition for associative strength is an important influence on the strength of an instrumental response. They also indicate that this competition is responsible for the influence of the response–reinforcer contingency on the rate of instrumental responding.

The nature of the reinforcer

Perhaps the most important requirement for successful instrumental conditioning is that the response is followed by a reinforcer. But what makes a reinforcer? In nearly all the experiments that have been described thus far, the reinforcer has been food for a hungry animal, or water for a thirsty animal. As these stimuli are of obvious biological importance, it is hardly surprising to discover that animals are prepared to engage in an activity such as lever pressing in order to earn them. However, this does not mean that a reinforcer is necessarily a stimulus that is of biological significance to the animal. As Schwartz (1989) notes, animals will press a lever to turn on a light, and it is difficult to imagine the biological need that is satisfied on these occasions.

Thorndike (1911) was the first to appreciate the need to identify the defining characteristics of a reinforcer, and his solution was contained within the Law of Effect. He maintained that a reinforcer was a stimulus that resulted in a satisfying state of affairs. A satisfying state of affairs was then defined as " . . . one which the animal does nothing to avoid, often doing things which maintain or renew it" (Thorndike, 1913, p. 2). In other words, Thorndike effectively proposed that a stimulus would serve as a reinforcer (increase the likelihood of a response) if animals were willing to respond in order to receive that stimulus. The circularity in this definition should be obvious and has served as a valid source of criticism of the Law of Effect on more than one occasion (e.g. Meehl, 1950). Thorndike was not alone in providing a circular definition of a reinforcer. Skinner has been perhaps the most blatant in this respect, as the following quotation reveals (Skinner, 1953, pp. 72–73):

> *The only way to tell whether or not a given event is reinforcing to a given organism under given conditions is to make a direct test. We observe the frequency of a selected response, then make an event contingent upon it and observe any change in frequency. If there is a change, we classify the event as reinforcing.*

To be fair, for practical purposes this definition is quite adequate. It provides a useful and unambiguous terminology. At the same time, once we have decided that a stimulus, such as food, is a positive reinforcer, then we can turn to a study of a number of issues that are important to the analysis of instrumental learning. For instance, we have been able to study the role of the reinforcer in the associations that are formed during instrumental learning, without worrying unduly about what it is that makes a stimulus a reinforcer. But the definitions offered by Thorndike and

Skinner are not very helpful if a general statement is being sought about the characteristics of a stimulus that dictate whether or not it will function as a reinforcer. And the absence of such a general statement makes our understanding of the conditions that promote instrumental learning incomplete.

A particularly elegant solution to the problem of deciding whether a stimulus will function as a reinforcer is provided by the work of Premack (1959, 1962, 1965), who put forward what is now called the **Premack principle**. He proposed that reinforcers were not stimuli but opportunities to engage in behavior. Thus the activity of eating, not the stimulus of food, should be regarded as the reinforcer when an animal has been trained to lever press for food. To determine if one activity will serve as the reinforcer for another activity, Premack proposed that the animal should be allowed to engage freely in both activities. For example, a rat might be placed into a chamber containing a lever and some food pellets. If it shows a greater willingness to eat the food than to press the lever, then we can conclude that the opportunity to eat will reinforce lever pressing, but the opportunity to lever press will not reinforce eating.

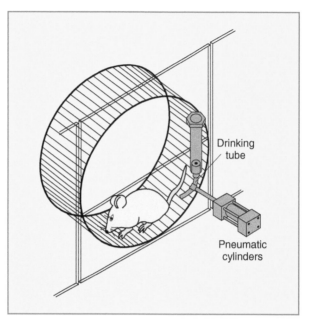

Drinking tube

Pneumatic cylinders

FIGURE 4.7 A sketch of the apparatus used by Premack (1971a) to determine if being given the opportunity to run could serve as a reinforcer for drinking in rats that were not thirsty (adapted from Premack, 1971a).

It is perhaps natural to think of the properties of a reinforcer as being absolute. That is, if eating is an effective reinforcer for one response, such as lever pressing, then it might be expected to serve as a reinforcer for any response. But Premack (1965) has argued this assumption is unjustified. An activity will only be reinforcing if subjects would rather engage in it than in the activity that is to be reinforced. To demonstrate this relative property of a reinforcer, Premack (1971a) placed rats into a running wheel, similar to the one sketched in Figure 4.7, for 15 minutes a day.

When the rats were thirsty, they preferred to drink rather than to run in the wheel, but when they were not thirsty, they preferred to run rather than to drink. For the test phase of the experiment, the wheel was locked and the rats had to lick the drinking tube to free it and so gain the opportunity to run for 5 seconds. Running is not normally regarded as a reinforcing activity but because rats that are not thirsty prefer to run rather than drink, it follows from Premack's (1965) argument that they should increase the amount they drink in the wheel in order to earn the opportunity to run. Conversely; running would not be expected to reinforce drinking for thirsty rats, because in this state of deprivation they prefer drinking to running. In clear support of this analysis, Premack (1971a) found that running could serve as a reinforcer for drinking, but only with rats that were not thirsty.

As Allison (1989) has pointed out, Premack's proposals can be expressed succinctly by paraphrasing Thorndike's Law of Effect. For instrumental conditioning to be effective it is necessary for a response to be followed not by a satisfying state of affairs, but by a preferred response. Despite the improvement this change affords with respect to the problem of defining a reinforcer, experiments have shown that it does not account adequately for all the circumstances where one activity will serve as a reinforcer for another.

Consider an experiment by Allison and Timberlake (1974) in which rats were first allowed to drink from two spouts that provided different concentrations of saccharin solution. This baseline test session revealed a preference for the sweeter solution. According to Premack's proposals, therefore, rats should be willing to increase their consumption of the weaker solution if drinking it is the only means by which they can gain access to the sweeter solution. By contrast, rats should *not* be willing to increase their consumption of the sweeter solution to gain access to the weaker one. To test this second prediction, rats were allowed to drink from the spout supplying the sweeter solution and, after every 10 licks, they were permitted one lick at the spout offering the less-sweet solution. This 10 : 1 ratio meant that, relative to the amount of sweet solution consumed, the rats received less of the weaker solution than they chose to consume in the baseline test session. As a consequence of this constraint imposed by the experiment, Allison and Timberlake (1974) found that rats increased their consumption of the stronger solution. It is important to emphasize that this increase occurred in order to allow the rats to gain access to the less preferred solution, which, according to Premack's theory, should not have taken place.

Timberlake and Allison (1974) explained their results in terms of an equilibrium theory of behavior. They argued that when an animal is able to engage in a variety of activities, it will have a natural tendency to allocate more time to some than others. The ideal amount of time that would be devoted to an activity is referred to as its bliss point, and each activity is assumed to have its own bliss point. By preventing an animal from engaging in even its least preferred activity, it will be displaced from the bliss point and do its best to restore responding to this point.

In the experiment by Allison and Timberlake (1974), therefore, forcing the subjects to drink much more of the strong than the weak solution meant that they were effectively deprived of the weak solution. As the only way to overcome this deficit was to drink more of the sweet solution, this is what they did. Of course, as the rats approached their bliss point for the consumption of the weak solution, they would go beyond their bliss point for the consumption of the sweet solution. To cope with this type of conflict, animals are believed to seek a compromise, or state of equilibrium, in which the amount of each activity they perform will lead them as close as possible to the bliss points for all activities. Thus the rats completed the experiment by drinking rather more than they would prefer of the strong solution, and rather less than they would prefer of the weak solution.

By referring to bliss points, we can thus predict when the opportunity to engage in one activity will serve as a reinforcer for another activity. But this does not mean that we have now identified completely the circumstances in which the delivery of a particular event will function as a reinforcer. Some reinforcers do not elicit responses that can be analyzed usefully by equilibrium theory. Rats will press a lever to receive stimulation to certain regions of the brain, or to turn on a light, or to turn off an electric shock to the feet. I find it difficult to envisage how any measure of baseline activity in the presence of these events would reveal that they will serve as reinforcers for lever pressing. In the next section we will find that a stimulus that has been paired with food can reinforce lever pressing in hungry rats. Again, simply by observing an animal's behavior in the presence of the stimulus, it is hard to imagine how one could predict that the stimulus will function as a reinforcer. Our understanding of the nature of a reinforcer has advanced considerably since Thorndike proposed the Law of Effect. However, if we wish to determine with confidence if a certain event will act as a reinforcer for a particular response, at times there will be no better alternative than to adopt Skinner's suggestion of testing for this property directly.

Conditioned reinforcement

The discussion has been concerned thus far with primary reinforcers, that is, with stimuli that do not need to be paired with another stimulus to function as reinforcers for instrumental conditioning. There are, in addition, numerous studies that have shown that even a neutral stimulus may serve as an instrumental reinforcer by virtue of being paired with a primary reinforcer. An experiment by Hyde (1976) provides a good example of a stimulus acting in this capacity as a **conditioned reinforcer**. In the first stage of the experiment, an experimental group of hungry rats had a number of sessions in which the occasional delivery of food was signaled by a brief tone. A control group was treated in much the same way except that the tone and food were presented randomly in respect to each other. Both groups were then given the opportunity to press the lever to present the tone. The results from the eight sessions of this testing are displayed in Figure 4.8. Even though no food was presented in this test phase, the experimental group initially showed a considerable willingness to press the lever. The superior rate of pressing by the experimental compared to the control group strongly suggests that pairing the tone with food resulted in it becoming a conditioned reinforcer.

In the previous experiment, the effect of the conditioned reinforcer was relatively short lasting, which should not be surprising because it will lose its properties by virtue of being presented in the absence of food. The effects of conditioned reinforcers can be considerably more robust if their relationship with the primary reinforcer is maintained, albeit intermittently. Experiments using **token reinforcers** provide a particularly forceful demonstration of how the influence of a conditioned reinforcer may be sustained in this way. Token reinforcers are typically small plastic discs that are earned by performing some response, and once earned they can be exchanged for food. In an experiment by Kelleher (1958), chimpanzees had to press a key 125 times to receive a single token. When they had collected 50 tokens they were allowed to push them all into a slot to receive food. In this experiment, therefore, the effect of the token reinforcers was sufficiently strong that they were able to reinforce a sequence of more than 6000 responses.

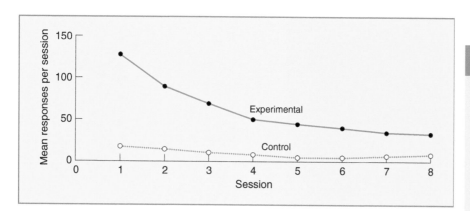

FIGURE 4.8 The mean rates of lever pressing for a brief tone by two groups of rats. For the experimental group the tone had previously been paired with food, whereas for the control group the tone and food had been presented randomly in respect to each other (adapted from Hyde, 1976).

A straightforward explanation for the results of the experiment by Hyde (1976) is that the tone became an appetitive Pavlovian CS and thus effectively served as a substitute for food. The results from experiments such as that by Kelleher (1958) have led Schwartz (1989) to argue that there are additional ways in which conditioned reinforcers can be effective (see also Golub, 1977):

- They provide feedback that the correct response has been made. Delivering a token after the completion of 125 responses would provide a useful signal that the subject is engaged in the correct activity.
- Conditioned reinforcers might act as a cue for the next response to be performed. Kelleher (1958) observed that his chimpanzees often waited for several hours before making their first response in a session. This delay was virtually eliminated by giving the subject some tokens at the start of the session, thus indicating that the tokens acted as a cue for key pressing.
- Conditioned reinforcers may be effective because they help to counteract the disruptive effects of imposing a long delay between a response and the delivery of a primary reinforcer. Interestingly, as far as tokens are concerned, this property of the token is seen only when the chimpanzee is allowed to hold it during the delay.

Taken together, these proposals imply that the properties of a conditioned reinforcer are considerably more complex than would be expected if they were based solely on its Pavlovian properties.

THE PERFORMANCE OF INSTRUMENTAL BEHAVIOR

The experiments considered so far have been concerned with revealing the knowledge that is acquired during the course of instrumental conditioning. They have also indicated some of the factors that influence the acquisition of this knowledge. We turn our attention now to examining the factors that determine the vigor with which an animal will perform an instrumental response. We have already seen that certain devaluation treatments can influence instrumental responding, and so too can manipulations designed to modify the strength of the instrumental association. But there remain a number of other factors that influence instrumental behavior. In the discussion that follows we shall consider two of these influences in some detail: deprivation state and the presence of Pavlovian CSs.

Deprivation

The level of food deprivation has been shown, up to a point, to be directly related to the vigor with which an animal responds for food. This is true when the response is running down an alley (Cotton, 1953) or pressing a lever (Clark, 1958). To explain this relationship, Hull (1943) suggested that motivational effects are mediated by activity in a drive center. Drive is a central state that is excited by needs and energizes behavior. It was proposed that the greater the level of drive, the more vigorous will be the response that the animal is currently performing. Thus, if a rat is pressing a lever for food, then hunger will excite drive, which, in turn, will invigorate this activity.

A serious shortcoming of Hull's (1943) account is the claim that drive is nonspecific, so that it can be enhanced by an increase in any need of the animal. A number of curious predictions follow from this basic aspect of his theorizing. For example, the pain produced by electric shock is assumed to increase drive, so that if animals are given shocks while lever pressing for food, they should respond more rapidly than in the absence of shock. By far the most frequent finding is that this manipulation has the opposite effect of decreasing appetitive instrumental responding (e.g. Boe & Church, 1967). Conversely, the theory predicts that enhancing drive by making animals hungrier should facilitate the rate at which they press a lever to escape or avoid shock. Again, it should not be surprising to discover that generally this prediction is not confirmed. Increases in deprivation have been found, in this respect, to be either without effect (Misanin & Campbell, 1969) or to reduce the rate of such behavior (Meyer, Adams, & Worthen, 1969; Leander, 1973).

In response to this problem, more recent theorists have proposed that animals possess two drive centers: One is concerned with energizing behavior that leads to reward, the other is responsible for invigorating activity that minimizes contact with aversive stimuli. These can be referred to, respectively, as the positive and negative motivational systems. A number of such **dual-system theories of motivation** have been proposed (Konorski, 1967; Rescorla & Solomon, 1967; Estes, 1969).

The assumption that there are two motivational systems rather than a single drive center allows these theories to overcome many of the problems encountered by Hull's (1943) theory. For example, it is believed that deprivation states like hunger and thirst will increase activity only in the positive system, so that a change in deprivation should not influence the vigor of behavior that minimizes contact with aversive stimuli such as shock. Conversely, electric shock should not invigorate responding for food as it will excite only the negative system.

But even this characterization of the way in which deprivation states influence behavior may be too simple. Suppose that an animal that has been trained to lever press for food when it is hungry is satiated by being granted unrestricted access to food before it is returned to the conditioning chamber. The account that has just been developed predicts that satiating the animal will reduce the motivational support for lever pressing by lowering the activity in the positive system. The animal would thus be expected to respond less vigorously than one that was still hungry. There is some evidence to support this prediction (e.g. Balleine, Garner, Gonzalez & Dickinson, 1995), but additional findings by Balleine (1992) demonstrate that dual-system theories of motivation are in need of elaboration if they are to provide a complete account of the way in which deprivation states influence responding.

In one experiment by Balleine (1992), two groups of rats were trained to press a bar for food while they were hungry (H). For reasons that will be made evident shortly, it is important to note that the food pellets used as the instrumental reinforcer were different to the food that was presented at all other times in this experiment. Group H–S was then satiated (S) by being allowed unrestricted access to their normal food for 24 hours, whereas Group H–H remained on the deprivation schedule. Finally, both groups were again given the opportunity to press the bar, but responding never resulted in the delivery of the reinforcer. Because of their different deprivation states, dual-system theories of motivation, as well as our intuitions, predict that Group H–H should respond more vigorously than Group H–S in this test session. But it seems that our intuitions are wrong on this occasion. The mean number of responses made by each group in the test session are shown in the two gray histograms on the left-hand side of Figure 4.9, which reveal that both groups responded quite vigorously, and at a similar rate.

The equivalent histograms on the right-hand side of Figure 4.9 show the results of two further groups from this study, which were trained to lever press for food while they were satiated by being fed unrestricted food in their home cages. Rats will learn to respond for food in these conditions, provided that the pellets are of a different flavor to that of the unrestricted food presented in the home cages. Group S–S was then tested while satiated, whereas Group S–H was tested while hungry. Once again, and contrary to our intuitions, both groups performed similarly in the test session despite their different levels of deprivation. When the results of the four groups are compared, it is evident that the groups that were trained hungry responded somewhat more on the test trials than those that were trained while they were satiated. But to labor the point, there is no indication that changing deprivation level for the test session had any influence on responding.

Balleine's (1992) explanation for these findings is that the incentive value, or attractiveness, of the reinforcer is an important determinant of how willing animals will be to press for it. If an animal consumes a reinforcer while it is hungry, then that reinforcer may well be more attractive than if it is consumed while the animal is satiated. Thus Group H–H and Group H–S may have responded rapidly in the test session because they anticipated a food that in the past had proved attractive, because they had only eaten it while they were hungry. By way of contrast, the slower responding by Groups S–S and S–H can be attributed to them anticipating food that in the past had not been particularly attractive, because they had eaten it only while they were not hungry.

This explanation was tested with two additional groups. Prior to the experiment, animals in Group Pre(S) H–S were given reward pellets while they were satiated to

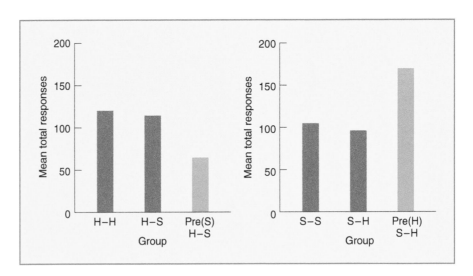

FIGURE 4.9 The mean number of responses made by six groups of rats in an extinction test session. The left-hand letter of each pair indicates the level of deprivation when subjects were trained to lever press for reward—either satiated (S) or hungry (H)—the right-hand letter indicates the deprivation level during test trials. Two of the groups were allowed to consume the reward either satiated, Pre(S), or hungry, Pre(H), prior to instrumental conditioning (adapted from Balleine, 1992).

demonstrate that the pellets are not particularly attractive in this deprivation state. The group was then trained to lever press while hungry and received test trials while satiated. On the test trials, the subjects should know that because, of their low level of deprivation, the reward pellets are no longer attractive and they should be reluctant to press the lever. The results, which are shown in the blue histogram in the left-hand side of Figure 4.9, confirmed this prediction. The final group to be considered, Group Pre(H) S–H, was first allowed to eat reward pellets in the home cage while hungry, instrumental conditioning was then conducted while the group was satiated and the test trials were conducted while the group was hungry. In contrast to Group S–H and Group S–S, this group should appreciate that the reward pellets are attractive while hungry and respond more rapidly than the other two groups during the test trials. Once again, the results confirmed this prediction—see the blue histogram on the right-hand side of Figure 4.9

By now it should be evident that no simple conclusion can be drawn concerning the way in which deprivation states influence the vigor of instrumental responding. On some occasions a change in deprivation state is able to modify directly the rate of responding, as dual-systems theories of motivation predict. On other occasions, this influence is more indirect by modifying the attractiveness of the reinforcer. An informative account of the way in which these findings may be integrated can be found in Balleine et al. (1995).

Pavlovian–instrumental interactions

For a long time, theorists have been interested in the way in which Pavlovian CSs influence the strength of instrumental responses that are performed in their presence. One reason for this interest is that Pavlovian and instrumental conditioning are regarded as two fundamental learning processes, and it is important to appreciate the way in which they work together to determine how an animal behaves. A second reason was mentioned at the end of Chapter 2, where we saw that Pavlovian CSs tend to elicit reflexive responses that may not always be in the best interests of the animal. If a Pavlovian CS was also able to modulate the vigor of instrumental responding, then this would allow it to have a more general, and more flexible, influence on behavior than has so far been implied. For example, if a CS for food were to invigorate instrumental responses that normally lead to food, then such responses would be strongest at a time when they are most needed, that is, in a context where food is likely to occur. The experiments described in this section show that Pavlovian stimuli can modulate the strength of instrumental responding. They also show that there are at least two ways in which this influence takes place.

Motivational influences

Konorski (1967), it should be recalled from Chapter 2, believed that a CS can excite an affective representation of the US that was responsible for arousing a preparatory CR. He further believed that a component of this CR consists of a change in the level of activity in a motivational system. A CS for food, say, was said to increase activity in the positive motivational system, whereas a CS for shock should excite the negative system. If these proposals are correct, then it should be possible to alter the strength of instrumental responding by presenting the appropriate Pavlovian CS (see also Rescorla & Solomon, 1967).

An experiment by Lovibond (1983), using **Pavlovian–instrumental transfer** design, provides good support for this prediction. Hungry rabbits were first trained to operate a lever with their snouts to receive a squirt of sucrose into the mouth. The levers were then withdrawn for a number of sessions of Pavlovian conditioning in which a clicker that lasted for 10 seconds signaled the delivery of sucrose. In a final test stage, subjects were again able to press the lever and, as they were doing so, the clicker was occasionally operated. The effect of this appetitive CS was to increase the rate of lever pressing both during its presence and for a short while after it was turned off. A similar effect has also been reported in a study using an aversive US. Rescorla and LoLordo (1965) found that the presentation of a CS previously paired with shock enhanced the rate at which dogs responded to avoid shock.

In addition to explaining the findings that have just been described, a further advantage of dual-system theories of motivation is that they are able to account for many of the effects of exposing animals simultaneously to both appetitive and aversive stimuli. For example, an animal may be exposed to one stimulus that signals reward and another indicating danger. In these circumstances, instead of the two systems working independently, they are assumed to be connected by mutually inhibitory links, so that activity in one will inhibit the other (Dickinson & Pearce, 1977).

To understand this relationship, consider the effect of presenting a signal for shock to a rat while it is lever pressing for food. Prior to the signal, the level of activity in the positive system will be solely responsible for the rate of pressing. When the aversive CS is presented, it will arouse the negative system. The existence of the inhibitory link will then allow the negative system to suppress activity in the positive system and weaken instrumental responding. As soon as the aversive CS is turned off, the inhibition will be removed and the original response rate restored. By assuming the existence of inhibitory links, dual-system theories can provide a very simple explanation for conditioned suppression. It occurs because the aversive CS reduces the positive motivational support for the instrumental response.

Response-cueing properties of Pavlovian CRs

In addition to modulating activity in motivational systems, Pavlovian stimuli can influence instrumental responding through a response-cueing process (Trapold & Overmier, 1972). To demonstrate this point we shall consider an experiment by Colwill and Rescorla (1988), which is very similar in design to an earlier study by Kruse, Overmier, Konz, and Rokke (1983).

In the first stage of the experiment, hungry rats received Pavlovian conditioning in which US1 was occasionally delivered during a 30-second CS. Training was then given, in separate sessions, in which R1 produced US1 and R2 produced US2. The two responses were chain pulling and lever pressing, and the two reinforcers were food pellets and sucrose solution. For the test stage, animals had the opportunity for the first time to perform R1 and R2 in the presence of the CS, but neither response led to a reinforcer. As Figure 4.10 shows, R1 was performed more vigorously than R2.

The first point to note is that it is not possible to explain these findings by appealing to the motivational properties of the CS. The CS should, of course, enhance the level of activity in the positive system. But this increase in activity should then invigorate R1 to exactly the same extent as R2 because the motivational support for both responses will be provided by the same, positive, system.

In developing an alternative explanation for the findings by Colwill and Rescorla (1988), note that instrumental conditioning with the two responses was conducted in separate sessions. Thus R1 was acquired against a background of presentations of US1 and, likewise, R2 was acquired against a background of US2 presentations. If we now accept that the training resulted in the development of S-R associations, it is conceivable that certain properties of the two rewards contributed towards the S component of these associations. For example, a memory of US1 might contribute to the set of stimuli that are responsible for eliciting R1. When the CS was presented for testing, it should activate a memory of US1, which in turn should elicit R1 rather than R2. In other words, the Pavlovian CS was able to invigorate the instrumental response by providing cues that had previously become associated with the instrumental response.

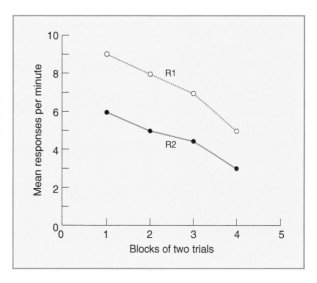

Concluding comments

The research reviewed so far in this chapter shows that we have discovered a considerable amount about the associations that are formed during instrumental conditioning. We have also discovered a great deal about the factors that influence the strength of instrumental responding. In Chapter 2 a simple memory model was developed to show how the associations formed during Pavlovian conditioning influence responding. It would be helpful if a similar model could be developed for instrumental conditioning, but this may not be an easy task. We would need to take account of three different associations that have been shown to be involved in instrumental behavior, S–R, R–US, S–(R–US). We would also need to take account of the motivational and response-cueing properties of any Pavlovian CS–US associations that may develop. Finally, the model would need to explain how changes in deprivation can influence responding. It hardly needs to be said that any model that is able to take account of all these factors satisfactorily will be complex and would not fit comfortably into an introductory text. The interested reader is, however, referred to Dickinson (1994) who shows how much of our knowledge about instrumental behavior can be explained by what he calls an associative-cybernetic model. In essence, this model is a more complex version of the dual-system theories of motivation that we have considered. The reader might also wish to consult Balleine (2001) for a more recent account of the influence of motivational processes on instrumental behavior.

Our discussion of the basic processes of instrumental conditioning is now complete, but there is one final topic to consider in this chapter. That is, whether the principles we have considered can provide a satisfactory account for the problem solving abilities of animals.

FIGURE 4.10 The mean rates of performing two responses, R1 and R2, in the presence of an established Pavlovian conditioned stimulus (CS). Prior to testing, instrumental conditioning had been given in which the reinforcer for R1 was the same as the Pavlovian unconditioned stimulus (US), and the reinforcer for R2 was different to the Pavlovian US. Testing was conducted in the absence of any reinforcers in a single session (adapted from Colwill & Rescorla, 1988).

THE LAW OF EFFECT AND PROBLEM SOLVING

Animals can be said to have solved a problem whenever they overcome an obstacle to attain a goal. The problem may be artificial, such as having to press a lever for reward, or it might be one that occurs naturally, such as having to locate a new source of food. Early studies of problem solving in animals were conducted by means of collecting anecdotes, but this unsatisfactory method was soon replaced by experimental tests in the laboratory (see Chapter 1). As a result of his experiments, Thorndike (1911) argued that despite the range of potential problems that can confront an animal, they are all solved in the same manner. Animals are assumed to behave randomly until by trial and error the correct response is made and reward is forthcoming. To capture this idea, Thorndike (1911) proposed the Law of Effect, which stipulates that one effect of reward is to strengthen the accidentally occurring response and to make its occurrence more likely in the future. This account may explain adequately the way cats learn to escape from puzzle boxes, but is it suitable for all aspects of problem solving? A number of researchers have argued that animals are more sophisticated at solving problems than is implied by the Law of Effect. It has been suggested that they are able to solve problems through **insight**. It has also been suggested that animals can solve problems because they have an understanding of the causal properties of the objects in their environment or, as it is sometimes described, an understanding of folk physics. We shall consider each of these possibilities.

Insight

An early objector to Thorndike's (1911) account of problem solving was Kohler (1925). Thorndike's experiments were so restrictive, he argued, that they prevented animals from revealing their capacity to solve problems by any means other than the most simple. Kohler spent the First World War on the Canary Islands, where he conducted a number of studies that were meant to reveal sophisticated intellectual processes in animals. He is best known for experiments that, he claimed, demonstrate the importance of insight in problem solving. Many of his findings are described in his book *The mentality of apes*, which documents some remarkable feats of problem solving by chimpanzees and other animals. Two examples should be sufficient to give an indication of his methodology. These example involve Sultan (Figure 4.11), whom Kohler (1925) regarded as the brightest of his chimpanzees. On one occasion Sultan, was in a cage in which there was also a small stick. Outside the cage was a longer stick, which was beyond Sultan's reach, and even further away was a reward of fruit (p. 151):

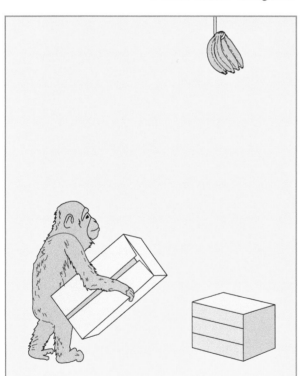

FIGURE 4.11 Sultan stacking boxes in an attempt to reach a banana (drawing based on Kohler, 1956).

Sultan tries to reach the fruit with the smaller of the sticks. Not succeeding, he tries a piece of wire that projects from the netting in his cage, but that, too, is in vain. Then he gazes about him (there are always in the course of these tests some long pauses, during which the animal scrutinizes the whole visible area). He suddenly picks up the little stick once more, goes to the bars directly opposite to the long stick, scratches it towards him with the auxiliary, seizes it and goes with it to the point opposite the objective which he secures. From the moment that his eyes fell upon the long stick, his procedure forms one consecutive whole.

In the other study, Kohler (1925) hung a piece of fruit from the ceiling of a cage housing six apes, including Sultan. There was a wooden box in the cage (p. 41):

All six apes vainly endeavored to reach the fruit by leaping up from the ground. Sultan soon relinquished this attempt, paced restlessly up and down, suddenly stood still in front of the box, seized it, tipped it hastily straight towards the objective, but began to climb upon it at a (horizontal) distance of ½ meter and springing upwards with all his force, tore down the banana.

In both examples there is a period when the animal responds incorrectly; this is then followed by activity that, as it is reported, suggests that the solution to the problem has suddenly occurred to the subject. There is certainly no hint in these reports that the problem was solved by trial and error. Does this mean, then, that Kohler (1925) was correct in his criticism of Thorndike's (1911) theorizing?

A problem with interpreting Kohler's (1925) findings is that all of the apes had played with boxes and sticks prior to the studies just described. The absence of trial-and-error responding may thus have been due to the previous experience of the animals. Sultan may, by accident, have learned about the consequences of jumping from boxes in earlier sessions, and he was perhaps doing no more than acting on the basis of his previous trial-and-error learning. This criticism of Kohler's (1925) work is by no means original. Birch (1945) and Schiller (1952) have both suggested that without prior experience with sticks and so forth, there is very little reason for believing that apes can solve Kohler's problems in the manner just described.

The absence of trial-and-error responses in Kohler's (1925) findings might have been due to the fact that most apes would have had prior experience of playing with sticks.

An amusing experiment by Epstein, Kirshnit, Lanza, and Rubin (1984) also shows the importance of past experience in problem solving and, at the same time, raises some important issues concerning the intellectual abilities of animals. Pigeons were given two different types of training. They were rewarded with food for pushing a box towards a spot randomly located at the base of a wall of the test chamber. Pushing in the absence of the spot was never rewarded. They were also trained to stand on the box when it was fixed to the floor and peck for food at a plastic banana suspended from the ceiling. Attempts to peck the banana when not standing on the box were never rewarded. Finally, on a test session they were confronted with a novel situation in which the banana was suspended from the ceiling and the box was placed some distance from beneath it. Epstein et al. (1984) report that (p. 61):

> At first each pigeon appeared to be "confused"; it stretched and turned beneath the banana, looked back and forth from banana to box, and so on. Then each subject began rather suddenly to push the box in what was clearly the direction of the banana. Each subject sighted the banana as it pushed and readjusted the box as necessary to move it towards the banana. Each subject stopped pushing it in the appropriate place, climbed and pecked the banana. This quite remarkable performance was achieved by one bird in 49 sec, which compares very favorably with the 5 min it took Sultan to solve his similar problem.

There can be no doubt from this study that the prior training of the pigeon played an important role in helping it solve the problem. Even so, the study clearly reveals that the pigeons performed on the test session in a manner that extends beyond trial-and-error responding. The act of pecking the banana might have been acquired by trial-and-error learning, and so, too, might the act of moving the box around. But the way in which the box was moved to below the banana does not seem to be compatible with this analysis.

The description by Epstein et al. (1984) of the pigeons' behavior bears a striking similarity to Kohler's (1925) account of Sultan's reaction to the similar problem. It might be thought, therefore, that it would be appropriate to account for the pigeons' success in terms of insight. In truth, this would not be a particularly useful approach as it really does not offer an account of the way in which the problem was solved. Other than indicating that the problem was solved suddenly, and not by trial and error, the term "insight" adds little else to our understanding of these results.

I regret that I find it impossible to offer, with confidence, any explanation for the findings by Epstein et al. (1984). But one possibility is that during their training with the blue spot, pigeons learned that certain responses moved the box towards the spot, and that the box by the spot was a signal for food. The combination of these associations would then result in them pushing the box towards the spot. During their training with the banana, one of the things the pigeons may have learned is that the banana is associated with food. Then, for the test session, although they would be unable to push the box towards the blue spot, generalization from their previous training might result in them pushing the box in the direction of another signal for food, the banana.

Causal inference and folk physics

The term "insight" is now rarely used in discussions of problem solving by animals. As an alternative, it has been proposed that animals have some understanding of causal relationships and that they can draw inferences based on this understanding to solve problems. When a problem is encountered, therefore, animals are believed to solve it through reasoning based on their understanding of the physical and causal properties of the objects at their disposal. To take the example of Sultan joining two sticks together to reach food, if he understood that this action would create a longer stick that would allow him to reach further, he would then be able to solve the problem in a manner that is considerably more sophisticated than relying on trial and error. Of course, we have just seen that the studies by Kohler (1925) do not provide evidence that animals can solve problems in this way, but the results from other experiments have been taken as evidence that animals are capable of making causal inferences. The following discussion will focus separately on this work with primates and birds.

Primates

Premack (1976, pp. 249–261) describes an experiment with chimpanzees in which a single subject would be shown an array of objects similar to the one in Figure 4.12. To gain reward, the chimpanzee was required to replace the strange shape in the upper row with the knife from the lower row. The choice of the knife was intended to reveal that the ape understood this object causes an apple to be cut in half. Two of the four subjects that were tested performed consistently well on this task. They received a novel problem on each trial, thus their success could not depend on them solving the problem by associating a given choice with a particular array of objects. An alternative explanation for the problem shown in Figure 4.12 is that the apes had repeatedly seen an apple being cut with a knife and they may have learned to select the object from the lower row that was most strongly associated with the one from the upper row. Although this explanation will work for many of the test trials, Premack (1976) argues there were certain occasions where it provides an implausible explanation for the successful choice. For instance, one trial was similar to that shown in Figure 4.12 except the apple was replaced by a whole ball and a ball cut into pieces. Even though the subjects had rarely seen a knife and a ball together, they still made the correct choice (see also Premack & Premack, 1994, pp. 354–357).

FIGURE 4.12 Sketch of an array of objects used by Premack (1976) to test for causal inference in chimpanzees (adapted from Premack, 1976).

The findings from the experiment are encouraging, but there is some doubt about how they should be interpreted. The two apes who performed well on the task had received extensive training on other tasks, and one of them, Sarah, had even been taught an artificial language (see Chapter 13). Perhaps the extensive training given to the chimpanzees resulted in them acquiring a rich array of associations that helped them perform correctly on the tests, without the need to understand the relevant causal relationships. It is also possible that because of the similarity between the shapes of an apple and a ball, stimulus generalization rather than a causal inference was responsible for the selection of the knife during the test with the ball. To properly evaluate the results from the experiment it would be necessary to have a complete account of the training that was given before it started. It would also be important to have a full description of the method and results from the experiment itself. Unfortunately, the information that is available is rather brief and the reader is left in some doubt as to how Premack's findings should be interpreted. Another possibility is that because of their extensive training, the two chimpanzees were able to appreciate causal relationships and to draw inferences from them in a way that is not open to relatively naïve chimpanzees. Once again, there is insufficient information available for this possibility to be assessed. There is no denying that the experiment by Premack has revealed some intriguing findings but, before its full significance can be appreciated, additional experiments are needed in order to pursue the issues that have just been raised.

Rather than study causal inference, some researchers have investigated what they call "folk physics", which refers to a common-sense appreciation of the causal properties of objects in the environment. Problems could then be solved by drawing inferences from the understanding about these properties. Povinelli (2000) has conducted a thorough series of experiments to explore whether chimpanzees make use of folk physics in problem solving, and they point to rather different conclusions to those drawn by Premack (1976).

In one of Povinelli's experiments, chimpanzees were confronted with a clear tube that contained a peanut. To retrieve the food, they were required to push it out of the tube with a stick. Once they had mastered this skill they were given the same task but this time there was a trap in the tube. Pushing the stick in one direction caused the peanut to fall out of the tube, pushing it in the other direction caused the peanut to fall in the trap where it was inaccessible. A sketch of this simple apparatus can be seen in Figure 4.13. Three of the four chimpanzees that were given this task never mastered it, and the fourth chimpanzee came to terms with it only after many practice trials. The conclusion to be drawn from this study is that chimpanzees did not have any appreciation of the problem created by the presence of the trap, that is, they lacked an understanding provided by folk physics concerning the properties of traps. Instead, the eventual success of the single chimpanzee can be explained by assuming that she learned through trial and error how to avoid pushing the food into the trap by inserting the stick into the end of the tube that was furthest from the peanut. A similar failure to find evidence of successful performance on the same problem has been found with capuchin monkeys (Visalberghi & Limongelli, 1994). Povinelli (2000) cites a total of 27 experiments, using a variety of tests, all of which show that chimpanzees have a complete lack of understanding of the physical properties of the problems that confront them. The interested reader might also refer to an article by Nissani (2006), which reports a failure by elephants to display causal reasoning in a tool-use task.

The negative results that have just been cited make it all the more important to determine whether Premack (1976) was correct in claiming that chimpanzees are

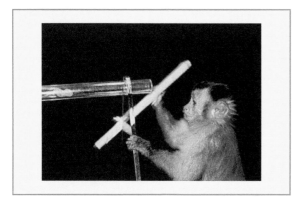 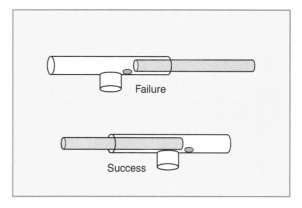

FIGURE 4.13 Right: Diagram of the apparatus used by Povinelli (2000) and by Visalberghi and Limongelli (1994) to test whether an animal will push a peanut in the direction that ensures it does not fall into a trap. From Visalberghi and Limongelli, 1994. Copyright © 1994 American Psychological Association. Reproduced with permission. Left: A monkey about to attempt to retrieve a nut from the apparatus. Photograph by Elisabetta Visalberghi.

capable of causal inference. For the present, it is perhaps wisest to keep an open mind about the capacity of primates to refer to folk physics when solving problems, but what about other species? Clayton and Dickinson (2006) have suggested that the most compelling evidence that animals have an appreciation of folk physics can be found in certain species of birds.

Birds

In one study, Seed, Tebbich, Emery, and Clayton (2006) presented a group of naïve rooks a version of the trap problem used by Povinelli (2000; described above). When first confronted with this problem, the direction in which the birds pushed the food was determined by chance but, as training progressed, they showed a marked improvement in avoiding the trap. To test whether this improvement reflected anything more than learning through trial and error, the birds were given a new problem where performance was not expected to be influenced by the effects of any prior trial-and-error learning. Six out of seven birds performed poorly on the new problem, but one bird performed extremely well from the outset. As the authors point out, it is hard to know what conclusions to draw when one bird passes a test that six others have failed, but the performance of the one successful bird encourages the view that future research with rooks might reveal promising results.

Another species of bird that might possess an understanding of folk physics is the raven. Heinrich (2000; see also Heinrich and Bugnyar, 2005) describes a series of experiments with hand-reared ravens in which the birds were presented with a piece of meat hanging from a perch (see the left-hand side of Figure 4.14). The meat could not be obtained by flying towards it and clasping it in the beak. Instead, to reach the meat some birds settled on the perch where the string was attached and grasped the string below the perch with their beak and pulled it upwards. To stop the meat falling back they placed a foot on the string and then let it drop from their beak whereupon they bent down to grasp again the string below the perch. This operation was repeated until the meat was near enough to be grasped directly with the beak. In another test, ravens were confronted with the arrangement shown in the right-hand side of Figure 4.14. On this occasion, meat could be retrieved by standing on the

FIGURE 4.14 Diagram of the apparatus used by Heinrich and Bugnyar (2005). A raven stood on the perch and was expected to retrieve food by pulling the string upwards (left-hand side) or downwards (right-hand side).

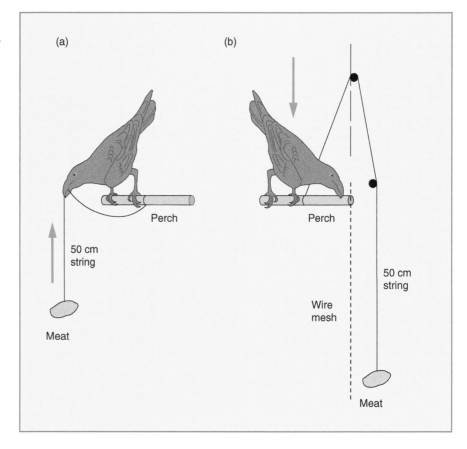

(a)

(b)

Perch

Perch

50 cm string

50 cm string

Wire mesh

Meat

Meat

perch and pulling the string downwards. Birds who had mastered the original task were also adept at mastering this new task, but birds without prior experience of pulling string never mastered this second task.

Heinrich and Bugnyar (2005) believe these results show that ravens have "some kind of understanding of means–end relationships, i.e. an apprehension of a cause-effect relation between string, food, and certain body parts" (p. 973). In other words, they have an appreciation of folk physics. This conclusion is based on the finding that birds spontaneously solved the first problem but not the second one. It was assumed that an understanding of cause–effect relations would allow the birds to appreciate that pulling food in one direction would result in the food moving in the same direction (Figure 4.15). Such knowledge would be beneficial when the birds had to pull the string upwards to make the meat rise upwards, but it would be a hindrance in the second problem in which the birds were required to pull the string downwards to make meat rise upwards.

Although the performance of the ravens is impressive, it does not necessarily demonstrate that the birds relied on folk physics to solve the problem that initially confronted them. As Heinrich and Bugnyar (2005) acknowledge, the solution to the first problem might have been a product of trial-and-error learning in which the sight of food being drawn ever closer served as the reward for the sequence of stepping and pulling that the birds engaged in. According to this analysis, the initial contact with the string would have to occur by chance, which seems plausible because the bird's

FIGURE 4.15 A raven solving the problem set by Heinrich and Bugnyar (2005). Photographs by Bernd Heinrich and Thomas Bugnyar. Reprinted with permission.

beak may have been close to the string as it peered down from the perch at the food. It is also worth noting that the birds had experience of eating road-kill carcasses, which may have allowed them to refine their skills of pulling and stepping to retrieve edible constituents. In the case of the second problem, the naïve birds would be unlikely to make contact with the string as they looked down on the food, and they would therefore be unlikely to initiate a response that would be rewarded by the sight of food being drawn upwards. In support of this claim, it is noteworthy that the authors observed the naïve birds make rather few contacts with the string in the second problem. The success on the second problem by birds with experience of the first problem can also be readily explained by assuming that the original experience increased the likelihood that they would pull on string attached to the perch in the new problem. A similar experiment has been conducted with elephants by Nissani (2004), who concluded that even their successful performance was a consequence of nothing more than learning through trial and error.

Before describing one final laboratory study, it is worth considering an example of tool use by birds in their natural environment. Woodpecker finches live on the Galapagos Islands, where many of them use twigs or cactus spines held in their beaks to extract insects from holes in trees. They will even modify these tools by shortening them if they are too long, and removing twiglets if they prevent the twig from being inserted into a hole. Although it might be thought that this behavior reflects an understanding of how sticks can be used as tools to extend the reach of the beak, and an understanding of how such tools can be modified to make them more effective, a careful study by Tebbich, Taborsky, Fessl, and Blomqvist (2001) provides a more mundane explanation for this behavior. It seems that juvenile woodpecker finches have a natural tendency to pick up twigs and cactus spines and to insert them in holes in trees. If this activity should result in food, then the particular action that has been performed will be repeated in other holes. Not all adult woodpecker finches display this skill, which has led Tebbich et al. (2001) to argue that tool use can be acquired only when the bird is young, and only if it is exposed to the appropriate environment. In other words, the skill of inserting twigs into holes is no more than a consequence of the interaction between learning through trial and error and the maturation of a species-typical behavior.

Perhaps the most dramatic example of tool use in birds has been shown in New Caledonian crows (Weir, Chappell and Kacelnik, 2002). These birds live on New Caledonia, an island about 1600 km east of the north-east coast of Australia.

They use long thin strips of leaf with barbs running down one edge to draw prey from cracks and holes in trees. It is not known if this ability is learned or inherited, but if the conclusions drawn from the study by Tebbich et al. (2001) have any generality, then it will be a mixture of the two.

In the experiment by Weir et al. (2002), a male and a female crow were expected to retrieve a piece of food from a bucket with a handle that was placed in a clear, vertical tube (Figure 4.16). The tube was so deep that it was impossible for the birds to reach the handle of the bucket with their beaks. A piece of straight wire and a piece of wire with a hook at one end were placed near the tube and the birds were expected to use the hooked wire to lift the bucket out of the tube by its handle. On one occasion, the male crow selected the hooked wire, which left the female with the straight wire. She picked up one end in her beak inserted the other end in a small opening and then bent the wire to create a hook which was of a suitable size to enable her to lift the bucket from the tube. A video clip of this sequence can be seen by going to the following web address http://www.sciencemag.org/cgi/content/full/297/5583/981/DC1. As one watches the female crow bend the wire it is hard not to agree with the authors that she was deliberately modifying the wire to create a tool, and that this modification relied on an understanding of "folk physics" and causality. However, appearances can be deceptive, and it would be a mistake to ignore the possibility that the bird's behavior was a consequence of less sophisticated processes. As with the woodpecker finches, it is possible that the skill displayed by the female crow was a consequence of the interaction between inherited tendencies and learning based on prior experience with sticks, twigs, and so on. Before this explanation can be rejected with complete confidence, more needs to be known about the development of tool use in New Caledonian crows in their natural habitat. It is also a pity that rather little is known about the prior experiences of the bird in question, which was captured in the wild.

The results from these tests for an understanding of folk physics in birds can perhaps most fairly be described as ambiguous in their theoretical significance. On the one hand, it is possible to explain most, if not all, of them in terms of the trial-and-error principles advocated by Thorndike (1911) almost a century ago.

FIGURE 4.16 A New Caledonian crow lifting a bucket out of a tube in order to retrieve food in an experiment by Weir, et al., (2002). Photograph by Alex Weir © Behavioural Ecology Research Group, University of Oxford.

However, a critic of this type of explanation would argue that it is so versatile that it can explain almost any result that is obtained. Moreover, although the trial-and-error explanations we have considered may be plausible, there is no evidence to confirm that they are necessarily correct. On the other hand, some of the behavior that has been discovered with birds is so impressive to watch that many researchers find it hard to believe they lack any understanding of the problem that confronts them.

For myself, my sympathies rest with an analysis of problem solving in terms of trial-and-error learning. The great advantage of this explanation is that it is based on firmly established principles of associative learning. Problem solving relies on the capacity for rewards to strengthen associations involving responses, and the transfer of the solution from one problem to another is explained through stimulus generalization. By contrast, much less is known about the mental processes that would permit animals to make causal inferences, or to reason using folk physics. Seed et al. (2006) note briefly that these processes may involve the capacity for acquiring abstract rules about simple, physical properties of the environment. Given such a proposal two questions arise: first, how is such knowledge about the environment acquired, and second, are animals capable of abstract thought? As far as I am aware, no-one has offered an answer to the first question and, as for the second question, we shall see in later chapters that whether or not animals are capable of abstract thought is a contentious issue that has yet to be fully resolved.

CHAPTER 5

CONTENTS

Extinction

The previous chapters have revealed that two different conditioning techniques can exert a profound influence on the behavior of animals. Using Pavlovian conditioning, in which a neutral conditioned stimulus (CS) is paired with a biologically significant unconditioned stimulus (US), animals can be trained to perform a new response to a stimulus. With instrumental conditioning, animals can be trained to increase the frequency with which they make a response if it leads to reward. The present chapter is concerned with considering what happens when circumstances change and a Pavlovian CS is no longer paired with the US, or an instrumental response no longer leads to reward. In both cases, the frequency with which the response is performed will gradually decline and eventually cease. The loss in the strength of a response in these conditions is referred to as extinction.

The fact that extinction takes place raises two fundamentally important questions: First, what is learned during extinction? Second, what are the conditions that promote extinction? In answer to the first question, we shall adopt the strategy that has proved so useful in previous chapters by assuming that Pavlovian and instrumental conditioning result in the formation of associations. As these associations are said to determine the vigor with which a response occurs, it is natural to think that extinction is effective by weakening previously formed associations. The obvious answer to the second question is that the omission of a US for Pavlovian conditioning, or a reward for instrumental conditioning, provides the necessary conditions for extinction. Contrary to intuition, we shall see that neither of these answers is satisfactory. There is abundant evidence to show that extinction does not result solely in the weakening of existing association. Instead, extinction often appears to be a consequence of the formation of new associations. As far as the second question is concerned, extinction takes place more rapidly in some circumstances than in others. This means that something more than just the omission of a US or reward is responsible for determining the effectiveness of an extinction treatment.

In attempting to answer the two questions posed above, we shall focus on the explanation for extinction offered by the Rescorla–Wagner (1972) theory, which, it will be recalled from Chapter 3, explains an impressive array of findings. According to this theory, Pavlovian conditioning results in the growth of CS–US associations. Extinction is seen quite simply as being the reverse of this process. That is, extinction is regarded as new learning—or perhaps more accurately, unlearning—which is characterized as a progressive weakening of a CS–US association. Although there is more to extinction than is implied by the Rescorla–Wagner (1972) theory, it provides a useful framework on which to base a discussion of this topic. Before exploring the application of the theory to extinction, however, we need to make sure that extinction does indeed depend upon new learning.

EXTINCTION AS GENERALIZATION DECREMENT

Although most, if not all theoretical accounts of extinction assume that it depends on some form of learning, extinction may occur for another reason:

generalization decrement. To appreciate this reason it might be helpful to consider briefly the results from two experiments. In the first study, which was conducted by Holz and Azrin (1963), pigeons were trained to peck a white key to receive food. After a fair amount of training, the color of the key was suddenly changed to green and there was an immediate drop in the rate of responding. In the second study, which was conducted by Brandon, Vogel, and Wagner (2000), rabbits received eye-blink conditioning in which a CS was paired with a shock. Test trials were then given in which the CS was presented by itself or in combination with either one or two novel stimuli. The strength of the response to the CS was reduced to some extent by the addition of one stimulus, and to a greater extent by the addition of two stimuli.

The important implication of these experiments is that the strength of conditioned responding can be weakened by changing the environment in which the response is performed, that is, through generalization decrement. The processes underlying generalization decrement are considered in Chapter 6; for the present, we will pursue the implications of this phenomenon for our understanding of extinction. If a subject has repeatedly received food for pressing a lever, and then food should no longer follow this response, it can be argued that the absence of food constitutes a change to the environment. The generalization decrement brought about by this change might then be responsible for the weakening of responding produced by the extinction treatment. That is, extinction may occur not because animals have learned something new about the relationship between lever pressing and food, but because of a generalization decrement produced by the omission of the food. According to this analysis, therefore, the answer to the first question posed at the start of this chapter is that nothing is learned during extinction.

A similar explanation can be developed for extinction in Pavlovian conditioning. If a rabbit should repeatedly receive a tone followed by shock, and then receive just the tone by itself, it will suddenly find itself in an environment where shock is no longer delivered. This change may weaken responding through generalization decrement, rather than through a change to the associations involving the tone.

If this trainer were to deny these dolphins their edible reward, the conditioned behavior would be weakened, resulting in extinction. In this instance, the likelihood is that the dolphins would be less likely to respond to signals from the trainer as desired.

The results from an experiment by Napier, Macrae, and Kehoe (1992) are relevant to this explanation. Two groups of rabbits first received eye-blink conditioning in which a tone signaled a brief shock to the cheek. Once a conditioned response of blinking was recorded on nearly every trial, the tone was presented for 60 trials in an extinction session. This was the only treatment that was given to Group Tone, but for Group Unpaired the presentations of the tone were intermingled with unsignaled presentations of the shock. The results from the test session are shown in Figure 5.1. Extinction occurred in both groups but it is apparent from the figure that responding was consistently more frequent in Group Unpaired than in Group Tone. The first point to make concerning this experiment relates to the substantial decline in responding by Group Unpaired as the extinction trials progressed. As this group received both the tone and the shock in the test session, it is hard to explain this pattern of results by appealing to generalization decrement. Put simply, the stimuli present during conditioning were also present during extinction, which should have resulted in little or no disruption of responding through generalization decrement. Thus the results from Group Unpaired imply that extinction is not just a consequence of generalization decrement. It must, instead, be a consequence of new learning based on the fact that the tone was no longer followed by shock.

The second point to make is that the foregoing conclusion does not mean the effects of generalization decrement can be ignored as far as extinction is concerned. On the contrary, a ready explanation for the difference between the results for the two groups is that the absence of the shock for Group Tone during the extinction session weakened responding through generalization decrement. If this explanation is correct, then the difference between the results from the two groups can be taken as a measure of the degree to which generalization decrement contributed to extinction in Group Tone. Similar findings to those by Napier et al. (1992) have been reported using instrumental conditioning with both pigeons (Boakes, 1973) and rats (Rescorla & Skucy, 1969). There are therefore good reasons for believing that extinction in a wide range of species, and in a variety of tasks, is at least in part due to learning about the omission of a US for Pavlovian conditioning, or a reward for instrumental conditioning. We now turn to consider the conditions that influence this learning.

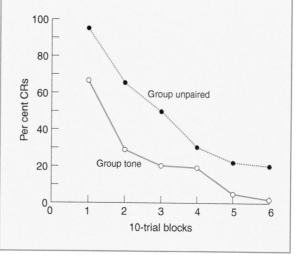

FIGURE 5.1 The mean frequency of an eye-blink conditioned response (CR) during extinction trials with a tone that had previously been a signal for shock, for a group that received the tone by itself (Group tone) or the tone unpaired with shock (Group unpaired) (adapted from Napier et al., 1992).

THE CONDITIONS FOR EXTINCTION

Surprise

In Chapter 3, we saw that according to the Rescorla–Wagner (1972) theory an important ingredient for successful conditioning is surprise. During the course of acquisition, the increment in associative strength of a CS was predicted to be greater if the US with which it is paired was surprising rather than expected. Surprise is predicted to play a similar role in extinction. Each extinction trial is assumed to result in the loss of associative strength by the CS, and the extent of this loss is believed to be directly related to the degree to which the omission of the US is unexpected. Suppose animals have received training in which a tone signals food. On the first trial of extinction, the tone will activate a representation of food and, according to the theory, considerable surprise will be generated when the food is not presented. The surprising omission of food will then result in a weakening of the tone–food association. As extinction continues, the progressive weakening of the associative strength of the tone will lead to the expectation of food during the tone being reduced, so that its omission will become less and less surprising, and the decrements in associative strength will be smaller and smaller. Eventually, the strength of the tone–food association will be reduced to zero and extinction will be complete. The graph in the right-hand side of Figure 3.2 (p. 66) shows the decline in the associative strength of the tone that is predicted by the Rescorla–Wagner (1972) equation. It is encouraging to note that this graph is similar in form to the results that were recorded with the two groups in the experiment by Napier et al. (1992) and which are shown in Figure 5.1. The results from two rather different experiments, which we will now consider, lend considerable support to the account for extinction provided by the Rescorla–Wagner (1972) theory.

Protection from extinction

One prediction that follows from the analysis of extinction provided by the Rescorla–Wagner (1972) theory is that it should be possible to **protect a CS from extinction** even if it is no longer paired with a US. To help clarify this statement, consider an autoshaping experiment by Rescorla (2003), the design of which is summarized in Table 5.1. During the conditioning stage of the experiment, pigeons received trials in which a visual stimulus O was presented on a response key either by itself and followed by food, or accompanied by a tone (T) and followed by nothing. As a result of this training, the birds pecked rapidly at the key during O by itself, but not during O and T together. The purpose of this training was to convert the tone into a signal for the absence of food or, more formally, into a conditioned inhibitor with negative associative strength (see Chapter 3). The pigeons also received conditioning trials in which two different visual stimuli, A and B, were presented on the key and followed by food. The next stage of experiment consisted of extinction trials without food. Stimulus B was repeatedly presented by itself, whereas A was presented in the company of the tone. The extinction stage lasted for two and a half sessions. Finally, test trials were given with A and B by themselves to compare the effects of the different extinction treatments.

The left-hand panel of Figure 5.2 shows the rates of key-pecking during AT and B during the extinction stage. There is a gradual weakening of responding on trials with B, which reflects the normal effects of extinction, but responding during AT is consistently weaker than during B. The results with AT can be understood when it

KEY TERM

Protect from extinction
The loss of effectiveness of extinction that occurs when a CS is presented without a US in the presence of a conditioned inhibitor.

TABLE 5.1 Summary of the training given to a single group of pigeons in an experiment by Rescorla (2003)

Conditioning stage	Extinction stage	Test stage
O+ OT− A+ B+	AT− B−	A− B−

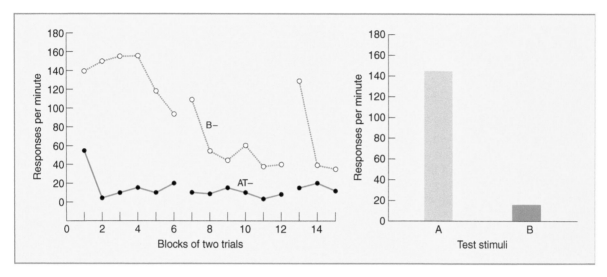

FIGURE 5.2 The mean rate of autoshaped key pecking for a group that received extinction trials with a visual stimulus in compound with a tone, AT−, or trials with a visual stimulus by itself, B− (left-hand panel), and the mean rate of key pecking that was recorded during subsequent test trials with A and B presented by themselves (right-hand panel) (adapted from Rescorla, 2003).

is recalled that the Rescorla–Wagner (1972) theory predicts that the strength of responding during a compound is determined by the sum of the associative strengths of its components. Thus the positive associative strength of A, together with the negative associative strength of T, will result in AT possessing rather little overall excitatory strength when it is first presented. One consequence of this low overall excitatory strength is that responding throughout extinction will be weak to the compound.

Of more interest are the implications of this analysis for the effects of the AT trials on extinction with A. Because AT comprises one element that signals food, and one that signals its absence, the combination of these stimuli will mean that subjects will not have a strong expectation of food when AT is first presented. The omission of food after AT will thus not be surprising and there should be little change to the associative strength of either A or T. The results from the test trials shown in the right-hand side of Figure 5.2 confirmed this prediction by revealing that responding during A was quite rapid when it was presented without T. In fact, despite having been presented for 30 trials during the extinction stage, responding to A was almost as rapid as when it was paired with food during conditioning. A rather different story concerns the fate of stimulus B. At the outset of extinction, because B was presented by itself animals should have a strong expectancy of food during this stimulus, which should make its omission particularly surprising. The extinction stage was thus predicted to result eventually in a considerable loss of associative strength by B and this was confirmed by the low response rate during the test trial.

The experiment by Rescorla (2003) demonstrates that the presence of a conditioned inhibitor, T, protected A from losing associative strength during the extinction stage of the experiment. In developing this explanation it was stated that responding during the extinction trials with AT was weak because T was a conditioned inhibitor with negative associative strength. Readers might wonder whether the poor responding during AT in the extinction stage was instead due to a generalization decrement brought about by the presence of T. Rescorla (2003) was aware of this possibility, and demonstrated in subsequent experiments that the pattern of results shown with AT and A in Figure 5.2 does not occur if T is a neutral stimulus, rather than one with negative associative strength.

Enhanced extinction

Another prediction from the Rescorla–Wagner (1972) theory concerns the effects of conducting extinction with two stimuli, A and B, that have separately been paired with a US. When the stimuli are presented together, the overall associative strength of the compound AB is predicted to be equal to the sum of the associative strengths of the two stimuli. The compound will therefore excite a very strong expectancy for the US and its omission should be a much greater surprise after A and B together than after A or B alone. If the amount of surprise determines the effectiveness of the extinction trial, then it follows that the components of the compound will lose more associative strength on each trial than if they were presented for extinction in isolation.

Table 5.2 summarizes the design of an experiment by Rescorla (2000), which was conducted to test the foregoing prediction. Two groups of rats first received conditioning in which two stimuli, A and B, were paired with food. During a subsequent extinction stage, Group AB received trials in which the compound AB was followed by nothing, whereas Group B received trials in which B was followed by nothing. The results from this stage are shown in the left-hand side of Figure 5.3, where it is evident that responding during AB was stronger than during B throughout extinction. This difference is in keeping with the prediction from the Rescorla–Wagner (1972) theory that the associative strength of a compound, and hence the strength of responding in its presence, is determined by the sum of the associative strengths of its constituents.

The right-hand side of Figure 5.3 shows the results from test trials in which both groups were presented with B by itself. In confirmation of the prediction made above, responding was weaker during B in Group AB than Group B. Thus the presence of A during extinction appears to have augmented the loss of associative strength by B in Group AB.

These two experiments show that extinction with a CS can be facilitated if it is accompanied by another stimulus that has been paired with a US, and slowed down if it is accompanied by a CS that signals the absence of the US. Taken together, the results provide compelling support for the claim that the effectiveness of extinction on any trial is influenced by the extent to which the omission of the US is surprising.

TABLE 5.2 Summary of the training given to two groups of rats in an experiment by Rescorla (2000)

	Conditioning stage	Extinction stage	Test stage
Group AB	A+ B+	AB–	B
Group B	A+ B+	B–	B

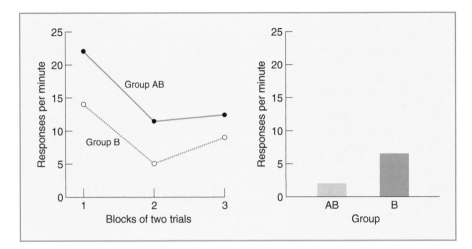

FIGURE 5.3 The mean rate of conditioned magazine activity during extinction either with a compound composed of two stimuli that had separately been paired with food, Group AB, or with a single stimulus that had been paired with food, Group B (left-hand panel), and the mean rates of this activity during a subsequent test trial in which both groups were tested with the same single stimulus (right-hand panel) (adapted from Rescorla, 2000).

Extinction with a US

A great benefit of the Rescorla–Wagner (1972) theory is that it has been presented formally so that precise predictions can be derived from it. The strength of the theory is revealed by the fact that many of these predictions have been confirmed, even if they seem unlikely. Extinction provides one particularly striking example of an unlikely prediction being confirmed. Consider a Pavlovian conditioning experiment in which two stimuli, A and B, are separately paired with a US, before they are presented together and again paired with the same US. Intuition might suggest that because the compound is followed by a US then there will be no change in the associative strength of either A or B. According to the theory, however, our intuition is wrong. The combination of the associative strengths of A and B will result in the expectancy for shock being twice as great as during either A or B alone. This will mean, effectively, that the shock that follows the compound will be half the size of the one anticipated and the theory predicts there will be a loss in the associative strength of A and B. Thus, according to the theory, extinction can occur in certain circumstances, even when a US is present. It further follows from the theory that extinction will not be complete but will cease when the combined associative strengths of A and B equal the value of the US. These counterintuitive predictions have been confirmed by Kremer (1978) and Wagner and Rescorla (1972).

Extinction of conditioned inhibition

At the start of this chapter, the question was posed: What are the conditions that promote extinction? According to the Rescorla–Wagner (1972) theory, the answer is that extinction is governed by the extent to which expectations concerning the magnitude of an anticipated US are not confirmed. The results from the three experiments that have just been described lend this answer considerable support, and it is likely that the answer will lie at the heart of any complete analysis of extinction. There are, however, findings that challenge the account of extinction offered by the Rescorla–Wagner (1972) theory.

One finding was reported by Zimmer-Hart and Rescorla (1974). Rats received conditioning with an A+ AB− discrimination in which one stimulus, A, signaled shock, and a compound of A with another stimulus, B, signaled the absence of shock. We have just seen that this treatment will result in B becoming a conditioned inhibitor with negative associative strength. Zimmer-Hart and Rescorla (1974) were interested in what would happen to the properties of B if it was then repeatedly presented by itself for a series of extinction trials. They found that even though B was presented alone for 96 trials, there was no hint that it had lost any of its inhibitory properties. For example, during a test in which B and a conditioned excitor were presented together, B was quite capable of weakening responding during the excitor. Moreover, the extent of this effect was no different to that seen in a control group that had received similar training but no extinction trials with B (for a related finding see Baker, 1974).

At first glance, the results of Zimmer-Hart and Rescorla (1974) might not seem problematic. During the discrimination, B signaled the absence of shock and it was followed by the absence of shock during the extinction trials. Why should the extinction treatment result in any change to the properties of B? The problem is that during the extinction trials the associative strength of B is predicted by the Rescorla–Wagner (1972) theory to be negative. It follows from the theory's equation that each extinction trial will gradually reduce the magnitude of this negative value until B has no negative associative strength and, at this point, it will fail to act as conditioned inhibitor.

The findings of Zimmer-Hart and Rescorla (1974) demonstrate that the Rescorla–Wagner (1972) theory does not provide a full explanation for extinction. But the problems posed by the experiment are not too serious. As far as extinction with conditioned excitors is concerned, the theory appears to provide a fair account of the conditions that promote extinction; it is when the theory is applied to the extinction of conditioned inhibition that it runs into difficulty. Rescorla (1979) has considered this difficulty and offered several suggestions for ways in which the Rescorla–Wagner (1972) theory might overcome it.

Partial reinforcement

One of the most enduring problems for the study of extinction has arisen from studies that have compared the effects of **partial reinforcement** and **continuous reinforcement**. Many experiments have revealed that these different training schedules result in different rates of extinction which has given rise to the term the **partial reinforcement effect (PRE)**. To provide a demonstration of the PRE, and to clarify why it poses a theoretical problem, we shall consider first a simple Pavlovian conditioning experiment by Pearce, Redhead, and Aydin (1997).

Pearce et al. (1997) conducted appetitive conditioning with two groups of rats for which occasional presentations of a CS were followed by food. The CS was followed by food on every trial for Group Continuous, and on a randomly selected half of the trials for Group Partial. On the remaining trials for Group Partial, the CS was followed by nothing. Figure 5.4 shows the results from the test phase of the experiment in which the CS was repeatedly presented without food. The measure of conditioning in this experiment was the time that subjects spent with their heads in the food magazine during each presentation of the CS. At the outset of the extinction trials, there was more magazine activity during the CS in Group Continuous than Group Partial but, as extinction progressed, this relationship reversed so that by the end of the test trials the amount of magazine activity was greater during the CS for Group Partial than Group Continuous. Extinction was thus slower for Group Partial than Group Continuous.

KEY TERMS

Partial reinforcement
A schedule in which a CS is occasionally followed by a US for Pavlovian conditioning, or a response is occasionally followed by a reinforcer for instrumental conditioning.

Continuous reinforcement
A schedule in which every CS is followed by a US for Pavlovian conditioning, or every response is followed by a reinforcer for instrumental conditioning

Partial reinforcement effect (PRE)
The slower loss of responding during extinction after conditioning with a partial than a continuous reinforcement schedule.

According to most theories, including Rescorla and Wagner (1972), pairing a stimulus with food on every trial will result in it gaining more associative strength than if it is paired with food on only half the trials. The reason for this prediction is that each trial with a continuous reinforcement schedule will provide the opportunity for a growth in the associative strength of the stimulus, whereas with a partial reinforcement schedule the trials without food will undo some of the good that was done on the trials with food. The greater amount of magazine activity by Group Continuous than Group Partial at the outset of extinction is consistent with this analysis. A further prediction from the theories is that the strength of responding throughout extinction will reflect the associative strength of the CS at the end of conditioning. If the associative strength of the CS was high before the first extinction trial, because of conditioning with continuous reinforcement, then throughout extinction, responding is predicted to be stronger than if the associative strength was low at the end of conditioning, because of training with partial reinforcement. This prediction is hard to justify without resorting to mathematics, but an intuitive feel for the reasoning behind it can be gained by imagining two baths of the same size, and with one bath filled with more water than the other. If the plugs are pulled simultaneously, then, until they are empty, the bath with more water originally will always contain more water than the other bath. Thus a common prediction for many theories of associative learning is that during extinction after conditioning with a partial reinforcement schedule, responding will be weaker than after conditioning with continuous reinforcement. Results of the kind reported by Pearce et al. (1997) thus pose a serious theoretical problem.

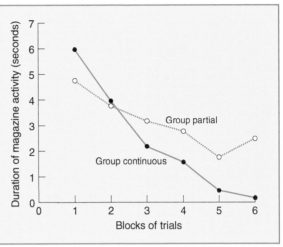

FIGURE 5.4 The mean duration of magazine activity during extinction trials with an auditory stimulus that had previously been paired with food on either a continuous (Group Continuous) or a partial (Group Partial) reinforcement schedule (adapted from Pearce et al., 1997).

A similar problem is posed by investigations into the effects of partial reinforcement using instrumental conditioning. According to Chapter 4, instrumental conditioning will result in a response entering into associations. If the strength of these associations determines how vigorously the response is performed then, for the reasons just outlined, a response that has been consistently followed by reward will be performed more often, or more vigorously, during extinction than one that has been intermittently followed by reward. The results from a large number of experiments contradict this prediction, and a discussion of two of them should give a flavor of the sort of research that has been conducted.

Weinstock (1954) trained rats to run down a 45-cm alley to gain food. Group Continuous received food on every trial, whereas Group Partial received food on half of the trials selected in a random sequence. The left half of Figure 5.5 shows the speed with which the animals ran down the alley to reach the goal. Both groups increased their speed of running as training progressed, but the effects of the different schedules are revealed by Group Continuous eventually running faster than Group Partial. One has to sympathize with Weinstock: During his experiment, two rats in Group Partial bit him and held on with such tenacity that it was apparently difficult for him to pry them loose.

The right half of Figure 5.5 shows speed of running down the alley for the extinction phase of the experiment in which food was no longer presented at the end of the alley. Group Continuous soon gave up running swiftly down the alley and took

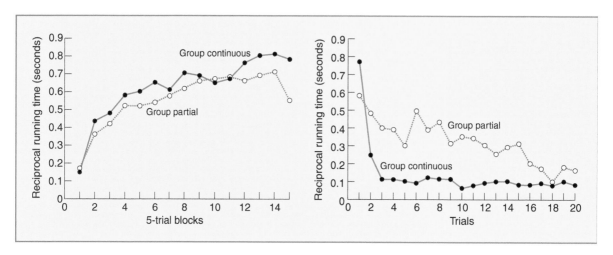

FIGURE 5.5 The mean speed of running down an alley for food that was presented on every trial, Group Continuous, or on a randomly selected half of the trials, Group Partial (left-hand panel), and the mean speed of running down the alley by the same two groups when food was no longer presented (right-hand panel) (adapted from Weinstock, 1954).

a considerable amount of time to reach the goal on each trial. Extinction thus occurred rapidly in this group. By contrast, a demonstration of the PRE was provided by Group Partial which persisted in running rapidly down the alley for many more trials than Group Continuous.

A rather different demonstration of the PRE was provided by Jenkins, McFann, & Clayton (1950), who required pigeons to peck a response key for food. Each peck resulted in food for Group Continuous, whereas for Group Partial pecks resulted in food on average once every minute. After both groups had earned 200 food rewards, they were placed in the test chamber for 6 hours and food was never presented. The average number of responses made by Group Continuous during this period was 638, whereas for Group Partial the number was over 2500.

During the middle of the twentieth century, considerable effort was invested into trying to understand why extinction is slower after partial than continuous reinforcement. At least seven different theories were developed to explain the PRE, and literally hundreds of experiments were conducted to test them. This effort was not in vain. An excellent review by Mackintosh (1974) concludes that two of the theories are superior to any of their competitors: Amsel's (1958, 1992) **frustration theory** and Capaldi's (1966, 1994) **sequential theory**. Although these theories differ substantially in how they are formulated, they provide a rather similar analysis of the PRE.

Both theories have their roots in the explanation for extinction offered earlier in terms of generalization decrement. Let us start by assuming animals have been trained to run down an alley for continuous reinforcement and that they then receive an extinction trial. Amsel (1958, 1992) and Capaldi (1966, 1994) assume that the omission of food during the extinction trials will leave an after-effect. Amsel (1958, 1992) regards the after-effect as an emotional state called frustration. Evidence that the omission of an anticipated reward can generate an emotional state comes from the finding that both extinction and intermittent reinforcement can make an animal aggressive (e.g. Azrin, Hutchinson, & Hake, 1966; Hutchinson, Azrin & Hunt, 1968). Aggression induced by frustration may also have been responsible for the unfortunate attacks on Weinstock (1954) by two of the rats that he trained. Capaldi

(1966, 1994), on the other hand, regards the after-effects as simply being the memory of nonreinforcement. For the sake of discussion, the after-effect of nonreinforcement will be referred to as stimulus N.

Normally, repeated extinction trials are given in each daily session. Once it has been generated, therefore, Amsel (1958, 1992) and Capaldi (1966, 1994) assume that N will persist for a short while and be present at the start of the next trial. The presence of N will then mean that the conditions in the start box from the second trial onwards will be different from those that prevailed during training and the tendency to run down the alley will, as a consequence, be weakened through generalization decrement.

Suppose, instead, that rats are trained to run down the alley for partial reinforcement. The occurrence of nonreinforced trials during this training will excite stimulus N, which will still be active when subjects are returned to the start box. As a result, there will be trials in which the presence of N in the start box is followed by reward in the goal box. As training with the partial reinforcement schedule progresses, the presence of N will become one of the constellation of cues in the start box that signal reward in the goal box. The start of extinction will result in N again being excited in the start box and rats should persist running for two reasons. First, the presence of N will be familiar and fail to weaken responding through generalization decrement. Second, the presence of N will elicit the same response that it elicited during acquisition, and encourage rats to run rapidly down the alley. It is impossible to do justice here to the many experiments that have been conducted to evaluate different explanations of the PRE. Instead, just one experiment will be described. Not only does this experiment provide a good example of the sort of design that was used to test theories of the PRE, but its results lend clear support to the analysis that has just been developed.

Spivey and Hess (1968) required two groups of rats to run down an alley four times a day. Food was in the goal box for two of these trials (R+), but not the other two (R−). One group was trained each day with the sequence of trials R+R+R−R− and the other group was trained with R−R−R+R+. After some initial training, both groups will expect food for running down the alley on any trial. At this point for rats in the R−R−R+R+ condition, the omission of food on the first two trials of a session will create the internal state N, which will persist for the remaining two trials. Because these trials lead to food, the presence of N will come to serve as a cue that indicates that running down the alley will be rewarded. The theories of Amsel (1958, 1992) and Capaldi (1966, 1994) therefore predict that rats in this group will demonstrate a PRE by running down the alley rapidly during subsequent extinction trials. A different outcome is predicted for the group trained with the R+R+R−R− schedule. The after-effects of the two R− trials of each session for this group can be expected to dissipate by the start of the next day. The group will therefore be denied the opportunity of learning that the presence of N in the start box serves as a cue for reward and the occurrence of this after-effect during the extinction trials should not have the beneficial effect that is predicted for the group trained with the R−R−R+R+ condition. The results supported this analysis by showing that extinction was slower for the group trained with the R−R−R+R+ than the R+R+R−R− condition. Thus, not every partial reinforcement schedule results in a PRE. A considerable strength of the explanations offered by Amsel 1958, 1992) and Capaldi (1966, 1994) for this effect is that they are able to make precise and accurate predictions about the effects of training schedules that differ in subtle ways.

Most of the theorizing about the effects of partial reinforcement has concerned instrumental conditioning, but Pearce et al. (1997) have suggested that the proposals of Amsel (1958, 1992) and Capaldi (1966, 1994) may also apply to Pavlovian conditioning. If conditioning is conducted with a continuous reinforcement schedule, then during a subsequent extinction phase the omission of the US after the CS will create an internal state N that may persist from one trial to the next. The presence of N can therefore be expected to weaken responding through generalization decrement, and to facilitate extinction. Training with a partial reinforcement schedule, however, will allow subjects to experience the after-effects of nonreinforced trials during trials in which the CS is paired with the US. As a consequence, the generalization decrement produced by the presence of N during extinction should be minimal and extinction will progress relatively slowly. This analysis is thus able to account for the results reported by Pearce et al. (1997) that are shown in Figure 5.4.

To test the above explanation, Pearce et al. (1997) conducted another Pavlovian conditioning experiment with rats, but this time they were trained with two different stimuli presented in a random sequence. One of the stimuli was paired with food on a continuous reinforcement schedule, CS C, and the other was paired with food on a partial reinforcement schedule, CS P. There were six trials with C and twelve with P in every session. As a result of this treatment, the after-effects of the nonreinforced trials with CS P were expected to persist until a subsequent trial with CS C as well as CS P. Reinforced trials with both stimuli would then take place in the presence of N, and the occurrence of this stimulus during extinction should not weaken responding through generalization decrement. The strength of responding during extinction can, therefore, be expected to be determined solely by the associative strength of the two stimuli. It was noted earlier that the associative strength of a stimulus is predicted to be stronger after continuous than partial reinforcement and we therefore expected that responding throughout extinction would be stronger during CS C than CS P. The results, which are shown in Figure 5.6, confirmed this prediction.

The results from the experiments that have just been reviewed lend considerable support to the claim that nonreinforced trials during both instrumental and Pavlovian conditioning generate after-effects that can influence the strength of conditioned behavior. By taking account of these after-effects it has proved possible to understand the paradoxical finding that extinction is often slower after a partial than a continuous reinforcement schedule.

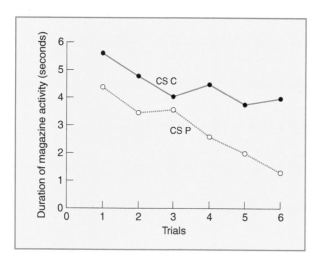

FIGURE 5.6 The mean duration of magazine activity for a single group during extinction trials with one stimulus that had been paired with food on a continuous reinforcement schedule (CS C) and with another stimulus that had been paired with food on a partial reinforcement schedule (CS P) (adapted from Pearce et al., 1997).

ASSOCIATIVE CHANGES DURING EXTINCTION

Associations with a no-US center

Thus far, we have assumed that extinction is due to the weakening of associations that were formed during conditioning. However, almost as soon as Pavlov (1927) started to study extinction it was evident that this assumption was either an oversimplification or wrong. Once a conditioned response had been weakened by repeatedly presenting the CS by itself, Pavlov (1927) found that presenting the CS again after an interval allowed the response to the CS to recover, but not completely. This effect is referred to as **spontaneous recovery**.

A relatively recent example of spontaneous recovery can be found in the experiment by Napier et al. (1992), which was described at the start of this chapter. Recall that rabbits received eye-blink conditioning with a tone, before the tone was presented by itself for extinction. To simplify the description of the experiment, the results from only the first extinction session were described, but five such sessions took place with each one occurring on a different day. The results from all five sessions can be seen in Figure 5.7 for Group Tone and Group Unpaired. Note particularly that at the start of the first few extinction sessions the frequency of responding recovered substantially from the relatively low level it reached at the end of the previous session. The rabbits did not receive tone–shock pairings during extinction and the spontaneous recovery must have been a consequence of the passage of time that elapsed between successive sessions.

The implication of spontaneous recovery is that extinction is not just a consequence of the weakening of associations. If it were, then it should not be possible to observe a recovery from extinction just by presenting the CS again after a delay. Instead, some other changes must take place during extinction. One suggestion is that extinction results not from the weakening of old associations, but from the establishment of new ones.

One of the first to put this idea forward was Konorski (1967). We saw in Chapter 2 that Konorski (1967) believed the omission of an anticipated US can elicit emotional reactions—frustration if the US is food or relief if it is shock. He further believed that stimuli that are present when these reactions occur enter into associations with a no-US center. Once activated, a no-US center can inhibit activation of the US center if it is aroused at the same time (see Figure 2.19). Konorski assumed that each extinction trial would result in the growth of a connection between the CS and the no-US center so that the CS would come to simultaneously activate both a US and a no-US center. Repeated extinction trials would then result in the CS activating the no-US center to a greater and greater extent, with the consequence that the no-US center would suppress the US center to a greater and greater extent and make it progressively harder for the CS to elicit a response. Spontaneous recovery can now be explained by assuming that the passage of time weakens the CS–no-US association. In other words, spontaneous recovery is

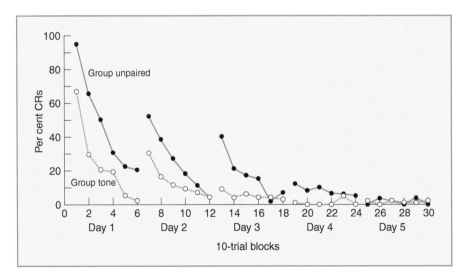

FIGURE 5.7 The mean frequency of an eye-blink conditioned response (CR) during extinction trials over successive daily sessions with a tone that had previously been a signal for shock, for a group that received the tone by itself (Group Tone) or the tone unpaired with shock (Group Unpaired) (adapted from Napier et al., 1992).

attributed to the CS–no-US association being stronger at the end of one extinction session than at the start of the next one.

Many researchers now accept that extinction results, at least in part, from the formation of new associations, but not all accept Konorski's claims concerning the nature of these associations. In the next section we examine a phenomenon known as **the renewal effect**, which is important because it suggests that the inhibitory influence acquired by a CS during extinction is more complex than that envisaged by Konorski. We shall then turn to an examination of experiments whose findings suggest that extinction does not affect the capacity of the CS to activate a representation of the US. Instead, they imply that the CS directly inhibits the response acquired during conditioning.

The renewal effect

A demonstration of the renewal effect can be found in an experiment by Bouton and Peck (1989). Appetitive conditioning took place in two contexts, A and B, that were conditioning chambers constructed from different materials and which had different smells. The treatment for the two groups is summarized in Table 5.3, and the results from the experiment are shown in Figure 5.8. Group AAA received, first, conditioning with a tone paired with food in Context A, second, extinction trials with the tone in Context A and, third, a renewal test in Context A which consisted of the tone again followed by nothing. Group ABA received the same treatment, except that the extinction trials with the tone took place in Context B.

Figure 5.8 shows that there was no difference between the groups during conditioning or during the extinction trials. However, there was a difference between the groups during the test stage. Group AAA showed a very weak response during this stage, which is hardly surprising because the renewal test was no more than a continuation of the extinction trials from the previous stage in the same context. Group ABA, however, showed a recovery, or renewal, of responding relative to that seen at the end of the extinction trials. We shall refer to this recovery of responding in the test stage as the A-B-A renewal effect, because it resulted from conditioning in Context A, extinction in Context B, and then testing in Context A. It hardly needs to be said that A-B-A renewal would not be expected if the extinction trials in Context B erased completely the tone–food association that was formed during the first stage of the experiment.

Bouton (1993) has explained A-B-A renewal by suggesting that extinction results in the formation of an inhibitory connection between representations of the CS and US in the manner depicted in the left-hand side of Figure 5.9. He could also have suggested that the new link developed between the CS and a no-US center as Konorski (1967) maintained. For the sake of being faithful to Bouton's ideas,

TABLE 5.3 Summary of the training given to two groups of rats in an experiment by Bouton and Peck (1989)

	Conditioning stage	Extinction stage	Test stage
Group AAA	Context A: Tone+	Context A: Tone−	Context A: Tone−
Group ABA	Context A: Tone+	Context B: Tone−	Context A: Tone−

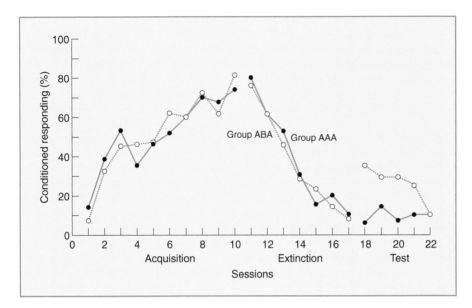

FIGURE 5.8 The frequency of conditioned responding during a tone that was paired with food for acquisition and presented without food for extinction and a renewal test. The three stages took place in the same context for Group AAA, and the extinction stage took place in a different context to the other two stages for Group ABA (adapted from Bouton & Peck, 1989).

however, we shall continue with his suggestion that the CS enters directly into an inhibitory association with the US.

Bouton (1993) further suggested that because the inhibitory association is acquired after the excitatory one, it will be more susceptible to disruption if there is a change of context. Thus, with an A-B-A treatment, the inhibitory association acquired in Context B in Group ABA is not expected to be very influential when animals are returned to Context A and a renewal of responding to the CS would be expected. A more explicit version of this proposal is shown in the right-hand half of Figure 5.9, where there is a modulatory link between the context and the inhibitory association that is formed during extinction (Bouton & Ricker, 1994). The modulatory link functions as a switch that allows the inhibitory association to be effective only in Context B, so that a strong conditioned response should be observed once subjects are returned to Context A.

The proposals of Bouton (1993) and Bouton and Ricker (1994) have been tested with a variety of renewal treatments. Harris, Jones, Bailey, and Westbrook (2000)

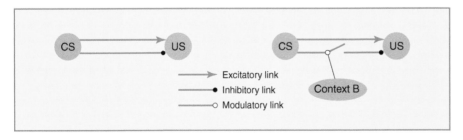

FIGURE 5.9 A model of the associations that control responding during extinction (left-hand panel). During conditioning an excitatory link will develop between the conditioned stimulus (CS) and unconditioned stimulus (US) centers, and during extinction an inhibitory link will develop between these centers. A modification of this model was proposed by Bouton and Ricker (1994) to account for the renewal effect (right-hand panel). The modulatory link allows the inhibitory link to be effective only in Context B (adapted from Bouton & Ricker, 1994).

compared an A-B-C treatment (conditioning with a CS in Context A, extinction in Context B, renewal test in Context C) with an A-B-B treatment. According to the theory, a strong response on the renewal test will be seen with the A-B-C treatment because the inhibitory link acquired in Context B will be ineffective in Context C. Conversely, the renewal test should result in a weak response during the renewal test with the A-B-B treatment. The results confirmed these predictions. Thomas, Larsen, and Ayres (2003) compared the effects of an A-B-C and an A-B-A treatment. With both methods of training, the change of context after the extinction trials in the second stage should permit a renewal of the extinguished response. Once again, the results confirmed this prediction.

Bouton (1993, 2004) has argued that the passage of time can act as a change in context in much the same way as a change to the external environment. This proposal has led to an explanation for spontaneous recovery that is very similar to that just put forward for the renewal effect. If animals receive conditioning, followed immediately by extinction and then a test trial, this can be characterized as an A-A-A treatment and there will not be a renewal of responding during the final test. Bouton (1993, 2004) has agued that placing an interval between the extinction stage and the renewal test will provide an opportunity for changes to internal stimuli, such as hormones and neurochemicals, and to external stimuli that are incidental to the experiment. The method of training can now be characterized as an A-A-B renewal treatment. The change of context for the final test will mean that the modulatory link based on Context A will no longer be effective and responding during the test trials will be restored and provide a demonstration of spontaneous recovery.

Despite the successes of the account offered by Bouton (1993) and Bouton and Ricker (1994), it provides at best an incomplete explanation for renewal. An inspection of Figure 5.8 indicates that the recovery of responding during the renewal test with the A-B-A treatment was far from complete. Bouton and Ricker's (1994) model implies that once the animals have been returned to Context A, they should behave as if they did not receive any treatment in Context B. Perhaps, therefore, the treatment in Context B resulted in some weakening of the original CS–US association, as well as the growth of an inhibitory association.

Another problem comes from studies that have examined the effects of an A-A-B renewal treatment (e.g. Thomas et al, 2003). Bouton and Ricker's (1994) model stipulates that the extinction trials in Context A during the second stage of the experiment will allow Context A to activate an inhibitory CS–US connection. When animals are tested in Context B, this activation will not take place and a renewal of the conditioned response is predicted. Although Thomas et al. (2003) found renewal, this was only slight and was substantially less than for a group that received an A-B-A treatment. The difference between the effects of these two treatments is not predicted by Bouton's (1993) and Bouton and Ricker's (1994) explanations for renewal.

Our understanding of renewal is thus incomplete. Nonetheless, the many demonstrations of this effect again point forcefully to the conclusion that extinction involves more than a weakening of previously formed associations. They also show that the context plays an important role in determining the effectiveness of new associations that are formed during extinction.

Extinction does not affect CS–US associations

The theories considered thus far have assumed that extinction after Pavlovian conditioning results from the weakening of previously formed CS–US associations

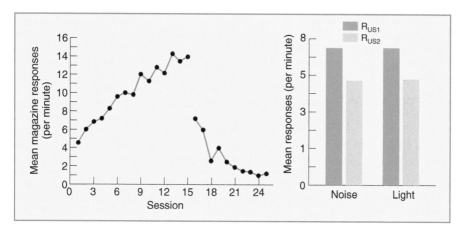

FIGURE 5.10 The acquisition and extinction of conditioned responding to a noise that was paired with food, US1, in an experiment by Delamater (1996) (left-hand panel), and the rate of performing two instrumental responses during subsequent test trials with the same noise, and with a light that had been paired with US1 (right-hand panel). One instrumental response had produced US1, and the other response had produced a different reward, US2 (adapted from Delamater, 1996).

(Rescorla & Wagner, 1972), or from the growth of new associations that either directly (Bouton & Ricker, 1994) or indirectly (Konorski, 1967) inhibit activity in a US center. Despite their differences, these theories all assume that extinction makes it more difficult for the CS to activate a representation, or memory of the US with which it was originally paired. We now consider the possibility that extinction does not affect the capacity of the CS to activate a representation of the US, but is effective for a different reason.

Any experimenter who wishes to demonstrate that extinction does not affect an existing CS–US association is immediately faced with a difficult challenge. How does one assess the strength of a CS–US association after extinction, when there is very little behavior to measure? Delamater (1996) devised an ingenious solution to this problem by making use of the fact that a Pavlovian CS for an outcome will increase the rate of instrumental responding for the same outcome. Rats were first trained to make one response for reward US1, R_{US1}, and a different response, R_{US2}, for reward US2. They were then given trials in which a noise signaled US1, followed by as many as 80 extinction trials with the noise presented in the absence of US1. The results of the conditioning and extinction trials with the noise are shown in the left-hand panel of Figure 5.10, from which it can be seen that responding during the noise was very weak by the end of extinction. After the extinction trials with the noise, rats were again given the opportunity to make the two responses, but now the noise was presented from time to time. The left-hand pair of histograms in the right-hand panel of Figure 5.10 shows the mean rate of making R_{US1} and R_{US2} in the presence of the noise. R_{US1} was performed more rapidly than R_{US2}, which implies that, despite 80 extinction trials with the noise, this stimulus was still able to exert some influence on instrumental behavior. Moreover, because this influence was greater on R_{US1} than R_{US2}, it follows that the extinction treatment had not abolished the noise-US1 association.

An interesting question at this point is whether the extinction trials had any effect on the noise–US1 association at all. Delamater (1996) included additional training in his experiment to address this question. During the conditioning trials with the noise, there were also trials in which a light was paired with US1. The light was not presented during the extinction stage, but it was presented to the animals while they were performing R_{US1} and R_{US2}. The results from these test trials, which were very similar to those obtained with the noise, can be seen in the right-hand pair of histograms. On the basis of these findings, therefore, it follows that the extinction treatment did not alter the capacity of the noise to invigorate R US1, and thus did not alter at all the strength of the noise–US1 association. This conclusion is reinforced by additional findings described by Delamater (1996) and from related experiments by Rescorla (1996).

There is also evidence to show that the extinction of an instrumental response does not affect the strength of associations formed during acquisition. Rescorla (1991) required rats to make two different responses for food. On the completion of this training, one of the responses was extinguished by no longer presenting food after it. During subsequent test trials, it was found that this response was performed more readily during a stimulus that signaled food than during a stimulus that signaled another reward. This finding indicates that, despite making nearly 200 responses in extinction, subjects had retained information about the fact that the response had previously been paired with food. Additional test trials, which were conducted with the response that had not been extinguished, also revealed more vigorous responding during the stimulus for food than for the other reward. Moreover, there was no indication that the magnitude of this preference was any different to that found with the extinguished response. In other words, on the basis of this test it would be concluded that the extinction treatment was ineffective.

The results from these experiments raise an obvious question. In the experiment by Delamater (1996), if the noise–US1 association remained intact after 80 extinction trials, why should magazine activity during the noise virtually disappear as a result of this treatment? Likewise, in the experiment by Rescorla (1991), if a response–food association remained intact when the response no longer resulted in food, why should the animal cease lever pressing? It is also difficult to understand Delamater's (1996) findings if extinction depends upon the growth of a new association that makes it hard for the CS to activate a representation of the US (Konorski, 1967; Bouton & Ricker, 1994). Once this association has developed, the CS should not only fail to elicit a conditioned response of magazine approach but it should also fail to energize an instrumental response for the same US. Given these issues, researchers have looked for an alternative account for the learning that takes place during extinction.

Associations that inhibit responses

To explain his results, Delamater (1996) proposed that extinction results in the growth of an inhibitory S–R connection (see also Delamater, 2004; Rescorla, 2003). One way of characterizing this connection is shown in Figure 5.11. The figure is based on Figure 2.15, which was developed to show the associations that form during excitatory Pavlovian conditioning. According to the original figure, conditioning results in the growth of a connection between representations of the CS and US. A subsequent presentation of the CS will then activate the US representation, which will activate a center in the response generator and lead to a conditioned response. Delamater (1996) suggested that during extinction an inhibitory connection will grow between the representation of the CS and the center in the response generator. As extinction progresses, therefore, the CS will continue to excite a representation of the US, which will continue to excite the response center. However, the growth of an inhibitory CS–R association between the representation of the CS and the response generator will make it increasingly more difficult for a response to occur. Eventually, the inhibitory connection will be of sufficient strength to suppress completely conditioned responding during the CS. However, if the animal should now be

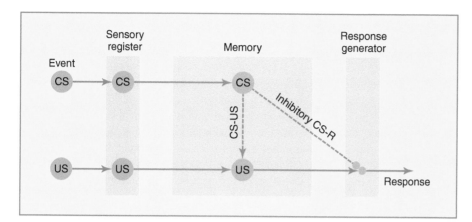

FIGURE 5.11 A modification of Figure 2.14 showing the inhibitory S–R link that was proposed by Delamater (1996) and Rescorla (1991) to develop during extinction. CS, conditioned stimulus; R, response; US, unconditioned stimulus.

allowed to lever press for the same US, a presentation of the CS should allow the memory of the US to be activated, which will then boost the frequency of lever pressing for reasons considered in the previous chapter.

A rather similar explanation has been proposed for extinction in instrumental conditioning. Suppose a rat has been trained to press a lever for food in a conditioning chamber and suddenly responses no longer lead to food. Rescorla (1993) has suggested that during extinction an inhibitory association will develop between the conditioning chamber and the center that is responsible for generating lever pressing. As this association gains in strength, so the animal will make fewer and fewer responses in the chamber.

Support for this explanation comes from an experiment by Rescorla (1993), the design of which is shown in Table 5.4. Hungry rats were trained in the dark to make two responses for food: pull a chain and press a lever. They then received extinction training in the presence of a light. For this training, the rats had access to the chain, but not the lever, and pulling the chain did not produce food. Because chain pulling had virtually ceased by the end of this stage, further training was given in the dark in which both chain pulling and lever pressing resulted again in food. Test trials were then conducted to examine the influence of the light on both responses. The rats were willing to press the lever during the light but reluctant to pull the chain. According to Rescorla (1993), one explanation for this reluctance to pull the chain is that the extinction treatment resulted in an inhibitory S–R association between the light and chain pulling.

TABLE 5.4 Summary of the training given to one group of rats in an experiment by Rescorla (1993)

Training in the dark	Extinction in the light	Recovery in the dark	Test in the light
Chain pull → Food	Chain pull → 0	Chain pull → Food	Chain pull
Lever press → Food		Lever press → Food	Lever press

At this point, we can conclude that extinction results in the growth of new, inhibitory S–R, associations which allow behavior to adapt to the conditions of extinction without the necessity of undoing previous associations. According to both Delamater (1996, 2004) and Rescorla (1996), the new associations are so effective that there is no good reason for believing that the associations formed during acquisition are weakened at all during extinction. This conclusion might seem implausible, so it is worth describing briefly two further studies that lends it additional support.

Harris, Shand, Carroll, and Westbrook (2004) allowed rats to drink a solution of sucrose mixed with salt for 5 minutes a day for 4 days. This treatment was intended to encourage rats to associate salt with sucrose and thus enhance the attractiveness of salt. The experiment was successful in this respect because a test revealed that after this treatment the rats had a stronger preference for salt, by itself, than a control group that had never experienced salt paired with sucrose. Of interest to the present discussion is the additional finding that there was no hint of this preference diminishing, even though rats were tested for 10 minutes a day over 7 days. A similar finding has been reported by Capaldi, Myers, Campbell, and Sheffer (1983), who found that drinking a solution of wintergreen mixed with saccharin resulted in a sustained increase in the preference for wintergreen over 28 days of testing. Although these results demonstrate that associations do not weaken during extinction, they also raise the question of why the acquired flavor preference was so unaffected by the extinction treatment. A satisfactory answer to this question remains to be found, but it seems there is something unusual about conditioned flavor preferences that make them particularly resistant to extinction.

It is too early to say whether extinction never affects the capacity of a CS to excite a representation of the US with which it was paired. It is possible that, during extinction, a CS inhibits a US center and a response center. The extent to which these influences develop, and the conditions under which they are effective, may vary according to factors that remain to be specified. Of course, if it should transpire that inhibitory CS–US associations do not develop during extinction, then the problem would arise of explaining the renewal effect. The simple solution to this problem would be to assume that the modulatory link involving the context shown in Figure 5.9 exerts its influence on an inhibitory CS–R association, rather than an inhibitory CS–US association. Once this change has been made, the predictions made concerning renewal would be the same as those that follow from the model shown in Figure 5.9.

ARE TRIALS IMPORTANT FOR PAVLOVIAN EXTINCTION?

The final topic to be discussed in this chapter can be introduced by examining another implication of the Rescorla–Wagner (1972) theory for extinction. The Rescorla–Wagner (1972) theory is said to be a trial-based theory because it is assumed that the associative strength of a CS changes on a trial-by-trial basis. As far as excitatory conditioning is concerned, the associative strength of the CS is held to be adjusted whenever the US occurs, which is normally at the end of each presentation of the CS or, in other words, at the end of each trial. The adjustment to the associative strength during extinction is said to take place at the time when the US is expected to occur, which—again—will normally be at the end of the trial. Thus, a major determinant of extinction is the number of trials that have been presented without the US. If there have been just a few of these trials then a stronger response is predicted to occur than after many extinction trials. The purpose of this section is to consider another possibility, that extinction is determined not by the number of extinction trials but by the amount of exposure to the CS. At first blush, there might seem to be rather little to choose between these points of view. Increasing the number of extinction trials will increase the amount of exposure to the CS and both factors should therefore be expected to exert the same influence on extinction. However, behind these different views of extinction rests a profoundly important theoretical issue.

Throughout the history of the study of animal learning and intelligence, it has been assumed that conditioning is effective because it results in the formation of associations (e.g. Thorndike, 1898; Mackintosh, 1974, Pearce & Bouton, 2001). Indeed, such an assumption constitutes a fundamental premise of the present text. Gallistel and Gibbon (2000, 2002) have argued that this assumption is mistaken. They suggested instead that, during the course of Pavlovian conditioning, animals compute the rate at which the US occurs during the presence of the CS, and the rate at which it occurs in its absence. The animal is then assumed to compare these rates to decide whether to make a response. This is a radical alternative to established theories of learning because it assumes that, rather than acquire associations, animals make calculations based on the number of USs they have experienced, on the duration of the CS, and so on. A detailed discussion of this new way of conceptualizing how animals learn is beyond the scope of this book. It is, however, appropriate to consider briefly the implications for extinction of Gallistel and Gibbon's (2000, 2002) proposals. These proposals have prompted a number of new experiments, which, to date, lend more support to trial-based theories than the proposed alternative. The experiments have also revealed some striking findings about the effects of different extinction treatments.

Gallistel and Gibbon (2000, 2002) maintain that the decision by an animal to cease responding during a CS is determined by a rather different comparison to that made during acquisition. Figure 5.12 portrays the sequence of events for a simple experiment in which the duration of the CS was t seconds. It shows the final two trials of conditioning with a continuous reinforcement schedule, and the first two trials of extinction. Gallistel and Gibbon (2000, 2002) maintain that extinction will depend on the relative values of two variables. One variable, Ics, is the amount of exposure to the CS between each presentation of the US—for the schedule in Figure 5.12 the value for this variable will be the same as t. The other variable, Iext is the amount of exposure to the CS that has occurred since the US was last presented—after one extinction trial this value will be t, after two trials it will be $2t$, and so on. Animals are assumed to calculate a ratio Iext/Ics and, when this ratio exceeds a predetermined value, then responding during the CS will cease.

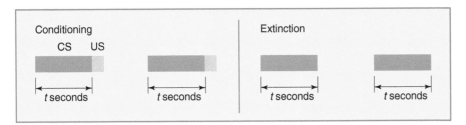

FIGURE 5.12 A diagram of the events that take place during two conditioning trials followed by two extinction trials with a conditioned stimulus (CS) of duration t seconds.

To test this account of extinction, Haselgrove and Pearce (2003) initially conditioned two groups of rats with a 10-second clicker followed on every trial by food. Both groups then received an extinction session in which the clicker was presented for a total of 270 seconds. The clicker was presented for 10 seconds at a time for 27 trials for Group 10, whereas for Group 270 it was presented once for 270 seconds. According to the proposals of Gallistel and Gibbon (2000), both groups should stop responding after similar amounts of exposure to the clicker during extinction, because they had the same value of Ics during conditioning. This prediction was not confirmed. Figure 5.13 shows the strength of the conditioned response for successive 30-second intervals of exposure to the clicker in a single session and it is quite evident that extinction occurred more rapidly in Group 270 than Group 10.

A plausible explanation for the dramatically different results from the two groups can be based on generalization decrement. As the clicker remained on for more and more time during the trial for Group 270, the difference between the conditions of acquisition and extinction presumably became more marked and responding would be weakened. By contrast, the pattern of trials with the CS during extinction was similar to that during acquisition for Group 10, and the disruptive effects of generalization decrement would be less for this group than for Group 270.

In another experiment by Haselgrove and Pearce (2003), two groups again received conditioning in which a 10-second clicker was paired with food on every trial. Both groups received the same number of extinction trials but the duration of each one was 10 seconds for Group 10 and 270 seconds for Group 270. To compare

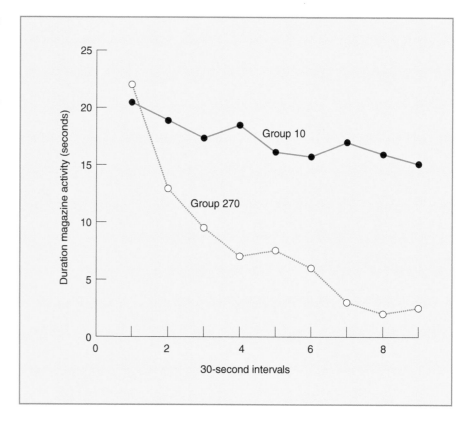

FIGURE 5.13 The mean duration of magazine activity during extinction trials with a clicker that was of 10 seconds duration when it was paired with food for conditioning. The clicker was presented for 10 seconds at a time during extinction for Group 10, and for a single period of 270 seconds for Group 270 (adapted from Haselgrove & Pearce, 2003).

the performance of the two groups, we recorded the duration of magazine activity during the first 10 seconds of each trial. With this measure, the theory of Gallistel and Gibbon (2000, 2002) predicts that responding will be weaker for Group 270 than Group 10 because, after the first trial, the former group will have received 27 times as much nonreinforced exposure to the clicker than the latter. In fact, we could detect no statistically significant difference between the performance of the two groups. Hence, after 25 extinction trials, Group 10 had received 4 minutes of exposure to the clicker, whereas Group 270 had received 1¾ hours. Despite this difference, responding during the first 10 seconds of this trial was remarkably similar for both groups.

The results of this experiment suggest that the effects of extinction take place on a trial-by-trial basis. If it is accepted that during training subjects come to expect the US 10 seconds after the start of the CS, then the effects due to nonreinforcement will take place 10 seconds after the start of each extinction trial, even though the CS might then remain on for a further 260 seconds. On this basis, therefore, responding during the first 10 seconds of the CS during extinction will be unaffected by how long it is presented for each trial.

Before leaving this discussion of Gallistel and Gibbon's (2000, 2002) theory, it is worth looking at its implications for the effect of partial reinforcement on extinction in Pavlovian conditioning. Figure 5.14 shows the events that take place during conditioning with a CS that is always presented for *t* seconds, and which is paired with a US on either a continuous reinforcement schedule (upper row) or a 50% partial reinforcement schedule (lower row). The amount of exposure to the CS between each presentation of the US is *t* seconds for the continuous reinforcement schedule and 2*t* seconds for the partial reinforcement schedule. We have just seen that the theory of Gallistel and Gibbon (2000, 2002) maintains that animals will cease responding during extinction when the ratio of (a) the amount of total exposure to the CS during extinction to (b) the amount of exposure to the CS between each presentation of the US, exceeds a certain value. The theory therefore predicts that before responding ceases it will be necessary for the group trained with the partial reinforcement schedule to receive twice as much exposure to the CS in extinction than the group trained with the continuous reinforcement schedule. That is, the theory predicts a PRE.

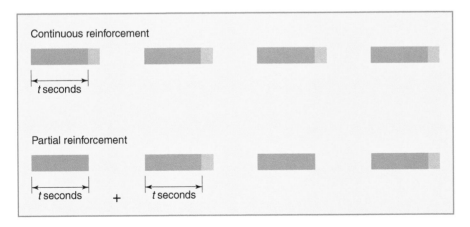

FIGURE 5.14 A diagram of the events that take place during Pavlovian conditioning with a continuous and a partial reinforcement schedule.

FIGURE 5.15 A diagram of the events that took place during Pavlovian conditioning in an experiment by Haselgrove et al. (2004) for groups trained with either a continuous or a partial reinforcement schedule. CS, conditioned stimulus; US, unconditioned stimulus.

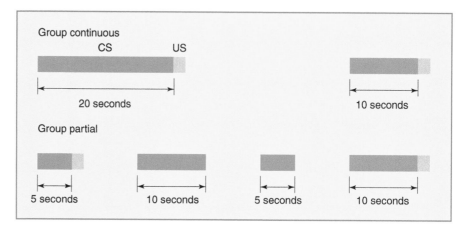

To test this explanation for the PRE, Haselgrove, Aydin, and Pearce (2004) trained two groups of rats with the two schedules depicted in Figure 5.15. Group Continuous received trials with a 10-second and a 20-second clicker, all of which were followed by food. Group Partial received trials with a 5-second and 10-second clicker, half of which were followed by food. Both groups then received extinction trials with a 10-second clicker. The average amount of exposure to the CS between each presentation of the US was 15 seconds in both groups and, according to the theory of Gallistel and Gibbon (2000, 2002), they should perform similarly during the extinction stage. In fact, as Figure 5.16 shows, extinction progressed more rapidly for Group Continuous than Group Partial. Gallistel and Gibbon's (2000, 2002) explanation for the PRE thus appears to be wrong, which is a pity because there is an attractive elegance to it.

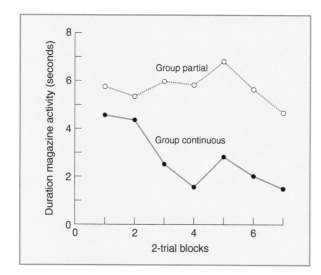

FIGURE 5.16 The mean duration of magazine activity during extinction trials with a 10-second stimulus for two groups that received the training depicted in Figure 5.15 (adapted from Haselgrove et al., 2004).

The results from the experiment can be explained with the explanation for the PRE that was put forward earlier in the chapter and which should by now be familiar. After training with a continuous reinforcement schedule, the after-effects of omitting the US for each extinction trial will alter the context in which the CS occurs and weaken responding through generalization decrement. The training with a partial reinforcement schedule, by contrast, will allow subjects during conditioning to experience the CS in the presence of these after-effects. The generalization decrement produced by the omission of the US during extinction will thus be minimal and will result in stronger responding than after continuous reinforcement. An important feature of this analysis is that it highlights the influence of the conditioning trial on extinction. That is, it is the experience of an entire trial with the CS—in the absence of the US—during training with a partial reinforcement schedule that is assumed to generate the after-effects that are held to be responsible for the PRE. The results from the experiment therefore not only challenge the theoretical proposals of Gallistel and Gibbon (2002) but also lend support to the trial-based theories of conditioning (e.g. Rescorla & Wagner, 1972), which the theory was intended to replace.

To summarize this chapter, for many years the principal reason for studying extinction was to find a satisfactory explanation for the PRE. During the last 20 years or so, research on other topics relating to extinction has revealed valuable new insights not only into the factors that promote extinction, such as surprise, but also into the associative changes that take place within the animal during the course of extinction.

CHAPTER 6

CONTENTS

Discrimination learning

Animals must be able to solve discriminations if they are to survive. They need to develop a diet whereby they select nutritious foods and avoid potentially poisonous substances. Predators have to be distinguished from less-threatening creatures. Animals that form bonds with a single member of the opposite sex must be able to differentiate this chosen individual from all others that belong to the same species. Infants often have to be able to distinguish between their parents and other adults. Social animals must be able to identify the group to which they belong.

Given this importance of the ability to acquire discriminations, it should not be surprising to discover that it is displayed by, if not all, then by very nearly all animals. We saw in Chapter 3, for example, that *Aplysia* will react more strongly to being stimulated on one part of the body than another if the former stimulation is consistently followed by an electric shock. There is also a report that paramecia, which consist of a single, complex cell, are capable of forming a discrimination between two tones that differ in frequency (Hennessey, Rucker, & McDiarmid, 1979).

The way in which animals solve discriminations has been the focus of interest now for nearly 100 years. Pavlov (1927) describes an experiment conducted in 1917 in which the presentation of an illuminated circle, but not an illuminated square, signaled the imminent delivery of food to a hungry dog. Initially, both stimuli were treated similarly, but with continued training a conditioned response (CR) of salivation was recorded predominantly in the presence of the circle. Since this study, there has been a persistent interest in the way discriminations are solved. Indeed, the analysis of discrimination learning constitutes one of the more enduring theoretical endeavors in psychology. The principal purpose of this chapter is to provide a summary of the fruits of this theoretical endeavor, and to reveal how our theoretical understanding of discrimination learning has gradually evolved.

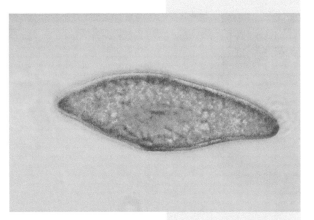

Paramecia consist of a single complex cell, and are capable of forming a discrimination between two tones that differ in frequency. Copyright © Lester V. Bergman/Corbis.

THEORIES OF DISCRIMINATION LEARNING

Relational learning and transposition

In many discriminations, the signals for reward and nonreward bear some relationship to each other. One of the earliest theoretical accounts of discrimination learning proposed that an appreciation of this relationship was essential if the discrimination was to be solved (Kinnaman, 1902; Kohler, 1918). Suppose that an animal must approach a white square, but not a black square, to obtain food. Kohler (1918) argued that, to solve this discrimination, animals inspected both stimuli on each trial and then selected the lighter of the two. As a test of this proposal, chickens were trained with two cards, one of which was darker than the other. Pecks at the light card (S+), but not the dark card (S−), were rewarded with food. A **transposition test** was then given in which the subjects had to choose between the original S+ and an even lighter card. If the original discrimination was solved on the basis of relational information, then Kohler reasoned that the new card would be chosen in preference to S+ on the test trials. This prediction was confirmed, even though it meant that subjects rejected the card that they had originally been trained to select. Despite the success of this experiment, we shall see shortly that a number of more recent theorists have preferred to interpret Kohler's findings in other ways.

Spence

The first formal theory of discrimination learning was presented in two classic papers by Spence (1936, 1937). He proposed that, if an animal is rewarded for approaching a stimulus, then the tendency to repeat the response in the presence of the stimulus will be increased. Conversely, if the animal should fail to receive reward for approaching a stimulus then the likelihood of repeating the response to the stimulus will be reduced.

Spence believed that animals learn about the absolute properties of stimuli. Given a choice between approaching a black or a white card to gain food, he argued that animals will not use relational information to decide where to jump. Instead, they will acquire an excitatory tendency to approach the one associated with reward (S+) and inhibitory tendency to avoid the one associated with the absence of reward (S−). In view of the transposition study by Kohler (1918), these proposals might well be regarded as mistaken but, by referring to the effects of stimulus generalization, Spence (1937) was able to explain transposition in a way that is both elegant and ingenious.

A fundamental characteristic of conditioning is that after being trained with one stimulus, animals will show a conditioned response to other stimuli, but to a lesser extent. This effect is referred to as stimulus generalization and it is determined by the degree of similarity between the training and the test stimuli (see p. 37). Spence argued that when a discrimination is conducted between two stimuli from the same dimension, say brightness, performance will inevitably be affected by generalization between them. The excitatory tendency to approach S+ (light) will also be elicited by S− (dark), but to a weaker extent; and the inhibitory tendency to avoid S− will be aroused, albeit slightly, by S+. The strength of approach to either stimulus will then be determined by the interaction between these sources of generalization. Spence (1937) characterized this interaction in the manner shown in Figure 6.1. The training stimuli are placed on the horizontal axis according to their brightness and together with a third stimulus, S′, which is even lighter than S+. The larger curve depicts the excitatory generalization gradient that will develop after a number of rewards have been received for selecting S+, and the smaller curve depicts the inhibitory generalization gradient that will develop around S−. The strength of approach to any stimulus will then be determined by the difference between these two gradients. As this

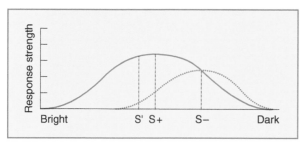

FIGURE 6.1 The gradients of excitation and inhibition that are predicted (by Spence's theory) to develop during a discrimination in which reward is presented in the presence of one stimulus (S+) but not another (S−). The stimuli are located on a dimension of brightness (adapted from Spence, 1937).

difference is greater for S+ than S−, the theory correctly predicts that discrimination training will result in a preference for S+ over S−. Now turn to S′, which is to the left of S+, the difference between the two generalization gradients for this new stimulus is greater than for S+. The theory thus predicts that after discrimination training with S+ and S−, if subjects are required to choose between S′ and S+, they will choose the lighter of the two and show transposition.

A test of Spence's (1936, 1937) theorizing was conducted by Hanson (1959) with a successive discrimination, in which the discriminative stimuli were presented at different times rather than simultaneously. Pigeons were first rewarded for pecking a response key when it was illuminated by light of 550 nanometers (nm) (S+) but not when it was illuminated by light of 590 nm (S−). Test trials were then conducted with different colors of light ranging in wavelength from 480 to 620 nm. The effects of this training can again be understood by referring to Figure 6.1, but now the difference between the excitatory and inhibitory gradients indicates the strength of responding during a stimulus. Responding during S+ is predicted to be faster than during S−. Of considerably more interest, however, is the prediction that can be derived from the figure that during a light with a wavelength that is slightly less than that of S+, responding should be faster than during S+ itself. In confirmation of this prediction, Hanson discovered that the highest rate of responding on the test trials occurred in the presence of light with a wavelength of 540 nm. The discovery of such a **peak shift** constitutes an outstanding success of Spence's theory. Further examination of Figure 6.1 suggests that as the wavelength of the test stimuli is reduced below 540 nm, so the peak shift will disappear and responding should eventually decline to a lower rate than during S+. Hanson (1959) was also able to confirm these predictions. A summary of the response rates that were recorded during his test trials is shown in Figure 6.2.

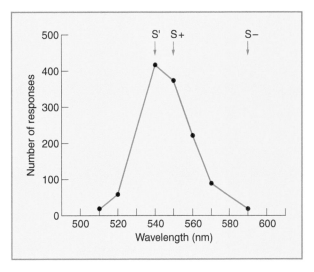

FIGURE 6.2 The number of responses recorded on test trials with key-lights of varying colors, after pigeons have been rewarded for pecking a key when it was illuminated with light of 550 nanometers (S+) but not when it was illuminated with light of 590 nanometers (S−) (adapted from Hanson, 1959).

Despite its early successes, it eventually became apparent that there was a fatal flaw in Spence's theorizing, which can be appreciated by considering the effects of what is known as a **feature-positive discrimination**. In an experiment by Wagner (1969), rats were rewarded for lever pressing when a tone and light were presented together for 2 minutes, but they were never rewarded for responding when the tone was presented by itself. The effects of this training are shown in Figure 6.3, which reveals that responding was vigorous during the compound and negligible during the tone. Indeed, responding during the tone was no faster than during the interval between trials, when responding never produced food. Spence's theory is unable to explain this pattern of results. In essence, his theory provides a nonselective account for the way in which discriminations are solved. This means that learning will take place about a stimulus independently of what has been learned about any other stimulus that is present during a trial. In the case of the feature-positive discrimination, therefore, the light will rapidly acquire excitatory strength because every time the light is presented it is paired with food. As a result, responding on

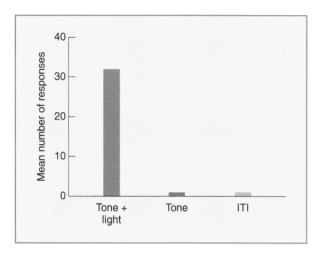

FIGURE 6.3 The mean number of responses that were recorded during a tone–light compound, a tone, and the intertrial interval (ITI) by a group of rats that had received food for lever pressing only during the compound. The results were collected after 25 sessions of training had been given (adapted from Wagner, 1969).

trials when the light is presented is predicted to be rapid. Turning now to the tone: Because this stimulus is paired with food on half the occasions that it occurs, the theory predicts that this stimulus too should acquire excitatory strength. The intermittent pairing of the tone with food will mean, however, that the tone acquires less excitatory strength than the light. Even so, the theory unequivocally predicts that the tone will elicit a relatively strong response whenever it is presented, and thus the discrimination will never be properly solved. The results in Figure 6.3 show, in contrast, that the training used by Wagner (1969) resulted in a perfect discrimination.

The Rescorla–Wagner theory

In terms of the profound influence it has exerted on the study of discrimination learning, the Rescorla–Wagner (1972) model of conditioning can be seen as the natural successor to Spence's theory. Indeed, there are a number of similarities between the two theories: They both assume that conditioning can result in the acquisition of either excitatory or inhibitory tendencies; they both assume that changes in these tendencies are gradual; and they both assume that animals learn about the absolute properties of stimuli. The major difference between the theories concerns the rule that is used to determine the extent to which the associative properties of a stimulus will change on any trial. Whereas Spence believed these changes took place independently of the properties of the other stimuli that were present, we saw in Chapter 3 that this is not true for the Rescorla–Wagner (1972) model. As a consequence, this theory is readily able to explain the successful solution of the feature-positive discrimination that poses such a problem for the theory of Spence.

Consider again the experiment by Wagner (1969). Equation 3.7 (p. 69) predicts that, initially, the compound trials will result in the tone and light each gaining associative strength. This strength will be lost to some extent by the tone on the nonreinforced trials, but the light will continue to acquire associative strength on each compound trial until it reaches the asymptotic value, λ. At this point, the light will block any additional increments in the associative strength of the tone on the compound trials, and the only effect of further training will be to reduce the associative strength of the tone on nonreinforced trials. Eventually, the tone will have no associative strength and responding during this stimulus by itself will be minimal, whereas responding during the tone–light compound will be vigorous.

It is not just the outcome of feature-positive discriminations that the Rescorla–Wagner theory is able to predict satisfactorily. There are many other types of discrimination in which the theory has proved to be a substantial improvement over its predecessors, particularly where the role of inhibition is concerned. Moreover, by making a few simple modifications to the theory it has been possible to extend its scope considerably.

One useful modification has been to assume that individual stimuli are composed of a variety of elements that represent its different characteristics

(Blough, 1975; Rescorla, 1976). These elements are then assumed to gain and lose their associative strength in a manner that is dictated by the Rescorla–Wagner equation. If it is accepted that the elements belonging to one stimulus are shared to some extent by other stimuli, the model is then able to explain stimulus generalization. In addition, as Blough (1975) has shown, such an extension of the Rescorla–Wagner (1972) theory allows it to explain a wide range of findings associated with discrimination learning, including peak shift.

A second modification was proposed to take account of the problem for the theory that is posed by the results from **negative patterning** discriminations (Woodbury, 1943). An example of this discrimination is provided by Rescorla (1972), who rewarded rats for pressing a lever in the presence of a tone (T), or a clicker (C), although lever pressing was never rewarded when these stimuli were presented together (C+ CT– T+). The course of acquisition of this discrimination is portrayed in Figure 6.4, which shows that, eventually, the rate of lever pressing for food was more rapid when the stimuli were presented alone rather than together. The trials in which C and T were individually paired with food can be expected to result in each of them acquiring positive associative strength. The Rescorla–Wagner (1972) theory assumes that responding during a compound is determined by the sum of the associative strengths of its components. Responding during CT is therefore predicted to be consistently stronger than during either C or T alone. The implication of this analysis is that a negative patterning discrimination will be insoluble.

To avoid making this incorrect prediction, Wagner and Rescorla (1972) suggested that when two stimuli are presented together they create a hypothetical, compound-unique, **configural cue** that is capable of taking part in associative learning just like any other stimulus. Thus the experimental design of Rescorla (1972) can be conceptualized as C+ T+ CTX–, where X is the hypothetical stimulus. In these circumstances, the theory now predicts that on the nonreinforced trials with the compound, X will acquire inhibitory properties that will counter the excitatory influence of C and T. As these inhibitory properties grow in strength, they will reduce the level of responding during the compound and result eventually in the discrimination being mastered.

KEY TERMS

Negative patterning
A discrimination in which an outcome is delivered during a compound of two stimuli, but not during either stimulus by itself.

Configural cue
A hypothetical stimulus that is assumed to be created by presenting two stimuli together. Different pairs of stimuli are assumed to create different configural cues.

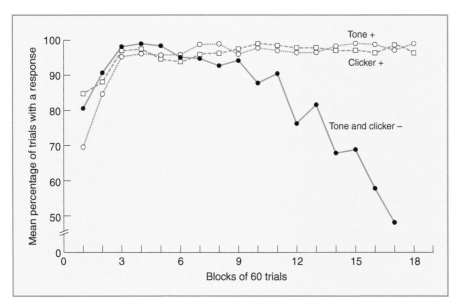

FIGURE 6.4 The mean percentage of trials in which an instrumental response was made for a group of rats that was rewarded for lever pressing during a tone and a clicker when they were presented individually, but not when they were presented together (adapted from Rescorla, 1972).

FIGURE 6.5 Left. The mean rates of responding during three different trials that were presented for eight sessions of discrimination training in an autoshaping experiment. Food was made available after trials with stimulus A, and compound BC, but food was never presented on trials with compound ABC (adapted from Redhead & Pearce, 1995a). Right. The response strengths for A, BC, and ABC that are predicted by the Rescorla–Wagner theory for the experiment by Redhead and Pearce (1995a).

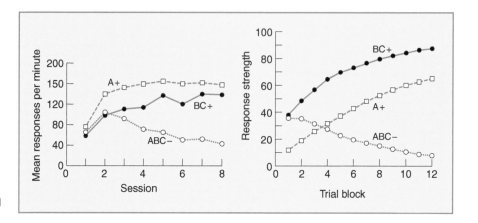

Other findings pose more of a problem for the theory. Redhead and Pearce (1995a; see also Pearce, 1994) trained pigeons with a discrimination in which the stimuli were dots of different colors. Food was delivered on trials when dots of one color (A) were shown, and when dots of two other colors (B and C) were shown together, but food was never delivered in the presence of dots of all three colors (A, B, and C), thus creating an A+ BC+ ABC– discrimination. The left-hand side of Figure 6.5 shows the results from this experiment, which makes it quite clear that eventually responding during ABC was slower than during either A or BC.

The right-hand side of Figure 6.5 shows the outcome of the discrimination that is predicted by the Rescorla–Wagner model. This prediction was derived from a computer simulation based on the Rescorla–Wagner equation that incorporated the assumption that compounds generate unique cues. An account of the way in which the simulation was conducted can be found in Pearce (1994). Although the figure shows that responding during ABC will eventually be slow, it also shows that responding during BC is predicted to be consistently stronger than during A. Such a pattern of results is anticipated because excitatory conditioning with a compound of two stimuli is expected to progress more readily than with a single stimulus.

The prediction that responding will be more vigorous during BC than A poses two serious problems for the Rescorla–Wagner model. First, this prediction was not confirmed: The left-hand side of Figure 6.5 shows that responding throughout the experiment was faster during A than BC. The second problem is perhaps more serious and requires us to consider the relationship between similarity and discrimination learning. In keeping with common sense, most theorists accept that the difficulty of a discrimination is determined by the similarity of the signals for reward and nonreward. The greater the similarity of these signals, the harder will be the discrimination. The results from the experiment by Redhead and Pearce (1995a) are entirely in keeping with this analysis. Because A has only one element in common with ABC, these signals for reward and nonreward can be regarded as being quite different and the discrimination between them should develop rapidly. However, BC shares two elements with ABC and these signals for reward and nonreward can be seen as quite similar, so that the discrimination between them should emerge slowly. If similarity exerts an important influence on the ease with which discriminations are solved, then the difference between the rates of responding during A and ABC will be greater than for BC and ABC. The results shown in the left-hand side of Figure 6.5 demonstrate that this was true throughout the experiment.

Turning now to the pattern of results predicted by the Rescorla–Wagner theory for the experiment, we can see that the discrimination between BC and ABC is predicted to develop more readily than between A and ABC. The theory thus makes the counterintuitive prediction that a discrimination between two sets of stimuli will be easier when they are similar (BC and ABC) than when they are different (A and ABC). I have argued (Pearce, 1994) that by making such a counterintuitive, and incorrect, prediction, the analysis of discrimination learning offered by the Rescorla–Wagner theory is seriously called into question. Moreover, it is not just the results from a single experiment that pose a problem for the theory. Pearce and Redhead (1993; see also Redhead & Pearce, 1995a,b) describe a number of experimental designs for which the Rescorla–Wagner theory predicts that a discrimination will be made easier by enhancing the similarity of the signals for reward and nonreward. The results from all of our experiments contradicted this prediction (see also Williams, Mehta, & Dumont, 2004).

There can be no denying that a large number of successful predictions have been derived from the Rescorla–Wagner model, and that it has thoroughly deserved its considerable influence during the last 35 years or so. None the less, the fact that it occasionally makes counterintuitive, and incorrect, predictions concerning the influence of similarity on discrimination learning suggests that there is a need to seek an alternative theoretical account for the way in which discriminations are solved.

Configural theory

Despite their differences, many theories share a common assumption that allows them to be classified as **elemental theories of discrimination learning**. In the case of the Rescorla–Wagner model, for example, if an unconditioned stimulus (US) is delivered after a compound, then it predicts that the associative strength of each element will be changed. It should be apparent that this elemental assumption can also be found in the theory of Spence. Despite the popularity of this assumption, the theories that have adopted it are unable to explain all that is known about discrimination learning. The possibility must be considered, therefore, that the elemental assumption on which these theories are based is wrong. The next theory to be considered does not incorporate the elemental assumption and, interestingly, it is able to provide an accurate account of the relationship between similarity and discrimination learning.

The alternative class of theory is referred to as configural theory. According to the theory of Pearce (1987, 1994, 2002), for example, conditioning will result in the gradual growth of an association between a single representation of all the stimuli that are present on the trial and the US. The strength of this association will determine the vigor of the CR that will occur to that particular pattern of stimulation. If the pattern of stimulation should change in any way, then a weaker CR will be performed with a vigor that is related to the similarity of the training and test pattern. Responding during the new pattern, in other words, will be determined by stimulus generalization from the original pattern.

The application of this theory to discrimination learning can be introduced by referring again to a feature-positive, AB+ B−, discrimination in which food is presented after AB but not B. When AB is first presented a representation of this compound will enter into an association with food. On a subsequent trial with B there will be a measure of generalization from AB, and a response will occur. Of course, this response will be inappropriate because B signals the absence of food and, as a consequence, B will enter into an inhibitory association to counter the excitation that generalizes from AB. The discrimination will be solved when the excitation

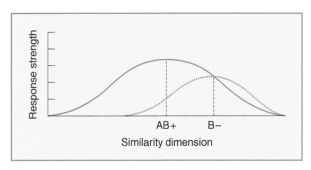

FIGURE 6.6 One way in which the theory of Spence (1937) could be developed to provide a configural explanation for the solution of an AB+ B− discrimination.

aroused by AB is sufficient to generate a normal response, and the inhibition associated with B is sufficient to counter completely the excitation that spreads to it from AB.

This account may seem complex but it is really no more than a modification of the analysis of discrimination learning developed by Spence (1937). Figure 6.6 shows the way in which these ideas can be accommodated within Spence's (1937) framework. In this figure, distance along the abscissa does not reflect the difference between two stimuli from the same dimension. This distance instead reflects the difference between configurations of stimuli measured in a more complex manner that need not concern us here. The figure demonstrates that an AB+ B− discrimination will result in an inhibitory generalization gradient around B (small curve) and an excitatory gradient around AB (large curve). If the difference between these gradients determines the strength of responding, then it follows that the compound AB, but not the element, B, will elicit a CR.

By emphasizing the importance of generalization between different patterns of stimuli, configural theory is able to provide a straightforward explanation of the results reported by Redhead and Pearce (1995a) that posed such a problem for the Rescorla–Wagner theory. Training with an A+ BC+ ABC− discrimination will result in A and BC entering into excitatory associations. The configuration of ABC will then have to enter into an inhibitory association to counter the generalization of excitation from A and BC. The inhibition that grows to ABC will generalize to both A and BC, and weaken responding in their presence. Because ABC is more similar to BC than A, more inhibition will generalize to BC than A and thus disrupt responding to a greater extent during BC than A. As the discrimination is being acquired, therefore, A is correctly predicted to elicit a stronger response than BC.

A further advantage of configural theory is that it can explain the solution to discriminations, such as negative patterning, without the need to make additional assumptions. Quite simply, a negative patterning discrimination (A+ B+ AB−) will result in A and B entering individually into excitatory associations. Although the effects of these associations will generalize to AB, the absence of any reward in its presence will result in this compound entering into an inhibitory association that will eventually serve to confine responding to trials with A and B alone.

In summary, configural theory differs from the other theories that have been considered because it is assumed that, when two or more stimuli are presented together for conditioning, only a single association will develop. This association is between a unitary, configural representation of all the stimuli and the US. By making the additional assumption that generalization will occur between configurations, configural theory can explain most of the findings from the discrimination studies that are described above. It has to be said that not everyone shares my enthusiasm for a **configural theory of discrimination learning**. Indeed, new accounts of associative learning have been proposed, which are based firmly on the assumption that discrimination learning depends on the growth of associations between each element of a compound stimulus and the trial outcome (e.g. McLaren & Mackintosh, 2000, 2002; Wagner, 2003; Harris, 2006). Others have argued that both elemental and configural associations may develop during the course of a discrimination (e.g. Kehoe, 1988; Schmajuk & DiCarlo, 1992). Great progress has been made in our understanding of how discriminations are solved during the last 100 years, but it

KEY TERM

Configural theory of discrimination learning A theory based on the assumption that during conditioning with a compound stimulus, a representation of the compound in its entirety enters into a single association with the US.

seems there is still room for theoretical debate, and a need for further experimental investigation, before our understanding is complete.

Stimulus preexposure and discrimination learning

The previous discussion has shown that one important influence on the ease with which a discrimination is solved is the similarity between the signals for reward and nonreward. Another—perhaps unexpected—factor that influences the acquisition of a discrimination is whether subjects receive preexposure to the stimuli before the discrimination commences. Several examples of this effect are described below, together with a discussion of how these effects may be explained. The explanations are somewhat complex but are based on associative learning principles that should be familiar.

Acquired equivalence and distinctiveness

Miller and Dollard (1941) argued that certain treatments can result in stimuli appearing to become more similar to each other, **acquired equivalence**, whereas other treatments can have the opposite effect of making the stimuli appear to be more different, **acquired distinctiveness**. A prediction from these proposals is that pairing two stimuli with the same outcome should make it difficult subsequently to solve a discrimination between them. Another prediction is that pairing two stimuli with different outcomes should have the opposite effect and facilitate the discrimination.

A test of these predictions was conducted by Delamater (1998), who presented two groups of rats with two visual stimuli, V1 and V2. During a preexposure phase of the experiment, the two stimuli signaled different types of food for Group Distinct, and the same type of food for Group Equivalent. A summary of the experimental design can be seen in Table 6.1. Both groups then received a discrimination in which V1 was paired with the same food that it was paired with originally, and V2 was followed by nothing. If the preexposure treatment received by Group Equivalent resulted in V1 and V2 being treated as if they were more similar to each other, the discrimination between them in the second phase should progress slowly. Conversely, this discrimination should be relatively easy for Group Distinct if the original treatment in this group resulted in V1 and V2 being regarded as more different to each other. In keeping with these predictions, the discrimination between these two stimuli developed more rapidly in Group Distinct (see the left-hand panel of Figure 6.7) than Group Equivalent (see the right-hand panel of Figure 6.7).

A slightly different demonstration of acquired equivalence and distinctiveness comes from a study involving two groups of rats by Honey and Hall (1991). Group Same received treatment designed to make two flavors, A and B, equivalent by pairing each of them with another flavor, X; whereas Group Different received treatment to

TABLE 6.1 Summary of the design of an experiment by Delamater (1998). Two experimental groups involved two different visual conditioned stimuli, V1 and V2, and two different unconditioned stimuli, + and *

	Acquisition	Test discrimination
Group Equivalent	V1+ V2+	V1+ V2−
Group Distinct	V1+ V2*	V1+ V2−

FIGURE 6.7 The
acquisition of a
discrimination between
two visual stimuli, one
of which signaled food,
V1, and the other of
which was followed by
nothing, V2. The two
stimuli had previously
been paired with
different outcomes for
Group Distinct, and the
same outcome for
Group Equivalent. The
measure of conditioning
was the frequency with
which rats put their
head in the magazine
where food was
delivered (adapted from
Delamater, 1998).

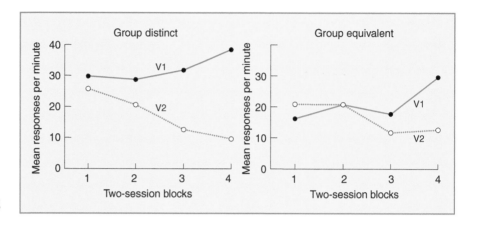

FIGURE 6.7 The
acquisition of a
discrimination between
two visual stimuli, one
of which signaled food,
V1, and the other of
which was followed by
nothing, V2. The two
stimuli had previously
been paired with
different outcomes for
Group Distinct, and the
same outcome for
Group Equivalent. The
measure of conditioning
was the frequency with
which rats put their
head in the magazine
where food was
delivered (adapted from
Delamater, 1998).

make A and B distinct by pairing one with flavor X and the other with flavor, Y. The groups then received taste aversion conditioning in which consumption of A was followed by the injection of a mild toxin. In a final test trial, in which both groups had the opportunity to drink flavor B, Group Same showed a greater reluctance to drink this fluid than Group Different. To explain this outcome, Honey and Hall (1991) suggested that when the taste aversion conditioning took place, Group Same regarded A and B as being equivalent, with the result that the aversion conditioned to A generalized strongly to B. However, during this conditioning Group Different saw A and B as being distinct from each other, which minimized the scope for generalization from A to B.

There is therefore good evidence for the effects of acquired equivalence and acquired distinctiveness, but do these effects really depend on changes in the similarity between stimuli? In fact, the explanation offered by Honey and Hall (1991; see also Honey and Hall, 1989) for their findings makes no appeal at all to changes in the similarity of the training stimuli. They explained their findings instead by referring to mediated conditioning. This phenomenon was described in Chapter 2 and to refresh our memories, we shall consider again an experiment by Holland (1981). Rats were first trained with a tone as a signal for food, and then the same tone served as a signal for illness by pairing it with the injection of a mild toxin. When the tone was paired with illness, Holland (1981) expected it to activate a representation of food, by virtue of the previous training, and that once activated the representation would then enter into an association with illness. In keeping with this analysis, a subsequent test trial revealed that rats were reluctant to eat the food that had been paired with the tone.

Honey and Hall (1991) suggested that a similar effect took place in their experiment. That is, when A was paired with illness it was expected to activate a memory of X, which would also enter into an association with illness. When B was presented by itself for the test trial in Group Same, it should a activate a memory of X, which should then activate an aversive CR and lead to a similar response to that observed during A. This effect would not be expected for the test trial in Group Different because there was no reason for B to activate a memory of X and hence excite the aversive CR. A rather more complex explanation, but based on the same principles, was developed by Delamater (1998) to explain the results of his experiment.

Perceptual learning

In the experiment by Delamater (1998), a discrimination between two stimuli was influenced by whether they had previously signaled the same or different outcomes.

FIGURE 6.8 Sketches of the two images of jungle fowl that were used in the study by Honey and Bateson (1996). To gain reward, young chicks had to approach one of the images, but not the other. Reproduced from Honey and Bateson, 1996. Copyright © Psychology Press.

The acquisition of a discrimination can also be affected by preexposure to stimuli if they are presented by themselves, as the following experiment by Honey and Bateson (1996) demonstrates. Young chicks were placed in a cool chamber in which the two pictures in Figure 6.8 were shown. To alleviate the chill, by turning on a stream of warm air, the chicks were expected to approach one of the images, but not the other. Group Control received just this training, but an experimental group was preexposed to the two pictures presented in an intermixed sequence before the start of the discrimination. Both groups solved the discrimination but, as Figure 6.9 shows, the control group required more training trials than the experimental group. Hence, being allowed to look at both pictures before the start of the discrimination training made it easier to tell the difference between them. **Perceptual learning** refers to this beneficial effect of preexposure (Hall, 1991, 2001).

Perceptual learning has also been demonstrated using more conventional laboratory stimuli and techniques. Two groups of rats in an experiment by Mackintosh, Kaye, and Bennett (1991) were allowed to drink a solution containing saline and lemon before being injected with lithium chloride to induce an aversion to the compound. They then received a test trial with the original solution of saline and lemon, and with a new solution containing sucrose and lemon. This was the only treatment that was given to the control group, which, as the left-hand pair of histograms in Figure 6.10 shows, was extremely reluctant to drink either solution during the test. The conditioning trial was obviously effective for this group and it is also evident that the control group failed to discriminate between the two solutions. A different outcome was observed in an experimental group, which received repeated preexposure to the two solutions in alternating sessions before the conditioning trial. The right-hand pair of histograms reveals that on the test trial there was again a strong aversion to the lemon–saline solution, but that this group was now willing to drink the lemon–sucrose solution. Preexposure to the two compounds resulted in perceptual learning and allowed the second group to discriminate between the two solutions in the final test.

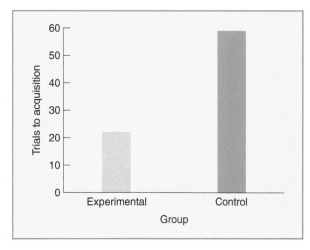

FIGURE 6.9 The mean number of trials needed to acquire a discrimination between the two images shown in Figure 6.8 by an experimental group, which received preexposure to the images prior to discrimination training, and by a control group, which received no preexposure to the images.

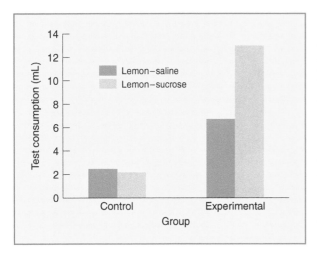

FIGURE 6.10 The mean amount drunk during test trials with lemon–sucrose and lemon–saline solution, after a taste aversion conditioning trial with lemon–saline solution. The experimental group received preexposure to the two test solutions prior to the conditioning trial (right-hand pair of histograms); the control group received no preexposure to the two solutions (left-hand pair of histograms) (adapted from Mackintosh et al., 1991).

An ingenious explanation for perceptual learning has been put forward by McLaren, Kaye, and Mackintosh (1989). Inspection of the two images in Figure 6.8 reveals that they have many features in common: two legs, a head, a base on which the bird is standing and so on. They also have many unique features: the legs are farther apart on one bird than the other, there is an eye and beak in one but not the other, and so on. To solve a discrimination between these pictures, it would be helpful to concentrate on the features that are unique to each picture and to ignore those that are common. The explanation offered by McLaren et al. (1989) for perceptual learning provides a mechanism that encourages subjects to attend to the unique features of stimuli, and to ignore their common features.

For the purposes of discussion, the left-hand image in Figure 6.8 can be regarded as a compound stimulus, AX, where A refers to all the features that are unique to it, and X refers to the features that it shares with the right-hand image. Likewise, the right-hand image can be regarded as BX, where B represents its unique features, and X represents the features it shares with the left-hand image. The preexposure treatment can now be characterized as the sequence of trials:

AX BX AX BX AX BX . . .

An obvious implication of this characterization is that by the end of the preexposure phase, subjects will have received twice as much exposure to the common features X, as to the unique features, A or B. We saw in Chapter 3 that animals will effectively reduce the amount of attention they pay to a stimulus if it is repeatedly presented without consequence. Hence, after the preexposure training the different amounts of exposure to the stimuli will result in rather little attention being paid to X, and rather more to A and B. These differences in attention will then mean that subjects learn rapidly about the significance of A and B, and slowly about X, which should help the discrimination to be solved swiftly. However, without preexposure to the training stimuli, subjects may pay considerable attention to X, at the expense of the attention they pay to A and B, which will make it hard to solve the discrimination. An important implication of this analysis is that it should not matter if preexposure takes place with the AX and BX presented as compounds, or with A, B, and X presented separately. All that is important is that subjects receive twice as much preexposure to X by itself as to A and B by themselves. When AX and BX are then introduced as compounds for the discrimination, animals will learn more slowly about X than A or B and the discrimination will progress more rapidly than when there is no preexposure treatment.

It would be difficult to test the foregoing prediction with the stimuli used by Honey and Bateson (1996) because they could not be broken down into their constituent features. Mackintosh, Kaye, and Bennett (1991) did, however, test the prediction in a further experiment by using flavored solutions made up of separable elements. One of the groups, Group Control, was trained and tested in the same way as its namesake in the study by Mackintosh et al. (1991) that has just been described. In keeping with the results from the earlier experiment, the right-hand pair of histograms in Figure 6.11 shows that subjects during the subsequent test trial were more reluctant to drink lemon–saline than lemon–sucrose solution. Group Element was also preexposed to sucrose, lemon, and saline but these flavors were presented separately and with twice as much preexposure to lemon as to the other flavors. After conditioning with lemon–saline solution, test trials revealed a similar pattern or results to that found with Group Control: a strong aversion to lemon–saline solution and a weaker aversion to lemon–sucrose. Thus, in keeping with the prediction drawn from the theory of McLaren et al. (1989), even though the preexposure treatment did not involve compound solutions, it nonetheless enabled subjects to discriminate between lemon–saline and lemon–sucrose during the test trial. Thus perceptual learning does not depend on preexposure to the compounds that are used for the test trials. It can also be found with preexposure to just the elements of the compounds, provided the common element receives more preexposure than the unique elements.

McLaren et al. (1989) have developed an additional explanation for perceptual learning, which lies beyond the scope of the present text because of its complexity. A discussion of this explanation can be found in Dwyer, Bennett, and Mackintosh (2001), who also describe an experiment that lends it support. In closing this section, we can note that the experiments that have been described have enhanced our understanding of the factors that determine how easy it is for an animal to tell the difference between two stimuli or two compounds. All of these factors can be understood by referring to the principles of learning that were developed in previous chapters.

CONNECTIONIST MODELS OF DISCRIMINATION LEARNING

An important development in the study of human learning and memory has been the growth of interest in connectionist—or neural net—theories, which have been used with considerable success to account for the results from a wide range of experiments. One reason for mentioning these theories now is that they bear more than a passing similarity to some of the theories that have been examined in this chapter. This raises the possibility that the mechanisms for learning in animals and humans might be quite similar, and it is certainly worth spending some time exploring this possibility. We might even hope that experiments that have aided the evaluation of theories of animal discrimination learning are of relevance to theories of learning in humans.

An attractive feature of connectionist network theories is that they operate in a way that bears at least a superficial resemblance to processes that take place in the brain. The brain consists of a very large number of interconnected elements that communicate with each other by means of excitatory and inhibitory signals. In essence, these properties can also be found in neural networks. To understand how these networks operate, we will start by examining a very simple network and then progress to ones that are more complex.

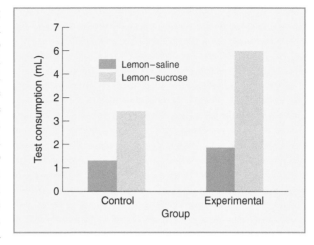

FIGURE 6.11 The mean amount drunk during test trials with lemon–sucrose and lemon–saline solution, after a taste aversion conditioning trial with lemon–saline solution. The experimental group received preexposure to the two test solutions prior to the conditioning trial (right-hand pair of histograms); the control group received preexposure to saline, sucrose, and lemon presented individually (left-hand pair of histograms) (adapted from Mackintosh et al., 1991).

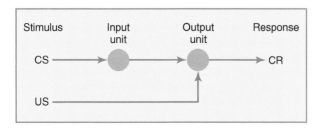

FIGURE 6.12 A simple connectionist network for representing the changes that occur during Pavlovian conditioning with a conditioned stimulus (CS) and unconditioned stimulus (US). The strength of the connection between the input and output unit increases with repeated pairings of the CS and US.

Single-layer networks

Learning in a single-layer network occurs when there is a change in the strength of a connection between an input and an output unit. For Pavlovian conditioning, the input unit would be activated by the conditioned stimulus (CS) and the output unit will be activated by the US. The output unit is also responsible for generating a response. These connections are shown in Figure 6.12. When the CS–US (input–output) connection is weak, activating the CS unit will have little impact on the US unit; when the connection is strong, the CS will strongly excite the output unit and lead to a response even if the US is not presented.

When more than one stimulus is used for an experiment, the simple model in Figure 6.12 must be elaborated to allow each stimulus to become connected with the US. Figure 6.13 shows the connections that this theory assumes will develop if four different stimuli are used to signal the presence, or absence, of a US. The level of activity in the output unit, and hence the strength of the CR, is given by the sum of the strengths of all the connections for those stimuli that are present. Normally, the rule that governs the change in strength of the CS–US connection is the same as the Rescorla–Wagner (1972) rule, which leads the network to make the same predictions as the theory (see Gluck & Bower, 1988). The networks in Figures 6.12 and 6.13 are referred to as a single-layer networks because there is only a single layer of connections.

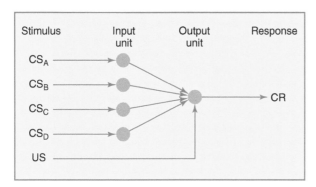

FIGURE 6.13 Development of the network shown in Figure 6.12 to represent the changes that can take place when as many as four stimuli are used for conditioning with a single unconditioned stimulus (US) (adapted from Gluck & Bower, 1988). CR, conditioned response; CS, conditioned stimulus.

The single-layer network shown in Figure 6.13 has been used by Gluck and Bower (1988) to account for learning by humans. The purpose of this network was to classify lists of four different symptoms on the basis of whether they were indicative of one of two illnesses. Each symptom activated a different input unit, and when the output unit had a value of $+\lambda$, the network was regarded as classifying a list as being symptomatic of one illness, whereas an output value of $-\lambda$ was construed as being indicative of the other illness. The predictions derived from the network were confirmed by the performance of the participants.

We noted earlier that in its most basic form the Rescorla–Wagner (1972) theory is unable to explain the ability of animals to solve a negative patterning discrimination (A+ B+ AB–). In fact, this problem is not unique to this particular theory. There have been other attempts to develop single-layer learning networks (e.g. Rosenblatt, 1962), and it has long been appreciated that they are unable to solve negative patterning discriminations or, as it is more generally known, the exclusive–or problem (Minsky & Papert, 1969). That is, many single-layer networks are unable to respond correctly when they are trained with a problem in which an outcome is signaled by either of two events when they are presented separately, but not when they are presented together. Indeed, the network shown in Figure 6.13 is unable to solve this type of problem.

Following the proposals made by Rescorla and Wagner (1972) to deal with this problem, Gluck (1991) has suggested that the network shown in Figure 6.13 can be modified to include compound-unique configural cues as input units.

Figure 6.14 shows a network that incorporates this proposal. The three input units are activated by three different stimuli: A, B, and C. There are also three input units, which are activated only by particular pairs of stimuli. Thus, if the compound AB should be presented to the network, then three input units will be activated by A, B, and AB. This network has also been expanded to include two output units. One is expected to fire maximally when one response is made and the other is expected to fire maximally when a different response is made. Although this network appears to be considerably more complex than the one shown in Figure 6.13, it works on exactly the same principles.

Although the network developed by Gluck (1991) can solve many discriminations, it has at least two shortcomings. First, because it is formally equivalent to the Rescorla–Wagner (1972) theory, the network makes the same erroneous predictions as that theory concerning the outcome of the experiment by Redhead and Pearce (1995a). When this network is presented with an A+ BC+ ABC– discrimination, it incorrectly predicts that the discrimination between the two similar signals, BC and ABC, will progress more readily than between the two different signals, A and ABC.

The second problem is one that is common to many network theories of learning (McCloskey & Cohen, 1989): The networks proposed by Gluck and Bower (1988) and Gluck (1991) are unduly sensitive to the effects of retroactive interference. That is, if the network is trained to solve one problem and it is then subsequently required to learn something new, this new learning can have a catastrophic effect on the original learning. An experiment by Pearce and Wilson (1991) will serve to demonstrate this problem; the design of the experiment is summarized in Table 6.2. Rats first received a feature-negative discrimination (A+ AB–) in which food was signaled by one stimulus, A, but not by AB. According to the network model of Gluck and Bower (1989), this training will enable A to excite the output unit to its maximum value of λ, whereas B will have the opposite effect of reducing the level of activation in the same output unit to $-\lambda$. When A and B are then presented together, these effects will cancel each other out, and no response will be observed. For a more detailed presentation of this analysis see pp. 70–71.

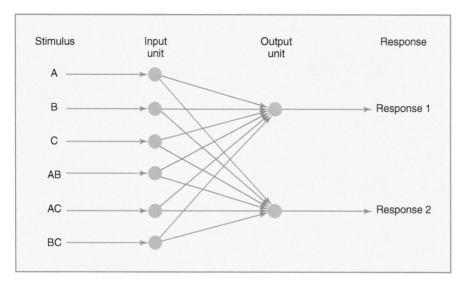

FIGURE 6.14 A development of the network shown in Figure 6.13 that allows for the possibility that pairs of stimuli create configural cues, and which allows for more than one output unit (adapted from Gluck, 1991).

TABLE 6.2 Summary of training given to a single group in an experiment by Pearce and Wilson (1991)

Stage 1	Stage 2	Test stage
A → Food	B → Food	A → Food
AB → Nothing		AB → Nothing

For the second stage of training, B was repeatedly paired with food until this stimulus elicited a CR of asymptotic magnitude. In terms of the network models of both Gluck and Bower (1988) and Gluck (1991), this training will result in the connection between B and the output unit acquiring an asymptotic value of λ, and thus erase entirely the effect of the original training. To test this interpretation, the subjects were reintroduced to the original discrimination. The first presentation of AB will now allow each of A and B to exert an excitatory influence on the output unit, and an unusually strong response should be observed. In formal terms, the level of activation of the output unit will initially have a magnitude of 2λ. The model thus predicts that not only should pairing B with food erase the effects of the original discrimination, but that it should actually result in stronger responding during AB than A. In fact, the effects of the excitatory conditioning were far less disruptive on the original discrimination than this prediction implies. There was no evidence of an unusually high level of responding during AB, and the A+ AB– discrimination was reacquired significantly more rapidly than by a control group.

Multi-layer networks

Another way of enabling a network to solve the exclusive–or problem is to add a second layer of connections. This strategy has been used to great effect with what is known as a two-layer back-propagation network (e.g. Rumelhart, Hinton, & Williams, 1988). A relatively simple version of this network (shown in the upper panel of Figure 6.15) was used by Maki and Abunawass (1991) to simulate the way in which discriminations are solved. A more elaborate example of a two-layer network is shown in the lower panel of Figure 6.15. In both networks, the input and output units perform in much the same way as in the networks that we have already considered. There is, in addition, a row of hidden units, each one of which is connected to every input unit and every output unit. Whenever the input layer is activated, each hidden unit will be excited to a level that is determined by the activation that it receives from all the input units. Likewise, the level of activation of each output unit is determined by the activation it receives from all the hidden units. The rules that determine the change in the strength of each connection are rather more complex than we have considered so far. There is also a more complex rule for determining the way in which each hidden unit and output unit is activated. Even so, there remains a close relationship between the Rescorla–Wagner (1972) model and this type of connectionist network model (Sutton & Barto, 1981; Gluck & Bower, 1988; Maki & Abunawass, 1991).

This relationship is not so close, however, that it prevents the two-layer network from solving the exclusive–or problem. The ability to solve this problem, as well as many other properties, has resulted in various versions of this network being used to explain the way in which humans categorize, read, acquire language, and so on. It has even been claimed that the effects of brain damage can be understood by reference to this type of multi-layer network.

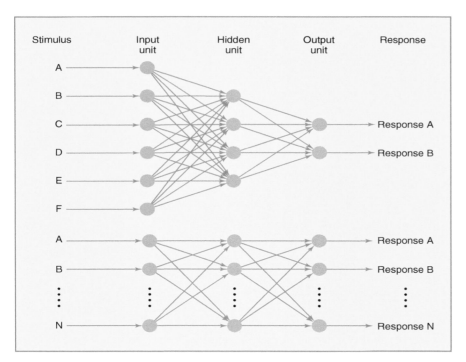

FIGURE 6.15 Upper panel. A simple two-layer, back-propagation network that was developed to account for the way in which pigeons solve discriminations (adapted from Maki & Abunawass, 1991). Lower panel: A complex two-layer, back-propagation network that has proved successful for explaining various aspects of human cognition.

None the less, given their relationship, albeit distant, with the Rescorla–Wagner (1972) model, networks based on the patterns of connections shown in Figure 6.15 have inherited at least some of its problems. Thus McCloskey and Cohen (1989) show forcefully that this type of network is unduly sensitive to the effects of retroactive interference, which means it is unable to explain the findings by Pearce and Wilson (1991) that have just been mentioned. In addition, Pearce (1994) has argued that a two-layer network based on the principles espoused by Maki and Abunawass (1991) occasionally makes the wrong predictions concerning the influence of similarity on discrimination learning.

Exemplar-based networks

I suspect that it will be possible to develop a back-propagation network that overcomes these shortcomings. Even so, a number of theorists have been encouraged to develop a rather different type of multi-layer network. These exemplar-based networks capture many of the principles of configural theories of conditioning (Pearce, 1994, 2002). Figure 6.16 shows one version of this type of configural, or exemplar-based, network that was proposed by Pearce (1994). In this network, the role of the units in the hidden layer is more specific than in the two-layer network of Rumelhart et al. (1988). As a result of being exposed to a particular pattern of stimulation, the network will select one hidden unit, or configural unit, which will be activated maximally whenever that pattern is presented again. If the pattern signals a US, then an association will develop between that configural unit and the US output unit. Subsequent presentations of the same pattern will then activate fully the configural unit, which will activate fully the US unit and lead to a CR. If the input pattern should change, then it will only partially activate the configural unit, and lead to a weaker CR. In addition, the new pattern will activate its own configural unit, which will then be capable of entering into its own associations with a US.

FIGURE 6.16 An exemplar-based connectionist network that has been exposed to trials in which a compound AC is paired with an unconditioned stimulus (US). The dashed lines depict potential connections that can become effective whenever a new pattern is presented to the input units (adapted from Pearce, 1994). CR, conditioned response.

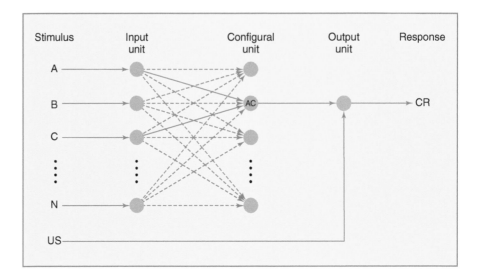

Kruschke (1992) shows how a network that is in principle similar to the one in Figure 6.16 is able to account for the outcome of many studies of learning with humans, including those reported in the study by Gluck and Bower (1988). Furthermore, Pearce (1994) has shown that such an exemplar-based connectionist network is less sensitive to the effects of retroactive interference than the other networks that we have considered. An exemplar-based network is also able to predict the correct influence of similarity on discrimination learning.

These are but a few of the network theories of learning that have been developed (see also Kehoe, 1988; McLaren et al., 1989; Schmajuk & DiCarlo, 1992; Gluck & Myers, 1993). In addition, a number of modifications have been proposed for the models that we have already considered. Until the predictions made by these different models and their variations have been thoroughly tested, it would be premature to conclude that one type of network is superior to another. For the present, the main conclusion to draw from this discussion is that there is a growing correspondence between network theories that have been developed to account for learning by animals on the one hand, and humans on the other. Such a development strongly suggests that there are some similarities between the ways in which humans and animals form associations and solve discriminations.

METACOGNITION AND DISCRIMINATION LEARNING

The final topic in this chapter examines a very different parallel that has been suggested to exist between the way in which humans and animals solve discriminations. If I have to make a difficult discrimination between two similar stimuli, then I am aware of this difficulty and may experience a state of uncertainty. **Metacognition** refers to the capacity of humans to be aware of, and to be able to report, the state of their mental processes. According to at least one group of researchers, monkeys may also be aware that they are uncertain about how to respond in a discrimination and thus capable of metacognition (Smith, Shields, Schull, and Washburn, 1997; see also Smith, Shields, & Washburn, 2003).

Monkeys were trained to move a cursor around on a television monitor by means of a joystick, before being given a visual density discrimination in which they were confronted with an array on the monitor similar to that shown in Figure 6.17. On any trial, the number of pixels in the top left-hand box would vary between 200 and 2950. To gain reward on dense trials, when there were exactly 2950 pixels in the box, the monkeys had to move the cursor to the box; but on sparse trials, when there were fewer than 2950 pixels in the box, then they were expected to move the cursor to the S for reward. The results from the experiment are presented in Figure 6.18, which shows that the percentage of trials on which a monkey moved the cursor to the box increased directly with the number of pixels it contained. The opposite pattern of results was found with the response of moving the cursor to the S. This response occurred often when there were relatively few pixels in the box, and became less frequent as the number of pixels approached 2950. These results indicate that the monkey found it difficult to tell when there were 2950 pixels in the box. The monkeys were also allowed to make a third response of moving the cursor to the star shown in Figure 6.17. This response had the effect of terminating the trial and moving the subject to a very simple problem for which it was rewarded on every trial. To prevent the subjects selecting the star on every trial, making this response had the adverse effect of postponing the start of the next trial of the density discrimination.

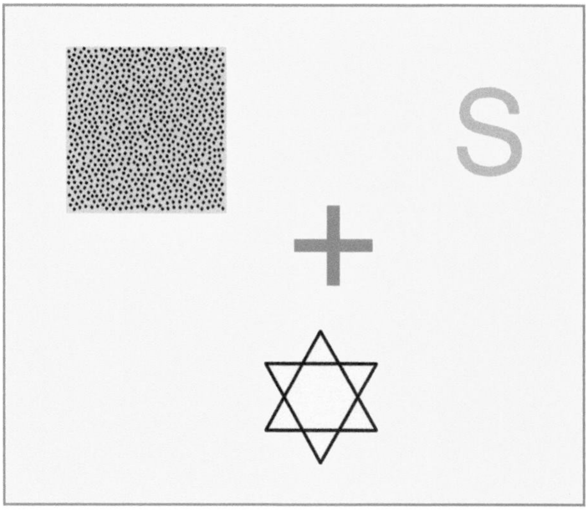

FIGURE 6.17 Sketch of the screen that was used for a visual discrimination with monkeys. When the number of dots in the display box in the top left-hand corner was 2950, moving the cursor—the cross in the center—to the display box resulted in reward. If the number of pixels in the display box was less than 2950 then moving the cursor to S resulted in reward. On any trial, moving the cursor to the star resulted in reward and a delay before the next trial. Subjects were expected to make this response when they were uncertain as to whether to select the display box or S (adapted from Smith et al., 1997).

The extra response was made available in the hope that subjects would use it when they were uncertain about whether to respond to the box or the S. The point where two dashed lines cross in Figure 6.18 indicates the point where the monkeys found it hardest to decide whether to move the cursor to the box or the S and thus the point where they were most likely to make an error. It is at this point that moving the cursor to the star would make most sense because this response would lead to certain reward. In keeping with this analysis, the solid line in Figure 6.18 shows that the third response was most likely on trials when each of the other two responses were equally likely to occur. Smith et al. (1997) refer to the act of moving the cursor to the star as the uncertain response because they assume subjects use it when they are uncertain about which of the other two responses to make.

Smith et al. (1997) conducted an experiment with humans that was very close in design to the one just described and which revealed an almost identical pattern of results. After the experiment, the participants said they chose the Uncertain response in response to feeling doubtful about the correct answer to the discrimination. Smith et al. (2003) infer from these reports that for humans the Uncertain response "may reveal not only metacognitive monitoring but also a reflexive awareness of the self as cognitive monitor" (p. 321). Their next step was to propose that because of

FIGURE 6.18 The percentage of responses to the display box, to the S, and to the star, according to the number of pixels in the displays box, for one monkey tested with the apparatus sketched in Figure 6.17 (adapted from Smith et al., 2003).

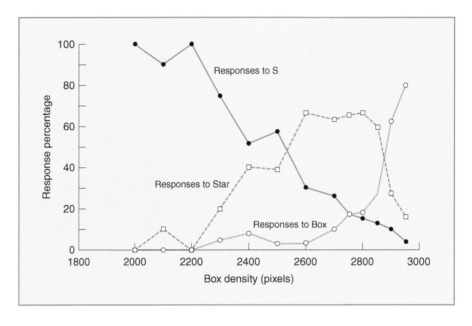

the similarity between the results obtained with monkeys and humans, then it follows that the monkeys solved the task in the same way as the humans:

> *Humans report that they are consciously uncertain and reflexively self aware as they produce these graphs. And humans and monkeys share evolutionary pasts, adaptive pressures, and homologous brain structures. Thus it is unparsimonious to interpret the same graph produced by humans and monkeys in different ways. (Smith et al., 2003, p. 335)*

Humans are capable of metacognition (an awareness of and an ability to report back on their own mental processes). This man, for example, might be unsure that the answer he has entered to a certain crossword clue is correct but he will concurrently be aware of this uncertainty.

This argument is original, and very bold. It certainly poses a challenge to the explanations for how animals solve discriminations. Thus far, we have assumed that discrimination learning results from the formation of associations, and none of the theories that have been considered—even the most complex connectionist theories—allows animals to reflect on their mental states and to make decisions based on these reflections. Do the results by Smith et al. (1997) therefore pose a challenge to conventional accounts of animal discrimination learning?

A serious obstacle to line of reasoning followed by Smith et al. (2003) was touched upon in Chapter 1, when the term "anthropomorphism" was introduced. This term refers to the strategy of inferring that animals solve problems in the same ways as humans if their performance on the problem is the same as that of humans. The trouble with this strategy is that it does not necessarily follow that because humans and animals behave in the same way then the mental processes responsible for the behavior must be the same. These processes might be identical, but they could be quite different. Thus the most that can be justifiably concluded from the similar performance of the monkeys and people is that they *might* have made the Uncertain response for the same reason; we are not justified in concluding that they *did* make this response for the same reason. As a commentator on the article by Smith et al. (2003) remarked: just because an electric car and a petrol car perform similarly does not mean that they have the same engine (Zentall, 2003).

If the monkeys did not make the Uncertain response because they were aware of being uncertain about how to respond, then why did they make it? A plausible explanation is that they learned through trial and error that in the presence of patterns with dots of a particular density, the most reliable method for obtaining reward, was to select the star. Even if this explanation should prove to be wrong, it would not mean that the explanation offered by Smith et al. (2003) is correct. The experience of a mental state, such as uncertainty, is a private event that is impossible for others to observe directly. In the case of humans, we infer that someone is experiencing a state of uncertainty by asking them. But we are unable to ask monkeys about their mental states and, even if we *were* able to ask them, it would be impossible to know if they were telling the truth in their responses to our questions. We are thus left in the tantalizing position of being confronted with a pattern of results that is consistent with the claim that monkeys are capable of metacognition, but our scientific tools are currently inadequate for the task of confirming this conclusion. Whether these tools will ever be adequate is a matter for debate, which—I suspect—will be waged for many years to come.

CHAPTER 7

CONTENTS

Category formation

7

Chapter 6 concentrated on discriminations using relatively simple stimuli in the hope that the interpretation of experimental findings would be more straightforward than if complex stimuli had been used. By focusing on relatively simple discriminations, there is a risk that important principles concerning the solution of complex discriminations will be overlooked. This possibility is made more plausible by the intriguing results of an experiment by Herrnstein, Loveland, and Cable (1976). In each session, pigeons were shown a set of eighty different photographic slides, half of which contained pictures of trees; the slides were selected from a pool containing more than 500 pictures. The trees were not especially prominent in the slides; rather, the slides were of scenes that contained trees. The remaining slides were of similar scenes but without trees. Slides were shown one at a time and pecks at a response key were rewarded with food only in the presence of pictures of trees. Eventually, subjects were able to discriminate accurately between the two sets, or categories, of slide. An impressive feature of this study is that the pigeons responded correctly even when they were shown novel photographs. Such a finding demonstrates that animals are capable of discriminating between stimuli on the basis of the category to which they belong, and has led some authors to propose that pigeons have the ability to acquire concepts (e.g. Herrnstein et al., 1976).

In this chapter we will examine in some detail how animals solve categorization problems. We will see that the theories that were developed to explain how simple discriminations are solved (which were considered in Chapter 6) can be used with considerable success to account for the results from experiments with more complex stimuli. Before turning to the theoretical analysis of categorization, however, some selected experimental findings merit attention. These add little in substance to the findings of Herrnstein et al. (1976) but they emphasize the remarkable ability of animals to utilize a broad range of categories.

EXAMPLES OF CATEGORIZATION

In one experiment by Cerella (1979), pigeons were shown the same set of eighty slides in each session. Reward was made available for responding in the presence of forty slides, which were all silhouettes of oak leaves (upper row, Figure 7.1) but reward was never presented for responding during the remaining slides, which were silhouettes of other leaves (lower row, Figure 7.1). Only twenty-four sessions were needed before the birds displayed a near perfect discrimination between the two sets of slides. The discrimination was also maintained when forty novel silhouettes of oak leaves replaced the original set. This last finding is particularly important because it shows that categorization does not depend merely on remembering how to respond to each training slide (see also Herrnstein et al., 1976; Schrier & Brady, 1987; Bhatt, Wasserman, Reynolds, & Knauss, 1988). However, there is a limit to the ability of pigeons. Cerella (1980) had difficulty training them to distinguish one oak leaf from forty other oak leaves; in fact, two of the four pigeons trained in this manner were unable to learn the discrimination.

FIGURE 7.1 Silhouettes of oak leaves (upper row) and leaves from other trees (lower row) that are representative of the stimuli used in a category learning experiment by Cerella (1979) (from Cerella, 1979).

There is now ample evidence showing that many species are capable of solving categorization problems. Indeed, after reviewing some of this evidence, Herrnstein (1990, p. 138) was led to conclude that categorization has "turned up at every level of the animal kingdom where it has been competently sought". Thus studies of categorization have involved monkeys (e.g. Schrier, Angarella, & Povar, 1984), chinchillas (Burdick & Miller, 1975), pigeons (e.g. Herrnstein et al., 1976), chickens (Ryan, 1982), quail (Kluender, Diehl, & Killeen, 1987), blue jays (Pietrewicz & Kamil, 1977) and an African grey parrot (Pepperberg, 1983).

A wide variety of categories has been studied in these experiments. Some categories have been based on natural objects: trees, water, people, cats, and flowers (e.g. Herrnstein et al., 1976; Bhatt et al., 1988), others have involved human-made objects: cars, chairs, the letter A in various typescripts, the cartoon character Charlie Brown, and even the paintings of Monet and Picasso (Morgan, Fitch, Holman, & Lea, 1976; Cerella, 1980; Bhatt et al., 1988; Watanabe, Sakamoto, & Wakita, 1995). Most categorization studies employ visual stimuli, but I want to describe two experiments because of the unconventional auditory stimuli they used.

Porter and Neuringer (1984) presented pigeons with excerpts of J.S. Bach's toccatas and fugues for organ, which alternated with Stravinsky's *Rite of spring* for orchestra. Pecks on one response key were occasionally rewarded during the music by Bach, whereas pecks on another key were rewarded during the *Rite of spring*. Even though the excerpts of music varied considerably from trial to trial, all subjects eventually displayed a clear discrimination between the two pieces of music.

Herrnstein (1990) stated that categorization has "turned up at every level of the animal kingdom where it has been competently sought". Experiments thus tend to be conducted across a broad variety of animals.

This training might have resulted in the pigeons discriminating between an organ (Bach) and an orchestra (Stravinsky), but the results from a series of generalization tests suggest this did not occur. The tests consisted of various novel pieces of music by a variety of composers. There was no indication that organ works necessarily resulted in responding on the "Bach" key, or orchestral works on the "Stravinsky" key. Instead, the fairest conclusion to be drawn from these test trials is that subjects were likely to respond on the "Stravinsky" key whenever they heard modern music and on the "Bach" key when they heard baroque music.

The second study involved carp, which were played intermixed excerpts of blues music played by John Lee Hooker and oboe concertos written by Bach (Chase, 2001). The fish were required to press a button during the former but not the latter to gain reward. Not only did they acquire the discrimination but they showed good transfer to novel examples from each category. In addition to being able to form musical categories, there is also evidence showing that some animals can discriminate between auditory categories based on the phonemes of human speech (Burdick & Miller, 1975; Kluender et al., 1987).

THEORIES OF CATEGORIZATION

Feature theory

When confronted with the stimuli shown in Figure 7.1, animals could solve the problem by looking for a unique feature that is present in oak leaves, but not in other leaves. For instance, a series of curved protuberances on the edge of the silhouette occurs with greater frequency in the oak leaves than the other leaves. By searching for this feature on every trial, the animal would be able to solve the discrimination without regard to the overall shape or nature of the entire pattern. **Feature theories** of categorization (e.g. Lea, 1984; D'Amato & Van Sant, 1988) assume that animals adopt this type of strategy, and there is a fair amount of evidence to support them. This evidence reveals that animals, at least occasionally, find ways of solving apparently complex problems in a relatively mundane way.

Huber, Troje, Loidolt, Aust, and Grass (2000) showed pigeons color pictures of fifty male and fifty female human faces. The problem was made difficult by using hairless faces but, even so, the birds were able to discriminate between the two sexes. Once the discrimination had been solved, test trials were conducted with transformed faces. If the faces were blurred, even quite considerably, the birds were able to tell the difference between males and females. At this point, it is tempting to think that the pigeons were displaying a remarkable skill, but this optimism is dashed by the finding that the discrimination was completely abolished when black and white pictures were used. Presumably, the female faces used for training shared a color that was different to the color shared by the male faces, and this was the feature the pigeons selected to distinguish between the two sets of pictures.

The results from a study by Aust and Huber (2001) point to a similar conclusion. Pigeons were trained to categorize eighty color pictures on the basis of whether they contained a person. Examples of the photographs that were used can be seen in Panel (a) of Figure 7.2. The birds were then given test trials with novel pictures—see Panel (b)—and demonstrated excellent transfer. Test trials were then conducted with scrambled images that were created by breaking the pictures into small squares and then moving some of the squares around. In addition, the size of the squares varied

KEY TERM

Feature theory
A theory of categorization that assumes instances are classified on the basis of whether or not they contain a particular feature, or set of features.

FIGURE 7.2 (a) Examples of the photographs showing a person (P) or no person (NP) from the training trials of a categorization experiment by Aust and Huber (2001). (b) Example of novel pictures that were presented for test trials in the same study. (c) Examples of a photograph from each category that were subjected to increasing degrees of scrambling; the numbers refer to the degree of scrambling (from Aust and Huber, 2001). Copyright © The Psychonomic Society. Reproduced with permission.

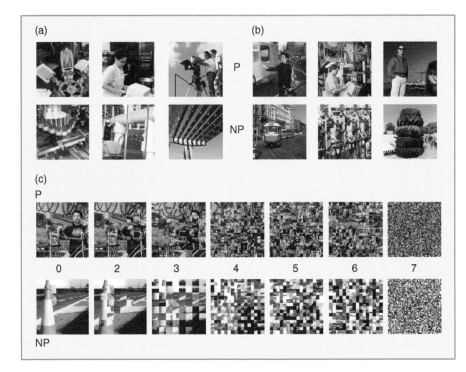

from being quite large to very small—Panel (c) of Figure 7.2. The birds were able to classify the test pictures correctly, even at level 5 of the sequence shown in the figure, but they were unable to classify the test patterns accurately when they were in black and white. Thus, the pigeons appear to have solved the person versus no-person discrimination on the basis of whether the photographs contained a small zone of a particular color.

Other studies have revealed that color is not the only feature that pigeons use when solving categorization problems based on faces. Jitsumori and Yoshihara (1997) initially trained birds with a categorization task involving Japanese faces that were happy or angry. Tests were then conducted with faces in which either the mouth or the eyes were removed and replaced by skin. The removal of these features resulted in a deterioration of the discrimination. It is interesting to note that the discrimination was not affected by inverting the eyes and mouth in a face. Humans find it very difficult to tell whether the person is happy or sad after the same transformation to a face, which implies that the birds solved the problem by looking for the presence or absence of local features—even if they were upside down, instead of paying heed to the overall pattern created by the features.

Rather different support for feature theories of categorization can be found in a study by Cerella (1980), who trained pigeons to peck a key for food in the presence of Charlie Brown cartoons but not other cartoon characters. Once this was achieved, albeit with considerable difficulty, they received generalization tests with unusual slides of Charlie Brown in which the parts of his body were rearranged (Figure 7.3). These were treated as if they were quite normal instances of the training category. Feature theory is able to explain this finding because the test stimuli contained all the features of the training stimuli, even though they were presented in a novel way.

FIGURE 7.3 Examples of the slides used in the generalization tests by Cerella (1980) after pigeons had received a categorization problem based on different images of the cartoon character Charlie Brown. From Cerella, 1986. Copyright © 1986 Elsevier. Reprinted with permission.

An experiment by Watanabe (2001) used a similar design to that of Cerella (1980), but failed to replicate his findings. Pigeons were trained to discriminate between photographs of one person from photographs of other people. They were then shown scrambled images of individual photographs in which the parts of the body were rearranged haphazardly. The birds were unable to tell the difference between the two categories in these circumstances, which implies that they classified the photographs on the basis of the overall configuration of the features they contained. Thus animals sometimes rely on individual features to solve a categorization problem, and at other times on the global pattern created by these features. The problem then arises of specifying the circumstances that determine which of these strategies will be adopted in a particular experiment. One factor that might be important is the number of pictures, or **exemplars**, that are used for the rewarded trials during training. Aust and Huber (2001) used forty photographs as signals for food and found a feature controlled the discrimination, whereas Watanabe (2001) used ten photographs and found that the overall arrangement of the features was important for successful categorization. Perhaps when animals are confronted with a large number of exemplars they seek to simplify the task by searching for a feature that is common to all of them, but when trained with only a few exemplars they may adopt the strategy of remembering each exemplar as a single configuration. Another factor is whether the image contains background cues. Matsukawa, Inoue, and Jitsumori (2004) have suggested that scrambling pictures is more likely to disrupt performance on a categorization task if the target for the task is presented against a background rather than a blank screen. Why this should be is something of a mystery.

If we accept that, at least in some circumstances, animals rely on no more than a few features to solve a categorization problem, then the way in which these features acquire their influence must be explained. One solution to this problem is to look to a theory such as the Rescorla–Wagner (1972) model. Suppose that animals receive trials in which photographs of trees signal food, whereas slides without trees are followed by nothing. Whenever a photograph is presented for a trial, the associative strength of each of its many features can be expected to change. The features that belong to trees will, in general, be present only on reinforced trials and they will steadily acquire associative strength. By contrast, the features that are irrelevant to the solution of the discrimination, for example, patches of sky, will occur on both reinforced and nonreinforced trials and the manner in which they acquire associative strength will be erratic. In other words, a categorization problem can be construed as feature-positive discrimination in which the features that are present only on

KEY TERM

Exemplar
A single item that is used for training or testing in a categorization task.

reinforced trials, specifically those belonging to trees, will gain considerably more associative strength than the features present on both types of trial. Once this has occurred, the discrimination will be solved and even novel photographs will be classified correctly.

Rigorous tests of the foregoing analysis have often proved difficult because of the complex nature of the stimuli that are typically employed in a categorization experiment. However, the results of an experiment by Huber and Lenz (1993) are entirely consistent with detailed predictions that can be derived from feature theory. Figure 7.4 shows three examples of the stimuli that were employed in this study. Inspection of these figures will reveal that the faces differ on four dimensions: the area above the eyes, the distance between the eyes, the length of the nose, and the area below the mouth. The figures also show, progressively from left to right, the three values that were used to represent each dimension. The features in the left-hand figure were assigned a value of -1, in the center figure 0, and in the right-hand figure $+1$.

Sixty-two different faces were used for the training stage of the experiment. Pigeons were rewarded for pecking a response key in the presence of any face for which the sum of the feature values was greater than zero. The birds eventually responded more rapidly during faces that signaled the availability, rather than the absence, of food. The advantage of using artificially created stimuli is that the experimenter knows which features the subjects must use to solve the discrimination. It is also possible to study performance in the presence of different faces, to gain an understanding of the control exerted by these features. Huber and Lenz (1993) adopted this strategy and found that there was an extremely orderly relationship between the sum of the feature values of a particular face and the rate of responding that it elicited. This relationship is shown for one pigeon in Figure 7.5, which makes it clear that the more features a face had in common with the right-hand face of Figure 7.4, the faster was responding in its presence.

The test results from this experiment demonstrate that not all members of a category are treated equally, with some being classified more readily than others. To explain this pattern of results in terms of a feature theory, such as the Rescorla–Wagner model, we must assume that each of the positive feature values gained positive associative strength during the course of training, and that each of the negative feature values gained negative associative strength. As the theory predicts that the strength of responding during a compound is determined by the sum of the associative strengths of its components, there will be a direct relationship between

FIGURE 7.4 Examples of three of the faces used by Huber and Lenz (1993) in a categorization study (adapted from Huber & Lenz, 1993).

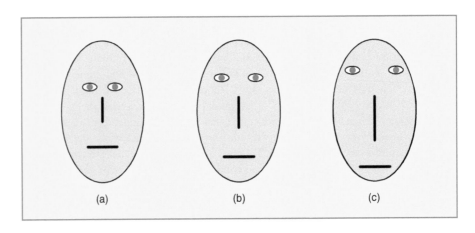

the rate of responding during a particular face and the sum of the values of its component features.

Exemplar theories

A number of authors have argued that the ability of both humans (Medin & Schaffer, 1978; Hintzman, 1986; Kruschke, 1992) and animals (Pearce, 1988, 1989, 1991; Astley & Wasserman, 1992) to categorize objects depends on them remembering each instance or exemplar and the category to which it belongs. Indeed, we have just come across support for this type of **exemplar theory** when considering the categorization experiment by Watanabe (2001). In that study, pigeons were shown scrambled versions of the images used for training and were unable to categorize them correctly. The implication of this outcome is that successful categorization was based on keeping a record of each training pattern. Such an account explains the ability to categorize familiar exemplars, but some additional mechanism is required if this account is to explain the successful categorization of novel stimuli. Both Pearce (1988, 1991) and Astley and Wasserman (1992) have proposed that this additional mechanism is based on the principles of stimulus generalization as envisaged by Spence (1937). When a stimulus is presented for the first time in a categorization problem, there will be generalization to it as a result of the training with the previous exemplars. Suppose the new stimulus belongs to the category associated with food—the positive category—then it will bear a strong similarity to many other stimuli that have already been shown and that have signaled food. There will, as a consequence, be a considerable generalization of the effects of the training with members of the positive category to the new pattern and the animal should respond rapidly in its presence. By contrast, if the new pattern belongs to the negative category, then it will not be similar to members of the positive category. There will be little generalization from the established members of the positive category and responding during the new stimulus will be slow.

Two points concerning this account of categorization merit brief consideration. The first relates to an argument that may occur to many readers: The account is implausible because it requires that animals remember an unreasonably large number of individual stimuli. In the case of the study by Herrnstein et al. (1976), this number would have to be a sizable proportion of 500. We shall see in Chapter 8, however, that pigeons are able to remember many hundreds of different photographs.

The second point concerns the finding that when the same pool of photographs is used for training with a category discrimination, performance in the presence of these photographs is often better than with novel photographs belonging to the same category (Schrier et al., 1984; Bhatt et al., 1988). This result has also been found in experiments with humans, where it is referred to as the **exemplar effect** (Homa, Dunbar, & Nohre, 1991). The implication of this result is that animals learn about individual training stimuli in a categorization task, and that this information is at least partially responsible for their successful performance.

Despite the very different assumptions on which they are based, it is often extremely difficult to differentiate between a feature and an exemplar theory in terms of the predictions they make. Consider, for example, the finding by Huber and

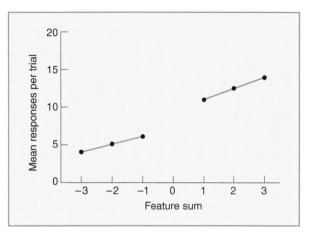

FIGURE 7.5 The mean number of responses on test trials in the categorization study by Huber and Lenz (1993). The test stimuli are arranged according to the sum of the values of their features (adapted from Huber & Lenz, 1993).

KEY TERMS

Exemplar theory
A theory of categorization which assumes instances are classified either by remembering the category to which they belong, or by their similarity to instances that have already been classified.

Exemplar effect
The finding that familiar exemplars of a category are easier to classify correctly than unfamiliar ones.

Lenz (1993) that faces with a net feature sum of, say, 3 elicited faster responding than those with a net feature sum of 1, even though they belonged to the same category. At first sight this finding might appear to be more compatible with a feature than an exemplar analysis of categorization, but it can be readily explained by the latter. Any face with a net feature sum of 1 will be more similar to the members of the negative category than a face with a net feature sum of 3. Generalization from members of the nonreinforced category will thus be greater to the former instance than the latter, and result in faces with a feature sum of 1 eliciting a weaker rate of responding than those with a feature sum of 3. In other words, the reason for the high rate of responding to a +3 face is essentially the same as that offered by Spence's (1937) theory of discrimination learning for the peak shift effect.

There are, therefore, two rather different types of theory available for explaining how animals solve categorization problems. We have just seen that it is difficult to differentiate between these theories on the basis of experimental evidence. It is also possible that in certain categorization tasks animals focus on the components of the stimuli, as feature theory predicts, whereas in other tasks they focus on more global aspects of the stimuli, as exemplar theory predicts (see Huber & Lenz, 1993). Perhaps the safest conclusion that can be drawn from this discussion is that the mechanisms that are believed to be responsible for the way animals solve relatively simple discriminations are also likely to be responsible for the way they solve categorization problems.

Prototype theory

The results from experimental studies of categorization by humans have encouraged the proposal that exposure to the members of a category results in the formation of a **prototype** (e.g. Posner & Keele, 1968; see also Shanks, 1994). The prototype of a category is supposed to be a summary representation that corresponds to the average, or central tendency, of all the exemplars that have been experienced. Once a prototype has been formed it is assumed to be activated whenever an exemplar is presented and, once activated, to elicit the response that is appropriate for the category. The likelihood of the response being performed is assumed to be determined by the extent to which the prototype is activated, which, in turn, is assumed to be related to the degree of similarity between the exemplar and the prototype.

Evidence in support of these proposals comes from the finding that exemplars bearing a close resemblance to the prototype are classified more easily than exemplars that are rather different to the prototype (Posner & Keele, 1968; Shanks, 1994). Although initial attempts to find a similar prototype effect with animals failed (see, for example, Lea & Harrison, 1978; Pearce, 1987; Watanabe, 1988), more recent experiments have been successful (Von Fersen & Lea, 1990; Aydin & Pearce, 1994). But even these successes do not necessarily mean that a prototypical representation is responsible for successful categorization by animals. It now seems that demonstrations of such an effect with humans can be explained by either a feature (McClelland & Rumelhart, 1985) or an exemplar (Hintzman, 1986; Shin & Nosofsky, 1992) theory of categorization, and the same may well be true for experiments with animals.

In terms of feature theory, for instance, a stimulus that corresponds to the average of all the members of a category is likely to be composed of elements that occur frequently in that category. If the category in question has been used to signal food, then each of these frequently occurring features will have considerable associative strength, and their combined influence will result in a high rate of responding during the prototypical stimulus. Furthermore, this level of responding is likely to be higher than during stimuli that are only distantly related to the prototype, and that can be expected to possess only a few features with high associative strength. Likewise, in terms of exemplar theory, an exemplar that corresponds to the average of the training patterns will bear a close similarity to these patterns. Responding in the presence of the exemplar can then be expected to be high because of the substantial spread of excitation to it from all the training patterns (see Aydin & Pearce, 1994).

ABSTRACT CATEGORIES

The results considered thus far have involved categories based on the presence or absence of one or more physical features. By way of example, in one of Herrnstein et al.'s (1976) experiments the physical features were provided by the presence or absence of a tree. Alternatively, in the case of the experiment of Huber and Lenz (1993) it was the presence or absence of a feature in a particular location that indicated the category to which an exemplar belonged. Moreover, by being based on the presence and absence of physical stimuli, the results from these studies have been easy to interpret in terms of the theories that have just been considered. It is, however, possible that animals can acquire categories on a more abstract basis than by concentrating on the presence and absence of physical features.

Categories as concepts

Schrier and Brady (1987, p. 142) made this point when they proposed that monkeys can categorize photographs of people because they possess a "concept 'humans' as we commonly understand it". Although it is easy to talk about concepts when they are used by humans, it is rather more difficult to specify what this term means when it applies to animals. Lea (1984) has considered this matter in some detail. He concludes that if animals acquire concepts, then successful categorization need not depend on the physical similarity of the members of the category but should also be successful when the exemplars bear no physical similarity to each other. To help clarify this point, consider the following experiment by Savage-Rumbaugh, Rumbaugh, Smith, and Lawson (1980). Chimpanzees were required to sort a mixed pile of tools and food into two separate piles. Initially, they were trained with the same objects, but when test trials were given with new objects they were able to categorize these successfully. It is not easy to argue that this problem was solved on the basis of the physical similarity of the test items to the training items because it is difficult to identify a set of physical features an object must possess to be classified as a tool or as food. Instead, these objects may have been categorized successfully because the subjects possessed the concepts "food" and "tool". In fact, the chimpanzees had received considerable language training (see Chapter 13) prior to this experiment and it is conceivable that this was responsible for their ability to acquire these concepts. There is, however, an alternative, theoretically less exciting explanation for the results of this experiment.

The successful categorization of food and tools shown by chimpanzees (Savage-Rumbaugh et al., 1980) might amount to no more than "mediated generalization", whereby salivation on the presentation of food (and lack thereof for tools) is the means by which the problem is solved.

When a chimpanzee picks up an item of food it may react in some consistent way, such as by salivating. To solve the discrimination, therefore, all the animal has to learn is that any object that elicits this reaction must be treated in one way, and objects that do not elicit this reaction must be treated in another way. Such a "mediated generalization" account is, admittedly, cumbersome but it has a long history (e.g. Osgood, 1953, p. 353) and there are good reasons for believing it to be true for both simple (Honey & Hall, 1989) and complex (Wasserman, DeVolder, & Coppage, 1992) discriminations. Researchers now rarely consider the question of whether animals can acquire concepts, partly because it is not entirely clear what is meant by this term. Instead, to understand if animals are capable of acquiring abstract categories, attention has focused on whether they can form categories on the basis of the relationship between two or more objects. This research is of interest because it highlights the intellectual limitations of certain species, and also because of its implications for our understanding of the way in which animals represent knowledge.

RELATIONSHIPS AS CATEGORIES

Sameness

One method that has been developed to study the way in which animals learn about relationships is known as **matching to sample**. For this technique, a sample stimulus is presented and, after the subject has directed a response at it, two comparison stimuli are shown, one of which is the same as the sample. To gain reward, the comparison stimulus that matches the sample must be selected. Panel (a) of Figure 7.6 portrays schematically the array of stimuli that might be presented for one trial of a typical matching experiment. There is a sample stimulus, which is red, and two comparison stimuli, one of which is red and the other of which is blue. To gain reward, the subject must respond to the comparison stimulus that corresponds to the sample. Figure 7.7 shows a sea lion selecting the correct comparison stimulus, after it has pressed the lever in front of the central, sample stimulus (Reichmuth-Kastak & Schusterman, 2002). The theoretically interesting account for successful matching is that animals can appreciate that the sample and comparison stimuli are the same, and that this relationship controls the choice of the correct comparison. As is so often the case, however, there are alternative accounts for successful matching, and these must be discounted before we accept that animals can detect and respond to a relationship.

A plausible account for matching can be developed in terms of configural (or exemplar) learning. The four panels in Figure 7.6 depict the possible configurations of stimuli that will confront an animal during a typical matching problem. To respond correctly, the left-hand comparison stimuli in panels (a) and (d) must be chosen, and so must the right-hand stimuli in panels (b) and (c). Note that these are the only possible trials, and that each panel contains a different configuration of sample and comparison stimuli. To solve the problem, then, all the animal must do is to associate a specific response with each configuration. For example, configuration b would be associated with the response of approaching top left. Once the four associations have been formed, the problem can be solved successfully on every trial.

To test this account of matching, it would be necessary to introduce a new set of sample and comparison stimuli. As there will have been no opportunity to associate the configurations of these stimuli with the correct choices, this change will result in a marked loss of accuracy if such associations are responsible for matching. On the other hand, if the original training resulted in subjects learning to respond according to the relationship between the sample and comparison stimuli, then changing their physical properties should not disrupt responding. Even when the stimuli are novel it will be possible to identify the comparison that is the same as the sample and respond correctly.

Experiments with chimpanzees (Nissen, Blum, & Blum, 1948; Oden, Thompson, & Premack, 1988), rhesus monkeys (Mishkin, Prockop, & Rosvold, 1962), dolphins (Herman & Gordon, 1974), sea lions (Kastak & Schusterman, 1994), and corvids (Wilson, Mackintosh, & Boakes, 1985a,b) have found that, after sufficient training on a variety of matching discriminations, these animals can respond correctly on the first trial with a novel set of stimuli. At least some species, therefore, seem capable of solving discriminations on the basis of relational information.

An experiment by Pepperberg (1987) provides rather different evidence that animals can classify novel stimuli on the basis of a judgment about sameness and

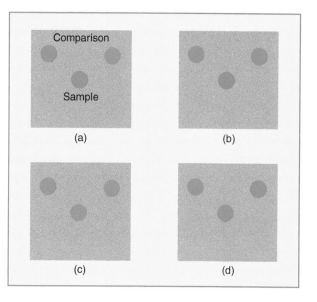

FIGURE 7.6 The four possible configurations of sample and comparison stimuli that can occur in a matching study.

FIGURE 7.7 A sea lion choosing the correct comparison stimulus in a matching study (photograph provided by Colleen Reichmuth-Kastak and Ron Schusterman).

FIGURE 7.8 Alex making a sameness/difference judgment about two stimuli presented to him by Irene Pepperberg (photograph by David Linden, courtesy of the Alex Foundation).

difference. The single subject in this experiment was Alex, an African grey parrot, who had been trained over many years to use vocal English labels to refer to a variety of objects in response to questions posed in spoken English by his trainers (a description of this training is presented in Chapter 13). He could also use such categorical labels as "color" and "shape". For the experiment under consideration, Alex was presented with two objects, such as a red pentagon and a red oval and was asked "What's same?" or "What's different?" (Figure 7.8). He was then expected to respond by saying the appropriate category label: "color" for the first question, and "shape" for the second. Performance on these tests, even when the objects had not previously been presented for testing, was considerably better than would be expected on the basis of chance.

Initial experiments with pigeons indicated that they fail to transfer successful matching from a familiar set of two stimuli to novel stimuli (e.g. Wilson et al., 1985a,b). To explain why pigeons are inferior, in this respect, to some other animals Wilson et al. (1985b) made use of the fact that there are two types of cue that can be used to solve a matching problem. One is based on individual training arrays, as described above, and the other is based on the relationship of sameness. They suggested that for species like corvids and apes, the relational cue is of relatively high salience and subjects readily learn to select the comparison stimulus that is the same as the sample. On the other hand, they further suggested that for pigeons the salience of the relational cue is relatively low, so that they will tend to solve matching problems by learning how to respond in the presence of individual training configurations. It has already been noted that this strategy would prevent subjects from responding correctly when new stimuli are introduced to the matching task. Thus according to Wilson et al. (1985b), the difference between species in their ability to solve matching problems with novel stimuli is not because some are able to appreciate relational information, and others are not; but because some can more readily use relational information than others. Put rather differently, learning based on relational cues is more likely to be overshadowed by learning based on individual configurations in pigeons than in corvids.

There is certainly support for the idea that pigeons find it difficult to make use of relational information. I have spent many frustrating hours attempting to train pigeons to judge whether two adjacent vertical bars were of the same or different heights (Pearce, 1988, 1991). Although I was eventually successful, the method I had to adopt makes it quite likely that the subjects remembered every possible configuration and whether or not it signaled food. A similar conclusion can be drawn from a study by Herrnstein, Vaughan, Mumford, and Kosslyn (1989), who presented pigeons with a discrimination in which a dot was located either inside or outside a hoop (Figure 7.9).

FIGURE 7.9 Four stimuli that are typical of those used in a categorization study by Herrnstein et al. (1989), based on the abstract relation of insideness (adapted from Herrnstein, 1990).

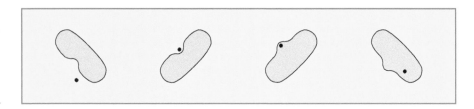

This was an extremely difficult problem for the birds and, once again, it is more than possible that their success was based solely on remembering the significance of individual training patterns.

Additional support for the proposals of Wilson et al. (1985b) can be found in experiments where the number of stimuli used for a matching task is increased. Normally, a matching to sample task involves only two stimuli and, as Figure 7.6 shows, this results in there being only four training configurations. Colombo, Cottle, and Frost (2003) used three stimuli during the initial training of a matching problem with pigeons. In contrast to previous studies, they were moderately successful in training birds to respond correctly on trials with novel stimuli. The use of three stimuli meant there were twelve different training configurations, and thus to perform accurately during the training trials it was necessary to remember how to respond to twelve different patterns. Even though the salience of the relational cue might be low, with so many patterns to remember, it is likely that this cue will gain more control over performance during the original training than when only two stimuli are used for the training trials. Indeed, theories of associative learning (e.g. Rescorla & Wagner, 1972) predict just this outcome.

An experiment by Katz and Wright (2006) makes the same point in a rather different way. Trials commenced with the presentation to pigeons of a single photograph, which they were required to peck. A second photograph and a white rectangle were then displayed below the first photograph (Figure 7.10). A peck to the second photograph resulted in food if it was the same as the first photograph, but if the two photographs were different then a peck to the white rectangle resulted in food. Eight photographs were used at first, which resulted in eight different configurations for trials when the two photographs were the same, and fifty-six different configurations when the two photographs were different. Despite this large number, once pigeons were performing accurately on the task, test trials revealed that subjects would respond correctly on no better than 50% of the trials when they were

FIGURE 7.10 The arrangement of the training stimuli on a television screen for the experiment by Katz and Wright (2006). On trials when the two photographs were the same, pecks to the lower photograph resulted in reward, but when the two photographs were different then pecks to the white rectangle were rewarded.

shown novel photographs. Thus, there was no evidence that the relational cue of sameness had acquired any influence. Katz and Wright (2006) then increased the size of the training set to thirty-six photographs (thirty-six same combinations and 1260 different combinations). After several thousand training trials, when subjects were performing accurately with the training photographs, test trials with new photographs revealed correct responding on nearly 60% of the trials.

Flushed with this success, Katz and Wright (2006) then increased the number of training photographs to 64, 128 and so on until the birds were being trained with 1024 photographs. Test trials were conducted when performance was accurate with each set size. The results from all the tests are portrayed by the solid line in Figure 7.11. It is apparent that as the set size increases so does the accuracy on the tests with the novel photographs. Indeed, for set sizes greater than 256, performance during the test trials was just as good as during the training trials. The results from this study can be readily understood, if it is accepted that the salience of the relational cue that can be used to solve the discrimination is very low, and requires many trials of training before it becomes effective.

The remaining lines on Figure 7.11 show the results from experiments by Katz, Wright, and Bachevalier (2002) using old-world rhesus monkeys and by Wright, Rivera, Katz, and Bachevalier (2003), using new-world capuchin monkeys. Both species were trained in a similar way to the pigeons, but it is evident that performance with the novel photographs was superior in the monkeys. The pattern of results in Figure 7.11 indicates that the monkeys found it easier to use the relational cue than the pigeons, which implies that the salience of this cue was higher for the monkeys than the pigeons. Wright et al. (2003) go further to suggest that if apes were tested with this task, then their performance would be even better than that of the monkeys.

The results discussed thus far indicate that pigeons find it difficult, but not impossible, to use relational information. With this conclusion in mind, it is necessary to consider some findings with this species that have been reported by Wasserman and colleagues (e.g. Wasserman, Hugart, & Kirkpatrick-Steger, 1995;

FIGURE 7.11 The results for three different species from the test trials of a matching discrimination. The discrimination was conducted in stages, with an increasing number of photographs used in each stage. Test trials, with novel photographs, took place at the end of each stage.

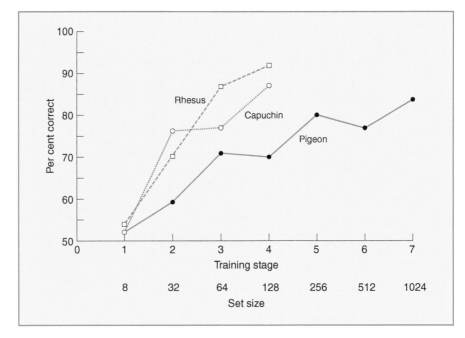

Young, Wasserman, & Garner, 1997; Young & Wasserman, 2001), which have been taken as evidence that pigeons can readily make use of relational cues for solving discriminations (see also Cook, Katz, & Cavoto, 1997). Wasserman et al. (1995) trained pigeons with arrays of icons similar to those shown in Figure 7.12. Each array was displayed on a screen with a response key on either side. Pecks to one response key resulted in food when the icons in the array were all the same, and pecks to another key resulted in food when they were different. Pigeons acquired this discrimination and, more importantly, they showed good transfer to novel arrays of icons. On the basis of these and related findings, Wasserman, Frank, and Young (2002) were led to conclude that for pigeons the salience of the relational cue is relatively high.

There is, however, at least one reason for questioning whether the choice of the correct response key was guided by an appreciation of the relationship among all the icons in an array (Katz and Wright, 2006). Young et al. (1997) and Wasserman et al. (2002) found that if the number of the icons presented in the test patterns was reduced then the accuracy of selecting the correct response key deteriorated dramatically. For example, in an experiment by Young et al. (1997) if there were two items in an array that were identical then approximately 90% of the responses were made to the incorrect key. If the discrimination was truly based on the relationship between the icons, then as long as there are two or more icons present the birds should be able to classify the array correctly. Shettleworth (1998) notes that it is possible that the findings described by Wasserman and colleagues depend on pigeons responding on the overall texture created by the arrays rather than the relationship between the icons. Certainly, the pattern in the left of Figure 7.12 appears more regular than the one in the right, and perhaps this difference between the patterns provided the cue on which pigeons based their responding. For the present therefore, it may be safest to conclude that pigeons find it difficult, but not impossible, to make use of relational information.

Second-order relationships

A stringent test for assessing whether an animal can detect a relationship between two objects is to ask whether it can appreciate **second-order relationships**.

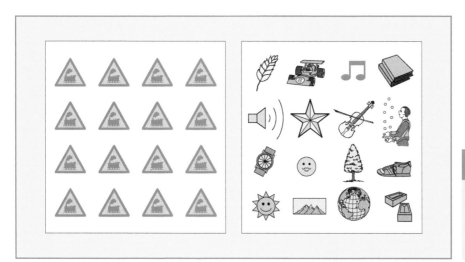

FIGURE 7.12 Examples of the arrays of patterns that were used by Wasserman et al. (2002) for a discrimination based on sameness and difference (adapted from Wasserman et al. 2002).

KEY TERM

Second-order relationship
The relationship between two other relationships.

Following a preliminary study by Premack (1983b), Oden, Thompson, and Premack (1988b, 1990) presented young chimpanzees with a pair of objects attached to a board for the sample of the matching problem depicted in Figure 7.13. The two objects might have been the same, AA, or they might have been different, CD. The chimpanzees were then given a choice between two pairs of new objects on boards, one pair consisted of two identical objects, BB, and the other pair consisted of two different objects, EF. If subjects had been presented with AA, they were meant to select BB, and if they were presented with CD they were meant to select EF. That is, they were required to select the pair of objects whose relationship matched the relationship between the two objects of the sample. The chimpanzees were therefore being asked to demonstrate the sophisticated skill of perceiving a second-order relationship, which means a relationship between two relationships. Despite receiving over a thousand trials, the chimpanzees failed completely on this problem. Perhaps their failure should not be surprising: even children under the age of five are unable to solve this type of problem (House, Brown, & Scott, 1974).

The obvious conclusion to draw from this experiment is that chimpanzees are unable to look at two relationships and make an inference about the relationship between them. Whereas it would be convenient at this point to conclude that we have now reached the frontier of the intellectual abilities of animals, a further study by Oden et al. (1990) implies that if we have reached the frontier then it is not yet particularly well defined. Oden et al.'s experiment made use of the finding that if chimpanzees are allowed to play with one object, and are then presented with another object, they will show more interest in the second object if it is different to the first one. In a similar way, chimpanzees were encouraged to hold and play with one of the pairs of objects used for the study just described, say AA. The pair was then replaced with another pair. Subjects found the new pair more interesting, by playing with it for longer, if the relationship between the new pair of objects was different, say CD, rather than the same, say BB, to that between the original pair. The clear implication of this finding is that the animals were able to appreciate whether the relationship between the first pair of objects was the same or different to that between the second pair.

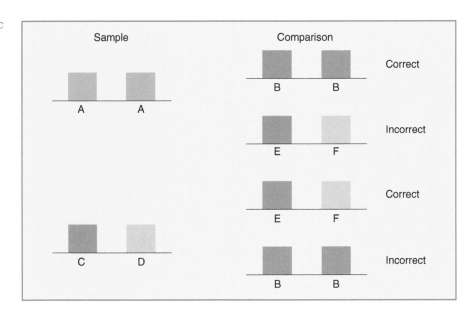

FIGURE 7.13 Schematic representation of the stimuli used for a discrimination based on second-order relationships in experiments by Oden and Thompson (1988, 1990).

Bolstered by this finding, Oden et al. (1988, 1990) conducted an additional study to assess whether, with special training, the chimpanzees might conquer the challenges posed by the original test. Chimpanzees received a discrimination in which they had to select a heart-shaped token for reward if they were shown two objects that were the same, and a diagonal-shaped token if they were shown two objects that were different. By using many different objects, it was hoped that the heart-shaped token would represent the relationship of same, and the other token the relationship of different. Once the chimpanzees were adept on this problem, they then received the matching problem based on second-order relationships. Unlike the chimpanzees studied by Oden et al. (1988, 1990), they solved this new problem with little difficulty. Quite why the training with the tokens was effective is not fully understood, but the fact that it *was* effective means that one species at least is able to make decisions based on second-order relationships. Thus far research with other species, notably monkeys (Thompson & Oden, 2000), has found no evidence that they can acquire this ability.

Analogical reasoning

A typical analogical reasoning experiment for humans would consist of the question "As dog is to puppy, so cow is to . . . ?" To reply correctly, it is necessary to identify the relationship between dog and puppy and then to select a word that bears the same relationship to cow—calf. Analogical reasoning, then, is the ability to judge the equivalence of the relationships between two sets of stimuli. This type of reasoning is therefore quite similar to that involved in making judgments concerning second-order relationships. Analogical reasoning is of interest because its existence in any animal would indicate that it can identify relationships that extend beyond sameness and difference.

We have just seen that only chimpanzees have been shown to be capable of responding on the basis of second-order relationships, and even then they required special training. It may come as no surprise, then, to learn that the only animal to have demonstrated a capacity for analogical reasoning is also a chimpanzee who had received special training. The chimpanzee in question was Sarah, who had been trained by Premack (1976) to communicate with her trainers through an artificial language (see Chapter 13). According to Premack (1988a), a particularly important aspect of this training was the use of two tokens to represent the relationships of same and different.

The stimuli used to study analogical reasoning by Sarah were of two basic types: In several experiments she was presented with a matrix of geometric shapes similar to those shown in the left-hand upper panel of Figure 7.14. Her task was to select a single shape from the bottom row and to place it in the vacant space in the matrix so that the relationship in the right-hand column matched that in the left-hand column. In this example the correct shape is the small triangle containing a dot. Sarah was able to perform a variety of problems based on this design with considerable ease. The other stimuli that Sarah was tested with consisted of household objects that were familiar to her. The example in the lower panel of Figure 7.14 is similar in principle to that in the upper panel, and in this instance the correct item to be placed in the space is the can-opener. Given her success with the geometric shapes, it might not be surprising to learn that Sarah was also very good at solving this sort of problem.

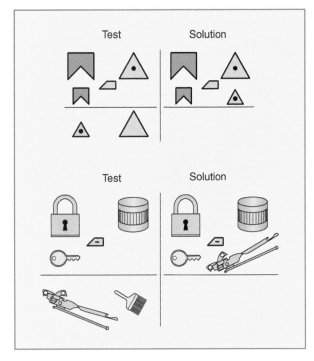

FIGURE 7.14 Two examples of the problems given to the chimpanzee, Sarah, in a study of analogical reasoning (adapted from Gillan et al., 1981).

THE REPRESENTATION OF KNOWLEDGE

Many of the findings that have just been discussed are fascinating in their own right, but they are also important because they have implications for our understanding of the way in which animals represent their knowledge. This is a difficult issue about which a great deal of controversy persists as far as human cognition is concerned. It is also a topic that is only infrequently considered in discussions of animal cognition (but see Premack, 1983a,b). None the less, I suspect that until we have discovered how information is stored by animals we shall remain a long way from understanding their cognitive abilities.

The simplest way in which information can be retained about a particular event is by storing a copy of it. The term "concrete code" can be used to refer to this means of storing information. Of course, the copy need not be perfect—a concrete copy may store only a fraction of the information that is available. Premack (1983a) talks about an "imaginal" code when he refers to information that is stored in a concrete way. By this, he implies that a memory of a stimulus is effectively equivalent to an image of it. In Chapter 2, we discussed some experiments by Holland (see pp. 48–49) that suggest that rats may use an imaginal code for retaining information about food. Premack (1983a) argues that an imaginal or concrete code is adequate for retaining information about any physical stimulus. A concrete code could also be used to represent the stimuli used for a categorization problem, provided it is based on specific objects, such as trees, water, or a person. However, Premack (1983a) maintains that a concrete code is of limited value when information of a more abstract nature must be retained.

One sort of information that is difficult to represent with a concrete code concerns relationships. I can form an image of a man, and of a boy, but I am unable to form an image of the relationship between the two. For example, the man might be the boy's stepfather, and it is impossible to form a concrete code, or image, of this relationship. The same is true for other relationships. Thus it is impossible to construct an image, or concrete code, that represents sameness. At first sight, therefore, showing that animals can solve discriminations on the basis of a relationship would appear to imply that they are able to represent knowledge in a more sophisticated manner than that allowed by a concrete code. Although this conclusion holds for certain types of discrimination, Premack (1983a) has argued that it does not necessarily apply to all experimental demonstrations of relational learning. To develop his argument Premack (1983a,b) focuses on the relationship of sameness, and proposes that it can hold at a number of levels. At the most fundamental, there is the similarity that pertains to objects that are physically identical. Suppose that an animal is briefly shown an object, which is presented again a short time later. On its first presentation, the object may leave an enduring concrete copy, or memory, of itself. This copy will then match the object when it is again presented; according to Premack this will result in a reaction of similarity.

Premack does not specify what this reaction consists of but, for want of a better expression, the second presentation of the object could be said to elicit a sensation of familiarity. In the case of physical identity, then, the sensation of familiarity could provide a concrete stimulus for use in solving simple matching problems. For the task summarized in Figure 7.6, a subject might look first at the sample and then at a comparison stimulus. If the latter should elicit a reaction of familiarity, then this could serve as the discriminative stimulus controlling the correct response. Thus, according to Premack (1983b), success on matching tasks, even with novel stimuli, does not require particularly sophisticated intellectual mechanisms.

At another level, Premack (1983a,b) argues there is similarity between relationships, for example, we can talk about the similarity between a dog-puppy and a cow-calf relationship. Premack (1983a) maintains that because of the physical difference between the four components of these two relationships, it is impossible to construct imaginal codes of the relationships that will allow us to conclude they are the same. These limitations of concrete representations led Premack (1983a) to propose that all relationships, apart from those of physical similarity and difference, must be represented in an abstract code. Premack (1983a) himself says very little about how the abstract code is formed, or about the information it may contain, but the absence of an obvious alternative method for storing information about relationships means that his ideas merit serious consideration.

A further proposal by Premack (1983a, 1988b) is that most animals are capable of forming concrete representations, but only chimpanzees possess the capacity to form abstract representations. Normally, this capacity is poorly developed but, as we have seen, given the right experience in the laboratory, they are able to make more use of it. Quite why the prior experience is so effective is hard to understand at the moment. Thompson and Oden (2000, p. 389) suggest that it provides the "representational scaffolding" for the complex computational judgments necessary for making abstract similarity judgments such as those in analogies. It is not possible to say why this scaffolding is necessary, or what it does, which is no more than to admit that we are reaching the limits of our understanding of animal cognition. Additional studies with chimpanzees that examine further the operation of their abstract thought processes will be essential if our knowledge about animal cognition is to be complete.

CHAPTER 8

CONTENTS

Short-term retention

8

The study of animal memory is concerned with understanding how information acquired at a particular time can influence future behavior. An example of the role of memory in a naturalistic setting is provided by certain birds that hide food when it is plentiful in the autumn and retrieve it in the winter when supplies are scarce. Unless the birds remembered where the food had been hidden, they would be unable to find it efficiently. An early demonstration of animal memory in the laboratory is provided by Hunter (1914), who allowed raccoons to observe three exits while they were retained in an observation chamber. A light above one exit was then briefly illuminated and some time later the animal was released. If it chose the exit that had been indicated by the light it received a reward. With sufficient training the subjects were able to tolerate a delay of as much as 25 seconds between the offset of the light and their release. Such a finding suggests that the raccoons could retain for nearly half a minute a memory of which light had been illuminated.

Once it is established that animals are able to retain information about past events, then a number of interesting questions arise. What sort of information can be retained? How much information can be retained? And for how long is it retained? In attempting to answer questions of this sort, a distinction is often made between two types of memory. One type lasts for relatively short periods of time and concerns information about the immediate past. The other type of memory is believed to endure for much longer periods of time. It may consist of the associations that are acquired during the course of either Pavlovian or instrumental conditioning, or it may consist of a representation of some particular event. A number of authors have made this distinction for humans, which is reflected by their use of such terms as primary and secondary memory (James, 1890; Waugh & Norman, 1965), short- and long-term memory (Peterson & Peterson, 1959; Atkinson & Shiffrin, 1968), working and reference memory (Baddeley & Hitch, 1974; Honig, 1978), and, finally, active and inactive memory (Lewis, 1979; Wagner, 1981).

The distinction between two types of memory is also adopted in this book, where they are referred to as short- and long-term retention. In this chapter we look at short-term retention; long-term retention is the focus of Chapter 9. The study of short-term retention in animals has been conducted with a variety of tasks. They reveal the common outcome that, after being exposed to a source of information, subjects are able to utilize it for only a restricted period.

The great spotted woodpecker stores food for winter, often pushing acorns through holes they have created in a tree trunk to produce an "acorn larder". The fact that the bird remembers where the food has been stored is evidence of retrieval of information from a long-term memory store.

METHODS OF STUDY

Tests of whether information about a previously presented stimulus has been retained for a short while involve presenting the stimulus on several occasions and looking for a change in the response to it. The repeated presentations could involve the stimulus by itself (habituation), or the stimulus could serve as a signal for a biologically important event (conditioning). These are very simple techniques, and one reason for discussing them is to demonstrate that even the most elementary behavioral phenomena rely on the involvement of memory processes. Of course, short-term memory processes are also influential in more complex tasks, and some of these are considered in the second part of this section.

Habituation

Hinde (1970, p. 577) defines habituation as "the relatively persistent waning of a response as a result of repeated stimulation which is not followed by any kind of reinforcement". To explain this effect, several authors have proposed that the initial exposure to the stimulus results in the formation of a memory or model of it (Sokolov, 1963; Wagner, 1976). If on subsequent trials the stimulus should match this model, then the reaction to it will be slight. The idea that the memory of a stimulus is important for habituation was raised in Chapter 3, where an experiment by Whitlow (1975) was said to support an account of habituation based on Wagner's (1981) "Standard Operating Procedures" (SOP) theory. In reality, it is more difficult than I implied in Chapter 3 to demonstrate the involvement of memory processes in habituation, as we shall see shortly when we discuss further Whitlow's (1975) experiment. First, a few examples should serve to demonstrate the ubiquity of habituation.

Jennings (1906) reports that paramecia—single-celled animals—react to being touched by contracting. With continued touching, however, the number of stimulations needed to produce this response increases to about twenty or thirty. In a study of the Pacific sea anemone, Logan (1975) has shown that the contractions produced by a novel strong stream of water are reduced considerably in magnitude after about thirty trials. The three-spined stickleback will respond aggressively to any territorial rivals, but this weakens with the continued presence of the same rival (Peeke & Veno, 1973). Finally, as Whitlow (1975) demonstrated, sounding a relatively loud tone to a rabbit will, among other reactions, produce a pronounced change in the rate of blood flow through the ear, brought about by vasoconstriction, which diminishes with repeated exposure to the tone.

In the experiment by Whitlow (1975) rabbits were placed into a sound- and light-proof chamber. After a while, a 1-second tone (S1) was presented, which was followed 30, 60, or 150 seconds later by another 1-second tone (S2). A resting period then followed (long enough for the effects of the first trial to dissipate), before the next trial began. This again consisted of the presentation of the pair of tones S1 and S2, separated by one of the three intervals. Training continued in this manner, with S1 and S2 on some trials being identical in frequency and on other trials being different.

The principal findings of the study are shown in Figure 8.1. The vertical axis represents the maximum change in vasoconstriction that was recorded on any trial. When S1 and S2 were identical (left-hand panel) and the interval between them was relatively short, the response to the second member of the pair was weaker than to the first. With a longer interval of 150 seconds, however, the response to the second tone recovered and was much the same as to the first. Thus the repetition of a tone can result in habituation, provided that the interval between its presentations is relatively short.

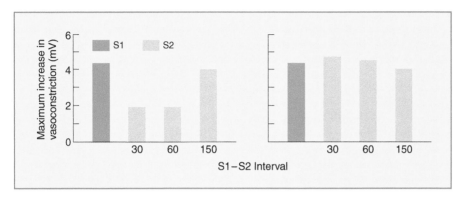

FIGURE 8.1 The maximum response to S1 and S2 in the study by Whitlow (1975) on trials when they were separated by intervals of 30, 60, or 150 seconds. The left-hand panel shows the results when S1 and S2 were identical, the right-hand panel when these stimuli were different. The measure of vasoconstriction is the increase from resting level in the output of a plethysmograph connected to the rabbit's ear (adapted from Whitlow, 1975).

As we saw in Chapter 3, Wagner (1976, 1981) explained these findings by proposing that the termination of S1 will leave a decaying representation of itself. If S2 is then presented before this decay is complete—that is, within 150 seconds—and it matches the representation of S1, habituation will be observed. But we need to consider alternative explanations for these results. For a short while after each response, the effector system may be fatigued, so that subsequent presentations of the tone will be unable to induce a large response. The simplicity of this account makes it attractive, and it may even be true for the findings with paramecia reported by Jennings (1906). But for the rabbit it is unlikely. The right-hand panel of Figure 8.1 indicates the maximum response to S1 and S2 for the trials when they differed. Although the two different tones elicited the same response in the same effector system, on these trials the response to S2 was as strong as that to S1, no matter how short the interval between them. This finding makes it difficult to believe that the weak response to S2, when it was the same as S1 and followed shortly after S1, was due to effector fatigue.

Yet another explanation for Whitlow's (1975) demonstration of habituation is that once a stimulus has been presented, the cells responsible for its reception become temporarily less sensitive. The occurrence of S2, when it is the same as S1, will then have less of an impact on the central nervous system and may produce a weaker response than S1. The results obtained when S1 and S2 were different are consistent with this interpretation, as the use of different stimuli will presumably excite different receptors.

Fortunately, an additional finding by Whitlow (1975) allows this account to be rejected. Subjects received similar training to that described previously, but the interval between S1 and S2 was always 60 seconds. On half the trials, a 2-second distractor, consisting of a flashing light followed by electrotactile stimulation, was presented 20 seconds after S1; on the remaining trials this complex stimulus was omitted. On trials when S1 and S2 were identical, the response to S2 was weak if the distractor was omitted; but when the distractor was presented, a much stronger response was elicited by S2. In other words, the distractor disrupted habituation with S2. This is usually referred to as **dishabituation**.

This example of dishabituation is important because it suggests that S2 is capable of eliciting a strong response, even though it is the same as S1 and the interval between them is short. This in turn implies that S2 is as well perceived as S1, even when they are the same, and that sensory adaptation is not an adequate explanation of habituation. One further possibility, however, is that the distractor enhances the responsiveness of the animal to any stimulus that is presented shortly after it (e.g. Thompson & Spencer, 1966). Thus S2 may have been poorly perceived by the rabbits but still elicited a strong response because of the arousing effects of the distractor. A reason for rejecting this possibility can be found in the impact of the distractor on trials when S1 and S2 were different. The arousing effects of the distractor should also be evident on these trials, yet the response to S2 was much the same on trials with and without the distractor. The account offered by Wagner (1976) for the dishabituating effect of the distractor when S1 and S2 were the same is quite straightforward. It assumes that this stimulus effectively erased the memory of Sl, or made subjects forget it, so that when S2 was presented it would not match a representation left by a preceding stimulus.

Whitlow's (1975) results strongly suggest that habituation in the rabbit depends on the existence of a memory of the repeatedly presented stimulus. The question is now raised as to whether all instances of habituation are due to the same process. Unfortunately, most investigations of habituation lack the necessary control conditions to enable unambiguous conclusions to be drawn from them. For the present, therefore, we must conclude that habituation, in at least some cases, depends on the ability of animals to remember stimuli for short periods of time. Whether this is true for all—or even the majority—of instances remains to be seen.

Trace conditioning

Typically, in Pavlovian conditioning, the conditioned stimulus (CS) remains on until at least the onset of the unconditioned stimulus (US); this technique is known as **delay conditioning**. With **trace conditioning**, the US is presented after the CS has been turned off, and for this training to be successful a memory of the CS must persist until the US occurs. Because trace conditioning is generally ineffective with relatively long **trace intervals**, it provides us with a method for studying short-term retention. In fact, it was thought originally that trace conditioning could only be effective with intervals extending up to a minute or so. Subsequent studies, however, have revealed that this is incorrect and that the short-term retention of some animals can extend up to several hours. An experiment by Smith and Roll (1967) demonstrates this point.

Thirsty rats were permitted to drink saccharin solution from a tube in a test chamber for several minutes. Later, at varying intervals, different groups were exposed to X-irradiation to induce illness. The animals were then returned to the chambers after 2 days and were allowed to drink either from a tube containing saccharin or from one containing water. Evidence of successful taste aversion conditioning was revealed by a low consumption of the saccharin solution. The results from this test are shown in Figure 8.2, which shows that even with a trace interval of 12 hours the consumption of saccharin was less than for a control group that was treated identically except that it never received X-irradiation.

In several experiments of this sort, rats have been given either water or some other flavor to drink in the interval between consumption of the flavor CS and the onset of illness, so it is quite implausible to suppose that the original flavor could have lingered in the mouth throughout the trace interval (Revusky, 1971). Instead, the more plausible interpretation of taste aversion learning over long delays is that a memory trace of the CS persists until the US occurs, and it is the existence of this trace that is responsible for successful conditioning.

The discovery that taste aversion conditioning is possible with extensive trace intervals prompted a number of authors to suggest that taste-aversion learning is not typical of conditioning in general. Seligman (1970) regards successful conditioning over such long delays as being due to the existence of a specialized taste learning process. According to Garcia, McGowan, and Green (1972), the mechanism responsible for this learning resides in a neural region that is relatively insulated from stimuli that do not arise from eating and drinking and is specialized to handle long trace intervals. Although these claims remain possible, it is certainly the case that the principles of associative learning that apply to conditioning, and which were discussed in Chapters 2 and 3, apply equally well to taste aversion conditioning (Mackintosh, 1974; Revusky, 1971, 1977). On the basis of this observation it would seem prudent to regard any differences between conditioning with stimuli such as tones, lights, and so on, rather than tastes, to be of degree rather than kind.

A further reason for believing that there is nothing special about taste aversion conditioning is that other, quite different, preparations have also resulted in learning over surprisingly long trace intervals. In an experiment by D'Amato and Buckiewicz (1980), monkeys were allowed to explore a T maze with a black arm and a striped arm. The next day they were confined in one arm for a minute and then placed into a holding chamber for 30 minutes. On their release they were put into the start box of the T maze and allowed to consume twelve raisins. The monkeys were then given a test in which they could choose between the two arms of the maze. A control group was treated identically, except that the raisins were not available on their return to the start box. On the choice trial the monkeys that had been fed the raisins showed a significantly greater preference than the controls for the arm in which they had been confined for a minute. The implication from this study is that the experimental group had retained, at least for 30 minutes, a memory of the arm in which they had been confined and that this then became associated with the raisins. D'Amato and Buckiewicz (1980) regarded the preference for the arm in which they had been confined as an example of conditioned attraction consequent on successful trace conditioning.

A similar finding has been reported by D'Amato, Safarjan, and Salmon (1981), except that the subjects were rats and they were held in a waste-paper basket before the choice trial in a T maze. One group was confined in an arm of the T maze for 40 minutes before being placed into the basket where they were fed after 2 hours. Once they had been fed, they were allowed to choose between the two arms of the maze. As with the monkeys, these subjects exhibited a greater preference for the arm in which they had been confined than a control group that was treated identically except that they were not fed in the waste-paper basket. Once again the explanation offered for this finding is that the memory of the arm of the maze was sustained for 2 hours and associated with the food that was eaten in the basket.

An intriguing study by Thomas, Lieberman, McIntosh, and Ronaldson (1983; see also Lieberman, McIntosh, & Thomas, 1979) identifies one factor that may be important for promoting learning across delays. Rats in Group Control were trained to run through a maze similar to that depicted in Figure 8.3. After entering the choice

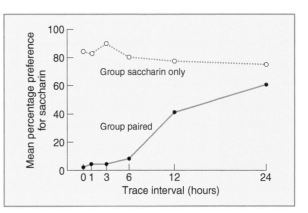

FIGURE 8.2 The preference of rats for drinking from a spout containing saccharin solution rather than water after they had previously received X-irradiation at different trace intervals following the consumption of saccharin solution (Group Paired). For Group Sacc. only, the consumption of saccharin was never followed by X-irradiation (adapted from Smith & Roll, 1967).

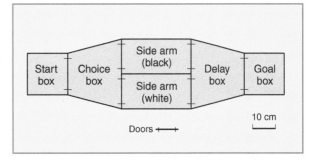

FIGURE 8.3 Plan of the maze used by Thomas et al. (1983). Copyright © American Psychological Association. Reproduced with permission.

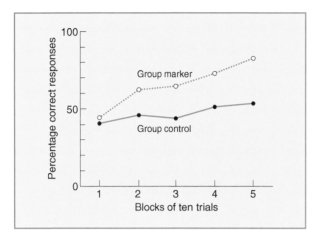

FIGURE 8.4 Percentage of correct responses by Group Control and Group Marker in ten-trial blocks in the marking study by Thomas et al. (1983) (adapted from Thomas et al., 1983).

box from the start box, they were permitted to enter either the black or the white side arm and then pass into the delay box, where they were confined for 2 minutes before being allowed to enter the goal box. Food was available in the goal box only on those trials when the rat had passed through the white arm. The results for this group are presented in Figure 8.4, which shows that despite a large amount of training there was virtually no increase in the preference for the white arm.

A second group in this study, Group Marker, was treated in much the same way except that both correct responses, of entering the white compartment, and incorrect responses, of entering the black compartment, were "marked" by being followed immediately with a burst of white noise for 2 seconds. This modest procedural change was sufficient to produce a substantial improvement in performance (see Figure 8.4). To explain this finding, Thomas et al. (1983) suggested that each burst of noise surprised the rat and resulted in the formation of a relatively salient memory of the response that had produced it. As a consequence, when food is delivered some 2 minutes later, subjects should be more likely in Group Marker than Group Control to remember their choice response and learn about its significance.

The radial maze

One task that has proved extremely popular for the study of short-term memory processes in animals is the radial maze. Figure 8.5 shows a radial maze, with a rat exploring it. A trial typically starts with a rat being placed into the arena at the center of the apparatus and with a pellet of food in a hole at the end of each arm. The rat is then allowed to explore the maze, where it remains until the food has been collected from each of the eight arms. During the preliminary trials a rat will often look at the landmarks beyond the maze when it reaches the end of an arm (Figure 8.6). After a number of trials, rats become very efficient at collecting food and rarely visit the same arm more than once per trial. It has been claimed that, to perform with this accuracy, the rat remembers either the arms that have been visited, or those that remain to be visited.

To examine how long information relevant to the solution of radial maze problems can be retained, Beatty and Shavalia (1980a) returned rats to their home cage after they had made four choices in an eight-arm maze. After a given period had elapsed, they were allowed to complete the trial. When this period of removal was 4 hours or less, subjects were still very accurate in selecting the arms they had not previously visited. There was, however, a marked and systematic decline in this accuracy when the delay was extended to 8, 12, and 24 hours. It is the fact—that the memory does not endure for longer than these periods—that points to the conclusion that performance on the radial maze is based on short-term retention of the arms that have been visited.

FIGURE 8.5 A rat exploring a radial maze.

There have also been attempts to establish how much information can be remembered when animals are solving radial maze problems. Olton (1978) has suggested that with an eight-arm maze the animal must remember seven locations to perform perfectly, but this might not be the limit of the rat's memory capacity. Olton, Collison, and Werz (1977) employed a seventeen-arm maze and found that, even in these circumstances, rats performed well above a level predicted by chance. Roberts (1979) constructed an eight-arm maze in which three subsidiary arms branched off from the end of the principal arms. On each trial, therefore, the subjects had to visit twenty-four different locations to collect food, and even in these circumstances they soon learned to perform with very few errors. Although these latter findings imply that rats can remember something approaching twenty-four different locations, an alternative explanation is possible. Observation of the rats in the maze revealed that they adopted stereotyped response patterns that may take the form, for example, of always turning right as they entered the central arena. Such a strategy, which is rarely evident in a more conventional eight-arm maze, would reduce considerably the number of locations that would have to be remembered in order to retrieve all the food efficiently. Thus, whereas the results show that rats are very good at performing in complex mazes, these results may not provide unambiguous information about the capacity of their memory.

FIGURE 8.6 A rat examining the landmarks beyond the end of one arm of a radial maze.

Delayed matching to sample

Chapter 7 introduced the technique of matching to sample as a means of studying relational learning. A simple modification of this task, known as **delayed matching to sample (DMTS)**, has proved extremely useful for the study of animal memory. However, unlike the robust effects just described, the implication of studies with DMTS is that short-term retention is rather poor.

Subjects are presented with one of two stimuli at the beginning of a trial. In the case of pigeons, this could be the illumination of a response key by either red or green light. After a while, this sample stimulus is turned off and nothing is presented for a period known as the **retention interval**. At the end of this interval, two different response keys are illuminated: one with red, the other with green light. These are referred to as the comparison stimuli. To gain reward, the pigeon must peck the comparison color that is the same as the sample presented on that particular trial. Pecks to the other color normally result in both keys being darkened and no reward. After the completion of the trial, whether the subject is correct or not, there is a period in which nothing happens—the **intertrial interval**—before the sample for the next trial is presented. To gain reward, then, the subject must store information at the time the sample is presented and make the correct choice between the two comparison stimuli.

Unlike the tasks already considered, DMTS is extremely difficult to learn. Subjects must first be trained with the single sample and two comparison stimuli presented simultaneously. Once they have learned to peck the comparison that matches the sample, the comparison stimuli are presented as soon as the sample is turned off. After considerable training, this 0-second retention interval is gradually extended, but rarely to very long intervals. For example, most researchers use delays of 5 to 10 seconds when pigeons are subjects. In one study, Grant (1976) obtained reasonably accurate performance by pigeons on DMTS with a 1-minute retention interval. This was achieved at the expense of considerable effort by both experimenter and subjects, as it required some 17,000 training trials.

Other species fare little better when this technique is adapted for them. D'Amato and O'Neill (1971) found with monkeys that accurate retention was possible for 2 minutes, and with careful training this can be extended to 9 minutes (D'Amato & Worsham, 1972). Using dolphins, accurate DMTS has been achieved with a retention interval of 4 minutes (Herman & Thompson, 1982).

A number of experiments have examined how much information can be stored during the retention interval with DMTS, and their findings suggest that it is relatively little. Riley and Roitblat (1978) employed a version of DMTS in which two samples were projected simultaneously onto the same key at the outset of a trial. Pigeons were required to remember information about both in order to perform accurately. Performance in this instance was inferior to that when only a single sample was used. The implication of this finding is that the memory of pigeons is stretched when they must retain simultaneously information about two items, even for short periods. Although this conclusion has been challenged (Cox & D'Amato, 1982), it is supported by more recent evidence (Langley & Riley, 1993).

The most obvious account of successful delayed matching is that subjects remember the sample until the comparison stimuli are presented, whereupon the comparison stimulus that matches the memory of the sample can be selected (see, for example, Roberts & Grant, 1976). The memory of the sample in this instance is referred to as a **retrospective code**, because it is of a stimulus that has already occurred. But this rather obvious view may be wrong, at least under certain circumstances (Gaffan, 1977; Honig, 1978; Roitblat, 1980). As an alternative, it may well be that at the time the sample is presented a **prospective code** is formed based on the instruction "peck the green comparison stimulus". Obviously, the memory of an inarticulate animal would not encode the information in precisely this way, but the point should be clear that it is knowledge about a mode of responding that is being stored.

Much of the evidence that relates to this proposal is based on experimental procedures that are not among the easiest to describe, or comprehend. In addition, as Grant (1981) concludes from his review of these studies, their interpretation is difficult as they occasionally yield ambiguous findings. Little space will therefore be devoted to this issue, except to note that at least one experiment provides good evidence that pigeons rely on a prospective code when engaged in a delayed matching to sample problem (Roitblat, 1980).

Theoretical interpretation

Relatively little has been said thus far about the processes that are responsible for the findings from studies of short-term retention in animals. The simplest approach would be to assume that there is a single system concerned with the short-term retention of information. If this is correct, then we might expect a given animal to remember similar amounts of information for similar intervals, irrespective of the task employed. But this has not proved to be the case. Using the radial maze, for example, the impression would be gained that short-term retention is both durable and of large capacity. In stark contrast, if the results from studies of DMTS are taken at face value, then short-term retention in animals would seem to be rather poor. The question is thus raised whether success on the different procedures that have been discussed depends on different memory processes. I do not believe it is possible to answer this question with complete certainty, but I favor the possibility that all the findings we have been reviewing are due to the operation of the same memory system. To account for the variety of outcomes that have been reported we must look to differences in the procedures that led to them.

One reason for the excellent memory revealed by the radial maze is that there are many features that enable the different arms to be identified. They occupy different spatial locations and they will be placed next to different features of the room housing the equipment. In contrast, with DMTS the samples are generally presented in a very similar manner and differ in only a single attribute: usually color. Perhaps it is easier to remember items that are composed of many distinctive attributes. Support for such a possibility comes from a study by Mazmanian and Roberts (1983) who trained two groups of rats on a radial maze. One group was permitted unrestricted views of the room while running in the maze; for the other, the careful placement of screens allowed only a restricted view of the room. In the latter case, the information available to identify the arms must have been considerably reduced, and, as indicated by the substantial number of errors, they were very much harder to remember.

A further difference between the various techniques we have discussed is the frequency with which the trials are conducted. Typically, conditioning with long trace intervals is successful only when there is a very long interval between the trials, or in the limiting case when only a single trial is given (e.g. Smith & Roll, 1967; Kaplan, 1984). Trials with the radial maze tend to be performed once a day. In the case of DMTS, sixty or more trials may be presented in a single session with an average intertrial interval of only 30 seconds. It turns out that massing trials in this way can have a profoundly disruptive effect on performance on this kind of task and may well contribute to the difference between DMTS and the other tasks. To understand why this should be, it is necessary to discuss the factors that are responsible for forgetting. We will turn to this issue shortly.

Surprisingly, the manner in which reward is delivered might also be responsible for the outcome of a memory experiment. For example, in the radial maze different choice responses lead to rewards in different locations, whereas for delayed matching to sample reward is normally delivered in the same location. Williams, Butler, and Overmier (1990) have shown that if DMTS is conducted with the two choice responses followed by reward delivered in different locations, then considerable delays can be tolerated between the end of the sample and the onset of the choice stimuli. Various reasons for this effect are reviewed by Linwick, Overmier, Peterson, and Mertens (1988) and by Williams et al. (1990). For the present, the important conclusion to draw is that the way in which reward is presented might be at least partially responsible for superior short-term retention that is seen with the radial maze rather than with delayed matching to sample.

FORGETTING

In all of the experiments considered in the previous section, the retention of information may be short-lived simply because it decays with the passage of time. More detailed consideration of such forgetting, however, suggests an alternative, or at least additional, explanation. Items are not remembered in isolation; instead, they are presented against a background of many other events. It may be that this additional material is responsible for forgetting, either because its presence in memory serves as a source of confusion or because it displaces the representation of the target from memory. In either case, the material can be said to induce forgetting by interference.

At a procedural level, it is possible to identify two potential sources of interference. **Proactive interference** is said to occur when information acquired prior to the target item disrupts its retention. **Retroactive interference** is used to describe the forgetting of information that occurs because it is followed by something distracting. Although both types of interference may be due to the same process, this distinction is useful, if only because it serves to organize a rather large body of diverse experimental findings. After examining a number of demonstrations of proactive and retroactive interference, we consider the various theories that have been offered to explain these effects.

Proactive interference

A modified DMTS design was adopted by Grant and Roberts (1973) to study proactive interference with pigeons. On control trials, straightforward DMTS with only a single sample was conducted, but at the start of other trials the two different samples were presented in succession, separated by a gap of either 0 or 10 seconds. For these trials, subjects were rewarded if they pecked the comparison stimulus that was the same as the more recently presented sample. When the interval between the two samples was 10 seconds, subjects chose the correct comparison with an accuracy equivalent to that when only a single sample was presented. But when the interval between the samples was 0 seconds, there was a significant reduction in the accuracy of matching. Thus the presence of the first sample can be said to have interfered proactively with the memory of the second one, but only when the interval between them was minimal.

A between-trials demonstration of proactive interference with DMTS is provided by Grant (1975). Pigeons were given a single delayed matching trial with two stimuli, X and Y, serving as the comparisons, and X as the sample. Immediately following this trial, they received another trial with the same comparison stimuli, but on this occasion Y served as the sample. Performance on the second trial was less accurate in these circumstances than when the first trial was omitted. There are at least two explanations for this finding. One is that the memory of the sample from the first trial persisted into the second trial and made it harder for subjects to identify the correct comparison because of the presence of a memory of each sample (Grant, 1975; Roberts & Grant, 1976). A second explanation is that the subject remembered the previously rewarded choice that it made (White, Parkinson, Brown, & Wixted, 2004). If the subject was correct on the first trial, which it generally was, then it would carry over to the second trial a tendency to repeat the response, which, on this occasion, would be incorrect. By studying carefully the errors that occur on one trial, in terms of which choice was rewarded on a previous trial, White et al. (2004), were able to reveal support for the second of these explanations.

Proactive interference has also been found in the radial maze by Olton (1978), who demonstrated that the choices on one trial with the radial maze can influence the errors made on the subsequent trial (remember that a trial is defined as being completed when all the arms have been visited). During a trial, the subject must keep a record of the arms it has already visited or has still to visit. If this information should be retained, then its presence at the start of a new trial could be extremely disruptive. Normally, trials with the radial maze are conducted at the rate of one a day, and this problem does not occur because the information about one trial is likely to have disappeared long before the start of the next trial. But if the interval between trials is reduced, then the potential for the memories of one trial to interfere proactively with performance on the next one will be increased. To test this possibility, Olton (1978) conducted eight radial maze trials a day with 1 minute between each trial. Figure 8.7 shows the results plotted for eight successive trials in one day. On Trial 1, rats made very few errors and it was only when they had visited seven of the eight arms that they occasionally made a mistake by revisiting one of the arms. With an increase in the number of trials, performance on the latter part of each trial showed more errors than on the first trial. This deterioration in performance can be regarded as an effect of proactive interference due to the initial training trials.

Retroactive interference

A straightforward demonstration of retroactive interference comes from the study by Whitlow (1975; discussed on p. 193), who found that the presentation of a 2-second distractor in the 60-second interval between two identical tones eliminated the habituation normally observed to the second tone. Because it has been argued that habituation results from the persistence of a memory for the first tone, the distractor can be said to have interfered with this memory. Such an effect is referred to as retroactive interference because the distractor disrupted the memory of a previous event.

Retroactive interference has been revealed with pigeons by Grant (1988) using DMTS. During the interval between the termination of the sample and the onset of the comparison stimuli, there was an increase in the illumination of the test chamber. This manipulation appears to have interfered retroactively with the memory of the sample because subjects found greater difficulty in identifying the correct comparison stimulus than when there was either no change or a reduction in the level of illumination. Similar effects have been observed with dolphins (Herman, 1975) and monkeys (D'Amato, 1973). A surprising finding is that for monkeys and pigeons the only effective distractor for DMTS is an increase in illumination (D'Amato, 1973;

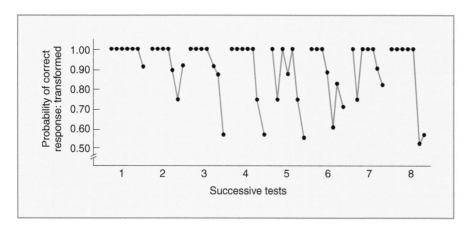

FIGURE 8.7 The corrected mean probability of a correct response for choices on an eight-arm radial maze when 8 test trials were given in succession (adapted from Olton, 1978).

Grant & Roberts, 1976; Kraemer & Roberts, 1984). Thus, for example, retroactive interference does not occur when sounds are presented in the retention interval. This is true for monkeys even when the sounds consist of the vocalizations of other members of the species.

Retroactive interference can also be observed with the radial maze, but here the distracting event must be quite substantial. A typical experiment involves confining a rat to the central arena after it has made four forced choices in an eight-arm maze (Maki, Brokofsky, & Berg, 1979; Beatty & Shavalia, 1980b). A variety of events—such as lights, sounds, odors, and food—are then presented before the subject can continue with the trial. Very often, such treatment has no influence at all on the four remaining choices, and more dramatic means of demonstrating retroactive interference are required. One technique that has been tried is to remove the animal from the radial maze after it has made four choices and to give it a trial with a different piece of apparatus. Such an interpolated trial can involve another eight-arm maze and be conducted in either the same or a different room. When conducted in the same room, the second maze may be physically superimposed on the first. Despite the similarity of the distracting interpolated trial with the original trial, it is still difficult to demonstrate retroactive interference. Indeed, Roberts (1981) reports that it is necessary to expose subjects to three identical mazes in different rooms before they display any significant decline in accuracy on the remaining four choices of the target trial.

THEORETICAL INTERPRETATION

Two accounts have dominated theorizing about short-term retention. According to **decay theory**, forgetting occurs because, once an event has been presented to an animal, information about it gradually, and spontaneously, decays. **Limited capacity theory**, on the other hand, asserts that animals are restricted in the amount of short-term information they are able to retain at the same time. Forgetting then occurs because information about an item is displaced by more recent events. Even though these simple principles can account for many of the effects outlined previously, I will argue that both accounts are contradicted by certain findings.

Decay theory

Roberts and Grant (1974, 1976) proposed that the presentation of a stimulus activates a representation, or trace, that persists after the stimulus has been removed. But traces do not last indefinitely; as soon as the stimulus ends, the trace starts to decay. The initial strength and persistence of this trace is determined by the intensity and duration of the stimulus concerned. An important feature of this theory is that the strength of a trace is not influenced at all by the presence of other short-term traces. The theory asserts, therefore, that short-term retention is of unrestricted capacity and the number of items stored is determined by the frequency with which they occur in the environment.

In a task such as DMTS it is assumed that if a number of items are in memory when the comparison stimuli are presented, then the one with the strongest trace will determine the subject's choice. Errors will occur if the traces of two samples are present and of equal strength, because it will be difficult to identify the relevant one. This outcome would be expected to occur in the study by Grant and Roberts (1973) when a target sample was preceded by one that was irrelevant. Increasing the interval between the two samples will enhance the discrepancy in the strength of their traces and make it easier to identify the trace of the correct sample. This account thus correctly explains the finding that a distracting sample produces most proactive interference when it is presented immediately before the sample. In a similar way, decay theory can also account for the proactive interference produced by one trial that shortly precedes another (Grant, 1975; Olton, 1978).

A problem with decay theory, as Grant (1981, p. 229) has pointed out, is that it does not provide a very good account of the sort of retroactive interference effects reported by Whitlow (1975). In that study, presentation of a distractor between a pair of identical tones attenuated habituation to the second tone. Because the distractor should not influence the memory of the preceding tone, it is hard to understand why it had this effect. For similar reasons, it is not clear why a change in illumination should interfere retroactively with DMTS. Another problem with decay theory is that it is not clear why animals should find it harder to remember two samples when they are presented together, rather than one sample in a DMTS experiment. Such a finding, which was mentioned earlier, has been reported by Riley and Roitblat (1978). As we will see, limited capacity theories are able to explain these effects.

Limited capacity theory

Wagner (1976) has proposed that there is a limit to the number of traces of stimuli that can be retained simultaneously. The introduction of a stimulus, therefore, will not only result in a representation of itself being formed, it will also weaken or displace any previously formed traces. These principles explain the effects of the distractor in the habituation experiment with rabbits by Whitlow (1975).

The retroactive interference effects that posed a problem for decay theory can also be understood within this framework. Presenting a distractor after a target, such as a sample in DMTS, will weaken the trace of the target and make it that much harder for it to be effective at the time of testing. The retroactive interference observed with the radial maze is also consistent with this account. Furthermore, by adding the assumption that existing memory traces can restrict the strength of new traces, this theory can account for many of the effects of proactive interference. Thus it would be difficult to store a list of arms that have been visited during a trial with the radial maze if there already exist numerous traces of arms visited in previous trials.

Wagner (1976) has suggested that the extent to which a distracting stimulus can displace other stimuli from active memory is determined by how surprising it is. Distractors that are surprising or unexpected are believed to disrupt the short-term retention of stimuli to a greater extent than distractors whose occurrence is fully expected. If this is correct, then surprising distractors should be especially good at promoting retroactive interference. To test this idea, Terry (1996) made use of a task known as serial delayed alternation. Consider the T-maze depicted in the left-hand side of Figure 8.8. A rat might be placed in the start box at the bottom and be required to turn left when it reaches the choice point in order to obtain food. A barrier has been inserted at the choice point to prevent the animal from choosing the wrong arm. Shortly after this trial, the rat is returned to the start box with no barriers in the maze. To gain reward, the rat at the choice point must select the arm opposite to the one selected on the previous trial (right-hand side of Figure 8.8). Rats find this task remarkably easy. To perform correctly on the second trial, the rat must remember

FIGURE 8.8 Sketch of the T-maze used by Terry (1996) to study short-term retention in rats. A rat was placed in the bottom of the maze shown on the left and had to collect food from the left-hand arm. The solid line represents a barrier that prevented rats from entering the other arm. They were then placed in the bottom of the maze shown to the right and had to collect food from the right-hand arm.

the direction in which it turned during the first trial until it reaches the choice point. In his experiment, Terry (1996) arranged for food to be presented to the rat during the interval between the first and second trial. He found that performance on the second trial was unimpaired if the food was expected during this interval, but was seriously affected if the food was unexpected. The obvious implication of this result is that the unexpected food disrupted the short-term retention of information acquired during the first trial, and thus made it hard for the rat to determine the direction in which to head on the second trial.

Despite its successes, there remain problems for limited capacity theory. It does not explain why, for pigeons and monkeys, DMTS is susceptible to retroactive interference only when the distractor is a change of illumination. The use of other distractors should also reduce the trace strength of the sample and result in forgetting. In addition, it is not immediately clear why immunity to retroactive interference should be so much greater for tasks such as the radial maze than, say, habituation.

Deliberate forgetting

As it has been described, animal memory is a rather passive repository for information, with the short-term duration of a memory trace being determined by its intensity and, perhaps, the number of other traces that are present. Recently, a number of authors have suggested that the storage of information may be more flexible than this account implies, and when information is irrelevant to a task it might be discarded by a process of deliberate or active forgetting.

Olton (1978) was among the first to suggest that rats actively forget information that is no longer relevant, supporting this claim by his study of proactive interference that we considered earlier. Olton (1978) was impressed by the small amount of proactive interference when rats were given a series of massed trials on the radial maze, that is, by the accuracy of his rats when they were given several trials in succession (see Figure 8.7). Accordingly, he proposed that rats can erase or reset the contents of memory at the end of each trial. In this way the memory of arms visited on one trial would not be able to interfere with the task of trying to remember which arms had already been visited on a subsequent trial.

Subsequent findings suggest that Olton (1978) may have greatly exaggerated his rats' efficiency. Roberts and Dale (1981) repeated Olton's study, and at the same time they kept a record of the pattern of responding within each trial. Although they were able essentially to replicate Olton's (1978) findings, they discovered that the use of massed trials resulted in rats adopting a response strategy of always choosing the adjacent arm. This outcome indicates that the memories formed on one trial may not be reset at the end of a trial. Instead, to overcome the potentially interfering effects of these memories, the rats were forced to find a method that did not involve remembering the arms they had visited. A further observation by Roberts and Dale (1981) is consistent with this interpretation. At the start of a trial rats showed a marked tendency to avoid the arm selected last on the preceding trial. This bias should not be evident if information about the preceding trial had been erased from memory on its completion.

Although there may be little evidence for the deliberate forgetting of information from one trial to the next, it is possible that rats employ deliberate memory strategies within a radial maze trial. Thus far, I have followed Olton (1978) and others in assuming that the radial maze task imposes an increasing burden on memory as each trial progresses. After seven choices, for example, the rat must remember seven arms if it is to choose the one unvisited arm. A moment's thought, however, suggests that this is an uneconomical strategy. At this point in the trial, the rat need only remember the one unvisited arm. The most efficient strategy, in terms of minimizing the burden on memory, is to remember the arms already visited, in order to avoid them, for the first half of the trial, and the arms that have not been visited, in order to select them, for the second half of the trial. In this way the subject could perform the entire task without having to remember more than half the arms of the maze.

Evidence that rats do indeed adopt this sensible strategy can be found in a study by Cook, Brown, and Riley (1985), using a twelve-arm radial maze. Once they had learned the problem, they were occasionally removed from the apparatus for a period of 15 minutes after the second, fourth, sixth, eighth, or tenth choice. If they always remembered the arms they had already visited on a trial, then this additional delay should be most difficult to cope with when their memory is most overburdened, that is, after ten choices. However, if they remembered the arms that remained to be visited, then the delay should be most disruptive after two choices. Instead, they made most errors when the delay was imposed after six choices. The implication of this finding is that the subject's memory is most burdened at the half-way point in a trial, and this is exactly what would be expected if they adopted the strategy just outlined. There are also reasons for believing that, like rats, pigeons remember the choices that have been made during the early trials of a radial maze problem, but later in the trial they remember the choices that remain to be made (Zentall, Steirn, & Jackson-Smith, 1990).

Turning now to the pigeon, it has also been suggested that this species is capable of deliberate forgetting. After giving subjects standard DMTS training, Maki and Hegvik (1980) introduced trials in which the sample was immediately followed by one of two stimuli. One stimulus, known as the remember cue, signaled that the comparison stimuli would be presented at the end of the retention interval. The other stimulus, the forget cue, signaled that the comparison stimuli would not be presented. On these latter trials, then, there was no need to remember the sample, and the forget cue could serve as a signal for the sample to be forgotten. To examine whether the forget cue served this function, subjects were occasionally tricked by being presented with the comparison stimuli at the end of the forget cue trials. If this cue makes pigeons actively forget the sample, then on these test trials they should be very poor at identifying the correct comparison. The results were consistent with this prediction (see also Grant & Soldat, 1995).

The issue of whether animals are capable of deliberately forgetting information has been raised only recently. We should not be surprised, therefore, to find that the interpretation of many of the results in this area is still a matter for debate (e.g. Roper & Zentall, 1993). But if it should be discovered that animals are capable of deliberately forgetting, and perhaps also deliberately remembering, then this would have important implications for our understanding of forgetting in general. We should have to acknowledge that neither decay nor interference theory by themselves can provide an adequate account of forgetting because superimposed on these processes would be deliberate memory strategies that greatly influenced their outcome.

SERIAL POSITION EFFECTS

Thompson and Herman's (1977) test with bottle-nosed dolphins revealed a recency effect of remembering accurately the later items of a list. There was no indication of a primacy effect in which the early items would have been remembered well.

When humans are given a list of words and asked to recall them immediately in any order, they typically recall the first and last items more accurately than those in the middle. This pattern is referred to as the serial position curve. The good recall of early items is referred to as **primacy**; the term **recency** refers to the good recall of the later items. Recency is said to occur because the items are held in a limited capacity short-term memory store. The most recently presented item should be the most prominent in this store, and thus the easiest to retrieve (Baddeley, 1997). Primacy, on the other hand, is normally explained by assuming that the initial items of a list become memorable by being rehearsed verbally to a greater extent than the later items (Rundus, 1971; Baddeley, 1997). The reliability with which serial position effects are found with humans has led researchers to investigate whether they can also be found with animals. We have seen that animals can be assumed to have a limited capacity short-term memory, which implies that they too should reveal recency effects. However, it is unreasonable to suppose that animals rehearse materially verbally and they might not be expected to reveal primacy effects.

In support of the first of these predictions, recency effects have been relatively easy to demonstrate with a variety of species. Thompson and Herman (1977) presented bottle-nosed dolphins with a list of six sounds, after which they were presented with a test sound. On some trials the test sound was different to those in the list; on others, it was identical to a member of the list, but the position of the one to which it corresponded varied from trial to trial. The task confronting the dolphin was to indicate whether or not the test sound had occurred in the list.

Figure 8.9 shows the accuracy with which this task was performed for the various list positions. When the test sound was identical to the last member of the list, a recency effect of responding very accurately was revealed. This accuracy declined, however, as the serial position of the sound that matched the test sound moved towards the front of the list. There was, however, no indication of a primacy effect, as performance was very poor when the test sound matched the initial member of the list. Using variations of this technique, similar effects have been revealed with rhesus monkeys (Gaffan, 1977; Gaffan & Weiskrantz, 1980), squirrel monkeys (Roberts & Kraemer, 1981), pigeons (Macphail, 1980), and rats (Roberts & Smythe, 1979).

In keeping with the prediction concerning primacy, this effect has been reported only rarely (e.g. Dimattia & Kesner, 1984; Wright et al., 2003), and some controversy surrounds the way in which several of these findings should be interpreted (D. Gaffan, 1983; E. A. Gaffan, 1992; but see Wright & Rivera, 1997). However, a study by Harper, McLean, and Dalrymple-Alford (1993) shows that it is possible to obtain a robust primacy effect with rats tested in a twelve-arm radial maze. Experienced rats were placed into the central arena of the maze with their access to each arm blocked by a door. The experimenter then opened the door for one arm and allowed the rat to run to the end to retrieve a chocolate chip. On returning to the central arena, the door was closed behind the rat and another was opened. Training continued in this manner until the rat had visited seven arms. Testing then began with the rat being confined to the central arena for 5 seconds before it was offered a choice between two open doors: One provided access to an arm that had just been visited; the other led to an arm that had not been visited on this particular trial. To earn food, the subject was required to select the arm that had already been visited. Testing took place over a number of sessions, with a different set of seven arms being selected by the experimenter for each session.

The curve with solid circles in the left-hand panel of Figure 8.10 shows the accuracy with which subjects selected the familiar rather than the novel arm on the test trials. These results are plotted according to the serial position with which the familiar arm was entered in the training list. When the familiar arm was experienced either early or late in the list of seven arms, subjects selected it with confidence. But when the arm occupied an intermediate position in the training list, subjects were less likely to select the familiar arm. These results thus constitute a clear demonstration of both a primacy and a recency effect in list learning by rats.

Harper et al.'s (1993) results show that serial position curves are not unique to humans. Moreover, some of the factors that are known to influence the shape of the serial position curve with humans have been shown by Harper et al. (1993) to have a similar influence with rats. If delay is allowed to elapse between the learning of a list and the test trial for humans, then the primacy effect remains but the recency effect is reduced (Glanzer & Cunitz, 1966). Likewise, if humans engage in some activity, such as counting backwards, immediately after they have been exposed to a list then once again testing reveals a disruption in the effect of recency but not primacy (Roediger & Crowder, 1975).

To test for these effects with rats, Harper et al. (1993) trained a group in the manner described above, but a delay of 30 seconds elapsed before they received the test trial. The results from these trials are shown by the curve with the open circles in the left-hand panel of Figure 8.10. Extending the interval between training and testing from 5 to 30 seconds reduced the recency effect, and left the primacy effect more or less unaffected. In a second study, the gap between the end of training and testing was always 10 seconds. For a control condition, subjects were simply retained in the central arena for this period, whereas for the experimental condition they were allowed to eat chocolate freely during this period. The results in the right-hand panel of Figure 8.10 show that the control condition (solid circles) resulted in the typical serial position curve, but eating chocolate in the experimental condition (open circles) eliminated the recency component of this curve.

Harper et al. (1993) admit to being unable to offer a convincing explanation for their findings. They are certainly unwilling to consider that their rats indulged in verbal rehearsal. Instead, they focused on the similarity between their results and those obtained with humans. This similarity, they suggest, should enable us to use animals as models to help us understand the neurobiology of normal memory processes in humans, and to devise new treatments when these processes go wrong.

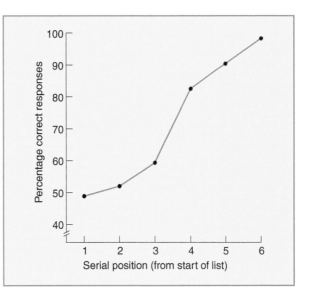

FIGURE 8.9 Percentage of correct recognitions by dolphins of a sound that had previously been presented in a list of six items, according to its serial position (adapted from Thompson & Herman, 1977).

METAMEMORY

Humans are able not only to recall particular items of information, we can also comment on the quality of our memory for the item and how confident we are that it is accurate. For example, we are quite comfortable using phrases such as "it's on the tip of my tongue" to indicate our belief about how readily we believe we can retrieve

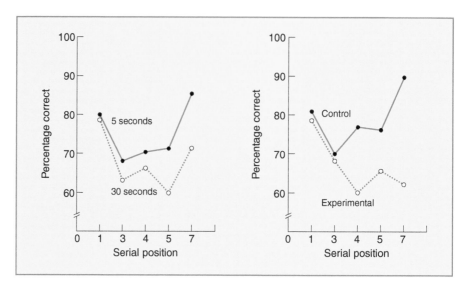

FIGURE 8.10 Mean percentages of correct choices of a previously visited arm in a radial maze, from one that had not been visited, as a function of the position of the correct arm in a sequence of seven previously visited arms. In one experiment (left-hand panel) the choice trial for one group was given 5 seconds after the seven arms had been visited, but for another group this interval was 30 seconds. In a second experiment (right-hand panel) the choice trial was delayed for 10 seconds during which an experimental, but not a control group was allowed to eat chocolate (adapted from Harper et al., 1993).

a memory for a particular event. This ability to comment on how accessible a memory is, or how confident we are that the memory is true, is referred to as **metamemory**, and demonstrating its existence in humans is made easy by the use of language. The experiments in this section were conducted to establish whether animals are able to demonstrate their confidence in how accurately they are able to remember an event. Their lack of language means that designing a suitable experiment poses a much greater challenge than for similar work with humans.

Hampton (2001) used a particularly ingenious experiment to study metamemory in two rhesus monkeys. It was based on delayed matching to sample but each of four different photographs could serve as the sample. In a conventional task based on this design, subjects would be shown one of the four pictures as the sample for a study phase. This picture would then be removed and, after a retention interval, all four pictures would be shown together and reward would be given for touching the picture that matched the sample. The procedure used by Hampton (2001) was made more complicated by presenting one of two different displays at the end of the retention interval (Figure 8.11). For forced-choice trials, the display at the end of the retention interval consisted of only Pattern A. Touching Pattern A produced the four pictures and a touch to the correct picture resulted in food. On free trials, the display consisted of two patterns, Pattern A and Pattern B. A touch to Pattern A had the same effect as touching this pattern on forced-choice trials, but a touch to Pattern B resulted in a new picture being displayed. A touch to this picture yielded food, but it was less attractive than the reward that was delivered whenever the correct picture from the array of four was selected.

KEY TERM

Metamemory
An individual's knowledge about the strength, accuracy, and ease of accessibility of a specific memory.

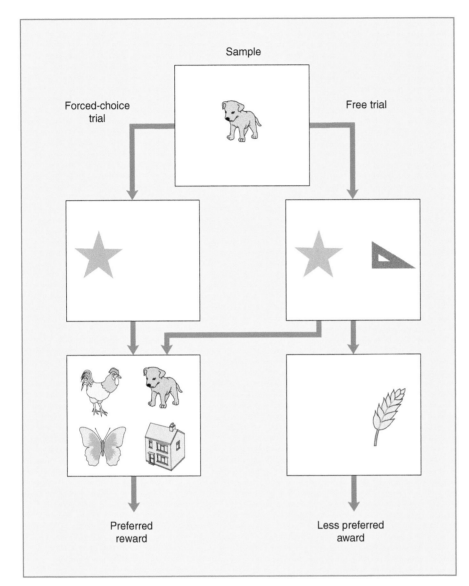

Sample

Forced-choice
trial

Free trial

Preferred
reward

Less preferred
award

FIGURE 8.11 Diagram showing the sequence of events in a study of metamemory by Hampton (2001). Trials started with the display of a sample stimulus. On some occasions, a short while after this stimulus had been turned off a single stimulus was shown for a forced-choice trial. Touching this stimulus resulted in four stimuli being shown, and a touch to the one matching the sample produced a preferred reward. On other occasions, two stimuli were shown a short while after the sample was turned off. Responses to the stimulus on these free trials that was the same as the one shown on the forced-choice trials had the same effect as on those trials. Responses to the other stimulus produced a new stimulus on the screen and touching this stimulus produced a less preferred reward (adapted from Hampton, 2001).

Suppose a monkey could remember perfectly the sample that had just been presented whenever he was required to choose between Patterns A and B on a free trial. By choosing Pattern A he would gain access to the four pictures, select the correct one and receive his preferred reward. Thus a well-trained monkey with a perfect memory should always choose Pattern A over Pattern B. But suppose the monkey's memory was variable and that on some trials it had forgotten the sample by the time Patterns A and B were presented. On these occasions, if he selected Pattern A he would be unable to select the correct picture from the array of four and would be forced to choose one of them at random. The chances of receiving reward for adopting this strategy are one in four. On the other hand, if he selected Pattern B he would receive reward even though it was not his favorite kind. In keeping with this analysis, the two monkeys when confronted with Patterns A and B together would sometimes choose one and sometimes choose the other. An explanation for this outcome is that the monkeys appreciated on some trials that their memory of the sample was good—in which case they would select A—and on other trials that their memory of the sample was poor—in which case they would select B.

Another explanation for the foregoing result is that the monkeys selected A and B at random. Fortunately, the results from the forced-choice trials allow the second of these explanations to be rejected. On these trials, a monkey's memory for the sample can be expected to be occasionally good and occasionally poor. The overall accuracy with which the sample can be identified from the pool of four pictures can therefore be expected to reflect an average of both the good and poor performance of the subject. Turning now to the free trials, if Pattern A is selected only when the memory of the sample is good, then the monkey should be able to identify the sample in the array of four pictures with greater accuracy than its average performance on the forced-choice trials. The pattern of results confirmed this prediction. For example, one monkey was correct on approximately 90% of the occasions that it selected A on the free trials, but on only 65% of the trials when it was forced to select A. The implication of these results is that through trial and error on the free trials the monkeys learned to press Pattern A when the memory for the sample was strong, and to press Pattern B when the memory for the sample was weak. This clever experiment thus demonstrates that the strength of a memory trace or, in other words, the strength of a reaction to a previously presented stimulus, can serve as a cue for discriminating between patterns A and B.

Hampton (2001) takes the interpretation of his findings a step further by suggesting that the monkeys knew whether they could remember the sample, and decided to select either Pattern A or B on the basis of this knowledge. He further suggested that this type of decision is associated with conscious thought in humans and raises the possibility that his findings might be a consequence of conscious thought in animals. We saw at the end of Chapter 6 that a similar conclusion was reached by Smith et al. (2003) concerning their study of metacognition in

Hampton's (2001) study delivered findings that suggested that rhesus monkeys had the capacity to make a type of decision that is associated with conscious thought in humans.

monkeys when solving discriminations. As in that case, Hampton's evidence is certainly consistent with the claim that monkeys are conscious of some of their mental processes, but we are frustrated by the lack of methodology to determine if this is actually true because it is not possible to observe directly the mental states of an animal. Hampton (2001) acknowledges that the evidence in support of his proposal is not watertight and offers an alternative, more conventional, explanation for his findings. For a variety of reasons, the sample might leave a memory trace that is stronger on some trials than others. Hampton (2001) suggests that a strong trace would create an internal cue that would be different to that created by a weak trace. Through a combination of trial and error and associative learning, the monkey could then learn to select Pattern A on free trials when the cue for the strong trace was present, because this leads to more reward than selecting Pattern B. Likewise, it would learn to select Pattern B, rather than A, on free trials when the cue created by the weak trace was present. Even if we opt for this explanation, the experiment is still important because it is one of the few to demonstrate that animals are able to solve discriminations based on the strength of their reaction to a previously presented stimulus (see also Cowey & Stoerig, 1995). To close this chapter on a comparative note, attempts to reveal metamemory in species other than primates, such as pigeons (e.g. Inman & Shettleworth, 1999), have not been successful.

CHAPTER 9

CONTENTS

Long-term retention

The two outstanding features of long-term retention in humans are its capacity and durability. A moment's reflection will reveal its large capacity when it is appreciated that it holds the memories of our entire life. And the durability of human memory is revealed most forcefully by an elderly person's recollections of childhood. These characteristics of large capacity and durability can also be found in studies of long-term retention in animals.

When talking about long-term memory in animals, the adage "an elephant never forgets" inevitably comes to mind. Whether this is true is hard to tell because of the dearth of studies of elephant memory. Rensch (1956, 1957) found that elephants mastered a simple discrimination with difficulty, but then remembered it for a year. Nissani (2004) cites a study, described in Stevens (1978), which revealed that an elephant could learn a simple discrimination and remember it for 8 years. On the basis of this slender evidence, Nissani (2004) cautiously agreed with the delightful claim of Carrington (1958) that "elephants are not sufficiently intelligence to grasp an idea easily or quickly in the early stages, but once it has penetrated their somewhat slow brains it is virtually ineradicable". Given that elephants can live for nearly 70 years, the existing studies can hardly be said to have tested these conclusions rigorously. We turn now to consider long-term retention in other animals where, in general, there is a greater body of evidence on which to base our discussion.

Rensch (1956, 1957) found that elephants were capable of mastering a simple discrimination, albeit with some difficulty, but they would then go on to remember it for a whole year, supporting the old adage "an elephant never forgets".

CAPACITY

As far as the amount of information that can be retained by an animal is concerned, the record, at present, is held by Clark's nutcracker. Every autumn, these birds collect as many as 33,000 pine seeds and bury them in shallow holes (caches) at an average of four seeds per cache. Throughout the winter and spring the birds retrieve these hidden supplies to feed both themselves and their offspring. According to Vander Wall (1982), this requires the nutcrackers to revisit between 2500 and 3750 different caches. Because the seeds are most frequently recovered from caches made by the retriever, these birds are believed to store sufficient information to identify well over 3000 different locations. Even though strategies might be employed to reduce the amount that must be remembered, for instance, by burying a number of seeds close to one another, this still provides a most impressive demonstration of animal memory.

Almost equally remarkable are the results of a series of laboratory experiments involving pigeons (Vaughan & Greene, 1984). Subjects were placed into a conditioning chamber with a clear response key that was about 5 cm in diameter. They then received discrimination training in which a series of different slides was projected onto the key. Responding in the presence of some (S+) resulted in the delivery of food, whereas responding in the presence of the remainder (S−) did not. When the slides were first introduced, subjects naturally responded at a similar rate to all of them, but as training progressed, the pigeons came to peck more rapidly at those designated as S+ and more slowly at those designated as S−. This discrimination can only be possible if the pigeons remembered the slides and whether they signaled food.

In one study, the slides between which pigeons successfully discriminated were complex random squiggles of the sort depicted in Figure 9.1. Despite the large number of slides employed (eighty S+ and eighty S−), performance was extremely accurate by the end of training, although, it must be admitted, training continued for just on 1000 sessions.

In another experiment, the pigeons were shown a large number of ordinary snapshots. Initially, the birds were trained with forty S+ and forty S− snapshots, but this does not appear to be close to the upper limit of the number of pictures that pigeons can remember. Once they were discriminating accurately between the original slides a new set of eighty slides was introduced. Training with these was continued until the discrimination had been learned, whereupon a further set of eighty slides was introduced. The experiment continued in this way until the pigeons had been exposed to 320 different pictures, half of which were associated with food. At this point the birds were exposed to all 320 slides—separately of course—and their discrimination between them was very accurate indeed.

The results from the experiment by Vaughan and Greene (1984) may lie well short of the capacity of pigeons for remembering photographs. Using a slightly different test, Cook, Levison, Gillett, and Blaisdell (2005) required pigeons to select

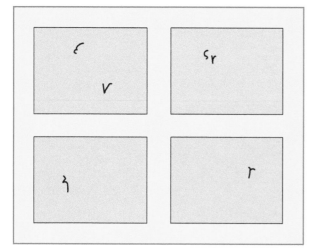

FIGURE 9.1 Examples of the slides used in a study by Vaughan and Greene (1984). Slides in the left-hand column signaled the availability of food, whereas those in the right-hand column signaled its absence (adapted from Vaughan & Greene, 1984).

one of two food magazines on the basis of photographs that were shown. Approach to one magazine was rewarded in the presence of half of the photographs; approach to the other magazine was rewarded in the presence of the remaining photographs. Approach to the incorrect magazine resulted in the trial terminating without reward. Training started with a few photographs, and as the birds became adept at making the correct choices, new ones were added. After 700 sessions of training, which took 3 years, the birds had been exposed to 1600 photographs, and were correct on about 75% of the trials. By taking account of the likelihood that some of the correct responses were a result of guessing, the authors estimated the number of pictures that the birds had remembered after increasing amounts of training. Figure 9.2 shows the results of this calculation for the two birds that participated in the experiment. The estimated number of pictures that the birds remembered increased as they were exposed to more and more of them. Of particular interest is that this gradual increase ceases and stabilizes at just over 800. Cook et al. (2005) suggest that this number represents the capacity of long-term memory for pigeons.

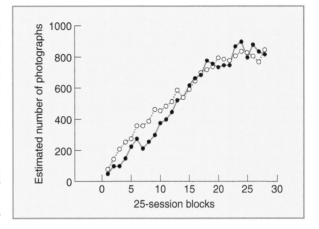

FIGURE 9.2 The number of photographs that two pigeons were estimated to have remembered in an experiment by Cook et al. (2005). They were exposed to an increasing number of photographs as training progressed.

This finding that there may be an upper limit to long-term memory in animals is original and the reasons for it have yet to be discovered. It is unlikely that the memory of the two birds was full because, as the authors point out, they would probably have been capable of solving a new discrimination with different stimuli. Perhaps, as they further suggest, the capacity may reflect an inability to distinguish new items from old when they have been exposed to many pictures. In view of the amount of training that was needed before the limit to long-term memory became evident, progress towards understanding the factors responsible for this limit is likely to be slow.

DURABILITY

Animals can, therefore, retain large amounts of information. But how is retention affected by the passage of time? To my knowledge, the record for long-term retention in an experimental setting is held by a sea lion (Reichmuth-Kastak & Schusterman, 2002). The subject, Rio, was originally trained to solve matching discriminations (see p. 181) before she was given a wide range of different tests. When Rio was returned to the matching task, some 10 years later, her performance was not significantly different from that recorded originally. It thus appears that Rio was able to remember how to match to sample for at least 10 years.

Another demonstration of substantial long-term retention can be found in a report by Vaughan and Greene (1984). After the experiment described in the previous section was completed, the pigeons were retained in their home cages for 2 years before being returned to the experimental apparatus. Even after this interval the discrimination between the two categories of pictures was still far in excess of that expected by chance. Further evidence of the durability of pigeon memory is provided by Skinner (1950), who demonstrated that they may retain information for as long as 5 years.

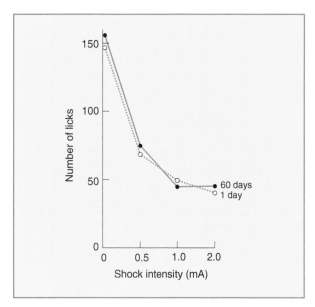

FIGURE 9.3 The retention of conditioned fear as a function of the intensity of shock during conditioning (adapted from Hendersen, 1985).

In Miller and Berk's (1977) experiment, both the tadpoles and young of the African claw-toed frog seemed to learn the given task with equal facility. Furthermore, they went on to show an excellent retention of the task when tested 35 days later, even after the tadpoles had turned into frogs. Copyright © Chris Mattison; Frank Lane Picture Agency/Corbis.

The considerably shorter life-span of the rat (2–3 years) compared with that of the pigeon (more than 15 years) or the sea lion (20 years) means that demonstrations of a long memory with rats are of necessity less impressive. None the less, there is ample evidence that they are capable of storing information for considerable periods. In an experiment by Hendersen (1985), rats were conditioned with a conditioned stimulus (CS) signaling shock that varied in intensity among different groups. To test how well subjects remembered this training, they were made thirsty and placed in chambers where they could lick a tube for water. Once they were licking at a consistent rate the CS was presented without the shock. Figure 9.3 shows the number of licks that were recorded in the presence of the CS for some subjects who were tested 1 day after conditioning and for others who were tested 60 days after conditioning. There is a clear indication that rats were more reluctant to lick when the CS had signaled a strong rather than a weak shock. But what is more important is that there is no hint that the retention interval had any influence on responding. Thus rats are able to remember very accurately for at least 60 days the magnitude of an aversive event that was paired with a CS. A rather similar experiment with rats by Gleitman (1971) found no forgetting of a conditioned response they had acquired 90 days previously.

A very different demonstration of the robustness of animal memory comes from the African claw-toed frog. This animal undergoes a metamorphosis, over a period of 35 days, from a limbless tadpole to a young frog that differs only in size from an adult, and this change is accompanied by considerable neural growth. In one study, Miller and Berk (1977) trained subjects to move from a black to a white compartment to reduce the severity of an electric shock. Both tadpoles and young frogs learned this task with equal facility, but the remarkable finding is that they also showed excellent retention of the task when tested 35 days later. In the former case, of course, they had metamorphosed into frogs by the time of the retention test, but the changes associated with this metamorphosis did nothing to disrupt memory.

Animals can therefore remember for a remarkably long time. But is there any loss of the information that is stored over such periods? One study to look for such forgetting is by Thomas and Lopez (1962), who trained pigeons to peck a key illuminated by a monochromatic light of a wavelength of 550 nanometers for food. The memory for this training stimulus was then tested in different groups after retention intervals of 1 minute, 1 day, or 1 week. The method of testing was to present the subjects with the key illuminated by light varying in wavelength from 500 to 600 nanometers. The results from this study are shown in Figure 9.4.

The group tested within a minute of being trained responded more rapidly to the original training color than to any other employed during testing. This indicates that the memory for the original training stimulus remained undiminished for at least 1 minute. The results from the other groups show that this memory soon decays to some extent. Both groups responded no more rapidly to the original training color than to its nearest neighbors (540 and 560 nanometers), which suggests that with the passage of time the exact value of the stimulus employed during training was forgotten. This conclusion has been confirmed with a variety of species and training procedures (e.g. Thomas & Riccio, 1979). The implication from this study is that with the passage of time subjects forget the specific attributes of the training stimulus but not its general significance.

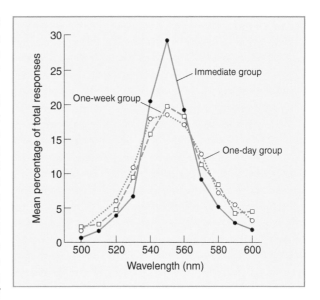

FIGURE 9.4 Mean stimulus generalization gradients for three groups of pigeons tested at different intervals after they had been trained to peck a key for food when it was illuminated with light of a wavelength of 550 nanometers (adapted from Thomas, 1981).

The previous conclusion applies to a discriminative stimulus that was used for instrumental conditioning. A report by Hendersen, Peterson, and Jackson (1980) suggests that it may also be true for the unconditioned stimulus (US) in Pavlovian conditioning. Although the results portrayed in Figure 9.3 show that rats are very good at remembering the severity of an aversive event, Hendersen at al. (1980) found that they are not so good at remembering its quality. Rats received conditioning in which a CS was paired for many trials with an aversive airblast. The CS was then presented after a retention interval while the animals were responding in order to avoid shock. With a retention interval of 1 day, the CS had little impact on responding, whereas after 45 days the CS augmented substantially the rate of responding. To explain these results Hendersen et al. (1980) proposed that over the course of the retention interval the memory of the precise nature of the air blast deteriorated. Thus the CS would not be expected to have an effect after a short retention interval because it would retrieve information about an event that is very different to the one that subjects were seeking to avoid. But after a longer retention interval, the CS would simply signal the imminent delivery of an unspecified aversive event (of certain magnitude), which would encourage responding to avoid any aversive stimulus.

The final experiments to be considered in this section show that forgetting may have a more disruptive effect on inhibitory than excitatory conditioning. Hendersen (1978) and Thomas (1979) trained rats so that one stimulus served as an excitatory CS signaling the delivery of shock, and another stimulus served as an inhibitory CS signaling the omission of shock. The rats then received test trials 25 days after the completion of the initial training. There was no effect of this interval on the strength of responding during the excitatory CS, but there was a considerable loss of influence by the inhibitory CS.

In addition to the passage of time, a number of other factors have been shown to influence how well material is remembered or recalled. These demonstrations have generally been conducted with the aim of evaluating different theories of long-term retention and will be considered next, along with the theories they were designed to test.

THEORETICAL INTERPRETATION

Two rather different theoretical frameworks have been developed to explain the way in which long-term storage of information takes place. Consolidation or rehearsal theory stresses that information must be rehearsed immediately after it has been presented if it is to be stored adequately. Retrieval theory, on the other hand, holds that information is stored virtually instantaneously and assumes that forgetting is due principally to a failure to find the information at the time of testing.

Consolidation theory

One reason for studying animal memory has been the hope that it will lead to an understanding of the neural processes subserving the acquisition and storage of knowledge in both humans and animals. The assumption underlying much of this work has been that any long-term retention of information must be due to an equally long-term change in the nervous system. According to Hebb (1949), memory storage depends on the virtually permanent formation of circuits of interconnected neurons. These circuits were assumed to be only partially formed at the end of a training trial, and for learning to be complete a period of sustained reverberatory activity (consolidation) in the neural circuit after the trial was deemed essential. Should this activity not occur, or be disrupted, then permanent links in the network would not be formed, and the memory of the trial would be incomplete.

Evidence to support this type of theory came from studies investigating the influence of electroconvulsive shock (ECS) on animal memory. ECS involves the passage through the brain of an electric current of sufficient intensity that it would presumably disrupt any reverberatory activity in a localized collection of cells. Administration of ECS shortly after a training trial should, therefore, inhibit the processes necessary for producing a normal memory of that trial. An experiment by Duncan (1949) was among the first to test this prediction. Rats were placed into a box with a metal grid floor that could be electrified. A light was then turned on for 10 seconds, and this was followed by foot shock (which is not part of the ECS treatment that involves a shock only to the brain). To prevent the foot shock occurring, the rat was required to move from one end of the box to the other while the light was still on, and, unless this response was made, foot shock was automatically delivered as soon as the light was turned off. There were nine groups in the study, eight of which received ECS at intervals varying from 20 seconds to 14 hours after each daily trial. A control group, which did not receive ECS, quickly learned to avoid the shock, but this learning was very much poorer for the group that received ECS 20 seconds after each trial. Moreover, as the interval between the end of each trial and the administration of ECS was extended, the disruptive influence of this treatment diminished (Figure 9.5). One explanation for these findings is that ECS immediately after a trial prevents the consolidation of the learning necessary for the successful prevention of shock. Postponing the ECS for a period after each trial would allow

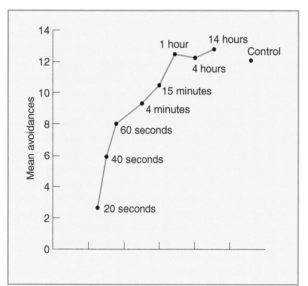

FIGURE 9.5 Mean number of avoidance responses made by groups of rats that differed in the interval for which the delivery of electroconvulsive shock (ECS) was delayed after each of eighteen avoidance training trials. Group Control did not receive ECS (adapted from Duncan, 1949).

some time for consolidation after the trial and hence reduce the disruptive influence of the treatment. A review of experiments on this topic is presented in Lewis (1979).

A prediction that follows from **consolidation theory** is that protracted exposure to a stimulus, by virtue of permitting more time for consolidation to take place, will result in a more accurate memory of it than a brief exposure, especially if the stimulus is complex. The outcome of an experiment by Fanselow (1990) is consistent with this prediction. Different groups of rats received a single footshock that was presented at intervals varying from 0 to 162 seconds after they had been placed in a novel conditioning chamber. With only a few seconds of exposure to the chamber before shock was delivered, it was anticipated that there would be insufficient time for an accurate representation of the chamber to consolidate, and this poor representation would be all that was available to enter into an association with shock. With a longer interval, there should be time for this representation to develop, which would then enable a rich representation of the chamber to enter into an association with shock. A conditioned fear of the chamber was therefore expected to develop more readily when the interval before the shock was delivered was long rather than short. This prediction was tested by returning the rats to the chamber the following day and recording the amount of time they were immobile, or freezing, during 5 minutes. The results labeled No Tone in the left-hand panel of Figure 9.6 show that the percentage of time spent freezing by the different groups was directly related to the amount of exposure they received to the chamber before shock was delivered.

A novel conditioning chamber is a complex environment and it is hardly surprising that a few seconds are required before a rich memory of it can consolidate. It seems possible, however, that if a simpler cue signals the delivery of shock, then less time might be required before an adequate memory for it develops. To test this prediction, Fanselow (1990) included additional groups in his experiment for which a tone was presented while they were in the chamber throughout the training and test trial. With short intervals before shock, animals would still find it difficult to associate the chamber with shock, but they may be able to associate the tone with shock. In support of this prediction, the results labeled Tone in Figure 9.6 show that

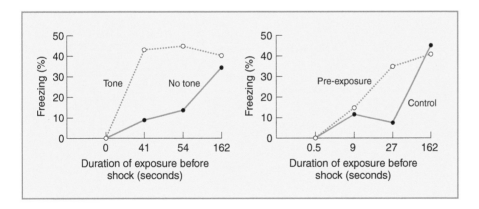

FIGURE 9.6 The mean amount of freezing that was observed in a context where a single shock had been delivered for groups of rats that had been exposed to the context for different durations before shock delivery. In one experiment, a tone was present throughout the experiment for the tone groups, but not for the No Tone groups (left-hand panel). In another experiment, 2 minutes of exposure to the context was given on the day before the conditioning trial for the preexposure, but not the control groups (right-hand panel) (adapted from Fanselow, 1990).

the presence of the tone resulted in effective conditioning when the interval before shock was delivered was relatively short.

According to the principles of consolidation, another method for helping subjects associate the chamber with shock, when the interval before shock is delivered is short, would be to provide some exposure to the chamber before the conditioning trial. Such exposure would allow an accurate representation of the chamber to develop. On being returned to the chamber for the conditioning trial, even a brief interval before shock is delivered should be sufficient to activate a rich memory of the chamber and enable conditioning to be effective. The results shown in the right-hand panel of Figure 9.6 were from another experiment by Fanselow (1990) that was based on this rationale. Four control groups received similar treatment to that described above for the No Tone groups, with four different intervals before shock was delivered. Another four, preexposure, groups received the same treatment, but on the day before the conditioning trial they were placed in the chamber for 2 minutes in the absence of shock. From the results shown in the right-hand panel of Figure 9.6 it is evident that conditioning with the chamber was more effective at short intervals before the delivery of shock if subjects had previously been exposed to the chamber.

Retrieval theory

The long-term retention of information can be subdivided into three stages. First, it is necessary to form a memory trace of a particular training episode; second, this trace must be stored until it is needed; and third, the trace must be retrieved at the appropriate time. Consolidation theories place most emphasis on the first two of these stages. They assume that a poor memory is due either to an inadequate trace being formed at the time of training, or to a decay of the memory trace due to the passage of time. In contrast, **retrieval theories** of memory (Lewis, 1979; Spear, 1973) maintain that the formation of memories is more or less instantaneous and that once formed they remain permanently intact. To account for forgetting and the amnesic effects of ECS, these theories place greatest emphasis on the retrieval process.

Of the various accounts of a retrieval theory of memory that have been proposed, the one considered here is that by Lewis (1979) because it provides the most explicit framework into which a variety of experimental findings can be accommodated. He maintains that the formation of the memory trace is very rapid and once formed it can reside in either **active memory** or **inactive memory**. At the time of acquisition, information is held in active memory, where it is assumed to be swiftly coded and elaborated before being stored permanently in inactive memory. The purpose of this coding and elaboration is to aid the efficient retrieval of the information from inactive memory when it is needed. For this retrieval to take place, subjects must be in the presence of some of the stimuli that were present at the time of the training trial. These stimuli serve to retrieve the memory of the entire trial into active memory, and once in this state the information can be further elaborated as well as influence the subject's behavior. It is important to emphasize that unless information is retrieved from inactive into active memory, it will be of no use to the animal. In some respects these ideas are similar to the views of Wagner that were discussed in Chapter 3.

A simple study supporting many of these proposals, and also showing that the room in which the training was conducted can serve as a retrieval cue, is reported by Spear, Smith, Bryan, Gordon, Timmons, and Chiszar (1980). The apparatus was a two-compartment shuttle box with an open top so that subjects could observe the room in which the experiment was conducted. One compartment was white with

KEY TERMS

Retrieval theory
The proposal that a failure to retrieve a memory of an event is not due to inadequate consolidation at the time of the event but to the absence of suitable cues to retrieve the memory.

Active memory
The state of a representation for a previous event in which it can influence behavior and be modified by experience.

Inactive memory
The state of a representation for a previous event in which it is unable to influence behavior and it is unable to be modified by experience.

a grid floor through which an electric shock could be passed, the other compartment was black; to cross between the two it was necessary to jump over a small hurdle. For the initial stage of the experiment, all animals received avoidance training in which they were placed into the white compartment and were given an electric shock if they did not step into the black compartment within 5 seconds. After a number of such trials, subjects rapidly jumped from the white compartment whenever they were placed into it. Some time after the completion of this training the rats were again placed into the white compartment, and the time taken to leave it was recorded. For Group Same, the test trials were conducted with the apparatus in the same room as that used during training, whereas for Group Different another room was used for the test trial. According to retrieval theory, the sight of the features of the room, which were visible during training, should immediately retrieve the memory of their training for Group Same and result in a rapid exit from the white compartment. However, the cues provided by the new room for Group Different will not aid such efficient retrieval, and these subjects should take longer than those in Group Same to escape from the white compartment; this is exactly what Spear et al. (1980) observed.

Reactivation effects

Some surprising results that are consistent with retrieval theory concern the effects of what have come to be known as **reactivation** treatments. Retrieval theory asserts that after training on a particular task, exposure to even a fraction of the cues that were present at the time of training will retrieve or reactivate information about that episode into Active Memory. Once reactivated, this information can be modified in a variety of ways and thus effectively alter the animal's memory of the original training. The results from a series of experiments summarized by Gordon (1981) are consistent with this analysis.

In one experiment, rats were trained with a procedure identical to that used by Spear et al. (1980) to leave a white compartment to avoid shock (Gordon, Frankl, & Hamberg, 1979, Experiment 1). Three days after the successful completion of this training, two groups were returned to the experimental room for what may be termed reactivation treatment, which consisted of being confined in the white compartment for either 15 or 75 seconds; a third group did not receive this treatment. Finally, on the following day the three groups received a single test trial in which they were placed into the white compartment and the time taken to cross to the black side was recorded.

The reactivation treatment had a profound effect (Figure 9.7). Subjects that had received exposure to the apparatus for 15 seconds were faster to leave the white compartment than those receiving either no exposure or exposure for 75 seconds. Gordon (1981) interpreted these findings in the following way: Exposure to the apparatus for 15 seconds should reactivate the memory of the avoidance training and may very well result in further elaboration and coding of this memory. On the test trial, the memory of the original training should then be retrieved easily and accurately, and result in a swifter avoidance response than for the group that did not receive the reactivation treatment. A similar effect would not be expected for the group that received the reactivation treatment for 75 seconds, as the extended exposure to the white compartment will have modified the memory of the original training to incorporate the information that shocks are now unlikely to occur in the apparatus. The retrieval of this modified memory on the test trial would not produce a particularly vigorous avoidance response.

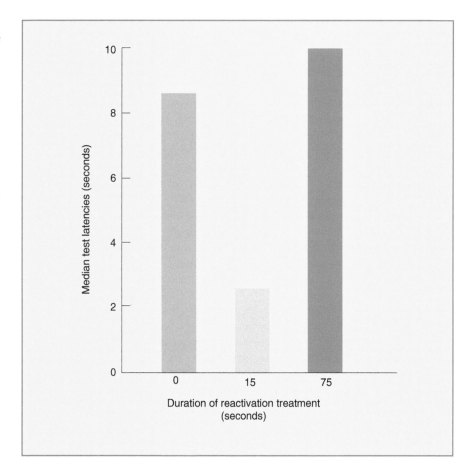

Another way of looking at the results from the experiment is to assume that the relatively poor performance on the test trial, in the absence of any reactivation treatment, was a consequence of forgetting that occurred during the 3 days between training and testing. The 15 seconds of reactivation treatment could then have worked by counteracting the effects of this forgetting. The implication of this analysis is that if a group had been tested immediately after the training trial, its performance should have been similar to that of the group that received the reactivation treatment for 15 seconds. Unfortunately, the above experiment did not include a group to test this prediction, but such a group was included in a rather different study of the effects of reactivation treatments by Deweer, Sara, and Hars (1980, Experiment 2).

Rats were initially trained to run through a maze containing six choice points to collect food. After only five trials the three groups were making as few as two errors per trial, and the time to run through the maze had fallen from some 300 seconds on the first trial to about 50 seconds on the fifth trial. One group (Group Immediate) was given a test trial on the next day, whereas the remaining subjects were not exposed to the apparatus for 25 days. Then, on the test session, one of the remaining groups (Group Delay) was run in the maze in the same manner as during training. The other group also received this test procedure, but just before it the rats were placed into a wire mesh cage beside the maze for 90 seconds (Group Reactivate).

The results from the study are depicted in Figure 9.8, which shows the average time it took the three groups to run through the maze on the final training trial and

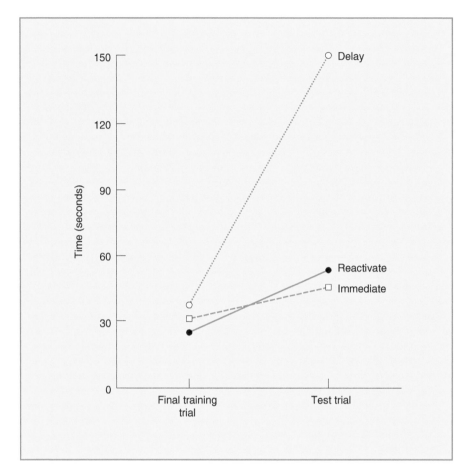

FIGURE 9.8 Mean time taken by three groups of rats to run through a maze on the final training trial and on a subsequent test trial. For Group Immediate, the interval between these trials was 1 day; for the other two groups it was 25 days. Group Reactivate was given reactivation treatment immediately before the test trial (adapted from Deweer et al., 1980).

on the test trial. The first feature to note is that on the test trial Group Immediate ran through the maze considerably more rapidly than Group Delay. This difference demonstrates forgetting by Group Delay. The more important point to note is that there was a similar difference between Group Delay and Group Reactivate on this trial, which indicates that the exposure to the room cues at the time of testing was, indeed, effective in overcoming the effects of forgetting. The results also indicate that the forgetting observed in Group Delay was not due to the loss of the memory of the original training, but to the effects of the original training being difficult to retrieve.

Why was it difficult for Group Delay to retrieve a memory of the original training when it received its test trial? As stated earlier, according to retrieval theory, a memory will be retrieved if the subject is exposed to a portion of the cues that were present at the time of training. Moreover, the more cues that are present the easier it will be to retrieve the memory. One possibility is that the internal state of an animal provides a component of the stimulation that can retrieve the memory of a training episode (e.g. Riccio & Ebner, 1981; Spear, 1981; Bouton, 1993). When the interval between the training and test episodes is short, there will be little change in the subject's internal state and the presence of this state will help to retrieve the memory. However, when there is a longer interval between the two episodes, the animal's internal state is likely to change and make it more difficult to retrieve the memory of training by reducing the number of suitable retrieval cues that are present. In support of this claim,

Spear et al. (1980) have shown that drugs such as pentobarbitol, which can alter an animal's anxiety level, can serve as influential retrieval cues in memory tasks.

In the experiment by Deweer et al. (1980), therefore, it is possible that when Group Delay was returned to the apparatus for the test trial the passage of 25 days resulted in a substantial change in the internal cues from those present during the training trials. This change would make it difficult to retrieve the memory of the original training and account for the relative poor outcome of the test trial. In the case of the Group Reactivate, exposure to the apparatus for 90 seconds before the test trial would reactivate the training memory and enable it to incorporate information about the current internal state. The internal state on the test trial will then correspond closely with the internal state just incorporated into the memory of the training trial, and facilitate the retrieval of the training memory relative to Group Delay.

Another form of forgetting that can be alleviated by a reactivation treatment is that which results from the application of ECS. Gordon and Mowrer (1980) trained rats to jump from a white compartment with an avoidance task similar to that described previously and tested their retention 3 days later. Animals that received ECS immediately after the initial training were much slower to respond on this retention test than controls given no ECS. But the deleterious effects of this ECS treatment were completely abolished if animals received a reactivation trial, consisting of brief exposure to the test apparatus, 15 minutes before the retention test.

According to retrieval theory, ECS acts by reducing the elaboration of memory necessary to ensure successful retrieval. The reactivation trial should, albeit with difficulty, have retrieved a memory of the original training and thus allowed it to undergo further elaboration to make it readily available at the time of testing. In keeping with this analysis, it was found that reactivation not only alleviated the effects of ECS but also improved performance relative to the group that had received neither ECS nor the reactivation treatment.

From the discussion so far, it should be apparent that when the memory of a training episode is reactivated it is in a labile state that allows the memory to be modified. A series of experiments by Nader and colleagues provides impressive support for this point of view by showing that once reactivated, memories in certain circumstances can be modified to such an extent that they are effectively erased (Nader, Schafe, & Le Doux, 2000; Nader, 2003; Duvarci & Nader, 2004). The experiments made use of the drug **anisomycin**, which is a protein inhibitor. If anisomycin is injected into the amygdala of rats immediately after a fear conditioning trial then it prevents a memory of the trial being formed. In one experiment by Nader et al. (2000), rats first received fear conditioning in which a tone was paired with shock. Twenty-four hours later they received Test Trial 1, which consisted of the tone being presented without the shock. Considerable fear, as measured by freezing, was recorded. This trial was followed immediately by an injection of anisomycin and then on the next day Test Trial 2 was conducted. The second test was the same as the first but now rats showed virtually no fear of the tone.

The lack of fear on Test Trial 2 could have resulted from extinction brought about by presenting the tone by itself during Test Trial 1. This possibility can be dismissed, however, because a control group that received the same treatment throughout the experiment, but no injection of anisomycin, displayed considerable fear of the tone during the second test. In view of this result, the absence of a response during Test Trial 2 must be attributed to the influence of the anisomycin. During Test Trial 1, the tone was assumed to reactivate a memory of the original training episode. Once activated, the neural basis of the memory was then assumed to be in a similar state to that which occurred during the training trial, which meant it was in a state that was susceptible to the amnesic influence of the drug injection. Thus, the drug was believed to erase the reactivated memory of the training trial, and destroy the memory of the training trial itself. The findings by Nader et al. (2000) have led to a renewal of interest into retrieval theories of memory, as well as into the neural mechanisms of memory retrieval. They have also raised the possibility that drugs can be used to manipulate the extent to which previous experiences can be remembered in both animals and humans.

Concluding comments concerning theories of memory

The foregoing results provide impressive evidence that reactivation treatments can influence the efficiency of memory recall. We should admit, however, that our understanding of the way retrieval operates is still incomplete. Thus, although efficient memory retrieval might depend on a period of elaboration after a training trial, it is not yet clear how this elaboration should be characterized. There is also some uncertainty about the way in which reactivation is effective. If exposure to the apparatus just before a test trial can activate a training memory, why should this not also occur on the test trial and result in normal performance?

Finally, we should acknowledge that it may not be as easy as I have implied to decide whether a particular pattern of results should be interpreted in terms of consolidation theory or retrieval theory. Suppose that a reactivation treatment improves performance on a subsequent memory test. According to retrieval theory, this improvement is due to the reactivation treatment making it easier to recover information about the original training. But it is quite conceivable that the reactivation treatment allowed the memory for the original training to be enriched. This proposal, which is more in keeping with consolidation than retrieval theory, would also be expected to enhance performance on the test trial. Unfortunately, it is not easy to choose between these accounts, because there is no clear-cut test for deciding whether an experimental manipulation has affected a consolidation or a retrieval process. Until such a test is developed, we should be cautious about interpreting any of the findings considered in this section as providing unequivocal support for one theory or the other. Instead, the greatest value of this research is for the insights it provides into the factors that influence the ease with which animals can recall information about prior events.

EPISODIC MEMORY

Humans are able to recall specific episodes from their past. For example, I am able to remember that this morning I ate toast and marmalade in my kitchen while listening to a particular piece of music. This ability is referred to as episodic memory, which, according to Tulving (1983) allows, "a person to be consciously aware of an earlier experience in a certain situation at a certain time" (p. 67). A common belief is that episodic memory is unique to humans and that animals are unable to recall specific episodes from their past (Suddendorf & Corballis, 1997). In one sense, this claim is impossible to test because, as noted in previous chapters, no method exists for determining whether an animal can consciously reexperience a previous event. In other words, the ability to record the mental experiences of animals or, indeed, to determine whether they have the capacity for such experiences, lies beyond the scope of the techniques available to the experimental psychologist. In another sense, however, it may be possible to test experimentally whether animals have episodic memory providing we are careful with how this term is defined. Clayton and Dickinson (1998; see also de Kort, Dickinson, & Clayton, 2005) use the term **episodic-like memories** to refer to memories that capture information about when an event occurred, where an event occurred, and what the event consisted of. Note that no mention of conscious awareness is made in this definition. If it could be shown that an animal is capable of remembering each of these components about a previous experience, then we might be able to say that the animal is demonstrating all the behavioral characteristics of episodic memory. A clear demonstration that animals can remember the what, where, and when of a particular experience is provided in a series of cleverly designed experiments by Clayton and Dickinson (1998).

The experiments were conducted with Western scrub jays, which inhabit California. On finding food, these birds will often **cache** it, to retrieve it for eating at a later time. The question of interest is whether, at the time of retrieval, the birds can remember not only where they had buried the food but what they had buried and when they had buried it. To address this question, Clayton and Dickinson (1999) tested a group of birds in the laboratory using the apparatus shown in Figure 9.9. The picture shows a scrub jay caching food in a tray filled with a material such as sand. The Lego Duplo™ building bricks behind the tray serve as a landmark to allow the bird to identify where the food has been hidden. To test whether the birds could remember what they hid, where they hid it, and when, the experiment was made more complex by allowing them to cache two types of food: peanuts and wax worms. Thus, during a caching trial a bird would be given a bowl of peanuts. It was then allowed 15 minutes to hide the nuts in a tray that was in a certain location in the cage and with a particular Lego™ landmark beside it. After 15 minutes, the bowl of peanuts was replaced with a bowl of wax worms, and the tray and landmark were replaced with a new tray and landmark in a different location. After a further 15 minutes these items were also removed from the cage.

Following an interval of either 4 or 124 hours, the birds were presented with both trays in their original locations and beside their original landmarks; the trays contained the food that was originally buried in them. However, the wax worms were fresh if only 4 hours had elapsed since the caching episode; they were no longer fresh

FIGURE 9.9 A female Western scrub jay, Sweetie Pie, caching wax worms (photograph by Dean Alexis and Ian Cannell of the University of Cambridge). Reproduced with permission.

and had deteriorated considerably if 124 hours has elapsed since caching. Scrub jays prefer fresh wax worms to peanuts, but they prefer peanuts to decayed wax worms. After only a few trials of training, a clear pattern of responding emerged. When birds were allowed to retrieve food 4 hours after they had buried it they showed a strong preference for searching where the wax worms had been hidden, but when this interval was 124 hours then they showed a strong preference for searching where the peanuts had been hidden.

Clayton and Dickinson (1999) accounted for this pattern of results by proposing that, at the time of retrieving food the birds remember what they buried, where they buried it, and how long ago it had been buried. Given access to this information, they should then search for wax worms in preference to peanuts if a relatively brief amount of time has elapsed since caching, but if this interval is extended to 124 hours then the knowledge that wax worms will be inedible will result in a preference for peanuts. Readers may wonder whether a simpler explanation can be developed for these results based on the supposition that the birds could smell the food buried in the trays, and that their choice of tray is guided by their sense of smell. To counter this possibility, Clayton and Dickinson (1999) kept a record during caching of what food was hidden, and where. They then conducted test trials with no food hidden in the tray. Despite the absence of food, the birds performed in the same way as on the normal trials. It would seem that the birds genuinely relied on their memory of the caching episode when deciding where to search at the time of testing.

There are, then, good grounds for believing that scrub jays can retrieve information about what, where, and when a particular episode occurred. In the sense used by Clayton and Dickinson (1998; see also de Kort et al., 2005), these findings demonstrate episodic-like memory in scrub jays. This conclusion does not mean that scrub jays can remember what, where, and when about every episode in their past. It is possible that this ability is confined to caching food, for which a rich memory of the episode would seem to be of particular importance to their survival.

One question raised by this impressive ability of scrub jays concerns the way in which they represent the time at which an event occurred. De Kort et al. (2005) raise the possibility that animals have a life-time clock that records when every event occurs and then allows them to compute the length of time that has elapsed since that event and the current time. Another possibility is that animals possess a clock that is triggered by an event, such as caching, and the value of which will then indicate how long ago it was that the event occurred. Roberts (2002) has suggested as an alternative that scrub jays keep a record of the number of diurnal cycles that have elapsed since food was hidden. They might then learn that wax worms do not decay in the absence of a diurnal cycle, but that after four such cycles wax worms are not particularly attractive. There is currently no evidence that would allow a choice to be made among these alternatives, which indicates that we do not fully understand how an animal knows when an event occurred. More will be said about how animals measure the passage of time in Chapter 10.

After the demonstration by Clayton and Dickinson (1999) of episodic-like memory in scrub jays, researchers began to look for evidence of this type of memory in other species. At first, the search was in vain. Tests in which rats (Bird, Roberts, Abroms, Kit, & Crupi, 2003) and monkeys (Hampton, Hampstead, & Murray, 2005) were required to retrieve food revealed that they could remember the type of food that was hidden, and where, but were unable to show that the animals remembered when the food was hidden. In the case of pigeons, Skov-Rackette, Miller, and Shettleworth (2006) describe an unpublished failure to demonstrate episodic-like memory. These findings point to the conclusion that episodic-like memory may be restricted to only a few species of birds. However, recent papers by Babb and Crystal (2005, 2006) describe episodic-like memory in rats, which were able to remember where different types of food could be found at different times. On the basis of this finding, it would seem that episodic-like memory might be quite widespread among animals, but additional experiments will be needed before this conclusion can be evaluated seriously.

The comparative study of animal memory

There has been considerable interest in comparing the performance of different species on a variety of memory tests. One strong motivation for this research has been to test what Macphail and Bolhuis (2001) refer to as the **ecological view of animal intelligence**. This view assumes that different species have evolved different cognitive abilities to cope with the demands of the different environment that they inhabit (e.g. Shettleworth, 1998). Before we consider whether this is the case, it is worth summarizing briefly some of the findings from the comparative study of memory to give a feel for the results that have been found. The summary will cover findings from studies of both short- and long-term retention.

On the one hand, there are number of striking similarities between the performance of a wide range of species on a variety of tests. Using spatial learning tasks, such as the radial maze, short-term retention has been found to be both capacious and durable for rats (Olton, 1978), a variety of birds (Kamil, 1978; Moore & Osadchuk, 1982; Roberts & Van Veldhuizen, 1985; Spetch & Edwards, 1986; Healy & Hurly, 1995), chimpanzees (Menzel, 1978), monkeys (Platt, Brannon, Briese, & French, 1996), at least two species of fish (Hughes & Blight, 1999), cows (Bailey et al., 1996) and even honey-bees (Brown & Demas, 1994). Moreover, it has been found that many of these species are still able to select the remaining arms of the maze accurately if they are interrupted mid-way through a trial. When short-term retention is investigated with delayed matching to sample, the results are not very different for species as diverse as pigeons and dolphins. Perhaps even more remarkable is the finding by Menzel (1979) that ECS has the same sort of disruptive influence on learning in bees as it has in rats. Finally, similar serial position curves have now been obtained in experiments with monkeys (Wright et al., 1984; 2003; Castro & Larsen, 1992), rats (Dimattia & Kesner, 1984; Harper et al., 1993), and pigeons (Wright et al., 1984).

On the other hand, there are many occasions when species differ in how they perform on tests of their memory. We saw at the start of this chapter that Clark's nutcracker can remember over 3000 spatial locations, but it would be surprising if this were true of all other animals. There is also evidence that animals may differ in the details of their performance on certain memory tests. For example, many experiments have examined the effect of preventing subjects from making further choices for a period when they are half way through a trial in the radial maze. Although most species that have been tested are able to cope with such an interruption, they differ in the length of the delay they can tolerate before they forget which arms remain to be visited. Both sticklebacks and wrasse (Hughes & Blight, 1999), and pigeons (Roberts & Van Veldhuizen, 1985) can tolerate delays of 30 seconds or so, but their performance is significantly impaired when this interval is increased to 5 or 6 minutes. Some mammals appear to be better than birds or fish at coping with these delays. Rats can identify the unvisited arms after an interruption

KEY TERM

Ecological view of animal intelligence
The claim that different species will have different mechanisms of intelligence, or different cognitive processes, to cope with the unique demands posed by the environments they inhabit.

of 4 hours (Beatty & Shavalia, 1980a), cows after a delay of 8 hours (Bailey et al., 1989), and tamarin monkeys after a delay of 24 hours (Platt et al., 1996). There are, by way of contrast, examples of some species appearing to be unable to rely on short-term retention when confronted with the radial-maze task. Roitblat, Tham, and Golub (1982) trained Siamese fighting fish in an aquatic version of an eight-arm radial maze and found that successful performance depended entirely on the strategy of swimming down adjacent arms in a clockwise or anti-clockwise direction. Lipp et al. (2001) report that hedgehogs and chickens perform rather poorly in the radial maze.

When confronted with the results just described, many readers might find it naturally interesting that, say, hedgehogs perform more poorly on the radial-arm maze test of memory than cows. The reader might also be tempted to go one step further and speculate that the memory of the hedgehog is different, perhaps inferior, to that of the cow, and that this is a consequence of the different demands they face in their fight for survival. Unfortunately, for reasons touched on in Chapter 1, such speculation is fraught with difficulty. The main problem is to ensure that the test imposes exactly the same demands on both species. When an animal is being tested in the radial maze, its performance will not just be influenced by its memory, but also by how readily it can discriminate between the different arms, by how willing it is to work for the reward that is available, by how easy it is to move around the apparatus, and so on. With species as different as cows and hedgehogs, it is obviously going to be difficult to ensure that the tasks are equated in all these respects, but unless they are equated it would be unreasonable to conclude that the difference in performance is a reflection of the different memory abilities of the two species. How then can we equate a memory test for two very different species? One solution was proposed by Bitterman (1975), who referred to the additional influences that might affect the outcome of the experiment as contextual variables. Bitterman proposed that the experiment should be repeated many times with different values for each contextual variable. If the performance of one species should consistently be better than the other, then it might be safe to conclude that the memory processes of the two species also differ. The trouble with this strategy is that it is time consuming, and it is not clear how the experimenter can be certain that all the relevant manipulations to the experimental design have been tried. For these reasons, researchers tend not to adopt the strategy advocated by Bitterman (1975), and comparisons concerning the memories of different species are rarely drawn.

One method for dealing with the foregoing problem is to compare the performance of closely related species on tests of memory. Birds that do, or do not, store food have proved particularly popular for this line of research (but see also Platt et al., 1996, for a related study using monkeys). The rationale behind this research is that by using closely related species it is likely that they will have similar perceptual, motivational, and motor processes, and the chances of the experimental outcome being influenced by contextual variables will be less than if radically different species are used. Furthermore, by comparing birds that do and do not store food, it should be possible to test the ecological view that cognitive processes, in this instance memory, are shaped by evolutionary pressures. Birds that depend on finding food they have buried for their survival might have better memories than birds that do not bury food. Despite the intuitive appeal of this argument, the evidence that relates to it is conflicting and not easy to interpret.

A number of studies have indeed shown that the performance of food storers is better than of nonstorers on tests of memory. For example, McGregor and Healy (1999) required birds to peck a stimulus in a particular location, and then some time later they had to select this stimulus when it was presented in the same location and reject it when it was presented in another location. Reward was thus presented for returning to the same location, which must depend on the short-term retention of spatial information. McGregor and Healy (1999) found that coal tits, who store tens or hundreds of items of food for up to a few weeks, outperformed blue tits, who rarely store food. However, when Clark's nutcrackers and Mexican jays (the former are considerably more dependent on stored food than the latter) were compared on a similar task no differences were found (Olson, Kamil, Balda, & Nims, 1995). Even more troubling is the discovery that on certain tests the memory of nonstoring birds for spatial locations is superior to that of their food storing counterparts (e.g. Hampton & Shettleworth, 1996). Given these disparate findings, it should not be surprising that in a thorough review by Macphail and Bolhuis (2001) of some twenty studies of birds on a variety of memory tests, no clear pattern of results emerged (see also Papini, 2002). Furthermore, as Macphail and Bolhuis (2001) note, on those occasions when birds that store food display a superior memory to birds that do not store food, there is no evidence of this superiority being enhanced by increasing the delay over which memory is tested, or the number of items that must be remembered (e.g. McGregor & Healy, 1999). If the food storers have a specially developed memory system then it is in these circumstances that the advantage it confers should be most evident.

There are, therefore, differences in the performance of closely related species of bird, but these differences do not appear to correspond with the need to store food, which makes it difficult to know how these differences might be explained. One possibility is to point to aspects of the life style of the species concerned other than their tendency to store food. Hence when discussing their findings, Olson et al. (1995, p. 178) drew attention to the fact that Clark's nutcrackers live in pairs whereas Mexican jays live in relatively permanent flocks. They then argued that the need to recognize other members of the flock would result in evolutionary pressures boosting the memory of the Mexican jays so that it was comparable with that of Clark's nutcracker. The problem with this argument is that not only is it hard to test, but it is also possible that any pattern of results can be explained by focusing selectively on aspects of the particular environment to which the species is adapted.

Another possibility, which is favored by Macphail and Bolhuis (2001), is that evolution has not resulted in the mechanisms of memory in some species being different to others. Instead, all birds, and perhaps all vertebrates, are assumed to have similar memory processes. This is referred to as the **general process view of animal intelligence** for the obvious reason that the same memory processes are assumed to be general to a wide range of species. Macphail and Bolhuis (2001) acknowledge that salient stimuli are more likely to be remembered than nonsalient stimuli, and that perhaps some species pay more attention to spatial cues than others. Such a bias in attention would then explain why some animals are better at remembering spatial information than others but, to emphasize the point, the memory processes involved would operate according to the same principles in all cases. Of course, the possibility must always be kept in mind that contextual variables may play a role when even closely related species perform differently on the same task and that these were responsible for the different test results that were found.

There are two lessons to be drawn from this section. The first is that it is very difficult to compare the amount of information that different species can retain, and for how long. Strenuous steps must be taken to rule out the possibility that any differences are not a consequence of differences in perception, motivation or their capacity physically to negotiate the experimental apparatus. The second lesson is that more evidence is needed before we can judge whether the ecological view or the general process view concerning the nature of animal memory is correct. These are two very different theoretical positions, but on the basis of progress so far, it will not be easy to choose between them.

CHAPTER 10

CONTENTS

Time, number, and serial order

10

The previous chapters summarize our knowledge about the fundamental mechanisms of animal learning and cognition. These mechanisms are responsible for associative learning and memory and, by referring to them, the behavior of animals in a wide range of settings can be explained. One concern now is to determine if these principles are able to explain all aspects of animal intelligence. Towards this end, this and the next chapter explore an issue that was touched on in Chapter 7—the representation of knowledge.

We have seen that animals can retain information about concrete stimuli, and they may even be able to represent some of the relationships created by these stimuli. But is this the only information they are capable of using? Animals live in a world that changes with time, and where the same event may occur more than once. To deal with these more abstract properties of their environment, animals may develop the capacity to measure the passage of time, and to count. In a rather different vein, associative learning enables animals to learn that one event is paired with another. But it is quite conceivable that they will also benefit from being able to appreciate the order in which a succession of stimuli occurs, or in which a variety of responses must be performed. The question is thus raised as to whether animals have a capacity for representing the order in which events take place. Each of these issues will be considered in turn in the present chapter. Chapter 11 is devoted to the analysis of how animals use spatial information.

TIME

The behavior of many animals, both vertebrates and invertebrates, is regulated by time. To understand the way in which this regulation takes place, two types of timing have been identified: periodic and interval (Church & Broadbent, 1991). **Periodic timing** refers to the ability of animals to respond at a particular time. **Interval timing** refers to the ability of animals to respond on the basis of specific durations.

Periodic timing

Many animals display periodic cycles of activity. Mice, for example, show enhanced levels of activity once every 24 hours. This **circadian rhythm** of their activity is unlikely to be controlled by such external factors as a change in illumination, because it is observed even when this source of stimulation remains constant. Instead, the timing of this change in activity is probably controlled by an internal clock, which cycles once every 24 hours (Aschoff, 1955). On a rather grander time scale, Berthold (1978) has proposed that the annual migration of many birds is controlled by a clock that indicates when a year has elapsed.

The properties of an internal, 24-hour clock have been clearly elucidated by Roberts (1965) in an experiment with cockroaches. These insects show an increased

KEY TERMS

Periodic timing
Timing that enables an animal to respond at regular periods, such as the same time every day.

Interval timing
Timing that enables animals to respond after a specific interval has elapsed since the occurrence of some event.

Circadian rhythm
The repeated occurrence of activity once every 24 hours that does not depend on external stimulation for it to be maintained.

level of activity at dusk. To determine if this change in behavior is controlled by an internal clock, a cockroach had a light-proof barrier placed over its eyes. Even though this eliminated any visual cues about the passage of time, the circadian rhythm in activity was sustained, albeit with the slightly shorter period of 23.5 hours. After 30 days of the experiment, therefore, the daily increase in activity was observed 15 hours before dusk. As it is hard to identify any external source of stimulation that would be responsible for this gradual shift in the activity cycle, it seems more than likely that it was controlled by an internal clock. Roberts further discovered that when the cockroach's sight was restored, by removing the barrier, the daily increase in activity did not suddenly revert to occurring just before dusk. Instead, it moved progressively closer to this time at the rate of about an hour a day. The implication of this observation is that even in normal circumstances an increase in activity is controlled by the clock, which required a number of days before it readjusted and again ensured that there was an increase in activity at dusk. A further implication of this finding is that in normal circumstances, any error in the measurement of time by the internal clock is adjusted by entraining it on the external light–dark cycle.

In addition to activity, there is ample evidence to show that feeding can be controlled by an internal clock. Wahl (1932) fed honey-bees at a feeding station every day between 3.00 and 5.00 p.m., and they soon concentrated their visits to the station to this 2-hour period. Of course, the timing of these visits could have been due to the bees being insufficiently motivated to seek food until 22 hours had elapsed since their last visit to the feeder. An experiment by Kolterman (1971), however, makes this explanation unlikely. Bees were trained to fly to a feeding station where food was continuously available. For one day only, the feeding beaker was placed on paper that had been soaked in geraniol (an extract from geranium flowers) for two periods of 15 minutes, one at 10.00 a.m. and the other at 11.00 a.m. Throughout the following day, the bees were confronted with a choice between two empty beakers that were scented either with geraniol or with thyme. They consistently preferred the geraniol beaker. The magnitude of this preference, however, was most marked at 10.00 a.m. and 11.00 a.m., and considerably weaker at other test times, including 10.30 a.m. The marked preference for the geraniol at 10.00 a.m. and 11.00 a.m. must have resulted from the bees' prior experience with the extract at these times. Moreover, it is not at all obvious how the results could be explained by referring to changes in the intensity of an internal state, such as hunger.

These findings can be explained if visits by bees to a feeding station are controlled by some external cue, such as the position of the sun. By making a note of its position whenever food is available, the experiences of one day would enable a return visit to the feeding table at the appropriate times on a subsequent day. Once again, there are good reasons for believing that this explanation is at best incomplete. Wahl (1932) trained bees to leave their hive at the same time every day for food that was a short distance away. Even when this experiment was conducted indoors, and in constant light, the bees reappeared at the feeder 24 hours after their last daily feeding. This result has also been replicated in a salt mine, where the sun could not possibly serve as a cue for the passage of time. Finally, in a study that commenced in France, Renner (1960) trained bees to leave an experimental chamber at a certain time each day for food. They were then flown in their chamber to New York, where it was discovered that they next reappeared for food 24 hours after their last feeding, rather than 29 hours later, which would have been the correct time in New York, as defined by the position of the sun.

There is ample experimental evidence, such as Wahl's (1932) honey-bee study, which shows that feeding can be controlled by an internal clock.

If it is accepted that animals have a 24-hour internal clock, then a series of experiments by Bolles and colleagues has revealed that the use of such a clock is not without its limitations for indicating the time of occurrence of a meal. When rats are reared and housed in conditions that eliminate fluctuations in light, temperature, and so on, they will show an increase in activity prior to meals that occur regularly once every 24 hours (Bolles & Moot, 1973). However, if the meals are presented regularly every 19 hours, or 29 hours, then this increase in anticipatory activity does not take place, even in animals that are reared in an environment where the light-dark cycle is set to these values (Bolles & de Lorge, 1962; Bolles & Stokes, 1965).

Gallistel (1990) has proposed that this pattern of results can be most readily explained by assuming that rats possess an internal clock that cycles once every 24 hours. If rats are fed every 24 hours, it will be possible for a particular state of the internal clock to be associated with food and, as this state approaches each day, so their activity will increase. There is abundant evidence that shows that although the internal clock can adapt to slight changes in the length of each day (between about 21 and 27 hours), the clock is unable to adapt to the size of change that was adopted in the experiments by Bolles. As a consequence, the state of the clock will be different on each day that the animal is fed. For example, if the internal clock cycles once every 24 hours, and food is delivered every 19 hours, then each meal will be associated with a state of the clock that occurs 5 hours in advance of the state associated with the previous meal. No particular state of the internal clock will thus be reliably associated with food, and there will be no cue to regulate anticipatory feeding activity.

A further interesting conclusion that can be drawn from this research is that the internal clock can be used only to indicate times of day, but not intervals of time. If the clock could be used to measure intervals, then rats would be able to identify when a period such as 19 hours had elapsed, and anticipatory activity with this interval between meals should be possible. This conclusion may not be surprising. Our everyday experience with clocks reveals that it is much easier to identify the time than it is to calculate the time that has elapsed since a previous reading of the clock. Even so, we shall see shortly that animals are able to perform this sort of calculation, provided that the intervals are considerably shorter than 19 hours.

There is evidence that animals are able to use an internal clock to identify a time of day with considerable precision. Gallistel (1990, pp. 258, 283–286) has argued that for both rats and bees the clock can regulate their daily activities to within 5 or 10 minutes. Unfortunately, very little is known about the way in which the clock can be used so accurately. Both Gallistel (1990) and Church and Broadbent (1991) consider that periodic timing can be achieved with the use of oscillators. By this they mean that timing is based on changes that occur in the animal on a regular basis. The changes could take place within the central nervous system, but regular changes that occur in the circulatory system, hormonal system, or the behavioral system could also be used for timing (Church & Broadbent, 1990; Mistlberger, 1994). If only a single oscillator were used, then it would have to change consistently throughout a 24-hour period and return to its original state at the end of this period. This would be akin to a clock with a single hand that rotated once every 24 hours. The use of such an oscillator would permit the identification of specific times on successive days, but it might be difficult to discriminate between times that are close together. However, Church and Broadbent (1991) show how a series of oscillators can measure time very precisely. One oscillator would alternate between two states, on and off, every 12 hours. A second oscillator would alternate between these states every 6 hours, and so on. A particular pattern of activation of the entire bank of oscillators would then permit a certain time to be read, with a precision that is determined by the oscillator with the shortest cycle time. The scant evidence that is available does not allow us to decide how many oscillators animals have at their disposal for timing. Indeed, the evidence does not really allow us to decide if timing is based on oscillators.

Interval timing

A clear demonstration of rats timing intervals can be found in the **temporal generalization** experiment by Church and Gibbon (1982). The rats were placed into an illuminated chamber in which the lights were occasionally turned off for periods that ranged from 0.8 to 7.2 seconds. The lights were then turned on and a lever was inserted into the chamber. Lever pressing was rewarded after an interval of darkness of 4 seconds, but not after intervals of darkness that were shorter or longer than this value. The center panel of Figure 10.1 summarizes the performance of the group after it had received extensive training on this task. A response on the lever was most probable after 4 seconds of darkness, but for periods that were either shorter or longer than this value there was an orderly decline in this measure of responding.

The additional training that was then given was similar to that just described, except food was presented after either a 2-second or an 8-second interval of darkness. The results for the rats trained with the 2-second signal are shown in the left-hand panel of Figure 10.1, and those for the other group in the right-hand panel. Responding was again most likely after the interval of darkness that signaled food but, relative to the 4-second signal, the slope of the generalization gradient is steeper for the 2-second signal and gentler for the 8-second signal.

These orderly findings forcefully demonstrate that rats are able to remember the durations of stimuli and whether or not a specific duration signals the availability

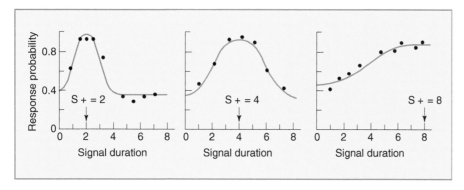

FIGURE 10.1 Mean probability of making a response after a period of darkness that varied in its duration. Responses were followed by food when the preceding period of darkness had been 2 seconds (left-hand panel), 4 seconds (center panel), and 8 seconds (right-hand panel) (adapted from Church & Gibbon, 1982).

of food. Indeed, the results shown in the left-hand panel indicate that the rats were able to discriminate between signals that were of either 2 or 3.2 seconds duration. How, then, is it possible for an animal to remember a specific interval of time? One answer to this question can be found in an information-processing model of timing that was developed by Gibbon, Church, and Meck (1984; see also Gibbon & Church, 1984; Church & Broadbent, 1990), and which is summarized in Figure 10.2.

FIGURE 10.2 An information-processing model for animal timing (adapted from Church & Broadbent, 1990).

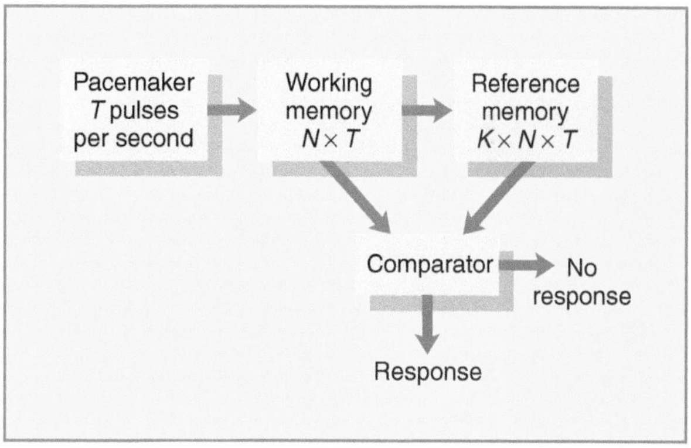

At the heart of the model lies a pacemaker that generates short-duration pulses at a constant rate. When a signal is presented, a switch directs these pulses to **working memory** until the signal is turned off. If the pacemaker generates T pulses per second, and the signal is of N seconds duration, then $N \times T$ pulses will be stored in working memory. At the end of the trial, this value is then transferred to **reference memory**, which will also contain information about whether or not the trial resulted in food. On subsequent trials, the number of pulses in working memory that have been generated during a test stimulus is compared, by means of the comparator, with the contents of reference memory. If the value in working memory should correspond closely with the number of pulses stored in reference memory for a stimulus that previously signaled food, then the animal will respond vigorously. But if these values in working and reference memory should differ, then the likelihood of a response after the test stimulus will be reduced.

An interesting conclusion about this decision process in the comparator can be drawn from the results shown in Figure 10.1. If the decision is based on the absolute difference between the values stored in working memory and reference memory, then the slopes of the gradients shown for the three durations of the signal should have been similar. For example, consider a trial with a 2-second test signal for the group trained with a 4-second food signal, and a trial with a 6-second test signal for the group trained with the 8-second food signal. In both cases the difference between the durations of the training and test signals is 2 seconds. If the magnitude of this difference is principally responsible for determining the response rate on a trial, then both groups should show an equivalent discrimination between the two types of signal. However, an inspection of the center and right-hand panels of Figure 10.1

KEY TERMS

Working memory
A short-lasting memory store that is broadly equivalent to active memory or short-term memory (see Chapters 8 and 9).

Reference memory
A long-lasting memory store that is broadly equivalent to inactive memory or long-term memory (see Chapter 9).

shows this was not the case. Responding after the 6-second test stimulus was similar to that after the 8-second training stimulus, whereas responding after the 2-second test stimulus was substantially slower than after the 4-second training stimulus. Church and Gibbon (1982; see also Gallistel, 1990) proposed, therefore, that the comparison process is based on the ratio of the values stored in working and reference memory. Specifically, when the ratio of the durations of the test and training stimuli is close to 1, which will be the case when these values are 6 and 8 seconds, then responding during the test stimulus will be similar to that during the training stimulus. But as the value of this ratio moves away from 1, which will be the case with a test stimulus duration of 2 seconds and a training stimulus duration of 4 seconds, then responding on the test trials will be progressively weaker than on the training trials.

Further insights into the way in which animals represent temporal intervals have been provided by **scalar timing** theory (Gallistel & Gibbon, 2000), which is based on the assumption that there is a constant relationship between each unit of remembered time and each unit of actual time. In other words, every interval of actual time is believed to be transformed by multiplying it by a constant, scalar factor, K, to determine the interval that is remembered. This fundamental assumption of scalar timing theory can be accommodated into the information-processing model shown in Figure 10.2, by allowing the value $N \times T$ in working memory to be transformed to $K \times N \times T$ when it is transferred to reference memory. Ideally, the value of K would be 1, so that each unit of remembered time will have the same value as each unit of actual time and timing by the animal will always be accurate. This relationship between remembered and actual time is depicted in the left-hand panel of Figure 10.3. In most cases, however, errors will creep into the timing process, and the value of K will differ from 1. If K is less than 1, then the remembered interval of time will be an underestimate of the actual interval, and this will result in the relationship between the two being similar to that shown in the center panel of Figure 10.3. However, if K is greater than 1, then remembered time will be an overestimate of actual time (see right-hand panel of Figure 10.3).

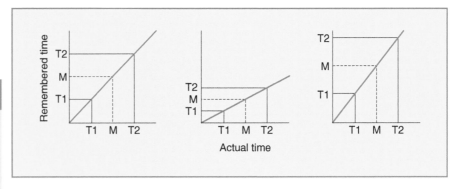

FIGURE 10.3 Three possible relationships between the duration of remembered time relative to the passage of actual time. In the left-hand panel, the duration of a remembered interval is the same as for the actual interval. In the remaining panels the duration of a remembered interval is either less than the actual interval (center panel), or greater than this interval (right-hand panel).

An example of the effects of an error in timing can be found in the **peak procedure** (Roberts, 1982). A single rat was trained to lever press for food in the presence of a distinctive stimulus, such as a white noise. On the majority of trials, the first response that occurred after 20 seconds from the onset of the stimulus resulted in the delivery of food and the stimulus was turned off. Responses prior to this point were without effect. In addition, there were occasional test trials in which the stimulus remained on for at least 40 seconds and all responses were without effect, except the last one, which turned the stimulus off. Figure 10.4 shows the results from the test trials after the rat had received considerable training with this procedure. At the outset of the trial, the rate of responding was slow, but it increased to a maximum at about 20 seconds, whereupon it returned to a low level after 40 seconds had elapsed. This pattern of results is similar to that obtained with the temporal generalization technique, and it can be explained in a similar way with the information-processing model of timing.

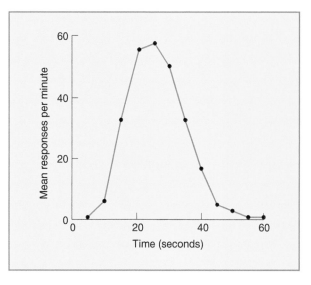

A careful inspection of the results in Figure 10.4 indicates that the peak rate of responding occurred at about 24 seconds, which implies that the rat anticipated food would be delivered later than when it was actually available. To explain this finding, scalar timing theory would assign a value of 1.2 to the scalar factor, K. An important implication of this type of analysis is that the absolute magnitude of errors in timing will increase as the interval being timed becomes larger. Gibbon et al. (1984) have shown that at least for the peak procedure this prediction is correct.

Further tests of scalar timing theory have examined the ability of animals to estimate the midpoint of a temporal interval. Figure 10.3 shows that the midpoint (M) of an interval between two actual times (T1 and T2) will also be the midpoint of the remembered interval. This relationship will be true if animals can time accurately (left-hand panel), or inaccurately (center and right-hand panels). If a way could therefore be found for a rat to show that it has calculated it is at the midpoint of a given interval, then, according to scalar timing theory, this midpoint should correspond to the actual midpoint. An ingenious experiment by Gibbon and Church (1981) was designed to test this prediction.

Rats were trained in conditioning chambers containing two levers. On some trials a light was presented, and 60 seconds later a response to the left lever produced food; on other trials a tone signaled the availability of food 30 seconds later for responses on the right lever. After extensive training with the stimuli presented separately, the preference exhibited for the levers when the stimuli were combined was examined. When the light and tone were switched on simultaneously, there was a marked preference for the right lever, which is to be expected because responding on this lever should produce food in 30 seconds, whereas a minute would have to elapse before food was made available for responding on the left lever. On other trials the tone commenced 45 seconds after the onset of the light, and here the preference was reversed. For this to have occurred, the rats must have calculated that the interval before food was available was less for the left (15 seconds) than the right (30 seconds) lever. Of particular interest is the finding that a preference for neither

FIGURE 10.4 Mean rate of responding during a 60-second test stimulus for rats who had been rewarded for making a response after 20 seconds from the onset of this stimulus (adapted from Roberts, 1982).

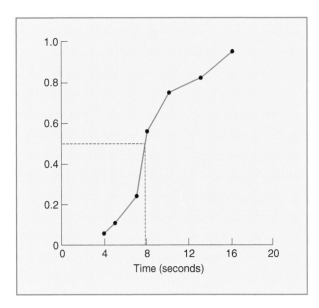

lever was revealed on trials when the tone commenced 30 seconds after the light, which suggests that the rats estimated they were at the midpoint of the light and that food would therefore be available on both levers in 30 seconds.

To be fair, not all experimental results lend such direct support to scalar timing theory. In a study described by Church (1978), rats in test boxes received either short (4 seconds) or long (16 seconds) signals. As soon as the signal had finished, two levers were inserted into the box. Presses on one, the "short" lever, resulted in food if the short signal had been presented, whereas after the long stimulus, presses on the alternative, "long", lever produced food. Once this discrimination had been acquired, test trials were conducted with signal durations that varied between the training values. With durations that were near one or other training value, responses tended to be directed towards the appropriate lever; but with intermediate values there was a reduction of this preference. A summary of the results can be seen in Figure 10.5, which shows how the probability of making a long response varied with the duration of the interval. The odd feature of the results is that the point at which the levers were equally preferred was not 10 seconds, where the value of the test signal was half way between the short and long training values—on these test trials there was a light preference for pressing the long lever. The point of equal preference occurred with test signals that lasted for 8 seconds.

With a little ingenuity, it turns out that these findings can be explained by scalar timing theory (Gibbon & Church, 1981). We saw earlier that comparisons between durations are based on their ratio, rather than their absolute difference. On this basis, the midpoint of the training values would not be given by their arithmetic mean of 10 seconds. Instead, it would be 8 seconds because this value is twice the value of the short duration signal and half the value of the long duration signal. In other words, the similarity between 4 and 8 seconds would be regarded as being the same as between 8 and 16 seconds.

A question that can be raised about the information-processing model of timing developed by Gibbon et al. (1984) concerns the way in which temporal information is stored in reference memory. This information could be intimately related to the experimental stimulus that was used to provide the temporal information. For example, in the temporal generalization experiment described at the beginning of this section the information about duration stored in reference memory could be that a period of darkness of a certain duration signaled the availability of food. However, the information could be more general, such that duration itself, rather than the duration of a particular stimulus, served as the signal for food. In this latter example, the term **amodal representation** is used, because the representation in reference memory is not confined to the modality of the original training stimulus.

One experiment that demonstrates that temporal information may be stored independently of the modality of the training stimulus was conducted by Meck and Church (1982). Rats were trained on a temporal generalization task in which they were rewarded for pressing a lever after they had been exposed to a light of medium, but not short or long duration. The solid line in Figure 10.6 indicates that, with sufficient training, rats learned the discrimination. Meck and Church (1982) then changed the procedure by using white noise rather than light as the temporal signal. The effects of this change, immediately after it was introduced, are shown by the dashed lines in Figure 10.6. It is quite evident that the discrimination was as good with this stimulus as with the light. Because there is physically little in common between a tone and a light, it is likely that an amodal representation of duration gained control over responding and permitted the excellent transfer between the two stimuli. For a similar finding with pigeons see Roberts, Cheng, and Cohen (1989).

Many more experiments could be described that bear on the analysis of animal timing developed by Gibbon et al. (1984). Church (1989), for instance, has reviewed a range of studies that shed light on the biological basis of timing and the way in which it is affected by certain drugs. There is a suggestion that the value of K can be reduced by injections of vasopressin, whereas the rate of the pacemaker can be enhanced by metamphetamine (Church, 1984). There is also evidence to suggest that rats are capable of timing two different intervals simultaneously (Meck & Church, 1984), which indicates that the information-processing model of timing is in need of elaboration. More recently, Church and Broadbent (1991) have developed a connectionist model of timing that captures many of the positive attributes of the information-processing model. In addition, this connectionist model can be shown to provide a good account of the way in which animals respond on a fixed interval schedule of reinforcement (Wearden & Doherty, 1995).

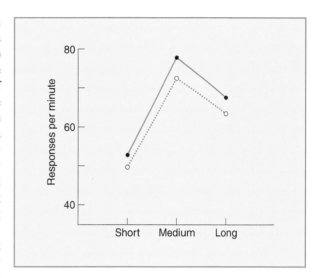

FIGURE 10.6 Average number of responses per minute following the short-, medium-, and long-duration stimuli in the experiment by Meck and Church (1982) (adapted from Meck & Church, 1982).

Alternatives to an internal clock

Even though the idea that animals possess an internal clock for interval timing can explain a variety of experimental findings, several authors have questioned whether animals do, in fact, possess such a clock (Killeen & Fetterman, 1988; Staddon & Higa, 1999). As an alternative, it has been suggested that the onset of a salient stimulus, such as the start of a trial, triggers a sequence of events that enable the animal to behave in a manner that implies it has an internal clock.

If pigeons receive food regularly—at, say, 60-second intervals—then, even though there is no signal to indicate when food will be delivered, there will be an increase in activity at the food magazine shortly before each presentation of food. One explanation for this activity, which does not appeal to timing, is that it is controlled by the memory of the preceding delivery of food. We saw in Chapter 8 that once a salient stimulus has been removed, it may leave a memory trace that will gradually decay. A presentation of food may, therefore, leave an initially strong memory that will weaken gradually as the time until the next delivery of food approaches. The next delivery of food will then take place in the context of a decayed trace of the previous delivery of food, and this decayed trace might enter into an association with food. If it is assumed that the rate of decay of the memory of food is roughly constant from one trial to the next, then a trace with a certain strength will be consistently associated with the delivery of food. This stimulus trace will then be

Killeen and Fetterman (1988) and Machado (1997) believe that the behavioral sequence that follows presentation of food to a hungry animal consists of fixed components.

able to serve as a Pavlovian CS and excite activity in the vicinity of the food hopper just before the end of each 60-second interval. One way of viewing this proposal is that physical time is coded not as value from an internal clock, but as the value of a memory trace (e.g. Sutton & Barto, 1981) or as a pattern of values created by a set of memory traces (e.g. Grossberg & Schmajuk, 1989; Staddon & Higa, 1999).

Another explanation for how animals are able to anticipate events that occur at regular intervals is that their behavior effectively functions as a clock (Killeen & Fetterman, 1988; Machado, 1997). Presenting food to a hungry animal, say a pigeon, will tend to elicit a fairly stereotyped sequence of responses. Obviously, the first of these will be eating, which will last until the food is withdrawn. At this point the bird will then spend some time in the vicinity of the food hopper, and perhaps peck at the floor, before it moves away from the hopper and paces about the chamber Both Killeen and Fetterman (1988) and Machado (1997) believe these activities occur in a fixed sequence and that each component lasts for approximately the same amount of time. If food should be presented at regular intervals then the subject will be engaged in much the same activity before each presentation of food. This activity could then serve as a cue for the forthcoming delivery of food and elicit responses in anticipation of food.

An experiment by Machado and Keen (1999) shows that this explanation need not apply just to experiments where the delivery of food indicates the start of an interval. Pigeons were trained in a task in which a central response key was illuminated white for either 4 or 16 seconds. This key was then turned off and two side keys were illuminated: one blue, the other yellow. To gain reward, it was necessary to peck the blue key if the center key had been illuminated for 4 seconds, and the yellow key if the center key had been illuminated for 16 seconds. Machado and Keen (1999) noticed that the illumination of the center key eventually elicited a similar sequence of responses in many of the birds. On first being illuminated they would move towards the center key and occasionally peck it. If the center key was illuminated for only 4 seconds, the birds ceased pecking it when it was turned off and selected the blue rather then the yellow key when the side keys were illuminated. On the remaining trials the birds would cease pecking the center key after about 6 seconds and then different birds engaged in different activities (some moved about the box, others looked at the house light) until the center key went dark and the side keys were illuminated. At this point they would generally select the yellow key. Thus there was a very close correspondence between the activity in which the pigeons were engaged and the side key that they selected. Using a rather different task, Machado and Keen (2003) have found additional evidence that the choices made by an animal in a temporal discrimination can be predicted on the basis of the behavior in which an animal is engaged when the choice stimuli are presented.

There is, therefore, a wide range of findings to show that animals can make judgments based on the passage of an interval of time. It would be convenient to conclude that these findings demonstrate that the judgments are based on an internal clock, or a decaying memory trace, or responses made by the animal. However, quite how animals measure the passage of time remains a matter of debate. An indication of the vigor of this debate can found in pages 253–301 of volume 71 of the *Journal of the Experimental Analysis of Behavior* (1999), where various commentators express contrasting opinions in response to the argument by Staddon and Higa (1999) that interval timing is based on decaying memory traces, not an internal clock. Some support this argument, others do not; and there is little indication as to how, or when, this debate will be resolved.

NUMBER

At the turn of the twentieth century, a horse named Clever Hans was said to possess remarkable intellectual skills (Pfungst, 1965/1908). A photograph of Hans with his trainer is shown in Figure 10.7. In response to being posed an arithmetic question by his trainer, Hans would tap a hoof on the ground for the number of times that corresponded to the correct answer. The problems that Hans solved were not always simple. For example, in response to seeing the expression ½ + ⅖ written on a blackboard, he correctly tapped 9, followed after a pause by 10 to indicate the solution ⁹⁄₁₀. He was not confined to replying to questions written on the blackboard.

FIGURE 10.7 Clever Hans (from Pfungst, 1965).

When in the presence of a large audience, his trainer might ask Hans to identify the number of people carrying an umbrella and the horse would again reply correctly. For a while, this behavior was taken as evidence that horses are capable of mental arithmetic, but a detailed examination of the conditions in which Hans performed yielded a different interpretation. Apparently, Hans' trainer calculated the answer to the problem, and after the correct number of taps he unconsciously moved. This movement, albeit slight, was a sufficient cue for Hans to stop tapping his hoof and coincidentally provide the correct answer.[1]

One of Hans' intriguing abilities is that he was often correct even when the questions were posed by people other than his trainer. It seems that once they have posed a question to an animal, humans commonly adopt a tense posture, which is relaxed as soon as the correct answer has been reached. Hans was evidently sensitive to these subtle changes in behavior. Of course, Hans was never correct if the questioner did not know the answer.

The study of counting in animals did not cease with Clever Hans. During the last 100 years or so, well over 100 experimental studies of counting by animals have been reported. In the following section a few of these experiments will be described with the aim of revealing what is known about the numerical competence of animals.

Relative numerosity

An examination of the center array in Figure 10.8 will reveal that it contains more red than blue circles. In fact the ratio of red to blue is 26 : 10 and our ability to tell there is more of one element than the other indicates that we are sensitive to relative numerosity. Honig and Stewart (1989) conducted an experiment to determine if pigeons are also sensitive to relative numerosity. A single group was initially trained with the pattern in the left-hand array of Figure 10.8 (the red array) as a signal for food, and with the pattern in the right-hand array (the blue array) as a signal for the absence of food. Once the discrimination had been solved, the birds received test trials with patterns containing different mixtures of the two colors. The results from the test

---

[1] Hans' trainer is said to have believed firmly in the arithmetic ability of his horse. When eventually he was persuaded that this was not the case, he became severely depressed and died a short time later.

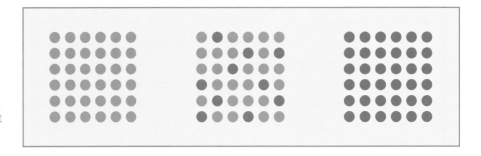

FIGURE 10.8 Three patterns that were used to study a relative numerosity discrimination in pigeons. Training was conducted initially with the patterns on the left and right, and then test trials were conducted with patterns containing mixtures of red and blue circles, such as the pattern in the center (adapted from Honig & Stewart, 1989).

are depicted by the solid line in Figure 10.9. The vertical axis depicts the rate of responding during a trial, which is shown in a rather unusual way—the response rate during a pattern is expressed as a proportion of the rate of responding to that during the red array. The horizontal axis depicts the proportion of red to blue circles in a test pattern ranging from 0 (the blue array) through .62 (the central square in Figure 10.8) to 1 (the red array). There is a direct relationship between the proportion of red circles in a test pattern and the rate of responding in the presence of that pattern.

The results can be explained in two ways, which make different assumptions about the numerical abilities of pigeons. One explanation is that the birds were aware that the red array contained 36 red circles. The rate of responding during a test pattern could then be determined by the number of red circles it contained. Patterns with few or no red circles would be responded to slowly, whereas those containing red circles numbering close to 36 would excite high response rates. The other explanation is that the birds were insensitive to the absolute number of items within a square, but were more interested in the relative proportions of the items. Squares containing entirely red circles, or a large proportion of red to blue circles, would be responded to rapidly, whereas those containing a low proportion of red to blue circles would be responded to slowly.

Honig and Stewart (1989) used a very simple method for choosing between these explanations. The same birds were given the same test trials again, except that now there were 16 rather than 36 elements in each pattern. If the training resulted in the birds basing their responding during the test patterns on the number of red circles that were present, then for each red : blue ratio, responding should be slower during the patterns with 16 elements than with 36 elements. The results from the tests with the 16-element patterns, which are shown by the dashed line in Figure 10.9, failed to confirm this prediction because performance was identical to that with the 36-element test patterns. Thus the results imply that during the test trials the birds responded principally on the relative numerosities of the red and blue circles, not the absolute number of red circles. Later, we will consider an explanation for how the relative numerosity of two items can influence behavior in the manner shown in Figure 10.9, but first we shall examine whether animals can, in other circumstances, determine the absolute number of times that a single item occurs.

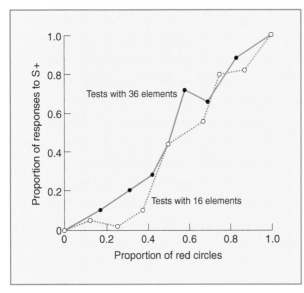

FIGURE 10.9 Relative numerosity generalization gradients for a group of pigeons who were tested with patterns containing either sixteen or thirty-six elements (adapted from Honig & Stewart, 1989).

Absolute number

A wide range of experiments has tested whether animals are sensitive to the number of times that some event takes place. In essence, these experiments have studied whether animals are capable of counting responses, counting sequentially presented stimuli, and counting simultaneously presented stimuli. After considering examples of each type of study, we shall review the various ways in which their findings can be explained. There are reasonable grounds for believing that some animals are able to count in a more honest way than Clever Hans.

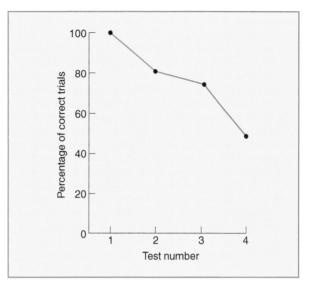

Responses

Mechner (1958; Mechner & Guevrekian, 1962) required a rat to press a lever for a specified number of times, before pressing another lever in order to earn food. Although subjects were able to earn reward when the criterion number for first lever presses was as high as 24, they also made many errors. A rather different study of counting responses was conducted by Rumbaugh and Washburn (1993) with a chimpanzee that had been trained to move a cursor on a computer monitor with a joystick. At the start of a trial, an Arabic numeral (1, 2, 3, or 4) was presented on the screen together with an array of colored rectangles, of which there were often considerably more than four. The chimpanzee was then required to delete the rectangles, by placing the cursor on them, until the number that had disappeared from the screen corresponded to the Arabic numeral. After extensive training, the chimpanzee achieved a consistently high level of accuracy on this task. Figure 10.10 shows her performance for each of the numbers with which she was tested. Even though her accuracy declined as the number of rectangles to be deleted increased, the chimpanzee's performance was still in excess of chance for every number.

FIGURE 10.10 The percentage of correct trials by a chimpanzee who was required to delete a specified number, from 1 to 4, of rectangles from a computer monitor. The results are from all test trials; chance performance was calculated to be at 20% (adapted from Rumbaugh & Washburn, 1993).

Sequential stimuli

Capaldi and Miller (1988) devised an ingeniously simple experiment to study the counting of sequential stimuli by rats. The subjects were placed into the start box of a straight alley, about 200 centimeters in length, and required to run to a goal box to gain food that was available only intermittently. The trials were conducted in blocks of two different sequences. For the RRRN sequence there were four trials, with reward occurring on all but the last trial. There were five trials in the NRRRN block, of which the middle three led to reward. Typically the interval between each trial of a block was about 15 seconds, and each block was separated by about 15 minutes. The blocks were presented randomly, with the consequence that on the first trial of a block the rat would be unable to anticipate whether or not it would receive food. The speed of running down the alley to the goal box for each trial of the two kinds of block is shown in Figure 10.11. In both blocks, subjects ran rapidly on every trial except the last. To explain this pattern of results, Capaldi and Miller (1988) argued that the rats counted the number of rewards they had received within a block, and that once they had received three, this served as a cue that the next trial would not result

FIGURE 10.11 The mean speed of running down an alley by a group of rats for successive trials within a block. On five-trial blocks (NRRRN) reward was available on trials two, three, and four; on four-trial blocks (RRRN) reward was available on trials one, two, and three (adapted from Capaldi & Miller, 1988).

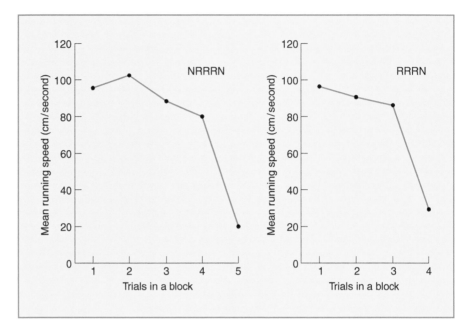

FIGURE 10.11 The mean speed of running down an alley by a group of rats for successive trials within a block. On five-trial blocks (NRRRN) reward was available on trials two, three, and four; on four-trial blocks (RRRN) reward was available on trials one, two, and three (adapted from Capaldi & Miller, 1988).

in food. One obvious effect of such a cue would be to reduce the running speed in the final trial of each block.

Another method for studying counting with sequentially presented stimuli was developed by Meck and Church (1983). Rats in a conditioning chamber were presented with either a few signal composed of two pulses of white noise, or a many signal composed of eight pulses. Two levers were then inserted into the chamber and food was delivered for pressing the left lever after the few signal, or the right lever after the many lever. The discrimination was mastered with little difficulty.

An explanation that comes to mind for the outcome of this last experiment is based on the ability of rats to time rather than count. Both signals consisted of 0.5-second pulses of white noise, separated by an equivalent period of silence. Thus the duration of the few signal was 2 seconds, whereas the many signal lasted 8 seconds and it is possible that rats referred to this difference to solve the discrimination. In order to confirm that rats can discriminate between few and many sequentially presented stimuli on the basis of numerical information, Breukelaar and Dalrymple-Alford (1998) conducted an experiment based on the design of Meck and Church (1983). On this occasion, however, the duration of each component of the few and the many signals varied randomly from trial to trial. Thus the only information that could be used to solve the discrimination was the number of pulses in each signal, and this was sufficient to enable rats to perform accurately.

Simultaneous stimuli

An excellent example of the ability of animals to count simultaneously presented stimuli is provided by Brannon and Terrace (2000). Monkeys were presented with an array of four discrete patterns on a computer monitor. Each pattern contained one, two, three or four objects (sketches of two possible arrays are shown in Figure 10.12). To gain reward, each pattern had to be touched in turn, starting with the one containing a single object, then the one containing two objects, and so on. To make matters more complicated, the positions of the four patterns on the screen, and the positions of the objects within a pattern, varied randomly from trial to trial. In addition, the size of the objects varied randomly across the four items, and so did their shape and orientation. It was thus impossible to solve this task by referring to some cue such as the total area occupied by all the objects in a pattern. Rather, the only cue that the monkeys could use was the number of objects. With careful training, the monkeys eventually solved the problem and touched the patterns in the correct order with a high degree of accuracy. Moreover, this accuracy was observed with sets of novel patterns. A related study has been conducted with crows that apparently were able to tell the difference between two patterns containing eleven and twelve objects (Zorina & Smirnova, 1996).

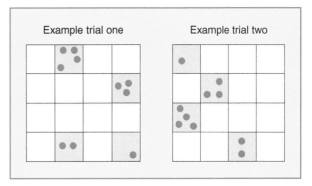

FIGURE 10.12
Sketches of two possible arrangements of the stimuli used in an experiment to study counting in monkeys. Subjects were required to touch the four arrays in each panel in ascending order of the number of dots they contained (adapted from Brannon & Terrace, 2000).

The representation of number

The foregoing experiments demonstrate that animals can identify the number of responses they have made, the number of times an item has been repeatedly presented, and the number of items present in an array. But how is this numerical information represented? A glance at any statistics textbook will reveal that number can be represented in a variety of ways. At its most basic, a number can be represented on a **nominal scale** as nothing more than a label for a particular item (which is not really a scale). A frequently cited example is the number on the back of a footballer's shirt. If humans were to adopt this level of measurement then they might solve the problem set by Brannon and Terrace (2000) by assigning four arbitrary labels to the four items, say A through D, and learn to select A first, then B and so on. An important property of nominal measurement is that it does not permit any inference to be made about the relative magnitudes of the items represented by the arbitrary labels. To make this inference, it is necessary for the number of objects in an item to be represented on an **ordinal scale**. Ordinal scales allow items to be ordered in a rank so that it can be inferred that an item higher in the rank contains more objects than one lower in the rank.

As they have been described, the experiments in this section do not allow a choice to be made as to whether subjects were responding on the basis of the nominal or ordinal properties of the numerosities to which they were exposed. By default, therefore, we should conclude that the numbers were represented nominally. However, additional trials in the experiment by Brannon and Terrace (2000) imply that monkeys, at least, are able to represent number on an ordinal scale (see also Brannon, Cantlon, & Terrace, 2006). Each trial consisted of the presentation of a novel pair of patterns and they both contained more than four objects. On these trials, the monkeys showed a strong tendency to select the pattern with the fewer objects first, and then the one containing the greater number of objects. If monkeys solved the original training by assigning the four patterns to four nominal categories, then they should not know how to respond to the two new patterns because the original categories will not apply to them. On the other hand, if they used ordinal categories to classify the four training patterns, then they might

KEY TERMS

Nominal scale
A set of numbers that serves to label different objects.

Ordinal scale
A set of numbers that denote different positions in sequence.

have learned to select the item with the fewest objects first, and then move on to the item with the next fewest objects, and so on. The results from the test trial therefore imply that the monkeys had indeed adopted this strategy and that it transferred to the test trials.

Although these results suggest that monkeys appreciate the ordinal properties of the quantities they are comparing, additional findings by Brannon and Terrace (2000; see also Brannon et al., 2006) are not consistent with this conclusion. Monkeys were trained in a similar manner to that just described, except that they had to touch the four training patterns in descending rather than ascending order. Despite being successful with this training, they were unsuccessful when they received test trials with pairs of patterns, each containing more than four objects, and were expected to select first the one with the larger number of objects. The reasons for this failure to confirm the conclusions drawn from the original study are complex and not fully understood (see Brannon & Terrace, 2000; Brannon et al., 2006). For the present, it is probably safe to say that the experiment by Brannon and Terrace (2000) suggests, but does not confirm, an appreciation of the ordinal properties of different quantities by monkeys.

Numerical symbols

If you or I had been given the task set by Brannon and Terrace (2000) for their monkeys, then we would probably solve it by using numbers to identify the four training patterns, and the test patterns. Indeed, it hardly needs to be said that a crucial aspect of counting for humans is our ability to use arbitrary symbols to represent specific numbers of objects. No-one has suggested that the success of the monkeys in the study by Brannon and Terrace (2000) depends on them using arbitrary symbols. Rather little is known, in fact, about how they translated the four different quantities used in the training patterns into a numerical representation. But evidence is beginning to grow which shows that certain animals can be trained to refer to different quantities by different symbols.

Boysen and Berntson (1989) describe a study with a chimpanzee called Sheba. In one stage of her training, Sheba would be shown Arabic numerals ranging from 0 to 4 in a row behind a tray containing from zero to four items of food. If she selected the numeral that corresponded with the number of food items then she was allowed to eat the food. After this training she was then tested by being shown a collection of everyday objects; she was expected to select the numeral that indicated the number of objects she had just seen. Despite not being trained on this last task, she correctly selected the appropriate numeral on thirteen out of fifteen trials (for a similar study see Matsuzawa, 1985).

FIGURE 10.13 Alex participating in a trial in which he is asked to identify the number of blocks that are of a particular color (photograph by Arlene Levin-Rowe, courtesy of the Alex Foundation).

Pepperberg (1994; see also Pepperberg & Gordon, 2005) tested an African grey parrot (called Alex, who we met in Chapter 7) that had been trained over many years to respond with spoken words to questions that were addressed to him. A more detailed account of this training can be found in Chapter 13, for the present it is sufficient to know that he was able to say in English the numbers one to six. Figure 10.13 shows Alex taking part in a typical trial in which he might be asked "How

TABLE 10.1 Examples of the different types of test trial used for a study of counting by a parrot. Note singular labels were used for all the questions to avoid cueing *one* (adapted from Pepperberg, 1994)

Objects	Question	Alex's reply
1 orange chalk, 2 orange wood, 4 purple wood, 5 purple chalk	How many purple wood?	4
1 yellow block, 2 grey block, 4 yellow wool, 6 gray wool	How many yellow block?	1
1 rose wood, 2 blue nail, 3 blue wood, 5 rose nail	How many rose nail?	5
2 grey truck, 3 grey key, 4 orange key, 5 orange truck	How many grey key?	2, 3
1 blue box, 3 green box, 4 blue cup, 6 green cup	How many green cup?	6
1 blue box, 2 green rock, 3 purple plastic key, 4 green plastic key	How many green rock?	2

many red wood?" and Alex would be expected to reply with the correct number. A sample of the questions that were posed to Alex, together with his answers, are shown in Table 10.1. Even though a novel array was presented on each test trial, his answers were considerably better than would be expected on the basis of chance.

These two studies suggest that animals can use numerical symbols to refer to specific quantities. What remains to be determined is whether these symbols have any additional properties. To address this question, Pepperberg (2006b) continued Alex's training by teaching him to label correctly the Arabic numerals 1 to 6. A typical trial for this training might consist of him being presented with an array of the six numerals, each one a different color, and then being asked "What number red?". It is important to stress that during this stage Alex did not associate the labels with the relevant physical quantities. He was then given a test—see Figure 10.14—in which he was shown two Arabic numerals of different colors, but the same area, and asked "What color bigger?". Even on the first test with each pair of numerals, Alex's answers were correct significantly more often than would be expected on the basis of chance. The implication of this impressive study is that Alex was indeed able to appreciate the relative magnitudes, and hence the ordinal properties, of the quantities referred to by the numbers one to six.

FIGURE 10.14 Alex participating in a trial in which he has to identify the color of the numeral with the larger value (photograph by Arlene Levin-Rowe, courtesy of the Alex Foundation).

Addition with quantities and symbols

Some time after Alex had been trained to pronounce numbers, he was given a new problem (Pepperberg, 2006a). He would be shown two inverted cups. One of the

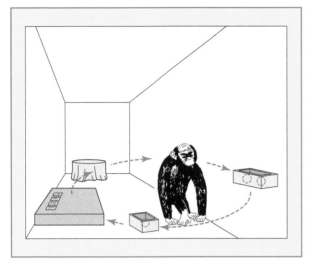

FIGURE 10.15
Experimental setting for a symbol counting task (adapted from Boysen & Berntson, 1989).

cups was lifted for a few seconds to reveal a small number of the same object, e.g. nuts. After the first cup had been replaced over the nuts, the second cup was lifted for a few seconds to reveal another small quantity of nuts. Alex was then asked "How many nut total?". He replied correctly considerably more often than would be expected if he just guessed the answer. A similar finding has been reported with Sheba (Boysen & Berntson, 1989). After the training that has just been described, Sheba was allowed into the room depicted in Figure 10.15, in which oranges were hidden in as many as three different places. To gain reward, Sheba was expected to inspect the three locations, and then select the numeral that corresponded to the total number of oranges that she had seen. From the outset of this testing, her performance was very accurate. The authors of both of these studies claim that they demonstrate that an animal can sum small quantities. These are intriguing findings but, as we shall see shortly, they are not easy to explain.

An even more intriguing finding comes from a final test that was conducted with Sheba. She was again allowed into the room depicted in Figure 10.15 but instead of oranges she found Arabic numerals in the two locations. From the first session of testing onwards, Sheba responded correctly by selecting the Arabic numeral that corresponded to the sum of the two numerals that she had just inspected. The number of trials that she received with each total, the number of times that she was correct with these totals, and the numerals she was shown to create the totals are shown in Table 10.2. The implication of this finding is that Sheba was capable of summing small quantities with numerical symbols to identify the quantities concerned.

This last result has implications for our understanding of the information that is represented by the numerical symbols that Sheba used. As well as nominal and ordinal scales, quantities can be measured according to an **interval scale**. This scale has the same properties as a nominal and ordinal scale, but in addition, the distances between any two adjacent points on the scale are equal. As a result of this property, it is possible to conduct addition and subtraction with values from an interval scale. The ability of Sheba to add correctly with the symbols that she used, therefore implies that they represented quantities measured according to an interval scale.

TABLE 10.2 Details of the different types of test trial used for a study of counting by a chimpanzee (adapted from Boysen & Berntson, 1989)

Sum	Test items	Number of trials	Number of correct trials
1	1 + 0	8	7
2	0 + 2	11	10
	1 + 1		
3	0 + 3	12	10
	1 + 2		
4	0 + 4	12	11
	1 + 3		

Theoretical interpretation

The experiments considered in this section have revealed that animals can respond on the basis of the numerical attributes of stimuli. But how are they able to use this numerical information?

Subitizing

When humans are asked to report the number of items in an array, they are able to respond both rapidly and accurately for numbers up to 6. This performance is said to depend on the ability to **subitize**. Subitizing can be contrasted with either estimating, which is less accurate but can be applied to much larger numbers, or counting, which again can be applied to large numbers but which involves the slow process of enumerating one by one. A number of authors have proposed that subitizing does not depend on counting; instead, it is regarded as more of a perceptual process where a frequently recurring pattern of stimulation elicits the appropriate numerical response. Although subitizing has been offered as an explanation for counting in animals (Davis & Perusse, 1988), others are less than enthusiastic about this proposal (Capaldi, 1993; Miller, 1993; Brannon & Terrace, 2000). They point to the fact that there is no clear test to determine whether subitizing has taken place. There is also the problem of specifying how a particular pattern becomes associated with a given number. At present, it is not possible to decide whether or not animals are capable of subitizing. However, we can note that subitizing is normally said to occur with simultaneously presented events. It would thus be unreasonable to apply this account to the results obtained with sequentially presented stimuli. Furthermore, the capacity of monkeys (Brannon & Terrace, 2000) and crows (Zorina & Smirnova, 1996) to discriminate between pairs of patterns that contain different, relatively large, numbers of objects is difficult to explain by reference to subitizing. Finally, subitizing is normally assumed to take place when the items to be counted are presented by themselves. The ability of Alex to count the members of one class of objects, when they were intermixed with members of a different class of objects, further demonstrates that, at best, subitizing provides an incomplete explanation for the way in which animals count.

Perceptual matching

Rumbaugh and Washburn (1993) and Thomas and Lorden (1993) have proposed that perceptual matching may be responsible for the outcome of many demonstrations of counting by animals. According to this explanation, animals take a "snapshot" of the training stimulus that contains numerical information. They are then assumed to compare this snapshot with a test pattern in order to determine how to respond on a subsequent test trial. To take a simple example, in the relative numerosity discrimination studied by Honig and Stewart (1989), it is possible that pigeons acquired snapshots of the two training arrays shown in Figure 10.8. The presentation of a test pattern, formed from a mixture of red and blue circles, would then result in it being compared with both snapshots. If the test pattern contained many more red than blue circles, for example, then it would be quite similar to the all red pattern (and quite different to the all blue pattern), and elicit a response that was similar to the one normally directed to the all red pattern.

Additional findings can be explained by a perceptual matching account, if it is accepted that animals can remember sequences of events. For example, the rats in the study by Meck and Church (1983) might have formed a memory of the sequence noise–silence–noise, and associated this with pressing the left lever. Subsequent presentations of the stimulus *few* would then activate this memory and lead to the correct response being performed. It is not unreasonable to suppose that explanations based on this type of analysis can also explain the findings by Capaldi and Miller (1988) and Rumbaugh and Washburn (1993).

A clear prediction of a perceptual matching explanation for counting is that animals will be able to respond correctly only with familiar training stimuli. If they are presented with a novel test stimulus, they should not know how to react to it. The results of the experiment by Brannon and Terrace (2000) provide mixed support for this prediction. They found that monkeys were able to perform correctly with some novel numerical arrays but not others. Whether a perceptual matching account can be developed to explain their findings satisfactorily remains to be seen. Another problem for a perceptual matching explanation for counting is that it is unable to explain how Alex and Sheba were able to perform addition.

Counting

If Alex or Sheba were human, we would happily explain their behavior by saying that they counted the number of items that they were shown by using numerical symbols. But we should be very cautious about using this explanation for animals that have either no, or at best limited, linguistic ability. At the very least, if we are to say that an animal is capable of counting, then we should specify precisely what is meant by this term.

To explain successful counting Gelman and Gallistel (1978) made use of the term "numerons". Numerons are labels that represent numerosities, they are not necessarily written or spoken, and they form an essential part of the counting process. The role of numerons in counting is revealed in the following quotation (Gallistel, 1993, pp. 217–218):

> *Counting processes obey three constraints:*
>
> *(a) The one–one principle: Each item in the set is assigned one and only one numeron.*
> *(b) The stable-ordering principle: The order in which numerons are assigned is always the same.*
> *(c) The cardinal principle: The final numeron assigned, and only the final numeron, is used as the representative of the numerosity of the set.*

Thus all groups of things that are represented by the same numeron will contain the same number of items. By virtue of being represented by the same numeron, the groups can then be treated in the same way, and categorization on the basis of number will be successful.

The clear way in which this analysis of counting by Gallistel (1993) is presented draws attention to a number of its deficiencies. It does not explain what a numeron is, how a numeron can be acquired, or how one numeron differs from another. At present, the results from studies of counting by animals barely allow us to speculate as to how these issues will be resolved in the future. None the less, a valuable contribution of the analysis of counting developed by Gallistel (1993; Gelman & Gallistel, 1978) is that it provides a framework to guide further research on this topic.

SERIAL ORDER

The aim of this section is to consider how animals represent serial order. A number of relatively simple experiments have shown that animals can remember the order in which a sequence of stimuli has been presented, or a sequence of responses must be performed. Using a **serial recognition** task Weisman, Wasserman, Dodd, and Larew (1980) presented pigeons with sequences of two colors: red–green, green–red, green–green, and red–red. Pecks on a response key after the first of these sequences resulted in the delivery of food, but reward was never presented after the remaining three sequences. Not many sessions were required before the birds were responding more rapidly after the red-green sequence than any other sequence, which confirms that they were influenced by the order in which the stimuli were presented. Similar results have been reported with sequences of three stimuli by Terrace (1986) and Roitblat, Bever, Helweg, and Harley (1991). In a response-chaining study, Balleine et al. (1995) required rats to press a lever and then pull a chain that was suspended from the ceiling in order to gain reward. Subjects had little trouble with learning to execute this sequence.

Successful performance on the serial recognition task has been taken as evidence that animals are able to represent the sequence with which stimuli are presented (Weisman et al., 1980; Terrace, 1986). One way of characterizing this knowledge is to assume, using terminology introduced in previous chapters, that a representation of the first element of the correct sequence enters into an association with a representation of the next element and that this chain is retained in long-term memory. By comparing the memory of the chain on subsequent trials with the sequence that is presented, it would be possible to determine whether or not responding will produce reward.

Successful **response chaining** can be most easily explained if it is accepted that instrumental conditioning results in the growth of stimulus–response (S–R) associations. In the experiment by Balleine et al. (1995), the conditioning chamber might serve as a discriminative stimulus that elicits the response of lever pressing. A press on the lever will then generate a specific pattern of feedback, which could serve as the stimulus that elicits the next component in the sequence, chain pulling.

The ability of animals to learn chains of responses, and to recognize certain sequences of stimuli, can thus be explained by principles that we encountered in earlier chapters. But the use of a rather different task for studying sequence learning has revealed findings that are not so readily explained by these principles. In this task, an animal is presented with an array of, say, four stimuli and it must make the same response to each of them in the correct sequence in order to gain reward (Terrace, Straub, Bever & Seidenberg, 1977). Terrace (1986) refers to this task as **simultaneous chaining**. Evidence is accumulating that suggests pigeons and monkeys solve this problem in different ways. Because of this possibility, we shall examine separately the results from these species.

Pigeons

Studies of simultaneous chaining with pigeons are typically conducted in a test chamber containing a response panel composed of eight response locations arranged in a 4 × 2 matrix (Terrace, 1987, 1991). Each response location is about 2.5 cm in diameter and a colored circle—which can be red (A), green (B), blue (C), yellow (D), or violet (E)—can be projected onto any response location. On a typical trial for

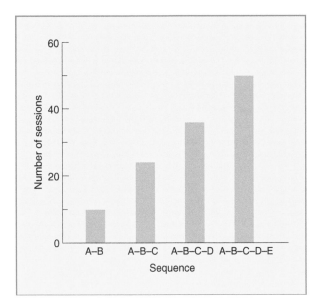

FIGURE 10.16 The mean number of sessions of training required for the various stages of a simultaneous chaining experiment with pigeons (adapted from Terrace, 1987).

a well-trained pigeon, five randomly selected locations are simultaneously illuminated with the five colors and the bird must peck the colors in a predetermined sequence, A–B–C–D–E, to obtain reward. As the bird progresses through the sequence, there is no change to the array. Thus the five colors remain present until the final one had been pecked. At this point, the entire array is extinguished and food delivered. Any errors of pecking a color out of sequence result in the array being extinguished and no food is presented.

Those with little experience of training pigeons may be surprised to discover that this is not an easy task for them to learn. Their training must commence with the first pair of items from the list A–B, and when they are able to peck A before B, they are introduced to the triad A–B–C. Training is then continued with A–B–C–D and finally A–B–C–D–E. The histograms in Figure 10.16 show the mean number of sessions (with forty trials in a session) that a group of five pigeons required to master each stage of training. In all, some 120 daily sessions were needed before a satisfactory level of performance was obtained with the five-item list.

The most widely accepted explanation for the way in which pigeons solve this serial problem is by assuming they treat it as a sequence of discriminations (D'Amato & Colombo, 1988; Terrace, 1991). The onset of the array might serve as a cue for pecking A. Once A has been pecked, the action of withdrawing the beak from A would provide a unique pattern of stimulation that could then serve as a cue for pecking B. The feedback generated by withdrawing from B could then serve as a discriminative stimulus for pecking at C, and so forth, until E is pecked. In other words, pigeons are believed to solve the serial learning task by acquiring a chain of responses, where the feedback from one response serves as the cue for the next response.

The merits of this analysis are revealed by further results reported by Terrace (1987). Once pigeons had been trained on a five-item series, they received test trials with pairs of items from the training sequence, such as AC, CD, and so on. The results from these tests can be seen in Figure 10.15, which shows the percentage of trials on which the members of each pair were pecked in the correct sequence. Thus A was pecked before B on more than 80% of the trials with AB, whereas B and C were pecked first equally often on trials with BC. The results in Figure 10.17 can be summarized by saying that responding was accurate on any pair that contained either the first item, A, or the last item, E, whereas performance was poor with pairs that were composed of two intermediate items, B, C, or D.

According to the account that has just been developed, the onset of any test array will serve as a discriminative stimulus for pecking A. Subjects should thus peck this stimulus first whenever it occurs in a test pair. Having pecked A, subjects will have no option but to peck its partner second, which will then ensure successful completion of the test sequence. The results from the test trials with AB, AC, AD, and AE are consistent with this analysis. Turning now to the trials with BC, BD, and CD, their onset might also elicit a tendency to peck at A. But in the absence of any opportunity to peck this key, the pigeons will lack the stimulation to guide their first response and they should thus choose an item at random. Once again, the results from the trials with these pairs are consistent with a response-chaining analysis. Of course, this analysis

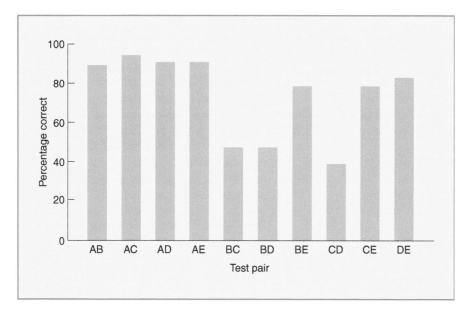

FIGURE 10.17 The mean percentage of correct responses on test trials with pairs of stimuli, after pigeons have been trained with the simultaneous chain A–B–C–D–E (adapted from Terrace, 1987).

also predicts poor performance with the pairs BE, CE, and DE, but the level of accuracy on these trials was much the same as with the pairs containing A. To explain these results, therefore, it is generally accepted that the serial training results in a tendency to refrain from pecking E until all the other keys have been pecked (D'Amato & Colombo, 1988; Straub & Terrace, 1981).

In summary, the results of the test trials with the intermediate pairs are important because they suggest that pigeons lacked any detailed knowledge about the structure of the list. If they possessed that knowledge, then they should have preferred, for example, to peck C before D with the pair CD. Their failure to respond in this manner lends considerable support to the overall principles of a response-chaining analysis for serial learning.

Chunking

The results thus far suggest that pigeons perform rather poorly on simultaneous chaining tasks, but a considerable improvement can be brought about if the method of training is changed slightly. Terrace (1991) trained a group in the same way as that just described, but the stimuli were different. Instead of receiving five colors, the birds were presented with an array composed of three colors (A, B, C) and two geometric shapes (X, Y). Food was delivered after these stimuli had been pecked in the sequence A–B–C–X–Y. Figure 10.18 shows the number of sessions that were required for each of the training stages in this experiment.

The differences between these results and those reported by Terrace (1987) are striking. Training in the new experiment with the four- and five-item sequence was much more efficient than in the original study, with the result that there was a total of

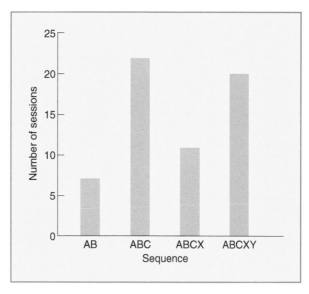

FIGURE 10.18 The mean number of sessions of training required in the various stages of a simultaneous chaining experiment with pigeons. Stimuli A, B, and C were colors, and stimuli X and Y were geometric shapes (adapted from Terrace, 1991).

around sixty training sessions. Furthermore, when test trials were conducted with pairs of stimuli, performance was accurate with each of the ten possible pairs. In one respect, this pattern of results is not surprising. Many studies of human memory show that changing the nature of the items part of the way through a list will facilitate considerably the memory for that list (Watkins, 1977; Brooks & Watkins, 1990).

Although these findings might not be surprising, they are hard to explain with a response-chaining analysis for serial learning. According to this analysis, it should not matter whether the items from a list belong to the same or different categories. Providing the items are easy to distinguish, the only factor that will determine how long it will take to master the problem is the number of items in the list.

Terrace (1991) interprets these findings in terms of chunking. By this he means that the use of two types of stimuli encouraged the pigeons to regard the serial task as being composed of two lists, the first containing three items and the second two. Additional studies by Terrace and Chen (1991a,b) lend this proposal considerable support. But why should chunking help pigeons to learn a list of five items? We shall see shortly that, compared with pigeons, monkeys find simultaneous chaining problems with five similar elements relatively easy. To explain this outcome, it has been suggested that monkeys are able to remember lists of five items. Perhaps, therefore, pigeons can remember a list of no more than three items. In which case, they could then reduce the A–B–C–X–Y sequence to two manageable lists, and there would be no need to rely on response chaining to solve the problem.

Monkeys

D'Amato and Colombo (1988) describe a single experiment with monkeys, which was effectively of the same design as the first of the pigeon studies. Of course, the monkeys were not expected to peck at the stimuli; they had to touch them instead. Figure 10.19 shows the mean number of trials that were required by a group of five cebus monkeys to pass through the various stages of training. The monkeys mastered their problem more readily than the pigeons, but this might have occurred because there were five rather than eight response locations for the monkeys. When they received their test trials with pairs of stimuli, the monkeys performed accurately with every possible test pair. The fact that the monkeys were able to respond accurately with the pairs composed of the intermediate items (B, C, and D), whereas the pigeons were not suggests that these different species solved the serial-learning task in different ways.

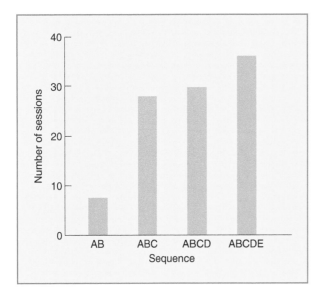

FIGURE 10.19 The mean number of sessions of training required for the various stages of a simultaneous chaining experiment with monkeys (adapted from D'Amato & Colombo, 1988).

Before we examine how monkeys represent serial order, it would be useful to consider some additional findings. During the test trials in the above experiment, a record was kept of the time that elapsed between the onset of the test array and when the first item was selected. The results in the left-hand panel of Figure 10.20 show that when the first item to be selected was near the top of the list then it was selected more rapidly than when it was near the end of the list. This effect has been found with humans when they are given a similar task, and is referred to as the **magnitude effect** (Terrace, Son, & Brannon, 2003).

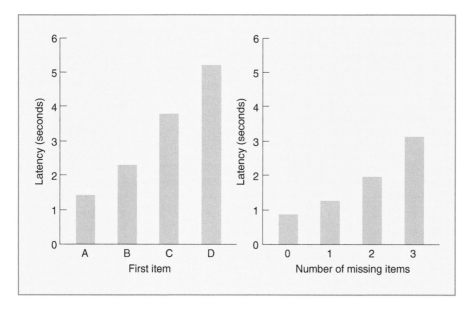

FIGURE 10.20 Left-hand panel: The mean time taken to select the first item of a test pair of stimuli by monkeys, after they had been trained with the simultaneous chain A–B–C–D–E. Right-hand panel: The mean time to select the second item of the test pairs by the same monkeys as function of the number of items that separate the members of the pair in the training list (adapted from D'Amato & Colombo, 1988).

A record was also taken in this experiment of the time that elapsed between the selection of the first and second member of the test pair. From the right-hand panel of Figure 10.20 it can be seen that this interval was influenced by the number of missing items between the members. The results for 0 missing items were for trials with AB, BC, CD, and DE and the response to the second item occurred fairly soon after the response to the first item. But as the number of missing items increased, so it took longer to respond to the second item, with the consequence that responding to the pair with three missing items, AE, was particularly slow. The trends depicted in both panels of Figure 10.20 have been replicated by Swartz, Chen, and Terrace (1991) with rhesus monkeys and a four-item list (see also Terrace et al., 2003).[2] The study by Terrace et al. (2003) is of some interest because after initial training with lists of three and four items, the monkeys were able to master a simultaneous chaining problem with seven items (A–B–C–D–E–F–G). This success was achieved even though the items, which consisted of photographs, had not been used for the previous lists. The experiment included tests with all possible pairs of items from the seven-item list. It was found that as the number of missing items between the two members of the pair increased, the latency to select the first item of the pair declined, and the frequency with which the first item was identified correctly increased. For example, using both measures, performance was superior with the pair BF than the pair BC. This effect has again been found with humans and is referred to as the **distance effect** (Terrace et al., 2003).

The final finding to consider is perhaps the most intriguing because it implies more forcefully than any other that monkeys appreciate the order in which the items of a simultaneously presented array must be selected. Experiments by Terrace and colleagues will be described (Chen, Swartz, & Terrace, 1997; Terrace et al., 2003) but similar findings have been reported using a different procedure by Orlov, Yakovlev,

Some animals, such as rhesus moneys, are able to remember the order of items when they are presented as a list.

KEY TERM

Distance effect
The finding that the latency to select the first of two items taken from a list is shorter when the distance between the items is large rather than small.

---

[2] Further evidence of a difference between the way monkeys and pigeons solve serial-order problems can be found in the report by Terrace (1991) that pigeons do not show these effects. Thus they respond equally rapidly to the first item of a test pair, no matter what position in the list it occupies; they also respond equally rapidly to the second item with no influence at all of the number of missing items (see also D'Amato, 1991, pp. 168–171).

Hochstein, and Zohary (2000) and Orlov, Yakovlev, Amit, Hochstein, and Zohary (2002). Experienced rhesus monkeys were trained to touch, in a certain order, four pictures that were presented simultaneously on a touch screen. Rather than being trained with just one list, they were trained with four lists that were shown at different times and with different items in each list. Rows 1 to 4 in Table 10.3 show the composition of these lists. Testing, which commenced after the four lists had been mastered, consisted of presenting novel arrays of four items selected from the original lists. The composition of two of these lists can be seen in the remaining rows of Table 10.3. One of the test lists is referred to as the Maintained List because the position of each item corresponds with its position in the original lists. Thus the item to be selected first in the new list was the first item from List 2, the item to be selected second in the new list was the second item from List 4, and so on. Quite surprisingly, performance on the Maintained List was almost perfect from the moment it was introduced. The other list is referred to as the Changed List because there was no correspondence between the position of an item in this list and the position it occupied in its original list. The two monkeys that were tested needed many hundreds of trials to master this list.

The implication of these results is that during their original training monkeys acquired knowledge about the position of each item in each of the four lists. By using this information they would then be able to select the four items of the Maintained List in the correct sequence, even when it was introduced for the first time. On the other hand, any knowledge about the original positions of the items in the Changed List would encourage subjects to select them in the incorrect sequence and make it very difficult to come to terms with the demands of this test series.

Once the correct explanation for these findings has been found, it will no doubt lie at the heart of our understanding of how monkeys represent serial order. Chen et al. (1997; see also Terrace et al., 2003) argue that the absence of any evidence that monkeys use arbitrary symbols to represent numbers makes it highly unlikely that they identified the position of an item by counting in the way that humans might do. Instead, they suggest that animals construct an analogical, or spatial, representation that could consist of four slots arranged in sequence, with each item of the list occupying, in the appropriate order, the four slots. Provided subjects started at the same end of the slots from one trial to the next, they would be able to work through this representation and select the items to be touched in the correct sequence. An implication of the study by Chen et al. (1997) is that monkeys can retain four such

TABLE 10.3 The four lists (numbered 1 through 4) that were used during the training stage of the experiment and two of the lists that were used for the test trials in the experiment by Terrace et al. (1997). Letters (A through D) indicate the position of a particular item in the list, numbers (1 through 4) indicate the training list to which a particular item belonged (adapted from Terrace et al., 1997)

List		Composition
1	A1 → B1 → C1 → D1	bird → flower → frog → shells
2	A2 → B2 → C2 → D2	tree → weasel → dragonfly → water
3	A3 → B3 → C3 → D3	elk → rocks → leaves → person
4	A4 → B4 → C4 → D4	mountain → fish → monkey → tomato
Maintained	A2 → B4 → C1 → D3	tree → fish → frog → person
Changed	B3 → A1 → D4 → C2	rocks → bird → tomato → dragonfly

spatial representations at the same time, and consult all of them, in order to decide how to respond when confronted with a novel combination of familiar items.

It is not too difficult to understand how these theoretical ideas could explain the magnitude and distance effects that were mentioned earlier. Once the spatial representation has been constructed, assume, first, that it can only be accessed from the beginning; second, that the slots can be inspected in a fixed order; and, third, that it takes time to move from one slot to the next. If a test trial is conducted with two items from a list, then the first item will be selected more rapidly the closer it is to the start of the list, the magnitude effect; and the time taken to select the second item will be determined by the number of items that separate them (as reported by D'Amato & Colombo, 1988). The explanation for the distance effect is then based on the supposition that the representation of the list has spatial properties which will make it easier to identify the item that is nearer to the start of the list when the gap between the items is large, rather than small.

Concluding comments

The suggestion that animals use an analogical or spatial representation to indicate the order in which items must be selected is controversial. This possibility has, however, not been plucked out of the blue. Instead, it is based on the claim that humans use such a representation as a non-verbal method for representing serial order (Kosslyn, 1980). It is also difficult to think of a better explanation for the findings with monkeys that have been considered in this section. If one accepts the theoretical proposals of Chen et al. (1997) then additional findings described by Terrace et al. (2003) take on an intriguing significance. They found that monkeys became more adept at their list learning task with extended training, which implies that their skill at using a spatial representation of serial order can improve with practice. It is not at all clear how this improvement could be explained. They also found that experienced monkeys were able to remember the sequence in which seven simultaneously placed objects had to be selected. The implication of this finding is that the spatial representation of order is not restricted to four slots, and that its upper limit remains to be determined.

The experiments considered in this section point to important differences between species. Monkeys are much better at remembering lists than pigeons. This ability in monkeys has been said to be based on a capacity for storing the items in a spatial representation containing a number of slots. There is no evidence that pigeons are equipped with a similar representation, but even if they can represent lists in this way the maximum number of items that can be stored is likely to be considerably smaller than for monkeys.

TRANSITIVE INFERENCE

When told that A is bigger than B, and that B is bigger than C, few adults have difficulty in reaching the conclusion that A is bigger than C. This type of reasoning, which allows us to combine knowledge about specific relationships to infer another relationship, is known as transitive inference. The results from several experiments suggest that animals, too, are capable of solving transitive inference problems. The reason for discussing these experiments now is that their results have been said to depend on the formation of a transitive series, which is similar to the list that is thought to aid the solution of serial-order problems in monkeys (D'Amato, 1991).

In a study by Gillan (1981; see also McGonigle & Chalmers, 1977, 1986, 1992) three female chimpanzees first received training with five containers, A, B, C, D, and E, each of which was a different color. A pair of containers was presented to the subject on each trial and the chimpanzees' task was to identify the one in which food was hidden. The trials were of the following sort: A+B−, B+C−, C+D−, D+E−, where + denotes the container with food. The spatial relationship between the members of each pair varied irregularly, so that the discriminations could be solved only on the basis of color. After a number of training sessions, performance on all discriminations was consistently accurate, which can be taken to indicate that subjects preferred A to B, B to C, C to D, and D to E. To examine whether these relationships can be combined to lead to a novel inference, Gillan (1981) then gave test sessions that included, for the first time, the pair B and D. If chimpanzees are capable of transitive inference, then combining the knowledge that B is preferred to C with the knowledge that C is preferred to D should lead to the conclusion that B is preferred to D. One chimpanzee, Sadie, performed perfectly on this test by choosing B in preference to D on all twelve test trials. Although the results for the other two chimpanzees were not so good, Sadie's success shows that at least one chimpanzee can solve transitive inference problems.

KEY TERM

Symbolic distance effect
The distance effect (see above) when it is obtained after training with a transitive inference problem.

This clear demonstration of transitive inference raises the question of how it was achieved. One explanation assumes that chimpanzees have a means of encoding information that allows them to represent the relationship between each pair and also to combine this information. They perhaps learn that "B is preferred to C" and "C is preferred to D", so that the combination of this knowledge would then lead to the correct conclusion. Fortunately, we do not have to worry about presenting this account in detail, because there is already evidence that suggests it is wrong. McGonigle and Chalmers (1992) studied transitive inference in squirrel monkeys using a similar method to that of Gillan (1981). Test trials included novel pairs of items that were either closely or distantly related on the transitive series. When the members of the test pair were closely related on the transitive series (e.g. BD), information about only a few training pairs would be required to determine which test item should be selected. In contrast, for pairs that were distantly related on the transitive series (e.g. AE), information about many of the training pairs would need to be consulted before a decision could be made. It follows from the above analysis that subjects should be quicker at choosing between items that are close rather than far apart on the transitive series, whereas the results directly contradicted this prediction.

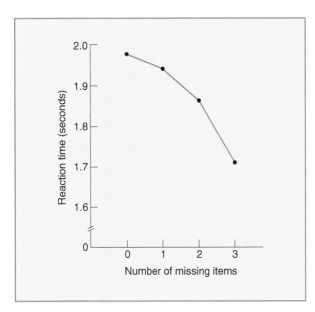

Figure 10.21 shows the time it took subjects to choose a cup on the test trials. The results are arranged according to the number of missing items of the transitive series between the two test items. For example, there were no missing items for the test pair AB, and one missing item for the pair AC. As the figure shows, choice of the correct item was faster when the members of a pair were distantly related, with the result, paradoxically, that choices between pairs that had never been given during training—BD, for example—were made more swiftly than those between pairs that were familiar, BC. This finding is known as the **symbolic distance effect** and is often found in experiments with

FIGURE 10.21 The time taken to select one of two cups on test trials with stimuli selected from a transitive series comprising five items. The results are arranged according to the number of items that separate the test pair in the transitive series (adapted from McGonigle & Chalmers, 1992).

humans (Bryant & Trabasso, 1971; Woocher, Glass, & Holyoak, 1978). It also closely resembles findings with monkeys in the serial order studies by Terrace et al. (2003) that have just been considered.

One explanation for the symbolic distance effect is that the information provided during training is reorganized into a transitive series. This suggestion has been made for humans (e.g. Anderson, 1980) as well as animals (D'Amato, 1991; McGonigle & Chalmers, 1986; Roberts & Phelps, 1994), and is very similar to the explanation offered by Terrace et al. (2003) for how monkeys represent serial order. In the experiment by McGonigle and Chalmers (1992), for example, the training with individual pairs will eventually result in the acquisition of the sequence A–B–C–D–E. Once this has been learned, then on any trial all that the subject must do is select the member of the pair of items that is nearer to the start of the sequence. As noted for the distance effect, the representation of the series is meant to have spatial properties. As a consequence, decisions about which item of a pair is nearer to the start will be easier, and faster, when the items are far apart, rather than close together in the transitive series.

A worrying finding for this explanation is that pigeons can also solve transitive inference problems, even when five stimuli are involved (Von Fersen, Wynne, Delius, & Staddon, 1991). We have just seen that these animals may not be able to represent a list of five items, which then makes it hard to accept that they created a transitive list of five items. In fact, Von Fersen et al. (1991) proposed a relatively simple explanation for the way in which the pigeons solved their problem. Once this explanation has been considered, we shall examine whether it can be applied to the findings that have been obtained with monkeys.

Pigeons were trained by Von Fersen et al. (1991) in the apparatus shown in Figure 10.22. On any trial, different geometric shapes were presented on the two displays and the bird was required to peck one, but not the other, to receive food. In keeping with other studies of transitive inference in animals, the pigeons received the following discriminations: A+B−, B+C−, C+D−, and D+E−, followed at the end of the experiment by test trials with BD. On the test, there was a significant preference for pecking B rather than D. To explain this outcome, which is normally taken as evidence of successful transitive inference, Von Fersen et al. (1991) referred to a mechanism known as **value transfer**. At the heart of this explanation is the observation that the training treatment will result in the individual stimuli having different values. A will be most highly valued because it will lead to food whenever it is selected; B, C, and D, will have an intermediate value because selecting them on some trials will lead to food and on other trials to nothing; finally, E will have no value because selecting it will never lead to food. On this basis, it might be thought that B and D will have equal value and thus B should not be selected in preference to D on the test. If it is accepted that presenting a pair of stimuli together for the original discriminations results in an association forming between them, then a different outcome is predicted for the test with B and D. Specifically, the sight of B will activate a memory of A, and of the high value associated with A; whereas the

KEY TERM

Value transfer
The change in value to one stimulus as a result of being associated with a stimulus with a different value.

FIGURE 10.22 A sketch of the apparatus used by Von Fersen et al. (1991) to study transitive inference in pigeons. Food can be delivered to two cups through the vertical tubes, and the stimuli were projected onto circular keys in front of the cups (adapted from Von Fersen et al., 1991).

sight of D will activate a memory of E, and of its low value. If some of the high value of A were to transfer to B, and some of the low value of E were to transfer to D, then the birds would prefer B over D in the test trials.

Direct support for this subtle explanation can be found in a series of experiments by Zentall and colleagues (e.g. Dorrance & Zentall, 1999; see also Cohen, Drummond, & Terrelonge, 2001). In an experiment by Zentall and Sherburne (1994), pigeons received two simultaneous discriminations in which they were presented with two stimuli and received reward for selecting one of the pair. On some trials they were presented with A and B together, and were rewarded on every occasion that they pecked A; on other trials they were shown C and D together and were rewarded on only half the occasions that they pecked C. Because A was consistently paired with food and C intermittently paired with food, it was assumed that A would have high value and C would have intermediate value. It was also assumed that B and D would have equivalent low values because they were never paired with food. In addition, it was expected that because B was always paired with A, some of the high value of A would transfer to B and, likewise, some of the intermediate value of C was expected to transfer to D. As a result of the transfer of these different values, it was concluded that B should have more value than D. Tests trials with B and D presented together confirmed this prediction by revealing a stronger preference for B than D. This result provides firm grounds for believing that when two stimuli are presented together for a simultaneous discrimination, the value of one stimulus can transfer to the other. On the basis of this conclusion it would seem that the explanation offered by Von Fersen et al. (1991) for transitive inference in pigeons is fully justified.

The method of training pigeons used by Von Fersen et al. (1991) was similar to that for monkeys (McGonigle & Chalmers, 1977, 1986, 1992) and chimpanzees (Gillan, 1981), which raises the question of whether the results from all three species should be explained in the same manner. On the basis of Lloyd Morgan's canon (see Chapter 1), the explanation offered for the results with pigeons should also apply to monkeys and chimpanzees, until there is evidence to suggest otherwise. Having said that, the claim that monkeys and chimpanzees solve transitive inference problems by constructing a spatial representation of the transitive series is similar to the explanation that was offered for how monkeys represent serial order. On this basis, it would not be surprising if a spatial representation of a transitive series was indeed used by primates for transitive inference.

CONCLUDING COMMENTS

Considerable attention was paid in the first part of this chapter to the ability of insects to utilize temporal information. Cockroaches were said to time daily bursts of activity by virtue of possessing a 24-hour clock, and a similar claim was made to explain patterns of feeding by honey-bees. Such conclusions are of interest in their own right, but they also emphasize two related points concerning the study of animal cognition.

First, they indicate that cognitive processes play an important role in the behavior of so-called primitive animals, and in the most basic of experimental tasks. Animal cognition is thus not to be found in a restricted selection of species, nor is it confined to methods designed to tax the higher mental capacities. The concern of this area of study is, instead, with the mechanisms that enable animals to store and utilize information gained from their experiences, wherever this may occur.

The second point concerns the merits of conducting experiments on animals with relatively simple nervous systems. By using insects, for example, it may be possible to study the fundamental operation of such processes as timing in a way that would be impossible with more sophisticated animals. We have already encountered support for this argument in Chapter 2, where the merits of studying the physiological mechanisms of associative learning with *Aplysia* were presented. In Chapter 11 we will consider additional evidence that is in keeping with the spirit of this conclusion. In addition, the fact that periodic timing can be studied at all in insects suggests that this sort of timing does not depend on a particularly sophisticated nervous system.

Some comment is needed about the general conclusions that can be drawn from the experiments considered in this chapter. These clearly show that animals can respond on the basis of information about time, number, and serial order. The question is then raised as to how animals are able to achieve their success on these tasks and it is here that our lack of knowledge becomes woefully apparent. We have very little evidence to support the claim that periodic timing depends on oscillators, or that interval timing depends on a pacemaker. We know very little about the way in which animals are able to count, and the manner in which animals represent and use information about serial order remains a matter for debate. We have thus extended considerably our understanding of the information that animals are able to use, but we have discovered rather little about the mechanisms that enable them to make use of this information.

CHAPTER 11

CONTENTS

Navigation

A capacity for navigation should be invaluable for the majority of animals. They will often find themselves in one location and need to move to another to obtain food, seek a mate, return to their home, and so on. This journey could, of course, be haphazard and guided by nothing more than the principle of trial and error. But if the position of the goal is known then a more efficient way of traveling would be to plot, and then follow, a course to the goal. A variety of sources of information could be used to help an animal navigate in this way. In the first part of this chapter we will examine how animals use these sources of information when the distance that must be traveled is relatively short.

In addition to navigating successfully over short distances, some animals are able to complete journeys that cover considerable distances and that may last for long periods of time. Pigeons are famous for their skill at homing, which allows them to fly hundreds of miles back to their loft after they have been released from an unfamiliar location. Other animals migrate annually over vast distances to a specific location, even when they have never before made that journey. The second part of this chapter will consider how animals are able to travel successfully over such large distances.

A theme that runs through this chapter is that travel through the environment can be controlled by numerous cues and that animals take advantage of this redundancy. They will often refer to different sources of information, and adopt different strategies, depending on the nature of the task that confronts them.

PART 1: SHORT-DISTANCE TRAVEL

METHODS OF NAVIGATION

Pheromone trails

A simple way by which an animal can find its way is to make use of a scent trail. Some animals possess scent glands that release **pheromones**. This term was used first by Karlson and Luscher (1959) to refer to chemicals that are used for communication, through the sense of smell, among individuals of a given species. Pheromones can be released directly into the air. For example, the female silkworm moth releases the pheromone bombykol from a gland in her abdomen; the pheromone is then carried away by air currents. If the antenna of a male should detect the pheromone, he will fly upwind until he finds the female and they will copulate. The detection of a single molecule is sufficient to encourage the male to fly, which makes the release of this particular pheromone effective over several kilometers (Shorey, 1976).

Pheromone trails can also guide animals to food. Foraging ants that have discovered a source of food deposit a recruitment trail of pheromones on the ground as they return to the nest. When they reach the nest, the ants perform stereotyped responses that stimulate other ants to leave the nest and to pursue the trail. As the recruited ants return to the nest, they too deposit the same pheromone, which strengthens the trail and attracts yet more foragers. As soon as the food source is depleted, the returning ants cease to secrete pheromones and the trail will gradually disappear.

The laying of a pheromone trail leads certain animals into displaying a quite unpleasant behavior described as urine washing (Shorey, 1976). To mark their journey through the branches of a forest, the males of some species of loris urinate onto one hand, rub their hands together, and then rub their hands on their feet. The consequent scent trails that are deposited as they move through the branches of the forest allow the route to be retraced, and also permit travel at night. Even worse, the brown bear marks its territory by rolling in its urine and then rubbing itself against a tree. A more efficient method would be to urinate directly onto the tree, but bears have yet to discover this solution.

Dead reckoning

Dead reckoning, or path integration as it is now more commonly called, is the method of navigating where no reference is made to landmarks. Instead, a record is kept of one's position in respect to some reference point by taking account of the distance that has been traveled and the changes in direction that have been made. As long as these sources of information are correct, and are combined in an appropriate manner, they should permit the navigator to specify the direction and distance since the journey started. An obvious problem with navigating in this way is that if an error has entered into the calculations there is no means of detecting it and the navigator will have no indication of being lost. Such errors can have serious consequences. In the early years of the Second World War, the pilots of Bomber Command were compelled to use dead reckoning because they could fly with safety only at night when they had no visible landmarks to guide them. The errors that crept into their navigation were occasionally so severe that they bombed cities in England believing them to be in Germany (Hastings, 1979). A more successful example of dead reckoning is described by Gallistel (1990): A nineteenth-century sailor, Slocum, sailed 4500 miles across the Pacific without once sighting land and correctly estimated when he was within a few hours of his destination.

The calculations involved in determining position by dead reckoning would seem to be complex but, as the following experiments show, even ants are capable of using this method of navigation. Desert ants will search for food in a rather haphazard manner until they are some distance from their nest. Having discovered food, they do not return along the circuitous path of their outward journey but, instead, they head directly for the nest. There is good evidence to show that the animals do not find their way home by looking for a prominent feature near their nest, and then heading for it. If an ant is trapped as it emerges from the nest, and is then released about 5 meters away, it appears to be lost and searches for the nest in all directions (Wehner & Flatt, 1972). Such a reaction would not be expected if ants identified the location of their nest by referring to a nearby landmark. As Gallistel (1990, p. 60) suggests, "ants do not know where they are, unless they themselves get there". He further proposes that they learn where they are by a process of dead reckoning, which can take place with considerable accuracy as the next experiment shows.

Desert ants were trained on a featureless plain to travel about 20 meters from their nest to a food source (Wehner & Srinivasan, 1981). When they were familiar with this journey, individual ants were picked up as they left the food source and transported about 600 meters before being placed on the ground. At this point, the

KEY TERM

Dead reckoning or path integration
A method of navigation in which a record is kept of where the journey began in terms of its distance and direction from the current position.

ants behaved as if they had not been displaced at all. They headed in a compass direction that was the same as the direction of the nest from the food source. Moreover, they continued in this direction for a distance that was virtually the same as the distance between the food source and the nest. When this distance had been traveled they began to search, unsuccessfully of course, for the nest. If the ants had not been displaced, then this journey would have brought them to within half a meter of the nest. It is unreasonable to argue that the ants were following a pheromone trail in this experiment, or that they were orienting towards a particular landmark. Instead, their journey must have been guided by dead reckoning, with the distance and direction of travel being determined relative to the point of release.

A desert ant can return directly to its nest across a featureless plain by referring to the direction and distance it traveled on its outward journey.

The sun plays an important role in determining the direction in which ants travel. Santchi (1913) placed a shield between the sun and an ant that was marching in a given direction. By use of a mirror, the sun was then reflected onto the opposite side of the ant, who promptly turned round and marched in the direction from where it had just come. In the experiment by Wehner and Srinivasan (1981), it is thus likely that the ant used the position of the sun to determine in which direction it should head when it was eventually placed on the ground. Journeys based on the position of the sun must take account of its movement through the sky. Jander (1957) has shown that even ants are able to make allowances for this movement. He interrupted their straight-line journeys by retaining them in a light-proof box for a number of hours. When they were released, they continued to head in their original directions, despite a considerable change in the position of the sun.

As far as the determination of distance that has been covered is concerned, an unusual experiment by Wittlinger, Wehner, and Wolf (2006) indicates that desert ants effectively use a pedometer or, in other words, keep a record of the number of steps they have taken. Ants were trained to walk 10 meters down an alley from their nest to food. On reaching the food, they were picked up and the length of their legs was either lengthened by attaching stilts to them (made of pig's hair), or shortened by amputation. The ants were then released in a parallel test alley. Unoperated control ants walked about 10 meters down this alley before they started searching for their nest. Those who had their legs extended walked for about 15 meters before searching for the nest, while for the ants with shortened legs, this distance was reduced to 5 meters. The explanation for these results is that, by altering the lengths of the legs, the experimenters altered the length of each stride that an ant took. If ants made a fixed number of strides before searching for their nest, then lengthening their stride would result in them walking too far, whereas shortening their stride would result in them not walking far enough.

Thus far, dead reckoning has been assumed to provide information about the current position of an ant from its nest. There is also evidence that it can provide information about the ant's position relative to a recently visited goal. Collett, Collett, and Wehner (1999) trained ants to travel down a 15-meter alley for food at the end. The walls of the alley were sufficiently deep to prevent the ants from seeing any landmarks, but they were able to see the sky and presumably the sun. After they had returned to the nest, the ants were released into an alley for a test trial, but on this occasion the alley was pointing 38° to the east of its normal direction. On reaching the end of the alley the ants turned and headed in a direction that would take them to food. The implication of this remarkable finding is that as they returned to their nest after the previous visit to the food source, ants kept a record of their current distance and direction of the food source. This record must have been retained while they were in the nest and then updated during the journey down the alley on the test trial. By referring to this record when they reached the end of the alley it would be possible to compute the direction in which to head to reach the food.

Another example of dead reckoning is provided by honey-bees. These insects possess a sophisticated method of communication that permits a forager returning to the hive to indicate the distance and direction of the source of food it has just collected (see Chapter 13). Von Frisch (1950) was interested in the information that was conveyed when a forager took a detour to avoid a mountain when returning to the hive from the food source. On returning to the hive, the bee was expected to indicate the direction and distance of either the first or the second leg of its journey. Instead, it communicated the direct route to food, despite never having passed along it. The information for this communication was presumably derived from dead reckoning. Further evidence of dead reckoning in the honey-bee is provided by the fact that when bees have received the information about the location of a food supply they will fly to the food even though the course must be adjusted to take account of the obstacle. Dead reckoning must play a part in determining how far is left to travel, and in what direction, once the obstacle has been passed.

Dead reckoning in the ant and honey-bee is likely to depend on information acquired from the movements they initiate during their journey. Dead reckoning in other animals, gerbils and hamsters, for example, has also been said to be influenced by changes that take place in the vestibular system (Mittelstaedt & Mittelstaedt, 1982; Etienne, Lambert, Reverdin, & Teroni, 1993). Support for this proposal comes from the finding that lesions of the vestibular system disrupt dead reckoning in rats (Matthews, Ryu, & Bockaneck, 1989).

A series of experiments by Saint Paul (1982) provides evidence of dead reckoning when an animal is passively transported to a release point. Furthermore, her results indicate that information about the direction and distance of travel can be acquired visually. In one experiment, seven geese were taken individually in a cage similar to the one sketched in Figure 11.1 from their home (H) to a place with which they were unfamiliar (S). The blue line in Figure 11.2 shows this journey and the arrows show the direction in which each goose headed when it was released from S. Two subjects started to retrace their outward route, but the remainder walked in the direction of home. Of course, those that headed in the direction of home

FIGURE 11.1 A drawing of the cart that was used to transport geese in the study by Saint Paul (1982) (adapted from Saint Paul, 1982).

may have been guided by a landmark that was also visible from home. Such an explanation for the initial heading of the geese is made unlikely by the results of a second group. This was treated in exactly the same way as the first group, except that the cart was covered on the outward journey. When released, these subjects showed no systematic tendency to head towards home.

Further evidence that homing by geese does not depend on orientation towards visual landmarks can be found in a second experiment by Saint Paul (1982). Geese were again transported from their home in a wheeled cage. Their home is marked by H in Figure 11.3, and they were taken to A along the route marked by the dotted blue line. At this point, a cover was placed over the cage and they were wheeled to B. When they were released from B, they followed the route that is marked by the dashed line in Figure 11.3. That is, they headed in the direction that would have taken them from A to H. The implication of this finding is that while traveling from H to A, the geese kept a record of their direction and distance from H, based on what they saw. This record was not altered by the journey in the covered cart, so that when they were eventually released they headed in an entirely inappropriate direction.

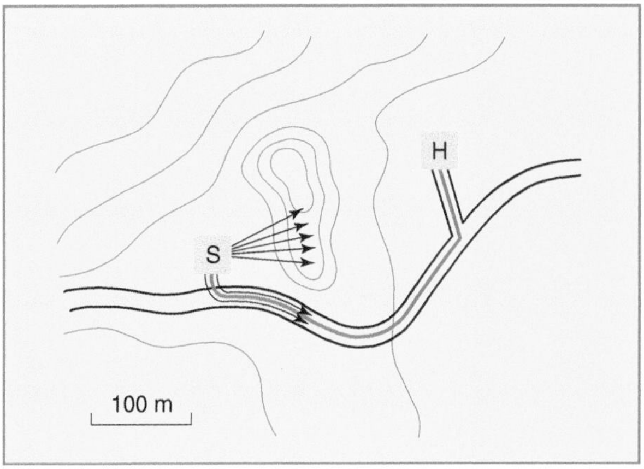

FIGURE 11.2 The departure direction of seven geese that were transported in an open cart along the route marked by the blue line from their home, H, to the release point, S (adapted from Saint Paul, 1982).

Piloting with a single landmark

We have already seen that animals may embark on journeys without making any reference to landmarks but, perhaps not surprisingly, animals can make use of landmarks to determine both the direction and the distance that they will travel. **Piloting** refers to this type of navigation.

The simplest form of piloting would be to navigate towards a feature that was located immediately by the goal—a beacon. But very often landmarks are not conveniently situated by a goal, and their use then becomes more complicated. Two related sets of experiments have provided considerable insight into the ways in which bees (Cartwright & Collett, 1983) and gerbils (Collett, Cartwright, & Smith, 1986) use landmarks that are located at a distance from a goal.

The bees were able to enter a white room (4 meters by 4 meters) through a small opening. A single landmark was provided by a black cylinder 4 centimeters wide and 40 centimeters high, and the goal consisted of a drop of sucrose solution placed on a glass slide. For the experiments with gerbils, a circular arena (3.5 meters in diameter) was used. Black chippings on the floor made it possible to hide a sprinkling of sunflower seeds just below the surface at a specific location. The landmark consisted of a white cylinder 6.3 centimeters wide and 40 centimeters high.

Both gerbils and bees were trained to find food when it was located at a given distance, for example 50 centimeters, and a given compass bearing, say due south from the landmark. Once they had been trained, then even when there was no food in the test area they persistently searched in the correct location. It is important to note that in these studies the position of the landmark moved from trial to trial, and that the gerbils were released from different points on the edge of the arena. Thus food could not be found simply by moving a fixed distance and at a fixed orientation from the release point. As a consequence, dead reckoning is unlikely to have guided the animals to their goal. The results suggest, instead, that the animals were using information that food was at a certain distance and compass bearing from the landmark.

The authors say very little about the way in which their subjects derived information about compass bearings. One possibility is that animals have a magnetic sense that allows them to determine directions such as north. Although there are

KEY TERM

Piloting
A method of navigation in which the course for a goal is set on the basis of landmarks that are in a known relation to the goal.

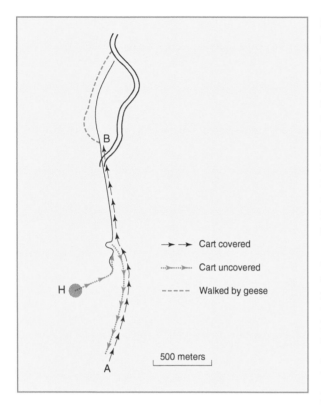

FIGURE 11.3 The dashed blue line shows the route taken by two geese as they walked together from their point of release at B. They had previously been taken from their home (H) to A in an uncovered cart, and then from A to B in a covered cart (adapted from Saint Paul, 1982).

Gerbils can return to a source of food by remembering the distance and direction it lies from a prominent landmark. Copyright © Louise Murray / Science Photo Library.

reasons for believing that bees possess a magnetic sense (Walker, Baird, & Bitterman, 1989), there is no good evidence that this source of information is available to gerbils. As an alternative, the animals may have derived their compass bearing from a relatively distant landmark, such as the entrance to the room. Suppose that food is always placed due south of the landmark, and that the entrance to the room is north of the landmark; food could then be found by searching on the side of the landmark that is furthest from the entrance. In any case, the fact the animals persistently searched in the correct location forcefully suggests that they were able to derive the direction of food in respect to the landmark.

As far as deriving information about distance is concerned, bees and gerbils appear to employ different methods. Once bees had been trained to find food at 35 centimeters from a single landmark, test trials were conducted in which the size of the landmark was varied. When the size of the landmark was halved, the bees concentrated their search in an area that was much closer to the landmark. But when the size of the landmark was doubled, they searched at a distance of greater than 35 centimeters from the landmark. On the basis of these findings Cartwright and Collett (1983) proposed that when bees are trained with a single landmark they make a record of the size of its retinal image at the goal. In other words, the bee takes a "retinal snapshot" of the landmark. On subsequent visits to the test area it will then approach the landmark from the appropriate direction and, as it does so, a comparison is made between the size of the image of the landmark on the retina and its size in the retinal snapshot. When there is a close correspondence between the two, the bee will then initiate its search for the goal. Providing that the retinal snapshot is reasonably accurate, this simple method should ensure that the bee consistently and accurately returns to the goal.

When a similar experiment was conducted with gerbils, changing the size of the landmark had relatively little effect on where the search for the goal was conducted. The account for the way that bees find food with a single landmark may not, therefore, be appropriate for gerbils. Further support for this conclusion comes from an experiment in which gerbils were again trained to find food near a certain landmark. On test trials, which were conducted in the absence of food, gerbils were released and as soon as they headed towards the goal all the lights in the room were extinguished. By monitoring the movement of the gerbil with the use of infrared light, it was found that the animal continued on its journey until it reached the correct location, whereupon it began to search for food. In some tests the gerbils covered as much as 2.5 meters yet they still managed to search in the correct region. In contrast to bees, therefore, gerbils appear to know how far they have to travel to food when they set their course on the basis of a landmark, and presumably dead reckoning can inform them when this distance has been traveled. At present we do not know how the distance that must be traveled is gauged.

Piloting with multiple landmarks

When multiple landmarks are located in a consistent relationship to a goal, a variety of strategies can be used to pilot towards that goal. Bees exploit a very simple method when they are presented with three landmarks (Cartwright & Collett, 1983). Figure 11.4 shows an array of three landmarks that are each 76 centimeters from the food source and whose compass bearings are 60°, 120°, and 180° from the food source (for the sake of discussion, these bearings are relative to the top of the page, which has a bearing of 0°). Bees were readily able to learn to locate food when they were trained with this configuration. It is important to note that although the location of the array was moved from one trial to the next, throughout the experiment, its orientation remained constant. That is, from the food site, the landmarks were always oriented with respect to north as shown in Figure 11.4. There were two types of test trial in this experiment. On some occasions, the distance of the landmarks from the goal was altered, while maintaining their size. On other occasions, the size of the landmarks was altered, while holding their distance from the goal constant. In the light of the results described in the previous section, it is interesting to note that neither of these manipulations had any substantial effect. The bees continued to search in a location that was defined simply by its compass bearings from the three landmarks.

The presence of multiple landmarks, therefore, appears to render their retinal size relatively unimportant as cues for navigation. What seems to be important is their compass bearing from the goal. Thus Cartwright and Collett (1983) have proposed that when a bee is at the goal, it makes a record of the compass bearing of each landmark. On returning to the area in the future, it will then search until it is in a position where the compass bearings of the landmarks match this record. An important feature of this account is that the bee is assumed to rely exclusively on compass bearings, that is, bearings in respect to a feature that lies beyond the landmarks themselves. This proposal was tested by repeating the experiment, with the simple change that the orientation of the array depicted in Figure 11.4 varied randomly during training. Thus only occasionally was the angle between the top landmark and north 60°. Each of the three bees trained in this way failed completely to show any sign of searching in the correct region for food. The failure of the bees to locate the food suggests that they were unable to use information about the relative position of one landmark to another to identify where food could be found.

An experiment with gerbils indicates that, in contrast to bees, they can use information about the relative position of a number of landmarks. Subjects were trained to find food at a point that was near two landmarks. This point is marked by F in the plan of the test apparatus shown Figure 11.5a; the positions of the landmarks are identified by two circles. Test trials were then given in which one landmark was removed (Figure 11.5b), or the landmarks were placed further apart (Figure 11.5c).

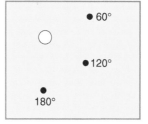

FIGURE 11.4 Plan of the room used by Cartwright and Collett (1983) to study the way in which bees use three landmarks to identify the location of food. The bees were able to enter the room through a small opening. The open circle depicts the location of food, the filled circles depict the three landmarks (adapted from Cartwright & Collett, 1983).

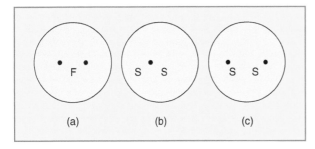

FIGURE 11.5 Plan of the test arena used by Collett et al. (1986) to study the way in which gerbils use two landmarks to locate a hidden source of food (F). One circle (a) depicts the arena used for training the gerbils. The two other circles depict where the gerbils searched (S) for food on test trials with a single landmark (circle b) or with the landmarks more widely separated than during training (circle c) (adapted from Collett et al., 1986).

With only a single landmark present, the subjects searched in the regions marked by S, which were either to the south-west or south-east of the landmark. This finding suggests that the animals knew about the direction and distance of food from the landmarks but they did not know which landmark they were being tested with. The results from the test trial with the separated landmarks show that the gerbils again searched in two places, which were defined by the direction and distance of the goal from each of the two landmarks during the training stage. An important implication of this outcome is that the landmarks were not treated independently. Thus the gerbils searched to the south-west of the eastern landmark, and to the south-east of the western landmark. Had the landmarks not been identified by their relative position, then the gerbils would have searched both to the south-west and south-east of each landmark.

These findings, together with those from related studies, led Collett et al. (1986) to conclude that gerbils use **heading vectors** based on individual landmarks to define the location of a goal. These vectors may be based on a compass bearing, so that they would be of the form "food is at a certain distance and in a certain direction from the landmark", or, when more than one landmark is available, they may be based on information about the relationship among landmarks. For the experiment just described, this might be of the form "food is at a certain distance to the south-west of the easternmost landmark and a certain distance to the south-east of the westernmost landmark". For similar findings with pigeons see Cheng (1994).

Use of geometric relations

When two or more landmarks are present, they create a geometric shape. Two landmarks create a line, three a triangle, and so on. A question that has been asked on a number of occasions is whether animals are able to detect this geometric information and to use it to define the location of a goal. For example, in the previous experiment, food in the training stage was near the midpoint of the line between the two landmarks. If this geometric information had been used to define the location of the goal, then on the test trial with the separated landmarks searching would have been concentrated on the region at the midpoint between them. The experiments described in this section were all conducted to explore whether animals can appreciate the geometric relationship between two or more landmarks.

Jones, Antoniadis, Shettleworth, and Kamil (2002) conducted an experiment to determine whether one species of bird—Clark's nutcracker—can appreciate a simple geometric relationship. A bird was released into a room and expected to find food that was hidden on the floor midway between a red and a blue cylindrical landmark. The distance between the landmarks varied from trial to trial, within the range 40 to 100 centimeters. As a result of this training, on being released subjects would search predominantly for food at the midpoint between the landmarks. An identical pattern of searching was also found during a test trial when the distance between the landmarks was increased to beyond 100 centimeters. According to Jones et al. (2002), these findings demonstrate that one species can appreciate the geometric relationship of halfway or middle. They further suggest that this appreciation was a consequence of being trained with a variety of distances between the landmarks. If the birds had just been trained with a single distance, then they might have identified the location of the platform with reference to a vector, and failed to locate the midpoint between the landmarks when the distance between them was increased.

Attempts to demonstrate that animals can appreciate more sophisticated geometric relations among landmarks than halfway have not been successful. Skov-Rackette and Shettleworth (2005) adopted a technique devised by Poucet, Chapuis, Durup, and Thinus-Blanc (1986) to study the information that animals acquire when they are exposed to an array of landmarks. A rat was released into a circular arena where it encountered an array of four landmarks in the shape of a square. Because the landmarks were novel, rats initially spent a considerable amount of time exploring in the vicinity of each of them but this activity soon habituated. The square was then expanded for a test trial, and the experimenters observed an increase in the amount of exploration directed towards each landmark. Skov-Rackette and Shettleworth (2005) concluded this dishabituation must have been a consequence of the change to the distance between one landmark and another, because the overall shape of the array remained constant.

To determine whether rats are also affected by changes to the shape of a landmark array, Skov-Rackette and Shettleworth (2005) conducted a further study. On this occasion, rats were released into a circular arena with three landmarks arranged in the form of the triangle shown in the left-hand panel of Figure 11.6. Once exploration of the landmarks had habituated, the rats were released into an arena from the same entrance as during the previous stage but with the landmarks creating the mirror image of the original triangle (see the right-hand panel of Figure 11.6). Despite the change to the shape of the triangle, there was no indication of a recovery of exploration to the landmarks. On this occasion, the distance between the landmarks remained the same. The results from the two experiments imply that when they are confronted with an array of landmarks, animals take note of the distance between pairs of landmarks, but they do not take note of the shape created by the landmarks.

An experiment by Esber, McGregor, Good, Hayward, and Pearce (2005) makes a similar point to that just drawn. Rats were trained to find a submerged platform near one of four identical landmarks that were arranged in the shape of a rectangle in a circular swimming pool (see left-hand side of Figure 11.7). Rats are natural swimmers and they soon learned to head directly for landmark A, where they found the platform, or for the diagonally opposite landmark, C. On failing to find the platform at C they would then head directly for landmark A. One explanation for these results is that the rats appreciated the landmarks created a rectangular shape, and that they searched for the platform in the corners where a short side was to the left of a long side. In the absence of any additional cues, this strategy would take them to corners A and C. A test trial was conducted to test this explanation by placing rats in the pool with only landmarks A and D present (see right-hand side of Figure 11.7). The rats showed a showed a strong tendency to swim towards landmark A rather than D. If rats originally identified the position of the platform by reference to the shape of the arena, then they should have not have shown this preference for landmark A. Instead, the results indicate that during their training the rats broke the array down into its components and learned to search for the goal in front of a landmark that was

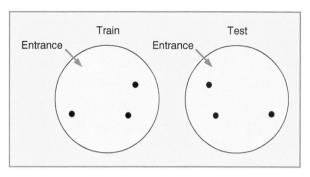

FIGURE 11.6 Plan of the arena, with three cylindrical landmarks, that was used during the training trials and the test trials in a study by Skov-Rackette and Shettleworth (2005). The arrow indicates the entrance into the arena (adapted from Skov-Rackette & Shettleworth, 2005).

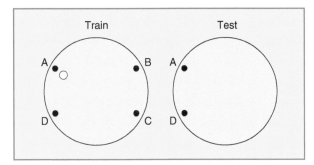

FIGURE 11.7 Left-hand side: Plan of the circular pool containing a rectangular array of four cylindrical landmarks (black circles) and an invisible, submerged escape platform (white circle) that were used for the training trials of an experiment by Esber et al. (2005). Right-hand side: Plan of the circular pool and two cylindrical landmarks that were used for the test trials in the experiment by Esber et al. (2005).

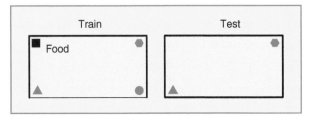

FIGURE 11.8 Left-hand side: Plan of the rectangular arena, with different landmarks in each corner and showing the location of food, that was used for the training trials of an experiment by Cheng (1986). Right-hand side: The same arena modified with the addition of a fourth black wall, and the removal of two landmarks, that was used for the test trials in the study by Cheng (1986) (adapted from Cheng, 1986).

the right-hand member of a pair with a relatively short distance between them. This strategy would take them either to landmark A or landmark C during the training trials, and to landmark A on the test trials.

The experiments in this section indicate that animals have a rudimentary appreciation of the geometric properties of an array of landmarks. They can appreciate the distance between two landmarks and one species has been shown to be capable of identifying the midpoint between a pair of landmarks. There is, however, very little evidence to suggest that animals can appreciate the shape created by three or more landmarks.

Navigation in an environment with a distinctive shape

Cheng (1986) conducted a relatively simple experiment with rats which has influenced considerably the study of navigation in both animals and humans and is thought by many to show that rats can appreciate quite complex geometric relations. The apparatus consisted of a rectangular chamber with three black walls and one white wall, and with a different landmark in each corner (see the left hand side of Figure 11.8). The rats were required to retrieve some food that was available only in one corner, say where a short wall was to the left of a long wall, and always in front of the same landmark. Once the rats were reliably heading directly for the correct corner after being released into the chamber, test trials were given in an arena with four black walls and with the landmarks in the correct corner and the diagonally opposite corner removed (see the right-hand side of Figure 11.8). The outcome of the test was that rats on approximately half the trials headed for the correct corner, and on the remaining trials they headed for the diagonally opposite corner. On the basis of these findings, Cheng (1986) concluded that rats had identified the correct corner by reference to the overall shape of the arena. They were also assumed to identify the correct corner by the landmarks and possibly by the color of the walls but, in the absence of these cues, were forced to reveal their knowledge about the significance of the arena's shape for finding the goal. It hardly needs to be added that by referring solely to the shape of the arena, rats would be unable to discriminate between the correct corner and the one that is diagonally opposite, which is exactly what Cheng (1986) found.

Cheng (1986) and Gallistel (1990) saw these results as evidence that a rat's brain contains a **geometric module** that is dedicated to encoding the shape of the environment, and to identifying where goals such as food can be found with reference to that shape. Subsequent experiments have revealed similar findings to those reported by Cheng (1986) with fish (Sovrano, Bisazza, & Vallortigara, 2003), birds (Kelly, Spetch, & Heth, 1998) nonhuman primates (Gouteux, Thinus-Blanc, & Vauclair, 2001), infant humans (Wang, Hermer, & Spelke, 1999), and adult humans (Hermer & Spelke, 1996). The majority of these researchers have gone along with the theoretical proposals of Cheng (1986). Some have even gone further to claim that the capacity to navigate with reference to the shape of the environment is widespread among vertebrates, and a fundamental cognitive process in animals and humans (Sovrano, Bisazza, & Vallortigara, 2002, pp. 56–57).

These conclusions, however, have been called into question by the findings of an experiment by Pearce, Good, Jones, and McGregor (2004). Rats were trained to escape from a rectangular pool by swimming to a submerged platform that was located in one corner (corner A in the left-hand panel of Figure 11.9). As with the study by Esber et al. (2005), the rats soon swam directly to corners A or C. The errors of searching in corner C can be readily understood because the appearance of this corner was in all respects the same as of corner A, and steps were taken to ensure that the arena provided the only information for finding the platform. On the completion of this training, the rats were tested in a kite-shaped arena (right-hand panel of Figure 11.9). The arena was built from the same walls as the rectangle, and corners E and G were each right angled. A record was taken of which corner rats headed for after being released into the pool.

If the platform in the rectangle was found by identifying its position relative to the overall shape of the pool then, on being placed in the kite, this arena should be treated as a totally new environment. Rats should thus be lost in the kite and lack a preference for any of the four corners. The results contradicted this prediction; the numbers within the kite in Figure 11.9 show the percentages of trials on which subjects swam directly to each of the four corners during a single test session. There was a similar strong tendency to swim to either the right-angled corner E, and the apex, corner H, and a weak tendency to swim to the other two corners. To explain these findings, Pearce et al. (2004) pointed out that during their training in the rectangle the rats did not necessarily have to rely on the global cue of the overall shape of the pool to find the platform. Instead, they might have used more local cues. They might, for example, have searched for the platform by looking for a corner where a short wall was to the right of a long wall. The transfer of this strategy to the kite would then encourage the rats to swim to corner E. Alternatively, in the rectangle the rats may have looked for a long wall and then headed to the corner at the right-hand end. The adoption of this strategy in the kite would then result in them swimming to corner E, if they selected long wall HE; or to corner H if they selected the other long wall, GH. In the absence of any tendency to select one long wall over the other then corners E and H should be approached first equally often, and more frequently than corners G and H. The results from the test trials are entirely consistent with this prediction and indicate that during their training in the rectangle rats navigated with reference to the second of the two local cues that have just been identified.

The explanation for the findings by Pearce et al. (2004) could apply equally well to the experiment by Cheng (1986). Rather than identify the position of food with reference to the rectangular shape of the arena, the rats may have used either of the local cues that have just been considered. Once it is accepted that rats can find

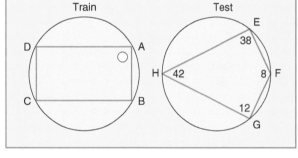

FIGURE 11.9 Left-hand side: Plan of the circular pool containing four walls arranged in the shape of a rectangle and an invisible, submerged escape platform (white circle) in one corner that was used for the training trials in an experiment by Pearce et al. (2004). Right-hand side: The same pool, with the walls re-arranged to create the shape of a kite for the test trials of the same experiment.

a hidden goal in an arena with a distinctive shape by reference to local rather than global cues, then the claim that animals possess a geometric module that is responsible for constructing a global representation of their environment is called into question. Indeed, such a claim can only be justified on the basis of evidence showing that animals navigate in a distinctively shaped environment with reference to global cues. To my knowledge, this evidence does not yet exist.

Cognitive maps

At this point it is natural to turn to a question that has been addressed for over sixty years: Do animals use cognitive maps? The suggestion that animals acquire such maps has been raised on several occasions (e.g. Gallistel, 1990; O'Keefe & Nadel, 1978; Tolman, Ritchie, & Kalish, 1946). According to Gallistel (1990, p. 103) a cognitive map is:

> *A record in the central nervous system of macroscopic geometric relations among surfaces in the environment used to plan movements through the environment.*

Rather than dwell on the interpretation of this definition, it would not be too misleading to suggest that a cognitive map is rather like an aerial view or plan of the space that is being represented. One property of a map is that it encodes information about the spatial relationship between objects in the environment. In view of the evidence cited in the previous sections that animals do not appear to have much knowledge of the overall shape created by the walls of their environment, or by the shape created by a set of landmarks within their environment, it would seem unlikely that animals construct a map based on these objects. In support of this conclusion, a number of authors have argued that there is little evidence to show that navigation by animals is based on information contained within a cognitive map (Benhamou, 1996; Bennett, 1996; Mackintosh, 2002; Healy, Hodgson, & Braithwaite, 2003). The purpose of the present section, therefore, is not to argue that animals construct cognitive maps. Instead, we shall review some of the evidence that has been said to support this claim and look at some of the problems that relate to interpreting this evidence.

Making a detour

One advantage of being in possession of a cognitive map is that enables a detour or novel route to be found to a goal if a familiar route should be blocked. An early attempt to demonstrate this benefit of a cognitive map was conducted by Tolman et al. (1946). A hungry rat was placed at point A in the maze shown on the left-hand side of Figure 11.10; it then had to pass points C, D, E, F, and G to reach the goal containing food. When subjects were practiced at running along this route, they were placed again at A for a trial in which the maze had been modified to the form depicted on the right-hand side of the figure. On this occasion the original exit from the maze was blocked and eighteen alternative exits had been added. Tolman et al. (1946) argued that if animals possessed a cognitive map of the maze, then on the test trial they should be able to deduce from it the direction of the goal relative to the arena and select the exit that most closely corresponded with this direction. On this basis animals were expected to leave the arena through exit 5.

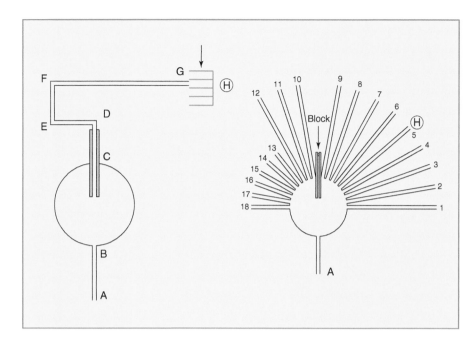

FIGURE 11.10 Plans of the mazes used in the two stages of the experiment by Tolman et al. (1946). Throughout the experiment a light bulb was located at H (from Tolman et al., 1946).

In support of the claim that rats possess cognitive maps, the majority of subjects did indeed leave by exit 5. However, there is a serious shortcoming with the design of this experiment. Throughout the study, a light bulb, H, was suspended over the goal; this was visible from all points of the maze. During their training, rats may have associated the light with food and, on the test trial, selected the path that led most directly to it. That is, navigating with reference to a single landmark, rather than taking advantage of a cognitive map, may have been responsible for the result of this experiment.

Although the experiment by Tolman et al. (1946) has never been repeated without the light bulb suspended above the goal, an experiment by Chapuis and Scardigli (1993) captures the essence of the design of that study while making it impossible for animals to find the goal by reference to a single landmark. A plan of their apparatus is shown in Figure 11.11, and this can best be described as a collection of alleyways and chambers joined together

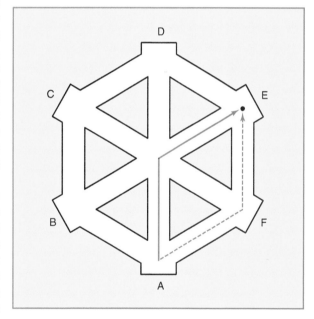

FIGURE 11.11 A plan of the circular maze used by Chapuis and Scardigli (1993) to study the way in which hamsters solve detour problems (adapted from Chapuis & Scardigli, 1993).

in the shape of a wagon wheel. In one experiment, a hamster was placed into chamber A; it had to pass along the route identified by the dashed line to obtain food in chamber E. Locked doors prevented the subject from deviating from this route. After a number of sessions of this training, all the doors in the apparatus were unlocked except the one that allowed the animal to leave chamber A on its normal route to food. If hamsters are able to identify a novel route to their goal, then they should pass along the route marked by the solid line in Figure 11.11. For the three test trials that were conducted, hamsters selected this route significantly more frequently than would be expected on the basis of chance.

An important feature of this experiment is that during the training phase, the maze was rotated relative to the room from one trial to the next. In addition, the chamber that served as the start of the route (chamber A) was varied from trial to trial. The success of the animals on this detour problem was thus not due to them orienting towards landmarks that lay beyond, or within the maze. Although this experiment constitutes a better design than the one used by Tolman et al. (1946), its findings do not allow us to conclude that the hamsters formed a cognitive map of the route they originally traveled. Instead, they could have learned through dead reckoning that the goal was a certain direction and distance from the start box. As they left the start box on the test trial, information about their current distance and direction from this box, together with the information about the direction and distance of the goal from the start box, would allow them to compute the direction in which to head when they arrived at the center of the apparatus. We saw in the section on dead reckoning that ants can make similar computations, and there is no reason to suppose that this sophisticated use of dead reckoning should be beyond a hamster.

Finding a goal from a novel release site

Another property of a map is that it should prevent its user from being lost if they should suddenly find themselves in unfamiliar territory. Provided the map encodes the position of landmarks that are visible from the novel location, then it should be possible to plot a course directly to a desired goal. An influential experiment by Morris (1981) was based on this rationale in order to demonstrate that rats use cognitive maps. To avoid the problem of giving the location of the goal away by a specific cue, a vat (1.3 meters in diameter) of milky water was used as the maze, and a platform submerged just below the surface was the goal. The apparatus was located in a room with a number of distinctive features that the rat could use as landmarks. After being released into the vat from the same point at the edge of the pool, rats soon learned to swim directly to the platform, which always remained in the same position (Figures 11.12 and 11.13). To explain this successful detection of the invisible goal, Morris (1981) argued that the rats acquired a cognitive map, which represented the position of the platform relative to the features of the experimental room. When placed into the vat, the subject would have to identify its location on the map and then deduce the direction in which to swim to reach the platform.

As a test of this argument, the rats were then divided into three groups. Group Control received the same treatment as for the previous stage; Group New-Place was released from the original release point but had to find the platform in a new location; and Group Same-Place was required to swim from a novel starting point to the platform, which was not moved. The routes taken by each rat from when it was released until the platform was discovered are shown in Figure 11.14.

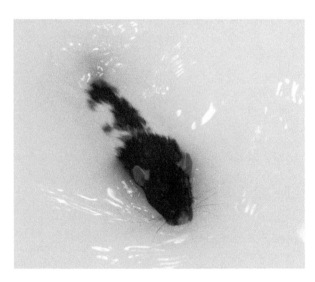

FIGURE 11.12 A rat exploring a water maze.

The control group performed the task without difficulty and swam directly to the platform. The performance for Group New-Place suggests that their problem was very difficult. After a period of swimming around the original location of the goal, the behavior of these animals was essentially without direction until they came upon the goal by chance. This finding confirms that there were no hidden cues to give away the position of the platform. The results for rats in Group Same-Place lie between these extremes. They located the platform without too much difficulty, which Morris (1981) regards as evidence that they possessed a cognitive map.

Examination of Figure 11.14 suggests, however, that this conclusion may be unwarranted. Apart from Subject 1, all the animals in Group Same-Place started off by swimming in the wrong direction, and there is no obvious reason why the possession of a cognitive map should result in this incorrect behavior. Admittedly, the rats soon adjusted their course, but this does not provide compelling evidence for the use of a cognitive map. During their training, rats will doubtless approach the platform from many angles, and they may well learn a variety of routes to the goal. The landmarks of these routes would be provided by the various configurations of external cues, and success in finding the platform would depend on nothing more than learning to swim in a certain direction relative to a specific landmark. In other words, learning to find the platform may involve nothing more than learning a number of different heading vectors. On the test trial, Group Same-Place might set off in a randomly determined direction and swim until a familiar landmark was perceived. At this point they could adjust their course and swim towards the platform. In support of this proposal, Sutherland, Chew, Baker, and Linggard (1987) report that rats find it hard to locate a hidden goal in a swimming pool if they are released from a region of the pool that they have not previously visited. Thus, if nothing else, the study by Morris (1981) demonstrates that even with a well-designed experiment, convincing evidence for the existence and operation of a cognitive map is hard to obtain.

FIGURE 11.13 A rat resting on a submerged platform after swimming to it from a release point at the side of a water maze.

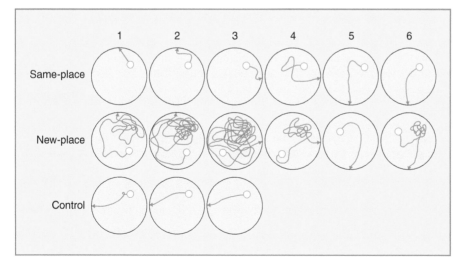

FIGURE 11.14 A vertical view of the routes taken on the first test trial by all the rats in the three groups of the study by Morris (1981) (from Morris, 1981). Copyright © Elsevier. Reproduced with permission.

Another experiment that has investigated whether animals can find their way when they are released from a novel place was conducted with bees (Menzel et al., 2005). Bees were settled into a hive in a novel location and allowed to spend some time exploring the area around the hive before being trained to fly to a feeding table for nutrient. Having consumed the nutrient they would fly directly back to the hive. The table was about 200 meters from the hive, and always in the same position. Once a bee was reliably foraging at the feeding table, she would be captured as she left the feeding platform, put in a lightproof container, and then taken to a new place where she was released. The bees would typically engage in a search flight, which appeared to be a rather slow meandering flight before suddenly changing direction and heading directly for home. The search flight suggests that the bees were initially lost, and the subsequent flight suggests that they were eventually able to determine a new route back to the hive. The evidence from individual flight paths indicated that the point where the direct flight to the hive commenced was situated near to a prominent landmark. It is thus possible that, during their flights around the hive, the bees identified a number of salient landmarks and associated each of them with their distance and direction from home. On being released from the container, the bees presumably searched for a familiar landmark and then used the associated information to determine in which direction to head for home. This is a remarkable feat because it depends on bees remembering the distance and direction to the hive from a variety of landmarks, but it does not force us to accept that the bees had a cognitive map of their environment. For this to be demonstrated it would be necessary to show that the bees had some record of the spatial relations among the various landmarks and, to the best of my knowledge, this has never been demonstrated. A number of other studies have been conducted with bees, often using extremely ingenious designs (e.g. Gould, 1984, 1986). Their findings, however, have been criticized as being open to a variety of interpretations (Dyer, 1991; Menzel, 1990) and they do not provide unambiguous evidence that bees use cognitive maps.

Studies designed to demonstrate that animals have cognitive maps have revealed that they are extremely good at finding their way to a goal by means of an unfamiliar route. However, this ability does not seem to depend on the use of a cognitive map. Instead, it depends on a capacity to remember the direction and distance to the goal of various landmarks in the surrounding environment. It also depends on a sophisticated use of dead reckoning.

The argument has occasionally been put forward that the possibility of animals using cognitive maps should be considered seriously because it provides a parsimonious, or simple, account of the animal's behavior (Menzel, 1978; Morris, 1981; Cheng & Gallistel, 2005). However, the ease of invoking a cognitive map as an explanation is partly illusory; the explanation seems simple only because it directs attention away from certain very important questions. If it is accepted that an animal possesses a cognitive map, then we need to know how it is constructed, how the animal knows where it is located on the map, and how the map is used to determine the route that is taken. Until these questions can be answered satisfactorily, accounts of behavior in terms of cognitive maps must be seen as incomplete. But even if they did not suffer from this shortcoming, these accounts should be viewed with caution until there is more compelling evidence than is currently available to support them.

Hippocampal place cells

The results that have been reviewed so far demonstrate forcefully that a specific location can be identified by animals in a variety of ways. This conclusion is further supported by some remarkable findings that have been obtained by recording the activity of nerve cells in a particular region of the brain—the hippocampus. By inserting a small electrode into a single hippocampal cell its electrical activity can be recorded as the animal, normally a rat or a rabbit, moves freely around its environment (O'Keefe, 1979). In a study by O'Keefe and Speakman (1987), rats were trained to find food in the simple maze depicted in Figure 11.15. The maze was an elevated wooden cross (Figure 11.16) located in a circular enclosure created from curtains. There were a number of landmarks in the enclosure, which included a cage of two rats, a white card, a light, a fan, a black towel, and an aromatic pen. On any trial, the relationship between the maze and these landmarks remained constant,

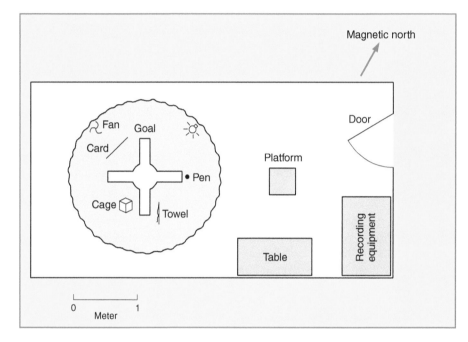

FIGURE 11.15 Plan of an elevated maze and the surrounding room used in the experiment by O'Keefe and Speakman (1987) to study the reaction of hippocampal place cells as rats moved through the maze (adapted from O'Keefe & Speakman, 1987).

FIGURE 11.16 A rat exploring an elevated cross maze (left-hand side) and a view of the maze showing the landmarks that the rat can use to identify the different arms.

so that food was always presented at the end of the arm that had the white card on its left and the light on its right. However, the entire configuration of landmarks and the maze itself was rotated from one trial to the next. On any trial a rat would be released from a randomly selected arm and it was expected to run to the goal in order to obtain food. Subjects became adept at this task, which indicates that they used the information provided by the landmarks to identify the location of the goal.

By recording the activity of different cells in the hippocampus, O'Keefe and Speakman (1987) were able to identify a number of **place cells**. These cells were normally inactive, but as the rat passed through a specific part of the maze they fired at a high rate. Figure 11.17 shows the regions of the maze that produced a high rate of firing in two different cells. For one cell, a high burst of activity was recorded only in the goal arm, whereas the second cell fired maximally when the rat was in the arm that was to the left of the goal arm. In both cases, it did not matter in which compass direction the arm was pointing. Thus the cues provided by the room, or the orientation of the maze in respect to the room, did not control the activity of the place cells. Instead, the determinant of responding was the position of the arm relative to the landmarks.

By selectively removing landmarks while the animal is in the goal arm, it should be possible to derive a more detailed understanding of the pattern of stimulation that controls the activity of the place cell. Although this strategy was not adopted in the study just referred to, it was employed in a very similar experiment in which there were four landmarks (O'Keefe & Conway, 1978). Removal of the landmarks revealed that some cells depended on one or two specific landmarks in order to be activated, whereas other cells would fire provided any two of the four landmarks were present. A subsequent study has shown that certain hippocampal cells are controlled by cues that lie beyond the immediate environment of the maze (O'Keefe & Speakman, 1987). For example, firing was observed whenever the rat entered a particular location in the room, no matter what the configuration of the local landmarks. If these findings have any implications for the way in which animals represent spatial information, then they confirm the conclusion that can be drawn from the previous sections of this chapter: A variety of potential sources of information can be used to define a specific location.

FIGURE 11.17 Regions of an elevated maze that produced activity in two different hippocampal cells of a rat. The regions extend further than the maze itself because the rat was able to move its head freely beyond the sides of the apparatus (from O'Keefe & Speakman, 1987). Copyright © 1987 Springer Science. Reproduced with permission.

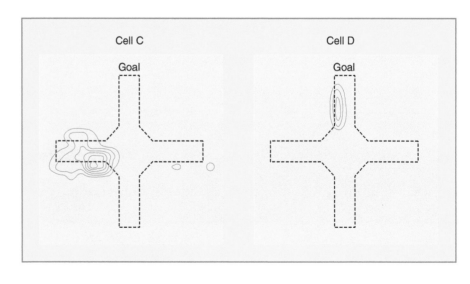

A further stage of the experiment by O'Keefe and Speakman (1987) demonstrates that the continued presence of the relevant landmarks is not always essential for the firing of place cells. In this stage, the rat was placed on the start arm and prevented from leaving it for about 90 seconds. During the first minute of this period the landmarks could be seen in their correct location, after which they were all removed from the apparatus. The animal was then allowed to leave the start arm, and to select the arm that led to the goal. Even though this choice was determined by cues that were no longer present, subjects were readily able to identify the correct arm. Of more importance, however, was the finding that some of the place cells that were normally controlled by the landmarks continued to fire when the rat entered the appropriate location in the maze. Note that the normal pattern of firing of the place cells was seriously disrupted if the animals were placed into the apparatus in the absence of any landmarks. The firing of the place cells on the memory trial was therefore not due to the influence of some additional landmark that the experimenters failed to remove.

These findings, more than any other, justify naming the relevant hippocampal cells as place cells. The findings indicate that the firing of a cell does not require the presence of a particular stimulus, or set of stimuli. Rather, these stimuli are necessary only to define a particular place in the animal's environment. Once this place has been identified it will serve to activate the relevant place cell whenever the animal enters it.

PART 2: LONG-DISTANCE TRAVEL

Some of the most remarkable feats of animal navigation are revealed by their capacity to travel long distances, often towards a localized goal. On some journeys, animals find their way to a specific goal even though they have never previously

Papi and Luschi (1996) describe how a green turtle astonishingly appeared at its birthplace of Ascension Island (a tiny island set in the vast Atlantic Ocean) 2 years after it had been tossed overboard into the English Channel.

visited it. They are also able to find their way home over hundreds of miles when they are released in unfamiliar territory. To demonstrate this ability it is hard to ignore the feats of a green turtle that is mentioned in a report Papi and Luschi (1996). The turtle was caught during the 1800s on a beach on Ascension Island in the middle of the Atlantic Ocean and taken by ship to the English Channel, where it was thrown overboard because the unfortunate animal looked unwell. It is most unlikely that the turtle had previously visited the English Channel, yet 2 years later this doughty mariner was found again on Ascension Island, possibly having swum there via the coast of Brazil.

To understand how animals are capable of this sort of achievement, the following discussion will look at studies of **homing** and **migration**. Both have been said to depend on the capacity of animals to detect sources of stimulation that are undetectable by humans. The first part of this section will therefore demonstrate that animals are indeed sensitive to these sources of information.

NAVIGATIONAL CUES

Magnetic fields

Animals might benefit from being able to detect magnetic fields because the magnetic properties of the earth provide a pervasive source of information for orientation. We have already come across the suggestion that this information would be useful for traveling short journeys, and a number of authors have suggested it would also help with navigation for longer journeys. Yeagley (1947) and Keeton (1974) both proposed that pigeon homing relies on information provided by the earth's magnetic field. In support of this proposal, pigeon homing is less accurate when there is a magnetic storm (Gould, 1982), when they are in the vicinity of anomalies in the earth's magnetic field (Walcott, 1978), and when they are carrying magnets (Keeton, 1974) or coils (Walcott & Green, 1974) that distort the earth's magnetic field. Given these, and related findings, it is now generally accepted that the earth's magnetic field plays a role in pigeon homing (e.g. Able, 1994; Gagliardo, Ioale, Savini, & Wild, 2006), but there is some debate about the exact nature of this role (Gagliardo et al., 2006; Walker, 1998).

In the hope of lending further support to the claim that pigeons are sensitive to magnetic fields, experiments have been conducted in conditioning chambers to discover if they can solve discriminations based on this cue. The results from this endeavor, it must be admitted, are far from clear cut. Mora, Davison, Wild, and Walker (2004) describe a successful experiment in which pigeons were trained to obtain food by occupying one platform when a magnetic field was on, and another platform, some 3 meters away, when the field was off. In contrast to this finding, Able (1994) summarizes nearly a dozen earlier studies in which only one, by Bookman (1977), provided a satisfactory demonstration of a successful discrimination. Furthermore, a subsequent attempt to replicate Bookman's experiment failed (Carman, Walker, & Lee, 1987). Mora et al. (2004) suggest that the type of magnetic field that is used as the discriminative stimulus determines whether or not the experiment will be successful, but why this should be the case is something of a mystery. It seems that magnetic fields can be used for conditioning with pigeons, but the circumstances in which they are effective remain obscure.

Air pressure

A change in altitude will necessarily be accompanied by a change in air pressure. Accordingly, any animals, but in particular birds, that possess the capacity to detect and remember levels of air pressure should be able to compute their altitude. To demonstrate that pigeons can detect changes in air pressure, Delius and Emmerton (1978) used a 10-second change to signal the delivery of electric shock. As conditioning progressed, a conditioned response of accelerated heart rate was recorded whenever this stimulus was presented. The change in pressure was slight and indicates that pigeons are sensitive to changes in air pressure that correspond to a vertical displacement of as little as 20 meters.

Rapid fluctuations in air pressure constitute sound, and if they are of sufficient intensity and within a range of 20–20,000 Hz, they will be heard by humans. Below the lower threshold of human hearing, animals may be able to detect sounds known as **infrasound**. They can be generated by thunderstorms, magnetic storms, earthquakes, and the impact of air currents on mountain ranges. One important property of infrasound is that it can travel many thousands of kilometers with little attenuation or distortion. Hence sonic booms generated by supersonic jets crossing the Atlantic have been recorded in New York from a distance of 1000 kilometers (Balachandran, Dunn, & Rind, 1977).

Kreithen (1978) has noted that an ability to detect infrasound would provide valuable meteorological and navigational information for animals. To test whether pigeons are sensitive to this sort of stimulation, Yodlowski, Kreithen, and Keeton (1977) conducted a Pavlovian conditioning study in which a burst of infrasound, with a frequency of 0.1 Hz, served as a signal for shock. The infrasound was inaudible to humans but conditioning with the pigeons was successful.

Pigeons are thus capable of detecting infrasound, but there may be limitations to the use of this source of information, especially for navigation. Infrasound is prone to severe interference by local winds and turbulence, and its source would also be extremely difficult for a stationary animal to localize. Unless animals possess mechanisms for circumventing these problems, infrasound would not be a useful tool for navigation. Nonetheless, as Baker (1984) points out, pigeons would be unlikely to be able to perceive infrasound unless it serves some purpose; and Quine (1982) shows how it would be possible for birds to use infrasound for navigation.

Polarized and ultraviolet light

Human sight is insensitive both to polarized and to ultraviolet light, and for a while it was thought that this constraint applied to all vertebrates. In contrast, insects such as bees have been known for some time to be able to detect both types of light (e.g. Von Frisch, 1950). But a report by Kreithen (1978) now suggests that one vertebrate—the pigeon again—can detect and be conditioned with ultraviolet as well as with polarized light. With both classes of stimuli a conditioned response of an accelerated heart rate was detected when they were used to signal the occurrence of an electric shock. An ability to perceive polarized light is of value for navigation, providing some blue sky is visible, because it allows the sun to be located when it is obscured by clouds. Whether pigeons use it in this way remains to be seen.

HOMING

Homing refers to the ability of animals to return to their nest or loft when they have been taken some distance from it and released. Very often this journey involves traveling across unfamiliar territory. Matthews (1955) has reported that a Manx shearwater released from Boston, Massachusetts, flew more than 3000 miles in 12 days to return to its nest in South Wales. The albatross has been known to home successfully over distances of greater than 4100 miles (Kenyon & Rice, 1958). The feats of the most famous homing bird, the pigeon, do not compare with these reports in terms of distance, but that they can return to their loft on the same day that they are released some 600 miles away is no small achievement (Keeton, 1974). However, homing is not confined to birds: Missouri cave bats were able to find their way back to the barn in which they nested after they had been released 75 miles away in unfamiliar territory (Gunier & Elder, 1971). Animals use a variety of strategies for homing. To give an indication of these, we will examine a number of explanations that have been developed to account for the homing skills of pigeons.

The use of landmarks

There is no doubt that pigeons make use of landmarks when returning to their loft. Biro, Meade, and Guilford (2004) released pigeons repeatedly from two sites that were about 10 kilometers from their lofts. By the use of miniaturized tracking equipment attached to the pigeons, they were able to discover that the birds adopted stereotyped routes from these release sites to their loft. Moreover, if the birds were released from a novel location that was as much as 1.5 kilometers from the familiar route then they would head for the familiar route before following it home. Careful inspection of the paths taken by the birds revealed that for some of their journeys they would even follow roads and railway lines that were oriented in roughly the correct direction (for similar findings, see Lipp et al., 2004). According to Biro et al. (2004), these findings imply that pigeons remember a sequence of landmarks and return home by flying from one to the other in a form of navigation that is referred to as steeple-chasing (Baker, 1984).

Equally, there is no doubt that pigeons are able to home accurately without the use of landmarks. In a study by Keeton (1974), great care was taken to ensure that pigeons were released more than 50 miles from familiar territory. It is highly unlikely that they could perceive any familiar landmarks when released, yet they were able to home without difficulty. In a more ingenious test of the hypothesis that use of landmarks is not essential for successful homing, Schlicte and Schmidt-Koenig (1971) fitted pigeons with frosted contact lenses. These allowed light to pass through but restricted the identification of landmarks to 6 meters. Despite this enormous handicap, when the pigeons were released 80 miles from their loft they rapidly oriented in the correct direction and a number actually managed to return. It is well worth reporting Keeton's (1974) observations of the behavior of the successful birds on their return home, because they strongly imply that homing is possible without the use of landmarks (p. 91):

It was a truly remarkable sight. The birds flew considerably higher than normal, and they did not swoop in for a landing on the loft like normal pigeons. Instead, they came almost straight down in a peculiar helicoptering or hovering flight. Being unable to see the loft itself, they landed in yards or fields in the vicinity, where we picked them up and carried them to the loft.

Retracing the outward route

When it is being transported to the release site, a pigeon might acquire information about the terrain through which it passes. This information could then be used to determine the correct direction in which to fly from the release point. In support of this proposal, homing can be affected by various manipulations to the birds as they are being transported to the release site. These manipulations include transporting birds along different routes to the same release site (Papi, Fiore, Fiaschi, & Benvenuti, 1972); preventing the animals from using their sense of smell (Baldaccini, Benvenuti, Fiaschi, Ioale, & Papi, 1982); and changing the magnetic field that surrounds the bird (Kiepenheuer, 1978). Furthermore, experiments have also shown that when pigeons are released from a particular site, their direction of flight from the site is very much influenced by their route to the site (Baker, 1984; see Figure 11.18).

However, pigeons are able to home effectively even when they are deeply anaesthetized on the journey to the release site (Walcott & Schmidt-Koenig, 1973). It is highly unlikely that pigeons learn much about the terrain through which they pass while asleep. Thus, although information acquired on the outward route can influence the return journey, this information is not always essential if the return journey is to be successful.

The map and compass hypothesis

According to Kramer (1952; see Wiltschko & Wiltschko, 2003, for a recent review), pigeons possess a map that allows them to determine the direction in which they must fly to return home. To be of any value, this information must be converted into a bearing that relates to the environment, which could be achieved, Kramer (1952) argues, if pigeons have a compass. For example, if it was inferred from the map that home lies due west of the release point, the use of a compass would then permit the subject to determine the direction in which it should fly. Obviously pigeons do not possess compasses of the sort that can be bought in shops, nor do they employ directions like due west, but the position of the sun appears to provide an excellent substitute. In fact, quite a lot is now known about the compass component of Kramer's hypothesis, whereas the map component is poorly understood.

The sun compass operates in the following way: On being released, the pigeon observes the position of the sun and by using the information supplied by an internal clock (see Chapter 10) it would then be able to compute any direction it requires. Suppose it needs to fly in a direction that is equivalent to south; this can be readily computed by extrapolating from the present position of the sun to where it should be at mid-day. Admittedly, this is a complex calculation but it does not appear to be beyond the capability of pigeons, as experiments on clock-shifting have shown.

An internal clock is generally considered to be set according to the light–dark cycle. Thus, by maintaining pigeons in an artificial environment with a light–dark cycle

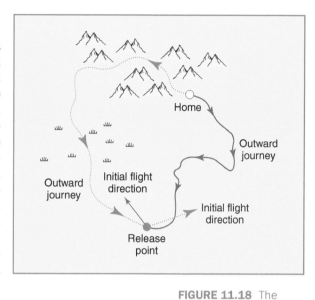

FIGURE 11.18 The initial direction of flight of two groups of pigeons that were taken from the same home to the same release point, along different routes. The different heading directions of the two groups indicate that information acquired on the outward journey can influence the return journey (adapted from Baker, 1980).

that is out of phase with the external cycle, it should be possible to change the internal clock and influence the accuracy of the sun compass. In a **clock-shift experiment**, then, pigeons are maintained for a while in a laboratory that receives no natural light. The lights might be turned on in the laboratory at midnight and turned off at midday. Assuming that dawn outside the laboratory is at 6 a.m., the internal clock of the pigeon will eventually be ahead of real time by 6 hours. If the pigeon is then released from the laboratory at, say, 9 a.m. real time, the internal clock will inform it that the time is 3 p.m. This will lead the bird to infer that the direction of the sun is equivalent to south-west, when in reality it will be south-east, and any computations involving this information will make the bird fly at right angles to the correct route home. A number of experiments have confirmed predictions of this sort (Keeton, 1969), which strongly implicates the involvement of the sun and the internal clock in homing.

Does this mean that pigeons can home only when the sun is shining? Not at all; accurate homing has been reported when the sky is overcast and, on occasions, at night (Keeton, 1974; Lipp, 1983). An obvious candidate for the source of compass information in these circumstances is the earth's magnetic field. Attempts to test this possibility have involved the placement of magnets, or coils that generate magnetic fields, on pigeons in the hope of distorting their magnetic sense. At first these manipulations did not disrupt homing, but Keeton (1974) has argued that this might be because the experiments were conducted on clear days when the sun compass can be used to home successfully. In support of this argument, Keeton (1974) has reported that carrying magnets can disrupt homing on overcast days. Similarly, the disruption to homing that is believed to be a consequence of magnetic storms (Gould, 1982) is not found on sunny days (Lednor & Walcott, 1983).

In contrast to the support for the compass component of Kramer's hypothesis, the evidence for the map component is much weaker. Kramer (1952) said rather little about this aspect of his model, which is perhaps not surprising. Because pigeons are capable of homing from a totally unfamiliar location, it is implausible that their success depends on a map that they can have had no opportunity to acquire. As it stands, then, the map and compass hypothesis must be regarded as an incomplete account of homing.

Bicoordinate navigation

Imagine that a pigeon is able to perceive two separate stimulus sources from its loft, and that it can also detect these sources from the release site. The direction and intensity of the sources will be different for these locations, and if the pigeon is sensitive to these differences then it will be in possession of sufficient information to compute the correct course home by means of bicoordinate navigation. The obvious advantage of this means of homing is that it can readily explain successful homing from unfamiliar territory. And a major obstacle is the specification of stimulus sources that can be detected over many hundreds of miles. As far as the pigeon is concerned, a number of possibilities have been examined. In addition to the earth's magnetic field (Walker, Dennis, & Kirschvink, 2002) researchers have investigated the information supplied by infrasound (Hagstrum, 2001), lines of coriolis force (Yeagley, 1947, 1951), and gravity (Lednor & Walcott, 1983). However, there is no evidence to show that these different sources of stimulation are used in the manner necessary for effective bicoordinate navigation.

Olfaction

The final theory of homing to consider may seem to be the one that is most implausible. According to this account, successful homing depends on the detection of odors at the release site that are also present at the home loft. The reason for questioning this account is that it might seem impossible for odors to be dispersed over the wide ranges that would be necessary to account for successful long-distance homing. The findings from a study by Wallraff and Andreae (2000), however, indicate that this expectation might be false. They measured the strength of various gases in the air at sites distributed over a circle with a radius of 200 kilometers. Not only was it possible to detect these gases over the entire area, but their intensity changed systematically across the region, and the location of their greatest intensity varied for different gases. On the basis of these findings, Wallraff (2004) has proposed that pigeons identify the proportions of different gases that are carried on the wind as they arrive at the loft. When the birds are then released some distance from the loft, these gases will be mixed in different proportions and to return home it is simply a matter of flying in a direction that alters this proportion until it matches that at the loft.

Additional support for the claim that homing depends upon olfaction comes from a variety of experiments. For example, homing is adversely affected by depriving pigeons of the sense of smell (Papi, Mariotti, Foa, & Fiaschi, 1980). A review of these and related experiments can be found in Wallraff (2004), who provides a detailed account of how homing could be based on olfaction. As this account has been presented thus far, it is not clear how it can explain the results considered earlier showing that homing involves the use of a compass that is provided either by the sun or by the earth's magnetic field. In brief, Wallraff (2004) has suggested that changes in the direction of the wind while they are in the loft will allow birds to infer the direction of the source of a particular odor, and this direction could be specified by the compass. If they are then released from a spot where, say, the odor is much weaker than at the loft, by referring to the compass they will know in which direction to head to get closer to the source of the odor and thereby closer to home. Additional experiments are needed to test the details of this explanation.

Some researchers doubt whether olfaction plays any role in pigeon homing (Wiltschko, 1996) but, at least for some instances of homing, the majority now accept that olfaction is important (e.g. Able, 1996; Bingman, 1998). The problem that remains is to understand how pigeons use their sense of smell to home efficiently and accurately. The theory offered by Wallraff (2004) is a step towards achieving this understanding but our knowledge is so scant that even he admits to being uncertain as to whether he is on the right track.

MIGRATION

Able (1980, p. 286) defines migration as the "oriented, long-distance, seasonal movement of individuals". Some feats of migration are quite spectacular. The Arctic tern, for instance, spends a fortnight each year at the North Pole, slightly longer at the South Pole, and the rest of the year traveling up to 50,000 kilometers between the two. Innate processes and learning both play an important role in successful migration, as the following discussion demonstrates.

Endogenous control

In many cases of migration, generations of the same species undertake much the same journey. It is thus possible, as Gwinner (1972) has noted, that the direction and duration of migration is largely under **endogenous** control, that is, it depends more on factors that originate within the animal, and rather little on learning. Migration by the loggerhead sea turtle provides an instance of this type of migration.

Loggerhead turtles hatch from eggs that are laid in underground nests on the Atlantic beaches of Florida. The hatchlings climb out of their nests and then scramble towards the sea, where they swim between 30 to 50 miles to the Gulf Stream. The Gulf Stream is attractive because it contains relatively few predators and yet provides an abundant supply of food. The turtles then spend the next few years swimming in loops around the Sargasso sea before returning to a beach in Florida, which may be the one on which they were born. A map of this voyage is presented in Figure 11.19.

A series of experiments has revealed how newly hatched turtles are able to find their way to the Gulf Stream. Young loggerhead turtles were placed into a large dish in which it was possible to measure their preferred direction of swimming (Lohman, 1992). When the experimental room was dark, except for the presence of a dim light source, the turtles were observed to swim towards the light. Apparently, newly hatched turtles emerge onto the beach at night, and reflected light from the moon and stars makes the sea brighter than the land. By being attracted to light, the turtles are thus led towards the ocean. When the room was completely dark, further testing revealed that the turtles had a tendency to swim head on into the waves, and also towards magnetic east (Lohman, 1991). Once they have reached the ocean, the joint influence of these tendencies would then lead to the comparative safety of the Gulf Stream.

As far as navigating around the Sargasso Sea is concerned, this could be accomplished by following the currents (see Figure 11.19). How the turtles are

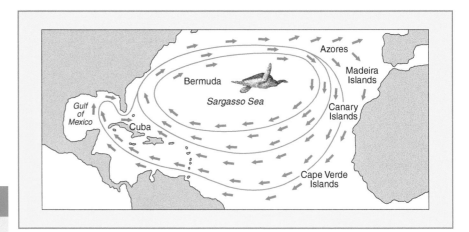

FIGURE 11.19 Migratory paths of sea turtles once they have left their nesting beaches in Florida. The arrows indicate the flow of ocean currents (the turtle is not drawn to scale).

then able to return to their hatching beaches remains a matter of speculation. The earth's magnetic field, patterns of wave propagation, and ocean swells have all been suggested as providing landmarks for the return journey, but none of these has received convincing support (see, for example, Lohman & Lohman, 1996).

To close this discussion of navigation by turtles, we return to the remarkable achievements of green turtles. Green turtles hatch on Ascension Island, which occupies 88 square kilometers and is located in the middle of the Atlantic Ocean. The turtles then migrate to the coast of Brazil, some 2200 kilometers away before returning to mate and nest on Ascension Island. After leaving Ascension Island, the coast of Brazil should be relatively easy to locate by using similar strategies to those possessed by loggerhead turtles, but it is almost impossible to believe that they are able to complete the return leg of the journey and find such a tiny island in such a vast ocean.

To assess whether green turtles use olfaction to help them in this task, Hays et al. (2003) captured adult turtles while they were on the beach of Ascension Island and then released them 50 kilometers away. By means of satellite, and a transmitter attached to the back of the turtle, they found that turtles released downwind of the island soon returned, whereas those released upwind took much longer, if they returned at all. Presumably, those released downwind of the island were able to detect odors from the island and swam towards their source. What remains to be explained is how the green turtles can navigate to a region from where they can detect the island's odors.

Endogenous factors also play an important role in bird migration, particularly on the first time that an individual undertakes its journey. As the time to migrate approaches, they start to build up fat deposits to provide energy reserves for the forthcoming journey. They also become restless and, if they are held in a cage, this restlessness is oriented towards the direction of migration. The restless activity is referred to as *Zugunruhe* and is assumed to result in the unrestrained bird embarking on its journey. According to Berthold (1998) endogenous circannual rhythms—or internal calendars—govern these and other aspects of migration. The annual rhythm is believed to be responsible for determining when the birds increase their food intake, which is essential if it is to have sufficient energy reserves to complete its journey. The annual rhythm is also believed to determine the time of departure, and the duration of the migration. Support for these claims comes from experiments in which birds are raised in a stable environment with a 12-hour, light–dark cycle. Despite the absence of any relevant environmental stimulation, these birds will show an increase in food intake at the same time as conspecifics (other birds from the same species) who are raised in more natural conditions. Furthermore, they will start to exhibit nocturnal restlessness in their cages as the time to migrate approaches; the duration of this restlessness corresponds with the duration that the migration would last if the bird had been released. If an endogenous rhythm determines when a bird starts and ends its migration, what determines the direction in which it should travel? To address this question, Wiltschko and Wiltschko (1996) studied the *Zugunruhe* of European robins. They found that captive subjects preferred to engage in this activity by the side of their cage that pointed in the direction of migration by their free-living conspecifics. They also demonstrated that this preference was controlled by the earth's magnetic field because the placement of a magnet by the cage altered the direction of the activity. Many species, including the European robin, migrate at night and at least some of these species refer to the stars to determine their direction of travel. As we shall now see, this ability depends to a certain degree on learning.

The role of learning

The migration of the indigo bunting provides a good example of the way in which learning interacts with endogenous processes in order to influence the direction of migration (Emlen, 1970). These North American birds migrate southwards in the autumn and northwards in the spring. Emlen (1970) hand-reared indigo buntings in an aviary that was entirely cut off from the outside world, except that the light–dark cycle coincided with the natural cycle. As autumn approached, two groups spent a number of nights in a planetarium, and a third group remained in the aviary. While they were in the planetarium, the buntings were exposed to a configuration of stars. For one group the configuration rotated around the normal north–south axis, but for the second group it rotated around a different axis. When it was time for the autumn migration, all three groups spent a test session of several hours in the planetarium with the stars motionless. The buntings were retained in small cages that indicated the orientation of their *Zugunruhe*.

The direction of their restless activity was essentially random for those birds that had remained in the aviary until the test session, which suggests they lacked a preferred direction for migration. The remaining birds, however, did express a preference, but this differed for the two groups. The group for which the stars had rotated around the north–south axis indicated a tendency to migrate southwards. The preferred direction for the other group was also along the axis of rotation they had experienced, but this was obviously not towards the south.

The interpretation of these results is complex yet fascinating. The random behavior of the buntings that spent all but the test session in the aviary indicates that extended exposure to the stars is essential if they are to migrate in the correct direction. As the groups that were exposed to the stars expressed different orientations of *Zugunruhe*, the movement of the stars must be an important influence on the direction of migration. Why should this be? The apparent movement of the stars is largely due to the rotation of the earth, so that the stars above the equator will seem to move a greater distance than those above the poles. Indeed, the stars that do not move at all, or at least very little, will indicate the direction of north (in the northern hemisphere). Thus, by remembering the position of the stars and comparing it with their position some time later, it would be possible to determine which stars have moved the least and therefore which indicate north. Emlen (1970) argues that buntings perform precisely this calculation when they are in the planetarium, and, by remembering the stars located above the pole, they are able to infer the direction for migration. Of course, this will be southwards only for those birds exposed to the normal rotation of the stars.

The orientation of migration is thus controlled by the stars, whereas the duration of the journey could be determined either by an internal clock, or when the energy reserves are depleted. Provided that the subject travels at a reasonably constant speed, these factors alone should be sufficient to ensure that it arrives at much the same place as its forefathers (see Able, 1980, for a review).

Obviously, the route will be unfamiliar to a bird on its first migration, but on subsequent journeys this will not be true. Experiments with starlings have revealed that the knowledge acquired on one journey can influence the course of a subsequent one. In an experiment by Perdeck (1958), starlings were taken from where they were born in Holland and released for migration from Switzerland. When juveniles without any experience of migration were released, the direction of their migration was appropriate for a release site in Holland rather than Switzerland. However, the adults that were released took account of their displacement and flew towards their usual winter quarters. Presumably this adjustment was possible because of information acquired during the course of previous migrations. But what this information might consist of remains a mystery—it is certainly unlikely to be based on a first-hand experience of Switzerland.

CONCLUDING COMMENTS

An obvious conclusion to draw from this chapter is that whether traveling over short or long distances, animals have a wide range of strategies at their disposal to help them reach their goal. The question is then raised of what will happen when more than one navigational cue is available to an animal while it is learning about the location of a new goal. According to theories of associative learning, such as the Rescorla–Wagner (1972) model, the cues will be in competition with each other so that the presence of one may overshadow or block learning about the other. By contrast, it is possible that animals do not select some cues at the expense of others but instead they make use of all the information that is available to them. O'Keefe and Nadel (1978), for instance, have argued that when learning about the location of a goal, animals make full use of all the landmarks in the environment. It may be a cause of some frustration to learn that there is evidence to support both points of view.

First, a few selected examples should serve to make the point that a reliance on one navigational cue does not automatically interfere with the control acquired by another cue. Hayward, McGregor, Good, and Pearce (2003) trained rats to find a hidden goal that was located beneath a landmark in one corner of a rectangular arena. There was no hint that the landmark restricted learning about the goal's position relative to cues provide by the walls of the arena (see also Wall, Botley, Black, & Shettleworth, 2004). In a rather different study, Shettleworth and Sutton (2005) required rats to enter a circular arena through one of sixteen identical doors to collect food before returning to their home box by passing through the same door. In one condition there were no cues to help the rats find the correct door for their return journey, which meant its location had to be identified by dead reckoning based on information acquired during the search for food. However, if the correct door was made distinctive by surrounding it with a black frame to act as a beacon, then test trials revealed that rats used both beacon homing and dead reckoning to find this door, and that the development of one strategy did not interfere with the other. On a grander scale, the experiment by Biro et al. (2004) considered earlier demonstrated that even though pigeons were able to home effectively when they were first released from an unfamiliar site, this strategy did not prevent them from acquiring the additional strategy during subsequent journeys of following a sequence of landmarks to their nest.

Next, a few experiments should make it clear that there are occasions when the presence of one cue can disrupt learning about other cues in a spatial task. A good example of this interaction comes from a study by Goodyear and Kamil (2004), who trained three groups of Clark's nutcrackers to find food hidden in the floor of a rectangular room. The food could be found by reference to an array of four different landmarks that surrounded it. As Figure 11.20 shows, the distance of the landmarks from the food varied in each of the groups, but all groups were trained with a landmark that was 70 centimeters due east of the food. Tests with individual landmarks at the end of the experiment revealed that the landmark that was 70 centimeters from the goal gained very little control over searching for the food in Group Close, a moderate amount of control in the Group Medium, and most control in Group Far. A ready explanation for this pattern of results is that animals tended to identify the position of the food with reference to the landmarks that were nearest to the goal. This strategy would lead them to pay little heed to the landmark that was 70 centimeters from food in Group Close, but more attention to this object in Group Far. In other words, the presence of landmarks close to food overshadowed learning about those that were more distant. For related findings, using a blocking design see Biegler and Morris (1999) and Roberts and Pearce (1999).

Another example of an interaction between cues in a spatial task is provided by Diez-Chamizo, Sterio, and Mackintosh (1985; see also March, Chamizo, & Mackintosh, 1992). Rats were trained in a rather unusual way in a radial maze. They were placed at the end of one arm and then had to go to the end of another arm in order to receive food. The correct arm was unique because it had a sandpaper floor. Throughout this training, the landmarks provided by various objects in the room, and the shape of the room itself, were made irrelevant by rotating the maze from one trial to the next. In a second stage of the experiment, food was again placed at the end of the sandpaper arm but the maze was *not* rotated, so that all the cues associated with the room were now relevant to the solution to the problem. Despite this change in training, subsequent testing revealed that the rats had learned very little about the significance of the cues that lay outside the maze. By contrast, a control group, which received just the second stage, learned a great deal about the significance of the extra-maze cues. One way of summarizing these results is to say that pretraining with the intra-maze cue of sandpaper blocked learning about the extra-maze cues in the second stage of the experiment.

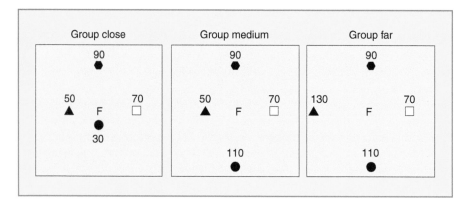

FIGURE 11.20 Plan of the three different training arenas that were used to train three groups of rats to find food (F) that was at a fixed distance from four different landmarks in the experiment by Goodyear and Kamil (2004). The numbers refer to the distance in cm of each landmark from the food (adapted from Goodyear & Kamil, 2004).

Taken together, these results pose something of a puzzle. It is quite clear that on some occasions the presence of certain cues will hinder the control acquired by other cues over searching for a hidden goal; whereas it is equally clear that on other occasions learning about two sets of cues will progress independently of each other. What is needed now is an explanation for why there is an interaction between cues in some conditions but not others. I regret to admit that this explanation is not obvious. We must close this chapter, therefore, with the unsatisfactory conclusion that we do not yet understand how animals choose among multiple sources of navigational information to find a goal.

CHAPTER 12

CONTENTS

Social learning

Until now we have concentrated on the behavior of animals in isolation, but many species live in groups and it is possible that the presence of one animal can influence greatly the knowledge that is acquired by another. The study of social learning is directed at exploring this possibility.

One obvious way in which social learning could benefit an animal is by allowing it to copy what other members of its group have learned through the potentially painful process of trial and error. By copying the diet of the adult members of a group, an infant will avoid poisonous substances without having to test them itself. An animal might also learn to avoid predators, not by interacting with them directly but by observing how other members of the species react to them. And if one member of a group should by chance solve a difficult problem, other members of the group would gain by copying the actions of the problem solver, rather than by having to work through the tedious problem-solving process themselves.

Social learning may not only allow an animal to profit from the experiences of others, it may be important in determining how a group of animals interacts. For example, in groups where some members are dominant over others, subordinate members may need to develop special strategies to outwit their superiors, who would otherwise restrict their access to such resources as food or a sexual partner. The proposal has been made that such strategies require an animal to learn about the intentions of other individuals. The purpose of this chapter is to examine these and other examples of social learning, in the hope of understanding how this type of learning takes place.

Social learning is often important for the development of young animals. By play-fighting with its mother, this tiger cub is given the opportunity to learn how to react to prey and predators in real life.

DIET SELECTION AND FORAGING

For most of us, the selection of a diet might seem to be very much a matter of personal choice that is guided by our own experiences with food. In the case of animals, however, the preferences and food-seeking behavior of one animal can exert a profound influence on the way in which another looks for food and chooses its diet.

An example of the way in which social learning can influence foraging for food is provided by a study of Burmese jungle fowl (McQuoid & Galef, 1992). Hungry fowl were allowed to explore an enclosure in which four bowls were placed in fixed positions. Food was consistently available in one of these bowls and eventually all the subjects approached this bowl whenever they entered the enclosure. Towards the end of this training, another group of fowl (observers) watched the first group (demonstrators) as they ate from the bowl. When the observers were themselves permitted into the enclosure, they showed a marked preference for the bowl from which the demonstrators had been seen to eat.

This experiment makes it quite clear that animals can learn something about a stimulus, a food bowl, simply by watching another animal eat from it. To explain this outcome, McQuoid and Galef (1992) refer to the mechanism of **stimulus enhancement**, which implies that as a result of watching the demonstrators as they ate, the attention of the observers was drawn to the bowl. This attention would then encourage the observers to approach the bowl and fortuitously lead them to food. Rather little is understood about the factors that promote stimulus enhancement, but we do know that its effects can persist for a relatively long time. The experiment by McQuoid and Galef (1992) was successful even when a period of 2 days elapsed between observational training and the test trial.

Stimulus enhancement effects are not unique to vertebrates. They have also been observed with octopuses (Fiorito & Scotto, 1992) and bumble-bees (Worden & Papaj, 2005). In the latter study, observer bees were allowed to watch demonstrators forage from green rather than orange flowers. When the observers were allowed access to the flowers they preferred to approach the green ones.

A rather different type of social learning can be shown to result in animals acquiring a preference for a particular food, even when they have no opportunity to consume it. In a series of experiments by Galef and colleagues (see Galef, 1988) a demonstrator rat was allowed to eat food with a distinctive flavor: either cocoa or cinnamon. An observer was then placed in the company of the demonstrator for 30 minutes, but in the absence of any food, before being allowed to choose between food flavored with either cocoa or cinnamon. The observers preferred the food that was of the same flavor as that consumed by the demonstrator. This preference has been shown to occur even if the demonstrator eats the flavored diet up to 4 hours before its encounter with the observer. After a single interaction with a demonstrator, the acquired preference endures for about 12 hours, but if the interaction between the observer and demonstrator is repeated on a number of occasions, or the interaction is repeated with a number of different demonstrators, then the preference lasts considerably longer (Galef & Whiskin, 1998). Other experiments have shown that animals can simultaneously acquire a preference through the above training for at least four different flavors, and that once acquired these preferences are hard to disrupt by subsequently exposing the animal to other types of food (Galef, Lee, & Whiskin, 2005).

An explanation for these findings can be based on the fact that rats are **neophobic**—they are reluctant to eat food with a novel flavor (Barnett, 1958;

Galef, 1970; see Galef, 1988, p. 131). In the experiments that have just been mentioned, the observers had no experience of cocoa- or cinnamon-flavored food prior to the test trial. The interaction between the rats might thus have allowed the observers to familiarize themselves with the food that the demonstrator has just eaten. Perhaps they detected the odor of the food on the demonstrator's breath, or they may have consumed particles of food that had stuck to the demonstrator's fur. At the time of testing, the observers would then be confronted with a choice between a familiar and a novel flavor, and their neophobia would lead them to select the former. Additional findings reported by Galef (1988) suggest that this explanation is unlikely. Before their encounter with a demonstrator, who had just eaten food flavored, say, with cinnamon, observer rats were allowed access to plentiful supplies of both cinnamon- and cocoa-flavored food for two days. Despite this opportunity to overcome their neophobia of both flavors, they still acquired a preference for the cinnamon as a result of their interaction with the demonstrator. The important conclusion to be drawn from this finding is that interacting with a rat that has just eaten food of a particular flavor results in a temporary enhancement of the attractiveness of that food.

A further experiment described by Galef (1988) identifies some of the critical features of the social interaction that are responsible for the acquired preference. The experiment employed the simple apparatus shown in Figure 12.1. An observer rat was placed into the bucket of the apparatus, and an anesthetized demonstrator was placed into the wire-mesh basket. Some demonstrators had food dusted on their faces and others had food placed directly into their stomachs through a tube. In both cases, the observers subsequently showed a preference for the flavored diet that had just been fed to the demonstrator. However, if the rear end of the demonstrator was dusted with food, and placed foremost in the basket, then only a slight preference for the food was demonstrated. Finally, if a wad of cotton wool, rather than a rat, was placed in the basket, then despite being dusted with food, there was no evidence that this resulted in a change in the attractiveness of the food. Thus the demonstrator does not need to be conscious if it is to encourage the development of a food preference in another rat. But the observer must interact with a rat, and preferably its front rather than its rear end.

The foregoing results suggest that a socially acquired food preference depends on the observer being able to smell food at the same time as it smells the demonstrator's breath (Galef, Mason, Preti, & Bean, 1988). Given such a conclusion, Galef and Durlach (1993) then proposed that the smell of the demonstrator serves as an unconditioned stimulus that enhances a preference for the relevant flavor through a process of Pavlovian conditioning. There is, however, no evidence that the socially acquired preference is susceptible to weakening by blocking, overshadowing, or latent inhibition (Galef & Durlach, 1993). These effects have come to be regarded as the hallmarks of Pavlovian conditioning, and in their absence it is hard to argue that a socially acquired preference is effectively a conditioned response. The breath of the demonstrator plays an important role in the acquisition of food preferences through social interaction, but it is not clear how.

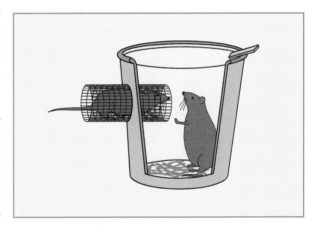

FIGURE 12.1 The apparatus used to allow one rat to smell food on an anesthetized demonstrator rat. From Galef and Stein, 1985. Reprinted by permission of the Psychonomic Society, Inc.

The ease with which rats acquire food preferences socially might lead one to expect that they can learn in a similar fashion to avoid food that is poisonous. In fact, Galef (1988; see also Galef, McQuoid, & Whiskin, 1990), was unable to demonstrate experimentally a social transfer of an acquired food aversion. Thus, whenever rats avoid poisoned bait that has been left for them, this must depend on their neophobia, together with their preference for food that has been eaten by other rats and that is presumably safe. A detailed discussion of the way in which rats avoid toxic food can be found in Galef and Clark (1971).

Galef (1996) states that social influences can affect diet selection in a variety of species including blackbirds, sheep, goats, cats, hyenas, pigs, rabbits, gerbils, mice, and monkeys. However, the principles that appear to control food selection in rats are not always true for these other species (Galef & Giraldeau, 2001). Capuchin monkeys tend to eat unfamiliar food if they come across it in the presence of other monkeys (Addessi & Visalberghi, 2001), but there is no evidence that diet selection in monkeys is affected by smelling the breath of a **conspecific** who has just consumed some food (see Fragaszy & Visalberghi, 2004). As far as avoiding toxic or noxious foods is concerned, Snowden and Boe (2003) found that if a tamarin monkey consumes a food laced with pepper then it will make an alarm call and exhibit visual signs of disgust. This reaction appears to be sufficient to discourage other members of the group from eating the food, even for lengthy periods of time. It is also possible that Japanese macaques learn an aversion to food from their mother (Hikami, Hasegawa, & Matsuzawa, 1990), and that adult wild squirrel monkeys prevent infants from approaching toxic prey (Boinski & Fragaszy, 1989).

The final study to consider in this section is one by Galef (1988), which indicates the potentially important role that socially acquired preferences may play in foraging. Figure 12.2 shows a maze with a start box connected to three goal boxes: A, B, and C. The rats were first trained by being required to run to a goal box to obtain food. The correct goal box varied from day to day, and food of different flavors was presented consistently in the different goals. Thus, depending on which goal box was correct, cheese would be presented in Goal A, cinnamon-flavored food in Goal B, or cocoa-flavored food in Goal C. After sufficient training, once a rat had discovered by chance which goal contained food, it developed a strong tendency to return to that goal box for the remainder of the session.

The test stage was conducted in much the same way as the training stage, except that prior to the first trial an experimental rat was confined in the start box with another rat. The second rat had just eaten food of the flavor that was available in the correct goal box. As a result of the interaction between the rats, the likelihood of the experimental rat running directly to the correct goal was enhanced considerably. The implication of these results for understanding the way in which rats find food should be obvious. When a rat returns to the colony after eating food, the information provided by this rat, together with

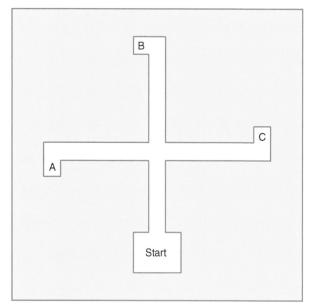

FIGURE 12.2 A plan of the maze used in an experiment by Galef (1988). Rats were allowed to leave the start box to find food in one of the three goal boxes. On different days they would find cheese in A, or cinnamon-flavored food in B, or cocoa-flavored food in C (adapted from Galef, 1988).

the knowledge that has been acquired of the area around the colony, will be sufficient to enable others to go to what is likely to be an abundant food supply.

CHOOSING A MATE

The selection of a mate in a variety of species can also be influenced by social factors. Female guppies were allowed to observe two males: one male was alone and the other with a female companion. When the female observer was given a choice between the two males, she preferred the one seen with the companion (Dugatkin, 1992; Dugatkin & Godin, 1992, 1993). A similar effect has been found with Japanese quail. White and Galef (1999a) allowed a female to choose between a male she had previously seen by himself and a male she had previously seen court and mate another female. She showed a clear preference for the latter. However, if the procedure is reversed so that a male is given a choice between a female he has seen in isolation and a female he has seen courting and mating with another male, then the observer will tend to prefer the female he had seen in isolation (White and Galef, 1999b).

The effect on females of seeing a male mate with another female can result in a male being in high demand. Male and female sage grouse meet at communal breeding grounds where activities commence with a few males mating with females. The remaining females on seeing this activity will then copy the mate choice of the original females with the result that a small number of males will have access to almost all the females (Gibson, Bradbury, & Vehrencamp, 1991). It is hard not to anthropomorphize by concluding that the chosen few will go to bed tired but happy. On a more serious note, we must also conclude that rather is little is known about the mechanism that is responsible for these changes in preferences for a member of the opposite sex.

FEAR OF PREDATORS

The experiments described in this section demonstrate the importance of social learning for acquiring a fear of potential predators. We will focus on the way in which monkeys acquire their fear of snakes.

When an adult free-ranging monkey suddenly encounters a snake its reaction is quite dramatic. It will attempt to flee from the snake, its facial expressions will indicate fear, it will look at the snake, and it will make specific alarm calls. A monkey that has been reared in the laboratory will, in stark contrast, show virtually none of these reactions. Clearly, a fear of snakes by monkeys is not innate but acquired through experience. To understand what this experience might be, experiments have been conducted in which laboratory-reared monkeys watch the reactions of a wild-reared monkey to a snake (Mineka & Cook, 1988). Typically, as soon as the wild-reared monkey sees the snake it becomes extremely agitated and, on seeing this reaction, the observer responds in a similar way. If the observer should subsequently be exposed to the snake by itself, it will then reveal all the manifestations of being afraid. Further studies have shown that this acquired fear of snakes can be passed on by allowing another laboratory-reared monkey to observe the originally trained monkey display its fear in the presence of a snake. The acquired fear is also extremely durable and has been shown to persist for at least a year. Mineka and Cook (1988) also report that if an observer watches a model that is unafraid of snakes, then the observer does not become afraid of the snake. Indeed, this treatment was found to immunize the observer so that

According to Mineka and Cook (1988), fear of snakes in monkeys is a Pavlovian conditioned response based on the sight of a snake (conditioned stimulus) while another monkey is displaying fear of the snake (unconditioned stimulus).

it failed to acquire a fear of snakes when it eventually saw a model react fearfully to a snake.

According to Mineka and Cook (1988), an acquired fear of snakes is a consequence of Pavlovian conditioning. The snake is the conditioned stimulus, the model's fear response is the unconditioned stimulus, and the subsequent fear shown by the observer is the conditioned response. Support for the claim that Pavlovian conditioning is responsible for the acquired fear of snakes comes from the additional finding of Mineka and Cook that the effectiveness of their training was directly related to the intensity of the model's reaction to the snake. If this reaction is regarded as an unconditioned stimulus, then it is in keeping with many studies of conventional Pavlovian conditioning that have shown that the strength of the conditioned response is directly related to the strength of the unconditioned stimulus. Because the fear of a snake is acquired through watching the behavior of another animal, it is said to be acquired through **observational conditioning**. For a demonstration of observational conditioning in blackbirds, see Curio (1988).

Mineka and Cook (1988) have argued that their successful demonstrations of observational conditioning result from an innate disposition of monkeys to acquire a fear of snakes. Support for this conclusion comes from an experiment in which laboratory-reared monkeys were able to watch a videotape of a monkey reacting fearfully. Through careful editing of this tape, the monkey appeared to be showing fear of either a live boa constrictor or brightly colored flowers. Subsequent testing revealed that the observers who watched the tape of the boa constrictor readily acquired a fear of snakes, whereas those who watched a monkey apparently display a fear of flowers did not themselves become afraid of flowers.

The alert reader might be concerned that this result does not necessarily mean that monkeys have an innate disposition to acquire a fear of snakes, but not flowers. During their lives, the observers may have seen many more flowers than snakes. If this were the case, then latent inhibition could be responsible for the poor conditioning with flowers. Alternatively, a snake might be a more salient stimulus than a flower for conditioning with any unconditioned stimulus. Although Cook and Mineka (1990) reject this second possibility, their arguments have not convinced everyone (Heyes, 1994a; Davey, 1995; Macphail & Bolhuis, 2001). It is also possible that monkeys have an innate fear of snakes that is slight until it is enhanced through observational conditioning. Mineka, Keir, and Price (1980) report that laboratory-reared monkeys display some unconditioned withdrawal responses to snakes, but these are considerably weaker than those displayed by wild-reared monkeys. Whether monkeys are innately disposed to learn readily to fear snakes thus remains an open question. None the less, these experiments provide a clear demonstration of observational conditioning. They also show how this conditioning can play an important role in learning to avoid predators.

COPYING BEHAVIOR: MIMICRY

The discussion thus far has focused on the way in which social learning can influence the reactions of an animal to a particular stimulus. We turn now to investigate how social learning can affect the responses that an animal makes. Topics that are of obvious relevance to this issue include **mimicry** and **imitation**. But what precisely is meant by these terms? Most psychologists would agree that imitation and mimicry result in animals performing new responses, and that these responses are arbitrary, rather than being closely tied to species-typical reactions to certain stimuli.

Given such a constraint, we can exclude contagious behavior as an example of imitation or mimicry. Contagious behavior is said to occur when the response of one animal triggers the same response in another animal. Chorusing in dogs and roosters provide two frequently encountered examples of this type of behavior where the response can hardly be said to be arbitrarily selected. Another example is yawning in humans.

For the purposes of the following discussion, we shall also distinguish between mimicry and imitation. Mimicry will be said to have occurred when the response that is copied does not lead to an immediate, tangible reward. Imitation will be used to refer to responses that have been copied, and that lead to reward.

Seals have been said to possess the ability to mimic human speech.

Mimicry is of interest in its own right, because it can result in animals behaving in an engaging fashion. Nearly 200 years ago Buffon (1818) reported that several orang-utans dined with humans and mimicked their use of silverware and cups, of pouring drinks, and even touching glasses with their hosts. More recent examples of mimicry by orang-utans can be found in Russon and Galdikas (1993), who observed these animals mimic the human actions of hanging up a hammock and then riding in it, untying a canoe and then using it, pouring fuel from a can, weeding a garden, and so on. A chimpanzee has been said to learn through mimicry how to sharpen pencils, use sandpaper, wash dishes (Hayes & Hayes, 1951; Hayes, 1961), and to wipe its bottom (Goodall, 1986, in Jolly, 1991). There is also ample evidence of vocal mimicry. Parrots and mynah birds are famous for their capacity to mimic human speech. What may not be so well known is that seals have also been said to possess this capacity. A harbor seal, Hoover, is reputed to have mimicked its human foster parents and produced phrases such as "Hello there" and "How are you?", which were occasionally followed by a belly laugh (cited in Moore, 1992).

Mimicry is important for theoretical reasons. The ability of an animal to acquire seemingly arbitrary responses, such as a rat pressing a lever, is generally attributed to the influence of instrumental conditioning. The animal is assumed to make the response, or some approximation to it, by trial and error. Should this response then be followed by reward, the likelihood of it being repeated is increased. If mimicry is possible, then it implies that this account of the way in which arbitrary responses are acquired is incomplete. First, it would seem that the form of the response can be acquired through observation, rather than by trial and error. Second, it would seem that reward is not necessary for the response to be performed repeatedly. Thus if mimicry can be reliably demonstrated, then our conclusions concerning the way in which arbitrary responses are acquired would have to be modified considerably.

Given the potential theoretical importance of mimicry, we need to be confident that it really exists. Many of the examples that have been cited were derived from casual observation of the animals, and care must be taken to ensure they are interpreted correctly. If a chimpanzee should be seen using sandpaper, does this reflect mimicry or does it merely reflect the fact that the animal was playing with an object in a way that the observer interprets as mimicry? Alternatively, if an animal should acquire the capacity to say "Hello there", is it mimicking its trainer, or have its vocalizations been shaped by reward to resemble this human phrase in much the same way as a rat can be trained to press a lever? Very often, insufficient details are provided in the report to allow these alternative explanations to be evaluated.

An experiment by Moore (1992, 1996) provides strong evidence that at least one species, the African grey parrot, has the capacity to mimic humans. The experimenter spent a few minutes every day with the parrot in its room. During this period the experimenter would utter a word or phrase, perform a stereotyped movement in front of the parrot, and then leave. A videotaped record of the parrot's behavior revealed that during the periods that it was alone it mimicked both the utterance and the action of the experimenter. For example, the experimenter would nod his head and say "nod". After a while the bird was heard to say "nod", and at the same time nod its head. As this action was never performed in the presence of the experimenter, its repeated occurrence is unlikely to be due to the influence of an extrinsic reward. Instead, this is but one of many examples reported by Moore (1992) that show that the parrot mimicked both the vocalizations and movements of its trainer.

The ability of the parrot to copy the spoken word "nod" can be understood if it is accepted that the parrot remembered how it sounded. To mimic the word, the parrot could then modify the sounds it produced until they matched the remembered sound. The ability of the parrot to copy the action of nodding, however, poses a greater theoretical challenge. The parrot might have stored a visual memory of the experimenter moving his head as he said "nod". However, because the parrot's view as it nodded its head would be totally unlike the sight of the experimenter nodding, this visual memory could not then be used to refine the response in the same way that vocal mimicry could be refined. In this instance the response of nodding is said to be perceptually opaque because it yields different visual input when it is performed by the subject rather than by a demonstrator (Heyes & Ray, 2000). The mimicry of perceptually opaque responses is particularly challenging to explain theoretically.

Another problem posed by these results is the explanation for why mimicry should occur at all. Moore (1992) has suggested tentatively that mimicry in primates helps them to acquire skills involving tools, whereas in parrots it serves a purely social function. Mimicry also plays an important role in communication. Certain birds, for example, learn their songs by mimicking adult birds. The way in which this learning takes place will be considered in the next chapter.

COPYING BEHAVIOR: IMITATION

If a problem is particularly hard for an animal to solve then it may take a considerable amount of time, or even generations, before the correct response is discovered. Once it has been discovered, other members of the group to which the animal belongs may well benefit from imitating the action of the successful problem solver. Imitation, therefore, can be viewed as a type of social learning that, theoretically, would be of value to many different species. In fact, despite the potential benefits of imitation, we shall see convincing demonstrations of imitation are relatively rare.

Naturalistic evidence

Birds

Blue tits and great tits in Britain are notorious for their ability to break through the foil tops of milk bottles to drink the cream at the top (Figure 12.3). This skill is believed to have originated in a small group (Fisher & Hinde, 1949), and its spread to the rest of the population has been attributed on more than one occasion to imitation (Bonner, 1980). However, the results from a series of experiments by Sherry and Galef (1984, 1990), using black-capped chickadees, suggest that the spread of this annoying habit was promoted by more mundane means than imitation. Sherry and Galef (1984) have shown that if a bird should come across a bottle that has already been opened, it will drink the milk and then be more likely to break through the foil tops in the future. Pavlovian conditioning provides one explanation for this outcome. While the bird is drinking, the sight of the foil top (conditioned stimulus) may be associated with the cream (unconditioned stimulus) beneath it. When the bird subsequently sees a foil top it would then be likely to approach and direct conditioned responses of pecking towards it. If these pecks should tear the foil, then the entire sequence of this activity is likely to be strengthened and result in the subject being more willing in the future to tear open foil tops for itself.

FIGURE 12.3 A great tit opening a milk bottle. © Michael Leech, Oxford Scientific Films.

Sherry and Galef (1990) report that their subjects were unlikely to open foil tops when they were naïve and tested in isolation. Such a finding then raises the question of how the birds came to open foil tops in the first place. In an attempt to answer this question, Sherry and Galef (1990) examined the behavior of a naïve bird that had access to a foil-covered container of cream when it could see another naïve bird in an adjacent cage. The mere presence of this second bird was sufficient to encourage the first bird to peck at the foil cap and eventually to open it. A possible explanation of such **social enhancement** is that the presence of the second bird reduced fear, or encouraged foraging responses, in the experimental subject. But whatever the reason, this type of social enhancement could well be responsible for the origins and perhaps spread of milk-bottle opening among certain birds. There can be little justification for believing that this skill is acquired through imitation.

Primates

The somewhat cumbersome phrase "population-specific behavioral traditions" is used to describe behaviors that have the following properties (Nagell, Olguin, & Tomasello, 1993):

1. They are acquired through experience, rather than being innate.
2. They are found throughout a well-defined population.
3. They persist from one generation to the next.
4. They are absent in other populations of the same species.

The spread of tearing foil tops by birds might be regarded as a population-specific behavioral tradition. An example of such a tradition in primates is provided

> **KEY TERM**
>
> **Social enhancement**
> An increase in the tendency to perform an established response because of the presence of one or more conspecifics.

by a group of fastidious Japanese macaque monkeys who wash sweet potatoes before eating them (Itani & Nishimura, 1973). Another behavioral tradition has been observed in a group of chimpanzees in the Ivory Coast who use stones to break open nuts (Boesch, 1991). From the point of view of the present discussion, these behavioral traditions are of interest because their widespread use within a group of primates has been attributed to imitation (Itani & Nishimura, 1973; Goodall, 1986).

There are, however, reasons for questioning whether these behavioral traditions depend on imitation (Galef, 2004). As far as potato washing is concerned, Nagell et al. (1993) have suggested that the spread of this habit is due in part to stimulus enhancement. The attention of a naïve monkey might be drawn to a potato when it sees another monkey pick one up. The naïve monkey might then pick up its own potato and for social reasons follow the experienced monkey into the river. At this point, the naïve monkey may learn by accident the benefits that accrue from placing the potato in the water. Although this account may seem contrived, it relies only on processes that are generally accepted to exist. Moreover, studies of complex skills that develop in colonies of primates have revealed that these skills do not spread easily. Kummer and Goodall (1985) state that "of the many [innovative] behaviors observed, only a few will be passed on to other individuals, and seldom will they spread through the whole troop" (p. 214, quoted in Nagell et al., 1993, p. 185). Such an observation is entirely understandable if the acquisition of a skill depends on the combination of a number of processes, including learning by trial and error. It is not so compatible, however, with the suggestion that primates are willing imitators. For an example of a population-specific behavioral tradition in rats see Parisi and Gandolfi (1974), and for a discussion of this finding see Galef (2004).

Laboratory studies

An obvious problem with attempts to study imitation in a naturalistic setting is that the history of individual animals is often unknown. Any particular action, or behavioral tradition, can thus be readily explained in a number of ways and often insufficient evidence is available to evaluate them. The experiments described in the next section examined imitation in a laboratory setting. Even though these experiments should be easier to interpret than more naturalistic studies, not all of them point to clear conclusions.

A straightforward test for learning by imitation in rats was conducted by Huang, Koski, and DeQuardo (1983). The apparatus consisted of a conventional conditioning chamber with a response lever and a food magazine. A diagonal, transparent partition divided the box into two halves. Three groups of rats were placed individually for 30 minutes into the half that did not contain the lever. Throughout this period, an experimental group was able to watch a rat in the other half of the chamber lever press for food. The remaining two groups were controls. For Group Control 1 the other half of the chamber was empty for the 30-minute period, whereas for Group Control 2 the other half of the chamber was occupied by a naïve rat that never received reward, even if it accidentally pressed the lever. After this observation period, the rats were permitted access to the lever, which, when pressed, resulted in the delivery of food. The graph in Figure 12.4 shows the mean number of lever presses that were performed in three successive daily sessions by each group. Lever pressing was clearly acquired more readily by the experimental group than by either control group.

The superior performance of the experimental rats may have been due to imitation, but there are at least two other possible explanations for the outcome of the experiment. One explanation appeals to the mechanism of stimulus enhancement that was mentioned earlier in this chapter. Watching a rat spend a great deal of time in the vicinity of the lever may have enhanced the salience of this stimulus for the experimental group. When this group was placed into the test compartment it may have approached the lever out of interest, and pressed it by chance. Any tendency to approach the lever in this way would obviously facilitate the acquisition of responding for food. The second explanation is based on observational appetitive conditioning. Browne (1976; see also Parisi & Matthews, 1975) allowed animals to observe, through a partition, an empty compartment where food was occasionally presented after a visual signal. When the animals were allowed access to the compartment, they approached and responded to the signal whenever it was shown. Conceivably, the experimental animals in the study by Huang et al. (1983) associated the sight of the movement of the response lever with the delivery of food. They would then be attracted to the lever when they were placed in the test chamber and this, again, would place them at an advantage over the control animals (see also Denny, Clos, & Bell, 1988). Three techniques have been developed to sidestep the objections that have just been raised concerning the above experiment and these will be considered in turn.

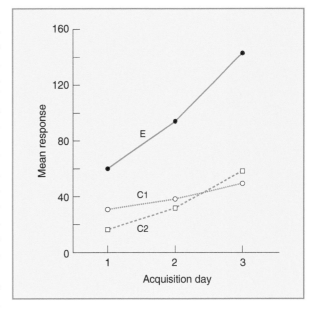

FIGURE 12.4 The mean number of rewarded lever presses made by three groups of rats in three successive test sessions. Prior to testing Group Experimental (E) had observed another rat lever pressing for food, Group Control 1 (C1) had observed an empty operant chamber, and Group Control 2 (C2) had observed a rat that was not rewarded for lever pressing (adapted from Huang et al., 1983).

The "Do as I do" test

Hayes and Hayes (1952) raised a chimpanzee called Viki in their home. As part of her training, Viki would be given the instruction "Do this" while her trainer was performing a particular response, say, touching his or her own chin. If Viki copied this action then she received reward. This example of copied behavior would be of little interest if Viki had received extensive training with the same action, because she may have learned through trial and error to make this response when she saw her trainer act in a certain way. There were, however, occasions when Viki was asked to "Do this" with a new action and apparently she immediately performed it correctly. In a more recent study, Custance, Whiten, and Bard (1995) were able to show that after being trained to respond correctly on the command of "Do this" to a limited set of actions, each of two chimpanzees would imitate correctly actions that they had never before been asked to perform. Examples of these actions include touching the back of the head, jumping, clapping hands, and flapping arms. As these acts are arbitrary gestures that were not directed towards a particular stimulus, it is hard to explain their occurrence in terms used to explain the findings by Huang et al. (1983). Instead, it appears that the chimpanzees were genuinely copying the behavior of the experimenter, presumably to gain reward, and thus these results provide a good demonstration of imitation.

The bidirectional control

The results from the "Do as I do" test may be easy to interpret but this test is of limited value for exploring the ability of many animals to imitate. For instance, this test is almost certain to fail with rats because they are unlikely to respond to spoken commands. Heyes and Dawson (1990) therefore developed an alternative method for testing whether this species is capable of imitation using what they called the bidirectional control. Their apparatus is depicted in Figure 12.5, which shows a demonstrator rat in the left compartment of a test chamber and an observer in the right compartment. To obtain food, the demonstrator had been trained to push the pole in a certain direction, to its left, for example. The position of the pole ensured that the demonstrator was always facing in the direction shown in the figure. After watching the demonstrators respond in this way to earn fifty food pellets, the observer rats were placed in the left-hand compartment where they pushed the pole in the same direction as the demonstrators had pushed it.

The observational training can reasonably be said to have taught the observers something about the pole. At the very least, their attention may have been drawn to this stimulus, or they may have learned that a movement of the pole was a signal for food. Although this learning might account for the observers approaching the pole in the test phase, through observational conditioning or stimulus enhancement, it does not explain why the observers preferred to push the pole in one direction rather than the other. A ready explanation for this preference is that it was acquired through imitating the demonstrators, which is how Heyes and Dawson (1990) explained their results.

Thus the essence of the bidirectional control is that the observer has an opportunity to respond in one of two directions, but only if the animal chooses the correct direction is the response regarded as imitation. Although the results by Heyes and Dawson (1990) meet this stipulation, there is a problem with

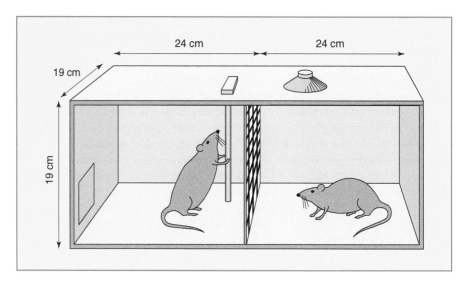

FIGURE 12.5 A sketch of the apparatus used to study observational learning in rats, showing the position and orientation of the demonstrator (left) and observer (right) (redrawn from Heyes & Dawson, 1990). Copyright © Psychology Press.

the experiment which makes its results difficult to interpret. Mitchell, Heyes, Gardner, and Dawson (1999) repeated the study just described and found that after eating food the demonstrators left odor cues on the side of the pole that they pushed during their efforts to gain reward. It is possible that when the observers were allowed into the test chamber they were attracted to these cues and, in investigating them, accidentally pushed the pole in the correct direction. Given this possibility it would be premature to conclude that the results of Heyes and Dawson (1990) provide a demonstration of imitation in the rat.

The experiment by Heyes and Dawson (1990) is important because it introduces the bidirectional control as a useful strategy for studying imitation, it also shows how careful an experimenter must be to rule out theoretically uninteresting explanations for their findings. There are, in fact, no reports of well-controlled demonstrations of imitation in rats, but the bidirectional control has been used with some success to demonstrate imitation in another species—Japanese quail—who are less sensitive to the influence of odor cues (Akins, Klein, & Zentall, 2002). A sketch of the apparatus used for this experiment is shown in Figure 12.6. To gain food, a demonstrator was placed in the right hand-chamber and required to push the screen with its beak in a particular direction, say to the left. After watching this activity from the adjacent chamber, an observer was then placed in the right-hand chamber where it showed a marked tendency to push the panel in the correct direction. Akins et al. (2002) argue that this preference for pushing the panel in a particular direction was a consequence of imitation.

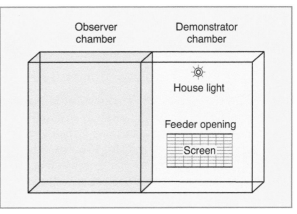

FIGURE 12.6 A sketch of the apparatus used to study observational learning in Japanese quail using the bidirectional control. The demonstrator was required to push the screen in a particular direction in the right-hand compartment while being observed by a bird in the left-hand compartment (adapted from Akins et al., 2002).

The two-action control

The final method for demonstrating imitation has its origins in an experiment by Dawson and Foss (1965) using budgerigars, but we shall examine a more recent study, using Japanese quail, by Akins and Zentall (1996). The apparatus for this experiment is shown in Figure 12.7. On this occasion, a demonstrator was trained either to peck or to step on the treadle in the right-hand compartment to gain food. When an observer was placed in this chamber it showed a strong preference for making the same response. Stimulus enhancement and observational conditioning would lead the observer to show an interest in the treadle, but neither of these processes would be expected to result in the observer preferring to make the response it had observed. To explain these biases, the most likely explanation is that the observer was imitating the response made by the demonstrator. The two-action control has also been used with success by Heyes and Saggerson (2002)

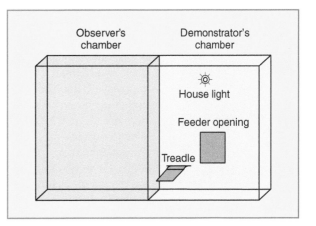

FIGURE 12.7 A sketch of the apparatus used to study observational learning in Japanese quail using the two-action control. The demonstrator was required to either peck or step on the treadle in the right-hand compartment while being observed by a bird in the left-hand compartment (adapted from Akins & Zentall, 1996).

with budgerigars, by Saggerson, George, and Honey (2005) with pigeons, and by Voelkl and Huber (2000) with marmosets.

The problem of emulation

The analysis of imitation in both humans and animals has been complicated by the need to determine whether an example of imitation can be attributed to something called **emulation learning** (Tomasello, 1996). Suppose that one budgerigar sees another budgerigar lift a stopper out of a container with its beak to gain access to food. If the observer makes the same response, then it might do so because it is imitating the response made by the demonstrator. Alternatively, by watching the demonstrator, the observer might have learned that stoppers can be removed from containers by moving them upwards. Emulation learning refers to the acquisition of this type of knowledge. Once such knowledge has been acquired, the observer when allowed access to the container and stopper may make a similar response to the demonstrator, not because it is copying the response but because of its knowledge about the properties of the container and stopper. A demonstration of emulation in chimpanzees is provided by Call, Carpenter, and Tomasello (2005). An observer watched a demonstrator open a tube by breaking it, or by removing caps at either end, to gain access to food. When the observers were given the tube they tended to open it using the method that was demonstrated, but the manner in which they performed this action was unrelated to the manner shown to them. For example, a demonstrator might have opened the tube by twisting the tops off, whereas the observer might have pulled them off. This result suggests that chimpanzees copy other chimpanzees through emulation, rather than through imitation. Once it is acknowledged that emulation can influence how an animal performs in an imitation experiment, it is then necessary to ask whether previous demonstrations of imitation can be explained in this way.

The results from the "Do as I do" study by Custance et al. (1995) are difficult to explain in terms of emulation because no object was involved. All that observers could learn about was the response made by the experimenter. It is also unlikely that emulation learning was responsible for the results from the study by Akins and Zentall (1996) using the two-action control. In that experiment, watching a demonstrator either pecking or stepping on the treadle might have taught the observer that the treadle could be depressed, but this knowledge would not then explain why the observer made the same response as its demonstrator in order to depress the treadle. A more obvious candidate for being explained in terms of emulation is the result from the bidirectional control study by Akins et al. (2002). Observers might have learned that the panel moved in only one direction on the basis of what they had seen, and this might have encouraged them to move the panel in the same direction. The results from an additional group in the experiment, however, lend little credence to this suggestion. Observers in this group were shown the panel moving in one direction in the absence of any demonstrator. When the observers were allowed into the test chamber they did not show a preference for pushing the panel in the direction that they had seen it move, which is what would be expected if their test behavior relied on emulation learning. For obvious reasons, this unusual, but sensible, control condition is referred to as the "ghost control".

Mechanisms of imitation

From a growing body of evidence it is apparent that a variety of animals are capable of imitation, which raises the important issue of explaining how imitation takes place. In Chapter 4, I argued that instrumental conditioning can result in the development of either stimulus–response (S–R) or response–unconditioned stimulus (R–US) associations. Are similar associations responsible for the successful acquisition of responses through imitation? If they are, then it is necessary to explain how they develop.

To deal with this problem, several researchers have suggested that the sight of a response being performed by another animal will excite a tendency to perform the same response in the observer (Heyes & Ray, 2000; Keysers & Perrett, 2004; Saggerson et al., 2005). In an imitation experiment, therefore, the sight of a demonstrator responding will encourage the observer to make the same response. If this response, or the tendency to make the response, is followed by the sight of demonstrator gaining reward then this might be sufficient to strengthen an S–R or an R–US association and increase the likelihood of the animal repeating the response it has observed.

Why should watching an animal respond encourage the observer to behave in the same way? One answer to this question can be based on the discovery in monkeys of mirror neurons, which have the property of firing either when the animal makes a particular action, or when it observes the same action being made (Rizzolatti, Fadiga, Gallese, & Fogassi, 1996; Rizzolatti, Fogassi, & Gallese, 2001). Hence, when one animal watches another perform a response, a mirror neuron will be activated and excite the neurons controlling the same response in the observer. One school of thought is that mirror neurons gain their properties through the experience of watching a demonstrator make a response, while the observer, by coincidence, performs the same response (Heyes & Ray, 2000, Keysers & Perrett, 2004; Saggerson et al., 2005). For instance, pigeons often feed in groups, which will mean that as one bird pecks at food it will see other birds engaged in the same activity. This combination of events would result in the sight of pecking and the action of pecking being associated via the same mirror neuron, so that the sight of a bird pecking in the future will elicit pecking in the observer.

Although the imitation of stereotyped responses, such as pecking by birds, can be explained in the above manner, this explanation may not be appropriate for imitation involving arbitrary responses. Recall that Custance et al. (1995) trained a chimpanzee to imitate a variety of responses made by a human. It seems far-fetched to suppose that this outcome depended on the prior experience of the chimpanzee accidentally making the chosen responses at the same time as the experimenter. In the absence of this experience, the sight of a person rubbing his or her head, for example, would fail to excite the same response in the chimpanzee who would then fail the "Do as I do" test. The ability of chimpanzees to pass this test suggests that if mirror neurons play a role in imitation, then we do not yet fully understand what it is.

Mirror neurons have also been used to explain the results from an experiment by Paukner, Anderson, Borelli, Visalberghi, and Ferrari (2005). Monkeys were given a wooden cube to play with while facing two experimenters who each held a similar cube. One of the experimenters copied the actions of the monkey as they were performed, while the other experimenter performed different actions. It was discovered that the monkeys spent most of their time looking at the experimenter

FIGURE 12.8 A capuchin monkey, on the right, inserting a stick into a tube to retrieve a peanut while being watched closely by a monkey who has received no training with the stick (from Fragaszy & Visalberghi, 2004). Photograph by Elisabetta Visalberghi.

who was imitating them. The explanation offered by Paukner et al. (2005) for this outcome is that mirror neurons detected the correspondence between the action of an experimenter and a monkey's own action, which then resulted in more attention being directed at the experimenter.

Mirror neurons were discovered relatively recently and it should not be surprising that a certain degree of controversy and uncertainty surrounds the foregoing explanations. For example, Gallese and Goldman (1998) have questioned whether mirror neurons even play a role in imitation. Nonetheless, these neurons provide a ready explanation for how one animal can recognize and copy the actions of another, and they are thus likely to feature in future attempts to unravel the mysteries of imitation in animals.

In closing this discussion of imitation and mimicry it is worth noting that although a variety of animals can copy the behavior of other animals, at least some of them are surprisingly reluctant to take advantage of this ability. Two examples should serve to reveal how animals fail to capitalize on any potential they may have for imitation. First, a cebus monkey was allowed to live in the house of a researcher (Gibson, 1989). It spent much of its time fastened to a leash and, despite observing on numerous occasions how the leash could be unfastened, the monkey never once performed this response for itself. Second, demonstrator cebus monkeys were trained by Visalberghi (1993) to push food out of a transparent tube with a rod in order to eat it (Figure 12.8). Other cebus monkeys then received lessons in this task by being allowed to watch a demonstrator. Despite receiving between fifty and seventy-five such lessons, there was no hint that the observers solved the problem or even appreciated how to insert the rod into the tube (Fragaszy & Visalberghi, 2004). These findings serve to emphasize that we know rather little about the circumstances that determine whether or not one animal will imitate another.

THEORY OF MIND

Humans have been said to possess a theory of mind, which we use to explain behavior by reference to mental states. To explain why I am walking into a restaurant, for example, I might say it is because I want food. A theory of mind further allows us to attribute mental states to others and then to use this attribution to make inferences about that person's behavior. To explain why my wife insists that we both go to a restaurant, I might say it is because she too wants to eat some food. Finally, a theory of mind allows us to influence the behavior of others by manipulating their beliefs. If I do not like the restaurant that my wife has selected, then I might attempt to change her behavior by informing her that rats were recently seen in its kitchen.

In 1978, Premack and Woodruff raised the challenging question of whether chimpanzees have a theory of mind. They wondered whether chimpanzees, like humans, have an ability to make inferences about the intentions, desires, knowledge, and states of minds of other animals. Of course, this question implies that animals possess mental states, which itself is contentious. For the present we shall ignore this issue, and focus on the evidence that has been said to demonstrate that animals possess a theory of mind. The two sorts of evidence that have been said to reveal a theory of mind, deception, and knowledge attribution, will be examined separately.

Deception

Once an animal can appreciate that the actions of other animals are influenced by their knowledge, then one animal could influence the behavior of another by manipulating the information it receives. Put slightly differently, the way is open for one animal to deceive another. In order to test whether or not chimpanzees possess a theory of mind, Woodruff and Premack (1979) attempted to determine experimentally if chimpanzees are capable of deception.

In their innovative study, a chimpanzee was able to observe a laboratory assistant hide food under one of two containers. The chimpanzee was then placed in such a position that it could not reach the containers and the assistant left the room. Either a cooperative or a competitive trainer then entered the room. The trainers were dressed differently, with the competitive trainer having the appearance of a bandit, and throughout all their interactions with the chimpanzee the cooperative trainer was friendly whereas the competitive trainer was hostile.

To obtain food with the help of the cooperative trainer, the chimpanzee had to direct the trainer towards the container in which the food was hidden. This was achieved by pointing or staring at the container. As soon as the trainer had identified the container, he or she took the food to the chimpanzee. If the chimpanzee directed the competitive trainer to the container with food, however, the trainer kept the food and the chimpanzee remained hungry. On the other hand, if the competitive trainer was directed to the empty container, then it was the chimpanzee who received food and the trainer who went unrewarded. At least some of the chimpanzees were able to earn food in the presence of both trainers, which suggests that they deliberately misinformed the competitive trainer. A justification for providing such misleading information is that the chimpanzee knew that the trainer would act on it and fail to obtain the food. This line of reasoning is clearly consistent with the proposal that chimpanzees possess a theory of mind.

Unfortunately, the results are open to more than one interpretation. Many training trials were required before the chimpanzees started to deceive the competitive trainer. During their training, therefore, subjects had ample time to learn that certain responses in the presence of the cooperative trainer always resulted in reward, whereas different responses resulted in reward in the presence of the competitive trainer. A discrimination of this sort can be readily explained with conventional principles of associative learning, and there is no reason to believe that this explanation would be inappropriate for the experimental findings. Mitchell and Anderson (1997) have put forward a similar explanation to the one just developed for the results reported by Woodruff and Premack (1979). They have also shown that capuchin monkeys perform on this task in a similar manner to chimpanzees, and explained their performance by referring to the principles of discrimination learning rather than to a theory of mind.

If chimpanzees possess a theory of mind, then it is unlikely to be of use only when they are in the psychological laboratory. They should also make use of this theory in more naturalistic settings. Indeed, some authors have argued that the need for a theory of mind has arisen out of the social interaction that occurs in a closely knit group of animals (Humphrey, 1982, 1983). Moreover, the potential for deception is said to be one of the more beneficial consequences of being endowed with a theory of mind (Whiten & Byrne, 1988).

Primates that live in social groups often have strict rules about mating. Dominant males, for example, will generally attempt to prevent their subordinates from mating with the females of a group. For the frustrated subordinates to fulfill their desires, therefore, they need to deceive their superiors by mating surreptitiously. Alternatively, at times when food is scarce, it may be of benefit to a subordinate member of a group to be secretive about any food that it discovers, so that it is not stolen by a more dominant member. There are numerous reports of individual primates acting in a way that appears to deceive other members of their group. Moreover, many of the perpetrators of these acts of deception have been said to behave in a way that suggests they possess a theory of mind (Byrne & Whiten, 1987; Jolly, 1991). The three examples that follow should help to clarify this line of reasoning.

While Byrne and Whiten (1985, 1987) observed a troop of baboons they noticed a strong adolescent, whom they called Melton, antagonize a younger one. A number of adults in the troop reacted to the screams of the youngster by moving rapidly towards Melton. Instead of fleeing, or showing submission, Melton stood on his hind legs and looked around in a way that is typical when one baboon suddenly notices a predator. The other members of the troop immediately ceased approaching Melton and instead looked in the same direction. As a consequence of this distraction, Melton avoided any punishment that he might have received had the adults reached him. Byrne and Whiten (1985) were unable to see any predator, and they concluded that Melton's behavior could have been designed to deceive the adults by pretending he had seen a predator. In other words, Melton might have made use of his theory of mind to avoid punishment by encouraging the belief in his chasers that a predator was nearby.

The second example is provided by Kummer (cited in Whiten & Byrne, 1988, p. 236), who also studied a troop of baboons. While he was observing the troop, he noticed an adult female gradually edge towards a rock where she began to groom a junior male. The leader of the troop was seated not too far away but the position of the rock prevented him from observing the young male that she was grooming. This was fortunate, because the leader rarely permitted such contact. According to Byrne and Whiten (1987), the female was able to appreciate the point of view of the leader and positioned herself in such a way that he would be unable to see the current object of her affections. The cartoon in Figure 12.9, which was taken from Byrne and Whiten (1987), characterizes the way in which the female might have used her theory of mind to achieve her goal.

The final example is a quote taken from the observations of de Waal (1982, cited in Whiten & Byrne, 1988):

Dandy and a female were courting each other surreptitiously. Dandy began to make advances to the female, whilst at the same time restlessly looking around

FIGURE 12.9 A cartoon from Byrne and Whiten (1987) depicting how baboon A might see herself from point of view of the dominant member of the troop, baboon T (from Byrne & Whiten, 1987). Copyright © 1987 New Scientist. Reproduced with permission.

to see if any of the other males were watching. Male chimpanzees start their advances by sitting with their legs wide apart revealing their erection. Precisely at this point when Dandy was exhibiting his sexual urge in this way, Luit, one of the older males, unexpectedly came round the corner. Dandy immediately dropped his hands over his penis concealing it from view.

In this example, Dandy might have been guided by his theory of mind to hide the offending part of his anatomy, and thus encourage the belief in Luit that his intentions towards the female were honorable.

For each example, the interpretation in terms of theory of mind is plausible, but at the same time, alternative explanations for the observed behavior are easy to develop. Melton may have genuinely seen something that he mistook for a predator, the position adopted by the female observed by Kummer may have served by coincidence to prevent the leader from observing what she was doing, and Dandy may have been doing nothing more than protecting his modesty. Alternatively, at least some of the animals may have learned from past experience that their respective strategies resulted in them avoiding punishment. In which case, associative learning theory, rather than a theory of mind, could account for the recorded observations. The absence of a detailed record of the previous experiences of these animals makes it impossible to choose between these different explanations. These reports thus provide evidence that suggests, but does not confirm, that some animals possess a theory of mind. A similar argument has been forcefully presented by Yoerg and Kamil (1991).

Perhaps researchers are being too ambitious in looking for evidence of a theory of mind in the deceptive behavior of animals. If deceptive behavior should derive from a theory of mind, then it will be the consequence of a complex reasoning process. Consider the example of Melton. The theory of mind interpretation for his behavior implies that Melton knew, first, that his pursuers intended to punish him, second, that it is possible to instill false beliefs about the presence of predators by adopting a certain posture, and, third, that once false beliefs have been instilled they will disrupt activities guided by previously formed intentions. Perhaps more convincing evidence that animals possess a theory of mind will come from tasks where the theory can be used in a more straightforward fashion.

Knowledge attribution

One potentially simple method for assessing whether chimpanzees possess a theory of mind is to determine whether or not they are capable of attributing knowledge to another animal. The design of an experiment that might test this possibility was first suggested by Premack (1988a), and put into practice by Povinelli, Nelson, and Boysen (1990). One of the four cups shown in Figure 12.10 contains a small piece of food that the chimpanzee is allowed to eat if she selects the correct cup. The chimpanzee does not know which cup hides the food, and to help her with her choice two of her trainers are pointing to two different cups. Immediately prior to this test, the chimpanzee had observed one of the trainers—the guesser—leave the room while the other trainer—the knower—placed food under one of the cups, which were hidden from the chimpanzee by a screen. For the test trial the knower pointed to the correct cup, whereas the guesser attempted to deceive the chimpanzee by pointing to one of the other three, empty cups. If animals are able to attribute mental states or knowledge to others, then the chimpanzee should infer that only the knower will be

FIGURE 12.10 A chimpanzee chooses one of four cups that might be covering a piece of food. Two trainers are pointing to the cups, one of whom knows where the food is hidden and the other has to guess (from Povinelli, Rulf, & Bierschwale, 1994) (photograph by Donna T. Bierschwale, courtesy of the University of Southwestern Louisiana New Iberia Research Center, Laboratory of Comparative Behavioral Biology).

able to identify correctly the cup containing food, and she should thus select the cup to which this person is pointing.

All four subjects tested on this problem showed a preference for the cup identified by the knower, but it required several hundred trials for this preference to be statistically significant in every subject. Although these results are consistent with the proposal that the chimpanzees attributed knowledge to the two trainers, there is, as might by now be expected, a simpler explanation for the successful performance. During their training, the chimpanzees would have often selected a cup that was pointed to by the guesser, and they would not be rewarded. In contrast, the chimpanzee would have received reward on the many trials that she selected the cup pointed to by the knower. The experiment is thus no more than a simple discrimination in which the person who has remained in the room for the longer time is the one who points to the correct cup. This is an unusual discrimination, but there is no reason why it should not be solved on the basis of the principles considered in Chapter 6 (see Heyes, 1998, Povinelli, 1994).

A simpler design for testing whether chimpanzees can appreciate what a human knows was used in a series of experiments by Povinelli and Eddy (1996; see also Povinelli, 2000). To gain a piece of food, the subjects were initially required to make a begging gesture in front of a trainer who was sitting beside the food. The chimpanzee was then presented with tests in which there were two trainers with the food between them. One of the trainers might have a bucket over her head, while the other would not. If the chimpanzee has a theory of mind then it would infer that the trainer with the bucket on her head would be unable to see the request for food and would therefore beg in front of the other trainer. In fact, in this test, and many similar ones, the chimpanzees failed to discriminate between the two trainers, which suggests they were unable to understand what a trainer could and could not see. It might be argued, however, that the chimpanzee did not know that buckets are opaque and that they would prevent anyone wearing them from seeing what was happening. As a counter to this possibility it is noteworthy that one of the favorite pastimes of the chimpanzees was to play by placing a bucket over their heads and then move cautiously around their enclosure until they bumped into something. Such play should have provided the necessary experience to allow the chimpanzee to discover that a bucket over the head prevents the wearer from seeing.

The simplicity of the experimental design makes it tempting to conclude from these results that chimpanzees do indeed lack a theory of mind. The problem with this conclusion, however, is that it is based on a null result and it is possible that if the experiment had been conducted differently then it would have revealed evidence of a theory of mind. For example, Nissani (2004) raised the possibility that the chimpanzees were too young (about 5 or 6 years old) to have developed a theory of mind and that a different outcome to the experiment would have been found with older chimpanzees. He therefore repeated the above experiment with chimpanzees ranging from 11 to 31 years old. He also conducted an equivalent study with elephants, who made a begging gesture with their trunk. In both cases, the subjects directed begging at the person without a bucket over their head. Although these results suggest that both species can acquire a theory of mind, another explanation is now possible. Because of the extensive experience of interacting with humans that the animals had received, they may have had ample opportunity to learn that begging from a person is worthwhile only when their eyes are visible. Thus once again, the principles of discrimination learning rather than a theory of mind might provide the correct explanation for these results. Nissani (2004) acknowledges this possibility and is unable to refute it.

Another explanation for the failure of Povinelli and Eddy (1996) to reveal evidence of a theory of mind in chimpanzees is that the experiments involved humans. If chimpanzees develop a theory of mind then they may be more disposed to applying it to other chimpanzees rather than to a completely different species. After all, given my own experiences, I am much more inclined to attribute a theory of mind to other humans than to any other species, including chimpanzees. With this possibility in mind, it is worth considering an experiment conducted by Hare, Call, and Tomasello (2001; see also Hare, Call, Agnetta, & Tomasello, 2000, and Tomasello, Call & Hare, 2003a). The experiment involved a dominant and a subordinate chimpanzee, who were tested with the apparatus sketched in Figure 12.11. The two chimpanzees were housed in cages that were on opposite sides of a test area in which there were two opaque barriers.

On some trials, both chimpanzees watched a trainer place food on the subordinate's side of one of the barriers before they were allowed into the arena.
The subordinate was reluctant in this condition to approach the food and left it for the dominant chimpanzee who headed directly towards the food. It is important to note that, through bitter experience, subordinate chimpanzees have learned not to take food if it is about to be eaten by a dominant chimpanzee. According to Tomasello et al. (2003a), the subordinate chimpanzee was able to appreciate that his superior saw where the food was hidden and inferred that the superior would head directly towards it when the doors into the arena were opened. To avoid antagonizing the superior, the subordinate therefore refrained from approaching the food.

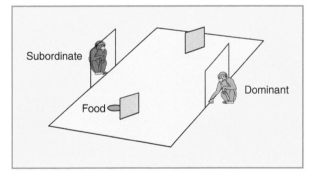

FIGURE 12.11 A sketch of the test environment in which a dominant and subordinate chimpanzee were able to watch a trainer place food on the subordinate's side of one of the opaque barriers (adapted from Tomasello et al., 2003a).

A similar procedure was used on other trials, except that a closed door prevented the dominant chimpanzee from watching where the food was hidden. When both animals were allowed into the arena, the subordinate would head directly for the food and eat it. Tomasello et al. (2003a) argue that because the dominant chimpanzee did not see where the food was hidden, the subordinate chimp inferred that the dominant chimpanzee did not know the location of the food and that it was therefore safe to approach the food. On the basis of these results, Tomasello et al. (2003a) concluded that chimpanzees know what others see, and also that barriers can prevent others from seeing an object such as food. They also know whether an individual has seen something happen and then draw an inference about how that individual will behave. That is, chimpanzees understand psychological states and thus possess a theory of mind.

Before accepting this bold interpretation, a simpler account for the behavior of the subordinate chimpanzee should be considered (Povinelli & Vonk, 2003). During the course of their previous interactions, it is likely that the subordinate learned how the dominant one would react in certain situations. The subordinate might have learned, for example, that she would suffer if she approached food if the dominant chimpanzee was visible when the food was introduced. Such learning would then result in the subordinate chimpanzee approaching the food during the experiment only if the dominant chimpanzee could not be seen when food was placed in the arena. Povinelli and Vonk (2003, p. 159) characterize the effects of this learning as the rule "Don't go after the food if the dominant was visible when it was placed in the arena". They further characterize the explanation offered by Tomasello et al. (2003a) as "Don't go after the food if the dominant was visible when it was placed in the arena, (because he has seen it and knows where it is)". It should be apparent that the phrase in brackets implies a theory of mind, whereas the rest of the sentence does not. Indeed, the knowledge implied by the first half of the sentence could be represented as an S–R habit acquired through discrimination learning. It should also be apparent that the phrase outside the brackets is sufficient to account for the subordinate's behavior. In this instance, therefore, there is no compelling reason to refer to a theory of mind to explain the outcome of the experiment. Furthermore, it is very difficult to think of any interaction between two chimpanzees using the design developed by Hare et al. (2000, 2001) that could not be explained in the plausible manner advocated by Povinelli and Vonk (2003).

Various experiments have been conducted to test whether one animal attributes knowledge to another. However, all of the findings that have been interpreted as being consistent with this claim can be explained in a simpler way by referring to the effects of discrimination based on the individual's prior experience. Given this conclusion, together with the negative results reported by Povinelli and Eddy (1996), it seems reasonable to conclude that chimpanzees, at least, lack a theory of mind insofar as it allows them to attribute knowledge to others (Heyes, 1998).

The final experiment to consider in this discussion of knowledge attribution involved scrub jays (Emery & Clayton, 2001). In Chapter 9, we saw that when scrub jays come across a new supply of food they may cache some of it for later consumption. If another scrub jay should observe where the food is hidden it will often steal the food before the bird who hid it returns (Emery & Clayton, 2004). In the experiment by Emery and Clayton (2001), scrub jays—the storers—were allowed to cache food while they were being observed by another scrub jay. Several hours later, the storers were returned to the apparatus, in the absence of another bird, and some of them moved the food to a new hiding place. The intriguing finding from this study is that most recaching was performed by birds that had themselves pilfered from the caches of other birds. Perhaps, therefore, when a storer was returned to the apparatus it remembered that it had been observed by another bird while it was hiding the food. If the storer had pilfered food in the past, it would then make the inference that the observer is also a pilferer and the storer would then be motivated to change the hiding place of food to protect it from being pilfered. The implication of this line of reasoning is that scrub jays have a rudimentary theory of mind that enables them to attribute knowledge based on their own experience to other scrub jays (see also Dally, Emery, & Clayton, 2006). If this interpretation is correct, then it should be possible for scrub jays to use their theory of mind in settings other than caching food. To my knowledge, there is no evidence of them using a theory of mind in this more general manner, and the results described by Emery and Clayton (2001) may reflect a specialization with limited applicability. Given this possibility, it would seem prudent to conclude this discussion with the observation that we are still some distance from showing that any animal has a full-blown theory of mind.

SELF-RECOGNITION

The discussion throughout this chapter has been based on the learning that takes places when one animal interacts with another. The final topic to be introduced is devoted to the learning that occurs when an animal interacts with itself by means of a mirror. As far as humans are concerned, some experience with mirrors is necessary before we appreciate that the image in the mirror is our own reflection. Thus congenitally blind people who have had their sight restored, and young children who have never seen a mirror, both react as if they were seeing another person when they first see a reflection of themselves (Povinelli, Rulf, Landau, & Bierschwale, 1993). But before too much time has passed this reaction is replaced with self-recognition. How do animals react if they see themselves in a mirror?

When chimpanzees first look in a mirror they treat their reflection as if it were another chimpanzee, but this reaction is soon replaced by more self-directed activities. Indeed, familiarity with a mirror appears to bring out the worst in chimpanzees. They use it to inspect closely the anal–genital area, as well as other hitherto unseen regions of their bodies. They also use the mirror for picking at their teeth, and extracting mucus from their eyes and nose. The photographs in Figure 12.12 indicate some of the less unpleasant ways in which chimpanzees interact with mirrors. Thus, like humans, chimpanzees seem to be able to learn that the image they see in a mirror is that of their own body. There is also evidence of similar learning in the two other great apes orang-utans (Suarez & Gallup, 1981; Miles, 1994), and gorillas (Patterson & Cohn, 1994). Figure 12.13, for example, shows a gorilla, Koko, using a mirror to examine herself (Patterson & Cohn, 1994).

The claim that the great apes can use mirrors in a similar way to humans has aroused surprisingly intense controversy. One objection to this claim is that the reports mentioned above do not provide convincing evidence that the chimpanzees used mirrors to direct responses towards themselves. It is possible, for example, that the various activities in which they engaged were not a response to the mirror but would have also occurred in its absence. According to this analysis it was only a coincidence that a chimpanzee, say, picked its teeth while facing the mirror. A variety of experiments have been conducted to address this type of criticism (e.g. Gallup, 1970), but perhaps the most convincing is reported by Povinelli et al. (1997). Seven chimpanzees were allowed to become familiar with their reflection in a mirror. A colored dye was then applied to one eyebrow and the top of one ear of each subject, as shown in Figure 12.14. During a subsequent 30-minute baseline period a record was taken of the number of occasions in which the chimpanzees touched the two marked regions, or two control regions, which consisted of the unmarked eyebrow and earlobe. This stage of the experiment was conducted in the absence of a mirror. From the left-hand side of Figure 12.15 it is evident that during this period the subjects rarely touched either the marked or unmarked regions. For the subsequent,

FIGURE 12.12 Examples of the ways in which some chimpanzees behave when they are accustomed to seeing their reflection in a mirror (from Povinelli et al., 1993). Photographs by Donna T. Bierschwale, courtesy of the University of Southwestern Louisiana New Iberia Research Center, Laboratory of Comparative Biology.

30-minute test stage of the experiment the chimpanzees were allowed to look at a mirror, and from the right-hand side of Figure 12.15 it is evident that the frequency of touching the marked regions, but not the unmarked regions, increased dramatically. Faced with these findings it is difficult not to accept that the chimpanzees, by virtue of the mirror, were able to see the dye on their heads and then use this information to guide their fingers to the strangely colored regions. Although not mentioned in the present report, Anderson and Gallup (1997) have remarked that chimpanzees will often inspect their fingers, and perhaps sniff them, after touching a dyed mark on their body that can be seen only by looking in a mirror.

FIGURE 12.13 Koko, a gorilla, making use of a mirror (from Patterson & Cohn, 1994). © Ronald Cohn/The Gorilla Foundation. Reproduced with permission of Cambridge University Press.

These results indicate that at least some species can behave as if they recognize themselves in mirrors, but it may be only some members of these species that can behave in this way. In the study by Povinelli et al. (1997), for instance, only three animals showed a strong response to the mirror. Rather little is known about the factors that determine whether an individual will progress from treating its reflection as that of another individual to that of itself. All that can be said is that the time to make this transition can take from a few minutes (Povinelli et al., 1993) to several days (Gallup, 1970). And as far as chimpanzees are concerned, the capacity to recognize their bodies in a mirror does not develop until they are more than 4 years old (Povinelli et al., 1993).

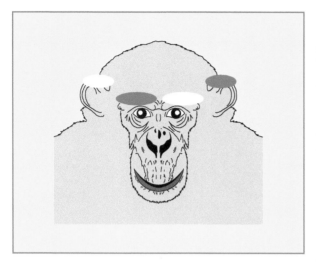

FIGURE 12.14 The marked (shaded) and unmarked (empty) regions on the head of a chimpanzee that were used for scoring a mark test in a self-recognition study (adapted from Povinelli et al., 1997).

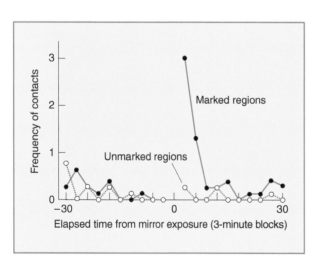

FIGURE 12.15 The frequency with which subjects touched the marked and unmarked regions of their heads shown in Figure 12.14 during a 30-minute baseline period in the absence of a mirror (left-hand side), and during a 30-minute test period in the presence of a mirror (right-hand side) (adapted from Povinelli et al., 1997).

There are, therefore, good reasons for believing that at least some animals are capable of using mirrors to provide information about their own bodies, but the controversy does not stop here. According to both Anderson and Gallup (1997) and Povinelli (2000), this ability is confined to the great apes: bonobos, chimpanzees, orang-utans, and gorillas. In general, the evidence supports this claim. Anderson (1983, 1984) found in more than a dozen species of Old and New World monkeys that they never progressed further than treating their reflection in a mirror as if it were another monkey. Other studies have shown a similar outcome with gibbons (Gallup, 1983), fish, sea lions, dogs, cats (see Gallup, 1975, for a review), and parrots (Pepperberg, Garcia, Jackson, & Marconi, 1995).

There have, however, been occasional reports of species other than the great apes using mirrors to provide information about their own bodies. Hauser, Kralik, Botto-Mahan, Garrett, and Oser (1995) reported evidence of this ability in cotton-top tamarin monkeys. Questions concerning this evidence can be found in a commentary by Anderson and Gallup (1997), and in a book by Povinelli (2000), who maintains that it has not been possible to replicate the original finding. More convincing evidence that a species other than a great ape can behave as if it recognizes itself in a mirror has been found with dolphins. By adopting a procedure based on the one used above by Povinelli et al. (1997), Reiss and Marino (2001) found that dolphins with considerable experience in pools with mirrored walls would more frequently expose a marked part of their body to a mirror than equivalent parts that had been marked with water rather than a dye. Of course, the dolphins were unable to touch the marks in the way demonstrated by chimpanzees, but their behavior suggests they were using the mirror to inspect the unfamiliar marks on their bodies. Despite an early failure (Povinelli, 1989), it now appears that elephants, too, can use mirrors to detect marks on their bodies, which they touch with their trunks (Plotnik, de Waal, & Reiss, 2006; a video clip of the elephants can be seen at: http://www.pnas.org/cgi/content/full/0608062103/DC1). There is also a report of pigeons using mirrors to direct a response towards their body (Epstein, Lanza, & Skinner, 1981), but this result has been difficult to replicate (Thompson & Contie, 1994), and there was no indication that the pigeons used the mirror in the way that other animals have done to inspect their body (Shettleworth, 1998).

The reason why some animals demonstrate recognition of themselves in mirrors and others do not remains something of a mystery. One possible explanation is that self-recognition is confined to animals that are able to use information provided by mirrors. However, examples are accumulating of animals being able to use mirrors even though they show no evidence of self-recognition with them. Itakura (1987) reports that monkeys can use a mirror to locate a plastic flower that was suspended above their heads by means of a specially adapted collar (see also Anderson, 1986), and Pepperberg et al. (1995) describe two different experiments in which African grey parrots were able to find hidden objects with a mirror. An obvious puzzle is created by these findings. If an animal such as a monkey is unable to recognize itself in a mirror, how then is it able to use a mirror to guide its own behavior? Perhaps the animal learns, by trial and error, to make certain movements that manipulate the image in the mirror until a goal is reached. Put rather differently, the animal may learn to move its image in the mirror in much the same way as humans learn to move a cursor to a particular point on a computer screen by use of a mouse.

What, then, is the difference between those animals that can use mirrors to direct responses towards their own bodies and those that do not? One proposal is that this activity depends on self-recognition, which, in turn, depends on the animal being self-aware (Gallup, 1970, 1975, 1983). Thus, a chimpanzee is assumed to be able to use a mirror to locate a spot on its forehead because it knows that it is looking at its own reflection. In addition, the capacity for self-awareness is said to be confined to great apes (chimpanzees, gorillas, orang-utans) and humans. The idea that even some animals are self-aware has by no means gained universal acceptance, with several authors putting forward alternative explanations for the results from self-recognition experiments (Heyes, 1994b, 1998; Macphail, 1998). Macphail, for instance, has suggested that if a chimpanzee touches a spot of dye on its forehead that it can see in a mirror, then it might be doing no more than exploring an unusual stimulus in an unexpected location. Of course, this explanation does not require that the animal is self-aware. For myself, I believe it is difficult to know for certain that an animal is self-aware because the existence of this mental state must be inferred, rather than observed directly. How can we, for example, be certain that a chimpanzee has an awareness of self, but a monkey does not? The use of a mirror for guiding self-directed responses might suggest, but it certainly does not confirm, that an animal is self-aware.

An alternative explanation for why some animals are able to use mirrors to direct responses towards themselves is based on the idea that this behavior depends on a "body concept" (Heyes, 1994b, 1998) or, as it has also been called, a "kinesthetic self concept" (Povinelli, 2000). Heyes has suggested that a body concept enables an animal to discriminate between sensory information emanating from its own body with that emanating from more external sources. This concept would then allow the animal to correlate the movements reflected in a mirror with its own movements, and thus appreciate that the reflection in the mirror is related to its "body concept". The failure of a particular chimpanzee to use a mirror to direct responses towards itself would then be explained by assuming that it had not drawn the link between its own movements and those it observes when looking at it reflection (Povinelli, 2000).

We need now to explain why some species but not others are capable of acquiring a body concept. Povinelli's (2000) answer to this question is couched in evolutionary terms. Chimpanzees and orang-utans swing from one branch to another as they move through a forest. To ensure they do not fall to the ground they need to make precise judgments based on their weight, their position, and the strength of the branches. Moreover, if they miscalculate the accident they suffer could have catastrophic consequences. These and related species are therefore assumed to have a particularly well-developed body concept to help them plan their movements through the forest. This is an intriguing proposal, but it is speculative and it fails to make clear how a body concept is represented by an animal. The reader might also wonder why it is that certain animals that do not swing through trees—elephants and dolphins—are able to use mirrors to direct responses towards themselves. Experiments that investigate how animals react to the sight of their reflection in a mirror have, on the whole, been very simple, but it is evident they have raised some fundamentally important issues that remain to be resolved satisfactorily.

We close this section with a brief discussion of an experiment by Emery and Clayton (2004). Its findings add little to the conclusion that birds do not recognize themselves in mirrors but their study merits mention because of its ingenious design. In the previous section, we saw that once they have hidden some food, scrub jays tend subsequently to change its hiding place if they were observed while originally caching it (providing the bird had previous experience of stealing food from other birds). Emery and Clayton (2004) replicated this earlier design except that while the bird was originally hiding the food, instead of being in the presence of another bird, it was accompanied by its own reflection in a mirror. If the bird appreciates that it is its own reflection in the mirror, then it should not bother about recaching the food when it is returned to the apparatus. But if the bird should regard its reflection as being another bird, then it should recache the food when subsequently given the opportunity. In keeping with the general claim that birds do not recognize themselves in mirrors, the storers were quite eager to move the food to new hiding places when they were returned to the test chamber.

CONCLUDING COMMENTS

The wide range of experiments reviewed in this chapter demonstrates convincingly that the presence of one animal can influence what another learns. This learning is dependent on a variety of mechanisms. Some of these mechanisms are relatively simple and included stimulus enhancement, social enhancement, and observational conditioning. Each of these mechanisms results in the behavior of one animal altering the reaction of another animal to a particular stimulus.

Other mechanisms for social learning are more complex. For instance, it is possible that imitation and mimicry depend on the influence of mirror neurons that respond either when an action is being observed or when it is being performed. It has even been suggested that mirror neurons enable one animal to detect the mental state of a conspecific (Gallese & Goldman, 1998). However, relatively little is known about the function of these neurons and how they acquire their properties, which means that these proposals should be regarded as speculative.

The most controversial issue in this chapter concerns the question of whether animals have a theory of mind and make inferences about the mental states of other animals. Some researchers believe that there is now ample evidence to show that animals have such a theory. Tomasello et al. (2003a), for example, have written an article entitled "Chimpanzees understand mental states – the question is which ones and to what extent" (see also Tomasello, Call, & Hare, 2003b). Others remain to be convinced (e.g. Povinelli & Vonk, 2003, 2004). It is probably evident that I, too, am not fully convinced that animals possess a full-blown theory of mind. One reason for my skepticism is that the processes involved in drawing inferences about one's own mental states, as well as the mental states of others, are complex and presumably require sophisticated thought processes based on an abstract or symbolic code. We saw in Chapter 7 that there is very little evidence to suggest that animals possess an abstract code and, if they do, it may be relatively simple and depend on special methods of training to develop. If this is correct, then animals will not be equipped with the necessary thought processes to engage in the reasoning that would allow a theory of mind to be effective. Future research will reveal whether this rather pessimistic view is justified.

CHAPTER 13

CONTENTS

Animal communication and language

13

Defining precisely what is meant by animal communication is a surprisingly difficult task that can readily lead to controversy. For present purposes, however, a useful definition is that communication occurs when one organism transmits a signal that another organism is capable of responding to appropriately. By interpreting this statement loosely, a wide range of species can be said to communicate. One of the simplest creatures, the protozoan, can influence the movement of others by secreting a chemical; during courtship, the male fruit-fly stimulates the female by producing a sound with its wings; and the chimpanzee uses a range of sounds, facial expressions, and smell to influence the behavior of other members of its social group.

The fact that animals are able to communicate with each other raises a variety of related questions. What sort of information do they communicate? How does the ability to communicate develop? Does one animal communicate with the intention of influencing another's behavior, or is the act of communication little more than a response to a certain stimulus? The purpose of the first part of this chapter is to address these questions by focusing on selected examples of communication by different species.

Other questions that are inevitably raised in discussions of animal communication concern their ability to use language. For example, to what extent does animal communication resemble language, and can animals be taught a language? The most important intellectual capacity possessed by humans is language. By use of the spoken word we are able to live together in large and more or less harmonious social groups; we can teach our children an enormous range of skills; and we can also express our feelings and our thoughts. By use of the written word we have benefited from the knowledge acquired by others over a period of more than 2500 years. The written word can also be used to create great works of art. Some have argued that language is unique to humans and that without it our lives would be little different to those of other animals (e.g. Chomsky, 1957; Macphail, 1982; Pinker, 1994). The purpose of the second, and larger, part of the chapter is to consider in some detail whether animals are capable of communicating by means of language.

ANIMAL COMMUNICATION

The range of information that may be communicated by animals is considerable. The identity of the sender can often be determined from its signals. This information may be rather general and indicate nothing more than the species of the sender, which is still worth knowing in the case of mating signals; alternatively, the identification can be more precise and allow an animal to return to its social group, or a parent to

identify and feed its offspring. The motivational state of the sender can also be inferred from the signals it sends. Aggression in cats is indicated by an arching of the back, and the change in bird song in the spring is a sure sign of the sexual readiness of males. Animals can also communicate about the environment. Many species, for example, have an alarm call that indicates the presence of a predator.

The manner in which communication takes place varies considerably in complexity. Acts of communication by animals can be relatively simple and may involve only a single feature. When the male stickleback is ready to breed, its belly turns red. Should he then enter the territory of another male, the sight of this stimulus will immediately elicit aggression (Tinbergen, 1953). But even a single feature can convey a variety of information. For instance, Stellar's jay raises its crest during aggressive encounters with other jays, and, according to Brown (1964), the degree to which the crest is raised is directly related to the ferocity of the opponent. A range of intensities of aggression can therefore be signaled by slight adjustments of the crest. Other acts of communication are more sophisticated, and a hint of this sophistication can be found in the way honey-bees communicate.

According to Brown (1964), the degree to which the Stellar's jay elevates its crest is directly proportional to the level of threat posed by its opponent.

Honey-bee communication

On returning to her hive, a worker will give the food she has collected to the other bees, prior to performing a dance on the vertical surface of a comb. If food is within 50 to 100 meters of the hive, then a round dance will be observed. The worker remains on the same spot and starts to turn, once to the left, once to the right, and so on for half a minute or more. A sketch of the dance can be seen in the left-hand side of Figure 13.1. This dance indicates to the other workers that food is nearby and the effect it has on them is described by Von Frisch (1950, p. 56):

> *During the dance the bees near the dancer become greatly excited; they troop behind her as she circles keeping their antennae close to her body. Suddenly one of them turns away and leaves the hive. Others do likewise, and soon some of the bees appear at the feeding place.*

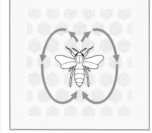

FIGURE 13.1 The round dance (left-hand side) and the waggle dance (right-hand side) of the honey-bee (adapted from Von Frisch, 1974).

When the food source is more than 100 meters from the hive the returning worker performs a waggle dance (see the right-hand side of Figure 13.1). After running a short distance in a straight line while wagging the abdomen rapidly, the bee turns through 360° to the left, and in doing so returns to the start of the straight run. She then again runs in the same straight line, wagging her abdomen, but this time at the end of it turns to the right. By repeating this routine, the waggle dance creates a figure-of-eight pattern. The impressive feature of the waggle dance is that it tells the other workers both the direction and the distance of the food. Distance is revealed by the length of the straight run—the further food is from the hive, the longer will be the straight run. As the rate of wagging the abdomen is constant throughout the straight run, it follows that the distance of food is also indicated by the number of wags that are performed on a straight run. Furthermore, because the length of the straight run determines the rate at which the figure of eight can be completed, this measure too provides an indication of the distance of food. An example of this last relationship is presented in Figure 13.2, which was constructed from the observation of 3885 dances performed after the bees had returned from food situated between 100 and 6000 meters from the hive. Apparently the experimenters had to run behind the bees for this study, which Von Frisch (1950, p. 73) described as "rather strenuous and exciting".

The way in which the direction of food is indicated is particularly ingenious. The waggle dance is performed on the vertical surface of a comb, with the direction of the waggle run being at a constant angle to the vertical. This angle corresponds directly to the angle, at the hive, between the direction of the food supply and the direction of the sun (Figure 13.3). Thus by observing the orientation of the waggle dance on the comb, the workers can calculate the direction in which they must fly from the hive, relative to the sun, to reach food.

The analysis offered by Von Frisch of the honey-bee dance has not gone unchallenged. When bees are close to a dancing forager they create squeaks that vibrate the comb and interrupt the dance. The forager then distributes small samples of her food to provide information about its taste and smell. Perhaps bees rely on olfactory information to identify the source of food that the dancer has just visited (Wenner, Wells, & Rohlf, 1969). Alternatively, it has been discovered that during her dance, the forager creates a sound like a motorboat by moving her wing muscles in short bursts. Wenner (1967) has argued that it is this sound, rather than the dance,

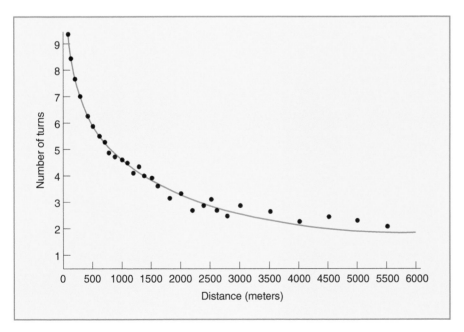

FIGURE 13.2 The relationship between the number of turns of the waggle dance, performed during a period of 15 seconds, and the distance of the feeding place (adapted from Von Frisch, 1950).

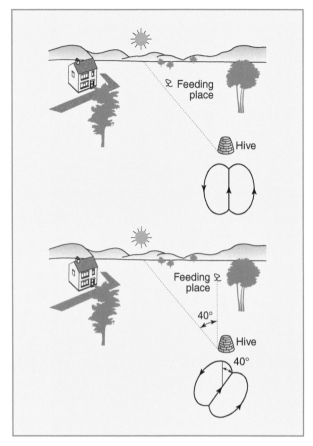

FIGURE 13.3 The way
in which the waggle
dance indicates the
direction of a food
source. The angle
between the orientation
of the dance and the
vertical is the same as
that between the sun
and the food source,
as measured at the
entrance to the hive
(adapted from Von
Frisch, 1974).

that provides the necessary information about the location of food.

Kirchner and Towne (1994) used a computer-controlled model bee to test these different accounts of how bees communicate. The model possessed artificial wings and was able to dispense small samples of food. By simulating a dance, and at the same time dispensing food and vibrating the wings so that they made the appropriate sounds, the model was able to encourage real bees to leave the hive and search for food in the place indicated by the dance. However, when any one of the three potential sources of information—food, wing sound, or dance—was not available, the number of bees influenced by the model declined dramatically. Thus it seems that the sounds the dancer makes are important for attracting bees to observe the dance. The sounds may also allow the bees to determine the orientation of the dance if it is performed in the dark. The dance itself provides important information about the direction and distance of food. Additional hints about the taste, smell, and quality of food are then provided by the small samples that are distributed.

Gould (1986) conducted an experiment whose findings led him to conclude that when a recruit observes the waggle dance she identifies on a cognitive map where food is located, and then uses the map to determine in which direction to head when she leaves the hive. This proposal has been criticized on several occasions (e.g. Dyer, 1991; Kirchner & Braun, 1994) but the best evidence against it can be found in a study by Riley, Greggers, Smith, Reynolds, and Menzel (2005). Bees were captured as they left their hive after watching a waggle dance, and then transported some 200 meters to a release point. If the bees had identified on a cognitive map where food was located, then they should have headed towards the source of food that was being referred to by the forager. Instead, by using radar to track the bees, it was found that they flew in the same compass direction and distance that they would have done if they had been allowed to start their journey from the hive. This experiment confirms the claim made by Von Frisch (1974) that recruits use information provided by the waggle dance to determine the direction and distance they should head when they start their search for food.

The development of communication

An act of communication will be effective only if the receiver can interpret the signal that is transmitted by the sender. There are two ways in which the significance of a signal can be established. One is through innate processes. That is, the signal transmitted by the sender will be an unconditioned response to a particular stimulus, and the reaction of the receiver will be an unconditioned response to the signal. The other way is through learning. Not only will learning influence the form of the message that is transmitted by the sender, it will also influence how the receiver reacts to the message. Both genetic influences and learning govern the development of animal communication, as the following discussion concerning honey-bees, song birds, and vervet monkeys reveals.

Honey-bees

Bees from different regions perform slight variations of the waggle dance. For the bees studied by Von Frisch, each waggle of the dance indicated that food was located an extra 45 meters from the hive, for bees in Italy this figure is 20 meters, and for Egyptian bees this figure is 12 meters. These differences do not reflect any influence of learning. For example, if the pupae of one race of bees are placed into the colony of another, then when the bees hatch they persistently behave in a manner that is appropriate to their real sisters and they are not influenced at all by their foster sisters. The details of the way in which the dance is performed and interpreted is thus determined genetically (Gould & Gould, 1988). For the next two species to be considered, the development of communication is rather more complicated.

Song birds

The vocal communication of birds can be categorized into calls and songs. Bird calls tend to be brief, almost monosyllabic bursts of sound that last up to a second. They permit individual recognition, serve in courtship, indicate motivational states, and may even serve to convey quite specific information about predators. Domestic chickens have at least two types of alarm call, one for aerial predators and one for ground predators (Klump & Shalter, 1984). Both the form of these calls and their significance is largely determined by inheritance, rather than learning. As a result, there is very little change in the calls from one generation to the next. However, there is a certain flexibility in the use of the calls. As an aid to identification, pairs of American goldfinch are able to modify their flight calls so that they become more similar to each other.

Despite the greater complexity of bird song—it involves the repetition of a sequence of syllables and notes—the messages it contains appear to be no more complex than those transmitted by bird calls. Singing is an almost exclusively male activity that serves the purpose of defending their territory from other males, or of attracting females for mating. In contrast to bird calls, learning is important for song acquisition. This was first made clear in an experiment by Thorpe (1963), who demonstrated that unless young chaffinches heard the song of an adult male chaffinch they could only make a raucous noise when they reached sexual maturity. Subsequent experiments with the white-crowned sparrow by Marler (1970) have shed light on the way in which the song is learned.

The song of the white-crowned sparrow consists of two components: A whistle, which lasts for about 500 to 1000 milliseconds, followed by a trill of much the same length. For sparrows living in the same area there is little variation in the structure of either the whistle or the trill. In the case of groups of sparrows from different areas, however, the construction of these components varies quite considerably. As a consequence, groups of sparrows can be said to possess their own dialects.

The young male white-crowned sparrow leaves the nest at about 10 days of age and for the next 20–100 days he is exposed repeatedly to the adult male song of his father and neighbors. This singing declines in the autumn and winter. The following spring, when he is about a year old and has reached sexual maturity, the young sparrow produces for the first time a good approximation of the local dialect of the adult male song. By acoustically isolating birds of different ages for various intervals, Marler (1970) has shown that the development of the adult song depends on the bird being exposed to it for a period between the ages of 10 and 50 days. A bird that hears the adult song during this period will produce a good copy of it on reaching sexual maturity. One that is not exposed to the adult song at all, or only after the age of 50 days, produces a song that does not correspond to even the basic structure of the species' song.

For the experiments that have been described, the songs were presented to the isolated birds through a loudspeaker. Rather different conclusions about song learning follow if the experimental subject receives its education from a live tutor that shares the same room. In these conditions, Baptista and Petrinovich (1984, 1986) have shown that song learning by white-crowned sparrows may be more flexible than was originally envisaged. Even if the young bird is older than 50 days when it first hears a song, it may still be able to learn the live tutor's song. In addition, if the live tutor is of a different species, then the subject may acquire the song. Baptista and Petrinovich (1984), for example, found that white-crowned sparrows were able to learn the song of the strawberry finch in this way.

The beneficial effect of a live tutor is important because of its implications for at least one influential account of how song learning takes place. Marler (1970) has proposed that white-crowned sparrows are born with an auditory template that permits only songs of its own species to pass through into long-term memory. If this were correct, then there should be no reason for a live tutor being more effective than a recording played through a loudspeaker. As an alternative explanation for these results, Petrinovich (1988) has proposed that white-crowned sparrows will learn any song to which they attend. An innate tuning of the sensory pathways is then believed to be responsible for birds paying more attention to the songs of their own, rather than other species. The reason for the superiority of live tutors over tape recordings as a means of teaching is attributed to the different patterns of stimulation that they produce. Live tutors provide a constantly changing pattern of stimulation that makes their songs difficult to ignore. By contrast, the repeated and stereotyped song that is characteristic of a tape recording will be less likely to capture the subject's attention. If this is correct, then it would imply that the presence of a tutor serves no other purpose than to ensure a constantly varying pattern of auditory stimulation. Whatever the merits of this conclusion, it is quite clear that bird song development is a consequence of an interaction between learning and the innate disposition of the male song bird.

In closing this discussion of bird-song learning, the achievements of the marsh warbler should not be overlooked. This bird constructs its own idiosyncratic song by mimicking and combining the components of the songs of an average of seventy-six different species of birds (Dowsett-Lemaire, 1979). Some birds are thus more constrained than others in the songs they learn.

Vervet monkeys

Birds are not the only animals to produce alarm calls. A variety of different species, including squirrels, South African mongoose, marmots, and monkeys are known to emit alarm calls in response to the presence of a predator. Sometimes these calls are remarkably specific. Vervet monkeys, which live in troops and inhabit savannah areas of Africa south of the Sahara, use a variety of alarm calls, each of which refers to a specific threat and elicits a different reaction from the receiver (Struhsaker, 1967;

see Figures 13.4 and 13.5). If an aerial predator such as an eagle should be spotted, then the alarm call resembles a chuckle that results in the troop either looking up or fleeing into a bush for cover. A threat posed by the appearance of a leopard results in an alarm call of a loud bark that causes the troop to flee for safety in a tree. Any individual that encounters a snake, particularly a python, will call with high-pitched chuttering, whereupon the members of the troop look around and perhaps mob the snake. The approach of baboons, which attack young vervets, also elicits separate and distinctive alarm calls. By playing recordings of these calls to a troop, Cheney and Seyfarth (1988; Seyfarth & Cheney, 1993)

FIGURE 13.4 An alert monkey responding to an alarm call.

revealed that calls in the absence of the relevant predator would still elicit the appropriate response. Thus the possibility can be ruled out that the call serves to elicit a general orienting reaction, which is followed by a specific response as soon as the source of the threat has been identified.

Vervet monkeys have been heard to produce the full repertoire of alarm calls from a very early age, which suggests that the physical properties of the call are genetically determined. Infants also start off by being relatively indiscriminate in the use of alarm calls. They have been heard to produce an eagle alarm call not only to eagles and other aerial predators, but also to pigeons, and even a falling leaf. Erroneous calls by infants are not entirely inappropriate. Eagle alarm calls, for example, were normally given to objects in the air and rarely to terrestrial predators. Vervet monkeys may thus be genetically predisposed to respond to certain classes of stimuli with specific alarm calls. There is, in addition, good reason to believe that learning plays an important role in refining the use of alarm calls. Moreover, this learning can be understood with principles that should already be familiar because they are based on associative learning (Seyfarth & Cheney, 2003).

To investigate the way in which vervet monkeys learn how to respond to the different alarm calls, Seyfarth and Cheney (1986) played a tape of an eagle alarm call whenever they saw an infant wander from its mother. At first, the infant appeared startled, or confused, and searched for its parent. Subsequent presentations of the alarm call then resulted in the infant watching its mother, and eventually the infant copied the mother's reaction to the call of looking up to the sky. It was as if the infant modeled its behavior on that of its mother through observational conditioning.

A further role for learning, this time in the production of calls, is indicated by the finding that the indiscriminate production of calls referred to earlier declines as the infant develops. When an infant was heard to make an eagle alarm call, other members of the troop looked up and, if they saw an eagle, they also made eagle alarm calls. If the infant's call was inappropriate, perhaps in response to a pigeon, then the adults did not call out. The feedback provided by the adults' calls may thus have served to strengthen correct, but not incorrect, calls by the infant. A report by Caro and Hauser (1992) suggests that additional factors may also influence this process of discrimination learning. Inappropriate alarm calls by infants have been observed to cause their mothers to flee, and then to return and punish the infant by biting or slapping. Whether this punishment was for making an incorrect call, or whether it was for some other reason, is not known.

FIGURE 13.5 The
different responses by
vervet monkeys that
are elicited by alarm
calls for three types of
predator (from Bright,
1984).

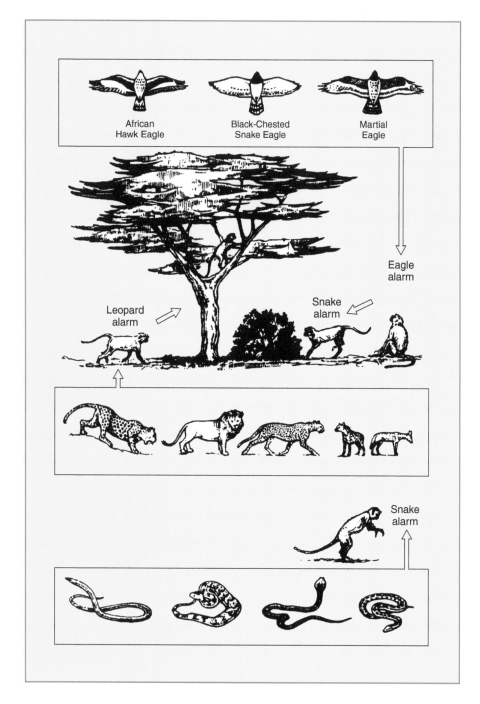

FIGURE 13.5 The different responses by vervet monkeys that are elicited by alarm calls for three types of predator (from Bright, 1984).

The significance of signals

When a male stickleback sees the red stomach of another male stickleback, its aggressive reaction is no doubt an unconditioned response to the sight of the red signal. The majority of signals are probably effective in this way. When it comes to the alarm calls of monkeys, however, it is possible that instead of just eliciting a response (either conditioned or unconditioned) they have some meaning to the sender. Seyfarth and

Cheney (2003) have pursued this possibility by suggesting that the alarm call for a predator activates in those who hear it a representation of the predator, which then has the same effect as if the predator were actually present. Support for this conclusion can be found in experiments by Cheney and Seyfarth (1988; see also Seyfarth & Cheney, 1993) and by Zuberbuhler, Cheney, and Seyfarth (1999). The study by Zuberbuhler et al. (1999) was conducted with diana monkeys, who inhabit the rain forests of West Africa, and its design was quite straightforward. A loudspeaker was used to present recordings of two stimuli separated by 5 minutes to groups of monkeys in their natural habitat. There were two types of recording: calls made by predators, which consisted of either the growls of a leopard, or the shrieks of an eagle; and the different alarm calls made by a male diana monkey in response to these predators. On baseline trials the two stimuli were the same, for example, the shriek of an eagle may have been played on both occasions. Baseline trials resulted in frequent alarm calls by the group on first hearing the predator, but no response on hearing it for the second time. For test trials, the first stimulus consisted of an alarm call made by a monkey, perhaps for an eagle, followed 5 minutes later by the sound made by the same predator. In keeping with the results from the baseline condition, there was no response to the second stimulus.

According to Seyfarth and Cheney (2003), during the baseline condition, the actual sound made by a predator will result in the monkeys giving alarm calls and storing the information that a particular predator is present. The repeat of this sound will not provide any new information, and thus the monkeys on this occasion will be reluctant to make an alarm call. Bear in mind that there may be a cost to making an alarm call by giving away one's location to the predator. In the test condition, the alarm call for a particular predator made by a monkey is assumed to activate a representation of the predator, so that when the sound made by the predator is subsequently heard it will provide no new information and there will be no need to make an alarm call. Of course, if the monkey should hear an alarm call for one predator followed by the sound made by the other predator, then it would now be expected to react to the second sound by making appropriate alarm calls. The results from a control condition in the experiment confirmed this prediction. Thus, as far as the receiver is concerned, alarm calls by vervet monkeys can, at least in certain circumstances, activate a representation of the relevant predator.

Communication and intention

The majority of human communication takes place because the speaker has the intention of influencing the knowledge possessed by the hearer. A speaker is therefore likely to have some idea of the knowledge possessed by the audience, and have a desire to add to or change this knowledge. Are the communications by animals also made with the intention of passing on knowledge to the receiver? If animals communicate intentionally then they should produce more signals when they are near conspecifics than when they are alone. Studies of the alarm calls of jungle fowl (Marler, Karakashian, & Gyger, 1990), ground squirrels (Sherman, 1977) and vervet monkeys (Cheney & Seyfarth, 1990) have all revealed such an **audience effect**, but this result is open to a variety of interpretations. It is possible that the signal was transmitted with the intention of warning conspecifics, but it is also possible that animals are innately disposed to making alarm calls in the presence rather than absence of conspecifics. An audience effect has also been found in the laboratory with apes that have been taught to communicate with their trainers by means of making gestures with their hands. They are much more likely to make these gestures in the presence than in the absence of

KEY TERM

Audience effect
The tendency to produce a signal more in the presence than in the absence of an audience.

a trainer (Leavens, Hopkins, & Bard, 1996). We shall see later in this chapter that one function of these gestures is to request a reward, and it is possible that the animals had learned through trial and error that the gestures were effective only when the trainer was present. Thus learning based on reward, rather than the intention to convey information may have been responsible for this example of the audience effect.

A rather different test for whether animals communicate with the intention of informing other animals is provided by Hostetter, Cantero, and Hopkins (2001). A human held a banana that was clearly visible to a chimpanzee, but just beyond its reach. If the human had his or her back to the chimpanzee, then the chimpanzee was most likely to produce a vocalization in an attempt to gain the banana, but if the human was facing the chimpanzee then it was most likely to communicate with a gesture of the hand. The authors suggest these results show that the different gestures were used for the intentional communicative purpose of gaining the attention of the human. Once again, however, it is possible to devise a more mundane explanation for the outcome of the experiment. Past experience may have taught the apes that begging with a gesture of the hand is more effective when directed towards the front rather than the back of a person. We need to know more about the way in which begging behaviors develop before these different interpretations can be evaluated.

The final findings to be considered in this section indicate that vervet monkeys do not use alarm calls intentionally. Baboons prey on young, but not adult, vervet monkeys with the consequence that only infants make alarm calls on seeing a baboon. This reluctance by adults to express alarm is found even if young vervet monkeys are nearby (Bright, 1984). If the alarm calls were made intentionally, then adults should make alarm call in these circumstances. Turning now to an experimental study, Seyfarth and Cheney (1993) allowed a mother to watch a threatening individual hide in an enclosure. The mother's child was then released into the enclosure and the mother made no effort to warn her infant of the imminent danger. A warning would be expected if alarms calls are used intentionally.

All in all, these results fail to provide any convincing evidence that the acts of communication by animals are made with the intention of conveying information to another individual. Instead, they may be an innate reaction to a particular set of circumstances, or a response that has been learned through trial and error as an effective means for gaining reward. This conclusion should not be too surprising in the light of findings discussed in the previous chapter. We found little reason to suppose that animals have a theory of mind, and such a theory would seem to be a natural requirement if an animal communicates with the intention of conveying knowledge to another individual.

The examples referred to above constitute only a fraction of what is known about animal communication, yet they serve to demonstrate many of the characteristics of the way in which animals exchange information. We now consider the extent to which animals are capable of communicating by means of language.

COMMUNICATION AND LANGUAGE

A definition of language

To determine if animals are capable of using language, we must first define what is meant by this term. Several authors have done this by listing a set of criteria that an act of communication must fulfill if it is to be regarded as language (Hockett, 1960;

Anderson, 2005). Although the following list is by no means exhaustive, it provides a useful framework for evaluating the linguistic skills of animals.

Arbitrariness of units

Language is composed of discrete units—words—which in general are arbitrarily related to the events to which they refer. This characteristic enables different languages to refer to the same object with different words. In certain cases, such as alarm calls, animal communication is also composed of discrete units, but in others the signal consists of a coherent unified pattern, as with the dance of the honey-bee. As far as the arbitrariness of the signal is concerned, some instances of communication manifest this property and some do not. Two examples that fail to meet this criterion are shown in Figure 13.6. The dogs are displaying submission and aggression, and it is quite apparent that the actions are related to the state they are signaling. An example of a more

FIGURE 13.6 The posture of dogs displaying submission (top) and aggression (bottom) (adapted from Darwin, 1872).

arbitrary relationship between a signal and the information it conveys was encountered in the previous section. Vervet monkeys were shown to give different alarm calls to different predators and it is most unlikely that the nature of the predator determines the precise form of the call. In support of this claim, recall that infants must, to some extent, learn the significance of the calls.

Semanticity

Language allows the transfer of information from one person to another because each word has a specific meaning. We shall presume that a signal, for an animal, has meaning if it can activate a representation of the event to which it relates. We have just seen that vervet monkeys appreciate the meaning of the alarm calls that they hear.

Displacement

Language allows people to communicate about events that are displaced either in time or in space. The bulk of animal communication lacks this property, because a signal is usually an immediate reaction to an internal state, such as an increase in certain hormones, or an external event, such as the sight of a predator. An obvious exception to this claim is the dance of the honey-bee, in which the precise form of the signal is governed by food that may be several kilometers from the hive.

Productivity

A powerful property of language derives from the fact that it is structured according to rules of grammar, or syntax. By using these rules an almost infinite number of sentences can be constructed, each of which will convey a different meaning. The productivity criterion refers to this ability to create a large number of meaningful utterances from a limited vocabulary. Examples of animal communication that meet this requirement are scarce, but they exist. The way in which Stellar's jay signals the intensity of aggression could be said to demonstrate productivity; so, too, could the way in which the honey-bee waggle dance is able to convey information about an almost unlimited number of spatial locations. None the less, in both these cases the range of information that can be transmitted is far more restricted than in human language. In these examples the animals are constrained to communicating about food and aggression. Their rules of production are not sufficiently sophisticated to permit them to converse about a wider range of topics. This may be slightly unfair to the honey-bee, which is able to communicate about the merits of potential sites for a new hive (McFarland, 1985, p. 416).

In addition, to my knowledge, natural communication by animals has never met the productivity criterion by combining discrete units, and this may be one characteristic that sets human language apart from the natural communication of every other animal. Where productivity is demonstrated by animals, it is always achieved by varying an attribute of the signal, such as its orientation or intensity.

Language and cooperation

Animal communication therefore differs from human language in a number of important ways. But this does not necessarily mean that all animal communication is inferior to language. Much remains to be discovered about the way in which animals communicate, and future research could reveal impressive capacities in this respect. Bottle-nosed dolphins, for instance, are believed to communicate with whistles that are relatively short and vary considerably in frequency (Herman, 2002; Richards, Wolz, & Herman, 1984). Rather little is known about the function of these signals, and conceivably they may be manifestations of a system approximating language. We should thus acknowledge the possibility that some animal communication meets all the criteria of language, but this has yet to be revealed because of our inability to translate it.

Even though this argument is extremely difficult to refute, because we do not understand the way in which all species communicate, there may be grounds for not taking it too seriously. An important influence of language is that it allows humans to cooperate in extremely complex ways. If it could be shown, therefore, that animals cooperate in complex ways, and that this depends on communication, then we might conclude that the animals concerned possess something akin to language. Of course, there would still remain the task of understanding the communications that passed between the individuals, but at least we could be reasonably confident that our labors in this respect might reveal something of interest. There have been a few studies of cooperation between animals in the laboratory, but none has yet revealed clear evidence that animals possess language.

In 1972, the BBC transmitted a *Horizon* program that demonstrated cooperation between a male and a female dolphin, possibly by means of an intelligent communication (details of this and related studies can be found in Bastian, 1961, and Wood, 1973, pp. 113–118). The two dolphins were situated in adjacent pools that allowed them to hear but not see each other. The female was occasionally shown either a steady or an intermittent light. If she saw a steady light then presses by the male on a panel resulted in them both receiving food, but if she saw an intermittent light then the male had to press a second panel for them both to receive food. Despite being unable to see the light, the male eventually selected the correct panel on the majority of trials. This success was accompanied by the female making different sounds in the presence of the two lights, which is consistent with the claim that the male's choices were the results of a complex exchange of information between the two animals.

Boakes and Gaertner (1977) discuss this experiment in some detail and propose that the performance of the dolphins can be explained in a rather different way. Suppose that the female, by chance, should make a sound in the presence of one of the lights, and the male should press the correct paddle. Then the female will be rewarded for making the sound during that particular light, and the male will be rewarded for making the response during that particular sound. The next time that the light is presented, the female will be disposed towards making the same sound again and the male will be disposed towards making the correct response. All that is now needed is for the female to make a different sound in the presence of the other light, and the process will repeat itself for the other paddle.

To support their analysis, Boakes and Gaertner (1977) were able to train pairs of pigeons to interact in a similar way to the dolphins. They were also able to show that this was achieved in the manner just described. There have been other studies of cooperation between animals (Savage-Rumbaugh, Rumbaugh, & Boysen, 1978; Epstein, Lanza, & Skinner, 1980; Lubinski & MacCorquodale, 1984), but these too appear to depend on the behavior of one animal serving as a discriminative cue for a certain response from another.

Of course, the possibility remains that the laboratory tests have been inadequate and that animals communicate in sophisticated ways in more naturalistic settings. If this were true, their complex communications should be accompanied by a correspondingly intricate pattern of cooperation. After all, there is little point in engaging in a complex dialogue if it leads nowhere. But to my knowledge there is no naturalistic evidence that groups of animals interact in ways that could be said to be a consequence of a complex communication. For this reason alone, the communications of animals would seem to be very much simpler than that permitted by language.

CAN AN APE CREATE A SENTENCE?

The evidence reviewed thus far provides scant support for anyone wishing to claim that animals possess an intellectual skill akin to language. There remains, however, one line of enquiry to be considered before we can reach any firm conclusions about their linguistic abilities. There has been a variety of attempts to teach animals an artificial language. Although this type of research will reveal little about the way animals communicate naturally, it should provide important insights into their linguistic potential. There is now little doubt that animals can be taught certain features of a language, but there is much dispute as to where the limit of this ability lies. Indeed, the question posed as the title for this section, which is taken from an article by Terrace, Petitto, Sanders, and Bever (1979), captures very precisely a major theoretical issue that occupies this area of research.

There have been a number of attempts in this century to teach language to all of the great apes: chimpanzee, orang-utan, and gorilla. After a brief account of the methods that have been used and the results they have produced, we shall examine critically the conclusions that have been drawn from these studies.

Training methods

One of the earliest attempts to teach an ape language was by William Furness (1916), and the rewards for his endeavors were slight. For many hours he attempted to teach a female orang-utan to speak English, but she was only able to pronounce "papa",

William Furness(1916) attempted to teach a female orang-utan to speak English, but the efforts were rather fruitless. The only words she successfully pronounced, hindered by a limited vocal tract, were "papa", "cup", and "th".

"cup", and "th". These were used as the trainer intended, and the ape is reported to have uttered the words "cup cup" shortly before dying of influenza. Some decades later Hayes and Hayes (1952; Hayes, 1961) raised a chimpanzee, Vicki, as if she were a human child, but again despite careful training she was able to speak just four words: "mama", "papa", "cup", "up".

This virtual failure to teach apes to speak is due in part to the fact that their vocal tracts are incapable of producing all the sounds of human speech. Figure 13.7 shows the vocal tracts of a human and a chimpanzee. The structures between the lips and the larynx are of great importance in producing speech, and it is apparent that they differ greatly for the two species. According to Duchin (1990), a major constraint on the ability of the chimpanzee to produce the sounds of human speech is its tongue which is unable to move to the correct positions to create the necessary sounds. By way of example, the vowel sounds [a], [i], and [u] are said to be impossible for the chimpanzee to produce. A possible means for overcoming this barrier to teaching apes a language is to use a medium for communication that does not involve speech. A variety of methods have been tried.

FIGURE 13.7 The adult vocal tract of a human (left-hand side) and a chimpanzee (right-hand side) (adapted from Lieberman, 1975).

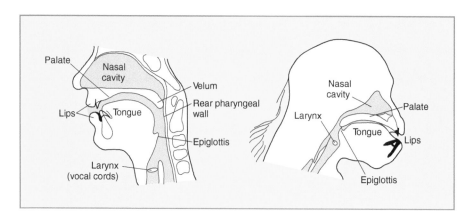

American sign language

Gardner and Gardner (1969; see also Gardner, Gardner, & Van Cantfort, 1989) trained a chimpanzee, Washoe, to communicate by using her hands in much the same way as deaf people do. In fact, Washoe was taught Ameslan, which is the principal method for conversation among deaf people in North America. Just as spoken words can be broken down into one or more units—phonemes—so words in Ameslan are constructed from a combination of one or more gestures—cheremes. Each chereme consists of a configuration of the hands placed in a specific position and making a particular action. The words can then be combined to produce sentences by the use of grammatical rules, which differ to some extent from those governing English. Ameslan meets all the requirements for language that were enumerated previously.

By using a variety of techniques, considerable success was achieved with Washoe. At the age of five, after 4 years of training, she was able to sign 132 different words, which included nouns ("sweet", "key"), pronouns ("me", "you"), and verbs ("tickle", "open"). She was also able to combine these words into strings of up to five in length and used them to give commands to her trainer: "you tickle me", "open key food" (an instruction to open the refrigerator). Washoe was capable of replying to questions posed by her trainer in Ameslan. On one occasion her trainer asked her "What's that?" in the presence of a swan, and was told "Water bird". Following this pioneering work, there have been other attempts to teach apes Ameslan. The most systematic of these has been by Terrace (1979; see especially Terrace et al., 1979), who trained a chimpanzee, Neam Chimpsky—nicknamed Nim. During the course of his training Nim learned 125 different signs and was observed to combine them into more than 19,000 utterances. Throughout the study a record was kept of these combinations and of the context in which they occurred.

Another way of teaching a chimpanzee to use Ameslan was to place an infant in the care of Washoe. This line of research had a rather sad start. When she was about fifteen, with a vocabularly of 180 signs, Washoe had a child. Her baby became very ill and had to be taken from her to receive special care. The treatment was unsuccessful and the baby died. The next day, Washoe's first question to the trainer was the sign "Baby?". The trainer replied "Baby gone, baby finished". Washoe then behaved in a manner that can best be described as grief (Fouts, Hirsch, & Fouts, 1982, p. 170):

> *She dropped her arms . . . to her lap and she broke eye contact and slowly moved away to a corner of the cage. She was demonstrating all the clinical signs of depression. She continued for the next several days to isolate herself from any interactions with the humans and her signing dropped off to almost nothing. Her eyes appeared to be vacant or distant.*

There is, fortunately, a happy ending to this story. A short time later, Washoe was introduced to a 10-month-old infant, Loulis, and rapidly adopted him as her son (Figure 13.8). They spent a great deal of time together and very soon Loulis started to copy the signs of Washoe. At first, the signs were used in play, but they were eventually used to make spontaneous requests to the trainers, such as "tickle", "drink", "hug". Loulis learned twenty-two signs from Washoe. Many of the signs were acquired by copying Washoe, but there are one or two reports of Washoe attempting to teach Loulis a sign. On one occasion, Washoe was repeatedly signing "food" as she was being brought some food. She then took Loulis' hand and molded

it into the correct configuration for the food sign. Reports of the development of Loulis as a sign user can be found in Fouts et al. (1982); Fouts and Fouts (1989); and Fouts, Fouts, and Van Cantfort (1989).

There is no doubt that Loulis learned about Ameslan from Washoe, because the trainers were instructed to refrain from signing in his presence. It also seems probable that this learning was based on mimicry and imitation. But how Washoe's role as a teacher should be interpreted remains open to question. She may have been attempting to teach her adopted son to use signs or she may have been playing with his hands for any one of a number of other reasons.

Plastic tokens

Premack's (1971b, 1976) solution to the problem of the ape's reluctance to speak was to create an artificial language in which the words were plastic objects that varied in shape, size, color, and texture. Sarah, Premack's brightest chimpanzee, became proficient in the use of about 130 words; these included nouns ("Sarah", "apple", "knife"), verbs ("wash", "draw", "give"), adjectives ("brown"), quantifiers ("all", "none"), and conditionals ("if", "then"). To create a sentence, the words, which had a metal backing, could be placed in a vertical column on a magnetic board (Figure 13.9). For the sentences to be acceptable, the words had to be placed in a grammatically correct sequence.

On some occasions, words were placed on the table beside the magnetic board and the chimpanzee was expected to construct a sentence. If it was correct, then the trainer would place a word representing "correct" on the board, praise Sarah verbally, and perhaps give her a jelly bean or similar reward. On trials when the sentence was wrong, an "incorrect" token was placed on the board, and the trainer might say "No, you dummy".

At other times the trainer placed a sentence on the board, and if it was an instruction, the subject was supposed to obey it, for example, "Sarah give Mary apple". The sentence could also take the form of a question. Two colored cards might be placed one on top of the other, on the table, and a sentence on the board would ask "? red on green" (is red on green?). The subject was then required to reply by placing a token for either "yes" or "no" on the board.

Lexigrams

Premack's technique has been developed a step further in a project supervised by Rumbaugh (1977),

FIGURE 13.9 One of the chimpanzees, Elizabeth, trained by Premack. The message on the board says, "Elizabeth give apple Amy" (adapted from Premack, 1976).

in which the symbols serving as words—or lexigrams, as they were called—were displayed on a keyboard connected to a computer. Pressing a key resulted in its symbol being projected onto a screen above the console. To create a sentence, the chimpanzee, originally Lana, had to press a sequence of keys that resulted in the display of a string of lexigrams. The sentence had to be structured according to a set of grammatical rules, known as Yerkish, which are not too dissimilar to those governing English. Hence, to receive a drink, Lana had to press the lexigrams for "Please machine give juice", in that sequence. Figure 13.10 shows a selection of lexigrams as they are typically arranged on a keyboard. The purpose of the computer was to keep a record of Lana's statements and to dispense films, slides, music, food, sweets, and liquids, when requested. The computer screen could also be used to present instructions to Lana in lexigrams.

Lana is a common chimpanzee (*Pan troglodytes*) but there is another species of chimpanzee, the bonobo (*Pan paniscus*), which is said to be able to modulate its

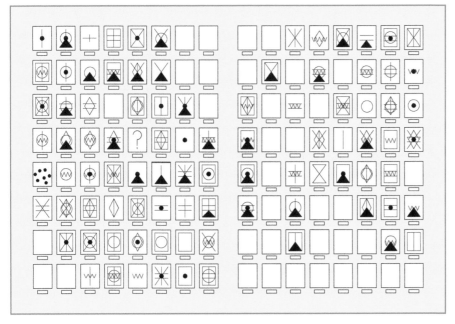

FIGURE 13.10 The arrangement of lexigrams on a keyboard. Blank spaces were nonfunctioning keys, or displayed photographs of trainers (from Savage-Rumbaugh et al., 1983). Copyright © 1983 American Psychological Association. Reproduced with permission.

vocalizations to a much greater extent than its near relative. Rumbaugh and Savage-Rumbaugh (1994) attempted to teach an adult bonobo, Matata, to use lexigrams, but they failed dismally. While she was being trained, however, Matata was accompanied by her adopted son, Kanzi. Even though no attempt was made to teach Kanzi, he started to communicate by means of the lexigrams on the keyboard. He requested things, named things, and announced what he was about to do (Figure 13.11).

Spoken English

Although apes are very poor at speaking English, they may well be able to comprehend statements that are spoken in English. Fouts et al. (1982) mention in passing that Washoe understood some spoken English, and additional experiments with Kanzi make this point forcefully.

As soon as Kanzi started to use the lexigram keyboard, he received special training. Instead of taking part in formal training sessions for a restricted amount of time each day, he received constant attention and spent his waking hours as a full member of the human social group that worked in the laboratory. He was also spoken to in much the same way as many human parents speak to their children before they can talk. That is, he was spoken to as if he understood everything that was being said.

FIGURE 13.11 Kanzi using lexigrams on a portable keyboard to communicate with his trainer Sue Savage-Rumbaugh (from *Kanzi: At the brink of the human mind* by E.S. Savage-Rumbaugh & R. Lewin).

Kanzi continued to receive training in the use of lexigrams, but these were now associated with the appropriate speech sounds. This method of training obviously required a great deal of patience, because it persisted for a number of years. Eventually, however, formal testing with single words and sentences confirmed that Kanzi could understand human speech. In some of the tests he was instructed to "take the can opener to the bedroom", "take the potato outdoors", "go outdoors and get the potato", or "take the potato outdoors and get the apple". He was also tested, and responded correctly, with statements of the sort "get item X from location Y", even if there was an identical item X in front of him. On the basis of his performance Rumbaugh and Savage-Rumbaugh (1994) proposed that Kanzi's comprehension skills are equivalent to those of a two-and-a-half-year-old child. An engaging account of Kanzi's achievements is provided by Savage-Rumbaugh and Lewin (1994).

Experiments by Sue Savage-Rumbaugh and her colleagues have started to reveal some of the reasons for Kanzi's sophisticated comprehension of speech. Kanzi's training commenced when he was about 6 months old. Williams, Brakke, and Savage-Rumbaugh (1997) found that a bonobo that received language training at an early age was much better at comprehending commands than one that started similar training at the age of 3.5 years. There is a need for caution when interpreting the results from a study based on just two individuals, but the implication of these results is that bonobos are more disposed to learn a language when they are young than when they are old. It seems that this disposition to comprehend speech may also apply to chimpanzees, but possibly to a lesser extent. Brakke and Savage-Rumbaugh (1995) found that by training a chimpanzee and a bonobo in a similar manner to that used with Kanzi, and at a very early age, both animals acquired a large vocabulary and were able to respond to multi-word commands. However, the bonobo was able to respond more accurately to more complex commands than the chimpanzee, and the size of the bonbo's vocabulary was greater than that of the chimpanzee. Once again, the small number of subjects makes it difficult to draw strong conclusions, but it appears that bonobos are more naturally disposed to understanding language than chimpanzees.

Assessment of language training with apes

Discreteness and displacement

Of the various criteria that were listed as requisites for language, both displacement and discreteness have been well demonstrated as being met by apes using an unnatural system of communication. Discreteness is revealed by the use of specific gestures or symbols to represent words, and displacement is revealed by conversations involving objects that are not in view. An excellent example of a conversation that meets both of these criteria is provided by Savage-Rumbaugh, Pate, Lawson, Smith, and Rosenbaum (1983). They tested two chimpanzees, Austin and Sherman, who were trained to communicate with an experimenter by a method based on that devised by Rumbaugh (1977). After examining a table of different items of food, the chimpanzee had to walk around a partition to a keyboard, from where the food could not be seen. He then had to request one of the items and wait for permission from the trainer to collect it. Once permission had been granted the chimpanzee returned to the table, picked up the specified food, and took it to the trainer, where it was shared. By requesting food that was out of sight, the subject is clearly communicating about a spatially displaced object.

Semanticity

Considerable effort has been expended in establishing whether or not apes know the meaning of the words they use. It would be as well to establish at the outset, therefore, what precisely is implied when we say that a word means, or symbolizes, something else. In the discussion of natural communication by animals a signal was said to be meaningful if it activated a representation of a particular event. An alternative way of expressing this idea is to say that a signal has meaning if it can serve as a cue for the retrieval of information about the event to which it relates. At this point it is perhaps worth drawing attention to the conclusion drawn in Chapter 2 that after pairing a signal, such as a tone or light, with an unconditioned stimulus (US), such as food, the signal may acquire the capacity to activate a representation of the US. As these results were obtained with rats it should not be surprising to discover that apes too can learn the "meaning" of signals.

Indeed, we have already come across evidence that supports this conclusion. The poignant reaction of Washoe to the news of her baby's death, and the ability of Kanzi to execute correctly the instructions he heard, provides compelling evidence that they understood what they were told. Premack (1976, pp. 473–474) describes an experiment that also demonstrates that Sarah understood the meaning of at least one of the words she used. Her training with the word "brown" consisted solely of being told that "Brown color of chocolate" in the absence of any chocolate. When she was then given four disks of different colors, she responded correctly to the command "Take brown" (Premack, 1976, p. 353). Unless the symbol for chocolate was capable of retrieving information about chocolate, she would not know to which color the word brown referred.

Particularly good evidence of chimpanzees being able to understand the words they use comes from a test conducted by Savage-Rumbaugh, Sevcik, and Hopkins (1988). The subjects—Austin and Sherman—had been trained in a similar way to Lana to communicate by means of lexigrams (see Savage-Rumbaugh et al., 1983, for details). The test consisted of showing the chimpanzees a lexigram for an object. They were then expected to retrieve the object from a box, into which they could not see, and which contained a number of different objects. They were both able to find the correct object, which is difficult to explain unless they knew the meaning of the lexigram.

There are, by contrast, occasions when chimpanzees do not appear to understand the words they use. A clear example was provided by Nim. He was quite capable of signing correctly "apple" or "banana" when these fruits were presented one at a time, but when they were given together he was unable to respond correctly if requested to give the trainer an apple. This confusion would not be expected if he understood the meaning of the words he used (Savage-Rumbaugh, 1984).

Productivity

Very often, the meaning of a sentence is not just governed by the words it contains; the order in which they occur is also very important. "Jessica hit Tim" is thus completely different in meaning to "Tim hit Jessica", even though both sentences contain the same words. This is possible because all sentences are constructed according to grammatical rules. Not only do these rules constrain the way a sentence can be constructed or interpreted, they also enable a speaker to create an almost unlimited number of meaningful statements from a finite vocabulary. Given the importance of grammar to language, it is understandable that a considerable amount of interest has been directed at the issue of whether or not apes can master these rules. In the following discussion their ability in this respect will be considered separately for language comprehension and production.

Sentence comprehension

We will first consider whether chimpanzees can comprehend sentences on the basis of their structure. For some of her training, Sarah was required to respond on the basis of information provided in the following form of sentence: "Debby give apple Mary ⊃ Sarah insert cracker dish", which is an instruction for Sarah to put a biscuit in a dish if Debby gives Mary an apple. After training with a variety of such sentences, Sarah responded to them correctly, even when they were novel. Because of the statement's complexity, her success might be taken as evidence that she had used grammatical rules to decode it. Premack (1976) points out, however, that instead of understanding the sentence, Sarah's training could have taught her an alternative means for solving this problem. In all the sentences of this sort that she was given, the first part was always true; in the quoted example Debby, as a matter of course, gave Mary the apple. Thus, to receive reward, Sarah needed only to fulfill the command in the second half of the sentence, and there was no reason for her even to look at the first half. A better test of Sarah's linguistic abilities would have been to examine her response on probe trials in which the "if" condition was not true. Regrettably, as is so often the case with good ideas, this one did not occur to Premack (1976) until it was too late to test it.

Even in the absence of this test, Sarah might be said to have understood grammatical rules, because in the example mentioned she put the biscuit in the dish. But Sarah had received extensive training with instructions such as "Sarah insert cracker dish", and she may simply have learned to perform the appropriate action in the presence of a certain configuration of shapes in order to gain reward. These are not isolated criticisms, a thorough review by Ristau and Robbins (1982) points to the conclusion that those sentences from studies before 1982 that have been claimed to reveal the use of grammatical rules by apes are open to alternative explanation. However, more encouraging findings can be found in more recent tests with bonobos. I mentioned earlier that one bonobo, Kanzi, was able to respond correctly to spoken instructions. Many of the novel instructions that Kanzi obeyed would have been ambiguous if he was insensitive to their syntactic structure. Even so, he was able to show that he understood them to a degree that is far greater than would be expected on the basis of chance (Savage-Rumbaugh et al., 1993). For some of these tests, Kanzi was required to wear headphones to prevent the person who was assessing his performance from hearing the commands (Figure 13.12). Examples of instructions that he executed correctly when he first heard them are:

"Make the snake bite Linda."

"Can you throw a potato at the turtle."

"Go outdoors and find the carrot."

"Take the carrot outdoors."

"Pour the Coke in the lemonade."

"Pour the lemonade in the Coke."

FIGURE 13.12 Kanzi listening to spoken instructions as he participates in a test of language comprehension (photograph by Mike Nichols).

Kanzi's success with this type of test shows that he can respond correctly to commands containing a good number of words, but it is not easy to understand how he was able to interpret the commands. Several sentences might have been interpreted without the use of any syntactic rules at all, because they could mean only one thing given the words they contained, for example, "Take the carrot outdoors". In addition, other sentences could have been interpreted correctly by using the simple rule of moving the first object in the sentence to the second object. Thus we can conclude that Kanzi was able to respond correctly to reasonably complex sentences using at least simple rules, but additional research will have to be conducted if we are to understand the full extent to which apes can master syntactic rules on which the commands they respond to are based.

Sentence production

We now turn to ask whether chimpanzees can create grammatically structured sentences. While being rowed across a pond by Fouts (1975), her trainer, Washoe was shown a swan and asked "What that?" Despite never having been taught the phrase, she replied "Water bird". On another occasion, Washoe's trainer placed a doll in a cup and asked the ape to sign about it. Washoe's reply is quite impressive: "Baby in my drink". These constitute but two of many examples where an ape has provided a novel utterance that is appropriate to the situation in which it occurred. Moreover, as they consist of a string of words that, for English, are correctly structured, it seems as if Washoe can use grammatical rules to produce sentences. Or does it? Terrace et al. (1979) have argued that they do not justify any sophisticated claims about the linguistic ability of apes. As far as the water-bird example is concerned, it is conceivable that Washoe was replying to the question by identifying, first, a body of water and, second, a bird:

"Before concluding that Washoe was relating the sign water to the sign bird, one must know whether she regularly placed an adjective (water) before,

or after, a noun (bird). That cannot be decided on the basis of a single anecdote, no matter how compelling the anecdote may seem to an English-speaking observer" (Terrace et al., 1979, pp. 895–896)

On examining a film of the "Baby in my drink" incident, Terrace et al. (1979, p. 898) discovered that, perhaps unwittingly, the trainer pointed first to the doll and then to the cup before Washoe started her reply. This information, rather than rules of grammar, was possibly responsible for the way in which Washoe structured her answer.

As well as analyzing the utterances of apes trained by other researchers, Terrace et al. (1979) also conducted a thorough examination of the strings of words produced by Nim. In total, over an 18-month period, Nim signed 19,203 multi-word utterances, of which there were 5235 different types. Despite this number and variety, the experimenters were unable to conclude that these statements were structured according to a set of rules.

One problem was posed by the limited variety of certain classes of utterance. For example, when the word "more" was used in a two-word utterance, it consistently occupied the first position. Unfortunately, it is impossible to determine whether this particular pattern reflects a grammatical rule or, more fundamentally, a general habit of starting statements with "more". Another difficulty is that Nim often copied the signs of the trainer. He may thus have created grammatically correct sequences by cheating.

It is also instructive to compare the multi-word utterances of Nim with those of children. The term **mean length of utterance (mlu)** refers to the average length of the utterances made by an individual. Figure 13.13 shows that for a normal child, as well as for one that is deaf and uses Ameslan, there is a sharp increase in mlu with age. In stark contrast, Nim's mlu was maintained at much the same value of about 1.5 throughout his training. If Nim had mastered the rules of grammar, then they would have allowed him to produce increasingly longer sentences. It is interesting to note that according to Savage-Rumbaugh et al. (1993), the mlu for Kanzi when communicating with lexigrams was also about 1.5. A further difference between Nim and children is that for the latter a long utterance is more informative than a short one. Thus "Sit Daddy" might be elaborated to "Sit Daddy chair". This was very rarely true for Nim, who generated long utterances principally by repeating words. The following utterance by Nim makes it hard to believe that he was grammatical in his use of language: "Give orange me give eat orange me eat orange give me eat orange give me you" (Terrace et al., 1979, p. 895).

Despite these arguments, there is no doubt that apes can produce reliably statements that are grammatically correct. Sarah would consistently write sentences of the form "Give Sarah grape" to indicate that she was to receive, and not give, a grape. But it is quite possible that these sentences were a consequence of Sarah remembering each of the strings of symbols that had previously led to reward. In other words, the sight of a grape might have served as a discriminative stimulus controlling the response of placing certain shapes in a fixed sequence.

KEY TERM

Mean length of utterance (mlu)
The mean number of meaningful linguistic units per utterance. Normally, mlu is based on a sample of 100 utterances.

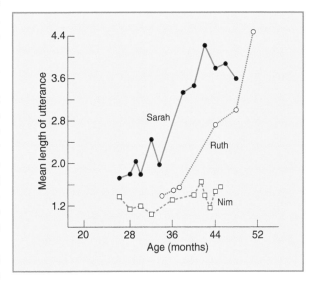

FIGURE 13.13 The change in the length of utterance with age for a normal child, Sara, a deaf child, Ruth, and Nim (adapted from Terrace et al., 1979).

Considerable emphasis has been placed on Nim's failure to acquire grammatical rules because of the detailed way in which the study was conducted and analyzed. There are, however, grounds for being cautious when interpreting the performance of this subject. Undoubtedly, the intellectual abilities of individual chimpanzees vary, as they do for humans. Nim may not have been an especially gifted subject and it would be unwise to regard his results as representative of chimpanzees in general. To support this point, it is noteworthy that Nim had a succession of trainers, which resulted in his repeatedly forming and then breaking close attachments. The influence of these emotional disturbances on his intellectual development is difficult to assess (see Lieberman, 1984, pp. 244–246). There has also been a suggestion that the social context in which Nim was tested was far from perfect (Fouts et al., 1982; O'Sullivan & Yeager, 1989).

In view of these criticisms, it is reassuring to note that a study by Rivas (2005) has replicated many of the important findings described by Terrace et al. (1979). The study included five chimpanzees, including Washoe and Loulis, and involved a careful examination of videotapes of sessions in which these chimpanzees used sign language to communicate with a trainer. Despite studying nearly 800 utterances consisting of combinations of two or more signs, Rivas (2005) was unable to find any evidence that the order of signs was used to convey meaning, or that the order was structured according to syntactic rules. It was also found that at least 44% of the utterances produced by each individual, including nearly 1600 single-sign utterances, involved the same four words. There were of course, individual differences in the preferred four words that were selected. By way of example, Loulis used only four signs which stood for Gimme, Chase, Hurry, and That/There/You. The maximum number of signs produced by a chimpanzee was fifty-five. In keeping with the findings described by Terrace et al. (1979), Rivas (2005) discovered that multi-sign utterances were repetitive and added little to the meaning of shorter strings. An example of a sixteen-sign utterance by Washoe is: "Flower hurry flower hug go flower book flower gimme flower gimme flower hug hurry drink gimme", which is very similar in style to the long utterance by Nim quoted above. The majority of utterances, 86%, were requests, which suggests that the signs were used as instrumental responses to gain reward. On the basis of these findings, therefore, it would seem that chimpanzees are not able to produce grammatically structured sequences of signs, and that they do not use signs in the same way as humans.

LANGUAGE TRAINING WITH OTHER SPECIES

Attempts to teach language to animals have not been confined to the apes. In this section the methods employed for this research, and the results it has revealed, are briefly examined.

Can a dog learn a word?

This question was posed by Bloom (2004) in response to the finding that some dogs are surprisingly good at responding to a large number of spoken commands. An early demonstration of this skill was provided by a German shepherd dog, called Fellow. Fellow appeared in a number of films during the 1920s and was reputed to respond to a large number of spoken commands. In a carefully controlled study of his abilities, Warden and Warner (1928) discovered that Fellow responded to a total of fifty-three different commands, including "sit", "stand up", "roll over", "turn around", "lay down" , "lie still", and "put your foot on the chair". If he was told "do that once more" he repeated the last action. To eliminate any possibility that Fellow was reacting to subtle actions by his trainer, rather than to spoken commands, he was tested on one occasion in a hotel room while his trainer shouted instructions through the closed door of the adjoining bathroom.

The performance of another dog—Rico, a border collie—is also worthy of mention. His training commenced with him being asked to fetch one object from an array of three that were placed near him, and he received reward for fetching the correct item. New items were then introduced into the array by their names being spoken several times before Rico was then allowed to play with them. Another method for teaching Rico the name of a new object was to place the new object among an array of familiar objects and ask him to "Fetch X", where X stands for the name of the new object. Apparently this method was particularly effective (Kaminski, Call, & Fischer, 2004). Over time, Rico became adept at collecting correctly over 200 items. Although one can not help but be impressed by the performance of Fellow and Rico, it is not clear that they are showing a sophisticated linguistic skill. Young children soon appreciate that words are not just used as commands for action, but they also have a referential function. That is, children can request an object, point out an object, or even comment on the absence of an object by using the word for that object. By contrast, as Bloom (2004) and Markman and Abelev (2004) point out, there is no evidence that dogs appreciate the referential function of words. In other words, Fellow and Rico could have learned through associative learning that the commands were auditory discriminative stimuli that required a particular response to be made in order to gain reward (Markman and Abelev, 2004).

A parrot

Parrots are famous for their capacity to mimic human speech, although normally they say only a few words. In a series of articles Pepperberg (1981, 1983, 1987, 1993) has shown that they can, in fact, acquire a relatively large vocabulary of spoken words, which can be combined to form meaningful multi-word utterances. Her principal subject has been an African grey parrot, Alex, but other parrots have been trained successfully using a similar method (Pepperberg & Shive, 2001). Alex was trained first to speak in English the names of objects (e.g. "paper", "key", "grain", "chair", "back", "gym"). Of some interest is the fact that the manner in which correct responses were rewarded differed from that used in the majority of studies with apes. Whenever Alex named an object correctly, he was praised and then allowed to eat it or to play with it. The method of training is also of interest. Alex would be in a position that allowed him to see two trainers. One trainer then asked the other, who adopted the role of a parrot, to name an object; if the trainer's reply was correct, then he or she was praised and expected to play with the object. Merely as a result of watching these interactions, Alex soon entered into the proceedings, as the following extract from a typical session shows (Pepperberg, 1981).

Irene (Pepperberg): Bruce, what's this?

Bruce (a trainer): Pasta. (loudly)

Irene: Good boy! Here you go. (Hands over a piece of pasta)

Alex: (interrupting) Ah-ah.

Bruce: Do you want this, Alex? What is it?

Alex: Pah-ah.

Bruce: Better . . .

Alex: Pah-ah.

Bruce: No. Irene, what's this?

Irene: Pah-ah.

Bruce: Better!

Irene: Pas-ta. (Emphasizing the "s" and "t")

Bruce: That's right, tell me what it is again. (Offers pasta)

Irene: Pasta! (Takes pasta) Pasta! (Alex stretches from his perch on top of the cage, appears to reach for pasta)

Alex: Pa!

Irene: Better . . . what is it?

Alex: Pah-ah.

Irene: Better!

Alex: Pah-ta.

Irene: OK, here's the pasta. Good try.

Training in this manner soon became more elaborate, so that Alex's speech eventually included colors, shapes, and numbers, which were often combined with object names. Thus when shown a piece of computer paper for the first time, he was able to identify it as "Four-corner paper". On other trials an object such as a blue triangle might be presented accompanied by the question "What color?" or "What shape?" His answers were correct with an accuracy that was far in excess of that predicted by chance. These findings are particularly impressive when it is appreciated that Lana was unable to respond correctly on this sort of problem (Savage-Rumbaugh et al., 1983). Subsequent studies have revealed the importance of the above method of training for the success with Alex. Pepperberg and McLaughlin (1996) report that if social interaction is kept to a minimum during the course of training then African grey parrots make very little progress with learning to speak the names of objects that are presented to them.

Intriguing as these findings may be, they do not show that Alex was capable of understanding or creating sentences. As an alternative, his sentences may have been the product of rote learning sequences of sounds that were produced in the presence of the appropriate discriminative stimuli. Evidence that Alex's linguistic skills might extend beyond this interpretation comes from his use of the phrase "Wanna go". At the outset of his training Alex was unhappy in novel places and consequently spent most of the time in either his cage or his gym, which contained a collection of rods and ropes. When in his cage he was often asked "Wanna go gym?" and this frequently produced a squeaky "Yeah" in reply. After a while he spontaneously uttered the phrase "Wanna go gym" and was immediately carried to it. He even modified this phrase to "Wanna go gym—no" when he was in the gym and appeared to want to leave it (as indicated by stretching towards something else).

As he gained in confidence, Alex would sit on chairs, shelves, and a trainer's knee. During this time he often heard the names of these perches, but care was taken to ensure that he never heard them in conjunction with the phrase "Wanna go". Despite this constraint, Alex started to say phrases like "Wanna go chair". And if he was taken to a different place he responded either with a "No" or with a repeat of the request.

These findings indicate that Alex was capable of generating novel, meaningful, multi-word utterances (although it is arguable that "wanna go" should be regarded as a single word). Unfortunately, the limited number of these utterances makes it difficult to be sure of their origins. They may have been the production of a primitive grammar that contains a rule of the form: "Wanna go" is followed by an object. Alternatively, they may have been produced by chance and strengthened because of the reward that followed.

Dolphins

Herman, Richards, and Wolz (1984; see also Herman, Pack, & Morrel-Samuels, 1993) have presented a carefully documented report of an investigation into the linguistic ability of two dolphins. The results from a very similar study using sea lions, which revealed much the same findings as with dolphins, can be found in Schusterman and Gisiner (1988). Whereas the training for apes, as well as that for Alex, involved both the comprehension and the production of sentences, only the former was tested with dolphins and sea lions.

Herman et al. (1984) trained two bottle-nosed dolphins—Akeakamai and Phoenix—to behave in specific ways according to sequences of signals. For Akeakamai, the signals were gestures performed by a person standing by the pool in which the dolphins were tested (Figure 13.14). The signals for Phoenix were short, discrete noises generated by a computer. The training for the two animals differed in a number of other respects, and for the sake of brevity the account that follows concentrates on Akeakamai's treatment and results.

Table 13.1 shows the words to which Akeakamai responded correctly. The list includes objects, actions, agents, and modifiers. After preliminary training, she was instructed in the comprehension of two-word sentences. Examples of these, and the longer sentences that were eventually used, can be seen in Table 13.2, together with the rules of the artificial syntax that governed their construction. The table also includes a translation of the sentences. Thus two-word sentences were structured according to the rule of object before action, which means that "Phoenix over" is an instruction for Akeakamai to jump over Phoenix. On the most recent test reported, Akeakamai responded correctly to 85% of the possible sentences that can be constructed from this language.

One enormous advantage of this type of training is that it is possible to conduct test trials that provide unambiguous results. For example, during the course of her training Akeakamai was tested with 193 novel sentences when all the objects listed in Table 13.1 were in the pool. The objects thus provided no clue as to how she should respond, yet her performance on these trials was extremely accurate. The most plausible explanation for this outcome is that she had understood the rules that structured the artificial language and could use them to interpret novel sequences

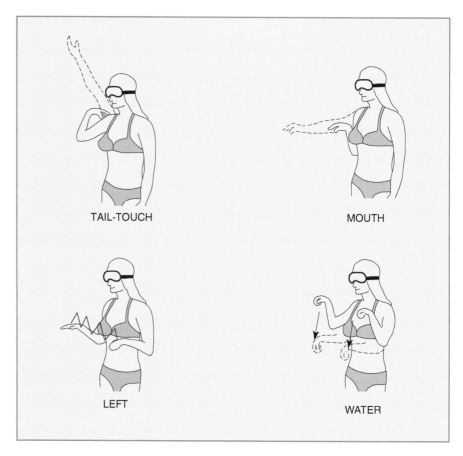

FIGURE 13.14 Examples of some of the gestural signs used for the sentence-comprehension studies with a dolphin, Akeakamai (adapted from Herman et al., 1984).

of signals. Support for this important conclusion can be found in other aspects of Akeakamai's performance.

After experiencing many two- and three-word sentences, Akeakamai was suddenly given one containing four words, and she responded correctly. The implication of this finding is that she was able to use the rules relevant to the shorter sentences to understand a more complex syntactic structure. This is precisely the sort of skill that should be demonstrated by an animal that is grammatically competent.

The sample of sentences in Table 13.2 makes it apparent that in some cases their meaning is very much dependent on word order. Although composed of the same signals, the string "Pipe hoop fetch" is a very different instruction to "Hoop pipe fetch". Despite this added complexity, Akeakamai was able to react appropriately when given a novel sentence of this sort. In fact, the likelihood of responding correctly was the same as for equivalent sentences with which she was familiar. Once again, such an outcome strongly suggests that she was sensitive to the grammatical rules of her language.

The dolphins also demonstrated that they were able to meet some of the other requirements of a linguistic ability. Mastery of the displacement criterion was

TABLE 13.1 The comprehension vocabulary of the dolphin Akeakamai (adapted from Herman et al., 1984)

Objects

Window	Speaker	Basket	Person
Net	Ball	Pipe	Frisbee
Water	Hoopfish	Surfboard	
Phoenix			

Actions

Tail touch	Pectoral touch	Mouth (grasp) with mouth	(Go) over
(Go) under	(Go) through	Spit (squirt water from mouth at object)	Fetch (take one named object to another named object)
In (place one named object in another named object)	Toss (throw object)		

Agent
Akeakamai (prefix for each sentence)

Modifiers

Left	Right

Other

No	Yes	Erase

TABLE 13.2 The rules of syntax of the gestural language for the dolphin, Akeakamai (adapted from Herman et al., 1984)

Rule	Example
2-word	
Object + Action	Basket toss (Throw the basket)
	Window tail-touch (Touch the window in the tank with your tail)
3-word	
Modifier + Object + Action	Left person mouth (Touch the person on your left with your mouth)
IO + DO + Action	Pipe hoop fetch (Take the hoop to the pipe)
	Hoop pipe fetch (Take the pipe to the hoop)
4-word	
IO + Modifier + DO + Action	Ball right frisbee fetch (Take the frisbee on your right to the ball)
Modifier + IO + DO + Action	Right basket pipe fetch (Take the pipe to the basket on your right)

DO, direct object; IO, indirect object.

revealed on numerous occasions. On some trials, the instruction related to an object that was hidden from view (spatial displacement), and the dolphin had to find it before responding. On other trials, the command was issued as much as 30 seconds before the objects to which it related were thrown into the pool (temporal displacement). Neither of these variants caused much difficulty. A rather different version of this type of test consisted of placing all the objects but one in the pool and then giving a two-word sentence that related to the missing object. Akeakamai would often search for up to nearly a minute for the missing item and then stop, without responding to the other objects. She also rapidly learned to press a paddle to indicate that the designated item was missing.

The way in which dolphins are able to react to sophisticated commands is most impressive and suggests at least a rudimentary understanding of grammatical rules, but some caution is needed when drawing conclusions from this study. As a component of language, production is certainly of equal importance to comprehension and, as yet, there is no evidence that dolphins can produce even the simplest sentence.

THE REQUIREMENTS FOR LEARNING A LANGUAGE

There is, therefore, a need for further research with animals before their ability to use language can be fully appreciated. As a way of gaining an insight into the likely outcome of this research, we can examine the requirements that might be considered necessary if an animal, either human or nonhuman, is to be linguistically proficient. In the discussion that follows we shall examine the role of innate factors, motivation, and thought, for the acquisition of language.

Language acquisition device

From the point of view advocated by Chomsky (1972; see also Pinker, 1994), the reason for the absence of a clear demonstration of linguistic competence by animals is quite simple. The languages of the world share a striking similarity in the way in which their grammars operate. This suggested to Chomsky (1972) that humans possess an innate **language acquisition device** for generating a "universal grammar", from which the grammars of these languages are derived. As apes and other animals do not naturally use language, it would be reasonable to conclude that they do not possess such a device, and this would explain their limitations in sentence construction. Macphail (1982) has also argued that language is a uniquely human phenomenon, but for reasons that are rather different from those of Chomsky (1972). After considering much of the evidence summarized previously, Macphail (1982, p. 312) concluded that: "humans acquire language (and non-humans do not) not because humans are (quantitatively) more intelligent, but because humans possess some species-specific mechanism (or mechanisms) which is a prerequisite of language-acquisition".

Plausible as these arguments may be, they should not be accepted without further thought. Currently, very little is known about the properties of the device that is said to provide humans with their universal grammar. We should, therefore, be cautious in accepting the existence of such a device until we know what it is and how it operates. Furthermore, Chomsky's (1972) proposals have not gone unchallenged. Anderson (2005), for example, maintains that there are constraints on the way in which our cognitive processes operate, and these, in turn, are responsible for the structure of language. Thus it is natural to think of the subject of an action before considering the object, and this constraint may explain why, for three-word sentences, the majority of the world's languages place the subject before the object (Greenberg, 1963). If there are grounds for doubting the existence of a specific language-acquisition device, then we should also doubt the claim that its absence is the reason for the inability of apes to produce a sentence.

Motivation

The claim that humans possess an innate language-acquisition device may not, therefore, be wholly justifiable. But even if it were, the possibility remains that with the right sort of training animals could acquire at least rudimentary language skills. There may, however, be another barrier that restricts animals in their use of language: They may simply be unwilling to communicate with humans, that is, their linguistic shortcomings may be due to a motivational rather than intellectual deficit.

There can be little doubt that young children are extremely willing communicators. In the early stages of language development, they frequently point to objects and name them without any prompting (Locke, 1980). At a later stage they will often initiate a conversation that bears no relevance to what has just been said. Apes, by contrast, have shown themselves to be much more reluctant to engage in spontaneous acts of communication. Hence, rather than to start a conversation, a high proportion of Nim's utterances were imitations of the trainer's previous signs, which is relatively rare in children (Terrace, 1979). Acts of spontaneous pointing and naming are also reported to be uncommon for many language-trained apes (Savage-Rumbaugh, 1984).

Despite what has just been said, there are a number of reports of apes communicating spontaneously, given the appropriate circumstances. A clear example concerns Austin and Sherman, who began to use spontaneously the names of objects they had learned. Thus one of the apes would name an object on the keyboard, for instance, "blanket", and then point to it or give it to the trainer. This behavior was not trained but, maintains Savage-Rumbaugh (1984), was a consequence of the type of language training they had received. There is also a report concerning Nim, which shows that when he was in a more informal setting than the one used for his training, there was a marked increase in the number of his spontaneous utterances (O'Sullivan & Yeager, 1989). Kanzi, too, would often offer an unsolicited multi-word utterance (Savage-Rumbaugh, McDonald, Sevcik, Hopkins, & Rubert, 1986). On this basis, then, it is likely that an unwillingness to communicate will not prove an impenetrable barrier for training apes to use language.

Some observations by Gardner and Gardner (1974) provide further support for this conclusion. They noticed that Washoe often signed to herself in play, or when looking through a book. "Washoe also signed to herself about her ongoing or impending actions. We have often seen Washoe moving stealthily to a forbidden part of the yard, signing quiet to herself" (Gardner & Gardner, 1974, p. 20). Furthermore, these instances of what have been called private signing occur quite frequently. In a detailed investigation of private signing that lasted for 56 hours, Washoe and four other chimpanzees were observed to sign to themselves on more than 350 occasions, using nearly sixty different signs. Finally, the way in which Loulis learned to use signs by copying Washoe suggests at least a rudimentary enthusiasm for communicating in this acquired manner.

Cognition

Language and cognition are intimately related. Without the capacity to think, people would have little need for a language, as they would not have any ideas to communicate; and without certain mental processes we would be unable to produce grammatically correct sentences that are comprehensible to others. Ultimately, therefore, the constraints on language use by animals may be imposed by the limitations of their thought processes. Discussions concerning the nature of animal thought are rare, principally because so little is known about it. We can, however, identify some thought processes that are essential for language and ask whether animals possess them.

Sentence production

Turning first to sentence production, two aspects of thought would seem to be essential. The language user must be able to construct sentences in a correct order. For example, to express the idea in three words that "Tim likes Alex", it is necessary to know that the subject of an English sentence precedes the verb, which, in turn, precedes the object. In Chapter 10, monkeys were shown to be capable of learning to touch in the correct order a number of colored keys that were displayed simultaneously. Moreover, this ability was sustained when they were tested with a novel subset of the array. Taken together with other findings cited in that chapter, these results provide convincing evidence that monkeys, at least, can represent information about serial order.

A capacity to learn about serial order will, however, be of little use for language if each member of the series is a specific item. Instead, the members of the series need to be categories, so that different exemplars of each category can be placed in the correct position in the sequence and thus allow the creation of novel sentences. In Chapter 7, a number of studies were described that show that animals can classify objects into categories. For example, once a pigeon has been trained to peck a key whenever it is shown a picture of water, then it will do so even in the presence of an unfamiliar picture of water. In general, the categories that have been studied are of objects that share common physical attributes—trees, a particular person, etc.—and this may be insufficient for language. The rules of grammar require that the categories are more abstract, so that events can be classified as subject or object, for example. At present, the evidence concerning the ability of animals to acquire abstract categories is, at best, promising rather than convincing (see pp. 180–189).

The representation of knowledge

We can now turn to the question of whether animals are capable of representing ideas that merit communication by language. All transitive sentences convey information about the relationship between a subject and an object, for instance, "Alex likes Tim". The same can also be said for intransitive sentences, except that here the relationship is implied: The sentence "Jessica fell over" can be interpreted as an expression of a relationship between Jessica and the ground. To produce a sentence, therefore, animals should be able to represent objects and, more importantly, they should be able to represent the relationships that exist between these objects.

The extent to which animals are capable of comprehending relationships is dealt with in some detail in Chapter 7. According to Premack (1983a,b), the ability to represent any but the most fundamental relationships depends on the possession of an abstract mental code. If his argument is correct, then it follows that language training will only be successful with animals that possess this code because without it they would be incapable of comprehending the relationships on which all sentences are based. Sarah's success with analogical reasoning tasks suggests that she is capable of understanding a wide range of relationships.

On the basis of the slender evidence that is available, some animals have shown that they may possess the fundamental thought processes necessary for language comprehension and production. If further research should confirm this conclusion, then future attempts to train animals in the use of language may well be more successful than the attempts thus far.

CHAPTER 14

CONTENTS

The distribution of intelligence

14

Two contrasting views of the way in which intelligence is distributed throughout the animal kingdom were presented in the opening chapter of this book. One of these makes the assumption that intelligence is related to brain size or, more precisely, to a cephalization index (K), which is based on a ratio of the weight of the brain to that of the body. The other, which has been referred to as the null hypothesis (Macphail, 1982, 1985), asserts that, apart from humans, all vertebrates are of equal intelligence. We are now in a position to evaluate these different proposals.

INTELLIGENCE AND BRAIN SIZE

The suggestion that a cephalization index can provide an indication of intelligence is appealing; after all, it is presumably in the brain that most of the information processing by animals takes place. Moreover, there have been occasional reports that claim to demonstrate a high correspondence between intelligence and some measure of brain size.

One of the earlier sources of support for this claim comes from an experimental method that we have not yet considered: learning-set formation. Experiments that study the formation of **learning sets** involve a succession of discriminations with different stimuli, and the focus of interest is whether there is an improvement in the rate at which each discrimination is solved. To measure this improvement, a record is kept of the accuracy of responding on the second trial of each problem. With the first trial of each discrimination, subjects will be forced to choose at random between the two alternatives, but with experience they could theoretically perform with complete accuracy on the second trial. To gain reward consistently on the second trial they would need to repeat their previous choice, if it was successful, otherwise they should select the alternative stimulus. If performance on the second trial improves with continued exposure to new discriminations, then the subject is said to have formed a learning set (Harlow, 1949).

Figure 14.1 shows, for a variety of species, the accuracy on the second trial of a discrimination, as a function of the number of problems that have been given. All six species show an improved performance as their exposure to additional discriminations increases, but this improvement is more marked for some species than others. Passingham (1982) has shown that ranking the species on the basis of their ability to form a learning set corresponds to a ranking based on an index of brain size that is related to the cephalization index (Riddell, 1979). If it is now assumed that the ability to form learning sets is related to intelligence (McFarland, 1985), then the pattern of results depicted in Figure 14.1 suggests that intelligence depends on brain size.

The foregoing argument is of particular interest to the present discussion because it highlights two pitfalls that will be encountered by any attempt to relate intelligence in animals to their brain size. First, Macphail (1982) and Warren (1973), among

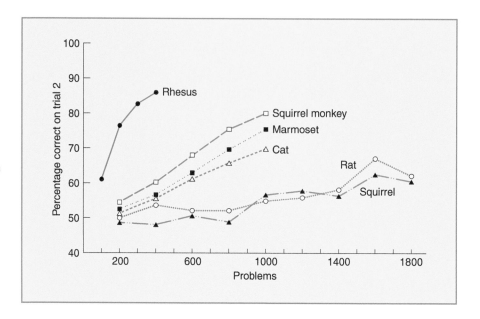

others, have argued that comparing results such as those summarized in Figure 14.1 can be very misleading. The reasons why such a comparison can be misleading were dealt with, in general terms, in Chapter 1 (see pp. 13–15). Comparing the speed at which species form learning sets is hampered not only because they possess different perceptual skills and motivational processes, but also because the apparatus in which they are trained is necessarily different. These differences in contextual variables, rather than variations in intelligence, may well be responsible for the pattern of results summarized in Figure 14.1.

To emphasize this point, it is worth looking at the results from two learning-set experiments with dolphins. When a single bottle-nosed dolphin was trained with a series of visual discriminations in which the stimuli differed in shape, Herman, Beach, Pepper, and Stalling (1969) found very little evidence for the formation of a learning set. By contrast, Herman and Arbeit (1973) had little difficulty in training another dolphin to form a learning set when the discriminations involved auditory stimuli. Indeed, by the end of her training, the dolphin was responding with an accuracy of greater than 85% on the second trial of each new discrimination. Thus, for dolphins, the way in which a learning-set experiment is conducted can have a profound influence on the outcome it reveals. This conclusion is also bound to be true for other species (see, for example, Zeldin & Olton, 1986, who found that learning-set performance in rats can be considerably better than that indicated in Figure 14.1). Consequently, when an animal shows a reluctance to form a learning set, we should be aware that this may be due to a poorly designed experiment, rather than to a lack of intelligence.

The second reason why the study of learning sets may not be a justifiable means for comparing animal intelligence rests with the way intelligence is defined. I argue in Chapter 1 that instead of regarding animal intelligence as a unitary mechanism it may be more useful to see it as being the product of a number of different cognitive processes. Moreover, these processes may take place in different regions of the brain. If this is correct, then a more accurate approach to the study of brain size and intelligence would be to explore how the size of specific brain regions is related to particular intellectual abilities. Evidence that this approach might be successful can be found in study by Spencer, Buchanan, Leitner, Goldsmith, and Catchpole (2005) who report that the size of a brain region known as the higher vocal center in adult male canaries is correlated with the complexity of their songs. They also report that there was no correlation between the overall size of the brain and song complexity, which reinforces the view that measuring the size of the entire brain will provide an insensitive measure for relating brain to behavior and intelligence.

Other research, however, has been less successful at revealing a relationship between the size of a particular brain region and the function it is supposed to serve. To make this point, we will examine in some detail studies based on the hippocampus. This region is believed to be important for spatial memory (see Chapter 11) and it has been found that the relative size of the hippocampus is generally larger in birds that store a large amount of food than in birds that store little or no food. For example, the hippocampus is larger relative to the rest of the forebrain in marsh tits, which store food, than in great tits, which do not store food (Healy, Clayton, & Krebs, 1994). Accordingly, Krebs (1990) has suggested that this difference between the size of the hippocampus of storers and nonstorers may reflect differences in memory capacity. Attractive as this suggestion may seem, it should be treated with a measure of caution in the light of a report by Healy (1995). Two food-storing and two nonstoring species of tit were trained in a delayed nonmatching to sample task. Subjects were shown a sample stimulus and then after a retention interval shown the sample together with another stimulus. To gain reward they had to select the stimulus that had not served as the sample, which obviously depends on them remembering the sample throughout the retention interval. There was no hint in any measure of memory that the species differed in their abilities on this task. For instance, both storers and nonstorers were able to tolerate delays of up to 100 seconds between the termination of the sample and the onset of the comparison stimuli.

Results reported by Hampton and Shettleworth (1996) complicate matters even further. Their subjects were two species of bird—dark-eyed juncos and black-capped chickadees—and the hippocampus is proportionally smaller in the former than the latter. When one spatial memory test was given to the birds, the black-capped chickadees came top, but when another type of spatial memory test was given it was the dark-eyed juncos that shone. It should also be added that not all birds who store food have a large hippocampus. Basil, Kamil, Balda, & Fite (1996) report that the size of the hippocampus in the pinyon jay is relatively small, yet this species caches a large amount of food each year, and performs well on tests of memory in the laboratory.

Hampton and Shettleworth (1996) reported that despite the fact that the black-capped chickadee (left) has a relatively large hippocampus in comparison to the dark-eyed junco (right) it was outperformed by the latter in a given spatial memory test.

Findings such as these make it unlikely that there is a simple relationship between the size of the hippocampus and the properties of spatial memory (Macphail & Bolhuis, 2001). One likely reason why no clear relationship between the size of the hippocampus and spatial memory has been found is that the hippocampus fulfils a variety of functions. In addition to being involved in spatial memory, it is also involved in non-spatial memory and probably many other aspects of behavior (Macphail, 1993). If the hippocampus serves a number of functions then it might be unduly optimistic to expect its size to correlate directly with a single intellectual ability such as spatial memory. This note of caution applies not only to the hippocampus. A number of researchers have examined the relationship between other brain regions, such as the neocortex, and other aspects of intelligence (e.g. Reader & Laland, 2002). As Healy and Rowe (2007) note, it is often difficult to draw clear conclusions from these studies because the regions concerned carry out multiple functions, and because the behavior under consideration is often complex and likely to be the product of activity in a number of different brain regions. Until our understanding of the function of individual brain regions improves, any attempt to relate the size of a brain region to an ability to perform a particular task is obviously going to be difficult.

THE NULL HYPOTHESIS

After reviewing a large body of experimental findings, Macphail (1982) concluded that all vertebrates (with the exception of humans) are of equal intelligence. Implausible as this proposal might seem, Macphail (1982, 1985) cites an impressive body of evidence in its support. We turn now to examine the implications of the results cited in the preceding chapters, as well as some others, for the null hypothesis. Because there are so many problems with identifying the general intelligence of a species, we shall not use this measure to evaluate the hypothesis. Instead, we shall look at the extent to which the null hypothesis can be justified for the various intellectual skills that have been the focus of attention throughout the book.

Associative learning

Macphail (1982) shows that both instrumental and Pavlovian conditioning are effective with an extremely wide range of vertebrate species. It is also possible to add that, as far as I am aware, no vertebrate has ever been shown to be incapable of solving discriminations. On this basis we could conclude, in keeping with the null hypothesis, that all vertebrates are capable of associative learning.

But even if this were true, the possibility would remain that the way in which associative learning takes place varies among different species. The effectiveness of Pavlovian conditioning was attributed in Chapter 2 to the development of either conditioned stimulus–unconditioned stimulus (CS–US), or CS–response (R) associations. Perhaps CS–R associations are responsible for successful Pavlovian conditioning with some species, whereas for others this success may depend on the growth of CS–US associations, or even both types of association. Brandon and Bitterman (1979) have drawn just such a conclusion by arguing that Pavlovian conditioning results in the formation of only CS–R associations in goldfish. Bitterman (1984) subsequently acknowledged that goldfish can acquire stimulus–stimulus associations, but this does not mean that all vertebrates are capable of forming both types of association. For this conclusion to be accepted, it will be necessary to conduct many well-controlled experiments with a far wider range of species than has hitherto been tested.

Turning now to instrumental conditioning, we saw in Chapter 4 that this can result in the growth of either S–R or R–US associations. Most of this research was conducted with rats and it is far too early to argue with any confidence that a similar conclusion will hold for all vertebrates. We might find, for example, that some vertebrates are capable of acquiring only S–R associations.

Instead of focusing on the types of association that are formed during Pavlovian and instrumental conditioning, a comparison of different species could consider whether they all share the same processes of association formation. Chapter 3 demonstrated the importance of surprise and attention for successful associative learning but, once again, we do not know whether the conclusions drawn in that chapter apply to all vertebrates. The slender evidence that is available suggests they do not.

When a rat is repeatedly exposed to a neutral stimulus, subsequent conditioning is slower than with a novel stimulus. This latent inhibition effect is said to reflect a loss of attention to the familiar stimulus. Although there is little difficulty in demonstrating latent inhibition with many mammals, to my knowledge it has never been demonstrated with goldfish. Indeed, Shishimi (1985) specifically tested them for latent inhibition and was unable to detect it either with excitatory or with inhibitory conditioning, and when both appetitive and aversive unconditioned stimuli were used. This failure also occurred whether the stimulus was auditory or visual. There seem to be strong grounds for concluding, therefore, that latent inhibition cannot be found in goldfish.

Of course, the possibility remains that Shishimi (1985) did not design his experiments properly. With mammals, a minimum of about twenty trials of exposure to the stimulus are necessary before latent inhibition can be demonstrated. Perhaps goldfish need more exposure than this, and even more than the 160 trials employed in one of the studies by Shishimi (1985). Despite this word of caution, the procedures for both generating and detecting latent inhibition are very simple, and it would be surprising if the various techniques used by Shishimi (1985) were inadequate. There is a possibility that other species are also not susceptible to latent inhibition. Mackintosh (1973) describes an experiment where he failed to demonstrate latent inhibition with pigeons; I have experienced a similar failure in my laboratory on a number of occasions.

If latent inhibition is a consequence of a change in the attention paid to a stimulus, then the mechanisms of attention in rats may differ from those in goldfish and pigeons. Interestingly, another source of evidence, based on a different experimental design, also suggests that the attentional processes of rats and goldfish differ. Chapter 2 shows that, for rats, the effects of blocking can be modified by the surprising omission of a US after each compound conditioning trial (Dickinson et al., 1976). Although there is some dispute about the interpretation of blocking, at least two theories (Mackintosh, 1975a; Pearce & Hall, 1980) attribute the effects of surprising events to their influence on attentional processes. Accordingly, if the mechanisms of attention for goldfish and rats differ, they might be affected in different ways when a US is unexpectedly omitted after a blocking trial. This prediction has been tested by Gonzalez (R. C. Gonzalez, 1985, personal communication), who conducted a blocking experiment with goldfish that was similar in design to the one conducted with rats by Dickinson et al. (1976).

Although he was able to demonstrate blocking, Gonzalez found that this effect was not at all disrupted by the surprising omission of a US during compound conditioning. Because of the difficulty of demonstrating latent inhibition with pigeons, it would be interesting to know how they would perform in a blocking experiment similar to that conducted by Gonzalez.

Thus, for associative learning, the null hypothesis is correct as far as the susceptibility of vertebrates to the techniques of instrumental and Pavlovian conditioning are concerned. But there is insufficient evidence to evaluate this hypothesis when interest is focused on the types of association that are formed as a result of these training methods. By contrast, there is some evidence to suggest that the hypothesis may be wrong as far as the role of attentional processes in learning are concerned.

Memory

There has been a tremendous growth in the comparative study of animal memory during the last 20 years or so, and a brief review of this research can be found at the end of Chapter 9. It was found that the performance of some species of animals on tests of memory is superior to that of others, but it was not clear whether this difference was a result of them possessing different mechanisms of memory. The results may, instead, have been a consequence of the different species reacting in different ways to aspects of the tasks that did not tax their memory; alternatively, some species may have been more disposed than others to pay attention to the relevant training stimuli. On the basis of the findings that were reviewed, therefore, it was impossible to accept or reject the null hypothesis.

There is, however, one study whose findings suggest that the short-term memory processes of two species of monkey are different (Platt et al., 1996). Tamarin and marmoset monkeys were trained in an open-field analog of an eight-arm radial maze, where they were allowed to visit four feeders before being prevented from visiting the remaining four until an interval varying between 5 minutes and 24 hours had elapsed. The proportion of correct choices that were made by the two groups after they were returned to the open field can be seen in Figure 14.2. It is evident that the marmosets were more accurate than the tamarins at identifying the correct locations when the retention interval was 5 minutes, but when it was 24 hours the performance of the tamarins was superior to that of the marmosets. This difference between the relative performances of the two groups at the two retention intervals makes it difficult to explain the results by appealing to contextual variables. For instance, if marmosets are able to perceive more readily than tamarins the relevant cues for solving the spatial problem, then the performance of the former group should have been better than the latter at both retention intervals. A similar prediction is made for many other contextual variables that might influence the outcome of the experiment. As an alternative explanation, Platt et al. (1996) noted that maromosets tend to revisit within the same day sources of food that renew rapidly, which presumably requires a good memory for recently visited locations.

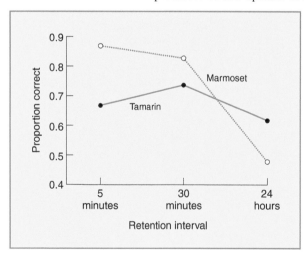

FIGURE 14.2 The mean proportion of correct choices in a test of spatial memory at varying retention intervals for two species of monkey (adapted from Platt et al., 1996).

On the other hand, tamarins return after days or weeks to places where food sources tend to renew rather slowly, which presumably depends on a durable rather than transient memory for where food has previously been found. Thus, because the availability of food with respect to the passage of time is different for these two species, they suggested evolution will result in marmosets being better at retaining information over short intervals than tamarins, but the opposite will be true for long intervals.

Navigation

One ability in which animals are bound to differ is navigation. Differences will arise because some animals engage in feats of navigation, such as migrating over vast distances that have no counterpart in other species. However, migration appears to be guided by innate mechanisms, and it is more questionable whether animals also differ in the types of spatial knowledge they acquire as a result of moving through an environment. The experiments reviewed in Chapter 11 revealed that there is rather little difference between a wide range of animals in this respect. Many animals are capable of navigating by means of dead reckoning, although the cues used to determine the direction and distance in which they have traveled will differ among species. A similarly wide range of species is also able to navigate with reference to a single landmark that is either beside the goal, or in a known position relative to the goal. When it comes to navigating by means of multiple landmarks, the important issue is whether animals can appreciate the geometric properties of the overall shape that is created. In Chapter 11 it was argued that there is no clear evidence to suggest that animals appreciate any but the simplest geometric relationship among landmarks. These observations together suggest that animals share relatively simple mechanisms for learning about the position of a goal and that in this respect the null hypothesis is correct. Of course, this conclusion might be premature and some animals may be capable of grasping more complex geometric relations among landmarks than other animals. We will have to wait and see.

Social learning

Animals differ in the degree to which they live in social groups, which, it has been argued, will result in some species possessing more sophisticated skills of social learning and social cognition than other species. Humphrey (1982, 1983) has proposed that as a result of living in groups, primates are likely to possess mental processes that allow them to interpret and manipulate the actions of other members of their group. If it could be shown that some species can develop a theory of mind, for example, then this finding would pose a serious challenge to the null hypothesis because such an ability is unlikely to be found in animals who lead solitary lives. However, as we saw in Chapter 12, the question of whether chimpanzees have a theory of mind is a matter of current dispute.

A likely candidate for revealing differences in social leaning among species is imitation. Results from "Do as I do" experiments strongly suggest that chimpanzees are capable of imitation, and results from investigations using the two-action control imply that quail, budgerigars, and marmosets are capable of imitation. Evidence of imitation with other species has proved more elusive. It has been claimed on several occasions that rats are capable of imitation, but close scrutiny reveals flaws with the experimental design which make this claim unjustified. There are also striking demonstrations of a failure to imitate by monkeys, even though they received training that was designed to encourage the observer to copy the actions of the demonstrator. Despite the necessary caveat about drawing conclusions from null results, future research may well reveal that some species are capable of imitation while others are not.

The representation of knowledge

Another, and perhaps more profound, way in which the intelligence of animals may differ is with the sort of knowledge they acquire. The discussion in Chapter 7 focused in some depth on the way in which animals are able to represent knowledge about relationships. In a matching to sample task, animals are required to select one of two comparison stimuli if it is the same as a sample stimulus. Although a wide range of species is able to solve this problem if repeated training is given with a restricted set of stimuli, differences begin to emerge when the transfer of this training to new stimuli is examined. We saw that transfer to new stimuli is poor with pigeons, whereas corvids, monkeys, and chimpanzees are much better in this respect. According to Premack (1983a,b), successful transfer of matching depends on subjects being able to appreciate the familiarity and novelty of the comparison stimuli in respect to the sample stimulus. Thus, either pigeons are less able than the other species to solve discriminations on the basis of familiarity and novelty, or they are very poor at transferring this strategy from one set of stimuli to a new set. In either case, research is beginning to suggest that there is a difference in the way some species solve matching to sample discriminations.

A further proposal of Premack (1983a,b) is that for a true appreciation of the relationship between two stimuli to develop, an animal must possess an abstract code. There are, however, very few demonstrations that suggest any vertebrate possesses such a code. The capacity of Sarah, a chimpanzee, to solve analogical reasoning problems is one such example. Another example is provided by Alex, a parrot. Recall that Alex might be presented with a red triangle and a red square and be asked "What's same?" or "What's different?". His ability to answer these questions correctly was difficult to explain, unless one accepts that Alex appreciated the relationships of sameness and difference. Thus experiments with Alex and Sarah suggest that at least two species are capable of using an abstract code to represent their knowledge. The lack of relevant research with other species means that it is not strictly justifiable to draw any conclusions about the generality of this skill, but on the basis of results considered in Chapter 7 my suspicion is that it will be shown by relatively few vertebrates and then only after special training.

Other types of knowledge that animals could differ in their capacity to represent are time, number, and serial order, which were considered in Chapter 10. There is, in fact, little reason at present for believing that vertebrates differ in their capacity to represent temporal information. And as far as the representation of numerical information is concerned, too few studies have been conducted to permit any firm conclusions to be drawn. Even so, it would be surprising to discover that all vertebrates can match the numerical abilities that have been claimed to be displayed by Sheba, a chimpanzee, and, again, Alex. A particularly strong indication of a difference between species is with the representation of serial order. The work of both Terrace and D'Amato implies that monkeys have much better-developed abilities than pigeons in this respect.

The final way in which vertebrates may differ in their representation of knowledge is revealed by their use of mirrors. The only species to have shown a capacity for self-recognition when they see their reflection are the great apes together with dolphins and elephants. Unfortunately, we know very little about the knowledge an animal must possess if it is to direct responses towards itself by means of a mirror. The suggestion by a number of authors that it is based on self-awareness is not particularly useful, because it is so difficult to verify.

Language

Only a few species have received language training, which means, yet again, that it is unreasonable to draw conclusions about the generality of the findings of this research to other vertebrates. Moreover, given the amount of time and effort that must be devoted to training an animal in the use of language, comparative studies on this topic are likely to be rare.

Conclusions

There are, then, occasions when the intellectual skills of one animal appear to differ from those of another but, as noted previously, this does not necessarily mean that we can reject the null hypothesis. Whenever one species fails on a test that is passed by another species, a proponent of the hypothesis can argue that the result is due to a failure of the experimenter rather than to the intelligence of the animal. Given such an argument, the null hypothesis becomes impossible to refute. Even so, if evidence that some species possess an intellectual skill that is absent in other species should continue to grow, then at the very least the plausibility of this hypothesis will be drawn into question. Perhaps as the comparative study of animal cognition develops, so too will demonstrations of animals differing in their intellectual abilities. If this should be the case, then despite the logical difficulty of refuting the null hypothesis it is likely to gain few adherents. On the other hand, if this research should reveal only small differences among the intellectual skills of different species, there will be good grounds for taking the hypothesis seriously.

INTELLIGENCE AND EVOLUTION

The final topic to be considered concerns an argument that leads to a conclusion that is diametrically opposite to that of the null hypothesis. That is, because of evolutionary pressures, different species will have rather little in common intellectually. During the course of evolution, the characteristics of a species will be changed according to the demands imposed on its members by the ecological niche they occupy. This niche can be identified by the relationship of the animal both with other organisms and with its physical environment. Because the problems that confront an animal differ markedly from one niche to another, it is understandable that species differ profoundly in their physical characteristics. Of course, it is not just physical characteristics that are influenced in this way; mental processes will also be modified as a result of evolutionary pressures.

One implication of this discussion is that animals occupying different niches will possess different mental processes (Shettleworth, 1998). For instance, a capacity to communicate about the location of food will be required only by those animals that need to forage for food cooperatively. We therefore should not expect to find this skill in more solitary animals. Alternatively, an ability to construct a cognitive map may be most likely in animals that forage over distances and must return to a specific location, such as a nest or hive.

A further implication is that even where animals have similar mental processes, evolutionary processes may result in them becoming specialized in some way. To avoid starving during the winter, Clark's nutcrackers must remember where they have stored a large number of pine seeds. Obviously the birds that are most likely to survive a winter are those with a large and accurate memory. It is therefore plausible that over successive generations there has been an improvement in the memory capacity of this species. Such an improvement would not be expected in species of birds for which the role played by memory in their survival is less critical.

Studies of learning provide a further indication of the way the characteristics of an ecological niche can influence a specific cognitive process. Many animals are capable of associative learning, but very often it is found that a particular species is able to learn more readily about some relationships than about others. Moreover, these relationships, such as that between illness and poison, are those that are most likely to occur naturally and are important to the animal's survival. The associative learning mechanisms could therefore be said to be biased in a way that facilitates the acquisition of knowledge that is most likely to be of importance to the animal. The way in which the white-crowned sparrow is restricted in its song learning provides a further example of the influence of evolution on the learning processes.

On the basis of the foregoing examples and discussion, the argument might be made that Macphail (1982, 1985) is wholly unjustified in proposing that all vertebrates other than humans are of equal intelligence, as they live in such a variety of environments. However, this criticism overlooks the fact that many niches have common characteristics that may be responsible for their occupants possessing similar mental processes (Dickinson, 1980; Revusky, 1977). This point is made in Chapter 1 with the example of Pavlovian conditioning. In many different environments a stimulus will signal the imminent occurrence of an event that is of significance to the animals that live in them. If these relationships can be learned

The capacity of communicate about the location of food might be found only in those animals that need to scavenge or forage for food cooperatively, such as the hyena. Solitary creatures will have little need for this communication skill.

about, then animals will be able to anticipate and prepare themselves for the events. Such a learning ability would be of as much value to insects as to chimpanzees, and we might expect a very wide range of animals to possess this ability. In addition, a number of authors argue convincingly that the laws governing associative learning in many animals are the same (Domjan, 1983; Roper, 1983). Hence, because they face a common problem of needing to predict what will happen to them, many species appear to possess a similar mechanism of associative learning. This argument does not only apply to associative learning; many other cognitive processes that would be of value to a wide range of species can be identified. We are thus in the position of anticipating, on the basis of evolutionary considerations, that animals will possess similar or different cognitive processes, or a mixture of both. Obviously this conclusion is of little help if we wish to draw conclusions about the distribution of different intellectual skills throughout the animal kingdom, as it is impossible to study the environment of an animal and then draw accurate conclusions about its intellectual processes. Instead, as we have seen, the way to understand the intelligence of animals is to experiment on them directly.

Before closing this discussion, some attention should be paid to our own species. Occasionally in this book, evidence is cited to suggest that the cognitive processes of humans and animals have much in common. As far as memory is concerned, the distinction between short- and long-term memory is valid for both humans and animals; and when the recall of a list is required, the primacy and recency effects that have been well established with humans can also be reliably shown in animals (see Chapter 10). Further evidence of a similarity in the intellectual processes of humans and animals may be found in the impressive concept-learning skills of animals, which appear to match at least some of those shown by humans. The attentional processes of humans and animals may also operate in fundamentally similar ways: For both it has proved useful to distinguish between two sorts of attention, which may be referred to as automatic and controlled (see Chapter 3). In studies of problem solving it is striking that both animals and humans can find it easier to choose between two members of a transitive series the more distantly they are related. Sarah's ability to reason analogically also hints at there being something in common in the way humans and animals solve problems. Finally, Premack's (1983a,b) suggestion that primates possess both a concrete and an abstract code for representing knowledge is a claim that has often been made about human cognition (e.g. Anderson, 1980).

How, then, do the cognitive processes of humans and animals differ? Language undoubtedly provides us with a tremendous intellectual advantage over our fellow creatures. I have also been struck by research, including my own (Pearce, 1987), which show that animals find it difficult to appreciate abstract relations and they may thus have, at best, a poorly developed capacity for abstract thought. Abstract thought is important because it might underlie our ability to use language (Anderson, 2005) and also serve as the foundation on which many of our other intellectual skills are based, including the development of a theory of mind.

Not everyone shares my pessimistic view that animals have a limited ability to engage in abstract thought; further research is needed before we have a full understanding of the degree to which animals possess this important ability. No doubt, as this research is conducted, and as additional research is directed at the many other unresolved issues raised in this book, we shall not only gain a deeper understanding of animal intelligence, we shall also learn more about the origins of human intelligence and the ways in which it is unique.

References

Able, K. P. (1980). Mechanisms of orientation, navigation, and homing. In S. A. Gauthreaux (Ed.), *Animal migration, orientation, and navigation* (pp. 284–373). New York: Academic Press.

Able, K. P. (1994). Magnetic orientation and magnetoreception in birds. *Progress in Neurobiology, 42*, 449–473.

Able, K. P. (1996). The debate over olfactory navigation by homing pigeons. *Journal of Experimental Biology, 199*, 121–124.

Adams, C. D., & Dickinson, A. (1981). Actions and habits: Variations in representations during instrumental learning. In N. E. Spear & R. R. Miller (Eds.), *Information processing in animals: Memory mechanisms* (pp. 143–165). Hillsdale, NJ: Lawrence Erlbaum Associates, Inc.

Addessi, E., & Visalberghi, E. (2001). Social facilitation of eating novel food in tufted capuchin monkeys (*Cebus apella*): Input provided by group members and responses affected in the observer. *Animal Cognition, 4*, 297–303.

Aggleton, J. P., & Brown, M. W. (1999). Episodic memory, amnesia, and the hippocampal–anterior thalamic axis. *Behavioral and Brain Sciences, 22*, 425–489.

Akins, C. K., & Zentall, T. R. (1996). Imitative learning in male Japanese quail (*Coturnix japonica*) using the two-action method. *Journal of Comparative Psychology, 110*, 316–320.

Akins, C. K., Klein, E. D., & Zentall, T. R. (2002). Imitative control in Japanese quail (*Coturnix japonica*) using the bidirectional control procedure. *Animal Learning and Behavior, 30*, 275–281.

Allison, J. (1989). The nature of reinforcement. In Mowrer, R. R. & Klein, S. B. (Eds.), *Contemporary learning theories: Instrumental conditioning theory and impact of biological constraints on learning* (pp. 13–39). Hillsdale, NJ: Lawrence Erlbaum Associates, Inc.

Allison, J., & Timberlake, W. (1974). Instrumental and contingent saccharine-licking in rats: Response deprivation and reinforcement. *Learning and Motivation, 5*, 231–247.

Amsel, A. (1958). The role of frustrative nonreward in noncontinuous reward situations. *Psychological Bulletin, 55*, 102–119.

Amsel, A. (1992). *Frustration theory*. Cambridge: Cambridge University Press.

Anderson, J. R. (1980). *Cognitive psychology and its implications*. San Francisco: Freeman.

Anderson, J. R. (1983). Response to mirror image stimulation and assessment of self-recognition in mirror- and peer-reared stumptail macaques. *Quarterly Journal of Experimental Psychology, 35B*, 201–212.

Anderson, J. R. (1984). The development of self-recognition: A review. *Developmental Psychobiology, 17*, 35–49.

Anderson, J. R. (1986). Mirror-mediated finding of hidden food by monkeys (*Macaca tonkeana* and *M. fascicularis*). *Journal of Comparative Psychology, 100*, 237–242.

Anderson, J. R. (2005). *Cognitive psychology and its implications* (6th edn). New York: Worth Publishers.

Anderson, J. R., & Gallup, G. G. (1997). Self recognition in Saguinus? A critical essay. *Animal Behaviour, 54*, 1563–1567.

Angermeier, W. F. (1984). *The evolution of operant learning and memory*. Basel: Karger.

Annau, Z., & Kamin, L. J. (1961). The conditioned emotional response as a function of intensity of the US. *Journal of Comparative and Physiological Psychology, 54*, 428–432.

Aschoff, J. (1955). Exogene und endogene Komponente der 24 Stunden-Periodik bei Tier und Mensche. *Naturwiss, 42*, 569–575.

Astley, S. L., & Wasserman, E. A. (1992). Categorical discrimination and generalization in pigeons: All negative stimuli are not created equal. *Journal of Experimental Psychology: Animal Behavior Processes, 18*, 193–207.

Atkinson, R. C., & Shiffrin, R. M. (1968). Human memory: A proposed system and its control processes. In K. W. Spence & J. T. Spence (Eds.), *The psychology of learning and motivation* (Vol. 2, pp. 89–195). New York: Academic Press.

Aust, U., & Huber, L. (2001). The role of item- and category-specific information in the discrimination of people versus nonpeople images by pigeons. *Animal Learning and Behavior, 29*, 107–119.

Aydin, A., & Pearce, J. M. (1994). Prototype effects in categorization by pigeons. *Journal of Experimental Psychology: Animal Behavior Processes, 20*, 264–277.

Azrin, N. H., Hutchinson, R. R., & Hake, D. F. (1966). Extinction-induced aggression. *Journal of the Experimental Analysis of Behavior, 9*, 191–204.

Babb, S. J., & Crystal, J. D. (2005). Discrimination of what, when and where: Implications for episodic-like memory in rats. *Learning and Motivation, 36*, 177–189.

Babb, S. J., & Crystal, J. D. (2006). Discrimination of what, when and where is not based on time of day. *Learning and Behavior, 34*, 124–130.

Baddeley, A. D. (1997). *Human memory: Theory and practice*. Hove, UK: Psychology Press.

Baddeley, A. D., & Hitch, G. (1974). Working memory. In G. H. Bower (Ed.), *The psychology of learning and motivation* (Vol. 8, pp. 47–90). New York: Academic Press.

Bailey, D. W., Gross, J. E., Laca, E. A., Rittenhouse, L. R., Coughenour, M. B., Swift, D. M., et al. (1996). Mechanisms that result in large herbivore grazing distribution patterns. *Journal of Range Management, 49*, 386–400.

Bailey, D. W., Rittenhouse, L. R., Hart, R. H., & Richards, R. W. (1989). Characteristics of spatial memory in cattle. *Applied Animal Behavior Sciences, 23*, 331–340.

Baker, A. G. (1974). Conditioned inhibition is not the symmetrical opposite of conditioned excitation: A test of the Rescorla–Wagner model. *Learning and Motivation, 5*, 369–379.

Baker, R. R. (1980). *The mystery of migration*. London: Macdonald Futura Books.

Baker, R. R. (1984). *Bird navigation: The solution of a mystery?* London: Hodder & Stoughton.

Balachandran, N. K., Dunn, W. L., & Rind, D. H. (1977). Concorde sonic booms as an atmospheric probe. *Science, 197*, 47–49.

Baldaccini, N., Benvenuti, S., Fiaschi, V., Ioale, P., & Papi, F. (1982). Pigeon orientation: Experiments on the role of olfactory stimuli perceived during the outward journey. In F. Papi & H. Wallraff (Eds.), *Avian navigation* (pp. 160–169). Berlin: Springer.

Balleine, B. (1992). Instrumental performance following a shift in primary motivation depends on incentive learning. *Journal of Experimental Psychology: Animal Behavior Processes, 18*, 236–250.

Balleine, B. W. (2001). Incentive processes in instrumental conditioning. In R. R. Mowrer & S. B. Klein (Eds.), *Handbook of contemporary learning theories* (pp. 307–366). Mahwah, NJ: Lawrence Erlbaum Associates, Inc.

Balleine, B. W., Garner, C., Gonzalez, F., & Dickinson, A. (1995). Motivational control of heterogenous instrumental chains. *Journal of Experimental Psychology: Animal Behavior Processes, 21*, 203–217.

Baptista, L. F., & Petrinovich, L. (1984). Social interaction, sensitive phases and the song template hypothesis in white-crowned sparrows. *Auk, 99*, 537–547.

Baptista, L. F., & Petrinovich, L. (1986). Song development in the white-crowned sparrow: Social factors and sex differences. *Animal Behaviour, 32*, 172–181.

Barnett, S. A. (1958). Experiments on "neophobia" in wild and laboratory rats. *British Journal of Psychology, 49*, 195–201.

Barnett, S. A. (1970). *Instinct and intelligence*. Harmondsworth, UK: Penguin.

Basil, J. A., Kamil, A. C., Balda, R. P., & Fite, K. V. (1996). Differences in hippocampal volume among food storing corvids. *Brain Behavior and Evolution, 47*, 156–164.

Bastian, J. (1961). *Proceedings of the symposium on bionic models of animal sonar systems*. Italy: Frascati.

Batson, J. D., & Best, M. R. (1981). Single-element assessment of conditioned inhibition. *Bulletin of the Psychonomic Society, 18*, 328–330.

Baum, M. (1966). Rapid extinction of an avoidance response following a period of response prevention in the avoidance apparatus. *Psychological Reports, 18*, 59–64.

Baum, W. M. (1973). The correlation based law of effect. *Journal of the Experimental Analysis of Behavior, 20*, 137–153.

Beatty, W. W., & Shavalia, D. A. (1980a). Rat spatial memory: Resistance to retroactive interference at long retention intervals. *Animal Learning and Behavior, 8*, 550–552.

Beatty, W. W., & Shavalia, D. A. (1980b). Spatial memory in rats: time course of working memory and effect of anaesthetics. *Behavioral and Neural Biology, 28*, 454–462.

Benhamou, S. (1996). No evidence of cognitive mapping in rats. *Animal Behaviour, 52*, 201–212.

Bennett, A. T. (1996). Do animals have cognitive maps? *Journal of Experimental Biology, 199*, 219–224.

Bennett, C. H., Maldonado, A., & Mackintosh, N. J. (1995). Learned irrelevance is not the sum of exposure to CS and US. *Quarterly Journal of Experimental Psychology, 48B*, 117–128.

Berthold, P. (1978). Concept of endogenous control of migration in warblers. In K. Schmidt-Koenig & W. T. Keeton (Eds.), *Animal migration, navigation, and homing* (pp. 275–282). Berlin: Springer-Verlag.

Berthold, P. (1998). Spatiotemporal aspects of avian long-distance migration. In S. Healy (Ed.), *Spatial representation in animals* (pp. 103–118). Oxford: Oxford University Press.

Best, M. R., & Gemberling, G. A. (1977). Role of short-term processes in the conditioned stimulus preexposure effect and the delay of reinforcement gradient in long-delay taste-aversion learning. *Journal of Experimental Psychology: Animal Behavior Processes, 3*, 253–263.

Best, M. R., Dunn, D. P., Batson, J. D., Meachum, C. I., & Nash, S. M. (1985). Extinguishing conditioned inhibition in flavour-aversion learning: Effects of repeated testing and extinction of the excitatory element. *Quarterly Journal of Experimental Psychology, 37B*, 359–378.

Bhatt, R. S., Wasserman, E. A., Reynolds, W. F., & Knauss, K. S. (1988). Conceptual behavior in pigeons: Categorization of both familiar and novel examples from four classes of natural and artificial stimuli. *Journal of Experimental Psychology: Animal Behavior Processes, 14*, 219–234.

Biegler, R., & Morris, R. G. M. (1999). Blocking in the spatial domain with arrays of discrete landmarks. *Journal of Experimental Psychology: Animal Behavior Processes, 25*, 341–351.

Bingman, V. (1998). Spatial representations and homing pigeon navigation. In S. Healy (Ed.), *Spatial representation in animals* (pp. 69–85). Oxford: Oxford University Press.

Birch, H. G. (1945). The relation of previous experience to insightful problem solving. *Journal of Comparative Psychology, 38*, 367–383.

Bird, L. R., Roberts, W. A., Abroms, B., Kit, K. A., & Crupi, C. (2003). Spatial memory for food hidden by rats (*Rattus norvegicus*) on the radial maze: Studies of memory for where, what and when. *Journal of Comparative Psychology, 117*, 176–187.

Biro, D., Meade, J., & Guilford, T. (2004). Familiar route loyalty implies visual pilotage in the homing pigeon. *Proceedings of the National Academy of Sciences, 101*, 17440–17443.

Bitterman, J. E. (1984). Learning in man and other animals. In V. Sarris & A. Parducci (Eds.), *Perspectives in psychological experimentation* (pp. 59–70). Hillsdale, NJ: Lawrence Erlbaum Associates, Inc.

Bitterman, M. E. (1965). The evolution of intelligence. *Scientific American, 212*, 92–100.

Bitterman, M. E. (1975). The comparative analysis of learning. *Science, 188*, 699–709.

Bitterman, M. E. (2000). Cognitive evolution: a psychological perspective. In C. Heyes & L. Huber (Eds.), *The evolution of cognition* (pp. 61–79). Cambridge, MA: MIT Press.

Bitterman, M. E., Menzel, R., Fietz, A., & Schafer, S. (1983). Classical conditioning of proboscis extension in honeybees (*Apis mellifera*). *Journal of Comparative Psychology, 97*, 107–119.

Bliss, T., Collingridge, G., & Morris, R. (2003). Introduction. *Philosophical Transactions of the Royal Society of London, B, 358*, 607–611.

Bloom, P. (2004). Can a dog learn a word? *Science, 304*, 1605–1606.

Blough, D. S. (1975). Steady state data and a quantitative model of operant generalization and discrimination. *Journal of Experimental Psychology: Animal Behavior Processes, 1*, 3–21.

Boakes, R. A. (1973). Response decrements produced by extinction and by response-independent reinforcements. *Journal of the Experimental Analysis of Behavaior, 19*, 293–302.

Boakes, R. A. (1984). *From Darwin to behaviorism*. Cambridge: Cambridge University Press.

Boakes, R. A., & Gaertner, I. (1977). The development of a simple form of communication. *Quarterly Journal of Experimental Psychology, 29*, 561–575.

Boakes, R. A., Poli, M., Lockwood, M. J., & Goodall, G. (1978). A study of misbehavior: Token reinforcement in the rat. *Journal of the Experimental Analysis of Behavior, 29*, 115–134.

Boe, E. E., & Church, R. M. (1967). Permanent effects of punishment during extinction. *Journal of Comparative and Physiological Psychology, 63*, 486–492.

Boesch, C. (1991). Teaching among wild primates. *Animal Behaviour, 41*, 530–532.

Boinski, S., & Fragaszy, D. M. (1989). The ontogeny of foraging in squirrel monkeys. *Animal Behaviour, 37*, 415–428.

Bolles, R. C. (1971). Species-specific defense reactions. In F. R. Brush (Ed.), *Aversive conditioning and learning* (pp. 183–233). New York: Academic Press.

Bolles, R. C. (1972). Reinforcement, expectancy and learning. *Psychological Review, 79*, 394–401.

Bolles, R. C. (1975). *Theory of motivation* (2nd ed). New York: Harper & Row.

Bolles, R. C., & de Lorge, J. (1962). The rat's adjustment to a diurnal feeding cycle. *Journal of Comparative and Physiological Psychology, 55*, 760–762.

Bolles, R. C., & Moot, S. A. (1973). The rat's anticipation of two meals a day. *Journal of Comparative and Physiological Psychology, 83*, 510–514.

Bolles, R. C., & Stokes, L. W. (1965). Rat's anticipation of diurnal and a-diurnal feeding. *Journal of Comparative and Physiological Psychology, 60*, 290–294.

Bond, A. B. (1983). Visual search and selection of natural stimuli in the pigeon: The attention threshold hypothesis. *Journal of Experimental Psychology: Animal Behavior Processes, 9*, 292–306.

Bonner, J. T. (1980). *The evolution of culture in animals*. Princeton, NJ: Princeton University Press.

Bookman, M. A. (1977). Sensitivity of the homing pigeon to an Earth-strength magnetic field. *Nature, 267*, 340–342.

Bouton, M. E. (1993). Context, time, and memory retrieval in the interference paradigms of Pavlovian learning. *Psychological Bulletin, 114*, 80–99.

Bouton, M. E. (2004). Context and behavioral processes in extinction. *Learning and Memory, 11*, 485–494.

Bouton, M. E., & Moody, E. W. (2004). Memory processes in classical conditioning. *Neuroscience and Behavioral Reviews, 28*, 663–674.

Bouton, M. E., & Peck, C. A. (1989). Context effects on conditioning, extinction, and reinstatement in an appetitive conditioning preparation. *Animal Learning and Behavior, 17*, 188–198.

Bouton, M. E., & Ricker, S. T. (1994). Renewal of extinguished responding in a second context. *Animal Learning and Behavior, 22*, 317–324.

Boysen, S. T., & Berntson, G. G. (1989). The development of numerical competence in the chimpanzee (*Pan troglodytes*). *Journal of Comparative Psychology, 103*, 23–31.

Brakke, K. E., & Savage-Rumbaugh, E. S. (1995). The development of language skills in bonobo and chimpanzee–I. Comprehension. *Language and communication, 15*, 121–148.

Brandon, S. E., & Bitterman, J. E. (1979). Analysis of autoshaping in goldfish. *Animal Learning and Behavior, 7*, 57–62.

Brandon, S. E., & Wagner, A. R. (1998). Occasion setting: Influences of conditional emotional responses and configural cues. In N. A. Schmajuk & P. C. Holland (Eds.), *Occasion setting: Associative learning and cognition in animals* (pp. 343–382). Washington, DC: American Psychological Association.

Brandon, S. E., Vogel, E. H., & Wagner, A. R. (2000). A componential view of configural cues in generalization and discrimination in Pavlovian conditioning. *Behavioral Brain Research, 110*, 67–72.

Brannon, E. M., & Terrace, H. S. (2000). Representation of numerosities 1–9 by rhesus macaques (*Macaca mulatta*). *Journal of Experimental Psychology: Animal Behavior Processes, 26*, 31–49.

Brannon, E. M., Cantlon, J. F., & Terrace, H. S. (2006). The role of reference points in ordinal numerical comparisons by rhesus macaques (*Macaca mulatta*). *Journal of Experimental Psychology: Animal Behavior Processes, 32*, 120–134.

Breland, K., & Breland, M. (1961). The misbehavior of organisms. *American Psychologist, 16*, 661–664.

Breukelaar, J. W. C., & Dalrymple-Alford, J. C. (1998). Timing ability and numerical competence in rats. *Journal of Experimental Psychology: Animal Behavior Processes, 24*, 84–97.

Bright, M. (1984). *Animal communication*. London: British Broadcasting Coporation.

Brooks, J. O., & Watkins, M. J. (1990). Further evidence of the intricacy of memory span. *Journal of Experimental Psychology: Learning, Memory, and Cognition, 16*, 1134–1141.

Brown, I. D., & Poulton, E. C. (1961). Measuring the spare "mental capacity" of drivers by a subsidiary task. *Ergonomics, 3*, 35–40.

Brown, J. L. (1964). The integration of agonistic behavior in Stellar's jay *Cyanocitta stelleri*. *University of California Publications in Psychology, 60*, 223–328.

Brown, M. F., & Demas, G. E. (1994). Evidence for spatial working memory in honeybees (*Apis mellifera*). *Journal of Comparative Psychology, 108*, 344–352.

Browne, M. P. (1976). The role of primary reinforcement and overt movements in autoshaping in the pigeon. *Animal Learning and Behavior, 4*, 287–292.

Bryant, P. E., & Trabasso, T. (1971). Transitive inference and memory in young children. *Nature, 232*, 456–458.

Buffon, G. L. C., Comte de, (1818). *Oeuvres completes de Buffon*. Paris: Rapet.

Bullard, J., & Bullard, M. (2000). *Inside Stalin's Russia: The diaries of Reader Bullard 1930–1934*. Oxfordshire: Day Books.

Burdick, C. K., & Miller, J. D. (1975). Speech perception by the chinchilla: Discrimination of sustained /a/ and /i/. *Journal of the Acoustical Society of America, 58*, 415–427.

Byrne, R., & Whiten, A. (1985). Tactical deception of familiar individuals in baboons (*Papio ursinus*). *Animal Behaviour, 33*, 669–673.

Byrne, R., & Whiten, A. (1987). A thinking primate's guide to deception. *New Scientist, 3 December*, 54–57.

Call, J., Carpenter, M., & Tomasello, M. (2005). Copying results and copying actions in the process of social learning: chimpanzee (*Pan troglodytes*) and human children (*Homo sapiens*). *Animal Cognition, 8*, 151–163.

Capaldi, E. D., Myers, D. E., Campbell, D. H., & Sheffer, J. D. (1983). Conditioned flavor preferences based on hunger level during original flavor exposure. *Animal Learning and Behavior, 11*, 107–115.

Capaldi, E. J. (1966). Partial reinforcement: A hypothesis of sequential effects. *Psychological Review, 73*, 459–477.

Capaldi, E. J. (1993). Animal number abilities: Implications for a hierarchical approach to instrumental learning. In S. J. Boysen & E. J. Capaldi (Eds.) *The development of numerical competence: Animal and human models* (pp. 191–209). Hillsdale, NJ: Lawrence Erlbaum Associates, Inc.

Capaldi, E. J. (1994). The sequential view: From rapidly fading stimulus traces to the organization of memory and the abstract concept of number. *Psychonomic Bulletin and Review, 1*, 156–181.

Capaldi, E. J., & Miller, D. J. (1988). Counting in rats: Its functional significance and the independent cognitive processes that constitute it. *Journal of Experimental Psychology: Animal Behavior Processes, 14*, 3–17.

Capaldi, E. J., Hovancik, J. R., & Lamb, E. O. (1975). The effects of strong irrelevant thirst on food-rewarded instrumental performance. *Animal Learning and Behavior, 3*, 172–178.

Carew, T. J., Hawkins, R. D., & Kandel, E. R. (1983). Differential classical conditioning of a defensive withdrawal reflex in *Aplysia californica*. *Science, 219*, 397–400.

Carew, T. J., Pinsker, H., & Kandel, E. R. (1972). Long-term habituation of a defensive withdrawal reflex in *Aplysia*. *Science, 175*, 451–454.

Carman, G. J., Walker, M. M., & Lee, A. K. (1987). Attempts to demonstrate magnetic discrimination by homing pigeons in flight. *Animal Learning and Behavior, 15*, 124–129.

Caro, T. M., & Hauser, M. D. (1992). Is there teaching in nonhuman animals? *The Quarterly Review of Biology, 67*, 151–174.

Carrington, R. (1958). *Elephants*. London: Chatto and Windus.

Cartwright, B. A., & Collett, T. S. (1983). Landmark learning in bees: Experiments and models. *Journal of Comparative Physiology A, 151*, 521–543.

Castro, C. A., & Larsen, T. (1992). Primacy and recency effects in nonhuman primates. *Journal of Experimental Psychology: Animal Behavior Processes, 18*, 335–340.

Catania, A. C., & Laties, V. G. (1999). Pavlov and Skinner: Two lives in science (An introduction to B. F. Skinner's "Some responses to the stimulus 'Pavlov' "). *Journal of the Experimental Analysis of Behavaior, 72*, 455–461.

Cerella, J. (1979). Visual classes and natural categories in the pigeon. *Journal of Experimental Psychology: Human Perception and Performance, 5*, 68–77.

Cerella, J. (1980). The pigeon's analysis of pictures. *Pattern Recognition, 12*, 1–6.

Cerella, J. (1982). Mechanisms of concept formation in the pigeon. In D. J. Ingle, M. A. Goodale, & R. J. W. Mansfield (Eds.), *Analysis of visual behaviour*, pp. 241–262. Cambridge, Mass.: M.I.T. Press.

Cerella, J. (1986). Pigeons and perceptrons. *Pattern Recognition, 19*, 431–438.

Chapuis, N., & Scardigli, P. (1993). Shortcut ability in hamsters (*Mesocricetus auratus*): The role of environmental and kinaesthetic information. *Animal Learning and Behavior, 21*, 255–265.

Chase, A. R. (2001). Music discrimination by carp (*Cyprinus carpio*). *Animal Learning and Behavior, 29*, 336–353.

Chen, S., Swartz, K. B., & Terrace, H. S. (1997). Knowledge of the ordinal position of list items in rhesus monkeys. *Psychological Science, 8*, 80–86.

Cheney, D. L., & Seyfarth, R. M. (1988). Assessment of meaning and the detection of unreliable signals by vervet monkeys. *Animal Behaviour, 36*, 477–486.

Cheney, D. L., & Seyfarth, R. M. (1990). *How monkeys see the world*. Chicago: University of Chicago Press.

Cheng, K. (1986). A purely geometric module in the rat's spatial representation. *Cognition, 23*, 149–178.

Cheng, K. (1994). The determination of direction in landmark-based spatial search in pigeons: A further test of the vector sum model. *Animal Learning and Behavior, 22*, 291–301.

Cheng, K., & Gallistel, C. R. (2005). Shape parameters explain data from spatial transformations: Comment on Pearce et al. (2004) and Tommasi & Polli (2004). *Journal of Experimental Psychology: Animal Behavior Processes, 31*, 254–259.

Cherry-Garrard, A. (2003). *The worst journey in the world*. London: Pimlico.

Chomsky, N. (1957). *Syntactic structures*. The Hague: Mouton.

Chomsky, N. (1972). *Language and mind* (enlarged edn). New York: Harcourt Brace Jovanovich.

Church, R. M. (1978). The internal clock. In S. H. Hulse, H. Fowler & W. K. Honig (Eds.), *Cognitive processes in animal behavior* (pp.277–310). Hillsdale, NJ: Lawrence Erlbaum Associates, Inc.

Church, R. M. (1984). Properties of the internal clock. In J. Gibbon & L. Allan (Eds.), *Timing and time perception* (pp. 566–582). New York: New York Academy of Sciences.

Church, R. M. (1989). Theories of timing behavior. In Mowrer, R. R. & Klein, S. B. (Eds.), *Contemporary learning theories: Instrumental conditioning theory and impact of biological constraints on learning* (pp. 41–71). Hillsdale, NJ: Lawrence Erlbaum Associates, Inc.

Church, R. M., & Broadbent, H. A. (1990). Alternative representations of time, number, and rate. *Cognition, 37*, 55–81.

Church, R. M., & Broadbent, H. A. (1991). A connectionist model of timing. In M. L. Commons, S. Grossberg & J. E. R. Staddon (Eds.), *Neural network models of conditioning and action* (pp. 225–240). Hillsdale, NJ: Lawrence Erlbaum Associates, Inc.

Church, R. M., & Gibbon, J. (1982). Temporal generalization. *Journal of Experimental Psychology: Animal Behavior Processes, 8*, 165–186.

Clark, F. C. (1958). The effect of deprivation and frequency of reinforcement on variable-interval responding. *Journal of the Experimental Analysis of Behavior, 1*, 221–227.

Clayton, N. S., & Dickinson, A. (1998). Episodic-like memory during cache recovery by scrub jays. *Nature, 395*, 272–274.

Clayton, N. S., & Dickinson, A. (1999). Scrub jays (*Aphelocoma coerulescens*) remember the relative time of caching as well as the location and content of their caches. *Journal of Comparative Psychology, 113*, 403–416.

Clayton, N., & Dickinson, A. (2006). Rational rats. *Nature Neuroscience, 9*, 472–474.

Cohen, J. S., Drummond, C., & Terrrelonge, N. (2001). Value transfer in simultaneous object discrimination by rats. *Animal Learning and Behavior, 29*, 326–335.

Collett, M., Collett, T. S., & Wehner, R. (1999). Calibration of vector navigation in desert ants. *Current Biology, 9*, 1031–1034.

Collett, T. S., Cartwright, B. A., & Smith, B. A. (1986). Landmark learning and visuo-spatial memories in gerbils. *Journal of Comparative Physiology A, 158*, 835–851.

Colombo, M., Cottle, A., & Frost, N. (2003). Degree of representation of the matching concept in pigeons (*Columba livia*). *Journal of Comparative Psychology, 117*, 246–256.

Colwill, R. M., & Motzkin, D. K. (1994). Encoding of the unconditioned stimulus in Pavlovian conditioning. *Animal Learning and Behavior, 22*, 384–394.

Colwill, R. M., & Rescorla, R. A. (1985). Instrumental responding remains sensitive to reinforcer devaluation after extensive training. *Journal of Experimental Psychology: Animal Behavior Processes, 11*, 520–536.

Colwill, R. M., & Rescorla, R. A. (1988). Associations between the discriminative stimulus and the reinforcer in instrumental learning. *Journal of Experimental Psychology: Animal Behavior Processes, 14*, 155–164.

Cook, M., & Mineka, S. (1990). Selective associations in the observational conditioning of fear in rhesus monkeys. *Journal of Experimental Psychology: Animal Behavior Processes, 16*, 372–389.

Cook, R. G., Brown, M. F., & Riley, D. A. (1985). Flexible memory processing by rats: Use of prospective and retrospective information in the radial maze. *Journal of Experimental Psychology: Animal Behavior Processes, 11*, 453–469.

Cook, R. G., Katz, J. S., & Cavoto, B. R. (1997). Pigeon same–different concept learning with multiple stimulus classes. *Journal of Experimental Psychology: Animal Behavior Processes, 23*, 417–433.

Cook, R. G., Levison, D. G., Gillett, S. R., & Blaisdell, A. P. (2005). Capacity and limits of associative memory in pigeons. *Psychonomic Bulletin and Review, 12*, 350–358.

Cotton, J. W. (1953). Running time as a function of food deprivation. *Journal of Experimental Psychology, 46*, 188–198.

Cotton, M. M., Goodall, G., & Mackintosh, N. J. (1982). Inhibitory conditioning resulting from a reduction in the magnitude of reinforcement. *Quarterly Journal of Experimental Psychology, 34B*, 163–181.

Cowey, A., & Stoerig, P. (1995). Blindsight in monkeys. *Nature, 373*, 247–249.

Cox, J. K., & D'Amato, M. R. (1982). Matching to compound samples by monkeys (*Cebus apella*): Shared attention or generalization decrement. *Journal of Experimental Psychology: Animal Behavior Processes, 8*, 209–225.

Crowell, C., Hinson, R., & Siegel, S. (1981). The role of conditional drug responses in tolerance to the hypothermic effects of ethanol. *Psychopharmacologia, 73*, 51–54.

Curio, E. (1988). Cultural transimission of enemy recognition by birds. In T. R. Zentall, & B. G. Galef, Jr. (Eds.), *Social learning psychological and biological perspectives* (pp.75–98). Hillsdale, NJ: Lawrence Erlbaum Associates, Inc.

Custance, D. M., Whiten, A., & Bard, K. A. (1995). Can young chimpanzees imitate arbitrary actions? Hayes and Hayes (1952) revisited. *Behaviour, 132*, 839–858.

Dally, J. M., Emery, N. J., & Clayton, N. S. (2006). Food-caching western scrub-jays keep track of who was watching when. *Science, 312*, 1662–1665.

D'Amato, M. R. (1973). Delayed matching and short-term memory in monkeys. In G. H. Bower (Ed.), *The psychology of learning and motivation* (Vol. 7, pp. 227–269). New York: Academic Press.

D'Amato, M. R. (1991). Comparative cognition: Processing of serial order and serial pattern. In L. Dachowski & Flaherty, C.F. (Eds.), *Current issues in animal learning: Brain, emotion and cognition* (pp. 165–185). Hillsdale, NJ: Lawrence Erlbaum Associates, Inc.

D'Amato, M. R., & Buckiewicz, J. (1980). Long delay, one-trial conditioned preference and retention in monkeys (*Cebus apella*). *Animal Learning and Behavior, 8*, 359–362.

D'Amato, M. R., & Colombo, M. (1988). Representation of serial order in monkeys. *Journal of Experimental Psychology: Animal Behavior Processes, 14*, 131–139.

D'Amato, M. R., & O'Neill, W. (1971). Effect of delay-interval illumination on matching behavior in the capuchin monkey. *Journal of the Experimental Analysis of Behavaior, 15*, 327–333.

D'Amato, M. R., & Van Sant, P. (1988). The person concept in monkeys (*Cebus apella*). *Journal of Experimental Psychology: Animal Behavior Processes, 14*, 43–55.

D'Amato, M. R., & Worsham, R. W. (1972). Delayed matching in the capuchin monkey with brief sample durations. *Learning and Motivation, 3*, 304–312.

D'Amato, M. R., Safarjan, W. R., & Salmon, D. (1981). Long-delay conditioning and instrumental learning: Some new findings. In N. E. Spear & R. R. Miller (Eds.), *Information processing in animals: Memory mechanisms* (pp. 113–142). Hillsdale, NJ: Lawrence Erlbaum Associates, Inc.

Darwin, C. R. (1859). *On the origin of species by natural selection*. London: Murray.

Darwin, C. R. (1871). *The descent of man and selection in relation to sex*. London: Murray.

Darwin, C. (1872). *The expression of emotions in man and animal*. London: John Murray.

Davey, G. (1989). *Ecological learning theory*. London: Routledge.

Davey, G. C. L. (1995). Preparedness and phobias: Specific evolved associations or a generalized expectancy bias? *Behavioral and Brain Sciences, 18*, 289–325.

Davis, H., & Perusse, R. (1988). Numerical competence in animals: Definitional issues, current evidence and a new research agenda. *Behavioral and Brain Sciences, 11*, 566–574.

Dawkins, M. (1971a). Perceptual changes in chicks: Another look at the "search image" concept. *Animal Behaviour, 19*, 566–574.

Dawkins, M. (1971b). Shifts of "attention" in chicks during feeding. *Animal Behaviour, 19*, 575–582.

Dawson, B. V., & Foss, B. M. (1965). Observational learning in budgerigars. *Animal Behaviour, 13*, 470–474.

de Kort, S. D., Dickinson, A., & Clayton, N. S. (2005). Retrospective cognition by food-caching western scrub-jays. *Learning and Motivation, 36*, 159–176.

Delamater, A. (1996). Effects of several extinction treatments upon the integrity of Pavlovian stimulus–outcome associations. *Animal Learning and Behavior, 24*, 437–449.

Delamater, A. (1998). Associative and mediational processes in the acquired distinctiveness and equivalence of cues. *Journal of Experimental Psychology: Animal Behavior Processes, 24*, 467–482.

Delamater, A. R. (2004). Experimental extinction in Pavlovian conditioning: Behavioural and neuroscience perspectives. *Quarterly Journal of Experimental Psychology, 57B*, 97–132.

Delius, J. D., & Emmerton, J. (1978). Sensory mechanisms related to homing in pigeons. In K. Schmidt-Koening & W. T. Keeton (Eds.), *Animal migration, navigation, and homing* (pp. 35–41). Berlin: Springer.

Denny, M. R., Clos, C. F., & Bell, R. C. (1988). Learning in the rat of a choice response by observation of S–S contingencies. In T. R. Zentall, & B. G. Galef, Jr. (Eds.), *Social learning, psychological and biological perspectives* (pp. 207–223). Hillsdale, NJ: Lawrence Erlbaum Associates, Inc.

Deweer, B., Sara, S. J., & Hars, B. (1980). Contextual cues and memory retrieval in rats: Alleviation of forgetting by a pretest exposure to background stimuli. *Animal Learning and Behavior, 8*, 265–272.

Dias, R., Robbins, T. W., & Roberts, A. C. (1996). Dissociations of affective and attentional shifting by selective lesions of prefrontal cortex. *Nature, 380*, 69–72.

Dickinson, A. (1977). Appetitive–aversive interactions: Superconditioning of fear by an appetitive CS. *Quarterly Journal of Experimental Psychology, 29*, 71–83.

Dickinson, A. (1980). *Contemporary animal learning theory*. Cambridge: Cambridge University Press.

Dickinson, A. (1994). Instrumental conditioning. In N. J. Mackintosh (Ed.), *Animal learning and cognition* (pp. 45–79). San Diego, CA: Academic Press.

Dickinson, A., & Balleine, B. (1994). Motivational control of goal-directed action. *Animal Learning and Behavior, 22*, 1–18.

Dickinson, A., & Charnock, D. J. (1985). Contingency effects with maintained instrumental reinforcement. *Quarterly Journal of Experimental Psychology, 37B*, 397–416.

Dickinson, A., & Mackintosh, N. J. (1979). Reinforcer specificity in enhancement of conditioning by posttrial surprise. *Journal of Experimental Psychology: Animal Behavior Processes, 5*, 162–177.

Dickinson, A., & Pearce, J. M. (1977). Inhibitory interactions between appetitive and aversive stimuli. *Psychological Bulletin, 84*, 690–711.

Dickinson, A., Hall, G., & Mackintosh, N. J. (1976). Surprise and the attenuation of blocking. *Journal of Experimental Psychology: Animal Behavior Processes, 2*, 313–322.

Dickinson, A., Watt, A., & Griffiths, W. J. H. (1992). Free-operant acquisition with delayed reinforcement. *Quarterly Journal of Experimental Psychology, 45B*, 241–258.

Diez-Chamizo, V., Sterio, D., & Mackintosh, N. J. (1985). Blocking and overshadowing between intra-maze and extra-maze cues: A test of the independence of locale and guidance learning. *Quarterly Journal of Experimental Psychology, 37B*, 235–253.

Dimattia, B. V., & Kesner, R. P. (1984). Serial position curves in rats: Automatic versus effortful information processing. *Journal of Experimental Psychology: Animal Behavior Processes, 10*, 557–563.

Domjan, M. (1983). Biological constraints on instrumental and classical conditioning: Implications for general process theory. *The Psychology of Learning and Motivation, 17*, 215–277.

Domjan, M. (1998). *The principles of learning and behavior.* Pacific Grove, CA: Brooks/Cole.

Dorrance, B. R., & Zentall, T. R. (1999). Within-event learning contributes to value transfer in simultaneous instrumental discriminations in pigeons. *Animal Learning and Behavior, 27*, 206–210.

Dowsett-Lemaire, F. (1979). The imitative range of the song of the marsh warbler, *Acrocephalus palustris*, with special reference to imitations of African birds. *Ibis, 121*, 453–468.

Duchin, L. E. (1990). The evolution of speech: comparative anatomy of the oral cavity in (*Pan*) and (*Homo*). *Journal of Human Evolution, 19*, 687–697.

Dugatkin, L. A. (1992). Sexual selection and imitation: Females copy the mate choices of others. *American Naturalist, 139*, 1384–1389.

Dugatkin, L. A., & Godin, J. G. J. (1992). Reversal of female mate choice by copying. *Proceedings of the Royal Society of London B, 249*, 179–184.

Dugatkin, L. A., & Godin, J. G. J. (1993). Female mate copying in the guppy, (*Poecilia reticulata*): Age dependent effects. *Behavioral Ecology, 4*, 289–292.

Duncan, C. P. (1949). The retroactive effect of electroshock on learning. *Journal of Comparative and Physiological Psychology, 42*, 32–44.

Duvarci, S., & Nader, K. (2004). Characterization of fear memory reconsolidation. *Journal of Neuroscience, 24*, 9269–9275.

Dwyer, D. M., Bennett, C. H., & Mackintosh, N. J. (2001). Evidence for inhibitory associations between the unique elements of two compound flavours. *Quarterly Journal of Experimental Psychology, 54B*, 97–107.

Dyer, F. C. (1991). Bees acquire route-based memories but not cognitive maps in a familiar landscape. *Animal Behaviour, 41*, 239–246.

Elliott, M. H. (1928). The effect of change of reward on the maze performance of rats. *University of California Publications in Psychology, 4*, 19–30.

Emery, N. J., & Clayton, N. S. (2001). Effects of experience and social context on prospective caching strategies by scrub jays. *Nature, 414*, 443–446.

Emery, N. J., & Clayton, N. S. (2004). Comparing the complex cognition of birds and primates. In L. J. Rogers & G. Kaplan (Eds.), *Comparative vertebrate cognition: Are primates superior to non-primates?* (pp. 3–55). New York: Kluwer Academic/Plenum Publishers.

Emlen, S. T. (1970). Celestial rotation: Its importance in the development of migratory orientation. *Science, 170*, 1198–1201.

Epstein, R., Kirshnit, C. E., Lanza, R. P., & Rubin, L. C. (1984). "Insight" in the pigeon: Antecedents and determinants of an intelligent performance. *Nature, 308*, 61–62.

Epstein, R., Lanza, R. P., & Skinner, B. F. (1980). Symbolic communication between two pigeons (*Columba livia domestica*). *Science, 207*, 543–545.

Epstein, R., Lanza, R. P., & Skinner, B. F. (1981). "Self-awareness" in the pigeon. *Science, 212*, 695–696.

Esber, G. R., McGregor, A., Good, M. A., Hayward, A., & Pearce, J. M. (2005). Transfer of spatial behaviour controlled by a landmark array with a distinctive shape. *Quarterly Journal of Experimental Psychology, 58B*, 69–91.

Estes, W. K. (1969). New perspectives on some old issues in association theory. In N. J. Mackintosh & W. K. Honig (Eds.), *Fundamental issues in associative learning* (pp.162–189). Halifax, Canada: Dalhousie University Press.

Etienne, A. S., Lambert, S. J., Reverdin, B., & Teroni, E. (1993). Learning to recalibrate the role of dead reckoning and visual cues in spatial navigation. *Animal Learning and Behavior, 21*, 266–280.

Fanselow, M. S. (1990). Factors governing one-trial contextual conditioning. *Animal Learning and Behavior, 18*, 264–270.

Farah, M. J. (1985). Psychophysical evidence for a shared representational medium for mental images and percepts. *Journal of Experimental Psychology: General, 114*, 91–103.

Finke, R. A. (1980). Levels of equivalence in imagery and perception. *Psychological Review, 87*, 113–132.

Fiorito, G., & Scotto, P. (1992). Observational learning in *Octopus vulgaris. Nature, 256*, 347–357.

Fisher, J., & Hinde, R. A. (1949). The opening of milk bottles by birds. *British Birds, 42*, 347–357.

Fouts, R. (1997). *Next of kin.* New York: William Morrow.

Fouts, R. S. (1975). In R. H. Turtle (Ed.), *Society and psychology of primates.* The Hague: Mouton.

Fouts, R. S., & Fouts, D. H. (1989). Loulis in conversation with cross-fostered chimpanzees. In R. G. Gardner, B. T. Gardner & T. E. Van Canfort (Eds.), *Teaching sign *language to chimpanzees* (pp. 293–307). New York: State University of New York Press.

Fouts, R. S., Fouts, D. H., & Van Cantforth, T. E. (1989). The infant Loulis learns signs from cross-fostered chimpanzees. In R. G. Gardner, B. T. Gardner, & T. E. Van Canfort (Eds.) *Teaching sign language to chimpanzees* (pp. 281–292). New York: State University of New York Press.

Fouts, R. S., Hirsch, A. D., & Fouts, D. H. (1982). Cultural transmission of a human language in a chimpanzee mother–infant relationship. In H. E. Fitzgerald, J. A. Mullins, & P. Gage (Eds.) *Child nurturance: III, studies of development in nonhuman primates* (pp. 159–193). New York: Plenum Press.

Fowler, H., & Miller, N. E. (1963). Facilitation and inhibition of runway performance by hind- and forepaw shock of various intensities. *Journal of Comparative and Physiological Psychology, 56*, 801–805.

Fragaszy, D., & Visalberghi, E. (2004). Socially biased learning in monkeys. *Learning and Behavior, 32*, 24–35.

Furness, W. (1916). Observations on the mentality of chimpanzees and orangutans. *Proceedings of the American Philosophical Society, 65*, 281–290.

Gaffan, D. (1977). Response coding in recall of colours by monkeys. *Quarterly Journal of Experimental Psychology, 29*, 597–605.

Gaffan, D. (1983). A comment on primacy effects in monkeys' memory for lists. *Animal Learning and Behavior, 11*, 144–145.

Gaffan, D., & Weiskrantz, L. (1980). Recency effects and lesion effects in delayed non-matching to randomly baited samples by monkeys. *Brain Research, 19*, 373–386.

Gaffan, E. A. (1992). Primacy, recency, and the variability of data in studies of animals' working memory. *Animal Learning and Behavior, 20*, 240–252.

Gagliardo, A., Ioale, P., Savini, M., & Wild, J. M. (2006). Having the nerve to home: trigeminal magnetoreceptor *versus* olfactory mediation of homing in pigeons. *The Journal of Experimental Biology, 209*, 2888–2892.

Galef, B. G., Jr. (1970). Aggression and timidity: Responses to novelty in feral Norway rats. *Journal of Comparative and Physiological Psychology, 70*, 370–381.

Galef, B. G., Jr. (1988). Communication of information concerning diets in social central-place foraging species: *Rattus norvegicus*. In T. R. Zentall, & B. G. Galef, Jr. (Eds.), *Social learning psychological and biological perspectives* (pp. 119–140). Hillsdale, NJ: Lawrence Erlbaum Associates, Inc.

Galef, B. G., Jr. (1996). Tradition in animals: Field observation and laboratory analyses. In M. Bekoff & D. Jamieson (Eds.), *Interpretations and explanations in the study of behaviour: Comparative perspectives* (pp. 74–95). Boulder, CO: Westview Press.

Galef, B. G., Jr. (2004). Approaches to the study of traditional behaviors of free-living animals. *Learning and Behavior, 32*, 53–61.

Galef, B. G., Jr., & Clark, M. M. (1971). Social factors in the poison avoidance and feeding behavior of wild and domesticated rat pups. *Journal of Comparative and Physiological Psychology, 75*, 341–357.

Galef, B. G., Jr., & Durlach, P. J. (1993). Absence of blocking, overshadowing, and latent inhibition in social enhancement of food preferences. *Animal Learning and Behavior, 21*, 214–220.

Galef, B. G., Jr., & Giraldeau, L. A. (2001). Social influences on foraging in vertebrates: Causal mechanisms and adaptive functions. *Animal Behaviour, 61*, 3–15.

Galef, B. G. Jr., & Stein, M. (1985). Demonstrators influence on observer diet preference: Analyses of critical social interactions and olfactory signals. *Animal Learning and Behavior, 13*, 131–138.

Galef, B. G., Jr., & Whiskin, E. E. (1998). Determinants of the longevity of socially learned food preferences of Norway rats. *Animal Behaviour, 55*, 967–975.

Galef, B. G., Jr., Lee, W. Y., & Whiskin, E. E. (2005). Lack of interference in long-term memory for socially learned food preferences in rats (*Rattus norvegicus*). *Journal of Comparative Psychology, 119*, 131–135.

Galef, B. G., Jr., Mason, J. R., Preti, G., & Bean, N. J. (1988). Carbon disulfide: A semiochemical mediating socially induced diet choice in rats. *Physiology and Behavior, 42*, 119–124.

Galef, B. G., Jr., McQuoid, L. M., & Whiskin, E. E. (1990). Further evidence that Norway rats do not socially transmit learned aversions to toxic baits. *Animal Learning and Behavior, 18*, 199–205.

Gallagher, M., & Holland, P. (1994). The amygdala complex: Multiple roles in associative learning and attention. *Proceedings of the National Academy of Science of the USA, 91*, 11771–11776.

Gallese, V., & Goldman, A. (1998). Mirror-neurons and the simulation theory of mind-reading. *Trends in Cognitive Science, 2*, 493–501.

Gallistel, C. R. (1990). *The organization of learning*. Cambridge, MA: MIT Press.

Gallistel, C. R. (1993). A conceptual framework for the study of numerical estimation and aritithmetic reasoning in animals. In S. T. Boysen & E. J. Capaldi (Eds.), *The development of numerical competence: Animal and human models* (pp. 211–223). Hillsdale, NJ: Lawrence Erlbaum Associates, Inc.

Gallistel, C. R., & Gibbon, J. (2002). *The symbolic foundations of conditioned behavior*. Mahwah, NJ: Lawrence Erlbaum Associates, Inc.

Gallistel, R. C., & Gibbon, J. (2000). Time, rate, and conditioning. *Psychological Review, 107*, 289–344.

Gallup, G. G., Jr. (1970). Chimpanzees: Self-recognition. *Science, 167*, 86–87.

Gallup, G. G., Jr. (1975). Toward an operational definition of self-awareness. In R. H. Tuttle (Ed.), *Socioecology and psychology of primates* (pp. 309–341). The Hague, Netherlands: Mouton.

Gallup, G. G., Jr. (1983). Toward a comparative psychology of mind. In R.L. Mellgren (Ed.), *Animal cognition and behavior* (pp. 473–510). Amsterdam: North Holland Publishing Co.

Ganesan, R., & Pearce, J. M. (1988). Effect of changing the unconditioned stimulus on appetitive blocking. *Journal of Experimental Psychology: Animal Behavior Processes, 14*, 280–291.

Garcia, J., & Koelling, R. A. (1966). Relation of cue to consequence in avoidance learning. *Psychonomic Science, 4*, 123–124.

Garcia, J., McGowan, B. K., & Green, K. F. (1972). Biological constraints on conditioning. In A. H. Black & W. F. Prokasy (Eds.), *Classical conditioning II: Current research and theory* (pp. 3–27). New York: Appleton-Century-Crofts.

Garcia, J., Rusiniak, K. W., & Brett, L. P. (1977). Conditioning food-illness in wild animals: *Caveant canonici*. In H. Davis & H. M. B. Hurwitz (Eds.), *Operant-Pavlovian interactions* (pp. 273–316). Hillsdale, NJ: Lawrence Erlbaum Associates, Inc.

Gardner, R. A., & Gardner, B. T. (1969). Teaching sign language to a chimpanzee. *Science, 165*, 664–672.

Gardner, R. A., & Gardner, B. T. (1974). Comparing the early utterances of child and chimpanzee. In A. Pick (Ed.), *Minnesota symposium on child psychology, 8*. Minneapolis, MN: University of Minneapolis Press.

Gardner, R. A., Gardner, B. T., & Van Cantfort, T. E. (1989). *Teaching sign language to chimpanzees*. New York: State University of New York Press.

Gelman, R., & Gallistel, C. R. (1978). *The child's understanding of number*. Cambridge, MA: Harvard University Press.

Gemberling, G. A., & Domjan, M. (1982). Selective association in one-day old rats: Taste-toxicosis and texture-toxicosis aversion learning. *Journal of Comparative and Physiological Psychology, 96*, 105–113.

George, D. N., & Pearce, J. M. (1999). Acquired distinctiveness is controlled by stimulus relevance not correlation with reward. *Journal of Experimental Psychology: Animal Behavior Processes, 25*, 363–373.

Gibbon, J., & Church, R. M. (1981). Time left: Linear versus logarithmic. *Journal of Experimental Psychology: Animal Behavior Processes, 7*, 87–108.

Gibbon, J., & Church, R. M. (1984). Sources of variance in an information processing theory of timing. In H. L. Roitblat, T. G. Bever & H. S. Terrace (Eds.), *Animal cognition* (pp. 465–490). Hillsdale, NJ: Lawrence Erlbaum Associates, Inc.

Gibbon, J., Church, R. M., & Meck, W. H. (1984). Scalar timing in memory. In J. Gibbon & L. G. Allan (Eds.), *Timing and perception, Annals of the New York Academy of Sciences* (Vol. 423, pp. 52–77). New York: New York Academy of Sciences.

Gibbs, C. M., Latham, S. B., & Gormezano, I. (1978). Classical conditioning of the rabbit nictitating membrane response: Effects of reinforcement schedule of response maintenance and resistance to extinction. *Animal Learning and Behavior, 6*, 209–215.

Gibson, K. R. (1989). Tool use in cebus monkeys: Moving from orthodox to neo-Piagetian analyses. *Behavioral and Brain Sciences, 12*, 598–599.

Gibson, R. M., Bradbury, J. W., & Vehrencamp, S. L. (1991). Mate choice in lekking sagegrouse: The role of vocal display, female site fidelity and copying. *Behavioral Ecology, 2*, 165–180.

Gillan, D. J. (1981). Reasoning in the chimpanzee: II. Transitive inference. *Journal of Experimental Psychology: Animal Behvior Processes, 7*, 150–164.

Gillan, D. J., Premack, D., & Woodruff, G. (1981). Reasoning in the chimpanzee: I. Analogical reasoning. *Journal of Experimental Psychology: Animal Behavior Processes, 7*, 1–17.

Glanzer, M., & Cunitz, A. R. (1966). Two storage mechanisms in free recall. *Journal of verbal learning and verbal behavior, 5*, 351–360.

Gleitman, H. (1971). Forgetting of long-term memories in animals. In W. K. Honig & P. H. R. James (Eds.), *Animal memory* (pp. 1–44). New York: Academic Press.

Gluck, M. A. (1991). Stimulus generalization and representation in adaptive network models of category learning. *Psychological Science, 2*, 50–55.

Gluck, M. A., & Bower, G. H. (1988). From conditioning to category learning: An adaptive network model. *Journal of Experimental Psychology: General, 117*, 225–244.

Gluck, M. A., & Myers, C. E. (1993). Hippocampal mediation of stimulus representation: A computational theory. *Hippocampus, 3*, 491–516.

Golub, L. (1977). Conditioned reinforcement: Schedule effects. In W. K. Honig & J. E. R. Staddon (Eds.), *Handbook of operant behavior* (pp. 288–312). Englewood Cliffs, NJ: Prentice-Hall.

Goodall, J. (1986). *The chimpanzees of Gombe*. Cambridge, MA: Harvard University Press.

Goodyear, A. I., & Kamil, A. C. (2004). Clark's nutcrackers (*Nucifraga columbiana*) and the effects of goal-landmark distance on overshadowing. *Journal of Comparative Psychology, 118*, 258–264.

Gordon, W. C. (1981). Mechanisms of cue-induced retention enhancement. In N. E. Spear & R. R. Miller (Eds.), *Information processing in animals: Memory mechanisms* (pp. 319–340). Hillsdale, NJ: Lawrence Erlbaum Associates, Inc.

Gordon, W. C., & Mowrer, R. R. (1980). The use of an extinction trial as a reminder treatment following ECS. *Animal Learning and Behavior, 8*, 363–367.

Gordon, W. C., Frankl, S. E., & Hamberg, J. M. (1979). Reactivation-induced proactive interference in rats. *American Journal of Psychology, 92*, 693–702.

Gormezano, I. (1965). Yoked comparisons of classical and instrumental conditioning of the eyelid response: And an addendum on "voluntary responders". In W. F. Prokasy (Ed.), *Classical conditioning: A symposium* (pp. 48–70). New York: Appleton-Century-Crofts.

Gould, J. L. (1982). The map sense of pigeons. *Nature, 296*, 205–211.

Gould, J. L. (1984). Natural history of honeybee learning. In P. Marler & H. S. Terrace (Eds.), *The biology of learning* (pp. 149–180). Berlin: Springer-Verlag.

Gould, J. L. (1986). The locale map of honey bees: Do insects have cognitive maps? *Science, 232*, 861–863.

Gould, J. L., & Gould, C. G. (1988). *The honey bee*. New York: Scientific American Library.

Gould, S. J. (1996). *Life's grandeur: The spread of excellence from Plato to Darwin*. London: Jonathan Cape.

Gouteux, S., Thinus-Blanc, C., & Vauclair, J. (2001). Rhesus monkeys use geometric and nongeometric information during a reorientation task. *Journal of Experimental Psychology: General, 130*, 505–519.

Grant, D. (1988). Sources of visual interference in delayed matching-to-sample with pigeons. *Journal of Experimental Psychology: Animal Behavior Processes, 14*, 368–375.

Grant, D. S. (1975). Proactive interference in pigeon short-term memory. *Journal of Experimental Psychology: Animal Behavior Processes, 1*, 207–220.

Grant, D. S. (1976). Effect of sample presentation time on long-delay matching in the pigeon. *Learning and Motivation, 7*, 580–590.

Grant, D. S. (1981). Short-term memory in the pigeon. In N. E. Spear & R. R. Miller (Eds.), *Information processing in animals: Memory mechanisms* (pp. 227–256). Hillsdale, NJ: Lawrence Erlbaum Associates, Inc.

Grant, D. S., & Roberts, W. A. (1973). Trace interaction in pigeon short-term memory. *Journal of Experimental Psychology, 101*, 21–29.

Grant, D. S., & Roberts, W. A. (1976). Sources of retroactive inhibition in pigeon short-term memory. *Journal of Experimental Psychology: Animal Behavior Processes, 2*, 1–16.

Grant, D. S., & Soldat, A. S. (1995). A postsample cue to forget does initiate a forgetting process in pigeons. *Journal of Experimental Psychology: Animal Behavior Processes, 21*, 218–228.

Greenberg, J. H. (1963). *Universals of language*. Cambridge, MA: MIT Press.

Grossberg, S., & Schmajuk, N. A. (1989). Neural dynamics of adaptive timing and temporal discrimination during associative learning. *Neural Networks, 2*, 79–102.

Gunier, W. J., & Elder, W. H. (1971). Experimental homing of gray bats to a maternity colony in a Missouri barn. *American Midlands Naturalist, 86*, 502–506.

Guthrie, E. R. (1935). *The psychology of learning*. New York: Harper.

Gwinner, E. (1972). Endogenous timing factors in bird migration. In S. R. Galler, K. Schmidt-Koenig, G. J. Jacobs, & R. E. Belleville (Eds.), *Animal orientation and navigation* (pp. 321–338). Washington, DC: NASA.

Hagstrum, J. T. (2001). Infrasound and the avian navigational map. *Journal of Navigation, 54*, 377–391.

Hall, G. (1991). *Perceptual and associative learning*. Oxford: Clarendon Press.

Hall, G. (2001). Perceptual learning: association and differentiation. In R. R. Mowrer & S. B. Klein (Eds.), *Handbook of contemporary learning theories*. Mahwah, NJ: Lawrence Erlbaum Associates, Inc.

Hall, G., & Pearce, J. M. (1979). Latent inhibition of a CS during CS–US pairings. *Journal of Experimental Psychology: Animal Behavior Processes, 5*, 31–42.

Hall, G., & Pearce, J. M. (1982a). Changes in stimulus associability during conditioning: Implications for theories of acquisition. In M. L. Commons, R. J. Herrnstein & A. R. Wagner (Eds.), *Quantitative analyses of behavior* (Vol. 3, pp. 221–239). Cambridge, MA: Ballinger.

Hall, G., & Pearce, J. M. (1982b). Restoring the associability of a preexposed CS by a surprising event. *Quarterly Journal of Experimental Psychology, 34B*, 127–140.

Hammond, L. J. (1980). The effects of contingencies upon appetitive conditioning of free-operant behavior. *Journal of the Experimental Analysis of Behavior, 34*, 297–304.

Hammond, L. J., & Weinberg, M. (1984). Signaling unearned reinforcers removes suppression produced by a zero correlation in an operant paradigm. *Animal Learning and Behavior, 12*, 371–374.

Hampton, R. R. (2001). Rhesus monkeys know when they remember. *Proceedings of the National Academy of Sciences, 98*, 5359–5362.

Hampton, R. R., & Shettleworth, S. (1996). Hippocampus and memory in food-storing and nonstoring bird species. *Behavioral Neuroscience, 110*, 946–964.

Hampton, R. R., Hampstead, B. M., & Murray, E. A. (2005). Rhesus monkeys (*Macaca mulatta*) demonstrate robust memory for what and where, but not when in an open-field test of memory. *Learning and Motivation, 36*, 245–259.

Hanson, H. M. (1959). Effect of discrimination training on stimulus generalization. *Journal of Experimental Psychology, 58*, 321–334.

Hare, B., Call, J., & Tomasello, M. (2001). Do chimpanzees know what conspecifics know? *Animal Behaviour, 61*, 139–151.

Hare, B., Call, J., Agnetta, B., & Tomasello, M. (2000). Chimpanzees know what conspecifics do and do not see. *Animal Behaviour, 59*, 771–785.

Harlow, H. F. (1949). The formation of learning sets. *Psychological Review, 56*, 51–65.

Harper, D. N., McLean, A. P., & Dalrymple-Alford, J. C. (1993). List item memory in rats: Effects of delay and task. *Journal of Experimental Psychology: Animal Behavior Processes, 19*, 307–316.

Harris, J. A. (2006). Elemental representation of stimuli in associative learning. *Psychological Reveiw, 113*, 584–605.

Harris, J. A., Jones, M. L., Bailey, G. K., & Westbrook, R. F. (2000). Contextual control over conditioned responding in an extinction paradigm. *Journal of Experimental Psychology: Animal Behavior Processes, 26*, 174–185.

Harris, J. A., Shand, F. L., Carroll, L. Q., & Westbrook, R. F. (2004). Pesistence of preference for flavor presented in simultaneous compound with sucrose. *Journal of Experimental Psychology: Animal Behavior Processes, 30*, 177–189.

Haselgrove, M., Aydin, A., & Pearce, J. M. (2004). A partial reinforcement extinction effect despite equal rates of reinforcement during Pavlovian conditioning. *Journal of Experimental Psychology: Animal Behavior Processes, 30*, 240–250.

Haselgrove, M., & Pearce, J. M. (2003). Facilitation of extinction by an increase or a decrease in trial duration. *Journal of Experimental Psychology: Animal Behavior Processes, 29*, 153–166.

Hastings, M. (1979). *Bomber command.* London: Michael Joseph.

Hauser, M. D., Kralik, J., Botto-Mahan, C., Garrett, M., & Oser, J. (1995). Self-recognition in primates: Phylogeny and the salience of species-typical features. *Proceedings of the National Academy of Science of the USA, 92*, 10811–10814.

Hawkins, R. D., & Kandel, E. R. (1984). Is there a cell biological alphabet for simple forms of learning? *Psychological Review, 91*, 375–391.

Hawkins, R. D., Abrams, T. W., Carew, T. J., & Kandel, E. R. (1983). A cellular mechanism of classical conditioning in *Aplysia*: Activity-dependent amplification of presynaptic facilitation. *Science, 219*, 400–405.

Hayes, C. (1961). *The ape in our house.* New York: Harper.

Hayes, K., & Hayes, C. (1951). The intellectual development of a home-raised chimpanzee. *Proceedings of the American Philosophical Society, 95*, 105–109.

Hays, G. C., Akesson, S., Broderick, A., Glen, F., Godley, B. J., Papi, F., et al. (2003). Island-finding ability of marine turtles. *Proceedings of the Royal Society of London B, 270*, S5–S7.

Hayward, A., McGregor, A., Good, M. A., & Pearce, J. M. (2003). Absence of overshadowing and blocking between landmarks and geometric cues provided by the shape of a test arena. *Quarterly Journal of Experimental Psychology, 56B*, 114–126.

Healy, S. D. (1995). Memory for objects and positions: Delayed non-matching-to-sample in storing and non-storing tits. *Quarterly Journal of Experimental Psychology, 48B*, 179–191.

Healy, S. D., & Hurly, T. A. (1995). Spatial memory in rufus hummingbirds (*Selasphorus rufus*): A field test. *Animal Learning and Behavior, 23*, 63–68.

Healy, S. D., & Rowe, C. (2007). A critique of comparative studies of brain size. *Proceedings of the Royal Society, B, 274*, 453–464.

Healy, S. D., Clayton, N. S., & Krebs, J. R. (1994). Development of hippocampal specialization in two species of tit (*Parus* spp.). *Behavioural Brain Research, 61*, 23–28.

Healy, S., Hodgson, Z., & Braithwaite, V. (2003). Do animals use maps? In K. J. Jeffery (Ed.), *The Neurobiology of spatial behaviour* (pp. 104–118). Oxford: Oxford University Press.

Hearst, E., & Franklin, S. R. (1977). Positive and negative relations between a signal and food: Approach–withdrawal behavior. *Journal of Experimental Psychology: Animal Behavior Processes, 3*, 37–52.

Hearst, E., & Jenkins, H. M. (1974). *Sign tracking: The stimulus–reinforcer relation and directed action.* Austin, TX: Psychonomic Society.

Hebb, D. O. (1949). *The organization of behavior.* New York: Wiley.

Heinrich, B. (2000). Testing insight in ravens. In C. Heyese & L. Huber (Eds.), *The evolution of cognition* (pp. 289–305). Cambridge, MA: MIT Press.

Heinrich, B., & Bugnyar, T. (2005). Testing problem solving in ravens: String-pulling to reach food. *Ethology, 111*, 962–976.

Hendersen, R. W. (1978). Fogetting of conditioned fear inhibition. *Learning and Motivation, 9*, 16–30.

Hendersen, R. W. (1985). The motivational significance of forgetting. In F. R. Brush & J. B. Overmier (Eds.), *Affect, conditioning, and cognition: Essay on the determinants of behavior* (pp. 43–53). Hillsdale, NJ: Lawrence Erlbaum Associates, Inc.

Hendersen, R. W., Peterson, J. M., & Jackson, R. L. (1980). Acquisition and retention of control of instrumental behavior by a cue signaling an airblast: How specific are conditioned anticipations? *Learning and Motivation, 11*, 407–426.

Hennessey, T. M., Rucker, W. B., & McDiarmid, C. G. (1979). Classical conditioning in paramecia. *Animal Learning and Behavior, 7*, 417–423.

Herman, L. M. (1975). Interference and auditory short-term memory in the bottlenosed dolphin. *Animal Learning and Behavior, 3*, 43–48.

Herman, L. M. (2002). Vocal, social and self imitation by bottlenosed dophins. In K. Dautenhan & C. L. Nehanir (Eds.), *Imitation in animals and artifacts* (pp. 63–107). Boston, MA: Bradford Books.

Herman, L. M., & Arbeit, W. R. (1973). Stimulus control and auditory discrimination learning sets in the bottlenose dolphin. *Journal of the Experimental Analysis of Behavaior, 19*, 379–394.

Herman, L. M., & Gordon, J. A. (1974). Auditory delayed matching in the bottlenose dolphin. *Journal of the Experimental Analysis of Behavior, 21*, 19–29.

Herman, L. M., & Thompson, R. K. R. (1982). Symbolic identity, and probed delayed matching of sounds in the bottlenosed dolphin. *Animal Learning and Behavior, 10*, 22–34.

Herman, L. M., Beach, F. A., Pepper, R. L., & Stalling, R. B. (1969). Learning-set formation in the bottlenose dolphin. *Psychonomic Science, 14*, 98–99.

Herman, L. M., Pack, A. A., & Morrel-Samuels, P. (1993). Representational and conceptual skills of dolphins. In H. L. Roitblat, L. M. Herman, & P. E. Nachtigall (Eds.) *Language and communication: Comparative perspectives* (pp. 403–442). Hillsdale, NJ: Lawrence Erlbaum Associates, Inc.

Herman, L. M., Richards, D. G., & Wolz, J. P. (1984). Comprehension of sentences by bottlenosed dolphins. *Cognition, 16*, 129–219.

Hermer, L., & Spelke, E. (1996). Modularity and development: The case of spatial reorientation. *Cognition, 61*, 195–232.

Herrnstein, R. J. (1990). Levels of stimulus control. *Cognition, 37*, 133–166.

Herrnstein, R. J., Loveland, D. H., & Cable, C. (1976). Natural concepts in pigeons. *Journal of Experimental Psychology: Animal Behavior Processes, 2*, 285–311.

Herrnstein, R. J., Vaughan, W., Jr., Mumford, D. B., & Kosslyn, S. M. (1989). Teaching pigeons an abstract relational rule: Insideness. *Perception and Psychophysics, 46*, 56–64.

Heyes, C. M. (1994a). Reflections on self-recognition in primates. *Animal Behaviour, 47*, 909–919.

Heyes, C. M. (1994b). Social learning in animals: Categories and mechanisms. *Biological Review, 69*, 207–231.

Heyes, C. M. (1998). Theory of mind in nonhuman primates. *Behavioral and Brain Sciences, 21*, 101–148.

Heyes, C. M., & Dawson, G. R. (1990). A demonstration of observational learning using a bidirectional control. *Quarterly Journal of Experimental Psychology, 42B*, 59–71.

Heyes, C. M., & Saggerson, A. L. (2002). Testing for imitative and non-imitative social learning in the budgerigar using a two-object/two-action test. *Animal Behaviour, 64*, 851–859.

Heyes, C., & Ray, E. D. (2000). What is the significance of imitation in animals? *Advances in the Study of Behaviour, 29*, 215–245.

Hikami, K., Hasegawa, Y., & Matsuzawa, T. (1990). Social transmission of food preferences in Japanese monkeys (*Macaca fuscata*) after mere exposure or aversion training. *Journal of Comparative Psychology, 104*, 233–237.

Hinde, R. A. (1970). *Animal behaviour: A synthesis of ethology and comparative psychology*. New York: McGraw-Hill.

Hinde, R. A., & Stevenson-Hinde, J. (Eds.). (1973). *Constraints on learning*. London: Academic Press.

Hinson, R., Poulos, C., & Cappell, H. (1982). Effects of pentobarbital and cocaine in rats expecting pentobarbital. *Pharmacology Biochemistry and Behavior, 16*, 661–666.

Hintzman, D. L. (1986). 'Schema abstraction' in a multiple trace memory. *Psychological Review, 93*, 411–428.

Hockett, C. F. (1960). The origin of speech. *Scientific American, 203*, 89–96.

Holland, P. C. (1981). Acquisition of representation-mediated conditioned food aversions. *Learning and Motivation, 12*, 1–18.

Holland, P. C. (1990). Event representation in Pavlovian conditioning: Image and action. *Cognition, 37*, 105–131.

Holland, P. C. (1992). Occasion setting in Pavlovian conditioning. In D. L. Medin (Ed.), *The psychology of learning and motivation* (Vol 28, pp. 69–125). San Diego, CA: Academic Press.

Holland, P. C., & Fox, G. (2003). Effects of hippocampal lesions in overshadowing and blocking procedures. *Behavioral Neuroscience, 117*, 650–656.

Holland, P. C., & Kenmuir, C. (2005). Variations in unconditioned stimulus processing in unblocking. *Journal of Experimental Psychology: Animal Behavior Processes, 31*, 155–171.

Holland, P. C., & Rescorla, R. A. (1975). The effects of two ways of devaluing the unconditioned stimulus after first- and second-order appetitive conditioning. *Journal of Experimental Psychology: Animal Behavior Processes, 1*, 355–363.

Holland, P. C., & Ross, R. T. (1981). Within-compound associations in serial compound conditioning. *Journal of Experimental Psychology: Animal Behavior Processes, 7*, 228–241.

Holz, W. C., & Azrin, N. H. (1963). A comparison of several procedures for eliminating behavior. *Journal of the Experimental Analysis of Behavior, 6*, 399–412.

Homa, D., Dunbar, S., & Nohre, L. (1991). Instance frequency, categorization, and the modulating effect of experience. *Journal of Experimental Psychology: Learning, Memory, and Cognition, 17*, 444–458.

Honey, R. C., & Bateson, P. (1996). Stimulus comparison and perceptual learning: further evidence and evaluation from an imprinting perspective. *Quarterly Journal of Experimental Psychology, 49B*, 259–269.

Honey, R. C., & Hall, G. (1989). Acquired equivalence and distinctiveness of cues. *Journal of Experimental Psychology: Animal Behavior Processes, 15*, 338–446.

Honey, R. C., & Hall, G. (1991). Acquired equivalence and distinctiveness of cues using a sensory-preconditioning procedure. *Quarterly Journal of Experimental Psychology, 43B*, 121–135.

Honig, W. K. (1978). Studies of working memory in the pigeon. In S. H. Hulse, H. Fowler, & W. K. Honig (Eds.), *Cognitive processes in animal behavior* (pp. 211–248). Hillsdale, NJ: Lawrence Erlbaum Associates, Inc.

Honig, W. K., & Stewart, K. E. (1989). Discrimination of relative numerosity by pigeons. *Animal Learning and Behavior, 17*, 134–146.

Hostetter, A. B., Cantero, M., & Hopkins, W. D. (2001). Differential use of vocal and gestural communication by chimpanzees (*Pan troglodytes*) in response to the attentional status of a human (*Homo sapiens*). *Journal of Comparative Psychology, 115*, 337–343.

House, B. J., Brown, A. L., & Scott, M. S. (1974). Children's discrimination learning based on identity or difference. In H. W. Reese (Ed.), *Advances in child development and behavior* (Vol. 9, pp. 1–45). New York: Academic Press.

Huang, I., Koski, C. A., & DeQuardo, J. R. (1983). Observational learning of a bar-press by rats. *The Journal of General Psychology, 108*, 103–111.

Huber, L., & Lenz, R. (1993). A test of the linear feature model of polymorphous concept discrimination with pigeons. *Quarterly Journal of Experimental Psychology, 46B, 1–18.*

Huber, L., Troje, N. F., Loidolt, M., Aust, U., & Grass, D. (2000). Natural categorization through multiple feature learning in pigeons. *Quarterly Journal of Experimental Psychology, 53B*, 341–357.

Hughes, R. N., & Blight, C. M. (1999). Algorithmic behaviour and spatial memory are used by two intertidal fish species to solve the radial maze. *Animal Behaviour, 58*, 601–613.

Hull, C. L. (1943). *Principles of behavior*. New York: Appleton-Century-Crofts.

Humphrey, N. K. (1982). Consciousness: A just-so story. *New Scientist, 19 August*, 474–478.

Humphrey, N. K. (1983). *Consciousness regained*. Oxford: Oxford University Press.

Hunter, W. S. (1914). The delayed reaction in animals and children. *Behavior Monographs, 2*, No. 6.

Hutchinson, R. R., Azrin, N. H., & Hunt, G. M. (1968). Attack produced by intermittent reinforcement of a concurrent operant response. *Journal of the Experimental Analysis of Behavior, 11*, 489–495.

Hyde, T. S. (1976). The effect of Pavlovian stimuli on the acquisition of a new response. *Learning and Motivation, 7*, 223–239.

Inman, A., & Shettleworth, S. J. (1999). Detecting metamemory in nonverbal subjects: A test with pigeons. *Journal of Experimental Psychology: Animal Behavior Processes, 25*, 389–395.

Itakura, S. (1987). Mirror guided behavior in Japanese monkeys (*Macaca fuscata fuscata*). *Primates, 28*, 149–161.

Itani, J., & Nishimura, A. (1973). The study of infrahuman culture in Japan. In E. Menzel (Ed.), *Precultural primate behavior* (pp. 127–141). Basel: Karger.

Itani, M. (2004). Theory of mind and insight in chimpanzees, elephants, and other animals? In L. J. Rogers & G. Kaplan (Eds.), *Comparative vertebrate cognition: Are primates superior to non-primates?* New York: Kluwer Academic.

James, W. (1890). *The principles of psychology*. New York: Holt.

Jander, R. (1957). Die optische Richtungsorientierung der roten Waldameise (Formica rufa L.). *Zeitschrift fur vergleichende Physiologie, 40*, 162–238.

Jenkins, W. O., McFann, H., & Clayton, F. L. (1950). A methodological study of extinction following aperiodic and continuous reinforcement. *Journal of Comparative and Physiological Psychology, 43*, 155–167.

Jennings, H. S. (1906). *Behavior of the lower organisms*. New York: Columbia University Press.

Jerison, H. J. (1969). Brain evolution and dinosaur brains. *American Naturalist, 103*, 575–588.

Jerison, H. J. (1973). *Evolution of the brain and intelligence*. New York: Academic Press.

Jitsumori, M., & Yoshihara, M. (1997). Categorical discrimination of human facial expressions by pigeons: A test of the linear feature model. *Quarterly Journal of Experimental Psychology, 50B*, 253–268.

Jolly, A. (1991). Conscious chimpanzees? A review of recent literature. In C. A. Ristau (Ed.) *Cognitive ethology: The minds of other animals* (pp. 231–252). Hillsdale, NJ: Lawrence Erlbaum Associates, Inc.

Jones, J. E., Antoniadis, E., Shettleworth, S., & Kamil, A. C. (2002). A comparative study of geometric rule learning in nutcrackers (*Nucifraga columbiana*), pigeons (*Columba livia*) and jackdaws (*Corvus monedula*). *Journal of Comparative Psychology, 116*, 350–356.

Jordan, W., Strasser, H., & McHale, L. (2000). Contextual control of long-term habituation in rats. *Journal of Experimental Psychology: Animal Behavior Processes, 26*, 323–339.

Kamil, A. C. (1978). Systematic foraging by a nectar feeding bird, the amakihi (*Loxops virens*). *Journal of Comparative and Physiological Psychology, 92*, 388–396.

Kamin, L. J. (1969). Selective association and conditioning. In N. J. Mackintosh & W. K. Honig (Eds.), *Fundamental issues in associative learning* (pp. 42–64). Halifax, Canada: Dalhousie University Press.

Kamin, L. J., & Schaub, R. E. (1963). Effects of conditioned stimulus intensity on the conditioned emotional response. *Journal of Comparative and Physiological Psychology, 56*, 502–507.

Kaminski, J., Call, J., & Fischer, J. (2004). Word learning in a domestic dog: Evidence for "fast mapping". *Science, 304*, 1682–1683.

Kandel, E. R., & Hawkins, R. D. (1992). The biological basis of learning and individuality. *Scientific American, 267*, 62–71.

Kaplan, P. S. (1984). Importance of relative temporal parameters in trace autoshaping: From excitation to inhibition. *Journal of Experimental Psychology: Animal Behavior Processes, 10*, 113–126.

Karlson, P., & Luscher, M. (1959). "Pheromones": A new term for a class of biologically active substances. *Nature, 183*, 55–56.

Karpicke, J., Christoph, G., Peterson, G., & Hearst, E. (1977). Signal location and positive versus negative conditioned suppression in the rat. *Journal of Experimental Psychology: Animal Behavior Processes, 3*, 105–118.

Kastak, D., & Schusterman, R. J. (1994). Transfer of visual identity matching-to-sample in two Californian sea lions (*Zalophus californianus*). *Animal Learning and Behavior, 22*, 427–453.

Katz, J. S., & Wright, A. A. (2006). Same–different abstract-concept learning by pigeons. *Journal of Experimental Psychology: Animal Behavior Processes, 32*, 80–86.

Katz, J. S., Wright, A. A., & Bachevalier, J. (2002). Mechanisms of same/different abstract-concept learning by rhesus monkeys (*Macaca mulatta*). *Journal of Experimental Psychology: Animal Behavior Processes, 28*, 358–368.

Kaye, H., & Pearce, J. M. (1987). Hippocampal lesions attenuate latent inhibition of a CS and a neutral stimulus. *Quarterly Journal of Experimental Psychology, 39B*, 107–125.

Kaye, H., & Pearce, J. M. (1984). The strength of the orienting response during Pavlovian conditioning. *Journal of Experimental Psychology: Animal Behavior Processes, 10*, 90–109.

Keeton, W. T. (1969). Orientation by pigeons: Is the sun necessary? *Science, 165*, 922–928.

Keeton, W. T. (1974). The orientational and navigational basis of homing in birds. *Advances in the Study of Behaviour, 5*, 47–132.

Kehoe, E. J. (1988). A layered network model of associative learning: Learning to learn and configuration. *Psychological Review, 95*, 411–433.

Kehoe, E. J., Horne, A. J., Horne, P. S., & Macrae, M. (1994). Summation and configuration between and within sensory modalities in classical conditioning of the rabbit. *Animal Learning and Behavior, 22*, 19–26.

Kelleher, R. T. (1958). Fixed-ratio schedules of conditioned reinforcement with chimpanzees. *Journal of the Experimental Analysis of Behavior, 1*, 281–289.

Kelly, D. M., Spetch, M. L., & Heth, C. D. (1998). Pigeons (*Columba livia*) encoding of geometric and featural properties of a spatial environment. *Journal of Comparative Psychology, 112*, 259–269.

Kenyon, K. W., & Rice, D. W. (1958). Homing of Laysan albatrosses. *Condor, 60*, 3–6.

Kesner, R., Bolland, B., & Dakis, M. (1993). Memory for spatial locations, motor responses, and objects: Triple dissociation among the hippocampus, caudate nucleus, and extrastriate visual cortex. *Experimental Brain Research, 93*, 462–470.

Keysers, C., & Perrett, D. I. (2004). Demystifying social cognition: A Hebbian perspective. *Trends in Cognitive Science, 8*, 501–507.

Kiepenheuer, J. (1978). The effect of magnetic anomalies on the homing behavior of pigeons: An attempt to analyse the possible factors involved. In F. Papi & H. Wallraff (Eds.), *Avian navigation* (pp. 120–128). Berlin: Springer.

Killeen, P. R., & Fetterman, J. G. (1988). A behavioral theory of timing. *Psychological Review, 95*, 274–295.

Kinnaman, A. J. (1902). Mental life of two macacus rhesus monkeys in captivity. *American Journal of Psychology, 13*, 98–148.

Kirchner, W. H., & Braun, U. (1994). Dancing honey bees indicate the location of food sources using path integration rather than cognitive maps. *Animal Behaviour, 48*, 1437–1441.

Kirchner, W. K., & Towne, W. F. (1994). The sensory basis of the honeybee's dance language. *Scientific American, 277*(6), 52–59.

Kluender, K. R., Diehl, R. L., & Killeen, P. R. (1987). Japanese quail can learn phonetic categories. *Science, 237*, 1195–1197.

Klump, G. M., & Shalter, M. D. (1984). Acoustic behavior of birds and mammals in the predator context. *Zeitschrift fur Tierpsychologie, 66*, 189–226.

Kohler, W. (1918). Nachweis einfacher structurfunktionen beim schimpansen und beim haushuhn. Abh.d., Konig, Prouss.Ak. D. Wissen. *Phys. Math. Klasse, 2*, 1–101. Translated and condensed as "Simple structural functions in chimpanzee and chicken". In W. D. Ellis (Ed.) (1969). *A source book of Gestalt psychology*. London: Routledge and Kegan Paul.

Kohler, W. (1925). *The mentality of apes*. New York: Harcourt.

Kohler, W. (1956). *The mentality of apes*. London: Routledge & Kegan Paul.

Kolterman, R. (1971). 24-Std-Periodik in der Langzeiterrinerung an Duft-und Farbsignale bei der Honigbiene. *Zeitschrift fur vergleichende Physiologie, 75*, 49–68.

Konorski, J. (1948). *Conditioned reflexes and neuron organization*. Cambridge: Cambridge University Press.

Konorski, J. (1967). *Integrative activity of the brain*. Chicago: University of Chicago Press.

Kosslyn, S. (1980). *Image and mind*. Cambridge, MA: Harvard University Press.

Kraemer, P. J., & Roberts, W. A. (1984). Short-term memory for visual and auditory stimuli in pigeons. *Animal Learning and Behavior, 12*, 275–284.

Kramer, G. (1952). Experiments on bird orientation. *Ibis, 94*, 265–285.

Krebs, J. R. (1990). Food-storing in birds: Adaptive specialization in brain and behaviour? *Philosophical Transactions of the Royal Society of London, B, 329*, 153–160.

Kreithen, M. L. (1978). Sensory mechanisms for animal orientation – can any new ones be discovered? In K. Schmidt-Koenig & W. T. Keeton (Eds.), *Animal migration, navigation and homing* (pp. 25–34). Berlin: Springer Verlag.

Kremer, E. F. (1978). The Rescorla–Wagner model: Losses in associative strength in compound conditioned stimuli. *Journal of Experimental Psychology: Animal Behavior Processes, 4*, 22–36.

Kruschke, J. K. (1992). ALCOVE: An exemplar-based connectionist model of category learning. *Psychological Review, 99*, 22–44.

Kruse, J. M., Overmier, J. B., Konz, W. A., & Rokke, E. (1983). Pavlovian conditioned stimulus effects upon instrumental choice behaviour are reinforcer specific. *Learning and Motivation, 14*, 165–181.

Kummer, H., & Goodall, J. (1985). Conditions of innovative behavior in primates. *Philosophical Transactions of the Royal Society of London, B, 308*, 203–214.

Laberge, D., & Samuels, S. J. (1974). Towards a theory of automatic information processing in reading. *Cognitive Psychology, 6*, 293–323.

Langley, C. M., & Riley, D. A. (1993). Limited capacity information processing and pigeon matching-to-sample: Testing alternative hypotheses. *Animal Learning and Behavior, 21*, 226–232.

Lattal, K. A., & Gleeson, S. (1990). Response acquisition with delayed reinforcement. *Journal of Experimental Psychology: Animal Behavior Processes, 16*, 27–39.

Lawrence, D. H. (1949). Acquired distinctiveness of cues. I. Transfer between discriminations on the basis of familiarity with the stimulus. *Journal of Experimental Psychology, 39*, 770–784.

Lawrence, D. H. (1950). Acquired distinctiveness of cues: II. Selective association in a constant stimulus situation. *Journal of Experimental Psychology, 40*, 175–188.

Lea, S. E. G. (1984). In what sense do pigeons learn concepts? In H. T. Roitblat, T. G. Bever, & H. S. Terrace (Eds.), *Animal cognition* (pp. 263–276). Hillsdale, NJ: Lawrence Erlbaum Associates, Inc.

Lea, S. E. G., & Harrison, S. N. (1978). Discrimination of polymorphous stimulus sets by pigeons. *Quarterly Journal of Experimental Psychology, 30*, 521–537.

Leander, J. D. (1973). Effects of food deprivation on free-operant avoidance behavior. *Journal of the Experimental Analysis of Behavior, 19*, 17–24.

Leavens, D. A., Hopkins, W. D., & Bard, K. A. (1996). Indexical and referential pointing in chimpanzees (*Pan troglodytes*). *Journal of Comparative Psychology, 110*, 346–353.

Lednor, A. J., & Walcott, C. (1983). Homing pigeon navigation: The effects of in-flight exposure to varying magnetic field. *Comparative Biochemistry and Physiology, 76A*, 665–671.

LePelley, M. E. (2004). The role of associative history in models of associative learning: A selective review and a hybrid model. *Quarterly Journal of Experimental Psychology, 57B*, 193–243.

Lewis, D. J. (1979). Psychobiology of active and inactive memory. *Psychological Bulletin, 86*, 1054–1083.

Lieberman, D. A., McIntosh, D. C., & Thomas, G. V. (1979). Learning when reward is delayed: A marking hypothesis. *Journal of Experimental Psychology: Animal Behavior Processes, 5*, 224–242.

Lieberman, P. (1975). On the origins of language. *New York: Macmillan.*

Lieberman, P. (1984). *The biology and evolution of language.* Cambridge, MA: Harvard University Press.

Linwick, D., Overmier, J. B., Peterson, G. B., & Mertens, M. (1988). Interaction of memories and expectancies as mediators of choice behavior. *American Psychologist, 101*, 313–334.

Lipp, H. P. (1983). Nocturnal homing in pigeons. *Comparative Biochemistry and Physiology, 76A*, 743–749.

Lipp, H. P., Pleskacheva, M. G., Gossweiler, H., Ricceri, L., Smirnova, A. A., Garin, N. N., et al. (2001). A large outdoor radial maze for comparative studies in birds and mammals. *Neuroscience and Biobehavioral Reviews, 25*, 83–99.

Lipp, H. P., Vyssotski, A. L., Wolfer, D. P., Renaudineau, S., Savini, M., Troster, G., et al. (2004). Pigeon homing along highways and exits. *Current Biology, 14*, 1239–1249.

Locke, A. (1980). *The guided reinvention of language.* London: Academic Press.

Logan, C. (1975). Topographic changes in responding during habituation to waterstream stimulation in sea anemones (*Anthopleura elegentissima*). *Journal of Comparative and Physiological Psychology, 89*, 105–117.

Logan, F. A. (1960). *Incentive.* New Haven, CT: Yale University Press.

Lohman, K. J. (1991). Magnetic orientation by hatchling loggerhead sea turtles. *Journal of Experimental Biology, 155*, 37–49.

Lohman, K. J. (1992). How sea turtles navigate. *Scientific American, 266(1)*, 82–88.

Lohman, K. J., & Lohman, C. M. F. (1996). Detection of magnetic field intensity by sea turtles. *Nature, 380*, 59–61.

Lovibond, P. F. (1983). Facilitation of instrumental behavior by a Pavlovian appetitive conditioned stimulus. *Journal of Experimental Psychology: Animal Behavior Processes, 9*, 225–247.

Lovibond, P. F., Preston, G. C., & Mackintosh, N. J. (1984). Context specificity of conditioning, extinction and latent inhibition. *Journal of Experimental Psychology: Animal Behavior Processes, 10*, 360–375.

Lubinski, D., & MacCorquodale, K. (1984). "Symbolic communication" between two pigeons (*Columba livia*) without unconditioned reinforcement. *Journal of Comparative Psychology, 98*, 372–380.

Lubow, R. E. (1973). Latent inhibition. *Psychological Bulletin, 79*, 398–407.

Machado, A. (1997). Learning the temporal dynamics of behavior. *Psychological Review, 104*, 241–265.

Machado, A., & Keen, R. (1999). Learning to time (LET) or scalar expectancy theory (SET)? A critical test of two models of timing. *Psychological Science, 10*, 285–290.

Machado, A., & Keen, R. (2003). Temporal discrimination in a long operant chamber. *Behavioural Processes, 62*, 157–182.

Mackintosh, N. J. (1973). Stimulus selection: Learning to ignore stimuli that predict no change in reinforcement. In R. A. Hinde & J. Stevenson-Hinde (Eds.), *Constraints on learning* (pp. 75–100). London: Academic Press.

Mackintosh, N. J. (1974). *The psychology of animal learning.* London: Academic Press.

Mackintosh, N. J. (1975a). A theory of attention: Variations in the associability of stimuli with reinforcement. *Psychological Review, 82*, 276–298.

Mackintosh, N. J. (1975b). Blocking of conditioned suppression: Role of the first compound trial. *Journal of Experimental Psychology: Animal Behavior Processes, 1*, 335–345.

Mackintosh, N. J. (2002). Do not ask whether they have a cognitive map, but how they find their way about. *Psicologica, 23*, 165–185.

Mackintosh, N. J., Bygrave, D. J., & Picton, B. M. B. (1977). Locus of the effect of a surprising reinforcer in the attenuation of blocking. *Quarterly Journal of Experimental Psychology, 29*, 327–336.

Mackintosh, N. J., Kaye, H., & Bennett, C. H. (1991). Perceptual learning in flavour aversion conditioning. *Quarterly Journal of Experimental Psychology, 43B*, 297–322.

Macphail, E. M. (1980). Short-term visual recognition memory in pigeons. *Quarterly Journal of Experimental Psychology, 32*, 521–538.

Macphail, E. M. (1982). *Brain and intelligence in vertebrates.* Oxford: Clarendon.

Macphail, E. M. (1985). Vertebrate intelligence: The null hypothesis. In L. Weiskrantz (Ed.), *Animal intelligence* (pp. 37–51). Oxford: Clarendon.

Macphail, E. M. (1993). *The neuroscience of animal intelligence.* New York: Columbia University Press.

MacPhail, E. M. (1998). *The evolution of consciousness.* Oxford: Oxford University Press.

Macphail, E. M., & Bolhuis, J. J. (2001). The evolution of intelligence: adpative specializations versus general process. *Biological Review, 76*, 341–364.

Maki, W. S., & Abunawass, A. M. (1991). A connectionist approach to conditional discriminations: Learning, short-term memory, and attention. In M. L. Commons, S. Grossberg & J. E. R. Staddon (Eds.), *Neural network models of conditioning and action* (pp. 241–278). Hillsdale, NJ: Lawrence Erlbaum Associates, Inc.

Maki, W. S., & Hegvik, D. K. (1980). Directed forgetting in pigeons. *Animal Learning and Behavior, 8*, 567–574.

Maki, W. S., Brokofsky, S., & Berg, B. (1979). Spatial memory in rats: Resistance to retroactive interference. *Animal Learning and Behavior, 7*, 25–30.

March, J., Chamizo, V. D., & Mackintosh, N. J. (1992). Reciprocal overshadowing between intra-maze and extra-maze cues. *Quaterly Journal of Experimental Psychology, 45B*, 49–63.

Markman, E. M., & Abelev, M. (2004). Word learning in dogs? *Trends in Cognitive Science, 18*, 479–481.

Marler, P. (1970). A comparative approach to vocal learning: Song development in white-crowned sparrows. *Journal of Comparative and Physiological Psychology, 71*(Supplement), 1–25.

Marler, P., Karakashian, S. J., & Gyger, M. (1990). Do animals have the option of whitholding signals when communication is inappropriate? In C. A. Ristau (Ed.), *Cognitive ethology: The minds of other animals* (pp. 187–208). Hillsdale, NJ: Lawrence Erlbaum Associates, Inc.

Matsukawa, A., Inoue, S., & Jitsumori, M. (2004). Pigeon's recognition of cartoons: effects of fragmentation, scrambling, and deletion of elements. *Behavioural Processes, 65*, 25–34.

Matsuzawa, T. (1985). Use of numbers by a chimpanzee. *Nature, 315*, 57–59.

Matthews, B. L., Ryu, J. H., & Bockaneck, C. (1989). Vestibular contribution to spatial orientation: Evidence of vestibular navigation in an animal model. *Acta Otolaryngolica, 468*, 149–154.

Matthews, G. V. T. (1955). *Bird navigation*. London: Cambridge University Press.

Mazmanian, D. S., & Roberts, W. A. (1983). Spatial memory in rats under restricted viewing conditions. *Learning and Motivation, 12*, 261–281.

McClelland, J. L., & Rummelhart, D. E. (1985). Distributed memory and the representation of general and specific information. *Journal of Experimental Psychology: General, 114*, 159–188.

McCloskey, M., & Cohen, N. J. (1989). Catastrophic interference in connectionist networks: The sequential learning problem. In G. Bower (Ed.), *The psychology of learning and motivation* (Vol. 24, pp. 109–165). San Diego, CA: Academic Press.

McFarland, D. (1985). *Animal Behaviour*. Bath, UK: Pitman.

McGonigle, B. O., & Chalmers, M. (1977). Are monkeys logical? *Nature, 267*, 694–696.

McGonigle, B. O., & Chalmers, M. (1986). Representations and strategies during inference. In T. Myers, K. Brown & B. O. McGonigle (Eds.), *Reasoning and discourse processes* (pp. 141–164). London: Academic Press.

McGonigle, B. O., & Chalmers, M. (1992). Monkeys are rational. *Quarterly Journal of Experimental Psychology, 45B*, 189–228.

McGregor, A., & Healy, S. (1999). Spatial accuracy in food-storing and nonstoring birds. *Animal Behaviour, 58*, 727–734.

McLaren, I. P. L., & Mackintosh, N. J. (2000). An elemental model of associative learning: Latent inhibition and perceptual learning. *Animal Learning and Behavior, 28*, 211–246.

McLaren, I. P. L., & Mackintosh, N. J. (2002). Associative learning and elemental representation: II. Generalization and discrimination. *Animal Learning and Behavior, 30*, 177–200.

McLaren, I. P. L., Kaye, H., & Mackintosh, N. J. (1989). An associative theory of the representation of stimuli: Applications to perceptual learning and latent inhibition. In R. G. M. Morris (Ed.), *Parallel distributed processing: Implications for psychology and neurobiology* (pp. 102–130). Oxford: Clarendon Press.

McQuoid, L. M., & Galef, B. G., Jr. (1992). Social influences on feeding site selection by Burmese fowl (*Gallus gallus*). *Journal of Comparative Psychology, 106*, 136–141.

Mechner, F. (1958). Probability relations within response sequences under ratio reinforcement. *Journal of the Experimental Analysis of Behavior, 1*, 109–122.

Mechner, F., & Guevrekian, L. (1962). Effects of deprivation on counting and timing in rats. *Journal of the Experimental Analysis of Behavaior, 5*, 463–466.

Meck, W. H., & Church, R. M. (1982). Abstraction of temporal attributes. *Journal of Experimental Psychology: Animal Behavior Processes, 8*, 226–243.

Meck, W. H., & Church, R. M. (1983). A mode control model of counting and timing processes. *Journal of Experimental Psychology: Animal Behavior Processes, 9*, 320–334.

Medin, D. L., & Schaffer, M. M. (1978). A context theory of classification learning. *Psychological Review, 85*, 217–238.

Meehl, P. E. (1950). On the circularity of the law of effect. *Psychological Bulletin, 47*, 52–75.

Menzel, E. W. (1978). Cognitive mapping in chimpanzees. In S. H. Hulse, H. Fowler, & W. K. Honig (Eds.), *Cognitive processes in animal behavior* (pp. 375–422). Hillsdale, NJ: Lawrence Erlbaum Associates, Inc.

Menzel, R. (1979). Behavioural access to short-term memory in bees. *Nature, 241*, 477–478.

Menzel, R. (1990). Learning, memory, and "cognition" in honey bees. In R. P. Kesner, & D. S. Olton (Eds.), *Neurobiology of comparative cognition* (pp. 237–292). Hillsdale, NJ: Lawrence Erlbaum Associates, Inc.

Menzel, R. M., & Erber, J. (1978). Learning and memory in bees. *Scientific American, 239*, 80–88.

Menzel, R., Greggers, U., Smith, A., Berger, S., Brandt, R., Brunke, S., et al. (2005). Honey bees navigate according to a map-like spatial memory. *Proceedings of the National Academy of Sciences, 102*, 3040–3045.

Meyer, M. E., Adams, W. A., & Worthen, V. K. (1969). Deprivation and escape conditioning with various intensities of shock. *Psychonomic Science, 14*, 212–214.

Miles, H. L. W. (1994). ME CHANTEK: The development of self-awareness in the signing oragutan. In S. T. Taylor, R. W. Mitchell & M. L. Bocciam (Eds.), *Self-awareness in animals and humans* (pp. 254–272). New York: Cambridge University Press.

Miller, D. J. (1993). Do animals subitize? In S. J. Boysen & E. J. Capaldi (Eds.) *The development of numerical competence: Animal and human models* (pp. 149–169). Hillsdale, NJ: Lawrence Erlbaum Associates, Inc.

Miller, N. E., & Dollard, J. (1941). *Social learning and imitation.* New Haven, CT: Yale University Press.

Miller, R. R., & Berk, A. M. (1977). Retention over metamorphosis in the African claw-toed frog. *Journal of Experimental Psychology: Animal Behavior Processes, 3*, 343–356.

Miller, R. R., Barnet, R. C., & Grahame, N. J. (1995). Assessment of the Rescorla–Wagner model. *Psychological Bulletin, 117*, 363–386.

Mineka, S., & Cook, M. (1988). Social learning and the acquisition of snake fear in monkeys. In T. R. Zentall & B. G. Galef, Jr. (Eds.), *Social learning: Psychological and biological perspectives* (pp. 51–74). Hillsdale, NJ: Lawrence Erlbaum Associates, Inc.

Mineka, S., Keir, R., & Price, V. (1980). Fear of snakes in wild- and laboratory-reared rhesus monkeys (*Macaca mulatta*). *Animal Learning and Behavior, 8*, 653–663.

Minsky, M. L., & Papert, S. (1969). *Perceptrons: An introduction to computational geometry.* Cambridge, MA: MIT Press.

Misanin, J. R., & Cambell, B. A. (1969). Effects of hunger and thirst on sensitivity and reactivity to shock. *Journal of Comparative and Physiological Psychology, 69*, 207–213.

Mishkin, M., Prockop, E. S., & Rosvold, H. E. (1962). One-trial object-discrimination learning in monkeys with frontal lesions. *Journal of Comparative and Physiological Psychology, 55*, 178–181.

Mistlberger, R. E. (1994). Circadian food-anticipatory activity: Formal models and physiological mechanisms. *Neuroscience and Behavioral Reviews, 18*, 171–195.

Mitchell, C. J., Heyes, C. M., Gardner, M. R., & Dawson, G. R. (1999). Limitations of a bidirectional control procedure for the investigation of imitation in rats: Odour cues on the manipulandum. *Quarterly Journal of Experimental Psychology, 52B*, 193–202.

Mitchell, R. W., & Anderson, J. R. (1997). Pointing, withholding information, and deception in capuchin monkeys (*Cebus apella*). *Journal of Comparative Psychology, 111*, 351–361.

Mittelstaedt, H., & Mittelstaedt, M. L. (1982). Homing by path integration. In F. Papi & H. G. Wallraff (Eds.), *Avian navigation* (pp. 290–297). Berlin: Springer-Verlag.

Moore, B. R. (1973). The role of directed Pavlovian reactions in simple instrumental learning in the pigeon. In R. A. Hinde & J. Stevenson-Hinde (Eds.) *Constraints on learning* (pp. 159–186). London: Academic Press.

Moore, B. R. (1992). Avian imitation and a new form of mimicry: Tracing the evolution of complex learning. *Behavior, 122*, 231–263.

Moore, B. R. (1996). The evolution of imitative learning. In C. M. Heyes & B. G. J. Galef (Eds.), *Social learning in animals: The roots of culture* (pp. 245–265). New York: Academic Press.

Moore, F. R., & Osadchuk, T. E. (1982). Spatial memory in a passerine migrant. In F. Papi & H. G. Wallraff (Eds.), *Avian navigation* (pp. 319–325). Berlin: Springer-Verlag.

Moore, J. W. (1972). Stimulus control: Studies of auditory generalization in the rabbit. In A. H. Black & W. F. Prokasy (Eds.), *Classical Conditioning II: Current research and theory* (pp. 206–320). New York: Appleton-Century-Crofts.

Moore, J. W., & Stickney, K. J. (1980). Formation of attentional–associative networks in real time: Role of the hippocampus and implications for conditioning. *Physiological Psychology, 8*, 207–217.

Mora, C. V., Davison, M., Wild, J. M., & Walker, M. M. (2004). Magnetoreception and its trigeminal mediation in the homing pigeon. *Nature, 432*, 508–511.

Morgan, C. L. (1890). *Animal life and intelligence.* London: Edward Arnold.

Morgan, C. L. (1894). *An introduction to comparative psychology.* London: Scott.

Morgan, C. L. (1900). *Animal behaviour.* London: Edward Arnold.

Morgan, M. J., Fitch, M. D., Holman, J. G., & Lea, S. E. G. (1976). Pigeons learn the concept of an "A". *Perception, 5*, 57–66.

Morris, R. G. M. (1981). Spatial localization does not require the presence of local cue. *Learning and Motivation, 12*, 239–260.

Nader, K. (2003). Memory traces unbound. *Trends in Neurosciences, 26*, 65–72.

Nader, K., Schafe, G. E., & Le Doux, J. E. (2000). Fear memories require protein synthesis for reconsolidation after retrieval. *Nature, 406*, 722–726.

Nagell, K., Olguin, R. S., & Tomasello, M. (1993). Processes of social learning in the tool use of chimpanzees (*Pan troglodytes*) and human children (*Homo sapiens*). *Journal of Comparative Psychology, 107*, 174–186.

Nakajima, S., Arimitsu, K., & Lattal, K. M. (2002). Estimation of animal intelligence by university students in Japan and the United States. *Anthrozoos, 15*, 194–205.

Napier, R. M., Macrae, M., & Kehoe, E. J. (1992). Rapid reacquisition in conditioning of the rabbit's nictitating membrane response. *Journal of Experimental Psychology: Animal Behavior Processes, 18*, 182–192.

Nissani, M. (2004). Theory of mind and insight in chimpanzees, elephants, and other animals? In L. J. Rogers & G. Kaplan (Eds.), *Comparative vertebrate cognition* (pp. 227–261). New York: Kluwer Academic/Plenum Publishers.

Nissani, M. (2006). Do Asian elephants (*Elephas maximus*) apply causal reasoning to tool-use tasks? *Journal of Experimental Psychology: Animal Behavior Processes, 32*, 91–96.

Nissen, H. W., Blum, J. S., & Blum, R. A. (1948). Analysis of matching behavior in chimpanzees. *Journal of Comparative and Physiological Psychology, 41*, 62–74.

Oden, D. L., Thompson, J. K., & Premack, D. (1990). Infant chimpanzees (*Pan troglodytes*) spontaneously perceive both concrete and abstract same/different relations. *Child Development, 61*, 621–631.

Oden, D. L., Thompson, R. K. R., & Premack, D. (1988). Spoontaneous transfer of matching by infant chimpanzees (*Pan troglodytes*). *Journal of Experimental Psychology: Animal Behavior Processes, 14*, 140–145.

O'Keefe, J. (1979). A review of the hippocampal place cells. *Progress in Neurobiology, 13*, 419–439.

O'Keefe, J., & Conway, D. H. (1978). On the trail of the hippocampal engram. *Physiological Psychology, 8*, 229–238.

O'Keefe, J., & Nadel, L. (1978). *The hippocampus as a cognitive map*. Oxford: Clarendon Press.

O'Keefe, J., & Speakman, A. (1987). Single unit activity in the rat hippocampus during a spatial memory task. *Experimental Brain Research, 68*, 1–27.

Olds, J., & Milner, P. (1954). Positive reinforcement produced by electrical stimulation of septal area and other regions of the rat brain. *Journal of Comparative and Physiological Psychology, 47*, 419–427.

Olson, D. J., Kamil, A. C., Balda, R. P., & Nims, P. J. (1995). Performance of 4 seed-caching corvid species in operant tests of nonspatial and spatial memory. *Journal of Comparative Psychology, 109*, 173–181.

Olton, D. S. (1978). Characteristics of spatial memory. In S. H. Hulse, H. Fowler, & W. K. Honig (Eds.), *Cognitive processes in animal behavior* (pp. 341–373). Hillsdale, NJ: Lawrence Erlbaum Associates, Inc.

Olton, D. S., Collison, C., & Werz, M. (1977). Spatial memory and radial arm maze performance of rats. *Learning and Motivation, 8*, 289–314.

Orlov, T., Yakovlev, V., Amit, D., Hochstein, S., & Zohary, E. (2002). Serial memory strategies in macaque monkeys: Behavioral and theoretical aspects. *Cerebral Cortex, 12*, 306–317.

Orlov, T., Yakovlev, V., Hochstein, S., & Zohary, E. (2000). Macaque monkeys categorize images by their ordinal number. *Nature, 404*, 77–80.

Osgood, C. E. (1953). *Method and theory in experimental psychology*. New York: Oxford University Press.

O'Sullivan, C., & Yeager, C. P. (1989). Communication context and linguistic competence: The effects of social setting on a chimpanzee's conversational skill. In R. G. Gardner, B. T. Gardner & T. E. Van Canfort (Eds.), *Teaching sign language to chimpanzees* (pp. 281–292). New York: New York State University Press.

Papi, F., & Luschi, P. (1996). Pinpointing "Isla Meta": The case of sea turtles and albatrosses. *Journal of Experimental Biology, 199*, 65–71.

Papi, F., Fiore, l., Fiaschi, V., & Benvenuti, S. (1972). Pigeon homing: Outward journey detours influence the initial orientation. *Monitore Zoologico Italiano, 7*, 129–133.

Papi, F., Mariotti, G., Foa, A., & Fiaschi, V. (1980). Orientation of anosmatic pigeons. *Journal of Comparative Physiology, 135*, 227–232.

Papini, M. R. (2002). Pattern and process in the evolution of learning. *Psychological Review, 109*, 186–201.

Papousek, H. (1977). Entwicklung der Lernfahigkeit im Sauglingsalter. In Nissen (Ed.). *Intelligenz, lernen und lernstorungen*. Berlin: Springer.

Parisi, V., & Gandolfi, G. (1974). Further aspects of the predation by rats on various mollusc species. *Bollettino di Zoologia, 41*, 87–106.

Parisi, T., & Matthews, T. J. (1975). Pavlovian determinants of the autoshaped keypeck response. *Bulletin of the Psychonomic Society, 6*, 527–529.

Passingham, R. E. (1982). *The human primate*. San Francisco: Freeman.

Patterson, F. G. P., & Cohn, R. H. (1994). Self-recognition and self-awareness in lowland gorillas. In S. T. Parker, R. W. Mitchell & M. L. Boccia (Eds.), *Self-awareness in animals and humans* (pp. 273–290). New York: Cambridge University Press.

Paukner, A., Anderson, J. R., Borelli, E., Visalberghi, E., & Ferrari, P. F. (2005). Macaques (*Macaca nemestrina*) recognize when they are being imitated. *Biology Letters, 1*, 219–222.

Pavlov, I. P. (1927). *Conditioned reflexes* (G. V. Anrep, Trans.). London: Oxford University Press.

Pearce, J. M. (1987). A model for stimulus generalization in Pavlovian conditioning. *Psychological Review, 94*, 61–73.

Pearce, J. M. (1988). Stimulus generalization and the acquisition of categories by pigeons. In L.Weiskrantz (Ed.), *Thought without language* (pp. 132–152). Oxford: Oxford University Press.

Pearce, J. M. (1989). The acquisition of an artificial category by pigeons. *Quarterly Journal of Experimental Psychology, 41B*, 381–406.

Pearce, J. M. (1991). The acquisition of abstract and concrete categories by pigeons. In L. Dachowski, & C. Flaherty (Eds.), *Current topics in animal learning: Brain, emotion and, cognition* (pp. 141–164). New Jersey: L. Erlbaum.

Pearce, J. M. (1994). Similarity and discrimination: A selective review and a connectionist model. *Psychological Review, 101*, 587–607.

Pearce, J. M. (2002). Evaluation and development of a connectionist theory of configural learning. *Animal Learning and Behavior, 30*, 73–95.

Pearce, J. M., & Bouton, M. E. (2001). Theories of associative learning in animals. *Annual Review of Psychology, 52*, 111–131.

Pearce, J. M., & Hall, G. (1978). Overshadowing the instrumental conditioning of a lever-press response by a more valid predictor of reinforcement. *Journal of Experimental Psychology: Animal Behavior Processes, 4*, 356–367.

Pearce, J. M., & Hall, G. (1979). Loss of associability by a compound stimulus comprising excitatory and inhibitory elements. *Journal of Experimental Psychology: Animal Behavior Processes, 5*, 19–30.

Pearce, J. M., & Hall, G. (1980). A model for Pavlovian learning: Variations in the effectiveness of conditioned but not unconditioned stimuli. *Psychological Review, 87*, 532–552.

Pearce, J. M., & Redhead, E. S. (1993). The influence of an irrelevant stimulus on two discriminations. *Journal of Experimental Psychology: Animal Behavior Processes, 19*, 180–190.

Pearce, J. M., & Wilson, P. N. (1991). Failure of excitatory conditioning to extinguish the influence of a conditioned inhibitor. *Journal of Experimental Psychology: Animal Behavior Processes, 17*, 519–529.

Pearce, J. M., Colwill, R. M., & Hall, G. (1978). The instrumental conditioning of scratching in the laboratory rat. *Learning and Motivation, 9*, 255–271.

Pearce, J. M., Good, M. A., Jones, P. M., & McGregor, A. (2004). Transfer of spatial behavior between different environments: Implications for theories of spatial learning and for the role of the hippocampus in spatial learning. *Journal of Experimental Psychology: Animal Behavior Processes, 30*, 135–147.

Pearce, J. M., Montgomery, A., & Dickinson, A. (1981). Contralateral transfer of inhibitory and excitatory eyelid conditioning in the rabbit. *Quarterly Journal of Experimental Psychology, 33B, 45–61.*

Pearce, J. M., Nicholas, D. J., & Dickinson, A. (1982). Loss of associability by a conditioned inhibitor. *Quarterly Journal of Experimental Psychology, 33B, 149–162.*

Pearce, J. M., Redhead, E. S., & Aydin, A. (1997). Partial reinforcement in appetitive Pavlovian conditioning with rats. *Quarterly Journal of Experimental Psychology, 50B,* 273–294.

Peeke, H. V. S., & Veno, A. (1973). Stimulus specifity of habituated aggression in three-spined sticklebacks (*Gasterosteus aculeatus*). *Behavioral Biology, 8*, 427–432.

Pepperberg, I. (1994). Numerical competence in an African grey parrot. *Journal of Comparative Psychology, 108*, 36–44.

Pepperberg, I. M. (1981). Functional vocalizations by an African grey parrot (*Psittacus erithacus*). *Zeitschrift fur Tierpsychologie 55*, 139–160.

Pepperberg, I. M. (1983). Cognition in the African grey parrot: Preliminary evidence for auditory/vocal comprehension of the class concept. *Animal Learning and Behavior, 11*, 179–185.

Pepperberg, I. M. (1987). Acquisition of the same/different concept by an African grey parrot (*Psittacus erithacus*): Learning with respect to color, shape and material. *Animal Learning and Behavior, 15*, 423–432.

Pepperberg, I. M. (1993). Cognition and communication in an African grey parrot (*Psittacus erithacus*): Studies on a nonhuman, nonprimate, nonmammalian subject. In H. L. Roitblat, L. M. Herman, & P. E. Nachtigall (Eds.), *Language and communication: Comparative perspectives* (pp. 221–248). Hillsdale, NJ: Lawrence Erlbaum Associates, Inc.

Pepperberg, I. M. (2006a). Grey parrot (*Psittacus erithacus*) numerical abilities: Addition and further experiments on a zero-like concept. *Journal of Comparative Psychology, 120*, 1–11.

Pepperberg, I. M. (2006b). Ordinality and inferential abilities of a grey parrot (*Psittacus erithacus*). *Journal of Comparative Psychology, 120*, 205–216.

Pepperberg, I. M., & Gordon, J. D. (2005). Number comprehension by a grey parrot (*Psittacus erithacus*), including a zero-like concept. *Journal of Comparative Psychology, 119*, 197–209.

Pepperberg, I. M., & McLaughlin, M. A. (1996). Effects of avian–human attention on allospecific vocal learning by grey parrots (*Psittacus erithacus*). *Journal of Comparative Psychology, 110*, 286–297.

Pepperberg, I. M., & Shive, H. R. (2001). Simultaneous development of vocal and physical object combinations by a grey parrot (*Psittacus erithacus*): Bottle caps, lids, and labels. *Journal of Comparative Psychology, 115*, 376–384.

Pepperberg, I. M., Garcia, S. E., Jackson, E. C., & Marconi, S. (1995). Mirror use by African grey parrots (*Psittacus erithacus*). *Journal of Comparative Psychology, 109*, 182–195.

Perdeck, A. C. (1958). Two types of orientation in migratory starlings, *Sturnus vulgaris* L, and chaffinches, *Fringilla coelebs* L, as revealed by displacement experiments. *Ardea, 46*, 1–37.

Peterson, L., & Peterson, M. J. (1959). Short-term retention of individual verbal items. *Journal of Experimental Psychology, 58*, 193–198.

Petrinovich, L. (1988). The role of social factors in white-crowned sparrow song development. In T. R. Zentall & B. G. Galef, Jr. (Eds.) *Social learning: Psychological and biological perspectives* (pp. 255–278). Hillsdale, NJ: Lawrence Erlbaum Associates, Inc.

Pfungst, O. (1965). *Clever Hans: The horse of Mr Van Osten.* New York: Holt (German original, 1908).

Pietrewicz, A. T., & Kamil, A. C. (1977). Visual detection of cryptic prey by blue jays. *Science, 195*, 580–582.

Pinker, S. (1994). *The language instinct.* New York: Penguin.

Plaisted, K. (1997). The effect of interstimulus interval on the discrimination of cryptic targets. *Journal of Experimental Psychology: Animal Behavior Processes, 23*, 248–259.

Platt, M. L., Brannon, E. M., Briese, T. L., & French, J. A. (1996). Differences in feeding ecology predict differences in performance between golden lion tamarins (*Leontopithecus rosalia*) and Wied's marmosets (*Callithrix kubli*) on spatial and visual memory tasks. *Animal Learning and Behavior, 24*, 384–393.

Plotnik, J. M., de Waal, F. B. M., & Reiss, D. (2006). Self-recognition in an Asian elephant. *Proceedings of the National Academy of Science of the USA, 103*, 17053–17057.

Porter, D., & Neuringer, A. (1984). Music discrimination by pigeons. *Journal of Experimental Psychology: Animal Behavior Processes, 10*, 138–148.

Posner, M. I., & Keele, S. W. (1968). On the genesis of abstract ideas. *Journal of Experimental Psychology, 77*, 353–363.

Poucet, B., Chapuis, N., Durup, M., & Thinus-Blanc, C. (1986). A study of exploratory behavior as an index of spatial knowledge in hamsters. *Animal Learning and Behavior, 14*, 93–100.

Povinelli, D. J. (1989). Failure to find self-recognition in Asian elephants (*Elephas maximus*) in contrast to their use of mirror cues to discover hidden food. *Journal of Comparative Psychology, 103*, 122–131.

Povinelli, D. J. (1994). Comparative studies of animal mental attributions: A reply to Heyes. *Animal Behaviour, 48*, 239–241.

Povinelli, D. J. (2000). *Folk physics for apes.* Oxford: Oxford University Press.

Povinelli, D. J., & Eddy, T. J. (1996). What young chimpanzees know about seeing. *Monographs of the Society for Research in Child Development, 61*, 1–190.

Povinelli, D. J., & Vonk, J. (2003). Chimpanzee minds: Suspiciously human? *Trends in Cognitive Sciences, 7*, 157–160.

Povinelli, D. J., & Vonk, J. (2004). We don't need a microscope to explore the chimpanzee's mind. *Mind and Language, 19*, 1–28.

Povinelli, D. J., Gallup, G. G., Jr., Eddy, T. J., Bierschwale, D. T., Engstrom, M. C., Perilloux, H. K., et al. (1997). Chimpanzees recognize themselves in mirrors. *Animal Behaviour, 53*, 1083–1088.

Povinelli, D. J., Nelson, K. E., & Boysen, S. T. (1990). Inferences about guessing and knowing by chimpanzees (*Pan troglodytes*). *Journal of Comparative Psychology, 104*, 203–210.

Povinelli, D. J., Rulf, A. B., & Bierschwale, D. T. (1994). Absence of knowledge attribution and self-recognition in young chimpanzees (*Pan troglodytes*). *Journal of Comparative Psychology, 108*, 74–80.

Povinelli, D. J., Rulf, A. B., Landau, K. R., & Bierschwale, D. T. (1993). Self-recognition in chimpanzees (*Pan troglodytes*): Distribution, ontogeny, and patterns of emergence. *Journal of Comparative Psychology, 107*, 347–372.

Premack, D. (1959). Toward empirical behavior laws: I. positive reinforcement. *Psychological Review, 66*, 219–233.

Premack, D. (1962). Reversibility of the reinforcement relation. *Science, 136*, 235–237.

Premack, D. (1965). Reinforcement theory. In D. Levine (Ed.), *Nebraska symposium on motivation* (pp. 123–180). Lincoln: University of Nebraska Press.

Premack, D. (1971a). Catching up with common sense, or two sides of a generalization: Reinforcement and punishment. In R. Glaser (Ed.) *The nature of reinforcement* (pp. 121–150). New York: Academic Press.

Premack, D. (1971b). Language in chimpanzees? *Science, 172*, 808–822.

Premack, D. (1976). *Intelligence in ape and man.* Hillsdale, NJ: Lawrence Erlbaum Associates, Inc.

Premack, D. (1983a). Animal cognition. *Annual Review of Psychology, 34*, 351–362.

Premack, D. (1983b). The codes of man and beasts. *Behavioral and Brain Sciences, 6*, 125–167.

Premack, D. (1988a). "Does the chimpanzee have a theory of mind?" revisited. In R. W. Byrne, & A. Whiten (Eds.), *Machiavellian intelligence* (pp. 160–179). Oxford: Clarendon Press.

Premack, D. (1988b). Minds with and without language. In L. Weiskrantz (Ed.), *Thought without language* (pp. 46–65). Oxford: Clarendon Press.

Premack, D., & Premack, A. J. (1994). Levels of causal understanding in chimpanzees and children. *Cognition, 50*, 347–362.

Premack, D., & Woodruff, G. (1978). Does the chimpanzee have a theory of mind? *Behavioral and Brain Sciences, 4*, 515–526.

Quine, D. B. (1982). Infrasounds: A potential navigational cue for homing pigeons. In F. Papi & H. G. Wallraff (Eds.), *Avian navigation* (pp. 373–376). Berlin: Springer-Verlag.

Ramsay, D., & Woods, S. (1997). Biological consequences of drug administration: Implications for acute and chronic tolerance. *Psychological Reveiw, 104*, 170–193.

Rashotte, M. E., Griffin, R. W., & Sisk, C. L. (1977). Second-order conditioning of the pigeon's key peck. *Animal Learning and Behavior, 5*, 25–38.

Reader, S. M., & Laland, K. N. (2002). Social intelligence, innovation, and enhanced brain size in primates. *Proceedings of the National Academy of Sciences, 99*, 4436–4441.

Redhead, E. S., & Pearce, J. M. (1995a). Similarity and discrimination learning. *Quarterly Journal of Experimental Psychology, 48B*, 46–66.

Redhead, E. S., & Pearce, J. M. (1995b). Stimulus salience and negative patterning. *Quarterly Journal of Experimental Psychology, 48B*, 67–83.

Reichmuth-Kastak, C., & Schusterman, R. J. (2002). Long-term memory for concepts in a California sea lion (*Zalophus californianus*). *Animal Cognition, 5*, 225–232.

Reiss, D., & Marino, L. (2001). Mirror self-recognition in the bottlenose dolphin: A case of cognitive convergence. *Proceedings of the National Academy of Sciences, 98*, 5937–5942.

Reiss, S., & Wagner, A. R. (1972). CS habituation produces a "latent inhibition" effect but no active "conditioned inhibition". *Learning and Motivation, 3*, 237–245.

Renner, M. (1960). Contribution of the honey bee to the study of time sense and astronomical orientation. *Cold Spring Harbor Symposium on Quantitative Biology, 25*, 361–367.

Rensch, B. (1956). Increase of learning capability with increase of brain size. *American Naturalist, 90*, 81–95.

Rensch, B. (1957). The intelligence of elephants. *Scientific American, 196*, 44–49.

Rescorla, R. A. (1967). Pavlovian conditioning and its proper control procedures. *Psychological Review, 74*, 71–80.

Rescorla, R. A. (1968). Probability of shock in the presence and absence of CS in fear conditioning. *Journal of Comparative and Physiological Psychology, 66*, 1–5.

Rescorla, R. A. (1969). Pavlovian conditioned inhibition. *Psychological Bulletin, 72*, 77–94.

Rescorla, R. A. (1972). "Configural" conditioning in discrete-trial bar pressing. *Journal of Comparative and Physiological Psychology, 79*, 307–317.

Rescorla, R. A. (1976). Stimulus generalization: Some predictions from a model of Pavlovian conditioning. *Journal of Experimental Psychology: Animal Behavior Processes, 2*, 88–96.

Rescorla, R. A. (1979). Conditioned inhibition and extinction. In A. Dickinson & R. A. Boakes (Eds.), *Mechanisms of learning and motivation* (pp. 83–110). Hillsdale, NJ: Lawrence Erlbaum Associates, Inc.

Rescorla, R. A. (1980). *Pavlovian second-order conditioning*. Hillsdale, N. J.: Lawrence Erlbaum Associates, Inc.

Rescorla, R. A. (1991). Associative relations in instrumental learning: The eighteenth Bartlett memorial lecture. *Quarterly Journal of Experimental Psychology, 43B*, 1–23.

Rescorla, R. A. (1993). Inhibitory associations between S and R in extinction. *Animal Learning and Behavior, 21*, 327–336.

Rescorla, R. A. (1996). Preservation of Pavlovian associations through extinction. *Quarterly Journal of Experimental Psychology, 49B*, 245–258.

Rescorla, R. A. (2000). Extinction can be enhanced by a concurrent excitor. *Journal of Experimental Psychology: Animal Behavior Processes, 26*, 251–260.

Rescorla, R. A. (2003). Protection from extinction. *Animal Learning and Behavior, 31*, 124–132.

Rescorla, R. A., & LoLordo, V. M. (1965). Inhibition of avoidance behavior. *Journal of Comparative and Physiological Psychology, 59*, 406–412.

Rescorla, R. A., & Skucy, J. C. (1969). Effect of response-independent reinforcers during extinction. *Journal of Comparative and Physiological Psychology, 67*, 381–389.

Rescorla, R. A., & Solomon, R. L. (1967). Two-process learning theory: relationship between Pavlovian conditioning and instrumental learning. *Psychological Bulletin, 88*, 151–182.

Rescorla, R. A., & Wagner, A. R. (1972). A theory of Pavlovian conditioning: Variations in the effectiveness of reinforcement and nonreinforcement. In A. H. Black & W. F. Prokasy (Eds.), *Classical conditioning II: Current research and theory* (pp. 64–99). New York: Appleton-Century-Crofts.

Revusky, S. (1971). The role of interference in association over delay. In W. K. Honig & P. H. R. James (Eds.), *Animal memory* (pp. 155–213). New York: Academic Press.

Revusky, S. H. (1977). Learning as a general process with an emphasis on data from feeding experiments. In N. W. Milgram, L. Krames & T. M. Alloway (Eds.), *Food aversion learning* (pp. 1–51). New York: Plenum.

Riccio, D. C., & Ebner, D. L. (1981). Posatacquisition modifications of memory. In N. E. Spear & R. R. Miller (Eds.), *Information processing in animals: Memory mechanisms* (pp. 291–317). Hillsdale, NJ: Lawrence Erlbaum Associates, Inc.

Richards, D. G., Wolz, J. P., & Herman, L. M. (1984). Vocal mimicry of computer-generated sounds and vocal labelling of objects by a bottlenosed dolphin, *Tusiops truncatus. Journal of Comparative Psychology, 98*, 10–28.

Riddell, W. I. (1979). Cerebral indices and behavioral differences. In M. E. Hahn, C. Jensen, & B. C. Dudek (Eds.), *Development and evolution of brain size* (pp. 89–111). New York: Academic Press.

Riley, D. A., & Roitblat, H. L. (1978). Selective attention and related cognitive processes in pigeons. In S. H. Hulse, H. Fowler & W. K. Honig (Eds.), *Cognitive processes in animal behavior* (pp. 249–276). Hillsdale, NJ: Lawrence Erlbaum Associates, Inc.

Riley, J. R., Greggers, U., Smith, A. D., Reynolds, D. R., & Menzel, R. (2005). The flight paths of honeybees recruited by the waggle dance. *Nature, 435*, 205–207.

Ristau, C. A., & Robbins, D. (1982). Language in great apes: A critical review. *Advances in the Study of Behaviour, 12*, 141–255.

Rivas, E. (2005). Recent use of signs by chimnpanzees (*Pan troglodytes*) in interactions with humans. *Journal of Comparative Psychology, 119*, 404–417.

Rizley, R. C., & Rescorla, R. A. (1972). Associations in second-order conditioning and sensory preconditioning. *Journal of Comparative and Physiological Psychology, 81*, 1–11.

Rizzolatti, G., Fadiga, L., Fogassi, L., & Gallese, V. (1996). Premotor cortex and the recognition of actions. *Cognitive Brain Research, 3*, 131–141.

Rizzolatti, G., Fogassi, L., & Gallese, V. (2001). Neurophysiological mechanisms underlying the understanding and imitation of action. *Nature Reviews Neuroscience, 2*, 661–670.

Roberts, A. D. L., & Pearce, J. M. (1999). Blocking in the Morris swimming pool. *Journal of Experimental Psychology: Animal Behavior Processes, 25*, 225–235.

Roberts, S. (1982). Cross-modal use of an internal clock. *Journal of Experimental Psychology: Animal Behavior Processes, 8*, 2–22.

Roberts, S. K. (1965). Photreception and entrainment of cockroach activity rhythms. *Science, 148*, 958–960.

Roberts, W. A. (1979). Spatial memory in the rat on a hierarchical maze. *Learning and Motivation, 10*, 117–140.

Roberts, W. A. (1981). Retroactive inhibition in rat spatial memory. *Animal Learning and Behavior, 9*, 566–574.

Roberts, W. A. (2002). Are animals stuck in time? *Psychological Bulletin, 128*, 473–489.

Roberts, W. A., & Dale, R. H. I. (1981). Remembrance of places lasts: Proactive inhibition and patterns of choices in rat spatial memory. *Learning and Motivation, 12*, 261–281.

Roberts, W. A., & Grant, D. S. (1974). Short-term memory in the pigeon with presentation time precisely controlled. *Learning and Motivation, 5*, 393–408.

Roberts, W. A., & Grant, D. S. (1976). Studies of short-term memory in the pigeon using the delayed-matching-to-sample procedure. In D. L. Medin, W. A. Roberts & R. T. Davis (Eds.), *Processes in animal memory*. Hillsdale, NJ: Lawrence Erlbaum Associates, Inc.

Roberts, W. A., & Kraemer, P. J. (1981). Recognition memory for lists of visual stimuli in monkeys and humans. *Animal Learning and Behavior, 9*, 587–594.

Roberts, W. A., & Phelps, M. T. (1994). Transitive inference in rats: A test of the spatial coding hypothesis. *Psychological Science, 6*, 368–374.

Roberts, W. A., & Smythe, W. E. (1979). Memory for lists of spatial events in the rat. *Learning and Motivation, 10*, 313–336.

Roberts, W. A., & Van Veldhuizen, N. (1985). Spatial memory in pigeons on the radial maze. *Journal of Experimental Psychology: Animal Behavior Processes, 11*, 241–260.

Roberts, W. A., Cheng, K., & Cohen, J. S. (1989). Timing light and tone signals in pigeons. *Journal of Experimental Psychology: Animal Behavior Processes, 15*, 23–35.

Roediger, H. L., & Crowder, R. G. (1975). The spacing of lists in free recall. *Journal of Verbal Learning and Verbal Behavior, 14*, 580–602.

Roitblat, H. L. (1980). Codes and coding processes in pigeon short-term memory. *Animal Learning and Behavior, 8*, 341–351.

Roitblat, H. L., Bever, T. G., Helweg, D. A., & Harley, H. E. (1991). On-line choice and representation of serially structured stimuli. *Journal of Experimental Psychology: Animal Behavior Processes, 17*, 55–67.

Roitblat, H. L., Tham, W., & Golub, L. (1982). Performance of *Betta splendens* in a radial arm maze. *Animal Learning and Behavior, 10*, 108–114.

Romanes, G. J. (1882). *Animal intelligence*. London: Kegan, Paul, Trench & Co.

Roper, K. L., & Zentall, T. R. (1993). Directed forgetting in animals. *Psychological Bulletin, 113*, 513–532.

Roper, T. J. (1983). Learning as a biological phenomenon. In T. R. Halliday, & P. J. B. Slater (Eds.), *Animal behaviour: Genes, development and learning* (pp. 178–212). Oxford: Blackwell.

Rosenblatt, F. (1962). *Principles of neurodynamics*. Washington, DC: Spartan Books.

Rozin, P., & Kalat, J. W. (1971). Specific hungers and poisoning as adaptive specializations of learning. *Psychological Review, 78*, 459–486.

Rumbaugh, D. M. (1977). *Language learning by a chimpanzee*: The LANA project. New York: Academic Press.

Rumbaugh, D. M., & Savage-Rumbaugh, E. S. (1994). Language in comparative perspective. In N. J. Mackintosh (Ed.), *Animal learning and cognition* (pp. 307–333). San Diego, CA: Academic Press.

Rumbaugh, D. M., & Washburn, D. A. (1993). Counting by chimpanzees and ordinality judgements by macaques in video-formatted tasks. In S. T. Boysen & E. J. Capaldi (Eds.), *The development of numerical competence: Animal and human models* (pp. 87–106). Hillsdale, NJ: Lawrence Erlbaum Associates, Inc.

Rumelhart, D. E., Hinton, G. E., & Williams, R. J. (1988). Learning internal representations by error propagation. In D. E. Rummelhart & J. L. McClelland (Eds.), *Parallel distributed processing* (Vol. 1, pp. 318–362). Cambridge, MA: MIT Press.

Rundus, D. (1971). Analysis of rehearsal processes in free recall. *Journal of Experimental Psychology, 89*, 63–77.

Russell, I. S. (1979). Brain size and intelligence: A comparative perspective. In D. A. Oakley & H. C. Plotkin (Eds.), *Brain behaviour and evolution* (pp. 126–153). London: Methuen.

Russon, A. E., & Galdikas, B. M. F. (1993). Imitation in free-ranging orangutans (*Pongo pygmaeus*). *Journal of Comparative Psychology, 107*, 147–161.

Ryan, C. W. E. (1982). Concept formation and individual recognition in the domestic chicken (*Gallus gallus*). *Behavior Analysis Letters, 2*, 213–220.

Saggerson, A. L., George, D. N., & Honey, R. C. (2005). Imitative learning of stimulus–response and response–outcome associations in pigeons. *Journal of Experimental Psychology: Animal Behavior Processes, 31*, 289–300.

Saint Paul, U. V. (1982). Do geese use path integration for walking home? In F. Papi & H. G. Wallraff (Eds.), *Avian navigation* (pp. 298–307). Berlin: Springer-Verlag.

Santchi, F. (1913). Comment s'orient les fourmis? *Revue Suisse de Zoologie, 21*, 298–307.

Savage-Rumbaugh, E. S. (1984). Acquisition of functional symbol usage in apes and children. In H. L. Roitblat. T. G. Bever, & H. S. Terrace (Eds.), *Animal cognition* (pp. 291–310). Hillsdale, NJ: Lawrence Erlbaum Associates, Inc.

Savage-Rumbaugh, E. S., & Lewin, R. (1994). *Kanzi: At the brink of the human mind*. New York: Wiley.

Savage-Rumbaugh, E. S., McDonald, K., Sevcik, R. A., Hopkins, W. D., & Rubert, E. (1986). Spontaneous symbol acquisition and communication by pygmy chimpanzees (*Pan paniscus*). *Journal of Experimental Psychology: General, 115*, 211–235.

Savage-Rumbaugh, E. S., Murphy, J., Sevcik, R. A., Brakke, K. E., Williams, S. L., & Rumbaugh, D. M. (1993). Language comprehension in ape and child. *Monographs of the Society for Research in Child Development, 58*, 1–221.

Savage-Rumbaugh, E. S., Pate, J. L., Lawson, J., Smith, T., & Rosenbaum, S. (1983). Can a chimpanzee make a statement? *Journal of Experimental Psychology: General, 112*, 457–492.

Savage-Rumbaugh, E. S., Rumbaugh, D. M., & Boysen, S. T. (1978). Symbolic communication between two chimpanzees (*Pan troglodytes*). *Science, 201*, 641–644.

Savage-Rumbaugh, E. S., Rumbaugh, D. M., Smith, S. T., & Lawson, J. (1980). Reference – the linguistic essential. *Science, 210*, 922–925.

Savage-Rumbaugh, S., Sevcik, R. A., & Hopkins, W. D. (1988). Symbolic cross-modal transfer in two species of chimpanzees. *Child Development, 59*, 617–625.

Schiller, P. H. (1952). Innate constituents of complex responses in primates. *Psychological Review, 59*, 177–191.

Schlicte, H. J., & Schmidt-Koenig, K. (1971). Zum Heimfindevermogen der Brieftaube bei erschwerter optischer Wahrnehmung. *Naturwissenschaften, 58*, 329–330.

Schmajuk, N. A., & DiCarlo, J. J. (1992). Stimulus configuration, classical conditioning, and hippocampal function. *Psychological Review, 99*, 268–305.

Schrier, A. M., & Brady, P. M. (1987). Categorization of natural stimuli by monkeys (*Macaca mulatta*): Effects of stimulus set size and modification of exemplars. *Journal of Experimental Psychology: Animal Behavior Processes, 13*, 136–143.

Schrier, A. M., Angarella, R., & Povar, M. L. (1984). Studies of concept formation by stumptailed monkeys: Concepts humans, monkeys, monkeys, and letter A. *Journal of Experimental Psychology: Animal Behavior Processes, 10*, 564–584.

Schultz, W., & Dickinson, A. (2000). Neuronal coding of prediction errors. *Annual Review of Neuroscience, 23*, 473–500.

Schusterman, R. J., & Gisiner, R. (1988). Artificial language comprehension in dolphins and sea lions: The essential cognitive skills. *Psychological Record, 38*, 3–18.

Schwartz, B. (1989). *The Psychology of Learning and Behavior*. New York: W. H. Norton.

Seed, A. M., Tebbich, S., Emery, N. J., & Clayton, N. S. (2006). Investigating physical cognition in rooks, *Corvus frugilegus. Current Biology, 16*, 697–701.

Seligman, M. E. P. (1970). On the generality of the laws of learning. *Psychological Review, 77*, 406–418.

Seligman, M. E. P., & Hager, J. L. (1972). *Biological boundaries of learning*. New York: Appleton-Century-Crofts.

Seyfarth, R. M., & Cheney, D. (1993). Meaning, reference, and intentionality in the natural vocalizations of monkeys. In H. L. Roitblat, L. M. Herman & P. E. Nachtigall (Eds.), *Language and communication: Comparative perspectives* (pp. 195–219). Hillsdale, NJ: Lawrence Erlbaum Associates, Inc.

Seyfarth, R. M., & Cheney, D. L. (1986). Vocal development in vervet monkeys. *Animal Behavior, 34*, 1640–1658.

Seyfarth, R. M., & Cheney, D. L. (2003). Signalers and receivers in animal communication. *Annual Review of Psychology, 54*, 145–173.

Shanks, D. R. (1994). Human associative learning. In N. J. Mackintosh (Ed.) *Animal learning and cognition* (pp. 335–368). San Diego, CA: Academic Press.

Shapiro, K. L., Jacobs, W. J., & LoLordo, V. M. (1980). Stimulus–reinforcer interactions in Pavlovian conditioning of pigeons: Implications for selective associations. *Animal Learning and Behavior, 8*, 586–594.

Sheafor, P. J. (1975). "Pseudoconditioned" jaw movements of the rabbit reflect associations conditioned to contextual background cues. *Journal of Experimental Psychology: Animal Behavior Processes, 1*, 245–260.

Shepp, B. E., & Eimas, P. D. (1964). Intradimensional and extradimensional shifts in the rat. *Journal of Comparative and Physiological Psychology, 57*, 357–364.

Sherman, P. W. (1977). Nepotism and the evolution of alarm calls. *Science, 197*, 1070–1094.

Sherry, D. F., & Galef, B. G., Jr. (1984). Cultural transmission without imitation: Milk bottle opening by birds. *Animal Behaviour, 32*, 937–938.

Sherry, D. F., & Galef, B. G., Jr. (1990). Social learning without imitation: More about milk bottle opening by birds. *Animal Behaviour, 40*, 987–989.

Shettleworth, S. J. (1998). *Cognition, evolution, and behavior*. New York: Oxford University Press.

Shettleworth, S. J., & Sutton, J. E. (2005). Multiple systems for spatial learning: Dead reckoning and beacon homing in rats. *Journal of Experimental Psychology: Animal Behavior Processes, 31*, 125–141.

Shiffrin, R. W., & Schneider, W. (1977). Controlled and automatic human information processing: II. Perceptual learning, automatic attending, and a general theory. *Psychological Review, 84*, 127–190.

Shin, H. J., & Nosofsky, R. M. (1992). Similarity-scaling of dot-pattern classification and recognition. *Journal of Experimental Psychology: General, 121*, 278–304.

Shishimi, A. (1985). Latent inhibition experiments with goldfish (*Carassius auratus*). *Journal of Comparative Psychology, 99*, 316–327.

Shorey, H. H. (1976). *Animal communication by pheromones*. New York: Academic Press.

Siegel, S. (1967). Overtraining and transfer processes. *Journal of Comparative and Physiological Psychology, 64*, 471–477.

Siegel, S. (1975). Evidence from rats that morphine tolerance is a learned response. *Journal of Comparative and Physiological Psychology, 89*, 498–506.

Siegel, S. (1977). Morphine tolerance acquisition as an associative process. *Journal of Experimental Psychology: Animal Behavior Processes, 3*, 1–13.

Siegel, S., & Allan, L. G. (1996). The widespread influence of the Rescorla–Wagner model. *Psychonomic Bulletin and Review, 3*, 314–321.

Siegel, S., & Allan, L. G. (1998). Learning and homeostasis: Drug addiction and the McCollough effect. *Psychological Bulletin, 124*, 230–239.

Skard, O. (1950). A comparison of human and animal learning in the Stone multiple T-maze. *Acta Psychologica, 7*, 89–109.

Skinner, B. F. (1950). Are theories of learning necessary? *Psychological Review, 57*, 193–216.

Skinner, B. F. (1953). *Science and human behavior.* New York: Macmillan.

Skinner, B. F. (1976). *Particulars of my life.* New York: Knopf.

Skinner, B. F. (1979). *The shaping of a behaviorist.* New York: Knopf.

Skov-Rackette, S. I., & Shettleworth, S. J. (2005). What do rats learn about the geometry of object arrays? Tests with exploratory behavior. *Journal of Experimental Psychology: Animal Behavior Processes, 31*, 142–154.

Skov-Rackette, S. I., Miller, N. Y., & Shettleworth, S. J. (2006). What–where–when memory in pigeons. *Journal of Experimental Psychology: Animal Behavior Processes, 32*, 345–358.

Smith, J. C., & Roll, D. L. (1967). Trace conditioning with X-rays as the aversive stimulus. *Psychonomic Science, 9*, 11–12.

Smith, J. D., Shields, W. E., & Washburn, D. A. (2003). The comparative psychology of uncertainty monitoring and metacognition. *Behavioral and Brain Sciences, 26*, 317–373.

Smith, J. D., Shields, W. E., Schull, J., & Washburn, D. A. (1997). The uncertain response in humans and animals. *Cognition, 62*, 75–97.

Smith, M. C. (1968). CS–US interval and US intensity in classical conditioning of the rabbit's nictitating membrane response. *Journal of Comparative and Physiological Psychology, 69*, 226–231.

Snowden, C. T., & Boe, C. Y. (2003). Social communication about unpalatable foods in tamarins (*Saguinus oedipus*). *Journal of Comparative Psychology, 117*, 142–148.

Sokolov, Y. N. (1963). *Perception and the conditioned reflex.* Oxford: Pergamon Press.

Sovrano, V. A., Bisazza, A., & Vallortigara, G. (2002). Modularity and spatial reorientation in a simple mind: Encoding of geometric and nongeometric properties of a spatial environment by fish. *Cognition, 85*, 51–59.

Sovrano, V. A., Bisazza, A., & Vallortigara, G. (2003). Modularity as a fish (*Xenotoca eiseni*) views it: conjoining geometric and nongeometic information for spatial representation. *Journal of Experimental Psychology: Animal Behavior Processes, 29*, 199–210.

Spear, N. E. (1973). Retrieval of memory in animals. *Psychological Review, 80*, 163–194.

Spear, N. E. (1981). Extending the domain of memory retrieval. In N. E. Spear & R. R. Miller (Eds.), *Information processing in animals: Memory mechanisms* (pp. 341–378). Hillsdale, N. J.: Lawrence Erlbaum Associates.

Spear, N. E., Smith, G. J., Bryan, R., Gordon, W., Timmons, R., & Chiszar, D. (1980). Contextual influences on the interaction between conflicting memories in the rat. *Animal Learning and Behavior, 8*, 273–281.

Spence, K. W. (1936). The nature of discrimination learning in animals. *Psychological Review, 43*, 427–449.

Spence, K. W. (1937). The differential response in animals to stimuli varying within a single dimension. *Psychological Review, 44*, 430–444.

Spence, K. W. (1956). *Behavior theory and conditioning.* New Haven: Yale University Press.

Spencer, K. A., Buchanan, K. L., Leitner, S., Goldsmith, A. R., & Catchpole, C. K. (2005). Parasites affect song complexity and neural development in a songbird. *Proceedings of the Royal Society, B, 272*, 2037–2043.

Spetch, M. L., & Edwards, C. A. (1986). Spatial memory in pigeons (*Columba livia*) in an open-field feeding environment. *Journal of Comparative Psychology, 100*, 266–278.

Spivey, J. E., & Hess, D. T. (1968). Effect of partial reinforcement trial sequences on extinction performance. *Psychonomic Science, 10*, 375–376.

Staddon, J. E. R., & Higa, J. J. (1999). Time and memory: Towards a pacemaker-free theory of interval timing. *Journal of the Experimental Analysis of Behavior, 71*, 215–251.

Stevens, V. J. (1978). Basic operant research in the zoo. In H. Markowitz & V. J. Stevens (Eds.), *Behavior of captive wild animals.* Chicago: Nelson-Hall.

Straub, R. O., & Terrace, H. S. (1981). Generalization of serial learning in the pigeon. *Animal Learning and Behavior, 9*, 454–468.

Struhsaker, K. (1967). Auditory communication among vervet monkeys (*Cercopithecus aethiops*). In S. A. Altman (Ed.), *Social communication among primates* (pp. 281–324). Chicago: University of Chicago Press.

Suarez, D., & Gallup, G. G., Jr. (1981). Self-recognition in chimpanzees and orangutans but not gorillas. *Journal of Human Evolution, 10*, 175–188.

Suddendorf, T., & Corballis, M. C. (1997). Mental time travel and the evolution of the human mind. *Genetic and Social General Psychology Monographs, 123*, 133–167.

Sutherland, N. S., & Mackintosh, N. J. (1971). *Mechanisms of animal discrimination learning.* New York: Academic Press.

Sutherland, R. J., Chew, G. L., Baker, J. C., & Linggard, R. C. (1987). Some limitations on the use of distal cues in place navigation by rats. *Psychobiology, 15*, 48–57.

Sutton, R. S., & Barto, A. G. (1981). Toward a modern theory of adaptive networks: Expectation and prediction. *Psychological Review, 88*, 135–170.

Swartz, K. B., Chen, S., & Terrace, H. S. (1991). Serial learning by rhesus monkeys: I. Acquisition and retention of multiple four-item lists. *Journal of*

Experimental Psychology: Animal Behavior Processes, 17, 396–410.

Tebbich, S., Taborsky, M., Fessl, B., & Blomqvist, D. (2001). Do woodpecker finches acquire tool-use by social learning. *Proceedings of the Royal Society of London B, 268*, 2189–2193.

Terrace, H. S. (1979). *Nim*. New York: Knopf.

Terrace, H. S. (1986). A nonverbal organism's knowledge of ordinal position in a serial learning task. *Journal of Experimental Psychology: Animal Behavior Processes, 12*, 202–214.

Terrace, H. S. (1987). Chunking by a pigeon in a serial learning task. *Nature, 325*, 149–151.

Terrace, H. S. (1991). Chunking during serial learning by a pigeon: I. Basic evidence. *Journal of Experimental Psychology: Animal Behavior Processes, 17*, 81–93.

Terrace, H. S., & Chen, S. (1991a). Chunking during serial learning by a pigeon: II. Integrity of a chunk on a new list. *Journal of Experimental Psychology: Animal Behavior Processes, 17*, 94–106.

Terrace, H. S., & Chen, S. (1991b). Chunking during serial learning by a pigeon: III. What are the necessary conditions for establishing a chunk? *Journal of Experimental Psychology: Animal Behavior Processes, 17*, 107–118.

Terrace, H. S., Petitto, L. A., Sanders, R. J., & Bever, T. G. (1979). Can an ape create a sentence? *Science, 206*, 891–902.

Terrace, H. S., Son, L. K., & Brannon, E. M. (2003). Serial expertise of rhesus macaques. *Psychological Science, 14*, 66–73.

Terrace, H. S., Straub, R. O., Bever, T. G., & Seidenberg, M. S. (1977). Representation of a sequence by a pigeon. *Bulletin of the Psychonomic Society, 10*, 269.

Terry, W. S. (1996). Retroactive interference effects of surprising reward omission on serial spatial memory. *Journal of Experimental Psychology: Animal Behavior Processes, 22*, 472–479.

Theios, J., Lynch, A. D., & Lowe, W. F., Jr. (1966). Differential effects of shock intensity on one-way and shuttle avoidance conditioning. *Journal of Experimental Psychology, 72*, 294–299.

Thomas, B. L., Larsen, N., & Ayres, J. J. B. (2003). Role of context similarity in ABA, ABC, and AAB renewal paradigms: Implications for theories of renewal and for treating human phobias. *Learning and Motivation, 34*, 410–436.

Thomas, D. A. (1979). Retention of conditioned inhibition in a bar-press suppression paradigm. *Learning and Motivation, 10*, 161–177.

Thomas, D. A., & Riccio, D. C. (1979). Forgetting of a CS attribute in a conditioned suppression paradigm. *Animal Learning and Behavior, 7*, 191–195.

Thomas, D. R., & Lopez, L. J. (1962). The effect of delayed testing on the generalization slope. *Journal of Comparative and Physiological Psychology, 44*, 541–544.

Thomas, G. (1981). Contiguity, reinforcement rate, and the law of effect. *Quarterly Journal of Experimental Psychology, 33B*, 33–43.

Thomas, G. V., Lieberman, D. A., McIntosh, D. C., & Ronaldson, P. (1983). The role of marking when reward is delayed. *Journal of Experimental Psychology: Animal Behavior Processes, 17*, 394–410.

Thomas, R. K., & Lorden, R. B. (1993). Numerical competence in animals: A conservative view. In S. T. Boysen & E. J. Capaldi (Eds.), *The development of numerical competence: Animal and Human Models* (pp. 127–147). Hillsdale, NJ: Lawrence Erlbaum Associates, Inc.

Thompson, R. F. (1986). The neurobiology of learning and memory. *Science, 233*, 941–947.

Thompson, R. F., & Spencer, W. A. (1966). Habituation: A model phenomenon for the study of the neural substrates of behavior. *Psychological Review, 173*, 16–43.

Thompson, R. K. R., & Contie, C. L. (1994). Further reflections on mirror use by pigeons: Lessons from Winnie-the-Pooh and Pinocchio too. In S. T. Parker, R. W. Mitchell & M. L. Boccia (Eds.), *Self-awareness in animals and humans* (pp. 392–409). New York: Cambridge University Press.

Thompson, R. K. R., & Herman, L. M. (1977). Memory for lists of sounds by the bottle-nosed dolphin: Convergence of memory processes with humans? *Science, 195*, 501–503.

Thompson, R. K., & Oden, D. L. (2000). Categorical perception and conceptual judgements by nonhuman primates: The paleological monkey and the analogical ape. *Cognitive Science, 24*, 363–396.

Thorndike, E. L. (1898). Animal intelligence: An experimental study of the associative processes in animals. *Psychological Monographs, 2*(4, Whole No. 8).

Thorndike, E. L. (1911). *Animal intelligence: Experimental studies*. New York: Macmillan.

Thorndike, E. L. (1913). *The psychology of learning. (Educational Psychology, II)*. New York: Teacher's College.

Thorpe, W. H. (1963). *Animal intelligence: Experimental studies*. New York: Macmillan.

Timberlake, W. (1983). The functional organization of appetitive behavior: Behavior systems and learning. In M. D. Zeiler & P. Harzem (Eds.), *Advances in analysis of behavior*, Vol 3: *Biological factors in learning* (pp. 177–221), Chichester: Wiley.

Timberlake, W. (1994). Behavior systems, associationism, and Pavlovian conditioning. *Psychonomic Bulletin and Review, 1*, 405–420.

Timberlake, W. (2001). Motivational modes in behavioral systems. In R. R. Mowrer & S. B. Klein (Eds.), *Handbook of contemporary learning theories* (pp. 155–209). Hillsdale, NJ: Lawrence Erlbaum Associates, Inc.

Timberlake, W., & Allison, J. (1974). Response deprivation: an empirical approach to instrumental performance. *Psychological Review, 81*, 146–164.

Timberlake, W., & Grant, D. S. (1975). Autoshaping in rats to presentation of another rat predicting food. *Science, 190*, 690–692.

Tinbergen, N. (1953). *The herring gull's world*. London: Collins.

Tinkelpaugh, O. L. (1928). An experimental study of representative factors in monkeys. *Journal of Comparative Psychology, 8*, 197–236.

Tolman, E. C. (1932). *Purposive behavior in animals and men*. New York: Century.

Tolman, E. C. (1948). Cognitive maps in rats and men. *Psychological Review, 55*, 189–208.

Tolman, E. C., Ritchie, B. F., & Kalish, D. (1946). Studies in spatial learning. I. Orientation and the short-cut. *Journal of Experimental Psychology, 36*, 13–24.

Tomasello, M. (1996). Do apes ape? In C. M. Heyes & B. G. J. Galef (Eds.), *Social learning in animals: The roots of culture* (pp. 319–346). New York: Academic Press.

Tomasello, M., Call, J., & Hare, B. (2003a). Chimpanzees understand psychological states – the question is which ones and to what extent? *Trends in cognitive sciences, 7*, 153–156.

Tomasello, M., Call, J., & Hare, B. (2003b). Chimpanzees versus humans: It's not that simple. *Trends in Cognitive Science, 7*, 239–240.

Tracy, J. A., Thompson, J. K., Krupa, D. J., & Thompson, R. F. (1998). Evidence of plasticity in the pontocerebellar conditioned stimulus pathway during classical conditioning of the eyeblink response in the rabbit. *Behavioral Neuroscience, 112*, 267–285.

Tranberg, D. K., & Rilling, M. (1978). Latent inhibition in the autoshaping paradigm. *Bulletin of the Psychonomic Society, 11*, 273–276.

Trapold, M. A., & Overmier, J. B. (1972). The second learning process in instrumental learning. In A. H. Black & W. F. Prokasy (Eds.), *Classical conditioning II: Current research and theory* (pp. 427–452). New York: Appleton-Century-Croft.

Tulving, E. (1983). *Elements of episodic memory*. Oxford: Clarendon Press.

Vander Wall, S. B. (1982). An experimental analysis of cache recovery in Clark's nutcracker. *Animal Behaviour, 30*, 84–94.

Vaughan, W., Jr., & Greene, S. L. (1984). Pigeon visual memory capacity. *Journal of Experimental Psychology: Animal Behavior Processes, 10*, 256–271.

Visalberghi, E. (1993). Capuchin monkeys: A window into tool use activities by apes and humans. In K. Gibson & T. Ingold (Eds.), *Tools, language and cognition in human evolution* (pp. 138–150). Cambridge: Cambridge University Press.

Visalberghi, E., & Limongelli, L. (1994). Lack of comprehension of cause–effect relations in tool-using capuchin monkeys (*Cebus apella*). *Journal of Comparative Psychology, 108*, 15–22.

Voelkl, B., & Huber, L. (2000). True imitation in marmosets. *Animal Behaviour, 60*, 195–202.

Von Fersen, L., & Lea, S. E. G. (1990). Category discriminations by pigeons using five polymorphous features. *Journal of the Experimental Analysis of Behavaior, 54*, 69–84.

Von Fersen, L., Wynne, C. D. L., Delius, J. D., & Staddon, J. E. R. (1991). Transitive inference formation in pigeons. *Journal of Experimental Psychology: Animal Behavior Processes, 17*, 334–341.

Von Frisch, K. (1950). *Bees, their vision, chemical senses, and language*. Ithaca, NY: Cornell University Press.

Von Frisch, K. (1974). Decoding the language of the bee. *Science, 185*, 663–668.

Von Uexkull, J. (1934). Streifzuge durch die Urnwelten yon Tieren und Menschen. Berlin: Springer-Verlag. Translated in C. H. Schiller (Ed.), *Instinctive behavior*. London: Methuen.

Wagner, A. (2003). Context-sensitive elemental theory. *Quarterly Journal of Experimental Psychology, 56B*, 7–29.

Wagner, A. R. (1969). Stimulus validity and stimulus selection in associative learning. In N. J. Mackintosh & W. K. Honig (Eds.), *Fundamental issues in associative learning* (pp. 90–122). Halifax, Canada: Dalhousie University Press.

Wagner, A. R. (1976). Priming in STM: An information-processing mechanism for self-generated or retrieval-generated depression in performance. In T. J. Tighe & R. N. Leaton (Eds.), *Habituation: Perspectives from child development, animal behavior, and neuropsychology* (pp. 95–128). Hillsdale, NJ: Lawrence Erlbaum Associates, Inc.

Wagner, A. R. (1978). Expectancies and the priming of STM. In S. H. Hulse, H. Fowler, & W. K. Honing (Eds.) *Cognitive processes in animal behavior* (pp. 177–209). Hillsdale, NJ: Lawrence Erlbaum Associates, Inc.

Wagner, A. R. (1981). SOP: A model of automatic memory processing in animal behavior. In N. E. Spear & R. R. Miller (Eds.), *Information processing in animals: Memory mechanisms* (pp. 5–47). Hillsdale, NJ: Lawrence Erlbaum Associates, Inc.

Wagner, A. R., & Brandon, S. E. (1989). Evolution of a structured connectionist model of Pavlovian conditioning (AESOP). In S. B. Klein & R. R. Mowrer (Eds.), *Contemporary learning theories: Pavlovian conditioning and the status of traditional learning theory* (pp. 149–189). Hillsdale, NJ: Lawrence Erlbaum Associates, Inc.

Wagner, A. R., & Larew, M. B. (1985). Opponent processes and Pavlovian inhibition. In R. R. Miller & N. E. Spear (Eds.), *Information processing in animals: Conditioned inhibition* (pp. 223–265). Hillsdale, NJ: Lawrence Erlbaum Associates, Inc.

Wagner, A. R., & Rescorla, R. A. (1972). Inhibition in Pavlovian conditioning: Application of a theory. In R. A. Boakes & M. S. Halliday (Eds.), *Inhibition and Learning* (pp. 301–336). New York: Academic Press.

Wahl, O. (1932). Neue Unterschungen uber das Zeitgedachtnis der Beinen. *Zeitschrift fur Vergleichende Physiologie, 18*, 709–717.

Walcott, C. (1978). Anomalies in the Earth's magnetic field increase the scattcr of pigeon's vanishing bearings. In K. Schmidt-Koenig & W. T. Keeton (Eds.), *Animal migration, navigation, and homing* (pp. 143–151). Berlin: Springer-Verlag.

Walcott, C., & Green, P. R. (1974). Orientation of homing pigeons altered by a change in the direction of an applied magnetic field. *Science, 184*, 180–182.

Walcott, C., & Schmidt-Koenig, K. (1973). The effect of anaesthesia during displacement on the homing performance of pigeons. *Auk, 90*, 281–286.

Walker, M. E., Dennis, T. E., & Kirschvink, J. L. (2002). The magnetic sense and its use in long-distance navigation by animals. *Current Opinion in Neurobiology, 12*, 735–744.

Walker, M. M. (1998). On a wing and a vector: a model for magnetic navigation by homing pigeons. *Journal of Theoretical Biology, 192*, 341–349.

Walker, M. M., Baird, D. L., & Bitterman, M. E. (1989). Failure of stationary but not flying honeybees (*Apis mellifera*) to respond to magnetic field stimuli. *Journal of Comparative Psychology, 103*, 62–69.

Wall, P. L., Botly, L. C. P., Black, C. K., & Shettleworth, S. J. (2004). The geometric module in the rat: Independence of shape and feature learning in a food finding task. *Learning and Behavior, 32*, 289–298.

Wallraff, H. G. (2004). Avian olfaction: its empirical foundation and conceptual state. *Animal Behaviour, 67*, 189–204.

Wallraff, H. G., & Andrae, M. O. (2000). Spatial gradients in ratios of atmospheric trace gases: A study stimulated by experiments on bird navigation. *Tellus (Series B: Chemical and Physical Meteorology), 52B*, 1138–1157.

Wang, R. F., Hermer, L., & Spelke, E. S. (1999). Mechanisms of reorientation and localization by children: A comparison with rats. *Behavioral Neuroscience, 113*, 475–485.

Warden, C. J., & Warner, L. H. (1928). The sensory capacities and intelligence of dogs, with a report on the ability of the noted dog "Fellow" to respond to verbal stimuli. *The Quarterly Review of Biology, 3*, 1–28.

Warren, J. M. (1965). Primate learning in comparative perspective. In A. M. Schrier, H. F. Harlow. & F. Stollnitz (Eds.), *Behaviour of nonhuman primates: Modern research trends* (pp. 249–281). New York: Academic Press.

Warren, J. M. (1973). Learning in vertebrates. In D. A. Dewsbury & D. A. Rethlingshafer (Eds.), *Comparative psychology: A modern survey* (pp. 471–509). New York: McGraw-Hill.

Wasserman, E. A., DeVolder, C. L., & Coppage, D. J. (1992). Non similarity-based conceptualization in pigeons via secondary or mediated generalization. *Psychological Science, 3*, 374–379.

Wasserman, E. A., Frank, A. J., & Young, M. E. (2002). Stimulus control by same-versus-different relations among multiple visual stimuli. *Journal of Experimental Psychology: Animal Behavior Processes, 28*, 347–357.

Wasserman, E. A., Hugart, J. A., & Kirkpatrick-Steger, K. (1995). Pigeons show same-different conceptualization after training with complex visual stimuli. *Journal of Experimental Psychology: Animal Behavior Processes, 21*, 248–252.

Watanabe, S. (1988). Failure of visual prototype learning in the pigeon. *Animal Learning and Behavior, 16*, 147–152.

Watanabe, S. (2001). Discrimination of cartoons and photographs in pigeons: effect of scrambling elements. *Behavioural Processes, 53*, 3–9.

Watanabe, S., Sakamoto, J., & Wakita, M. (1995). Pigeon's discrimination of paintings by Monet and Picasso. *Journal of the Experimental Analysis of Behavior, 63*, 165–174.

Watkins, M. J. (1977). The intricacy of memory span. *Memory and Cognition, 5*, 529–534.

Watson, J. B. (1913). Psychology as the behaviorist views it. *Psychological Review, 20*, 158–177.

Watson, J. B. (1914). *Behavior: An introduction to comparative psychology*. Henry Holt: New York.

Waugh, N. C., & Norman, D. A. (1965). Primary memory. *Psychological Review, 72*, 529–534.

Wearden, J. H., & Doherty, M. F. (1995). Exploring and developing a connectionist theory of animal timing: Peak procedure and fixed-interval simulations. *Journal of Experimental Psychology: Animal Behavior Processes, 21*, 99–115.

Wehner, R., & Flatt, I. (1972). The visual orientation of desert ants. In R. Wehner (Ed.), *Information processing in the visual system of arthropods* (pp. 295–302). New York: Springer.

Wehner, R., & Srinivasan, M. V. (1981). Searching behavior of desert ants, genus Cataglyphis (*Formicidiae hymenoptera*). *Journal of Comparative Physiology, 142*, 315–338.

Weinstock, S. (1954). Resistance to extinction of a running response following partial reinforcement under widely spaced trials. *Journal of Comparative and Physiological Psychology, 47*, 318–322.

Weir, A. A. S., Chappell, J., & Kacelnik, A. (2002). Shaping of hooks in New Caledonian crows. *Science, 297*, 981.

Weisman, R. G., Wasserman, E. A., Dodd, P. W. D., & Larew, M. B. (1980). Representation and retention of two-event sequences in pigeons. *Journal of Experimental Psychology: Animal Behavior Processes, 6*, 312–325.

Wenner, A. M. (1967). Honeybees: Do they use distance information contained in their dance maneuver? *Science, 155*, 847–849.

Wenner, A. M., Wells, P. H., & Rohlf, F. J. (1969). Honeybee recruitment to food sources: Olfaction or language? *Science, 164*, 84–86.

Westbrook, R. F., Bond, N. W., & Feyer, A. M. (1981). Short- and long-term decrements in toxicosis-induced odor-aversion learning: The role of duration of exposure to an odor. *Journal of Experimental Psychology: Animal Behavior Processes, 7*, 362–381.

White, D. J., & Galef, B. G., Jr. (1999a). Mate choice copying and conspecific cueing in Japanese quail (*Coturnix coturnix japonica*). *Animal Behaviour, 57*, 465–473.

White, D. J., & Galef, B. G., Jr. (1999b). Social effecs on mate choices of male Japanese quail

(*Coturnix japonica*). *Animal Behaviour, 57,* 1005–1012.

White, K. G., Parkinson, A. E., Brown, G. S., & Wixted, J. T. (2004). Local proactive interference in delayed matching to sample: The role of reinforcement. *Journal of Experimental Psychology: Animal Behavior Processes, 30,* 83–95.

Whiten, A., & Byrne, R. W. (1988). Tactical deception in primates. *Behavioral and Brain Sciences, 11,* 233–273.

Whitlow, J. W., Jr. (1975). Short-term memory in habituation and dishabituation. *Journal of Experimental Psychology: Animal Behavior Processes, 104,* 189–206.

Williams, B. A. (1994). Blocking despite changes in reinforcer identity. *Animal Learning and Behavior, 22,* 442–457.

Williams, D. A., Butler, M. M., & Overmier, J. B. (1990). Expectancies of reinforcer location and quality as cues for a conditional discrimination. *Journal of Experimental Psychology: Animal Behavior Processes, 16,* 3–13.

Williams, D. A., Mehta, R., & Dumont, J. L. (2004). Conditions favoring superconditioning of irrelevant conditioned stimuli. *Journal of Experimental Psychology: Animal Behavior Processes, 30,* 139–148.

Williams, D. A., Overmier, J. B., & LoLordo, V. M. (1992). A reevaluation of Rescorla's early dictums about Pavlovian conditioned inhibition. *Psychological Bulletin, 111,* 275–290.

Williams, D. R., & Williams, H. (1969). Automaintenance in the pigeon: Sustained pecking despite contingent nonreinforcement. *Journal of the Experimental Analysis of Behavior, 12,* 511–520.

Williams, S. L., Brakke, K. E., & Savage-Rumbaugh, E. S. (1997). Comprehension skills of language-competent apes and nonlanguage competent apes. *Language and Communication, 17,* 301–317.

Wilson, B., Mackintosh, N. J., & Boakes, R. A. (1985a). Matching and oddity learning in the pigeon: Transfer effects and the absence of relational learning. *Quarterly Journal of Experimental Psychology, 37B,* 295–312.

Wilson, B., Mackintosh, N. J., & Boakes, R. A. (1985b). Transfer of relational rules in matching and oddity learning by pigeons and corvids. *Quarterly Journal of Experimental Psychology, 37B,* 313–332.

Wilson, P. N., Boumphrey, P., & Pearce, J. M. (1992). Restoration of the orienting response to a light by a change in its predictive accuracy. *Quarterly Journal of Experimental Psychology, 44B,* 17–36.

Wiltschko, R. (1996). The function of olfactory input in pigeon orientation: does it provide navigational information or play another role? *Journal of Experimental Biology, 199,* 113–119.

Wiltschko, R., & Wiltschko, W. (2003). Avian navigation: From historical to modern concepts. *Animal Behaviour, 65,* 257–272.

Wiltschko, W., & Wiltschko, R. (1996). Magnetic orientation in birds. *Journal of Experimental Biology, 199,* 29–38.

Wittlinger, M., Wehner, R., & Wolf, H. (2006). The ant odometer: Stepping on stilts and stumps. *Science, 312,* 1965–1967.

Woocher, F. D., Glass, A. L., & Holyoak, K. J. (1978). Positional discriminability in linear orderings. *Memory and Cognition, 6,* 165–175.

Wood, F. G. (1973). *Marine mammals and man, the Navy's porpoises and sea lions.* Washington, DC: R. B. Luce.

Woodbury, C. B. (1943). The learning of stimulus patterns in dogs. *Journal of Comparative Psychology, 35,* 29–40.

Woodruff, G., & Premack, D. (1979). Intentional communication in the chimpanzee: The development of deception. *Cognition, 7,* 333–362.

Worden, B. D., & Papaj, D. R. (2005). Flower choice copying in bumblebees. *Biology Letters, 1,* 504–507.

Wright, A. A., & Rivera, J. L. (1997). Memory of auditory lists by rhesus monkeys (*Macaca mulatta*). *Journal of Experimental Psychology: Animal Behavior Processes, 23,* 441–449.

Wright, A. A., Rivera, J. J., Katz, J. S., & Bachevalier, J. (2003). Abstract-concept learning and list-memory processing by capuchin and rhesus monkeys. *Journal of Experimental Psychology: Animal Behavior Processes, 29,* 184–198.

Wright, A. A., Santiago, H. C., Sands, S. F., & Urcuioli, P. J. (1984). Pigeon and monkey serial probe recognition: Acquisition, strategies, and serial position effects. In H. L. Roitblat, T. G. Bever, & H. S. Terrace (Eds.), *Animal cognition* (pp. 353–374). Hillsdale, NJ: Lawrence Erlbaum Associates, Inc.

Yeagley, H. L. (1947). A preliminary study of a physical basis of bird navigation. *Journal of Applied Physiology, 18,* 1035–1063.

Yeagley, H. L. (1951). A preliminary study of a physical basis of bird navigation. II. *Journal of Applied Physiology, 22,* 746–760.

Yerkes, R. M., & Morgulis, S. (1909). The method of Pavlov in animal psychology. *Psychological Bulletin, 6,* 257–273.

Yodlowksi, M. L., Kreithen, M. L., & Keeton, W. T. (1977). Detection of atmospheric infrasound by homing pigeons. *Nature, 265,* 725–726.

Yoerg, S. I., & Kamil, A. C. (1991). Inegrating cognitive ethology with cognitive psychology. In C. A. Ristau (Ed.), *Cognitive ethology: The minds of other animals* (pp. 271–290). Hillsdale, NJ: Lawrence Erlbaum Associates, Inc.

Young, M. E., & Wasserman, E. A. (2001). Evidence for a conceptual account of same–different discrimination learning in the pigeon. *Psychonomic Bulletin and Review, 8,* 677–684.

Young, M. E., Wasserman, E. A., & Garner, K. L. (1997). Effects of number of items on the pigeon's discrimination of same from different visual displays. *Journal of Experimental Psychology: Animal Behavior Processes, 23,* 491–501.

Zeldin, R. K., & Olton, D. S. (1986). Rats acquire spatial learning sets. *Journal of Experimental Psychology: Animal Behavior Processes, 12,* 412–419.

Zentall, T. R. (2003). Evidence both for and against metacognition is insufficient. *Behavioral and Brain Sciences, 26*, 357–358.

Zentall, T. R., & Sherburne, L. M. (1994). Transfer of value from S+ to S– in a simultaneous discrimination. *Journal of Experimental Psychology: Animal Behavior Processes, 20*, 176–183.

Zentall, T. R., Steirn, J. N., & Jackson-Smith, P. (1990). Memory strategies in pigeons' performance of a radial-arm-maze analog task. *Journal of Experimental Psychology: Animal Behavior Processes, 16*, 358–371.

Zimmer-Hart, C. L., & Rescorla, R. A. (1974). Extinction of Pavlovian conditioned inhibition. *Journal of Comparative and Physiological Psychology, 86*, 837–845.

Zorina, Z. A., & Smirnova, A. A. (1996). Quantitative evaluation in gray crows: Generalization of the relative attribute "larger set". *Neuroscience and Behavioral Physiology, 26*, 357–364.

Zuberbuhler, K., Cheney, D. L., & Seyfarth, R. M. (1999). Conceptual semantics in nonhuman primates. *Journal of Comparative Psychology, 113*, 33–42.

Author index

Subject index

Note: Page numbers in *italic* refer to information contained in tables and diagrams.